HUNT MICHIGAN!
·How To
·Where To
·When To

by Tom Huggler

Cover photo by Ben Graham

MUCC
Copyright ©1984
Michigan United Conservation Clubs
ISBN: 0-933112-12-2

CONTENTS

GUIDE TO HUNTING BY COUNTIES 226

INTRODUCTION

AS the state's largest group of organized sportsmen, the Michigan United Conservation Clubs has been keenly aware of the need for a definitive guide to hunting in Michigan. For, although no state has a stronger hunting tradition than Michigan, there has been no complete compilation in one volume of all the information a person would need to hunt in Michigan—until now, that is. We believe that "Hunt Michigan!" more than fills the void that has existed in this area for these many years. You need only thumb through these pages for a moment or two to realize that you are holding a treasure trove of information about hunting throughout this great state. The hundreds of thousands of people who hunt in Michigan each year—men and women, youngsters and old-timers, residents and nonresidents—will find between these covers a wealth of data on all of Michigan's game species and where and how to hunt them.

When MUCC decided to undertake a project of this magnitude, it turned to Tom Huggler, a veteran sportsman and writer, to gather the material and compose the text. He spent more than a year researching and writing "Hunt Michigan!" He traveled from one end of the state to the other interviewing wildlife authorities and collecting the facts that appear on these pages. Huggler also drew widely on his own considerable observations and experiences in writing many of the chapters that follow. The result is this unique volume that we believe is destined to become a required reference for all who hunt in Michigan—a welcome hunter's companion.

—Kenneth S. Lowe

FOREWORD

RESEARCHING this book was a great deal more fun than writing it: We come to know time and place only through experiencing both. And that "research" experience—30-odd years of outdoor sport in Michigan, followed over the past 15 months by several hundred letters, dozens of phone calls, hours of note-taking in claustrophobic cubicles known as governmental offices, and 15,000 extra miles on a lame pickup that should have been shot earlier when the rust-proofing warranty ran out—brings me to this time and this place.

I can tell you, from both road notes and foot travel, that Michigan has hunting opportunities surpassed maybe only by Alaska. That each day a sportsman could choose one of many game species, seek it in a different place, and not repeat himself. That hunters in Michigan can roam 3.8 million acres of state forest land, 2.6 million acres of federal forest land, over 2 million acres of Commercial Forest Act program land, 268,000 acres of state game areas, 86,000 acres of state recreation areas, thousands of acres of state parks and two national wildlife refuges, over 125,000 acres of Public Access Stamp program land, and countless acres of private land—the latter if they simply make a courteous request.

I can show you statistics that Michigan's one million-plus whitetails provide sport for over 700,000 firearm and 225,000 bow hunters each fall. That she offers some of the nation's finest hunting for deer, black bear, raccoon, snowshoe hare, fox squirrel, gray squirrel, Canada goose, ruffed grouse, and woodcock.

More figures will reveal that the economic value of legalized hunting sport, when coupled with trapping, is unbelievably high and contributes a tremendous share toward tourism, which, along with agriculture, follows the auto industry as our state's second and third leading products. In 1982, for example, Michigan hunters and trappers spent nearly $15 million on licenses and another $318 million on travel, food, lodging, and fees. The value of the meat they brought home was over $28 million and the hides and fur were worth more than $19 million.

I can prove all these things to you. Yet, unless you know the power of a Michigan river against your canoe paddle, and unless you feel her glaciated land forms through the tightness of your calves—and not just through the accelerator pedal—you will not have experienced the hunter's time and place.

Ten thousand years ago a hunting party of Mongolian men huddled by a smoking fire near present-day Bay City. Wrapped in animal skins, they burned fingers while tearing at freshly roasted elk meat. Their ancestors, also nomads, had descended south from Canada while mountain-high glaciers were retreating north, and generations of hunters before them had migrated from the Dakotas, British Columbia, the Yukon, and from the land bridge itself across the Bering Sea.

Today a few lucky hunters can once again thrill at downing a 700-pound bull elk. The place is still Michigan and the time is measured only by the march of history.

And what will the future bring? Hunting opportunities in the Great Lake State have changed and will continue to change according to the degree that habitats and life needs of wild creatures are met. Thus, early conservation laws were already too late to save the passenger pigeon. What grizzlies, buffalo, and mountain lions might have lived here were already doomed with the settler's first axe strokes.

Yet today there are wild turkeys and elk, two game creatures returned from recent extinction in this state. And there are more deer than ever before and coyotes are increasing. The rush of wings from migrant ducks and geese was nearly stilled earlier in this century; today they are heard once more. Who dared dream a century ago—an eyeblink of time immemorial—that within 50 years Michigan hunters would kill over one million pheasants each fall and that 50 years later they would take as many, if not more, ruffed grouse from those same southern Michigan lands?

Understanding game creatures' preferred habitats and then being able to locate them—county by county, public land by public land—throughout Michigan is the primary purpose of this book. Just as a good photographer learns to see the world through his camera lens, so too a successful hunter takes the critical, narrow view. He learns to look for and find the forest edge for woodcock, grouse, and hare; to place his tree stand near the compromise of upland and lowland cover although, topographically, the difference may be only five feet; to tell the white oaks that bear fruit each fall from the red oaks that yield mast every two years.

Even so, this book will not teach the reader everything he needs to know about habitat. Nor will it provide answers to all his questions about how to hunt each game animal and bird. That is partly because identifying good habitat and then hunting it effectively is something you do not easily explain. The ability comes from a combination of hundreds—maybe thousands—of mental photographs of what productive habitat looks like. You gain that knowledge by walking through countless covers that don't hold birds or don't yield turkeys or deer and by remembering those that do.

I believe I can look at a bird-hunter's pants and tell with reasonable certainty if he understands anything at all about habitat. My second pair of shooting pants are nearly as frayed, torn, and stained as the first pair was when I threw them out. After wearing out two more pairs, I might let someone call me a habitat expert.

However, we need hunters who at least make the effort to understand. Not merely so they will kill more game, but so they will come to realize the importance of living space and place to the game creatures they seek. The outdoorsman who knows that wood ducks nest in dead trees with den holes hollowed by woodpeckers to precision size will not cut those trees for his fireplace. If he understands that a hen pheasant may nest in ditch cover, he might curtail burning, mowing, or spraying that cover until late in the summer. Instead of burning the fencerow brushpile, he may elect to leave it as a hiding place for rabbits. When the downstate sportsman who owns 40 acres "Up North" realizes that his 50-year-old aspen or 50-foot-tall red pine is as unproductive for ruffed grouse, deer, hares, and woodcock as a drive-in movie parking lot, he might decide to thin some acres and clear-cut the rest.

And when his nonhunting neighbor sees the abundance of wildlife that results, he may follow the hunter's lead.

One need look no further than our own recent history to see the rewards that responsible stewardship of the land can bring. From 1870 to 1910, most of Michigan's vast timber resources fell to the lumberman's axe and saw. Then forest fires burned the leftover slashings and undergrowth so that by 1920 huge areas of blackened desolation remained with charred stumps pointing skyward like grotesque tombstones. Each year between 1910 and 1928, 3.8 to 9.1 million acres of land were declared tax-delinquent. Nobody seemed to want the burned-out land, fast eroding by wind and water.

Between 1921 and 1932, the state gained title to nearly 2 million acres of this abandoned wasteland. Today the tax reversions make up most of our state game and recreation areas, state parks, and state forests and are proof that intensive management can produce abundant natural resources, including game animals and birds.

Besides meeting the habitat needs of wildlife, the future of hunting in Michigan (and elsewhere) depends on the sportsman's ability to show nonhunters that he is responsible and ethical.

He has to take an active role in local sportsmen's clubs and to support the principles of the Michigan United Conservation Clubs, which for almost 50 years has championed nearly every progressive piece of conservation legislation in this state.

He needs to back such efforts as National Hunting and Fishing Day so that the large majority of American citizens—who do not hunt—will understand both the purposes and contributions of those who do. And he must be willing to contact the 24-hour RAP hotline (1-800-292-7800, toll-free) when he witnesses a game-law violation and to find new hunting partners who are true sportsmen if his present friends are not.

Let it be said of us who occupy this scratch mark in the sweep of time and place that we were not only consumer but both protector and friend of the very game we sought.

Tom Huggler
Otisville, Michigan
August 1984

ACKNOWLEDGMENTS

THIS book bears the influence of many people—fellow hunters and professionals alike. I would like to credit those who took a special interest, reaching deeply for resources to help make it, I hope, both accurate and enlightening. Many work—or have worked—for the Department of Natural Resources. They include:

•Joe Vogt, Ray Schofield, Jerry Martz, George Burgoyne, Marv Johnson, Marv Cooley, Tom Nederveld, Pete Squibb, and Harry Hill of the Wildlife Division.

•Bill Pierce and Bill Cornish of the Parks Division.

•Mike Moore and Brad Conklin of the Forest Management Division.

•Frank Dufon and Jim Dabb of the Law Enforcement Division.

•Bill Schmidt of the Lands Division.

•Bob Couvreur of the Recreational Services Division.

•Norris McDowell and Clyde Allison of the Office of Public Affairs.

•Glenn Belyea, Rob Aho, and Ed Langenau of the Rose Lake Wildlife Research Center.

•Wildlife biologists El Harger (Baraga District); Jim Hammill and Duaine Wenzel (Crystal Falls District); Dick Aartila (Escanaba District); Jack Cook and Gregg Stoll (Newberry District); Doug Whitcomb, Glen Matthews, and Tom Carlson (Gaylord District); Bob Huff, Bob Odom, and Fred Ignatoski (Cadillac District); Tom Havard, Chris Eder, Larry Robinson, and Ray Perez (Mio District); Tom Prawdzik and Larry Smith (Clare District); Bob Hess and Bill Rowell (Grand Rapids District); Howard (Bing) Greene and Virginia Pierce (Imlay City District); Bob Wood (Plainwell District); Ralph Anderson, Jeff Greene, and Jon Royer (Jackson District); and Tim Payne and Al Stewart (Pontiac District).

I want to thank Professor Delbert Mokma of the Department of Crop and Soil Sciences of Michigan State University for kindly loaning several rare and out-of-print county soil survey books. Jim Kesel and Joe Hardy at the two national wildlife refuges offered solid assistance. The state ASCS office was helpful too, as were many of the state parks and recreation area managers, chambers of commerce, and information and resources specialists at Michigan's three national forests and two national lakeshores.

Thanks to Richard Smith of Marquette for his photo contributions, to Randy Carrels of Flint for helping with manuscript preparation, and to Ben Graham, art director of the Michigan United Conservation Clubs, for laying out the book. Many sportsmen throughout the state deserve credit for sharing how-to, where-to tips. Ralph Holsinger of Millington was especially helpful with his 40 years of hound hunting experience for raccoon, predators, rabbits, hares, and bear.

And a special thanks to *Michigan Out-of-Doors* editor Ken Lowe, who shared this idea from the start and then worked with me through its completion.

—*Tom Huggler*

How To Use This Book

THIS book was written for two reasons: to help readers learn how to hunt Michigan's game animals and birds and know where to seek them throughout the state. It was not intended to be read cover to cover but in small segments while planning a hunting trip or wanting to know about a specific subject.

To get the most from this book, pick a chapter on how to hunt a particular species, then target a county and learn what opportunities await you. If you wish to hunt public land within that county, then refer to the special sections mentioned at the end of each county listing.

It is hoped that the book will prove to be a useful reference for the county in which you live as well as other places in Michigan where you might hunt and/or own land. It may prove useful for locating hunting spots on the spur of the moment—say, during an afternoon's drive or a weekend trip with something other than hunting as the primary purpose. A good idea is to carry the book in your vehicle when you travel, whether or not you intend to hunt, because much of the information it contains is invaluable when away from home.

The author's intention was not to pinpoint highly sensitive areas that cannot withstand added hunting pressure, although that is likely to be a criticism by those who find "private" places they like to hunt suddenly "exposed."

Rather, it is his purpose to give hunters a feel for the counties and public lands contained within—both as to habitat types and hunting/shooting opportunities—so that they might, with reasonable accuracy, find their own productive niches to hunt. That is why the how-to chapters should be read along with the where-to-go sections (they are cross-referenced with a "which-see" notation) you are most interested in. Choose a certain game species, then pick a place to seek it, and you will begin to realize the wealth of information this book contains.

Also, hunters willing to use both their imagination and energy can uncover a tremendous amount of additional data about where to go and how to do it. This usually involves one-on-one contacts with both professional and nonprofessional resource people.

Professional resource contacts include DNR and federal foresters, wildlife biologists, parks personnel, and law enforcement officers. They also include people who do not readily come to mind, such as MSU Cooperative Extension Services and Soil Conservation District personnel. While sometimes reluctant to broadcast information for general public consumption, many of these professionals are extremely responsive to courteous requests from responsible sportsmen. That is partly because many are aware that hunters often pay their salaries through buying licenses. It may also be because many are hunters themselves and therefore appreciate the value of good information. Remember that you can get solid, where-to-go advice if you ask specific questions. For example, instead of,

"Where are all the best deer hunting spots in Dickinson County?" ask, "Where is a good place to go in Dickinson County for a trophy buck?"

Names, addresses, and phone numbers of government offices are listed at the end of each county and within the text of each parcel of public land open to hunting.

The other resource, the nonprofessional people, are other hunters, farm bureau personnel, farmers, mailmen, delivery company drivers, school bus drivers, and so on. Anyone who is involved with agriculture or forestry or who has a driving beat throughout these areas is a possible source of hunting informaton. Again, many of these people are glad to share information if you ask.

Because maps are the basis of many successful hunts and are a key aid in helping hunters plan, they deserve special mention.

The Michigan United Conservation Clubs (MUCC) has *topographic* maps, *county* maps, and *lake* maps for sale. There are two sizes of topographic maps available. One is a 7½' quad or topo (scale 1:24,000), a 22-inch by 27-inch map with a cover area of six by nine miles. The other is a 15' quad (scale 1:62,500), a 17-inch by 21-inch map with a cover are of nine by 18 miles. Each quad costs $2.25. Order by the name of the quad and be sure to give the scale desired. In addition, 24 state sectional maps are available at $3.75 each. These topographic maps cover about 7,000 square miles each on a scale of one inch equals about four miles. Printed in six colors on paper measuring 22 by 32, the sectional maps feature contour intervals set at 50 feet. Another topographic map with a scale of 1:500,000 measures 52 by 66. It shows contours, highways, national parks and forests, urban areas, wildlife refuges, and Indian reservations. The cost is $5.60.

All 83 Michigan counties are bound in the 11-by-17 "Michigan County Maps and Outdoor Guide" for $10. Further, about 2,500 of the state's larger lakes have been charted on contour maps, which are available for $1 each.

All MUCC map orders require a $2 handling and postage charge, and deliveries within Michigan will need an additional four percent sales tax. For a free Index, or to order any maps, write to MUCC, Box 30235, Lansing, Mich. 48909.

The Department of Natural Resources has individual 11 x 17 county maps available for 25 cents each. To get them, stop in to the nearest DNR office (see the listings at the end of each county in this book). The DNR also has available black and white infrared aerial photography maps for each quarter-township in the state. They cost $6.25 each (postpaid) and may be ordered from DNR Lands Resource Programs Division, Box 30028, Lansing, Mich. 48909. Be sure to include the town and range with your order.

State forest maps are not available and are therefore not included in this book. Information about national forest topographic maps is listed with each of the three federal forests elswhere in this

1

publication. State park, game area, and recreation area maps are included within these pages. Refer to the table of contents.

MSU Cooperative Extension Services has county plat books for sale at various prices. Plat books are actually maps that list ownership of various parcels throughout the county. For costs and ordering information, refer to the listings at the end of each county chapter. Plat books are sometimes available from banks and other community businesses, but they are not always the most recent publications.

Chambers of commerce throughout the state often distribute regional, county, and local maps free of charge. For a listing of chamber addresses, again refer to the individual counties.

Soil Conservation District (ASCS) offices, while they do not usually stock maps, can sometimes be helpful about steering sportsmen to farmers who might allow hunting. They are also good sources for learning which farmers, if any, are experiencing crop damage by deer and other animals.

In summary, use "Hunt Michigan!" as a reference to discover and enjoy Michigan's tremendous hunting opportunities. Then apply your own enthusiasm and imagination to make your experience a rewarding one.

(A couple of words of caution. Hunters should inquire at state park or recreation area headquarters to make sure of where the safety zone and area boundaries lie in the facility in which they intend to hunt.

(Hunting regulations are changed from time to time by the Legislature or the Natural Resources Commission. The regulations noted in this book were considered accurate at the time of printing, but there is no guarantee that none of them have been subsequently changed. Always consult current state hunting guides or inquire at local DNR offices to make certain of regulations that are in force at the time and place in which you may be hunting.)

Armed with a topographic map, a copy of "Michigan County Maps and Outdoor Guide," and "Hunt Michigan!," a sportsman lays plans for a fall hunting trip.

Ben Graham

Michigan DNR

HOW TO HUNT

White-tailed Deer

TO many sportsmen in Michigan, hunting means Deer Hunting. These men and women save their vacation time from work to be in the woods from November 15 to 30, the traditional, two-week firearm hunting season. They don't hunt birds, rabbits, ducks, or turkeys. They hunt deer. So do thousands of others who happen to like the taste of venison along with other wild game.

Deer hunting is our most popular sport, drawing upwards of 700,000 gun hunters each fall. Archery and muzzleloader deer hunters are also on the increase. Why?

Tremendous hunting opportunities on public (and private) land for a healthy whitetail herd numbering more than a million animals are the main reasons. In 1935, 94,369 hunters shot 30,000 bucks. Deer hunting has certainly come a long way in the past 50 years.

Whitetails prefer young growth of aspen and hardwoods, brushlands and plenty of forest edge and openings. Michigan's climax forests of a century ago didn't provide optimum deer habitat. But when the forests were leveled and then forest fires raged throughout the state, the result was a regeneration of cover types. And an explosion in whitetail numbers.

This natural enhancement of habitat has been helped along in recent years by an aggressive DNR deer-range improvement program. And $1.50 from each deer hunting license sold in Michigan helps fuel this program, which has not only helped deer but grouse, woodcock, and snowshoe hares as well.

Michigan hunters can pursue whitetails with shotgun or rifle, bow or muzzleloader. For each of the past five firearm seasons, an average of 733,000 gun hunters took to the woods. They shot an average of 104,378 bucks and 41,280 antlerless deer for a total of 145,658 whitetails. Buck hunters scored at about a 14 percent success rate. When does are figured in, the success ratio climbs to 20 percent.

About 215,000 bow hunters (including some of the same firearm hunters as well as pure archers) shoot 33,000 deer during the long archery season season which currently begins October 1 and ends November 14, then runs throughout the month of December. Nearly half of the whitetails they tag are bucks. Archers, therefore, enjoy an overall success rate of about 14 to 15 percent with an average of six to seven percent success on bucks.

In 1975 muzzleloaders enjoyed their first special, 10-day December season. That year about 8,500 shot 150 bucks. Today the 30,000 that will enter December woods should tag about 2,000 bucks (does are permitted for hunters with unfilled hunter's-choice permits from the firearm season) for a six to seven percent success rate. Taken together, December hunters (archers and muzzleloaders) claim only about four percent of the total Michigan deer harvest each year.

Therefore, Michigan hunters have unprecedented opportunity to pursue deer from Indian summer until past Christmas. And they may choose a variety of weapons. Where they go depends upon whether or not they like company; an easy versus a rugged, wilderness hunt; a backyard adventure or one 500 miles from home; a spikehorn yearling or a trophy-racked animal. Michigan can supply nearly any deer hunter's wishes.

According to Commemorative Bucks of Michigan (CBM), each of the state's 83 counties, even populous Wayne County in the Detroit metropolitan area, has produced record-book deer. However, the 35 southern Michigan counties have yielded 483 bucks of the total 1,185 identified thus far. These are mostly fat, farmland bucks that outweigh their northern cousins by as much as 20 percent. Washtenaw, Jackson, Livingston, Hillsdale, and Lenawee counties have been the best ones. Public land is at a premium and hunting pressure runs from negligible impact in Wayne and Monroe counties to about 25 hunters per square mile in Montcalm County. The DNR estimates the southern Michigan deer herd at 300,000 animals and growing. The region produces about 35 percent of the total state harvest each fall.

The 15 Upper Peninsula counties have thus far furnished 454 CBM-scored bucks. These are two-and-a-half-year-old or older whitetails tagged in both farm country and wilderness areas. Top counties have been Delta, Iron, Marquette, Ontonagon, and Mackinac. Severe winters stress deer in this region and so many die. The U.P. herd is thought to number 200,000 to 250,000 animals. More than half the land base is open to hunting. About 17 percent of the statewide deer kill occurs here, and pressure varies from less than one hunter per square mile in remote Keweenaw County to about 14 per square mile in Dickinson County.

Nearly half of the deer harvest comes from the northern Lower Peninsula where the herd is thought to number from 500,000 to 550,000 whitetails. Typical bucks on hunt-camp meat poles will be yearling spikehorns, four- and six-pointers. There are big deer here too, but the odds of bagging one are not as good as in the U.P. or southern Michigan. CBM has identified 237 record bucks from the 33 counties of the northern Lower Peninsula. Pressure varies from three hunters per square mile in Bay County to 50 or more in Roscommon County.

Each of the counties is described, along with the best places to hunt deer, elsewhere in this publication. In addition, all units of public land open to hunting throughout the state are similarly described. For specific, where-to-go suggestions, refer to them.

Many experts consider the whitetail to be the most challenging of all big game, and heavy hunting pressure in recent years has served to only sharpen the wits of these savvy creatures. Deer have fairly good eyesight, tremendous hearing capabilities, and noses that never fail. To bag one, you either must be extremely lucky or a woods-wise hunter. Sometimes both ingredients are needed.

Entire books have been written on the subject of deer behavior and how to hunt the animals

Teri Leix of Fostoria bagged Michigan's second-best nontypical whitetail killed with a firearm in the 1982 season. Hunters on facing page team up to drag huge buck from Upper Peninsula woods.

Pair of hunters hoist small buck to meat pole. Waterways like the river bottomlands pictured at right are excellent places to hunt deer.

successfully. I put off writing this chapter for last because, for me, it is the hardest one to do. My trepidation stems from having killed only two whitetails—one with a gun and one with a bow—thus far. Therefore, I am no expert on deer and quite likely never will be. Fortunately, I was able to interview many veteran Michigan hunters, who freely imparted their philosophies and methods. Much of their wisdom and advice is contained in this chapter.

SCOUTING

Preseason scouting will not only give you a trump up on other hunters, it is an enjoyable pastime. The hunter who knows how to look for deer sign and where he is likely to find it gains valuable experience and will become more and more at home in the outdoors.

How soon you begin scouting depends upon the season in which you intend to hunt and how much time you have. A week or two before the opener is about right since deer often alter behavior patterns according to weather, changing habitat and food supplies, the advent of the rut, and hunting pressure. The hunter who begins scouting a month early may be disappointed when the season opens and he cannot find deer where they once were.

Remember that deer are creatures of the edge. In southern Michigan, this might be woods along an alfalfa field; in northern Michigan, an oak ridge heavy with acorns next to a jack-pine belt; in the remote U.P., a dense cedar swamp fringed with lowland brush.

Look in these forest-edge areas for buck rubs on saplings and staghorn sumac, for tracks and trails skirting heavy cover and following the contours of the land, for droppings and pawings under apple trees and mast-heavy hardwoods. Some deer sign is much more subtle. Examples are oval-shaped depressions in lowland alder grass where the animals bedded, tufts of hair on barbed wire, tine marks in the snow where a buck dragged his antlers, urine dribbles in snow where a buck may have paused, nipped buds from browsing deer, and an occasional track.

Farmland crops of corn, soybeans, alfalfa, potatoes, and sugar beets attract deer as do acorns. Deer are opportunistic animals, seeking meals wherever they can find them. Remember that certain oaks don't fruit every year and that even those that do can suffer losses from late frosts in spring. Deer will often form trails between such feeding spots and bedding areas in heavy cover.

The hunter who drives north from Livonia on November 14 to open the season from the same stand year after year will likely not tag a buck year after year. Because habitat changes, hunters must be willing to scout to find these changes.

As the rut approaches, bucks begin leaving scrapes—oval-shaped areas ranging in size from dinner plates to wash tubs. The animals paw the ground clean, then stand in the scrape and urinate over their rear hocks to emit tarsal-gland secretions into the scrape. Boundary scrapes are often a series of smaller pawings along a hillside or field edge and quite apt to be in the open. They are not made so much to attract does as to let other bucks know that a rival is standing at stud in the area. Breeding scrapes are much larger; located in heavier, security cover such as lowland thickets or swamp conifers; and are frequented by their makers more often.

As green vegetation dies, the deer's world changes drastically. Snow, cold weather, and crop harvesting are other factors that move deer from area to area. So does hunting pressure. The alert hunter will be aware of these changes throughout the season and will learn to scout and hunt more productive areas. For example, U.P. hunters have learned to post migration routes along river valleys late in the season and throughout December. They know that some northern deer, especially those along the Lake Superior watershed, slowly drift toward wintering yards of protective conifers. Likewise, downstate hunters who shoot bucks in December generally do so from thick, nearly impenetrable cover where big deer go to recuperate from the rigors of the rut and a pressured hunting season.

Being in the right place at the right time is often the result of determined scouting efforts and hard hunting. As with other aspects of successful deer hunting, that will come only with experience.

STAND HUNTING

Most deer are bagged by hunters who have deliberately chosen an effective stand and then had the patience to wait until the animal they wanted showed up. For one hunter, this might take five minutes on opening morning; for another, the entire season.

Properly choosing a stand involves second-guessing where a deer is likely to appear and then putting yourself in a position to ambush him. Careful scouting will help you find the right place. It might be on a hillside overlooking the edge between lowland conifers and upland aspen, perhaps a two-track road that cuts through a swamp, possibly a trail leading from a bedding area to a feeding spot.

Whatever the stand, choose a location that affords good visibility; then be sure to check out shooting lanes which offer unimpeded shots with gun or bow.

If building a ground blind, work it into the natural terrain, such as a depression; or construct it against a tree or stump, which will help break up your outline. Keep the wind in your face or at least blowing across your field of view, and do not enter and leave via the same avenue. Be in your blind well before daylight and try to defeat the temptation to leave when your feet get cold. Midmorning and noon are times when stand hunting can be especially rewarding because other hunters on the move sometimes send deer your way.

MOST veteran bow hunters will tell you to place your tree stand at least 20 feet above the ground (don't believe that myth about deer not looking up). Rather than spot it along a single tree that will cause a silhouette from two directions, anchor it in a cluster of trees—a triangle works best—to break up your outline. Similarly, keeping a crown of conifers or other protective cover behind you and over your head will eliminate the potential of skylighting yourself.

I learned that rule the hard way during my initial season of bow hunting. The first two days deer picked me right off in my tree stand against a straight section of beech. I was as noticeable as if I had put my stand on a telephone pole. There was no way to move the platform and still post a bait pile I had been replenishing for weeks. To solve the problem, I hoisted a hay bale into the stand and then

covered the bale with a black garbage bag. The resulting lump in the tree approximated a sitting hunter. I hunted elsewhere for the next three days, and then on the first night of my return filled my tag when a lone deer walked in without hesitation.

Always wear a safety belt while in your stand. Every autumn we read about bow hunters falling asleep and tumbling from their tree stands.

Since bow hunters are exempt from the state's hunter-orange law, they should take advantage of camouflage. Choose clothing that will be warm, quiet, and comfortable, allowing you to draw your compound without binding. Spring turkey-hunting overalls work great for fall bow hunting, especially if they are large enough to accommodate insulated clothing underneath, necessary to withstand cold nights on the stand.

Use camo grease paints on your face and hands or wear a headnet and gloves. By all means, keep movement to a minimum. Alerted to any motion, deer become suspicious of unnatural movement. Take a half-hour to get comfortable and to tune yourself into the forest sounds. Then, if you keep quiet, you'll probably see deer.

Can deer smell a tree-stand hunter? Yes, and often just as easily as if he stood on the ground. Tests have shown that human scent wanders downwind in the shape of an ever-increasing cone. Hunters in tree stands exude scent in cones that travel down and away.

You'll hear plenty about masking odors, such as skunk scents, and food attractors, such as acorn and apple smells. Those scents may work very well, but more than one veteran stand hunter has told me that the best smell is none at all.

To de-scent themselves, hunters should eliminate the use of tobacco, shaving lotion, and deodorant. They can bathe themselves and their hunting clothes in baking soda or deodorized soap such as Shaklee's Basic H. Other good tips include toting all clothing in a plastic garbage bag containing conifer boughs and wearing rubber instead of leather footwear.

Another suggestion regarding wind is to consider spotting several stands in the same potentially good area. Having two or three places to watch a hot scrape, for example, can pay off whereas an unfavorable wind might put the hunter out of business if he has limited himself to a single stand.

BAITING

You'll read few articles about baiting for deer, largely because the practice, although legal, is at best, controversial. This is usually an emotion-charged issue, causing hunters to sort through their own ethics as sportsmen. The bottom line is, "Did you give the animal a sporting chance?" Only you, the hunter, can decide if baiting is for you.

I once got into an argument with another fellow who claimed that baiting deer was unsporting. He then went on to tell me how he shot a six-pointer along a runway that led from deep woods to a potato field. The deer was en route to supper when the hunter intercepted him with a broadhead arrow through the heart. I maintained he was hunting over bait, although admittedly a natural one. He said he wasn't. Who was right? Actually we both were.

The position of the DNR is that as long as the resource is not exploited, baiting is okay. It will likely remain legal—and controversial.

Successful baiting involves more than merely dumping a truckload of carrots in a likely spot, then standing guard over it until a trophy comes along. A

Michigan DNR

Camp life adds an extra dimension to the deer-hunting experience.

Michigan DNR

9

This fine buck was shot behind hunter's farm home. Right: Some bow hunters prefer to shoot while sitting on tree stand.

Michigan DNR

friend hunted over bait nearly every night one fall for weeks in hopes of arrowing a 12-point buck that his scouting had proved to be in the area. Yet he never drew his compound.

Baiting will not assure you of tagging a deer, but when done correctly, it can definitely improve your odds.

It is best to begin the practice at least two weeks before the season opener. A full month is even better. This will give deer time to become used to the handouts and allow you to find their trails, check prevailing winds, and locate ideal blinds. At first, you'll want to check baits weekly, then biweekly, every other day, and even daily as the opener nears. Having the animals coming regularly, their movements down pat, and a blind or stand secured in the right location are all important.

OBVIOUSLY, baiting properly requires a tremendous outlay in terms of time, energy, and cost if you must drive far and if you have to buy your bait. You'll want to have at least one and possibly two or even three back-up baits in the event you spook game, hunting pressure causes feeding changes, or wind conditions are not favorable for the site you plan to hunt.

Hunter-placed bait can be nearly any vegetable. Sweet corn, apples, carrots, lettuce, cabbage, and potatoes will all draw deer. Later in the season, sugar beets are No. 1 if you can get them. Some hunters even use rutabagas, squash, and pumpkins.

Best time to hunt is the last two hours before dark—say, 4:30 to 6:30 p.m., although 3 p.m. is none too early. Mornings can be effective too.

You'll see far more does and fawns than bucks on bait piles. One reason is that rutting bucks are less interested in food. They also may be smarter, often circling the food site thoroughly to check for danger

and then feeding only after full darkness.

Hunters should also know that baiting is especially effective in areas where light hunting pressure does not upset the deer's normal behavior patterns.

STILL-HUNTING

Still-hunting is the practice of creeping through woods in search of deer. Some hunters call it stalking; others claim that stalking occurs when the hunter has spotted a deer and then tries to sneak up on it. Either way, the method requires the utmost in hunter skills. You are expecting to see a whitetail before he sees you, and the odds of that happening are usually not in the sportsman's favor.

The successful still-hunter is one who slips through woods as though he is an integral part of them, not some bungling intruder. He has learned to take a few steps, stop, and look around slowly. He has developed the ability to see a portion of a deer—the flick of an ear, a foreleg through the brush, the gleam of an antler tine—cutting across the lines of vegetation or terrain. Often, he will crouch to get a view of the woods from a deer's perspective, and he has learned to wear soft-soled boots or tennis shoes and wool or other quiet clothing.

Some hunters like to stand-hunt in morning and evening and then spend the midday hours still-hunting. When possible, they keep the sun to their backs and the wind, if any, in their faces. A still-hunter might take an hour to move only a couple hundred yards. He also must learn to be a crack shot at running deer because, in spite of his precautions, many shots come at fleeing animals.

Still-hunting is especially difficult to accomplish in areas of heavy hunting pressure because the whitetail's always-alert behavior will be honed even finer when hunters are in the woods.

DRIVING

Driving deer is an excellent tactic for two or more

Her brother
Wayne gives Teri
Leix a hand in
loading her huge
buck—Teri's first.

hunters to employ in areas where cover can be sectioned off. Roughly 20 percent of southern Michigan, for example, is wooded, a surprisingly high figure. Wooded areas, especially the small timbered sections on the "back forty" or river bottomlands, are ideal for driving deer. Fields of standing corn are tops too. Thumb-area hunters have been successfully driving deer from corn and woods for years. The tactic, which employs drivers and posters, can also be practiced in northern areas.

Posters want to look for escape routes that driven deer will likely use. These are often fingers of cover such as fencerows, a narrow strip of standing crops, or a gray-dogwood thicket. And the drivers should zig-zag, take their time to look around, and be quiet. Several farmland hunters have told me that driven deer will likely slip back through the drive and can be bagged by ever-watchful drivers.

One master hunter, Gary Gabbard of Lum, has tagged 26 southern Michigan bucks, all taken within 45 minutes of his home. He told me the best place on a drive is near the start of it.

"Many times I'll see a drive in progress, involving hunters I don't even know," Gabbard said. "Knowing that a buck will backtrack every chance he gets, I've shot several by just stepping into the woods, after the drivers have passed, and waiting."

CORN fields are especially good places to initiate a deer drive. To a buck, standing corn is just another example of security habitat, no different than a cattail marsh or grapevine tangle. Many times driven deer will appear at the edge of corn fields and then simply melt back into the rows rather than risk exposing themselves to adjacent bare fields.

There are two schools of thought regarding noise on a deer drive. Some hunters claim that the more noise made, the better it routs deer. Others argue that noisy drivers simply alert deer as to their whereabouts and that it is far better to move quietly. Silent drivers, they say, have as good a chance as posters at tagging a buck.

TRACKING

Tracking after a fresh snow is yet another method to put a buck on the meat pole. Some southern Michigan hunters drive country roads, most often neatly arranged by mile section, looking for tracks. Others in the U.P. and northern Lower Peninsula use the same method on logging roads. Deer tracks that lead into an area and don't come out on any perimeter roads mean the animal is in the middle somewhere, probably bedded down.

If it's a buck and in farming country, don't be surprised to see him lying down in scant cover out in the middle of a field somewhere, usually along a slope. Then a good pair of field glasses will aid the hunter. A deer in more wooded terrain will likely head for heavy lowland cover.

You can track a deer alone and drive it into posters. If hunting alone, though, a good trick is to track the deer until you jump him, then loop the other way. That is because many bucks will circle around like a hound-pushed rabbit.

Mark Hedrick, who lives only three miles from me, used this tactic to kill a 200-pound, eight-point backyard buck a few years ago, and several of Gabbard's bucks have been taken on the backtrack after being jumped.

Tracking works just as well in northern Michigan woods too and can be especially effective in areas where there is little hunting pressure and few deer to confuse the set of prints you wish to follow. The tactic is actually a specialized form of still-hunting or stalking.

However and wherever you plan to hunt deer, Michigan whitetails will likely provide all the challenge you need.

Black Bear

I won't soon forget the hard work required to tag the only Michigan bear I have ever shot. It will also be awhile until I can write about that evening of September 22 without feeling my neck hair begin to stand.

Night was descending fast on the conifer swamp in Roscommon County where I squatted in a ground blind made from rotted pine stumps and fresh boughs trimmed from some storm-dropped cedar. It was my fifth consecutive evening of patiently waiting for a black bear to lumber into the bait pile 60 feet away.

The air at ground level was cemetery-still, yet several five-minute showers had come and gone during the past hour. Bear like to be out and about in a misting rain, so I had been told by those who should know—expert bear hunters. Even so, with each successive downpour the cedar swamp seemed a little gloomier, its dark shapes a little less certain. A pair of barred owls began talking around me. Night Five was going down as another luckless evening in the blind.

My digital watch, hanging from a stump knob a half-yardstick away, flashed 7:18 in red numerals. Twelve minutes and I could stretch cramped muscles. Then a half-mile hike to the swamp edge and I would turn my waiting car south for the two-hour run home.

Just then I leaned forward to ease a slight charley horse in my thigh and in doing so had a view of the woods from a slightly different angle. There, not 40 feet away, a hulking black bear was heading for me and the bait pile. Shaking, I slunk back, sucking in breath as though caught eavesdropping on the telephone. Then I held my breath and at the same time eased the .35 Remington pump over a section of stump positioned earlier for that purpose.

Five seconds passed. Then five more. The bear had either seen me or was testing the owlish air for danger. Suddenly, it glided into view about 30 feet away. Bear don't lumber through the woods as I had imagined; they float through it like black ghosts, without effort, without noise.

Centering just below his front leg, I let out half a breath and squeezed off a shot. The bruin leaped up and bounded for the swamp. A second round caught him in the back and he went down for good. It had all happened too fast for me to think much about it at the time. The "he" turned out to be a 150-pound sow, average weight for an adult Michigan bear.

While speedily dressing her, I was startled by a sucking sound of feet lifting from the swamp. I whipped around in time to see a much larger bear a few yards away. He saw me at the same time, *woofed*, and thankfully melted away into the darkness. My only driving thought was to get out of that swamp as quickly as possible and to my Chevette. An hour later when I arrived, puffing and sweating, the swamp had turned as black as Dante's Hell. Putting the back seat down and spreading a piece of visqueen on the floor, I pulled the bear in the little car on her back where she just nicely fit.

Then on the drive home I thought about the dues required to tag this bear—four weeks of sweat lugging doughnuts through nearly impenetrable swamps and 2,500 miles logged on the car. I was proud of my accomplishment and knew how my partner had felt three nights earlier when he had bow-killed a 180-pound boar, also his first bruin. But to be truthful, I don't know if I'd bear-hunt like that again. Bear baiting, if you do it right, is some of the toughest outdoor sport going.

It is also fast becoming a popular sport in Michigan. During a recent hunting season between 8,000 and 9,000 bear hunters took to the woods in quest of the state's finest big-game trophy. In 16 counties of the northern Lower Peninsula, the DNR sealed 197 bear. Mandatory registrations were dropped in the Upper Peninsula (they have since been reinstated), but DNR officials estimate, through a postcard poll, that hunters killed 1,330 bear, a probable record.

From 1936 to 1957 voluntary statewide hunter reports swung from a 1936 low of 306 bear to a 1948 high of 988 animals. Mandatory registering from 1958 through 1981 revealed a previous high of 911 bear killed in the U.P. in 1975. One reason the kill has fluctuated so widely throughout Michigan is because of changing laws from no protection to full protection and from the former liberalization of allowing deer hunters to bag a bear on their whitetail license to outlawing the practice today.

That last postcard poll also showed that hunters want more information about bear. The most often asked questions were, "Where do I find bear and how do I hunt them?"

To begin, bear are shy creatures of the deep woods. When scouting them, look for droppings, game trails, and tracks along fire lanes, old logging roads, and other two-tracks near the edges of conifer swamps and aspen slashings. This is where my partner and I found bear signs in Roscommon and Missaukee counties prior to our hunt. Some of that sign is very subtle too, like hair rubbed off on logs that cross game trails. It is no secret that the best bear hunters are also good woodsmen.

Bear are mostly nocturnal, foraging the countryside by night for food and holing up in heavy cover by day. Particularly in the U.P., bear can be found nearly anywhere that food is available. Garbage dumps, orchards, campgrounds, roadside parks, beech forests, blackberry thickets, and chokecherry patches are likely spots to look for sign. Depending upon the seasons and weapons regulations, there are three ways to hunt bear: trail watching, dog tracking, and blind-hunting over bait.

Trail watching is the most challenging and least successful way to kill a bear. The object is to find a game trail leading from the "bedroom" to the "kitchen table," that a bear is likely to use. Such a trail might lead from a thick, cedar-clogged swamp to acorn-heavy hardwood ridges, to a farmer's cornfield, or to an orchard heavy with fruit. Possibly it could route bear to a garbage dump or to a well-supplied bait that hunters have replenished every few days.

The late Art Jackson of Roscommon with huge bear shot in the Deadstream Swamp in the 1940s. The bear was never weighed; too bad— it might have been a state record. Author photographed bear on facing page while it searched for ants in a rotten log.

Michigan DNR

Michigan Travel Commission

Hunter and dog close in on black bear. Center photo: Many find hunting bear with a bow more rewarding than using a high-powered rifle.

If you're lucky, you will see a bear nosing along such a game trail either just before dark or at first light, and if you're not scared completely out of your wits, you might have time to draw your bow or shoulder your rifle. Sometimes a trail-bound bear will grunt like a pig or break some brush, but don't count on hearing the animal first. Bear have that uncanny ability to glide through heavy cover without a sound.

The problems with trail watching, if a bear happens along, are that the hunter gets only a few seconds for a shot, and he must be positioned very close to the trail, sometimes within touching distance of the animal. Few bear show themselves in broad daylight, and you will need to pick a spot in heavy cover. Then prepare to wait long hours. You also should have developed nerves of steel.

Dog tracking is an excellent way to hunt bear and, although I've never done it, it sounds exciting and fun. Some dog men use a bait to attract the bear so they'll hang around and leave scent. Others drag back roads at dusk with a bedspring or some conifer boughs to wipe out all tracks. Then hunters return in morning with their dogs in the kennel box and strike hound in a rigger—a special basket mounted to the vehicle front. A first-rate strike dog is usually a cold tracker with the best nose in the pack. Sometimes money can't buy these dogs.

Hunters then drive the roads and when the strike hound bellows over scent, they release him. If the track is a good one and it is not too late in the day, they will put other dogs out. Top-notch bear dogs are trained not to bark (I have heard that some hunters even leave dogs unkenneled in the truck which they wouldn't dare leave) until released to the chase. The reason is that hounds barking in the truck make it impossible for hunters to follow the chase.

SOME dog men equip their animals with radio collars so that they can pinpoint the chase as well as avoid having to hunt lost dogs. It is not uncommon for a big bear to run through whole townships; sometimes the chase will last all day and into the night.

Each hunter has his own secrets for baiting, and the reason that some dog men do bait is so that bear will leave scent for their dogs to find. One fellow I

know buys date-expired candy bars, removes the wrappers, and allows the sweets to congeal in a hot sun. Then he breaks off a couple of fist-sized chunks and puts them into a wire container, the kind milkmen once used to deliver glass bottles. Next he makes a metal lid which he padlocks to the basket. A frustrated bruin licking through the grating is bound to leave plenty of sign.

When this hunter can't get candy bars, he makes his own treats by boiling powdered chocolate and corn syrup or condensed milk until it reaches caramel stage. Upon cooling, the mixture hardens into a sweet chunk that bear love.

Hunters need a special permit (free from DNR offices) to hunt bear with dogs. No more than 10 dogs may be registered on one permit, and no more than six dogs can be run as a pack with relaying of packs prohibited. All dogs must be immunized and licensed and must have a license or other form of identification affixed to their collars.

Bait hunters locate likely sites in swamp openings or along edges where bear are likely to travel. As the animals become accustomed to the weekly hand-outs, hunters increase the baiting frequency to twice weekly, then every other day, and finally to a daily basis. When bowhunting, they secure a tree stand nearby; if rifle hunting, they must locate blinds on the ground. Complete all blinds and secure all stands at least a week before the opener.

Although it sounds simple, the system involves hard work. A friend broke me into the bear-baiting game during the summer 10 years ago when I helped him replenish bait sites in the Marquette area. I was reminded more recently from my own experiences what tough, hot work bear baiting is, but if done right, it is an effective way to tag a bruin.

Begin baiting about a month before the season opener. You'll need to locate a dependable supply of goodies and be prepared to pay for it. I'm told, for example, that due to heavy baiting in the Crystal Falls area, bear chow is at a premium.

Because bruins are omnivorous critters, you can use nearly anything for bait. Apples, sweet corn, muskmelons, fresh fish, table scraps, clean chunks of suet, and unspoiled meat trimmings will all draw bear at certain times. The best attractor, though, is day-old pastries and other baked goods from doughnut shops. My partner and I were able to find a steady supply in the vicinity of our Flint-area

Butch Van Amburg (left) of Millington and author pack out Van Amburg's bear on one-wheeled game cart.

homes. Invariably, bear would paw through the other offerings to get at the sweet treats.

REMEMBER to dump bait in an area that bear frequent. Locate the actual site along the edge of heavy cover or in openings within heavy cover. We found that bait sites that were too open, though, were either bypassed or received only nocturnal visits.

Cover the bait with a plastic-lined, baker's flour bag to keep rain from turning treats into a soggy mess. Add a few logs or pine stumps to keep crows and small animals out. Bear will find your bait pile, especially if you squirt it and the area with a few ounces of honey and water mixed with molasses and vanilla or anise flavoring.

The more we baited that summer, the more innovative my partner and I became. We began to hang small burlap bags of doughnuts and meat scraps along the trunks of soft-barked trees a dozen or so feet from the ground. Climbing bear leave claw marks that indicate the animal's size. Of about a dozen baits put in, we had at least one bear dependent on seven of our sites with two weeks to go before the mid-September opener. One of these baits was holding a 250-pound-plus bear, judging from his two-inch wide claw marks. Although I hunted him for three straight nights, I never saw the animal. Yet each morning the doughnut pile was flattened.

The bigger the animal, the smarter they are. This one either knew I was in the blind or was just plain too shy to show his hide during daylight. Either way, I finally gave up, settling for the smaller bear at another bait two miles away.

Often more than one bruin will frequent bait piles. I also learned (while field dressing the sow that evening in the swamp) that larger bear usually arrive later and chase smaller animals off the pile. When my partner went back to clean up his bait site a couple days after scoring on his boar, he noticed that another bruin, probably a bigger animal, was visiting the bait. I have heard similar stories from other hunters.

Baiters are the least respected of the three types of bear hunters. I suspect that is because some people view the practice as unsporting, something like shooting fish in a barrel. There may be some truth to the charge, especially if you're hunting over bait with a rifle, but every hunter must answer to his own inner code of personal ethics. Giving the animal a sporting chance, hunting legally, and leaving the woods in the condition you found them are three critical ones. I have since hunted bear with a bow over bait and find it personally more rewarding than using a high-powered rifle.

Others look down on bear baiters because more and more people are getting into it for the money, since few hunters have the time or ambition to do it right. Many simply drop baits near roads instead of working into the interior for a quality hunt away from others. As a result of increased baiting for dollars, licensing of such practices for others may be forthcoming.

A third black eye is that some baiters litter the ground with cans, bottles, plastic, and paper. Bait hunters should remember that it is illegal to litter both public and private land with nonperishable materials, an offense punishable by a maximum $400 fine and/or 90 days in jail.

Whatever hunting method you use, remember that bear do not see well, but they have remarkable senses of hearing and smelling. One reason I think my partner and I were successful in our first effort at hunting them is that we went to great lengths to conceal human odor.

We washed our clothing in Basic H, a nonodorous cleaning product made by the Shaklee Company, and then stuffed them into garbage bags containing cedar and pine boughs. Only when we stepped into the woods did we shuck street clothes for hunting duds. We also took baths in Basic H, wore rubber footwear instead of leather boots, used no shampoos, toothpastes, after shaves, or deodorants. Also, neither of us smokes.

Over 1,500 Michigan sportsmen tagged bear in a recent hunting season, many for the first time in their lives. Hunting is currently allowed in 16 northern counties of the Lower Peninsula and throughout the Upper Peninsula (with the exception of Drummond Island). Consult a current "Hunting and Trapping Guide" for details. Hunters in western U.P. counties (Gogebic, Ontonagon, Baraga, and Marquette) harvest the most animals, but the central and eastern U.P. also provide good hunting. South of the Straits, Cheboygan and Presque Isle county hunters score most often.

15

Raccoon

DICK Juneac cut the engine and stepped from his pickup. He leaned against it, folded his arms, and listened. I too lent an ear to this crisp October night near West Branch in Ogemaw County. A cow lowed from the bowels of some barn, and a great-horned owl boomed an answer.

Then I heard them—the faint squeal and chop of coon hounds on a smoking track. Soon they grew louder in the still night. Dick had chosen the stand well; it was beginning to sound as though his blueticks would run this ringtail right past our noses. I looked at my host and partner, who lives in Meredith, and in the glare of his miner's headlamp I could see that his eyes were closed. He might have been at some packed symphony listening to a horn medley instead of standing in woods in the middle of the night.

"Ain't that beautiful?" he said. "That's 90 percent of why I run coon all fall. Just to hear my dogs."

Suddenly, the pack took on a staccato attack.

"Treed coon," Dick said. "Let's go."

And when we arrived at a small grove of oaks along the streamside hill, Dick swept the trees, still surprisingly full after two hard frosts, with his headlamp. Finally, he picked out a pair of red-yellow eyes that announced the location of our treed quarry. Unable to make out the animal, I had to go along with Dick's assessment that it was a "good coon, a fat coon."

My partner braced his single-shot .22-caliber rifle along an oak and squeezed off a shot. The fuss that came from that tree sounded like two cats hissing and fighting. Suddenly, everything went quiet for a moment, then the unmistakable sound of a big animal crashed through the branches. Dick's three-hound pack swarmed over the fallen coon, already dead, no doubt.

He pulled the dogs off and leashed them.

"How big?" I wondered.

"Probably 18, 20 pounds. They seem to run bigger up north. Maybe because it's colder. Come on. We've got time to try for another."

That was only the second time I have ever hunted raccoon. The first incident occurred a couple weeks earlier when a friend from Clio took me to some private land in Saginaw County and we hunted from mules, a truly unusual experience. But the dogs treed only two small animals that night, and so we passed them up. Just hearing the hounds working over a hot track was worth shivering through that cold night. It was easy for me to understand how this sport could get into a person's blood.

Raccoon hunting with dogs is a sport as old as America itself. The scene I just described is repeated thousands of times each fall throughout Michigan when some 30,000 to 40,000 coon hunters take to the fields and woods. During each of the past five seasons, they bagged from 200,000 to 400,000 ringtails.

In spite of high hunting pressure in some areas, coon populations remain fairly steady, rising in years of high fur value, dropping in years when prices are down.

Currently, the season opens statewide on October 1 and lasts until January 31, offering hunters a full four months to run their hounds. A longtime controversy ended a few years ago when nonresidents were shut out from hunting until November 1. A continuing argument waxes each fall between hunters and trappers. The trappers claim that hunters take too many animals, including many "unprime" coon before they can be legally trapped. The hunters counter that most dog men don't shoot early-October raccoon. They also complain about trappers catching their dogs.

This is a no-win situation as long as there are two sets of sportsmen targeting the same game animal.

A raccoon in fall is omnivorous but is usually found near wooded waterways and farm fields. Typically, they will wander over one to three miles of habitat looking for wild grapes, young corn, fruits, nuts, and clams. Raccoon also eat snails, insects, frogs, crayfish, mice, bird eggs, garden vegetables, and carrion. They really pack in the chow in autumn and appear to walk with a waddle, which can be attributed to the ringtail's nature and because some of them grow so fat.

Hunters scout dense, mature riverbottoms with plenty of cottonwoods, swamp oak, and basswood. Often the best areas feature these huge trees girdled with grapevines and berry thickets and flanked by crop fields. A good time to hunt is a still, frosty night when fog or dew is settling.

Coon dogs come in all sizes and colors, but the more popular breeds include Plotts, Walkers, redbones, blueticks, redticks, black and tans, and beagles. Sometimes a single dog, usually the one with the best nose—the cold tracker—is released on its own or rigged to a cage on a truck. When he strikes scent, the others are turned loose and the chase is on. A cold-tracked coon can lead dogs on a run of several miles. On a hot track, however, sometimes the chase is over soon after it starts.

Each dog has its own set of vocal chords, and few things are as stirring as a pack of trailing hounds in full cry. Hunters who know their animals can tell when the coon is running or treed. Some dog men, however, train their hounds to run silently, claiming that an alerted coon can often elude dogs, but one that is unaware of the chase can sometimes be made to tree quickly. These trained dogs cut loose then only at bay.

Ralph Holsinger of Millington has hunted raccoon throughout Michigan for over 40 years. Many coon have earned his respect by giving him and his hounds the slip. He recalls an all-night hunt for a single, huge raccoon in the Skidway Lake area of Ogemaw County. His dogs ran the coon into a small lake where it climbed atop a log and fended off his swimming attackers with claw and fang. Holsinger said one of his dogs, circling the animal like Indians around a covered wagon, was nearly drowned. The hunters called off the chase at dawn when the raccoon dove underwater and got away.

Few things are more exciting in the world of hunting than a hound baying on an October night. Facing page: In spite of high hunting pressure in some areas, coon populations remain fairly steady.

"I used to weigh all the big coon we shot," Holsinger said. "The biggest one we ever took weighed 29 pounds, but I believe that coon was bigger."

The Michigan record is a 45-pounder shot near Rock in the Upper Peninsula by Milo Peacock of Perkins in October 1978.

Such big raccoon, especially in southern Michigan, are often battle-scarred veterans. Holsinger said he has seen raccoon run along split-rail fences to elude the dogs and he has experienced other animals dive from trees into rivers, swim downstream a quarter-mile, and then escape up the opposite bank.

"I tried to get one smart, old raccoon for three seasons and probably treed him 12 times over that period," Ralph recalls. "But he always pulled that diving, swimming trick and got away."

Veteran coon hunters who run their dogs several times each week will often shoot 100 or more animals in a single season. When fur prices are high, some hunters augment family income by hunting ringtails. Most hunters, however, do it for the sport although they admit to appreciating a little extra money for truck gas and dog food.

HOLSINGER believes the most sporting way to hunt raccoon is by casting through the woods with dogs until one strikes scent. He does not believe in road hunting, nor does he like the tactic of having trained dogs skirt cornfields and then return to the truck if they don't pick up a hot tack. Both hit-and-run methods, however, are legal. They are also deadly effective, and it is possible to shoot 15 to 20 animals in a single night.

Raccoon apparently exude a strong scent because a good cold tracker can pick up the trail when it is hours old. Holsinger believes that is because the animals are fat and have an oily odor. He claims he has seen dogs run across shallow ponds of water,

Above: Hound makes sure fallen coon is dead. Center: Raccoon apparently exude a strong scent because a good dog can pick up a trail that is hours old. Far right: Jeff Gray with 20-pound raccoon he shot near West Branch with help of dogs.

Richard P. Smith

18

yelping on a hot "track" all the way. "They don't do that on a rabbit," he explains.

Coon are good eating whether baked, fried, or barbecued, especially when body fat is knifed away. They need that extra fat, however, to help them in the dead of winter when times are tough. Although they do not truly hibernate like bear, raccoon will stay denned up for weeks at a time.

Because of colder weather and possibly too because they are not hunted as much and may be older on the average, northern Michigan raccoon are larger than their downstate brethren. Hunted coon wise up fast and may be difficult to tree. Untested animals are usually the first to scramble to the safety of treetops.

Michigan has plenty of public land open to hunting, especially in the northern Lower Peninsula and throughout the Upper Peninsula. You must get written permission, however, to hunt private lands.

The stirring sound of a bevy of coon hounds giving full tongue to a hot chase is an experience you are not likely to soon forget.

Cottontails

AN abandoned 40-acre farm and a brushy fencerow overgrown with multiflora rose. Add two inches of fresh snow in early December. What more could a Michigan cottontail hunter want?

I thought about that as I stood on the fencerow corner where it T-intersected with a weed field to one side and a hardwoods patch complete with grapevine tangles on the other. Tom Johnson's pair of gutsy beagles were already sounding off in the woods before us. Trinka's long, bawling squeals made an exciting backdrop to her son Andy's machine-gun-like yelps.

Johnson, posting the woods edge 30 yards to my right, motioned to get my attention.

"Beautiful, huh?" he said in a hoarse whisper. "You know, I have those hounds on tape. Nobody ever composed a more beautiful sound." A big smile split his eager face.

I nodded in agreement. Just being here—at a gone-to-seed farm in Oakland County on a gray December day; the hefty, truck-stop breakfast tamped down with a pitcher of coffee; Johnson's tandem making beagle music—was ample reward for crawling out of the sack on a sleeping-in Sunday.

The dogs were working closer. They stopped barking for a minute or so, and I could hear them wheezing and sniffing as they puzzled out the rabbit track. Then a loud bawl from Trinka 20 yards away had me sliding a finger to the safety on my 12-gauge pump.

Suddenly, a gray-brown streak squirted from a blowdown tangle and bounded away along the field edge. I quick-shouldered the pump, fired, and tumbled the bunny end-over-end.

"Get it?" Johnson hollered. "You must have. The dogs quit bellerin'."

Trinka shuffled up to check out the rabbit with Andy right behind. Then something I had never seen a beagle do happened. The young male grabbed the rabbit by its neck and hauled it over to Tom, who was fast coming up the field edge. Dropping the cottontail at his feet, Andy seemed to say, "Nice job, Boss. Are you ready for the next one?"

"Told you I had good dogs," Johnson said, beaming.

"You also said your uncle's farm was full of rabbits," I added. "That's two times you've been right today."

"My wife's uncle, twice removed."

"Whatever," I grinned. "But this could be a habit. Let's have at it again!"

I think we shot five cottontails from the foreclosed farm, and I was home in time to catch the Lions' 1 o'clock kickoff. That kind of action could spoil a rabbit hunter fast. It is repeated in Michigan countless times during the long hunting season, currently from October 20 to March 1 in southern Michigan and from October 1 to March 31 elsewhere (because these dates are subject to change, check a current issue of the "Hunting and Trapping Guide").

According to DNR harvest estimates, the cottontail remains Michigan's number one quarry. During the most recent hunting season for which statistics are available, 213,780 rabbit hunters killed 852,980 cottontails, a heap of bunnies and yet the first time in five years that the kill had slid under 1 million. Even so, that figures out to four rabbits per hunter, who averaged 9.5 days afield. Rabbit populations are cyclical although not necessarily in 10-year up-and-down periods. Seven years prior to this writing sportsmen enjoyed excellent shooting, bagging just over 2 million bunnies.

Even in so-called poor years, there seems to be enough rabbits to go around, at least in the farm belt of southern Michigan. During the most recent season, 671,000, or 78 percent of the state harvest, was shot here. The northern Lower Peninsula tallied 155,850 (about 18 percent), and Upper Peninsula hunters shot 25,370 for the other four percent. Although only estimates, these figures are based on an 80 percent return of questionnaires sent to Michigan hunters after the season. Therefore, they are probably reliable.

Few hunters have not experienced the excitement of a rabbit hunt with beagles on a crisp fall morning or have not tracked rabbit prints to brushpiles and then jumped the critters into runaway action. Many a young Michigan sportsman made his hunting debut with cottontails. By November or December a coating of snow helps hunters see targets in the undergrowth now devoid of leaves. Fall populations still remain fairly high then and rabbits have not yet turned to poor-quality browse which occasionally makes them taste strong in late winter.

Hunting pressure does little to change rabbit numbers. Many more fall prey to owls, hawks, foxes, and other predators, as well as disease, than to hunters' guns. And the cottontail's reproductive ability is amazing. They can breed when only a few weeks old and often bear multiple litters in a long season. There are always some rabbits around, it seems. In fact, as I write this in early July, our lawn and barnyard is alive with rabbits of all sizes.

Cottontails like farmland habitat, differing greatly from their northern cousins, the snowshoe hare. Hares prefer young, dense aspen and new hardwood stands near cedar swamps. Hares and rabbits do not readily mix although sometimes their boundaries overlap. Rabbits like to inhabit the edge; that is, heavy cover of undergrowth (briars, weeds, vines, and grass) near openings such as farm fields, meadows, even lawns. But they are keenly aware of their many enemies—including man—and so heavy cover is only a bound away.

No. 6 shot in field loads through modified- or full-choke scatterguns will stop most cottontails cold. I use both a 20-gauge and 12-gauge, depending upon my mood and what I feel like carrying. My 20-gauge over-under is especially effective for close-in shots in tight areas when an improved cylinder barrel is needed. Actually, gauge makes little difference.

Some hunters use a .22-caliber rifle with or

Linda Chapman of Weidman with Isabella County farm-bred cottontail. Facing page: Even in so-called poor years, there seems to be enough rabbits to go around.

Hunter with plump cottontail shot near Gladwin. Near right: Pair of cottontail hunters head home with their beagles. Center right: Though largely nocturnal, cottontails love to sit idly in the sun on warm winter afternoons. Far right: Hunter with brace of cottontails has reason to smile.

without a scope to bag bunnies. It takes woodsman's skills to stalk a sun-soaking rabbit on a winter day, and hunters should keep in mind that these little rifles can travel up to one-and-a-half miles. Especially in populated regions of southern Michigan, great care should be exercised. If you really want to give bunnies a sporting chance, try them with bows or slingshots.

Though largely nocturnal, cottontails love to sit idly in the sun on a warm winter afternoon. The best time to hunt them, with or without dogs, is over a fresh tracking snow when the sun has just appeared and temperatures are at freezing. Then the animals move freely, leaving lots of tracks to amuse and confuse hunters. You can also pot them on cold days by picking protected fields and heavy cover out of the wind, but take your time and check out every hiding place.

Tracking rabbits over fresh snow is a game of skill and luck. You can do it alone or work in harness with a partner, taking turns at posting and driving. The key is to size up potential cottontail covers and then post one or more hunters at escape spots. These are likely to be brush piles; stacks of lumber or wood; strip cover of weeds or brush along fences; creek bottoms; and the edges of sloughs, cattail fringes, and berry thickets. The driver pushes rabbits out, much like driving deer.

If hunting alone, try to sort out one track from what will likely be a maze since rabbits are great nighttime wanderers. A good tip is to stop every few yards since bunnies always figure they are invisible to a moving predator unless it comes too close. Stopping often unnerves them into bounding flight.

A lot can be said too for hunting cottontails with

dogs. The long Michigan season and normal abundance of targets make owning a beagle a smart investment. Hunters are allowed generous daily, possession, and season bags of five, 10, and 50 rabbits, respectively. Plenty of downstate Michigan houndsmen run their dogs locally on cottontails and then transport them north for snowshoe hare action on the weekends.

I'VE never known a rabbit to run more than 100 yards in a straight line. Soon after being jumped by hunters or dogs, the animals veer off to left or right. The smart hunter follows the progress of a chase through his hounds' yelping and then takes a stand at a good ambush site. Farm lanes, creek bottoms, field edges, and fencerows are ideal.

Of course, some days are just too cold to hunt rabbits. How well I remember a New Year's Day when Dad and several of us boys trudged through farm fields and woods with the temperature hovering around zero. Our beagles spent much of the morning biting ice balls from their toes, and we hunters constantly blew into gloved hands to keep fingers from stiffening. I don't remember cleaning any bunnies that day.

A point to keep in mind too is that rabbits often experience local ups and downs in their numbers. One good-looking area will have plenty of cottontails and yet another be strangely devoid, at least for that season. I think back to a time in college when I was home for Christmas holidays. The farmer neighbor of a friend called the Saturday morning after Christmas to see if he and his dad wanted to help

Richard P. Smith

him rid his orchard of ''vermin,'' as he put it.

The poor guy had about 10 acres of dwarf fruit trees, many of which had been girdled by rabbits. ''I've always had a few problems with them,'' said the farmer, ''but this year I don't know where they're coming from. They're everywhere.''

My friend's younger brother had just received his first shotgun, a 20-gauge bolt-action Mossberg. He was excited as only a 14-year-old can get on his first real hunt. We drove back to the farmer's sprawling orchard on a haywagon, and he showed us the damage with a pointing finger and some language better left unprinted.

It was a balmy morning with a melting sun that would shrink the four inches of snow to puddles by nightfall. Now that I think back to that day, the farmer had contributed somewhat to his own problems by leaving huge piles of brush and limbs from pruned fruit trees. They were arranged in neat piles all over the orchard. Shoot, all a cottontail had to do was stick out his head from the bedroom and he was in the kitchen.

We took turns jumping on the brush piles and snap-shooting the targets that streaked out. Some rabbits merely ran from brush pile to brush pile; others lit for the safety of nearby woods. The four of us followed them there and bagged three more. I think altogether we shot 17 rabbits, including Bobby's (my friend's brother) first three of his life. It was great sport and the farmer profusely thanked us.

Especially in southern Michigan, rabbits appear to be nearly everywhere. They provide a lot of sport during a long season for Michigan hunters of all ages.

Snowshoe Hares

EVEN loud sounds don't carry far in the snow-plugged cedar swamps of Michigan's north country. A moment before I had heard the frenzied belling of Ralph Holsinger's prize beagle Freddie. Now the eager black-and-white hound lunged into sight.

He punched his muzzle deep into the loose snow, wheezed and squealed again, while his skinny tail quivered like a CB whip antenna. My eyes jumped ahead for the snowshoe hare, whose hot track Freddie fussed over, but I already knew this one had gotten away. Freddie churned by within 10 yards. His stocky legs scrambled for footing in the powdery fluff and his one ear flopped like an old boot sole nearly torn free.

Seconds later the other panting beagles, stocky Ginger and young Zack right behind, bounded through the deep snow like cats chasing yarn balls. Alternately baying and bellowing, they filed by in turn, plunging in and out of sight like fishing boats on a wave-tossed sea.

I wondered if their medley of yelps and howls was aimed at me. After all, they had done their jobs. I hadn't done mine. A weighty silence of a few seconds was punctuated by a dull *whump*, and I figured Ralph or son Mike had put the stop to that chase.

Soon Mike snowshoed up. A big, white hare was swinging from his mittened hand. "Gave you the slip, huh?" he laughingly said.

I felt a little embarrassed, as I sometimes do when a mouthy kid with braces hollers out my order for everyone to hear in a fast-food restaurant.

"Now you see them; now you don't," Mike grinned. "Just remember to look ahead of the hounds before you see them because by then it's too late."

Later the yelping beagles pushed another phantom-like hare toward the fire lane. I stood there, straining to make substance from the gloomy shapes and shadows of this cedar swamp near Houghton Lake in Roscommon County.

Then I saw it—the whispy outline of white on white and black-tipped ears. A snowshoe hare ambled atop the uncrusted snow as though it had little concern for the brown-and-white attackers only half a block away. This woods sprite stopped once to look back, and that's when I rolled him with a blast of No. 6 shot from my 12-gauge. I laid him on the branches of a low conifer, then caught and leashed the beagles as they dog-paddled close by.

"Now you see them; now you don't!" I grinned at Mike when he snowshoed up. He smiled and gave me a thumbs up sign.

Although that hunt occurred many years ago, I remember it as though it happened yesterday. Eight inches of new snow lay fluffed in northern woods and the December sun was warm enough for hares to sunbathe. Hardly a minute went by when one of the dogs wasn't bellowing on a hot track. I ate hare for a long time after that hunt.

The Holsingers still pursue snowshoes many weekends of the long Michigan season, just as Ralph has done since 1945, and the last 20 years with son Mike, 30, who began tagging along before entering junior high school.

That long season (usually October 1 to March 31 in the northern Lower Peninsula and throughout the Upper Peninsula—check a current "Hunting and Trapping Guide" to be certain) and fairly light competition are a couple of reasons for hunting the snowshoe or varying hare as he is called. Having an ear for a hound symphony in winter is certainly another. And if you like chasing cottontails with dogs, give these swamp ghosts a go just once. About the time it takes a cottontail to hole up, a snowshoe is just getting his second wind.

Hares almost seem to enjoy being chased and don't seek shelter until they're shot at or tire of the game. While frantic beagles plunge into the loose snow, the big, all-white hares skim along the soft surface, unconcerned, like ghosts on wide, hairy feet. Over crusted snow, while frustrated hounds sort out their weak scent, the snowshoes lope ahead with only an occasional peek back.

Hunters play a hide-and-seek game with them in dark cedar swamps where they hide and play during the long, cold winter. Sometimes you have to kneel under the canopy of snow-burdened boughs and peek through dead lower branches to see the hares. Shots have to be quick and accurate. Misses, at least for me, are common.

From 80,000 to 120,000 Michigan hunters killed between 313,000 and 650,000 hares during each of the past five years. Hare populations have been on a long slide during that period, reflected by the loss of about one-third of the hunters in that five-year span. But hare numbers historically appear to run in cycles covering several years, and there are signs of a rebound just beginning to occur. On the average, U.P. hunters take about 40 percent of the annual state bag while northern Lower Penisula sportsmen account for the other 60 percent. Very few hares are shot in southern Michigan and then only in northern-tier counties.

Most dedicated snowshoe hunters have a half-dozen or more favorite swamps, thickets, and pine plantations where they like to go. Getting information from some is like trying to pry a gopher from a weasel. Still, a hunter just starting out can have success if he finds the right cover, one of the keys to a bonus day in the woods.

Open farmlands and fencerows are alien territory to the snowshoe who prefers the dark tangles of conifer swamps—especially if young growths of choice food areas are nearby. The hares prefer yellow and white birch, white cedar, sugar maple, trembling aspen, jack pine, and red pine. Other good foods include black and white spruce, hemlock, white pine, and beaked hazel. When hard-pressed in the dead of winter, they turn to poorer browse foods like cedar.

Find a combiantion of good food—preferably in thickets of saplings such as popple (aspen) slashings—and heavy cover nearby, and you will find snowshoe hares. Many Christmas tree farms

Snowshoe hares are hunted in Michigan from October through March. Facing page: Pair of snowshoes has hunter well on his way to his daily limit of five.

Richard P. Smith

24

Hare numbers historically appear to run in cycles covering several years. Below: Hunters killed between 313,000 and 650,000 hares each year during a recent five-year period in Michigan.

dot the abandoned, open farmland of northern Michigan, for instance, around Gaylord and Traverse City. Snowshoes like the young trees, mostly spruce and pine, which also afford protection. Fire lanes and trails in the plantations make good watching stands while the hounds push their quarry in ever-widening circles.

THERE are a number of good hunting sites then in northern Michigan, and much of the best hare habitat is state-owned (and therefore open to hunting), largely because it is swampland covered with second-rate timber and of little value. On the other hand, those Christmas tree farms are privately owned, and hunters must ask permission to hunt them.

I have hunted hares with the Holsingers and others in the Houghton Lake area, around Rose City, Atlanta, St. Helen, Mikado, Cadillac, Mio, Lachine, and Manistee. Although I have never hunted swamp ghosts there, the Upper Peninsula has many places to go. In fact, in some western regions, like Dickinson and Iron counties, it might be easier to mention areas that don't host them. Refer to northern Michigan counties listed elsewhere in this book for tips on where to go.

When numbers rebound to former highs, keep Beaver Island in mind for that once-in-a-lifetime hunt. Located northwest of Charlevoix in the middle of Lake Michigan, Beaver Island boasts hare

populations that have been known to explode dramatically. (For details, see Beaver Islands Wildlife Research Area elsewhere in this book.)

In just two days of hunting the 55-square-mile Beaver Island one winter, the Holsingers and four friends came home four animals shy of a 60-hare limit. On another trip, Mike, his dad, and a friend had a two-day limit of 30 snowshoes in one afternoon and the following morning of hunting.

Bagging these cagey critters, though, requires more than simply being in an area where they are plentiful. Knowledge of their habits and habitat is also important. Hunters who intimately know the contour of the land can get into positions ahead of the dogs and then ambush hares as they come loping by. Likely spots are along a fire lane, road, edge of a clearing, or base of a hill, but each area is different. Some hunters use snowshoes, cross-country skis, snowmobiles, and even 4WD vehicles to get into remote areas away from roads and other sportsmen.

Snowshoes generally run in a looping pattern of a few hundred yards. But not always. If the thicket or swamp is finger-shaped, they will often lope up and down its length. Mike Holsinger told me about a hare that his dogs jumped one day near St. Helen. "It struck straight out," Mike recalled, "and when the dogs' barking grew faint, we jumped into the car and drove two miles to the end of the swamp. A few minutes later when the rabbit came through, we were waiting for him."

An old-time practice was to place hunters at

strategic points and leave them there all day. At day's end the hunters and their game were picked up. "That's the way I learned to hunt 40 years ago," the senior Holsinger recalls. "Now we move with the dogs and change locations often."

Besides knowing the terrain and hare habits, owning good dogs is at the core of most successful hunts. Unlike cottontails, snowshoe hares can't be easily tracked since they hear the hunter coming and just shuffle out of the way. Instead of squirming into brush piles and hiding in culverts—as their farmland cousins do—snowshoes stay on the move and out of sight.

SO gutsy beagles with lots of stamina are needed to push them into ambush sites. Hunters serious about this sport rely on a pack of two or more hounds in the 13- to 15-inch height range. Top ones are often barrel-chested, hard-charging animals that will run rabbits, ignoring cut paws and ice balls on their bellies, until they drop from exhaustion.

Most hare hunters agree that December is the best month of the long season. Then temperatures often climb into the 20s, hare scent holds well, and snow is not so deep as in later months. The worst conditions are zero weather and loose, deep snow. Crusted snow is nearly as bad. Best conditions of packing snow in depths of a foot or less often appear during thaws in the colder months, but December rates

tops, especially early in the month just after firearm deer hunters have vacated the woods.

Shotguns with short barrels and improved cylinder or modified choke are the choices of most hare hunters. Snowshoes are tougher than cottontails, and ammunition should be field loads in No. 4, 5, or 6 shot. Most hare hunters prefer double barrel, 12-gauge scatterguns with 26-inch barrels.

"We've found over the years," Mike Holsinger says, "that pump-action guns ice-up with snow. The double barrel is light and quick and trouble free."

Some hunters use the sporting .22 rifle, but this can be dangerous in the close confines of a cedar swamp. If hunting alone or perhaps with only one other buddy, however, the .22 is challenging to use on hares. A few hunters use pistols or bows.

Dress warmly and wear a parka or high-collared coat since there's nothing worse than getting a slug of wet snow, jiggled from a loaded branch, dumped down your back. Footwear should be insulated and waterproof as winter-pasted cedar swamps are usually waterlogged. Snowshoes are not needed unless the snow is loose and more than a foot deep.

The first small game I ever killed was a bounding snowshoe hare that I cut down with a 20-gauge in a small swamp near Lachine while hunting with my dad. The hare was so big that both its head and hind feet hung out from opposite ends of my hunting coat game pouch.

Yes, Michigan's hares provide good sport for young, beginning hunters. We older guys too.

Knowledge of hare habits and habitat is important for hunters of these sporting critters.

Richard P. Smith

Squirrels

ALTHOUGH squirrels make up the second-largest statistic (after cottontails) among Michigan's annual kill of small-game animals, these sporting gamesters are greatly underhunted. In a good year 200,000 squirrel hunters will bag over 1 million bushytails. But neither hunter numbers nor the bag has changed much in the 45 years that the DNR has been keeping records.

Michigan hosts two types of game squirrels: the fox and the gray (red squirrels may be hunted year-round without limits). Fox squirrels are 1.5- to 2.5-pound animals that prefer open hardwoods near farm fields. They have a buff to orange-colored belly, back of tawny brown, and long plumed tail of black-brown with rust-tipped guard hairs. Grays and their black phase—the so-called black squirrel—are smaller than fox squirrels, have a more generally round appearance, and feature ears that are more pointed than fox squirrels. Grays sport an overall gray rather than brown appearance, their bellies are generally white, and tail hairs are white-tipped. Black squirrels are simply melanistic phases of grays. The two commonly interbreed and litters may contain both color types. Grays and blacks prefer deep woods and river bottomlands.

Fox-squirrel range was originally limited to southwestern Michigan prairie openings, which varied in size from 80 acres to 25 square miles. The counties of St. Joseph, Cass, and Kalamazoo all had fox squirrels (and still offer good hunting) at the time of settlement 140 years ago, but they were considered rare elsewhere. Then, blacks and grays were everywhere, it seemed—that is, until the forests were cut. As homesteaders and lumbermen moved north, so did fox squirrels, to the overall detriment of grays.

Carefully-kept records by three veteran Eaton County squirrel hunters from 1866 to 1915 reveal that they shot 4,168 blacks, 1,357 grays, and 1,148 fox squirrels over this period. During the first five years of record keeping, all the squirrels shot were blacks. From 1886 to 1890, 57 percent were blacks, 31 percent were grays, and 12 percent were fox squirrels. By the end of the century, more than 60 percent were fox squirrels, and when the records stopped in 1915, the ratio was 100 percent in favor of the fox.

Southern Michigan today affords outstanding fox-squirrel hunting with very limited opportunities for blacks and grays. Because forests have come back after a series of forest fires early in this century, northern Lower Michigan populations are probably equal between species, although locally one type or the other will be predominate. Fox squirrels are extremely rare in the Upper Peninsula and grays abundant only in localized areas. Rarely do the two species share the same habitat. In fact, you may choose your habitat, depending upon which type you wish to hunt. Fox squirrels prefer farmland woodlots of oak, hickory, butternut, beech, and maple. Grays like dense stands of timber of these same species but will also frequent riverbottom cover of sycamore, swamp white oak, black maple, kingnut hickory, pin oak, ironwood, and elm. Fox squirrels frequent waterways too, but only if farm fields are nearby.

A squirrel hunter who wishes to be successful should know his tree types. During hunting season the most highly prized food is hickory nuts. When they are gone, squirrels turn to white, swamp-white, bur, black, and jack oaks; black and white walnuts (butternuts); and beech. They also like hazelnuts, Michigan's only mast-bearing shrub. Squirrels love corn too and begin raiding farm fields in late summer to chow down on milky ears. They will return all winter to eat the hardened, dented kernels.

Unlike red squirrels, which hoard nuts in large caches, fox squirrels bury nuts individually. They return in winter to dig them up. When mast and corn supplies run out, they turn to poorer fare—fruits like bittersweet, hackberry, haws, rose hips, and wild grape along with the bark of maple, elm, beech, and orchard trees. Hungry squirrels can do a lot of damage by girdling trees, a practice that can ultimately kill the plants. In Hoffmaster State Park a few years ago, DNR officials authorized a special hunt to remove about 300 squirrels that were killing maple trees there.

Assuming food needs are met, most squirrels live out their lives in 10- to 40-acre woodlots. Beginning each August and peaking in September, however, is the "annual shuffle"—the wandering of young-of-the-year in search of a new home. Some squirrels travel miles. During years of poor or no mast crop, Michigan fox squirrels, young and old alike, have been known to migrate up to 40 miles. Apparently grays and blacks do too, as evidenced by pioneer reports of huge numbers of these animals on the move. Squirrels usually produce double litters about 45 days after peak breeding activity in January-February and again in May. But when food supplies are poor, they will often skip the first breeding, nature's way of fitting her population to availble food supplies.

A good squirrel hunter will scout thoroughly before putting in his time on a stand or stalking through woods, the two most preferred methods of hunting. He will look for signs of bushytails—den trees evidenced by tennis ball-size holes; leaf nests in grapevine tangles 10 feet from the ground to the crown of black oaks 100 feet high; acorn shucks and corn leavings on limbs, stumps, logs, and tree crotches; tracks in mud or snow.

Also, learn to identify squirrel food preferences and keep in mind that mast crops vary from year to year, locale to locale. A spring frost, for instance, can kill fruiting oaks on a ridge, yet 20 feet lower spare those same trees. The result in fall is a shortage of upland acorns—and a scarcity of squirrels (deer and turkeys too). They will then move out to greener pastures. A hunter who knows where to look can find them. Mast failure is of particular importance the further north you plan to hunt and is a big reason that squirrel populations are

Squirrels may be hunted in Michigan from September 15 through November 10. Facing page: Gray squirrel, one of two species of game squirrels found in Michigan, the other being the fox squirrel.

Richard P. Smith

Richard P. Smith

Black squirrel above is actually a gray squirrel in black—or melanistic—phase. Fox squirrels are pictured with hunter in center photo. Hunter at far right is working wooded fence line in search of fox squirrels.

not as stable in northern Michigan as they are downstate.

White, swamp white, bur, and chinkapin oaks (those with rounded lobes on their leaves) bear acorns which mature each fall. By June you can tell if they will shortly produce a crop. Black-oak species (black, jack, red, and pin—those with sharply-tipped leaves) fruit every two years. Another way to tell the two main groups apart is by examining the young acorns. Annual-bearing oaks have acorns with green stalks; those producing every other year have tough, woody stems in the second summer.

If the Michigan squirrel season is ever lengthened from its current statewide dates of September 15-November 10 (and the possibility is good that it will eventually be lengthened to January 1), then hunters will want to know that tactics must change if they are to be successful. The more squirrels are hunted, the more wary they become. This is especially true of grays and blacks, who are also more flighty and acrobatic by nature than fox squirrels.

In early fall, for example, many hunters, armed with shotguns, stalk quietly through woods while scanning treetops for bushytail activity. An absence of leaves on the ground and the abundance of overhead cover make stalking rather easy. They wear camouflage (state law requires, however, that hunters on public lands also wear a hat, vest, or jacket of blaze orange) and move slowly, stopping every 10 steps or so. An alarmed squirrel will often sound off with *chirrrrrrrrrrp, chak, chak, chak,* thus giving his position away. Some hunters carry calls which they use periodically, not to lure chatterboxes, but to get them to reveal their location.

As leaves come down, many hunters take a stand under oaks, along split-rail or pine-stump fencelines or in edge cover next to a corn field in hopes of ambushing a foraging squirrel. A sporting weapon then, especially among deer hunters priming themselves for the November 15 firearm opener, is a .22 rifle equipped with 4x scope. Still others use modified- or full-choke shotguns stoked with field loads of 4, 5, or 6 shot. A tough, old fox squirrel can carry a surprising amount of lead and make good his escape to leaf nest or den tree. With either rifle or shotgun, try for head shots to stop him cold.

When hunting grays, the first hour after dawn is best as the gray squirrel is an early riser. Not so the fox squirrel who may lounge in bed an extra hour or two. Late afternoon until evening is another prime period, especially if there is little or no wind. During periods of high wind, squirrels make only brief appearances at best, and in bad storms won't come out at all. An exception is a light misting rain. For some reason that puts bushytails on the move, and it deadens ground cover, allowing a productive stalk.

ANOTHER excellent hunting technique is to float a river while watching the canopy of streamside cover to either side. Arming yourself with a county plat book will help you to identify landowners from whom you can ask permission. Many rivers, of course, flow through state-owned lands open to hunting.

Veteran squirrel hunters always have a trick or two up their sleeves. One to try if a squirrel has spotted you and disappeared around a tree, is to toss a stick beyond. Hyperactive by nature anyway, a startled bushytail will then usually race around the tree to the hunter's side. Some hunters use trained dogs for the same purpose—first to tree squirrels after scenting them on the ground and then either to post

or to chase squirrels around to the hunter. Because chatterboxes are likely to be less afraid of a dog than a hunter, sometimes the hunter can knock him off while he's chewing out his dog.

Another tactic is to tie a long rope to a bush 10 to 20 yards away. Shake the bush to frighten the squirrel into shooting position. You can even bait bushytails with apples or corn and then set up a blind nearby, as anyone who has tried to keep the rascals out of bird feeders in winter knows.

Although I'm not a dyed-in-the-wool squirrel hunter, I know a challenging game target when I see one. And squirrel hunting is an excellent sport to break in a young sportsman. The first animal to grace the cavernous pouch on my two-sizes-too-big hunting jacket was a plump cottontail. I was in seventh grade, but rabbits were not first targets. Nope, fox squirrels claimed my complete interest, especially that crisp morning of October 1.

A schoolmate named Noel Reid had been bragging for months about what a great squirrel hunter and crack shot his father was. Would I like to join them on a season-opener hunt—assuming I could get parental permission—and learn how transplanted Missourians hunt northern Michigan bushytails? You bet!

Noel and I grew up in the Flint area. Our own southern Michigan small-game season wouldn't open until October 20, a light-year away to first-year hunters. But in the northern Lower Peninsula the season opener came every October 1 with the assurance of school bells after Labor Day.

We took up positions at daybreak in the oak woods behind the Reids' Gladwin County cabin. Lester, Noel's dad, spotted me under a gnarled black oak. Twenty yards away two fencelines met in a corner. Beyond, a field of uncut corn rolled away in

flax-colored columns.

"Sit still," Mr. Reid advised. "Squirrels love to raid corn fields; you'll see some soon enough. If you hit one, mark it, fetch it up, and get back to this tree. Then sit still all over again."

He dropped off Noel at the other end of the woods, a quarter-mile away, and then disappeared into the burnt-orange hardwoods. I don't know which was harder to do—sit through Mr. Purdey's boring math lectures or wait patiently for the *chrrrrrrrrrup* of a fox squirrel with breakfast on its mind. Either way, the temptation to squirm was overwhelming. What seemed like hours and a half-million crow calls later a squirrel suddenly exploded from a tree two oaks distant. *Chirrrrrp, chak, chak, chak* had the same effect on me then that a 10-point buck would have years later: my heart pounded, my throat ached, and my fingers trembled.

Finally, I could see the squirrel, a blur of rust orange, coming down a gray-sided oak about 30 yards away. He would descend about five feet, cut loose with a few *chaks*, and then come down a few more feet. My 20-gauge field load of 6 shot could have nailed him to the tree, except that I would have had to shoulder it on my left side, completely unnatural, perhaps impossible for a 12-year-old. When he passed by on a scramble to the corn field, I figured I could then ground rake him.

But the bark of a .22 rifle from interior oaks where Noel's dad had disappeared put Mr. Heartstopper back into the upper reaches of his oak. Probably 20 minutes passed before he ventured down again, encouraged by the chattering of other squirrels between me and Noel. The squirrel's plume-like tail was as long as the critter himself. He hit the ground and then headed for the corn field, scampering through dried leaves like so many cornflakes spilled on the kitchen floor.

Suddenly, he appeared right in front of me at 20 yards, then saw me bring up the single-shot. That squirrel lit out of there as though his tail were on fire. I scattered a big passel of leaves at least the length of a Louisville Slugger behind him.

It was the only chance I had. I heard Noel's 16-gauge boom twice and Mr. Reid's rifle zing several other times during that long morning. At noon Noel had a big bushytail to parade around, and his father sported three fox squirrels swinging from a game carrier attached to his belt. Noel was sure full of the tease that weekend, but I got even later by bagging the first cottontail between us.

Noel's dad was a crack shot all right and a good squirrel hunter. Two things he said that day still stick clearly in my mind. "If you want to shoot squirrels, you have to sit still and wait 'em out," was one. The other was his comment that Michigan hunters don't take advantage of the good squirrel hunting they have.

"Down home in Missouri," Mr. Reid said, "everybody hunts squirrels. Up here you folks have 'em coming out your ears, but not too many hunters take advantage."

His observation was as true 25 years ago as it is today. A point worth making too is that squirrel populations and hunting opportunities exist all over the state. Each year southern Michigan hunters bag about 60 percent of the state total, northern Michigan sportsmen take 35 percent, and those in the U.P. shoot about five percent. And there are plenty of bushytails who never even see a squirrel hunter.

Woodchucks

IF you're looking for a game animal that is underhunted, prolific, challenging, and good to eat, look no further than the woodchuck, or groundhog as he is commonly called. If those aren't enough reasons to go after chucks, then consider (1) you may observe gentleman's hunting hours since the animals are most active from midmorning until late afternoon, (2) they are best sought in the off-season of late spring, summer, and early fall, and (3) they can help fine-tune stalking and shooting skills for upcoming hunting seasons.

With all these benefits, it is surprising that more Michigan hunters don't go after woodchucks. Though nearly everyone has scored on a chuck or two sometime in his hunting past, no one among the many sportsmen I know habitually seeks them.

Woodchucks are one of several game species (deer, coyotes, hares, grouse, woodcock, and crows being some others) that have benefitted from man's farming and other land-development practices. Groundhogs are found throughout the state and in some localities have proved to be a nuisance.

Look for them in rural areas containing grassy openings, large and small. Pastures and farm fields of alfalfa are prime hunting spots. So are powerline rights-of-way, clearings in woods, old orchards, golf courses, and other open areas. If you plan to hunt near roads, however, be sure to get permission of the landowner and then exercise great caution when discharging firearms.

Some landowners, farmers in particular, welcome the woodchuck hunter with open arms. My neighbor has twin alfalfa fields, one on each side of his home. The eastern field is especially overrun with these rodents who love few foods as much as tender, young alfalfa shoots. Periodically, on late summer afternoons I'll hear Norman's .22 rifle zinging away and figure he has dusted off another varmint.

A local dairy farmer has asked me a half-dozen times when I'm planning to get over to his rented hayfields and "get rid of those pesky critters." But, like most others, I just don't take advantage of this prime hunting opportunity. We should be more ambitious, like the young sportsman who recently ran an ad in a shopper's guide that is distributed where I live. The ad said, "Farmers: I will take care of your woodchuck problems. Call Bill."

An adult chuck will weigh about 10 pounds and carries a surprising amount of good-to-eat meat. The animals are active from early spring until late October or November when they finally depart to their burrows and sleep away the winter. Woodchucks do not den together until the mating season in March. There may, however, be several dens with two or more entrances to each one, within just a few acres of habitat. Young chucks usually leave home in midsummer, traveling an average of a few hundred yards (although some disperse much farther) until they find a likely spot to set up housekeeping. This ranging behavior is when many young-of-the-year animals end their lives as highway statistics.

Like other rodents, woodchucks are vegetarians that will eat nearly anything green and growing. Alfalfa, clover, garden vegetables and greens, corn, soybeans, fruits, and berries are high on their list of preferred foods. It is when animals are foraging that they are best hunted since they often wander 50 yards or more from their holes. Although sharp-eyed and ever alert, they can be stalked at intervals when they drop to all fours to lunch on the meal of the moment. Catch a woodchuck between the dining room and bedroom, however, and he will likely run for a tree. Certain that I was witnessing a rare spectacle, I once shot a roll of film on a treed woodchuck, but apparently that behavior is not at all unusual.

It is a smart idea to locate dens of these burrowing creatures before attempting to hunt them. The homesites are easily found: simply look for fresh earth piled near holes about eight inches in diameter. The entrances to dens are usually raised somewhat, giving the wary chuck an elevated posting spot for checking danger.

Don't shoot at woodchucks half out of their holes or even near them, if that can be avoided. Unless you place a killing head shot (and sometimes even when you do), the animals will dash into the burrow and die there, which necessitates a tough digging job. Head shots make more sense anyway if you plan to eat your quarry.

Chucks can be sporting targets with small-caliber, flat-shooting rifles. Consider the following: .22, .22 Hornet, .17 Remington, .222 Remington, .223 Remington, .22-250 Remington, .220 Swift, .243 Winchester, 6mm Remington, and .25-06 Remington, the latter especially for windy days and long-range shots. Scopes allow shots from 200 yards or greater, but the real challenge is to stalk a woodchuck within 50 yards and then try to put him down with an iron-sighted rifle. I know of one hunter who has tried (and failed) to pot chucks with a bow. Another fellow relied on a handgun and did manage to bag a single varmint over several days of effort.

When using a rifle, however, always exercise great caution, keeping in mind that a .22 long rifle will travel a mile and more. This is especially important when hunting populated downstate areas in flat farm country.

Woodchucks are suspicious by nature, maybe because they must face both ground and air predators. Red fox and coyotes are natural enemies as are hawks and owls, especially on young chucks. Although I've never seen it, I would bet that a full-grown woodchuck could give a good accounting of himself, especially with the smaller predators. Another enemy with which they sometimes must contend is farm dogs.

A good pair of binoculars will help you to find woodchucks feeding or sunning themselves on warm afternoons. They especially show up while standing on hind feet in freshly mowed fields. If you can't locate their burrows from a distance, consider walking through the field once to take mental notes of their locations. A badly frightened chuck may stay

Brian Pugh of Otisville with fat woodchuck shot on area farm. Facing page: Woodchucks are found throughout Michigan and in some localities have proved to be a nuisance.

Lothar E. Konietzko

in his hole the rest of the day, but most reappear within a quarter-hour. On our own farm I have walked to within 10 feet of animals backed into their holes with just their eyes and noses peering out.

Plan your stalk to include irregularities in the ground, trees, brush, or other obstacles which may help conceal or at least break up your outline. Small fields are usually easy to approach unnoticed, but the larger fields may pose problems. A good tip is to place hay bales at strategic places around the field so that you can sneak from one to the other. On your belly and with gun in hand, advance a few feet at a time while the chuck is on all fours, feeding. Then freeze when he looks up.

If you do spook him, get up and move into a shooting position fast. Consider selecting a site off to the side of your original approach because when Mr. Woodchuck pops up for a second look, he usually will concentrate on where you were, not where you are. If you were able to find cover, wait him out until he loses caution, strays from the hole, and begins feeding away. If there is no cover, get a bead on him quickly and touch off before he drops out of sight for good. Then prepare to dig.

Camouflage clothing and grease paints will help break up your outline when some cover is available and will eliminate the shine from face and hands. Another good stalking tip is to keep the sun at your back and in the quarry's eyes.

The woodchuck is a pretty adaptable critter, thriving side by side with man. He is also a challenging gamester to stalk. No trophy on the order of a whitetail buck or a black bear, but like those animals, he requires patience, skills, and sometimes even luck to bag.

That makes me wonder just how wary woodchucks would become if Michigan hunters grew more interested in shooting them.

Predators

IF I were meant to be a game animal living in Michigan, I guess I'd want to be a predator. Why? Well, one very good reason is that few people would bother me.

Many Michigan bobcats, coyotes, and fox live out their entire lives without having to outwit tracking dogs or dodge hunters' bullets. True, they may have to outsleuth the occasional trapper, especially during years when fur value is high. But hunters certainly don't cut very deeply into their populations.

According to results of a DNR postcard survey, hunters shot only 16,000 red fox, 2,600 gray fox, and 2,000 coyotes during a recent hunting season *in the whole state*. The annual kill of bobcats (admittedly lower in numbers than the other predators due to limited habitat) runs from 400 to 600 animals.

Numbers, then, overall are in good supply, and predators are found throughout the state. They are among the most secretive, savvy, challenging game animals the hunter can go up against. Yet few sportsmen in Michigan seek them. Why?

I don't know except that perhaps there is little tradition for the sport and that too few hunters know how to bag the wily critters. Then again other outdoor activities like rabbit hunting and ice fishing compete for the sportsman's time. Probably more coyotes and fox are shot during deer season, by opportunistic hunters, than at any other time of year.

I confess that I do not hunt predators, actually for all the reasons above, but after talking with hunters who do and upon recalling some incidents I've had regarding these shy creatures while in pursuit of other game, I admit to wanting to try it. Apparently there are four hunting tactics to consider. They are (1) using a call, (2) tracking, (3) hunting with hounds, and (4) baiting. We'll look at each as well as habits and habitat of Michigan's three major predators. Although an occasional wolf is sighted in remote reaches of the Upper Peninsula, wolves are protected and therefore not of immediate interest to the hunter.

USING A CALL

Indians are said to have squeaked like a mouse on the back of their hands to call in predators. Whether the animals' interest is due to curiosity or hunger, no one can probably say, but there is no doubt that sounds of an injured animal—such as a mouse squealing or a rabbit sounding off with *waaaaa, waaaaa, waaaaa* in distress—can bring a fox or coyote on the run. Bobcats, on the other hand, are more secretive and harder to call. The few hunters that have been successful usually report that they looked up and "there the cat was."

I have never seen a bobcat close up in Michigan woods, but the first coyote I experienced answered a call—a turkey box call of all things. It happened just a couple years ago in Alcona County when, as morning light gathered, I slipped through quiet woods of oak, yelping on my caller. I was skirting an open field and was about half-way around when suddenly I heard the crashing sounds of a large animal about a hundred yards away. I figured it must be a deer, so imagine my surprise when 40 yards away a huge coyote, with a shaggy coat the color of yellow smoke, suddenly materialized. I was wearing camouflaged clothing, my face was streaked with green and black paint, and a large tree was to my back.

The animal knew I was there yet didn't know what I was. Had I been able to squawk the box call again without alarming him, I might have drawn him even closer (it didn't register that I could have shot the coyote with a load of 12-gauge No. 2s from my full-choke pump—there is no closed hunting season). We stared each other down for perhaps a minute; then he floated off into the woods like a tawny vapor.

Another time I was hunting crows at a garbage dump in Tuscola County. At dawn on this bitter winter morning a half-dozen crows came sailing overhead, spotted me, and scrambled away as though on fire. Unable to get off a shot, I did the next best thing, turned on the charm with distress notes from my hand call, which not only turned the crows around but brought a red fox around the hill at a fast trot. The fox and I were equally surprised to see each other. He streaked off, head and body low, in a blur of rust on white while I rearranged the snow five feet behind him.

One time as a high-schooler, I bought a pair of predator calls from Burnham Brothers, the two Texans who revolutionized the sport some 25 years ago. One call was a short-range squeaker. Made of rubber bands stretched over plastic, the gadget was supposed to sound like an injured mouse. The other, a closed reed call, emitted the wailing notes of a dying rabbit. A friend and I called in blue jays, a pair of great horned owls, and the neighbor's cat but no fox. One time, however, we set up in the midnight woods near Fairview in Oscoda County and picked up a pair of spooky-looking eyes in our flashlight beam. I never did find out if that animal was a deer, coyote, or whatever.

Ron Spomer, a sportsman friend who grew up hunting predators in South Dakota and Kansas, offers some tips for talking Michigan fox and coyotes into range. Ron says that getting into position unseen and unheard is the key. The smart hunter parks his vehicle at least a quarter-mile from the hunting site, which can be a natural crossing area between farm fields, the edge of a clearing in woods, or along the side of a hill.

"The critters will come in regardless of cover, so you want a good view of, say, 200 yards when possible," Spomer advises. "Don't skylight (walking along a hilltop without background protection to break up your profile), and take care not to leave shadows or silhouettes in late afternoon. Always sit with your back against a tree or stump to help break up that outline."

Camouflage is another key. Wear green pattern, brown pattern, or white depending upon the time of

Ron Spomer hefts a large male coyote. Facing page: The red fox has a general range of only a square mile or so.

Richard P. Smith

Fox hunting is legal from October 15 to March 1 in northern two-thirds of state and from November 1 to March 1 in southern third. Below: An average-size Michigan bobcat will weigh 20 to 25 pounds.

year and ground cover. It is a good idea to remove watches and rings that will cast a glint of light if the sun catches them. Also, consider daubing camo grease paints to face and hands, even to a shiny gun barrel. Predators are extremely sharp-eyed and all too often see the hunter before the hunter sees them.

Veteran hunters are split on whether or not to call into the wind. Predators usually like to nose their game as they approach, which means they will generally head into the wind. Ron prefers calling with the wind, but that means he may be located by scent from a long distance. Some callers use skunk scent to mask human odor. Others simply don't hunt when the wind is blowing.

Call for about 30 seconds with a series of separate, yet closely-connected *waaaas* into the call. Wait a full minute, then repeat and do this for 10 to 15 minutes. Some animals rush in; others are more cautious and liable to creep in or stand off a couple hundred yards with ears cocked. If you see a predator, stop calling immediately and only resume if it needs additional coaxing.

Best results will usually come in late afternoon or evening as predators stir to begin the long night of hunting. Early mornings are okay too, but, in fact, they can be called during midday as well. Night hunters in Michigan may not shine with artificial lights between the hours of 11 p.m. and 6 a.m.

Some callers rely on full-choke shotguns stoked with magnum 2s or BBs. Others prefer the challenge of rifle shooting, while a few try pistols. Whatever the weapon, keep in mind that an educated predator won't be easily fooled into shooting range again.

In many areas of the West, where calling has become a tradition among hunters, coyotes in particular have grown very cautious of dying rabbit sounds. Some won't even answer calls any longer. That, however, is not the case in Michigan where most fox and coyotes have never heard the phoney scream of a dying rabbit. Most sporting goods dealers sell predator calls and you will find them advertised in hunting magazines. Records and tapes are now available, and if a hunter wants to make a $200 investment, he can buy—and legally use—an electronic game call.

TRACKING

The red fox has a general range of only a square mile or more and therefore can be successfully trailed and stalked when fresh snow blankets the ground (the hunting season currently runs from October 15 to March 1 in the northern Lower Peninsula and the Upper Peninsula and from November 1 to March 1 in southern Michigan).

Although fox are rather omnivorous much of the year—eating insects, fruits, berries, mice, and small mammals—in winter they are likely to turn to mice, rabbits, an occasional pheasant, and also carrion. The fox's neat, round punctures in snow generally tell the story: straight-stepping tracks through fields and along farm lanes mean the animal is headed somewhere; zigzag prints along the edge of woods, through cattails, weed fields, and thickets denote a hungry fox hunting for supper.

A white-clad hunter can follow these tracks, stopping occasionally to glass terrain ahead and kill unsuspecting foxes in their sleep. The animals like to sleep in the open, often along a hill with a southerly exposure to catch the lean warmth of a winter sun. With a full stomach and nothing on his mind, ol' red will curl into a ball with his plume-like

tail over his nose and feet.

Two hunters risk the chance of detection but can team up to waylay a routed fox who thinks he outsmarted them by doubling back. One hunter stays on the trail while the other takes a stand with a good view near the original track. He then shoots the predator when he comes loping around on the backtrack, much like a hound-driven rabbit. Tracking will likely work on coyotes too except that the range of the males in particular may be a township or more in size. And the problem with tracking bobcats is that their habitat of close conifer swamps makes it nearly impossible to sneak into range without being detected.

Flat-shooting rifles in small calibers with scopes are good predator medicine. A .22 will do the job, but some hunters like a little more firepower found in the .22 Hornet, .220 Swift, or even the .25-06 Remington. Aim for the head since the average weight of a fox is only 10 pounds and the body cavity is about the diameter of a two-pound coffee can—not a large target at all.

HUNTING WITH HOUNDS

Those who have done it tell me no method surpasses the excitement of predator hunting with hounds. Some hunters don't even carry weapons, content to listen to the music of a pack in full cry.

Over 40 years, Ralph Holsinger of Millington and his endless parade of hounds have hunted hares, rabbits, raccoon, bear, fox, coyotes, and bobcats throughout the state. Most of his success with predators has been on red fox in the farming country near his downstate home.

Ralph's method is to drive around rural roads after a fresh snowfall and look for tracks. Fox have regular crossing places, which the observant hunter will soon identify. These are likely to be frozen creek beds, open fields, farm lanes—all located some distance from houses. When he finds a good track, Holsinger puts a hound down, usually a good cold tracker, and if things warm up, he then releases the pack. They will join the strike dog within minutes, and the chase is on.

A male red fox, late in the winter, may lead dogs on a 15-mile romp. That is likely because the animal is out of his territory looking for a mate and is anxious to get back to home turf. How long the chase lasts also depends on the expertise of the hounds and the terrain. Holsinger says some fox run around and around in standing corn or lowland brush when

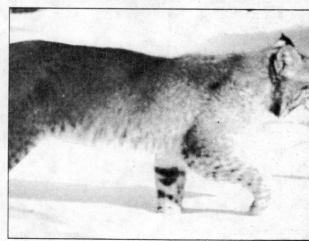

a slow pack is on their trail. Others, pushed by fast hounds, light out cross country like marathoners.

Once the running pattern is established, hunters try to get into position ahead of the fox. Once again, experience pays off, and Holsinger says he has shot several animals from the same crossing spots. Even a chased fox usually keeps his mind on what's ahead, and so hunters must learn to stay low and not move. Ralph likes to crouch behind a stump or disappear into thick cover where he can peer out.

"**M**OST hunters make the mistake of jumping up when the fox is twice out of range," he says. "The hardest part is lying still until he is right on top of you, then jump up and blaze away." When hunting with others, it is a good idea to use shotguns for safety's sake; besides, a dose of BBs in the face will stop any fox cold. Holsinger has a friend who shot five fox one winter with a pistol. Getting into position and remaining there undetected paid off with close-in shots.

Most fox hunters rely on Walker hounds, but any dog who goes nuts over a snootful of predator scent will work. Even beagles will run foxes if trained to do so.

Hound-hunting for coyotes makes use of the same tactics, but, once again, chases are apt to be long-winded affairs. This is especially true in deep snow, and that is why some hunters use teams of dogs, replacing worn-out hounds with fresh animals.

About 60 percent of the coyotes shot in Michigan are Upper Peninsula animals. According to the postcard survey mentioned earlier, 22 percent came from the northern Lower Peninsula and a surprising 18 percent were shot in southern Michigan.

Coyotes are often confused with timber wolves. In fact, the one that I saw while turkey hunting I was certain at first was a wolf. The animal appeared to weigh 90 to 100 pounds and stood higher and was longer than a German shepherd. However, I'm sure that I saw no wolf, just a very large, male coyote, probably 55 to 60 pounds in weight, that appeared much larger because of his winter coat.

According to noted animal expert Leonard Lee Rue, the eastern coyote found in Michigan and other states from the Midwest to the East is a crossbreed between the small, northeastern timber wolf and the western coyote. The animal likes brushy cover and edge cover near open spaces. In Michigan it is frequently found in young jack pines and slashings

where it seeks hares, its main source of winter fare. Coyotes also like mice, rabbits, muskrats, birds, whitetail fawns, and wild turkeys. The predators appear to be increasing throughout much of the state.

The few hunters who go after Michigan bobcats generally use hounds. Bobcats may be currently hunted throughout the Upper Peninsula (except for Drummond and Bois Blanc islands) from October 25 to March 31 and in eight northern Lower Peninsula counties from January 1 to March 1. All bobcats killed must be registered, whole, at a DNR office within 72 hours.

An average-size Michigan bobcat will weigh 20 to 25 pounds although much larger animals have been shot. Their gray-brown coats feature dark spots, and the tails are white-tipped with a black bar. These characteristics are important to note since the bobcat's larger cousin—the lynx—is protected. Lynx have pointed ears and black-tipped tails and are generally steely-gray in color. A few are found in the Upper Peninsula.

In winter, hunters drive two-track roads or walk hounds through swamp edges looking for fresh tracks of the shy, mysterious bobcats. The short-winded animals often tree rather easily, and so a fast hound is an advantage. However, cats are sharp-eared and don't often stay treed long enough for hunters to turn them into a statistic, and so the chase can go on and on.

BAITING

I mention this tactic because a few Upper Peninsula hunters report fairly good success on coyotes by using it. One such hunter is Jim Kesel of Germfask. The key is to place carrion—a car-struck deer (get a possession permit from a conservation officer or a DNR office first, however) or dead calf, for instance—in an open field or on a frozen lake during winter.

Coyotes ranging for food will smell the carrion and then hang around the area until it is devoured. A hunter with a high-powered rifle can take a stand in nearby cover in the evening and wait for one or more predators to show up at the bait site. A full moon will illuminate a snowscape brightly enough for killing shots with the aid of a good, light-gathering scope.

A final thought on hunting Michigan predators should contain mention of the gray fox. Although somewhat rare in the Upper Peninsula, grays are increasing downstate, especially in southern-tier counties fronting Indiana. Grays are more heavily built than red fox, they don't run as far, and they prefer plenty of thick cover. The top of a gray fox's back and tail is generally black descending to a salt and pepper gray along the flanks.

Gray fox are tree climbers. Their diet consists of red-fox foods as well as eggs and young of birds that live in brushy areas and the forest edge. This would include ruffed grouse, woodcock, and wild turkeys. Gray fox are most effectively hunted with predator calls.

Many people, including me, probably don't realize how abundant Michigan predators are. I was surprised, for example, when Ralph Holsinger recently told me that he and friends shot 33 red fox one winter between Otisville, where I presently live, and Genesee, where I used to teach high school. That distance is only seven miles.

If you want to try what many claim is a fascinating sport with little competition and plenty of targets, give predator hunting a go.

Grouse

AY "grouse," and "ruffed grouse" or "partridge" comes to the minds of most Michigan hunters. Each fall about 200,000 sportsmen take to brush and aspen covers from the downstate farming region to remote areas of the Upper Peninsula. During the most recent season for which records are complete, they spent 1.5 million days afield to bag 522,000 grouse—a "down" season considering that for each of the four previous years hunters had pocketed 700,000 birds or more.

The season has been opening statewide on September 15 and running through November 14. Then, Lower Peninsula hunters, in recent years at least, have been enjoying a special December season, which some observers claim is harmful to brood stocks. More on that in a moment. The point here is that hunters should check a current copy of the "Hunting and Trapping Guide" for season dates and regulations.

They should also be aware that Michigan has another grouse species legal to hunt in certain eastern U.P. counties. The sharp-tailed grouse, a bird of western prairies, is thought to number about 10,000 residents, probably 10 percent of which hunters harvest each fall. I'll cover sharpie habits, habitat, and hunting tactics later in this chapter.

Spruce grouse (also called "fool's hen" because of their lack of fear for man) are a conifer forest bird found infrequently in the western U.P. They are currently protected. A fourth grouse species—the prairie chicken—was once native to Michigan. Found in certain southern counties containing savanna prairies when the settlers arrived, "chickens" provided hunting sport and food well into this century. They also moved east from Wisconsin (along with sharptails) throughout much of the U.P. after loggers and fires depleted the vast forests and the land reverted to large, open areas containing prairies. Drumming males from Michigan's last remnant flock near Marion in Osceola County were last seen in the spring of 1982. Prairie chickens are now considered extinct in Michigan.

RUFFED GROUSE

Ruffed grouse have proved to be a versatile game bird for a whole range of Michigan hunters, from the brush-buster with ragged hunting coat, patch-colored mongrel, and cut-off single shot to the purist with pigeon-grade double barrel and matched English setters.

There seems to be no middle ground when it comes to grouse hunters. They either take birds incidentally (and usually call them "pats") when after pheasants or rabbits, or they seek them on their own merits with a peculiar kind of fever. During many years of hunting, I have grown from one extreme of hunter to the other.

I pocketed my first "ruff" as a sort of accident while tracking rabbits around Sand Lake in Iosco County years ago. Since that time the memories of whirring wings, the bittersweet tang of gunpowder, the appreciation for a bird as handsomely designed as a cock pheasant have worked like potions to make grouse hunting as close to an obsession as I dare allow it.

It is amazing how storm windows can lie waiting in the cellar, how rapidly leaves accumulate on the lawn, how dangerously low the antifreeze in my wife's car can become during Michigan's grouse-hunting season.

All the hours of practice with those fluorescent-orange skeet targets have failed to improve my shooting. Grouse simply refuse to fly like clay birds. Still, they are the only game bird I don't feel embarrassed about missing. Excuses are conveniently built into the sport: the shin tangle tripped you, wild-grape vines circled your shooting arm, a friendly birch got in the way of your shotgun blast, you just happened to be stepping over a log....

I could go on for pages about why I hunt grouse, but you will likely find out for yourself—if you haven't already. More importantly perhaps is to discuss how to hunt these magnificent game birds. Success begins with a knowledge of habitat.

When I began hunting, the woods all looked alike. I have since learned that just as certain portions of a lake will hold fish, so too niches of habitat type host the brunt of certain game animals and birds. Never is this more true than with ruffed grouse. I began to understand habitat when I found good shooting in certain covers and then made mental notes of what those covers contained. Locating similar habitats elsewhere became easier once I learned what to look for.

It pays to know that grouse are highly sensitive to their home turf, and what passed as excellent cover last year may decline to mediocrity the next and may well be worthless in another year or two. A grouse will spend his entire life in some 40 acres of woods if those woods contain drumming logs (for males), heavy density of aspen saplings (for nesting hens), a canopy of security cover from hawks and owls, and food.

Good grouse cover is usually thick. Young aspen (poplar or "popple") aged five to 15 years is a favorite, not only because of the large, nutritious male buds (which grouse eat, especially in winter) but also because the high stem density of youthful aspen protects them from raptors.

There are many other good covers in which to find grouse. Not surprisingly perhaps, most serve as understory to aspen. They include gray, silky, and red osier dogwood; witch and beaked hazel; blackberry, raspberry, and blueberry; grapevines; crab apples; old orchards gone to seed; willow, cherry, alder, birch, and sometimes pine. Several years ago Michigan DNR biologists found over 100 food types in the crops of birds they inspected. These foods included all types of berries, nuts, and seeds. Acorns, beechnuts, high bush cranberry, autumn olive, hawthorn, rose hips, and wintergreen berries are other examples of prime grouse fare and are worth locating in your search for prime habitat.

A good tip is to pick up a shirt-pocket size paperback on tree and wildflower identification.

English setter with Thumb-area ruffed grouse shot in December. Facing page: In recent years Michigan ruffed-grouse hunters have generally bagged 700,000 birds or more each year.

Al Stewart accepts grouse from his English setter, Bandit. Top center: Good grouse and woodcock habitat in Benzie County. Bottom center: Ruffed grouse are now the leading game bird in Michigan.

Also, check the crops of birds you kill. Be versatile and learn to hunt in many places, eliminating the unproductive ones. A friend has over 50 key covers that he hunts each year. Ones that have grown to maturity and no longer hold grouse are substituted for new spots. Hunt habitat first, then grouse.

You should also learn to seek birds under all conditions, which the current 90-day season allows. This same friend once hunted 89 days in a single season. His reason for missing one day? He remarried. Hunting even once weekly will go a long way toward unraveling the mysteries of ruffed grouse.

You will learn, for instance, that birds sit tightly on wet, rainy days and become jittery and flush wildly on windy days. In time, you will learn to watch the trees as well as the ground, and if you are like the rest of us who grew over the years into believers of the wing shot, you will likely shame yourself early by raking a bird or two from its perch or ground swatting a running target.

You will also watch your shooting chances improve from the green hell of mid-September to the leaf drop of late October/early November, then see them plummet again in December when birds seek the evergreen cloak of safety in swamp growth and pine plantations.

WITHIN the long season are actually three separate mini-seasons. Each has its advantages and disadvantages. Shooting is never tougher than in mid-September when Michigan woods rival a tropical jungle for thickness and tough going. Midday can be a sticky, hot affair, and dogs poop out, along with their out-of-shape masters, in an hour or two. One fall in Iron County three friends and I walked ourselves into a ferocious sweat during a three-day Indian-summer grouse hunt. It was more work than fun.

Another problem with early hunting is that the birds can be anywhere since food supplies are more abundant than at any other time of year. Further, the heavy ground cover of green bracken, coupled with full foliage on trees and shrubs, provides lots of protection, and clean shots are an impossibility. Small wonder that some veteran grouse hunters won't set foot in Michigan woods until October 1, which for years marked the traditional opener.

When you do find September grouse, though, multiple flushes from family units still intact are possible. Sometimes, it is a simple matter to follow up scattered birds to get reflushes. But as a general rule, you will earn every bird you pocket.

By mid-October, after the first freeze or two, dying bracken turns brown and wilts and trees become threadbare. The fall shuffle—that annual dispersal of young-of-the-year grouse to breeding territories—is in full swing, and birds again may be well scattered (though still usually found in the habitats described earlier). Most of the harvest comes during this period of mid-October until the regular-season closer the day before firearm deer hunting begins.

It is an excellent time to be in woods from standpoints of beautiful fall color, favorable temperatures, and shooting visibility. Many hunters then become leisurely about the sport, arriving in predetermined covers about midmorning—after birds have had a chance to forage and leave scent for the dogs—and hunting perhaps until midafternoon.

Someday I may hunt like that but for now I'm a ranger, used to covering 10 miles or more in a long hunting day. I travel as lightly as possible because every ounce I carry adds up. I wear a lightweight shooting cap, 25-ounce nylon-faced field pants, a long-sleeve flannel shirt, and a hunting vest with game pocket and shell holders (if they have protective flaps to keep the underbrush from ripping out my shells). For boots, I like the combination rubber sole and leather top in a lightweight model that weighs under three pounds for the pair. One pair of wool socks is all I wear.

If the weather is cold, I'll add lightweight fishnet underwear, another pair of wool socks, possibly a hunting jacket and left-handed glove, preferring to keep my shooting hand free. I remove the wallet and any coins from my pants pockets, replacing them with handkerchief, compass, dog whistle, and leash.

I hunt with gun halfway up, trigger finger lying along the guard, thumb on the safety. I try to put my boots down on solid, level ground, not resting on some wind-blown tree that is sure to offset my balance. I've long figured that grouse have the upper hand when I'm hunting their home range. They know about me and my setter long before we (or at least I) do. So if I hope to avoid discrediting myself, I have to be ready. It seems that the precise moment you let down your guard—to pick a burr or tie a shoe—grouse will thunder up and away.

Much has been written about proper grouse guns and loads. The rule is simple: use what works best under the conditions in which you hunt. This is almost always going to be light loads in small size shot and improved-cylinder shotguns. I've found that No. 7½, 8, or 9 shot in skeet loads pattern best in the lightweight over/under 20-gauge that I prefer for grouse. The top barrel is improved cylinder; the bottom tube is modified. A 40-yard shot is the maximum, but in actuality most shots average 20 yards or less.

December hunters might want to stoke up with more powerful shells, say No. 6 shot in a field load. Then, nervous birds flush farther away and may require the heavier load thrown from a tightly choked barrel to bring down.

Snow and cold weather, along with a shrinking dining table, tend to cluster grouse, sometimes in bunches of a dozen or so. Late in the year the last of the three seasons, you may spend hours walking and never see another concentration—then, suddenly, the roar of wings from a half-dozen birds that you hear but never see.

The best place to find December grouse is in what I call "green stuff," pockets of evergreen cover such as cedar or spruce swamps, pine plantations, and the like. Find green stuff that abuts to mature aspen or birch clumps and you will probably find grouse. Why? The conifers provide cover from weather and predators, and the aspens offer buds—as mentioned, the grouse's main winter fare. On only one occasion have I found December birds in food cover—a combination of sumac and gray dogwood tangles that rode a half-mile slope—without security cover, such as evergreens, nearby. It is likely that these grouse had flown a half-mile from a pine shelterbelt at the back of the farm we were hunting.

When hunting in snow, look for tracks since grouse often walk surprisingly long distances in their search for food. This is especially true on warmer winter days. On bitter cold ones, the birds seem more inclined to fly to feeding areas. I have

A grouse will spend his entire life in some 40 acres of woods if they contain proper food and cover.

41

Male ruffed grouse displaying. Center: Hunter moves in on Brittany spaniel's point in typical sharp-tailed grouse cover.

Richard P. Smith

followed their triple-toed prints (small, scale-like growths of skin between toes help grouse walk on loose snow) for up to a half-mile before wing prints said they took to the air. Sometimes, you will find several oval depressions in the snow where grouse roosted. Usually the depressions will feature green-yellow droppings.

In deep fluff grouse often burrow completely under the insulating snow, which keeps them both warm and safe from predators. When snow is nonexistent or too crusted for their use, we have found them roosting in conifers, a good place to hunt in early morning or late in the day. Peak hunting times are midmorning through late afternoon when grouse can be caught in either food or security habitat or en route to one or the other. Two other excellent times to hunt are just before or just after a winter storm as birds will then be on the move.

BECAUSE of both hunting pressure and the fact that their fall screening cover is mostly gone, grouse in December tend to be edgy. They don't usually hold well for dogs or hunters crackling through quiet woods, and on windy days they are even more skittish. I have learned that my setter helps little during December hunting and instead take my retriever at heel. Some hunters work in tandem to drive grouse from conifer belts. One hunter posts the escape route while the other drives, and then they switch roles at the next stop.

Another point to keep in mind, either during the regular or December season, is to watch for that first snowfall. First snow gives grouse a false sense of security, and they will often sit tightly like fall flight woodcock, offering excellent opportunities for nose-sticking work from your dog.

Because grouse left by December are true survivalists (biologists estimate that during the fall shuffle, which coincides with the hunting season, about one percent per day are lost), some observers think that winter hunting should be eliminated. They argue that by late in the year the males at least have established breeding territories. Killing a December grouse, they say, leaves a void that won't be filled for at least another year. They also claim that December hunters are determined, woods-wise sportsmen who probably take more birds than many realize. The DNR, currently assessing hunter kill in December, has no plans, in the immediate future at least, to scrap the special season.

Although the cyclical ruffed grouse is presently down somewhat, Michigan still produces large numbers that attract the attention of both state and nonresident hunters.

SHARP-TAILED GROUSE

Small numbers of sharp-tailed grouse probably always lived around bogs and marsh regions throughout Michigan. But it was not until loggers cleared vast areas of the Upper Peninsula of virgin timber and then forest fires roared through the leftover brush and debris that the land suddenly provided good habitat—sand prairie vegetation expanded from the small savanna openings of oak and pine—for these birds of the western prairies.

The earliest official report of a sharpie in the U.P. occurred in 1914 from Ewen in Ontonogon County.

That is because sharptails, along with prairie chickens, were expanding rapidly from Wisconsin into the newly created habitat. By the early 20s they were found in most of Gogebic, Iron, Ontonagon, and Keweenaw counties.

By 1942, prairie chickens also occurred throughout the U.P. Major trapping programs in the 30s by the Department of Conservation (now the DNR) helped them expand, and by 1952 they were most numerous in the eastern end.

In order to survive, both chickens and sharpies require huge areas (or many smaller areas linked together) of open prairie land. Effective fire protection, the failure of marginal farms, natural succession of plants that culminate in a mature climax forest, and deliberate planting programs to fill in openings have combined to squeeze the birds into smaller and smaller pieces of habitat. Wisconsin lost its prairie chicken population through reforestation of prairie lands. Michigan was soon to follow, with its last chicken-hunting season occurring in 1955. As mentioned, these birds are now extinct in Michigan.

As chicken habitat dwindled, so did sharp-tailed grouse habitat. The season on sharpies was closed for a couple years in the mid-70s and is open once again in a few eastern U.P. counties, thanks to some efforts at habitat improvement there. Remnant flocks still exist throughout much of the western U.P., but numbers are apparently too low to warrant hunting. Sharptails are also found on state-forest land on Drummond Island, which contains true prairie areas on limestone soils that have never grown trees since the last glacial period 8,000 to 12,000 years ago. However, Drummond Island birds are currently protected.

Successful hunting of sharptails requires a good pointing dog that ranges wide, has a good nose, and is staunch. Hunters will generally walk several miles to flush a flock (sharpies usually band together in fall). Since the birds can easily detect danger approaching through the short prairie grass, they often flush at 40 yards or farther. Full-choke shotguns loaded with No. 4 or 5 shot are required to bring them down.

FOR good hunting areas, refer to the following counties elsewhere in this book: Chippewa, Alger, Luce, Schoolcraft, and Delta. Large blocks of open, prairie-like land, surrounded by aspen or birch, are good places to seek them. Sharptails like the leaves of wild strawberries, sheep sorrel, and viburnums, and they devour grasshoppers and other insects as well as many kinds of seeds. Surviving in frigid temperatures in a region where three feet of snow may lie on the level plains is apparently no problem for sharptails. Their strong wings (the flesh is dark, like waterfowl) allow them to fly several miles without rest, and their toes have a fringe of horny growth which acts as snowshoes. And rather than scratch through snow, they eat the buds of willow and birch and their catkins in spring.

The sharp-tailed grouse is a remarkable game bird that offers hunting opportunities for a dedicated few sportsmen who seek this bird of the plains.

It is hoped that both ruffed and sharp-tailed grouse will figure high in Michigan hunters' game bags for years to come.

Woodcock

A woodcock is about as strange looking as a woman wrestler on a skateboard. The whole bird seems to be put together wrong. Insect eyes bug from the top of its head. That scissorlike bill could probably cut paper. And you call those tail feathers? The neighbors' chickens have more rump protection. How could such a goofy-looking bird that weighs a mere six ounces cause a grown man to kick his wife awake as he walks through alder tangles in his sleep?

The kids say, "Ugh, they taste like liver." Even the yellow Labrador, who fetches everything from cow chips to the neighbors' garbage, will wrinkle lips at a woodcock.

Yet Michigan has no other game bird that holds like flypaper for pointing dogs or that when met on its own terms—bamboo-thick jungles of aspen and alder—can humble the best wingshot. What other bird besides ducks and geese waxes strong as the season wanes? Is there another bird whose silent flight and secret comings and goings add more mystique to frost-fired Michigan woods? I don't think so.

Most hunters who chase pheasants and "pats" have bagged the incidental longbill. But learn the ways of woodcock; then hunt them with determination. You too will find yourself pleasantly addicted. And Michigan has some of the nation's finest woodcock hunting.

Like any other sport, woodcock hunting is something you learn through time and experience.

The most important thing to know is that habitat and timing are twin keys to a one-box-of-shells hunt. Most good shooting ground is in or near alder thickets, in cattle-cropped pastures, in abandoned orchards, near marsh edge uplands, or along old fencerows. Damp, rich earth attracts feeding birds that probe for worms in the evening and throughout the night. Resting areas, where woodcock spend daylight hours, may be traditional grouse habitat—aspen cover, witch hazel or hawthorn clumps, gray or red osier dogwood, sumac tangles, and even new conifers. Usually the best cover will resemble a park of young trees, quite open at ground level (get on hands and knees for a look) with just enough canopy protection to give birds a sense of security. Woodcock like to be mobile on the ground, both to escape danger and to scout for earthworms, their favorite food. That is why you'll never find timberdoodles, as they're often called, in grass. Bracken, on the other hand, is okay since they can see through it.

Whitewash streaks that look like a sloppy painter splashed paint from a too-full pail are a dead giveaway that woodcock are available or that they just moved on. Find borings where they drilled for worms and you have a feeding zone for sure. Whitewash splashes alone spell out a brief resting area. If there are no worms, the birds will move on.

You've probably heard it said, as I have, that woodcock are where you find them. To a degree, especially during the October migration, that's true.

Sometimes they are gunned in open fields by pheasant hunters. Sometimes they're found along edge cover a long way from water. A little pocket of cover in the middle of a barren field may hold birds. I have even shot them in leafless sumac tangles crawling up the side of hills and looking like hair on a horse's mane from a distance. A good tip to keep in mind is to hunt the bottomland cover during dry autumns; in wet years work the upland areas. Remember that woodcock want both food and cover, and where you find one bird there will almost always be another.

The best Michigan early-season gunning occurs in young aspen stands that have an understructure of ground cover such as witch hazel. Here is where the birds rest (and likely feed) by day. At night they seek more open areas, such as old pastures and abandoned orchards. Early-season flush rates after the September 15 statewide opener are excellent although birds in the bag may be another matter due to heavy foliage.

When low pressure systems combine with cold fronts, the aspen ground freezes, and that is when the real fun starts. Woodcock begin to stage in the last-to-freeze lowlands. Look for birds in balsam and spruce cover near alders or in areas of beaver activity. Although the longbills' general movement is southerly, there is plenty of east/west drifting as they travel in search of food. High nighttime winds with any kind of southern bent can postpone flights to stack up birds in tremendous concentrations. These conditions produce the 100 flushes per day and the 1,000-bird evening-flight stories we have all heard.

The migrations, up to 200 or even 300 miles nightly, occur over a period of several days or weeks. Young-of-the-year woodcock and females are the first to go, replaced by birds flying in from the north. The males, smaller than adult females, leave last; so if you are still shooting hens, it is a safe bet that flight gunning is not yet over.

Based on harvest figures, best overall shooting occurs from October 1 to 15 in west-central counties of the Upper Peninsula for local birds (there are likely few, if any, flight birds, however, in Dickinson and Iron counties, considered tops for woodcock). Peak hunting in the eastern U.P. for mixed bags of locals and Canadian flight birds occurs roughly during the same period. The northern Lower Peninsula produces the state's highest harvest figures (along with the heaviest gunning pressure) with peak hunting from October 8 to 21 most years. The best southern Michigan hunting comes during October 16 to 31.

If I had to mark the calendar early for a planned week's hunt, here is how I would do it: western U.P., October 3 to 10. Eastern U.P., October 5 to 12. Northern Lower Michigan, October 10 to 17. Southern Michigan, October 22 to 29. I base these conclusions on research, interviews with several Michigan DNR wildlife biologists (also avid woodcock hunters), and my own experiences.

The calendar, however, is far from absolute.

George Richey of Honor retrieves Benzie County woodcock. Facing page: The whole bird seems to be put together wrong.

Eldon Huggler and his grandson Brian examine Drummond Island woodcock. Below: Michigan woodcock limit of five longbills shot in Dickinson County.

Where I live in southeastern Michigan, the best local hunting occurred on October 29, 23, 27, 18, and 21 during each of the past five years that I have kept records. You cannot pin down woodcock movements with absolute precision year after year.

DURING a recent fall, for example, a friend and I shot two five-bird limits of what I believe were local birds in Roscommon County on October 13. On October 16, my wife and I, finding these same covers empty, drove 150 miles to the eastern U.P. Here we enjoyed our best day of the season — 35 productive points for our young setter. Yet the weekend before another friend with a good dog flushed only one timberdoodle in this same cover.

It was not coincidence that my wife and I found plenty of flight birds. After all, they were two weeks late. First freezes of that mild fall occurred during the nights of October 14 and 15, and a northerly wind had moved the birds south. We found them in lowland covers of mixed balsam and juniper and on dry humps in wet, red-willow tangles.

Therefore, I watch the calendar as critically as a chef checks the oven timer, yet, as we have seen, a date on the wall is not the end-all for deciding when to hunt Michigan's most mysterious game bird. Luckily, though, the forces that move woodcock are understood somewhat and even reasonably predictable.

Woodcock remain in an area as long as earthworms and other invertebrates rich in protein are availble. In order to put on precious flight fat, they eat huge amounts, cleaning out worm-rich areas quickly. A dry fall will put birds on the migration wing early while a wet one causes them to linger.

According to a 10-year harvest average, Michigan's top county is Gladwin, followed by Marquette, Dickinson, and Chippewa counties. These counties are rated fifth through ninth: Presque Isle, Lake, Midland, Newaygo, and Muskegon. Southern Michigan's St. Clair County ranks 10th. Woodcock can be found and hunted in every county. Numbers killed statewide for each of the past five years varied from 251,400 to 321,800, a surprisingly consistent harvest. Upper Peninsula and southern Michigan hunters shoot about 25 percent each of the total bag, while hunters in the northern Lower Peninsula pocket the other half.

Where woodcock were found last year, they will probably appear agin, give or take a few days. Woodcock habitat other than aspen fortunately changes little from year to year. No one harvests alder commercially, and such lowlands are usually marginal for agriculture or other development. Studies do show, however, that soil in really mature alder groves can become too acid for earthworms.

A friend and fellow addict of woodcock hunting once researched Michigan longbills as part of his graduate work in biology. He found that flight birds traveled tail winds along river valleys, particularly on starlit nights. East/west drifting, depending on the wind, was common along streams that flowed into larger south-running rivers. He used topographic maps to locate the junctures of east- and west-flowing streams with north/south rivers. Paying attention to wind and weather predictions has helped him to consistently good hunting in nearby covers.

I hunt woodcock throughout the state every chance I get. In addition to using my friend's theory with success, I have found that the flight birds apparently follow roads and highways which, from above, may well look like rivers to them in the dark. At any rate, I believe it is more than mere coincidence that some of my favorite covers are small aspen stands adjacent to roadways that may be miles from running water.

I remember a time back in high school when a buddy, David Pringle, who now lives in Cleveland, and I drove to his grandmother's house on Sand Lake in Iosco County. We had planned a weekend of grouse hunting and got started early Saturday morning. We shot a bird or two from conifer stands along the East Branch Au Gres River near National City. Then my partner disappeared into, of all places, a large sumac stand that topped a long slope and ran halfway down it toward the river.

I heard him fire once, then again, but no grouse came out. "Did you get him?" I hollered.

No answer but his gun went off again.

"Well, what are you shooting at?" I demanded.

Dave's double barrel sounded again.

"Get up here!" he commanded. "This place is full of woodcock and I can't hit 'em. Bring me some more shells!"

We shot that sumac stand from end to end and then started over. If I remember right, we ended up with six birds—four for Dave (on my shells) and two for me. That's flight woodcock shooting at its best.

Plenty has been written about proper woodcock guns and loads. Most hunters I know prefer twin barrels with the top or right-hand tube bored improved cylinder and the second barrel modified. Some use the lightest loads they can get—size 8 or 9—whereas others like size 7½, claiming they give a little more punch for knocking down grouse.

Yes, perhaps only the jacksnipe, a look-alike cousin of the marshes, is as strange looking as the woodcock. But few Michigan game birds, including the snipe, are as enjoyable to pursue. I have two English setters that would agree if they could only tell you.

A good dog makes for fun when hunting woodcock. This is a yellow Labrador retriever.

Pheasants

IF you haven't hunted Michigan pheasants lately, you're in for a surprise. The ball game has changed, mostly in favor of the pheasants. These colorful, exciting game birds are survival experts. They run, they hide, they flush early and low. They know all the hiding places on their home range, and they develop escape routes to elude hunters and dogs.

That does not mean they can't be hunted successfully, but the day when you could step into the backyard orchard and bust a two-rooster limit with or without a dog is long gone. And it likely won't return again.

The rare pheasant hunter who bags eight cocks (season limit) today holds as much respect in my eye as a guy taking a bear with a bow. Luck plays little part in the arsenal of the modern-day pheasant hunter. Hunting skills are required to put birds in the game bag day after day.

And scarcity of ringnecks is not the only reason. Pheasants today are the offspring of birds who learned how to thrive in a world of reduced habitat, predator harassment, and hunting pressure. Biologists call it the process of natural selection—the dumb birds get knocked off early—but what it means is that today's pheasant is no dummy. He has learned to run instead of fly, hide instead of flush, and skulk away instead of keeping his head up like a periscope. Fine-tuned hunting skills are required to bag him.

You must begin by sizing up the habitat you intend to work and you must hunt deliberately and hard. If I were hunting without a dog (and in the case of Michigan pheasants that isn't likely), I'd limit myself to strip cover, such as brushy fencerows often found along the flat, Thumb-area farms. Or I'd ambush birds as they crossed from roosting areas into crop fields to feed in early morning and back again at night. Sometimes roosters will crow at dawn, giving a clue to their whereabouts and helping a dogless hunter set up an ambush.

I've also shot pheasants without a dog just before dusk when they come sailing into weed stubble or cattail marshes to roost. But a good dog is so much more fun and efficient.

Sizing up cover is as important as remembering to sign your 1040 for a refund due. It involves finding pockets of untilled land—weed patches, river bottoms, railroad rights-of-way, brushchoked fencerows, thickets of dogwood and other shrubs, marsh areas, young timber with an understory, and abandoned crop fields. Once you find cover that looks birdy, figure out how best to hunt it.

That involves thinking like a pheasant. Where would you go if pressured when you know a flush means certain death? I like to play the game of deciding where a ringneck will burst from cover, and I'm right often enough to make it interesting. Successful hunting also means figuring out the best way to tackle the cover so that it is worked thoroughly.

One or two hunters can blanket a big weed field pretty well by zig-zagging in a drive to the corners, always trying to move birds into bottlenecks created by roads and open fields. A large group can still use the old-fashioned drive tactic with success if they walk slowly and keep in a loose horseshoe shape. Running birds that try to slip out the sides sometimes can be flushed by deliberate hunters who stop and go and zig-zag now and then as they move the drive along. Running pheasants passed over by the eager dogs will often turn back into the drive for a close flush.

One trick I've used in Michigan since hunting elsewhere in the Midwest is to post and block escape routes. Posting means spotting a hunter or two in the bottleneck areas you hope to create by the drive. Blocking involves placing hunters along the perimeter of cover to keep turning birds in until they reach the bottleneck.

You can post and block strip cover, small marshes, fencerows, and uncut crop fields such as corn. Two hunters working toward each other with an eye to safety can do surprisingly well. The idea is to pinch birds and pinch them hard, giving no option except to take to the air.

Fast hunters that push their dogs create sloppy and careless work. How well I learned this lesson years ago in the former pheasant-rich Thumb region. Our group of high schoolers fast-drove a long cornfield without result. Crossing an adjacent sugar beet field with our dogs, we took a break under some shade trees. Shortly, another hunter began to push through the beets with a slow methodical pace. His dog, a border collie, of all breeds, seemed to snoop under every green-leafed plant. The man shot a two-rooster limit, apparently skulkers that had sidestepped from the corn as we dashed through it.

Gary Irish of Flint is a slow, methodical pheasant hunter, but that is not necessarily his choice. A crippling back injury forces Gary to poke along while one or more of his Chesapeake Bay retrievers snoops through every foot of cover. It is not unusual for this determined hunter to bag eight cock birds in a season, but he will be the last one to tell you that it is easy.

Irish is a good example to illustrate two keys to the pheasant hunting success formula—find a pocket of birds and then hunt them slowly and deliberately. The time to hunt pheasants fast is when squeezing them into flight or when moving up on a bird dog. Hunters who race through fields otherwise to beat the next guy to the end are going to end up with short breath and nothing else. Cagey roosters just step out of their way.

It also pays to hunt quietly. Pheasants are exceptionally keen of hearing and have no problem detecting slammed car doors, loud talking, dog whistles, and shotguns being loaded. All too often they have proved to me that they usually know when someone is scooting down a field edge to post the other end. If you have ever experienced roosters flush twice out of range, double back on both dogs and hunters, or just seemingly disappear into the scantiest of cover, you can bet they have used their

Author retrieves ringneck he shot along Thumb-area fencerow. Facing page: Michigan pheasant hunters occasionally are treated to early snow, and such conditions tend to concentrate birds in heavy cover.

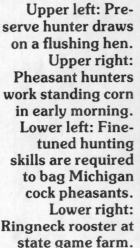

Upper left: Preserve hunter draws on a flushing hen. Upper right: Pheasant hunters work standing corn in early morning. Lower left: Fine-tuned hunting skills are required to bag Michigan cock pheasants. Lower right: Ringneck rooster at state game farm.

ears to escape being another statistic on someone's dinner table.

Pheasant biologists say the birds fare best when 80 percent of their environment is cultivated land. Unfortunately, most of that 80 percent does not hold birds, at least not for long. When corn and other grain crops are in the elevator, most farmers disk or chisel-plow burned-out stalks into the ground, thus creating a sterile environment for pheasants. I have yet to shoot a rooster from a chisel-plowed field.

ANOTHER key is trying to figure when pheasants will use certain covers, and then knowing how to hunt them effectively. Before season a cock bird will typically walk from grass-sloped roosting grounds to breakfast in a field of corn, beans, or late-season oats. When his crop fills by midmorning, he'll lounge in the sun or take dust baths along field edges. Security cover such as thick weeds, cattails, or woods will likely be nearby. Late afternoon finds him back at the dinner table. About sundown or a little later he will fly or walk to his roosting grounds.

If you know that pheasants frequent an area, you can use the above schedule to hunt them on opening day. Probably 50 percent of the season pressure occurs then, and fully 90 percent will come during the first three days. Pressured birds will change feeding schedules quickly, but I have noticed that during the second half of the season, when no one bothers them, they usually return to their preseason timetables.

It makes sense to hunt pheasants where your preseason scouting has shown them to be (another very important part of the success formula). And if they aren't in the immediate area, then head for the toughest, nastiest cover you can find. Pheasants will fly miles if necessary, to find protective cover. I'm talking about the kind of cover that could swallow a Roman legion. Riverbottom tangles, island jungles, cattail marshes thicker than woven basket—these are the covers to hunt when birds get cagey.

Those guys that bag eight birds don't all wear blue jeans and lightweight leather boots. Not at all. Some slap on brush-busting trousers, canvas hunting coats, and even hip boots to meet elusive ringnecks on their own terms. The sport then takes on the proportions of guerilla warfare and is a far cry from the leisurely hunting on some shirtsleeve afternoon in an alfalfa field. A good dog is a must.

The good pheasant hunters I know understand habitat and work at finding it. One friend is constantly scouting new places to hunt. He talks to UPS drivers, Michigan Milk Producers Association drivers, rural mail carriers, and anyone else with a driving beat in the country. Furthermore, he drives different routes to and from his job in the city. In short, he has done his homework long before the October 20 opener.

A good tip is to stop into a DNR field or district office and ask the wildlife biologist or a conservation officer if he has seen pheasant concentrations in his travels. Although reluctant to broadcast pheasant hot spots for publication, DNR personnel are usually helpful about guiding individuals or small hunting parties.

Hunter checks spurs on young rooster.

I have used county maps that denote state land to find my way into good pheasant hunting, and they are also useful for pinpointing Public Access Stamp Program leased lands. County maps cost a quarter each from DNR offices, or you can get all 83 in a special book put out by the Michigan United Conservation Clubs (refer to the beginning of this book for further information).

PHEASANT populations are currently the lowest on record since soon after the birds were first introduced near Holland in 1895. Million-ringneck harvest years in the mid-40s and again in the 50s have shrunk to a paltry 200,000 or less. The reasons are varied and complex but generally boil down to habitat loss. The DNR has finally launched its Southern Michigan Habitat Program, which (among other goals) hopes to put 700,000 roosters in hunters' coats and give them access to 400,000 acres of hunting land in the 35 southern counties.

That would be great, but it is going to take some doing.

Currently, birds have slipped badly and there seems to be little encouragement for immediate improvement. Best opportunities at this writing include the Thumb region of southern Huron, western Sanilac, southeastern Tuscola, northern Lapeer and northern St. Clair counties. Shiawassee and Livingston counties are still comparatively good as are a few key, southeastern counties: northern Hillsdale, Eaton, Lenawee, and Macomb. Barry and Berrien counties are best bets in southwestern Michigan. And there are still isolated pockets of pheasants (refer to the separate counties in this book) throughout southern Michigan, but hunters will have to use the above-described tactics to find them.

For all its good intentions, the 10-year put-take pheasant hunting program is no more, phased out due to high costs and declining hunter interest. In its stead and for the next couple of years (until the DNR habitat improvement programs take hold) look for special pheasant releases on some three dozen southern Michigan state game and recreation areas (all included separately in this book). Some of these releases will occur during the regular three-week pheasant hunting season. Others, at least in the immediate future, will take place from mid-September until mid-October.

In the past I used a 12-gauge, full-choke pump stoked with magnum 4s or 6s on pheasants. Since hunting these birds in other states where they are more prolific, I have changed my thinking. I now rely on Federal premium field loads in copper-plated No. 4 shot, and I push them through an over/under 20-gauge tubed improved cylinder and modified. By hunting hard and staying on top of the dogs, my friends and I get close-in shots (we pass up those low-percentage chances over 35-40 yards). And we experience few cripples—thanks to good patterns from cock-stopping loads.

Michigan pheasants are a whole new ball game today. They are as wily and challenging as any quarry you are likely to seek. And to my mind they are still worth going after.

Turkeys

ANYONE planning to hunt Michigan's wild turkeys should know he or she is up against what might well be the state's smartest, most challenging game creature. Some say gobblers' wits surpass those of bear and deer. Could be. I have tagged Michigan deer and a bear but have yet to seal my first tom turkey after four springs in the woods. Fortunately, there were morel mushrooms and brook trout to bring home from those luckless hunts. The more I seek these magnificent birds, at one time extinct in Michigan for the better part of a hundred years, the more I respect their savvy.

Here is a quarry which sees many times better than your corrected 20/20 vision. He hears an acorn hit the ground with the impact that you detect bowling ball strikes, and he is more suspicious by nature than Sherlock Holmes. He often moves about with a harem of up to 15 hens, giving him all the security of a hundred-eyed Argus. After "up periscoping" out of thin air, an old tom has the uncanny ability of slipping away while you count the trees he magically keeps between you and him. If spooked, he can spring at 20 miles an hour with ground-gobbling strides, and he has been clocked in level flight at speeds exceeding 50 mph—mallard velocity.

It is not my point to discourage anyone from going gobbler hunting. But if, like me, you want to experience one of hunting's greatest thrills—the satisfying weight of a 20-pound tom slung over your shoulder for the first time—it darn well pays to study up on turkeys before you step into the woods after them. You are going to need to know some things about wild-turkey habitat and habits as well as hunting and calling techniques. And, frankly, you won't learn it all from reading about it. The best experience is hands-on, and that you can do through preseason scouting and plenty of practice with a good call.

And as is true with most types of hunting, the success key is to become woods-wise.

Good woodsmanship begins with finding turkey terrain. Look for a balanced mixture of topography—some rolling ridges containing hardwoods, lowlands with conifers, a few fields bordered by open woods. Water systems such as seeps, bogs, and river bottomlands near openings with mature woods nearby offer choice habitat. Hunting oak woods along slopes tapering to lowlands is ideal during the spring Michigan season. Jack-pine woods are also good if they are free of heavy undergrowth. In fact, turkeys inhabit mature stands of most types of trees, so long as they have an open, parklike appearance and are free of underbrush. There are two reasons. First, turkeys rely upon their keen eyesight to elude coyotes, bobcats, and human hunters and are at a decided disadvantage in brush. Second, mature or nearly mature hardwoods produce mast, usually at the head of a long list of preferred foods.

Hens like to nest in these open woods from April through June at the bases of big trees such as beeches or oaks. Non-nesting hens and toms will often seek for their nightly roost a pine tree in a hardwood stand or a hardwood tree in a grove of pines. Maybe they select the odd tree because it aids their ability to see everything around them.

In the spring turkeys like to move slowly through such open woods. For this reason hunters must be well concealed and keep all movement to a minimum. Whether you set up a blind or take your stand at the base of a wide tree to break up your outline (then taking care to conceal minor movements with a few leafy branches stuck in the ground before you), you should be able to see 30 yards or better. A wise, old tom often won't come even that close, no matter how seductive you sound with a call. It doesn't hurt to be close to a field either as hens often nest near these insect-rich grounds, and gobblers will be in the area too, looking for yet another receptive female.

Turkeys eat a tremendous variety of foods, and the wise hunter will learn to identify as many types as possible. Of over 500 West Virginia turkey stomachs examined, researchers found 354 species of plants and 313 species of animals. Northern Michigan birds in spring are usually coming off poor-quality winter fare (winter mortality can run very high some years). In spring they scratch for protein among dead leaves. These include acorns and other mast, insects, and emerging green vegetation. They peck at unfurling buds and catkins from both the ground and while sitting in trees. As mentioned, hens with poults often frequent grassy fields, not far from escape cover. Here they seek weed seeds, grasshoppers, and other insects.

Good hunters learn to look for certain telltale turkey clues. V-shaped scratchings in leaves, for example, tell which direction (straight from the junction of the V) turkeys are heading as the adult birds search for food. White-green turkey droppings are another sign. Hens leave popcorn-sized round scat, whereas toms produce J-hooked droppings about an inch long.

Another way to tell the sexes apart from the sign they leave is the size of prints. If the distance from the back toe to the center front toe is longer than three-and-a-half inches, then a gobbler left the print. Even a yearling tom will weigh a dozen pounds and when fully mature with a six-inch beard will weigh considerably more than an adult hen.

Dusting bowls the size of dishpans (don't confuse them with the smaller depressions made by ruffed grouse) in sandy locations are further evidence of turkeys using an area. Breast feathers found here and elsewhere should be closely examined. If the tips are black, they were probably left by a tom. The breast feathers of hens are buff- or brown-tipped.

Preseason scouting to find likely habitat and then some detailed sleuthing to turn up examples of turkey use will pay big dividends during your hunt. Unless heavily pressured by weather or hunting conditions, turkeys pretty much follow a circuit of sorts and will show up in the same woods every few

Two keys to putting a tom over your shoulder are knowing turkey habits and habitat and learning to master calling tactics.

Turkey decoys (above) are legal in Michigan—and effective. Right: Flocks throughout Michigan presently total about 15,000 birds.

days. Hens do most of the wandering, especially if already part of a gobbler's harem. The big, fan-tailed toms move along with the flock, adding new breeders at every opportunity. On the other hand, gobblers without hens often seem to hang out together.

The best thing hunters have going for them during a spring hunt is the turkeys' mating season.

Normally the males gobble frequently during the early season, slack off in midseason, and then increase during the late season as fewer hens become available.

Weather plays a tremendous factor in the success or lack of it among Michigan spring turkey hunters. Normally by the mid- to late-April opener, birds are dispersed from wintering areas near stable food sources, such as farms. But not always. And during those four years of hunting, my partner and I have experienced only one season when turkeys were actively gobbling. Cold periods of wet or snowy weather can shut down their activities faster than a police raid on a blind pig. During inclement weather, turkeys sometimes will stay in the roost for a couple days.

AT other times they tend to flit through woods silently, scratching out quick meals and then returning to roost. Food availability is another factor that determines turkey movements. Localized failures of the acorn crop the previous spring, for example, will often disperse turkeys to new areas.

There are several successful ways to hunt them, none of which is very easy. One involves knowing the turkeys' home range as thoroughly as you might know your back yard. Turkeys have regular travel lines and places where they cross back and forth from fields and woods. As mentioned, they often forage in a loose circle and can be expected to return at some point. Topo maps available from the Michigan United Conservation Clubs (see the beginning of this book) are a big help toward gaining a familiarity with the area you plan to hunt.

Some hunters even wait near roosting sites, which they sometimes locate by walking woods late in the day and hooting like an owl or cawing with a crow call in hopes of getting a gobbler to respond and thus give up his whereabouts. The game plan involves returning the next morning to talk the tom into shooting range or coming back late in the afternoon (daily hunting closure has been 4 p.m.; check a current "Wild Turkey Gobbler Season" guide for changes) in hopes that the gobbler will roost early.

Another tactic is still-hunting, which involves stealthily creeping through woods until the hunter spots a flock before its sharp-eyed members see him. To still-hunt successfully, hunters must learn to move slowly and take care lest they snap twigs and rustle leaves, sounds that are sure to spook turkeys. They also must take advantage of the terrain, slipping through trees and keeping behind knolls and ridges. When you hear or see birds, take a stand and try calling the gobbler to you or try to get a fix on their direction and then head them off at a likely ambush site.

But calling is the ultimate in turkey hunting, and because I have not mastered these skills, I continue to go without tagging that first bird. Some hunters seem to have an innate ability to make love-sick hen

turkey music on homemade and manufactured calls. I tend to sound like an off-key yodeler at a Swiss Family Robinson reunion.

I wish I had learned even basic calling skills before my first hunt a few years ago. It was about 11 o'clock on the final morning of my partner's and my four-day special hunt. Joe was snoring away in a corner of our deer-hunting blind. He could afford to snooze, having already bagged a short-bearded jake (yearling tom) the previous morning. The warm, late-April sun kept causing me to nod off myself. A whitetail doe, her belly distended with one or more fawns, ambled by. With less than an hour left in our season, it didn't appear as though I would fill my turkey tag. Then a loud burst of gobbling came from just over a slope 100 yards away. Joe and I were instantly awake.

"Did you hear that?" he whispered, his eyes wide with excitement.

"I sure did. It came from over that knoll."

By now Joe had his box call out and was making the seductive yelps of a hen turkey in love. The gobbler answered. Then, stupidly, as I know now, I sounded off with a gigantic gobble, amplified, no doubt, by the tin roof of our blind. The original tom answered, as did a second gobbler!

In a few minutes a hen and then another materialized—the way turkeys so mysteriously do—on the ridge 100 yards away. They appeared to be in no hurry, tiptoeing through the woods, scratching in the leaves, and craning their long necks at intervals.

Every time the toms would gobble, we'd sound off on our calls. Eventually they too showed on the ridge. The boss gobbler sported a ruler-length beard and spread his fan tail in an impressive semi-circle, his red wattles gleaming like a splash of red paint. The other tom was considerably smaller with what looked like a five- or six-inch beard. They refused to come closer than 100 yards and even though our calling didn't seem to alarm them, they didn't break the world record 100-meter dash heading our way either.

I have since learned that to expect a gobbler who is already surrounded with a harem to come running would be contrary behavior. Hens normally go to the males, and so calling must be as seductive as possible.

The "gobble" itself is probably the most overrated call to use in spring woods. It is best reserved for the evening before a hunt when you are trying to locate a roosting tom. The idea is to walk through woods and gobble every five minutes or so. A response is what some veteran hunters call the defiant call. As mentioned earlier, a crow call, owl call or other loud, startling noise, such as a car door slamming, will often produce a defiant response from a gobbler. If you get an answer, mentally mark the location and return next morning in the dark. At first light give a quiet yelp or two to let the tom know a hen is in the area, but try to get the bird out of the tree before yelping away. Otherwise, you'll never get him down.

ONCE your gobbler is on the ground, you can turn on the charm with your call. Sometimes a bird will sound off all the way to your stand; other times he will come in silently. As a general rule, limit your yelps to three or four, interspersed with delays of a minute or more and then sweet-talk him into range with tantalizing softer notes. Remember that a single false note will send him packing. Good advice is to wait a half hour before leaving the area since all too often disappointed hunters have stood up to stretch, only to startle an incoming tom.

Good advice for a beginning hunter is to attend a turkey-hunting workshop (every spring several are held throughout the state), listen to a master caller give a demonstration, or pick up a good calling record.

Watching turkeys at a farm can help hunters to understand their intricate language of clucks, purrs, and gobbles. Clucks are little peeping noises that the birds use to let each other know where they are. Yelps are made by love-sick hens; purrs by feeding birds that are content. The assembly call is a series of quick yelps that denotes urgency.

For beginners, box and slate calls are probably the easiest to master, but they have the disadvantage of requiring movement on the hunter's part to operate. The diaphragm call, a half-moon shaped piece of metal covered with leather or vinyl and thin strip of latex rubber, fits nicely in the mouth and frees up both hands. For hunters with dentures, though, they

are tough to master. Innovative hunters can also make their own calls from pill or film canisters, turkey wing bones, even drinking straws.

Whatever call you choose, practice as though you planned to try out for the New York Philharmonic Symphony and try to learn all the nuances of turkey talk. Remember that to attract a harem-surrounded gobbler, you'll have to coax the hens to first come your way. And that is becoming harder to do, some veterans tell me, because the more Michigan turkeys are hunted, the smarter they are becoming.

If using a blind, be sure it blends into the environment and try to set it up a few days before the hunting season so that birds will become used to seeing it. Some sportsmen use two sets of camouflage clothes, brown and green, depending upon dominant color in the woods. It is also a good idea to carry a headnet and wear gloves or apply camo creams to mask the shine on skin. Remember to remove wristwatches and rings, as glint from the sun will send a turkey running. Some hunters even dull shotgun barrels or cover them with camo tape. Once in your blind or sitting at the base of a big tree, keep knees up to help hide face and movements and have your weapon ready.

Although decoys are presently legal, hunters should check the rules before trying them since there has been some effort to prohibit their use. As with baiting (also legal at this writing), the issue is one of controversy involving sportsmanship and ethics. Critics of decoys say they also add an element of danger to the sport, pointing out that although Michigan has thus far suffered no shooting accidents, other states have and it is only a matter of time here.

Wild turkeys were once abundant south of a line slanting from Saginaw Bay to Muskegon until about a hundred years ago. Habitat changes due to lumbering and farming, plus exploitation by people, forced their extinction. In 1954 the Department of Conservation (now the DNR) introduced 50 Pennsylvania birds at the Allegan State Game Area (*which see*). They are still found there in huntable numbers as well as in Menominee County in the Upper Peninsula and various places throughout the northern Lower Peninsula. Trap and transfer programs by the DNR are helping spread turkeys throughout transitional counties between northern forests and southern agricultural areas. Wild birds from Iowa, Pennsylvania, and Missouri also have recently been released at a dozen downstate public game and recreation areas. Presently, flocks throughout Michigan total about 15,000 birds with some 20,000 to 24,000 hunters turning out each spring for special seasons by areas. They bag about 1,800 birds for a success ratio of seven to 10 percent.

Hunters must use shotguns (no buckshot or slugs) or bows. A 12- or 10-gauge, full-choke scattergun, stoked with BBs or No. 2 shot, is solid firepower. Aim for the head if using a shotgun and for the body area if using a bow. And shoot twice as these birds can take a pounding and still get up and run off.

Just as you don't find many people simply walking into the woods and bagging a 12-point buck, so too there are few turkey hunters who kill their birds purely from luck (how well I know). Two keys to putting a tom over your shoulder are knowing turkey habits and habitat and learning to master calling tactics.

And you likely won't do that in a single season. Nor in four seasons, for that matter.

Ducks

MICHIGAN'S 55,000 to 60,000 duck hunters get what amounts to two seasons. Local birds are usually in good supply and make up most of the harvest in the early season (about 60 percent of which comes in the first two weeks). Over 36,000 miles of streams and 11,000 lakes, plus thousands of beaver floodings, borrow pits, and potholes throughout the state all contribute to bumper crops of locals. These are mostly puddle ducks—mallards, wood ducks, blue-winged teal, and black ducks.

Then, if weather permits, the flight ducks—puddlers and divers alike (blacks, goldeneyes, buffleheads, scaup, and many others)—stop over to provide good hunting from midseason on. Flight-duck hunting is based upon a couple of factors over which hunters have no control One is waterfowl production in the prairie provinces and plains states. The other is weather during the season itself. Winds with a southern bent tend to stack up birds on state waters whereas high northern or northwestern winds often push them through.

Michigan hunters have many opportunities for duck hunting throughout the state. Each of the 83 counties listed in this book includes specific, where-to-go information. In addition, refer to the following seven state waterfowl management areas and two national refuges detailed elsewhere in this book. All but the national refuge at Seney have controlled hunting by daily permit, usually determined by lottery.

- Fish Point Wildlife Area
- Nyanquing Point Wildlife Area
- Allegan State Game Area
- Muskegon County Wastewater Management System
- Pointe Mouillee State Game Area
- St. Clair Flats Wildlife Area
- Shiawassee River State Game Area
- Shiawassee National Wildlife Refuge
- Seney National Wildlife Refuge

In addition, four Upper Peninsula waterfowl management areas (also described elsewhere in this book) that do not operate on the daily lottery system include:

- Munuscong Waterofwl Management Area
- Baraga Plains Waterfowl Management Area
- Au Train Basin Waterfowl Project
- Sturgeon River Slouths Wildlife Area

Because duck hunting regulations are federally authorized and change frequently, hunters should consult a current "Waterfowl Hunting Guide" for details. There are many excellent methods for hunting ducks in Michigan. Here are the more popular ones:

JUMP-SHOOTING IN THE MARSHES

For years, I've been drawn to Saginaw Bay for the same reason the market hunters and Indians went there before me—good duck hunting. In low-water years when there is plenty of marsh, they serve up bumper crops of teal and mallards. When action slows by midday and the only things flying are red-winged blackbirds and insects, we turn to the marshes for jump-shooting fun.

Walking the thick tangle of cattails is tough, hot work. Hunters should strip down to travel as lightly as possible. It helps to be in shape as jump-shooting in the marshes is not for short-winded guys with weak legs.

There's no particular method involved except that we try to work upwind. That way we get closer to ducks, who can't hear as readily, and when they flush we get fast shots, up and into the wind. Some hunters, I've heard, tie tin cans to 100-foot lengths of clothesline to sweep the marsh of waterfowl between them.

We've found that the slapping, splashing sounds of wading hunters kick out sulking ducks, offering quick, open shots from 20 to 40 yards. It's surprising how close you can get to blacks, mallards, and teal by walking them up in the marsh, but you will work for every one you bag.

A few sportsmen also jump-shoot in the marshes for shorebirds. Here is some tremendously underutilized hunting for rails and snipe as early as mid-September and for coots and gallinules a little later.

JUMP-SHOOTING ALONG RIVERS AND STREAMS

I've shot enough ducks while seeking grouse along brush-choked stream banks to know that the sport offers further underutilized opportunity for waterfowlers. Many wood ducks, mallards, blacks, and teal often grow up along Michigan streams. Others seek refuge along such waterways when pressured from lakes or marshes by hunters.

To jump-shoot with success, try quietly stalking with gun at the ready. Shots will likely be fast and at close range. A good bet is to hunt toward a partner, perhaps on the opposite bank since routed ducks often fly up or down the stream.

DUCK HUNTING ON INLAND LAKES

Few waterfowlers give much thought to any of Michigan's 11,000 inland lakes, especially the smaller ones where vacationing cottagers water ski, fish, and swim in summer. Yet certain inland lakes can be gold mines for top duck hunting season after season.

Ducks that visit during the day are usually migrating birds or birds pressured off the nearby lakes or marshes. Where I live near Flint we sometimes see thousands of waterfowl in a single day, string after string of high-flying ducks and geese bending their wings south. Sometimes they can be talked down.

Two conditions help. Hunting pressure is one. For example, a favorite spot is Holloway Reservoir, which gets plenty of visitors from the burned-off marshes at Quanicassee, Fish Point, and Sebewaing, all on Saginaw Bay. Although wary, these birds can be decoyed with life-like spreads of decoys and artful calling.

As mentioned, the other condition that causes flight birds to stop at inland lakes is the weather. All

Layout hunting on Houghton Lake. Facing page: Mallards are Michigan's most abundant duck.

Michigan DNR

Waterfowlers who know their ducks can take low-point birds like these drake mallards (25 points) and let high-point birds go. Center: Decoys are often rigged in strings of a dozen each with a one-pound lead anchor on each end, a practice that speeds setting out and picking up. Far right: Layout hunters zero in on incoming divers on Houghton Lake.

too often big migrating masses of ducks and geese, hell-bent toward southern climes, bypass our state altogether. But choose a day with a south, southeast, or even a southwest wind, which the migrants have to buck, and they'll set down to wait for a better day. Rain will ground ducks too.

Small lakes only 50 or 100 acres in size, ringed with cottages and docks, often look as if they wouldn't interest a coot, but in spring these little lakes are dotted with northern migrants. They can be loaded in the fall as well.

A well-built blind that blends into the cover from which it was made is important. Streaking faces with camouflage paint is also a good idea. As with any type of waterfowl hunting, you must remain well hidden until the birds are within range.

Good calling is another key. Many times ducks need to be coaxed back into range. Remember that these are often wary, shotover birds, reluctant to drop into small lakes where homes, cars, and barking dogs don't offer much security.

Proper decoy setup goes a long way toward birds in the blind. One savvy hunter I know puts out a big spread—50 to 100 blocks—always taking care to create pockets for incoming birds to land. He includes goose decoys as initial attractors but never mixes them in with duck stools, which often begin with a lead string and end with a solid cluster, leaving an inside pocket 30 yards from the blind. This hunter is as fussy with his decoy placement as a grandmother is with her needlepoint. Wind direction determines how he arranges his spreads, and he'll often change formations in midday if the wind shifts.

If you ask a Michigan waterfowler to consider hunting the small inland lakes, he'll probably cite access problems and touchy residents as reasons why he doesn't. He figures homeowners are bound to complain about Sunday morning gunfire, safety concerns, and the slaughter of half-tame birds that are often hand-fed. These are often hurdles, to be sure, but certainly not insurmountable ones.

Many of Michigan's inland lakes have public-access sites, and although that in itself doesn't guarantee a place to hunt (Michigan law states that whoever owns the land, including the lake bottoms, retains hunting rights), they at least can put you on the water. A postcard to the DNR, Information Services Center, Box 30028, Lansing, Mich. 48909, will get you a free copy of ''Michigan's Water Access Sites.''

Accommodating homeowners would probably

appreciate a cleaned Canada goose for Thanksgiving, a face cord of firewood about Christmas time, or perhaps the use of the blind on off-hunting days.

Another tip is to check out private lakes, especially in southern Michigan. Many times landowners rent boats to summer bass and bluegill anglers. Before boats are mothballed for winter, duck hunters might be able to rent them. In short, there are inland-lake hunting opportunities for waterfowlers willing to do a little homework.

FLOAT THE RIVERS

The bigger Michigan rivers, like the Grand, St. Joseph, and Kalamazoo, offer some great float hunting. But big-river ducks wise up fast, and that's why hunters should also consider a float on small, out-of-the-way streams.

Fall water levels are usually high, and it's surprising the number of ducks, including the colorful woodies, that the little waterways produce. Small-stream ducks aren't exactly stupid, though. The brush-choked waterways where they grew up are haunted by predators, and the ducks have learned to use their wits to survive.

Wear drab or camouflage clothing to blend in with the autumn landscape. Shiny paddles should be painted a dead-grass green. We also cut branches from downed trees (otherwise you can kill a live tree) to break up the profile of our gliding canoe.

CANOES are light, fast, and easy to handle on the small rivers, such as the Flint, Shiawassee, and Cass, which course near my home. Floating for ducks is a silent sport, interrupted only by bankside wildlife or an occasional bass angler or squirrel hunter. We lie low in our canoe and stay quiet; you never know when ducks will explode in flight. Many times when entering a bend or straight, open section of river, I've stretched tense muscles only to have ducks burst from cover.

Sometimes we carry decoys and set them up in marshy areas, sand bars, or ponds. This is a good technique in early morning or late afternoon when river ducks are on the move. For more details about duck hunting on a river, refer to the chapter entitled ''Float Hunting.''

PUDDLERS OVER DECOYS

A well-placed set of decoys, coupled with good

calling, is probably the most exciting way to take early-season puddle ducks. The number of decoys is much less important than is their placement. A hunter with a half-dozen, lifelike mallard blocks spotted 20 to 40 yards from his blind can expect to draw singles and small bunches of puddlers. If hunting a marsh-fringed pond, spot the dekes in the middle so that ducks coming from any direction will be able to see them.

On wind-whipped days ducks will develop a flight line, usually into the blast. Then we put decoys along the marsh edge where incoming birds have the best chance to see them. If hunting open water, with two dozen or more decoys, a good trick is to make a J-hook pattern—a single file line of bobbing blocks with the top of the J about 50 yards from your blind. Locate the blind just outside the hook and you will have created a pocket for ducks to touch down. The more wary birds will land outside of the range; some will swim into the pocket. A few you may have to write off as college ducks.

Make your spread look lifelike, and you'll begin to shoot ducks over decoys. Some hunters are fussy about the small things. They're usually the ones to limit first. They stain anchor strings a dark green or brown; paint their decoys dull, muted colors rather than bright, glossy tones; weight them so they ride just so; and streak their own faces with dulling grease paints.

BIG-WATER DIVER-DUCK HUNTING

The peak joy in waterfowling, to me, is to hunt the flight ducks fresh down from the North. Although this can sometimes mean big strings of orange-legged mallards and ranging black ducks from Canada, many Michigan waterfowlers look ahead to the arrival of the divers. From late October until season's end they set up big spreads to welcome goldeneyes, buffleheads, mergansers, scaup, scoters, ruddy ducks, and oldsquaws among others.

I've seen bunches of 50 and 100 divers filter from a gray November sky, making queer *chucka, chucka* sounds as they dropped down into Saginaw Bay, Lake St. Clair, and Houghton Lake. One day, years ago, we were hunting a special period for geese after the duck season closed. That day we estimated that 15,000 ducks piled into a mile-long string far out on the bay. Not being able to hunt them did not lessen the excitement of that scene.

The most popular, and probably the most effective, hunting method to use on diving ducks is layout shooting. It's especially fun during the late

fall when big strings of ducks, heretofore unshot over, swarm into Michigan's Great Lakes bays, drowned rivermouths, and big inland lakes. They are usually suckers for a big spread.

Most hunters use up to 100 oversized cork decoys, a huge chore made simple by stringing them together in sets of 12 blocks, all connected with heavy-duty, three-foot strings, swivels, and snaps. One fellow I know anchors each with a one-pound lead weight. When laid out properly, the strings blend together, without tangle, and look just like a feeding raft of divers. He and a partner can pick up all their decoys in 15 minutes and pack and store them away, untangled, in compartments separated by plywood sheets in the pontoon boat they use for a blind. Other hunters rely on a two-boat system. The service boat is used for holding equipment and for transporting hunters to the low-profile layout boat.

These are oblong-shaped and about eight feet wide by 12 feet long. A boat of this size adequately holds two hunters. The boats are painted slate-gray like the big lakes in late fall. Incoming ducks can't spot the prone hunters whose profiles are as low to the water as their decoys. Hunters look down their noses at incoming ducks and when the birds punch feet forward and back-pump wings to brake for a landing, the shooters rise to a sitting position. It's mighty effective on diving ducks.

Many tips and hints help make layout hunting successful. One is to always anchor the layout boat upwind of the decoys since ducks will fly into the wind to land. Another is to spread decoys so that a pocket is left open. Twenty yards from the layout boat is about right because ducks that flare before and after shooting will still be within the magic 40-yard, safe-shooting limit.

Some hunters mix their decoys in with the layout boat and eliminate the pocket altogether. This method may improve pass-shooting chances, but if the ducks are wary, they will invariably set down out of range. For hunters with less than four-dozen decoys, the J-hook or V-shape method of setting decoys will work.

Diving ducks readily decoy, a trait that generations of hunters have used against them. Generally, the larger your spread of decoys, the better shooting you will get, but don't make the mistake of mixing divers and puddlers together, just for the sake of numbers. If you must use puddle-duck decoys, use them as an initial attractor only and keep them away from the layout boat and the diving-duck decoys.

Some friends and I once pooled all our decoys, putting out 105 off a Saginaw Bay cut. With every kind of decoy imaginable, we shot exactly one duck on a low-cloud ceiling, wind-blown day. Other guys were taking hefty limits. I figured that to the ducks, our mismatched collection of decoys must have looked about as real as a cigar-store Indian.

Layout shooting is a legal, modern version of the long-outlawed sinkbox that is particularly well-suited to the Great Lakes. Yet the method will work on any large inland body of water frequented by the divers.

It is one of many surefire methods to hunt Michigan ducks.

During the last year for which records are complete, Michigan hunters shot 391,000 ducks. The best year during recent seasons was a harvest of 488,000 ducks. That figures out to an average of eight or nine ducks per hunter per season.

Geese

IF you shot your first Canada goose 20 or more years ago, most likely you were hunting ducks and the honker was a "bonus" bird. If you have been bagging Canada geese in recent years, you might very well be a goose-hunting specialist, as more and more Michigan waterfowlers are concentrating on these big white-cheeked birds with the five-foot wingspreads. To these hunters, ducks—not geese—are incidental game in the bag.

And if you have never shot a Canada goose...well, you have missed one of hunting's greatest thrills. How well I know—I potted my first honker only recently after some 25 years of waterfowl hunting.

A wave of Canadas dropping to decoys, sable feet kicked out, and rocking left to right on back-pumping wings, can unnerve even the steadiest hunter. Then the big birds look like rudderless kites fluttering to earth. At 20 yards they appear as big as a fleet of Greyhound buses. The first time I saw geese suckering to decoys, I stood with mouth open and forgot to fire my gun. Goose fever. It paralleled the immobility I experienced on another hunt when I saw my first 10-pointer up close. Years would pass before I had another chance at close-up honkers.

Oh, I had pass-shot at plenty of geese, scrambling overhead like jets at an air show, but Canadas are deceptive birds, never as close as they look and appearing to hang in the air like a punted football does momentarily. And I learned that unless you go for head shots, after leading the length of a Lincoln Continental, you won't stop them. The fellow who termed C-130 cargo planes "flying fortresses" could have been a goose hunter.

Like most hunting sports, goose shooting requires specialized skills and equipment. The best hunters know how to call properly, how to conceal themselves, how and where to set up decoys, and they have proper firepower—a goose-hunting shotgun stoked with premium loads. But other than the kind of hoped-for thrill described above, why should someone consider hunting geese in the first place?

The answer is opportunity. According to one DNR estimate, Michigan hunters have now surpassed Wisconsin, with its famed Horicon Marsh and other excellent goose-hunting places, in annual harvest. Geese in Michigan are on the increase for at least three reasons: (1) Canada-bred birds, which contribute probably 90 percent of migrants passing through Michigan, have experienced good nesting seasons in recent years; (2) waterfowl management areas, especially those downstate, both lure and hold the big honkers; and (3) southeastern Michigan has become a hotbed of production for the giant strain of Canada geese.

Michigan hunters now bag close to 60,000 geese each fall. About 75 percent come from Region III (southern Michigan), which puts prime opportunity in the backyards of many sportsmen. About 15 percent of the total harvest occurs in the Upper Peninsula, with the northern Lower Peninsula contributing the other 10 percent. During the most recent season, downstaters averaged 1.6 geese per hunter and spent 7.7 days afield. In the U.P. the figures were 1.5 geese and 6.8 days; in Region II (northern Lower Peninsula), .78 and 5.6, respectively.

The DNR has apparently recognized that geese offer bonus opportunities for Michigan hunters. That is why in recent years the department has pushed for bag-limit and season liberalization. Waterfowl seasons and regulations are established each summer by the Mississippi Flyway Council and then must be approved by the U.S. Fish and Wildlife Service. Although they change annually, the following pattern has formed:

- Goose-kill quotas in state management zones have generally increased or have been eliminated altogether.
- Daily bag has been increased to two birds (one at Allegan, three during the special late season).
- Southeastern Michigan hunters have enjoyed a special 50- to 60-day season on giant Canadas, beginning in mid-December and lasting until mid-February.
- Western U.P. hunters recently received a special September season to take advantage of early-migrating geese.

Nuisance problems from giant Canadas prompted the special southeastern Michigan season that began a few years ago and in all likelihood will continue. Similar problems from too many resident geese have been increasing in southwestern Michigan, and so hunters may look for the special season to be extended here soon. For all the details, consult a current copy of the "Michigan Waterfowl Hunting Guide," available annually from DNR offices and licensing agents in early September.

There are many places in Michigan to hunt geese, with certain waterfowl management areas perhaps the best producers. At some, hunters bag upwards of 4,000 Canadas each fall. For details on best downstate sites, consult the following elsewhere in this book:

- Shiawassee National Wildlife Refuge
- Shiawassee River State Game Area
- Fish Point Wildlife Areas
- Allegan State Game Area
- Nayanquing Point State Game Area
- Muskegon County Wastewater Management System
- Lapeer State Game Area
- Wildfowl Bay Wildlife Area

For Upper Peninsula hunting, refer to:

- Sturgeon River Sloughs Wildlife Area
- Seney National Wildlife Refuge
- Au Train Basin Waterfowl Project
- Baraga Plains Waterfowl Management Area

In addition, many of the county references in this book include goose-hunting information. Plenty of geese come off private land too, and hunters willing to scout birds and then seek permission to hunt feed fields can get some fine shooting.

There are essentially two ways to hunt geese. One is to get on a flight line to pass-shoot birds flying en

Author with two young geese he shot at Shiawassee National Wildlife Refuge. Facing page: Black head and neck with white cheek patches readily set Canada goose apart from other species.

Hunter retrieves goose he shot in Oakland County cornfield during special season. Right: Fog shrouds goose-shooting layout at Shiawassee National Wildlife Refuge.

route to feeding or roosting areas. Hunters at the Highbanks Unit of Allegan State Game Area and around Long Lake in the Lapeer State Game Area score with this method. Private-land hunters can do the same thing. By scouting with binoculars while driving through areas that hold geese, they quickly learn the birds' habits and flight patterns.

Generally, geese require a secure roosting spot on water, with loafing fields, such as lawns or golf courses, nearby. So long as food is plentiful, birds are not overly harassed, and open water is available, they are content to stay; and the longer geese remain in one place, the easier it becomes for hunters to determine their habits. Once in morning and again in afternoon honkers leave roosting areas to feed. Hunters may then intercept them en route or employ a second gunning trick—decoying.

Since geese are primarily grazers, winter wheat, rye, and barley fields are ideal spots in which to set up decoys—again if you are able to secure permission from landowners or are hunting food patches on state or federal land. Geese are also opportunists; that is, they take advantage of what food they can find. That is why cornfields, either standing or cut, are also prime food zones in which to set up decoys.

Many hunters use a J- or U-shape pattern for decoys, taking care to leave a pocket for incoming birds to land. Sometimes two tight clusters of decoys work best with an opening between spreads. Keep dummies reasonably close to your blind; 20 to 40 yards is about right. On waterfowl management areas where blinds are likely to be 100 yards or so apart, you'll want decoys fairly close anyway or your efforts will only help neighboring gunners toward their own limits. Put a sentry (head up) decoy out to 40 yards, the maximum distance for killing shots.

If hunting from a pit blind or under a tarp, consider spreading decoys both in front and behind. Shot-over geese in particular are extremely wary and will often stop short of decoys. Spotting your blind within the spread itself may put short-stopping birds in range.

Always face decoys into the wind as honkers both land and take off with the wind in their faces. Some hunters believe that the bigger the spread of dummies, the better the shooting opportunity. That may be true when trying to lure big V-shaped strings flying high with a mission on their minds, but there

is no question that a half-dozen magnum-sized decoys, strategically placed, will sucker birds either looking for chow or companionship. I once saw a lone hunter at Shiawassee National Wildlife Refuge lure six geese to only three huge decoys.

Magnum and super-magnum (they are big enough for a hunter to crawl under) shell bodies are expensive and clumsy to tote, but if you're serious about goose hunting, consider buying at least a few. Some goose hunters pool their money to purchase a stool of 12 to 36 birds, which are then commonly-owned and can be used by everyone with a financial interest involved.

If hunting waterfowl management areas, check the daily-posted scoreboard to see how certain blinds have done thus far in the season. Consider too wind direction and proximity from the refuge when picking your spot. Many hunters think stands or blinds next to the refuge are best, but that is not necessarily so. Quite often, birds get up and fly over earlier spreads of artificials en route to setups in the middle of hunting areas. This is especially true if tree lines are evident between the refuge itself and hunters' locations. Gunned-over geese learn quickly to skirt cover areas such as tree lines that may shelter hunters.

I have not shot enough geese to qualify as an expert at this sport, but the how-to tips and points made here are from observations of, and interviews with, dyed-in-the-wool goose hunters. Some of these sportsmen show up daily at management-area drawings, and it is not uncommon for them to shoot 25 or more Canadas each fall.

ONE tip I picked up is to consider scheduling your hunt when the moon is dark as it is not uncommon for geese to feed during a moonlit night and then loaf all the next day in the refuge. Another tip one veteran passed along is to keep in mind choosing a blind downwind of other hunters. Since geese generally move into the wind, approaching birds will also hear calling from upwind hunters, which may aid in suckering birds into your own decoys. Consider too hunting the day of time change in late October because heavily-hunted birds sometimes learn to leave the refuge at the close of morning shooting hours. The fall time change gives gunners an extra hour that geese don't know about.

My first successful Canada goose hunt occurred while paired up with Al Stewart and Ray Rustem one fall while hunting at Shiawassee National Wildlife Refuge. Both Rustem—who also had never shot a Canada honker—and I killed two birds that day, thanks to top-notch calling from Stewart. I learned that hunters who can properly imitate the *hrrrrooooonnnnnkkkkk, hronk, hronk* of geese looking for friends or food are able to turn passing flocks for a second look.

As geese swing to approach, Al softens the *hronks* and mixes in a few gentle bursts of feeding chatter, which sounds like stuttering, *hronk—onk-onk-onk-onk-onk-onk.* The sound is similar to the feeding call for ducks, only it is not as fast nor as loud. A final soft *hronk* may suffice to get birds to lock wings. Stewart advises against calling at all when birds are within 100 yards.

Some hunters say the best time to wallop a goose is the instant it realizes it has been duped and starts pumping for the sky. Although a honker will appear to hang in midair at this point, swing past his bill in order to get a head shot. Unless you put pellets in a Canada's head or break his wing, you will likely not bring him down. This is especially true with late-season giants who are well-muscled and protected with dense feathering. Always pick a single target too instead of shooting for the whole flock.

A fellow could get into a no-win argument by recommending goose guns and loads. Let it suffice to say that most goose hunters rely on 12- or 10-gauge shotguns with 30- to 35-inch barrels tubed full choke. Size 2 or BB shot is preferred. If hunting with steel shot (required within the waterfowl management areas and in certain other zones—consult the "Waterfowl Hunting Guide" for details), go one size larger than if using lead. Generally, pass-shoot gunners need the longer guns. Some veterans who hunt over decoys and take no shots outside of 25 yards rely on 20-gauge guns with lighter doses of shot.

The first goose I finally killed was not going to get away. I put two rounds of 12-gauge No. 1 steel shot into him for insurance. When Holly, my 60-pound yellow Labrador, strained to bring the bird back, I figured it had to weigh 10 pounds. Stewart, who is a wildlife biologist, checked the honker's primary feathers.

"Juvenile bird," he said.

"But a giant Canada, right?" I wondered. "Probably weighs 10 or 11 pounds, don't you think?"

"Maybe eight pounds."

At the check station, the goose weighed in at five pounds, 12 ounces. The other one, also a young-of-the-year bird, measured an even six pounds. Even in the hand, Canada geese are not as large as they appear. A 12- or 15-pound giant looks as though it could plunge a butcher's scale to 25 pounds.

And speaking of giants, here is excellent late-season opportunity for southeastern Michigan hunters willing to scout birds, knock on doors, and spend cold hours in blinds or under burlap or bedsheet camouflage. Hunters kill about 1,500 birds each winter, but even when this kill figure is coupled with annual DNR goose roundups of 1,000 to 1,500 (in summer when the molting adults are flightless), there are still numerous complaints of nuisance geese.

In a sense, southeastern Michigan is one large management area (though not by design) for geese. Neatly-manicured lawns and golf courses attract and hold them here. So do food handouts by citizens and visitors to metroparks. Farm crops and scores of shallow-water lakes complete with nesting islands contribute to ideal goose habitat.

But too many geese cause problems. Droppings which make some homeowners and golfers irate can foul the water too, contributing to swimmer's itch and closed beaches. A horde of geese can cause crop and lawn depredation as well. Known as aggressive nesters, parent birds have even attacked children.

These problems prompted the DNR to establish a nuisance-goose policy, a portion of which allows controlled hunting.

The home-reared giants (a strain once thought extinct) contribute greatly to Michigan's Canada-goose population. Yet in truth only about 10 percent of honkers bagged each fall are Michigan-bred. The other 90 percent come from the James and Hudson bays region of Canada.

Birds that migrate through the western U.P. and into Wisconsin are Mississippi Flyway geese that nest in the northwestern corner of James Bay and in southern Hudson Bay. Eastern U.P. birds that move through the Lower Peninsula are usually Tennessee Valley flock members raised in northeastern James and Hudson bays. Honkers from both flocks mix in Illinois and Kentucky, and some migrate as far south as northern Alabama.

Then again, some geese, mostly giant Canadas, stay in southern Michigan all winter as long as food supplies last and open water prevails.

Our state also gets visitations from snow geese in both their white and gray phases, the latter often called "blue geese." However, in recent years, snows and blues have largely bypassed Michigan. During years when the Canadian hatch is late, a condition which puts weak juveniles on the migrant wing, young birds stopping to rest can provide excellent hunting opportunities. A stiff, three-day south or southeast wind helps bring them down. Occasionally, Great Lake State hunters also bag brant as well as white-fronted and Ross' geese.

To find goose hunting better than Michigan waterfowlers are currently enjoying, one might have to look back to a time when hunters carried bows and fashioned snares. Excellent hunting is now availble, and this sport still has room for new members.

CROWS

THE crow goes by many names—most of them unkind. Black devil, vermin, freebooter, nest-robber, pirate, marauder, cold-blooded killer, egg thief—whatever you call him, his reputation as a mischief-maker and gossiper is well established.

Western literature is peppered with references to crows and ravens, the crow's larger cousin (ravens, incidentally, are protected in Michigan). An ancient Greek myth says that the crow, at one time an all-white bird, was turned black when it told a secret on the gods. Ever since, these rascals have been no good.

Few have a good word for the crow. Farmers hate them because they eat their field seed and are a general nuisance. Many duck hunters and songbird lovers say the only good crow is a dead crow, since they destroy millions of eggs each year. Sixty years ago when pork chops cost a nickel each, Iosco County crows fetched a quarter apiece in bounty. With the possible exceptions of buzzards and vultures, the crow has to be the most maligned, most despised bird in North America. He's also one of the smartest and, to my mind, one of the most challenging to hunt.

I have been chasing crows for most of my life, and they have made a fool of me more times than ducks, geese, or even white-tailed deer. Their sharp eyes, suspicious nature and keen minds have helped keep them alive in a hostile world, which has all too often tried to wipe them out.

Crows used to be plentiful in Michigan. Although still found throughout every region of the state, the old-time roosts that used to hold thousands of birds are no more. Today it is unusual to see more than a couple hundred crows in one place. Stripped of all protection for many years (no bag limits, no closed season), Michigan crows took a hammering in the 60s and early 70s. Electronic game calls suckered huge flocks from up to a mile distant. Nighttime roost shooting increased too. In one spot I know, unsporting types dynamited the birds when they touched down to roost one winter evening. In Frankenmuth other killers wiped out an entire roost one moonlit night by raking the trees with shotgun blasts.

Crow numbers tumbled as a result of this "kill-the-crow" mentality. Then, several years ago, the U.S. government signed an agreement with Mexico to give the migratory crow some protection. Michigan was one of several states that adopted crow seasons. For many years hunters here enjoyed a split season—one in late summer/early fall and another in winter.

Unfortunately, Michigan in 1984 returned to the old practice of lifting all protection against crows (no closed season). The DNR believes that the birds may be hunted year around with no harm to existing numbers. I respectfully disagree and can only hope that other hunters will not shoot into roosts or kill the young of nesting crows, even though those tactics are legal.

When hunted with sporting methods, these birds are among the best "game birds" I know. Crows help me to keep my shooting eye sharp, and we have a lot of fun trying to outfox them.

Over the years, I've learned three things about crows: (1) they are always curious, (2) they are usually hungry, (3) they love company, cackling over gossip like cocktail party-goers. My friends and I use these habits against them. That's why we eagerly await late summer, one of the best times to hunt crows.

Young crows are on the wing by midsummer. Like hyperactive kids, they are full of spunk, just itching for something to tease or taunt. Food is plentiful and the lazy, waning days of summer are meant for loafing and goofing off. This is a good time to put a few decoys high in a bare tree and mount a stuffed or papier-mache owl on a nearby post or anywhere else it can be easily seen.

Crows are still bunched in families by late summer. When the kids hear fighting calls on the summer wind, Mom and Pop couldn't hold them back if they wanted to. We use a good wooden call—a Lohman, Olt, or Scotchman—to draw crows into battle. A series of loud, raucous calls in bursts of three or four (caw-caw-caw-caw) at five- or 10-second intervals usually turns cruising crows our way. Sometimes we mix it up a little, adding some longer wailing notes to our fighting caws. The wailing notes sound something like caaaaaaaw, caaaaaaaw.

Tone of the call must sound authentic or you'll chase crows away. Their alarm call is also a machine-gun burst of sharp caws, except that it is usually higher pitched. Crows know the difference, but unless you practice, the two are easily confused. Stick to deep, raucous tones for fighting calls.

To blow a crow call properly, make a circle around the call with your thumb and index finger, thus cupping it. Then grunt into it by tightening the stomach and clearing the throat. If your cheeks puff, you're not calling properly. You'll know you have it right when you get a sore throat after a half-hour or so.

When summer and fall hunting, we often streak our faces with camouflage paints to break up any brightness that might be easily spotted from above. We usually wear camouflage shirts or parkas and like to hunker down behind simple blinds made from mosquito netting, torn from a discarded tent.

Good set-up sites include farm field edges, small openings in the woods, on an island in a river or lake, in portions of state parks open to hunting, and along farm ponds and old gravel pits. Any area where you have watched crows trading on warm summer days is a good choice.

Decoys are not a must for this late summer/early fall hunting. In fact, I wonder sometimes if the crows, especially the younger ones spoiling for action, even spot the dummies. We've had good shooting by just floating down rivers and calling every mile or so.

Summer hunter folds a curious crow that made the mistake of passing into range. Facing page: The crow is one of the smartest of birds and, many scattergunners believe, one of the most challenging to hunt.

Michigan DNR

Cane pole is ideal for swinging aloft decoys into bare branches during winter hunting season. Below left: Crow calls and decoys help hunters boost their take of these birds.

You've probably heard stories about crows with their tail feathers just scorched charging right back into a mock rumble. This often happens with young birds. They're easily bluffed back into shotgun range by the distress call, a long wailing note. It can be made with the regular call by wailing out a single, long-drawn sound for up to three or four seconds.

A good trick to try with two hunters is to have one switch to the distress notes while the other chimes in with fighting caws. You can turn crows around fast with this double-team method.

I'll never forget the summer afternoon a friend and I floated the lower Flint River below the town of Flushing. We set up on a sandbar, after stashing our canoe in some nearby willows. I tuned up on a mouth call while Robert hooked two decoys to the spindly branches of a dead elm. A young crow zipped overhead and spotted my partner halfway up the tree. I dropped this nosey bird in the river before he could warn the others.

Then I mixed up the calling between distress calls and fighting caws, and an angry pack of brothers and sisters charged from downstream woods. Robert scratched a parent bird that hovered overhead, and I missed two easy shots. The others scattered on battering wings, but even after all the racket and gunfire, a juvenile just had to come back for a last look. I sent him crashing into the willows over our canoe.

By mid-September most of the crows are combining families to form larger bands. These fall gangs, which may number from 25 to several hundred birds, will stay in an area as long as food supplies hold and hunting pressure isn't too great.

Most of the fall crows we shoot are taken while upland gamebird hunting. I rarely enter fall woods without a crow call in my pocket. Many times crows have made the difference between a fine autumn hike and getting to clean the tubes on my double-barrel. Food is usually not a problem in fall, and most crows are as cocky as ever then. The same techniques of setting up with or without decoys, and with careful camouflage, work well.

Sometimes camouflage is not even needed. I remember a grand shoot we enjoyed in the Fairview area of Oscoda County some autumns ago. The reds, yellows, and oranges of frost-fired hardwoods rolled away in gentle swells. We had been hunting grouse all day with little success. Crows seemed to be trading throughout the area, and I noticed a flight pattern developing by late afternoon. We spread out in a long field between two woods and knelt down, our red and orange hunting jackets looking like just so many blazing trees. The crows never knew we were there until it was too late.

In anticipation of winter hunting, I start watching crow patterns after deer season, at the end of November, in the area around my home in northeastern Genesee County. Although we have good crow numbers here, they have learned not to bunch together in the huge flocks of former years. A good-size roost will now number 100 birds and is likely to be found in a county park closed to hunting. I begin keeping tabs on local crows to determine their patterns. Where are they first seen in the morning? How about in the late afternoon? What areas are they roosting in?

In most respects, wintertime crow hunting is quite different than fall hunting. Crows bunch together for warmth and security in the dead of winter, often picking small pine groves for their roosts. Streaks of whitewash droppings are a sure sign that crows are using a stand of evergreens.

T HE birds leave the roost at first light, often fanning out like the spokes of a bicycle wheel, in their daily search for food. While crows may fly up to 50 miles one way, slowly wending their way home by late afternoon, they will only go as far as they have to to find food. Because farmers often clean-pick their crops and since garbage dumps by law must now cover refuse, wintering crows often have to scrounge hard to find a meal. They are found

hanging out at school playgrounds, year-round drive-in theaters, cattle feedlots, and along road shoulders where they pick at car-struck animals.

Years ago, as junior high kids, my friends and I would pack our decoys, sheet blind, shells, and guns on a sled and tote it two miles along the railroad track to the Flint City Dump in rural Genesee County. Hundreds of crows used this area each day.

When winter hunting today, we still like to find a spot where crows have been dining. Early the next morning, assuming we've secured hunting permission, we'll often get set up in a sheet blind and wearing white parkas or sheets wrapped around us. We usually try to work the blind into some edge cover along a field or fencerow. If tall trees are nearby, we'll swing some papier-mache decoys, with the help of a long cane pole, high in the branches of stark trees. Coat-hanger hooks secured in the decoys' backs make it easy to swing and hook them up high.

Some winter crow hunters go so far as to cover their guns with white adhesive tape and to spray their faces with artificial Christmas tree snow.

Early in the morning when crows are prowling for food, I send out what I call greeting calls—a series of three or four deep caws. These lack the excitement of the fighting calls described earlier. When crows answer and turn my way, I quit calling as one off-key note will spook them.

Crows in my area get shot at enough during the fall to remember what guns are. By winter they are very wary. We try to kill the scout bird to keep him from warning others, and I usually don't try the distress call when hunting feeding sites as chances are good that others will appear on the flight line in due time anyway. On snow-driven days crows will pile in to these dinner spots and provide terrific shooting.

When a crow's belly is full, he'll turn to mischief. The owl and decoy trick will work well in afternoon as the lazy birds like to loiter on their slow way home. Crows have a wintertime habit of banding together at afternoon gathering points, usually a mile or two from their roost. Here they trade the day's gossip, chase one another, and otherwise "mix it up." Crows sitting in trees or hanging around farm fields by midafternoon are using the spot for an afternoon gathering place. Soon, others will join or the band will move to mix with others at another spot nearby.

Just before dark they will often lift as a single body and silently fly into the roost. If the roost is closed to hunting, they will sometimes fly in high, then spiral straight down to avoid being shot by perimeter hunters. Ducks and geese often do this too as they enter a refuge where perimeter shooting is allowed.

IT pays to be observant in your daily travels throughout Michigan as crows are habitual birds. Where you see them today they are likely to be tomorrow. We get some really good hunts at these afternoon gathering points, but we never hunt in the roost itself. This is not only unsporting, but it is also the quickest way to end some great winter shooting. Crows will simply pull out and may go 100 miles away for safety. It's a good practice to rest shooting areas at least a week for the same reason.

Crows are keen-eyed, savvy birds. Unless you're well camouflaged, you'll get few shots under 40 yards. For that reason I like a modified or full-choke bore shotgun. I use low brass loads in No. 8 shot since crows, which weigh only a pound or so, tumble pretty easily when hit. The 8s give a dense pattern and are cheaper than field or magnum loads. Although some hunters stalk crows with scoped .22 rifles, the area I hunt is too populated for this method. In unsettled areas of northern Michigan, I bet it would be a fun sport.

Sure, the crow has a criminal reputation, is ugly as sin, and none too palatable. But there are fairly good numbers of these birds throughout the state. Crows also happen to be one of the sharpest birds you will ever hunt. The first time a crow makes a fool of you, you'll know what I mean.

Leonard Lee Rue III

Like hyperactive kids, young crows are full of spunk, just itching for something to tease or taunt.

Quail

Few, if any, game birds hold tighter for a dog than quail.

QUAIL hunting in Michigan has been a history of ups and downs. Currently, bobwhite numbers are very low—based upon annual spring counts of singing males—and the season is closed.

The problem is that southern Michigan is the

northern boundary for these game birds, which suffer losses even during mild winters. When winters are prolonged and severe, up to 95 percent mortality may occur in a single season. The DNR has had a policy of offering a limited season when four or more contiguous counties revealed spring counts of 10 or more singing males. That has not happened since 1977 and is not likely to occur again soon.

Quail hunting was prohibited from 1911 to 1965, when the DNR allowed a four-bird limit in selected southern Michigan counties. The birds seemed to be coming back, and in 1973, when the limit was raised to five, roughly 148,000 quail were harvested. Then for the next four years numbers tumbled, resulting in the closure after 1977.

Pen-reared quail have a tough time making it in the wild although Ohio DNR biologists are having some success with hatchery birds raised in a wild environment. Michigan's last attempt at a similar effort was in 1982 when the DNR accepted 3,800 quail from Illinois and then stocked the birds in Lenawee, Berrien, and other selected downstate counties. However, during a special survey a short time later, biologists recorded no singing males.

In the foreseeable future, Michigan hunters will have to seek their bobwhites on shooting preserves or out-of-state.

Doves

Farm country offers ideal habitat for doves. Facing page: Nation's number one game bird in terms of numbers bagged is the mourning dove.

IT is presently illegal to hunt mourning doves in Michigan. However, a growing interest among sportsmen and the long-range possibility of a dove season occurring sometime in Michigan prompt us to include a few comments in this book.

Doves are the nation's number one game bird in terms of numbers bagged. Hunters kill about 50 million, or some 10 percent of the estimated national population, in the 35 states where dove hunting is allowed. States near Michigan with open seasons include Wisconsin, Illinois, Pennsylvania, and, most recently, Indiana.

Many Michigan hunters would like to see a dove

Michigan Travel Commission

season here for several reasons. First, federal law (the migratory dove comes under federal jurisdiction just as waterfowl do) would allow a generous season up to 70 days between September 1 and January 15, with bag and possession limits of 12 and 24, respectively. Second, Michigan has a large number of the prolific birds, in fact, more doves than at least five other states with open seasons. Third, Michigan doves are shot in other states as the birds migrate south, thus depriving state hunters of excellent shooting potential. Fourth, doves could help fill the sporting gap left by our declining pheasant population and could also help rebuild DNR Fish and Game Fund coffers, dwindling in part due to a drop in small-game hunters.

Perhaps most important, doves are challenging game birds to hunt. Tactics involve pass-shooting with No. 8 or 9 shot along flight routes and hunting from blinds and using decoys and calls. Many sportsmen find the elusive dove to be hard to hit, an excellent game bird for retrieving with dogs, and a real delight on the table.

When the Legislature passed the Licensing Act of 1980, it reclassified Michigan's birds and game animals. Because doves are now ''game birds,'' all that is needed is for sportsmen to convince legislators to draft a season. The time to hunt doves in Michigan is now.

Leonard Lee Rue III

Leonard Lee Rue III

Preserve Hunting

I remember reading as a kid in *Field & Stream* that preserve shooting was the probable future of American hunting and that perhaps in our lifetime we'd see the end of public hunting on public land. That threat always seemed to taint my thinking toward the preserves. Coupled with the feared high expense and the notion of shooting tame birds, preserve hunting just wasn't too high on my priority list of things to do.

But now that I've tried it a few times, I've changed my mind.

The memberships of many Michigan shooting preserves open to the public cut across lines of sex, age, and social status. An 86-year-old retired dentist, for example, might warm up on the skeet field next to a second shifter at the Saginaw Gray Iron Foundry. After you pay the annual membership fee ($100 to $300 at most preserves), costs are related to how much sport you demand. Two or three hunters can pool their resources to enjoy a six-bird pheasant hunt for $30 or $40 each. They'll pay that much and more on a charter boat for trout and salmon.

Another criticism I had heard is that preserve hunting is like shooting fish in a barrel. Limited habitat and tame birds equal poor sport, some say. That depends on the preserve. Some, like Hunter's Creek Club in Metamora or Willow Lake Sportsmen's Club in Three Rivers, have huge areas in which to roam. Weather and time of year determine how birds act, just as in the wild. One time in December, we hunted a preserve in a foot of snow and a frigid wind. Birds sat so tightly that a couple needed the toe to get airborne. True, I have never had to boot a wild ringneck to make it flush. Then another time in March (near the pheasant-breeding season when ringnecks become wild) a friend and I went after a 12-rooster release with a crackerjack dog and found exactly two birds after three hours.

One big advantage of preserve hunting is the long, eight-and-one-half-month Michigan season, which runs August 15 through April 30 for pheasants, bobwhite quail, Hungarian partridge, and mallards. Exotic birds, such as chukar partridges and coturnix (Japanese) quail, may be hunted through June 30 (check with a preserve or the DNR as these dates are subject to change). That's a lot of time to keep dogs sharp with regular field work.

Adding the month that dog men get (the earliest legal date that dogs can be taken afield is July 16) to the long preserve season makes training nearly year-round a possibility. Another plus is that Michigan and nonresident small game licenses cover preserve shooting. Hunters without the regular license must buy a shooting preserve license, however. Current cost is $8.75.

Most preserves operate by reservation, and sportsmen are practically guaranteed a private hunt. Many allow hunting by guests of members. In most cases, if you want to try it, you can do so for $10, plus birds. Generally, hunters pay for the number of birds they want released, and some clubs have a

minimum release figure.

Most Michigan hunting preserves have membership ceilings, taking on new members as others drop out. All but a few require membership as a prerequisite for hunting privileges. There are often a variety of ways to join; individual, limited, corporate, social, and associate memberships are some. Currently, there are 24 preserves in Michigan open to the public in one form or another. For addresses, phone numbers, and other details, see "Other Shooting Opportunities" toward the end of the county listings in this book.

Hunting birds is only a part of the offerings of the bigger, established preserves. Dog training and boarding, skeet and trap instruction, and shooting, fishing, camping, parties and meetings, dining, and

special European hunts can all be part of the atmosphere.

Most shooting preserves promote the use of dogs, since they add to the enjoyment of the hunt and greatly cut down on the needless waste of cripples. Some members belong to the North American Versatile Hunting Dog Association, a national organization whose main goal is to promote hunting-dog use. Most preserves offer club dogs and handlers for rent too.

I no longer think of shooting preserves as the future of American hunting. In Michigan at least, I view them as supplementing the wild-bird hunting that we already enjoy. There is no question that preserves fill a big need for many sportsmen.

Hunter below finds some fast shooting on Thumb-area preserve. A fine morning of shooting at Willow Lake Sportsmen's Club was enjoyed by hunters in photo at right. High-flushing rooster challenges scatter-gunner on facing page.

Float Hunting

FLOATING a Michigan river for hunting waterfowl, squirrels, deer, and other game takes a hunter back to basics. A quiet stalk in the ageless canoe, as old as North American hunting itself, is a rewarding day in the outdoors. Rivers have a timeless ability to soothe the soul, to make a hunter forget all about highway traffic, ringing phones, next month's rent payment. And a day spent float-hunting on a river will help tune you into the outdoors, making you a part of it.

Rivers offer an effective means of hunting, both for game spotted en route and as avenues of access to out-of-the-way places. A partner and I once cut two hours of hiking out of our daily bear-baiting and hunting schedule by relying upon a seven-mile run up and down a river. The wildlife we saw both coming and going was worth the float alone.

Michigan is blessed with some 36,000 miles of running water and although not all of its streams are floatable, a great many are. You can get a free copy of "Canoeing in Michigan," which lists the major flows, by contacting the DNR Information Services Center, Box 30028, Lansing, Mich. 48909 (517/373-1220). Or you can refer to the 83 separate counties listed in this book for information on floating opportunities. It's also fun to find your own streams to negotiate. After all, our country's early explorers were canoeists.

I don't float-hunt as much as I used to, but a good friend does and is always asking me along. He especially likes to hunt the small streams because few others do. Major rivers always seem to have duck hunters and squirrel hunters, as well as fall fishermen, on them. It's pretty difficult to sneak up again on a resting pair of blue-winged teal, for example, that have just been flushed by a party of hunters moments before. Likewise, it's not easy to find unwary ducks on the big streams where fall anglers line the banks to try for trout and spawning salmon.

Picking a good stream to float is not really difficult. My friend looks for water that is not too narrow—the size of a two-lane highway is about right for canoeing, he says—and yet the stream should not be so large that it will fill up with competition. If banks are heavily wooded, so much the better as this feature will afford good camouflage and allow a quiet stalk. Winding streams may be sometimes tough to negotiate, but they are best since drifting hunters can often surprise game just around curves.

Another feature the float hunter wants to look for is easy put-in and take-out points. Bridges are good bets and they help hunters to better time their float. Try to determine the average current speed and compute the distance between the put-in and take-out points as a straight line. Then double the float time to account for stops and a meandering stream.

Hunters should take care not to trespass on private property through which most Michigan streams flow. A good idea is to pick up a county plat book (see ordering information at the end of each county entry

in this book). Plat books tell who owns the land, and, coupled with your "Michigan County Maps and Outdoor Guide," will help you to follow the law. Many of these maps also mark public-access points.

I prefer a canoe for floating the streams because they are generally light, quiet, and easy to handle in tight spots. Some hunters use duck boats designed for marsh hunting, and these are fine too except there is a great weight difference between heavy, wooden duck boats and the lighter canoes. This difference will quickly show up if a portage is necessary, and it seems as though portaging is an integral part of floating the small streams.

Aluminum canoes are lighter than fiberglass or wooden models, but they are also noisier. So some hunters cushion the bottoms of metal canoes with plastic foam or burlap. A friend owns an ideal canoe for negotiating Michigan rivers. It's an 18-foot fiberglass model which he has painted a dead-grass color. A freighter style with motor mount attached, this craft has sponsons added to the sides as an antitipping device. Two men can easily handle it, and it fits nicely atop a full-size car.

A 14- or 15-foot canoe is large enough for one hunter, but I wouldn't want anything smaller, for safety's sake, than 16 feet for two hunters. Canoes are tippy at best and during the excitement of a hunt they can capsize.

Only the bowman should hunt. The stern paddler should keep his gun unloaded and occupy his mind on keeping the canoe upright and on course. When a bevy of puddle ducks bursts unexpectedly from the river, the stern hunter will be tempted to join the action, but he can't if his gun is unloaded.

As kids we once narrowly averted a terrible shooting accident, one which left an indelible mark on my mind about the potential dangers of float-hunting. A high-school friend and I were drifting the sluggish Flint River in lower Michigan when suddenly we jumped a small flock of teal in some pocket water around a sharp bend. I got off a couple of rounds when my friend's gun suddenly exploded, practically in my ear. I momentarily lost my sense of balance, and my ears rang for hours afterward. I could have easily been killed.

To repeat, *only one hunter—the one in the bow—should have a loaded gun.* The partners can switch off from time to time so both hunters get an equal chance. Incidentally, float-hunting is a good way to teach a youngster safe hunting habits, as well as patience and stalking techniques.

Sometimes you will get surprisingly close to game by carefully and quietly drifting along. Yet on other occasions ducks and other wild creatures seem to know they are being duped long before you drift into range. Maybe that is because the smaller streams in particular are often haunted by many predators. By early fall the survivors are plenty wary.

To stalk successfully, hunters have to lie low in their canoes and remain motionless, especially when approaching a bend. I well remember drifting through straight, open stretches of stream that

Duck hunters float a Michigan stream (facing page). Some floaters tote a few decoys and set up on islands in hopes of taking ducks or geese (below) early in the morning or late in the afternoon.

Gordon Charles

A float trip can offer a variety of shooting—for crows, ducks, even deer. Young hunters in bottom photo floated a northern Michigan river to bag some fox squirrels late in the season.

seemed empty of any life, only to stretch tense muscles and then experience ducks or geese bursting from behind a debris pile or storm-toppled tree. Such missed opportunities should remind the float hunter to be always alert.

WHEN hunting waterfowl, crows, or squirrels, it's a good idea to wear camouflage clothing (waterfowlers hunting from a boat or blind and bobcat, crow, wild turkey, and bow-and-arrow deer hunters are exempt from the law that requires hunters to wear a cap, vest, or jacket of blaze orange when hunting public lands). Some hunters even streak their faces with camo creams.

Camouflaging the canoe with branches and leaves will help to make it resemble a big log knocked into the stream by some recent storm. An important ecological tip is to cut branches from trees already in the water. Never kill a live tree just for the sake of a few branches for camouflage. My friend who floats the small streams also paints his paddles the same dull green color as his canoe. He says that shiny canoe paddles can give ducks downstream a distant early warning.

Incidentally, for some reason, jumped ducks will often fly upstream right at the canoe and offer easy passing shots. This is particularly true of migrating divers, such as scaup, redheads, goldeneyes, and buffleheads. Divers and dabblers alike often pile into rivers for a brief rest or to escape a storm or hunting pressure on nearby lakes and bigger rivers. Some days a river may seem to be full of waterfowl; other times you're sure they all flew south.

Not much equipment is needed to hunt ducks from canoes. Life preservers should be carried, of course, and if you like the vest-like, flotation type, they can be purchased in camouflage color. Consider carrying chest waders and keep a rain parka handy for sudden downpours. The waders are useful for getting out in tight places too. Some float hunters carry a dry change of clothes in a plastic bag and bring waterproof matches along just in case a fire is needed. Another good item is a small hand axe to chop away debris clogging the river. Sometimes a portage can be avoided on the smaller streams if hunters are able to hack their way through.

Some floaters tote a few decoys and set up early in the morning or late in the afternoon on islands or calm stretches of river. Wood ducks, mallards, blue-winged teal, and Canada geese often take to the air at these times and can be brought in with the right combination of calling and a proper decoy spread.

Calling is a real art, but it is not necessary to know everything about it to take waterfowl via the float method. Still, it's a handy back-up technique, according to my friend, who has turned some poor days into successful hunts by decoying ducks, especially mallards and woodies. The feeding call, a low, chuckling sound, is especially effective. Another trick is to couple occasional quacks of greeting with splashing water from a cupped hand or boot turned up in the stream. Many times ducks cruising the area come weaving in through bankside woods to join what they suppose is a duck feast.

Squirrel hunting is another sport that float hunters can enjoy. Lowland hardwoods mixed with conifers often contain gray/black species whereas beech, oak, and hickory stands usually hold fox squirrels, especially if a corn field is nearby. You will have to be

Michigan DNR

very still to catch sharp-eyed bushytails unaware of your presence. Sometimes you will surprise them far out on a limb over the river. At other times by slipping an anchor into the stream or tying up to a bankside log, you can outwait a spooked squirrel into showing itself again. If the adjoining property is state-owned or you have permission to go ashore, you can use your float as a means of access to squirrel woods which may never see another hunter.

A nice feature of float-hunting is that you are constantly moving through new habitat, and this is a perfect opportunity to slip a crow call into your hunting coat and a few decoys in the canoe. These black varmints are fond of trading up and down waterways while scouting for food and mischief. Every couple miles or so you can ditch the canoe and set up a papier mache owl in a visible spot—say on a dead tree limb on an island—along with a few crow decoys. Then, some fighting caws on the call will bring crows in a hurry. When action is over, stow your gear in the canoe and set up once more farther downstream.

The crow season in Michigan is now open year-around, but float-hunting is an especially good tactic to use in late summer or early fall when young-of-the-year crows are just earning their flight feathers. Lacking the savvy of older birds, they are easily talked into a mock fray.

I have never hunted deer from a canoe but know from others' experiences that it can be an effective technique. Being in the right place at the right time is the key, and that apparently may well require much patience. Where runways lead to the water, however, it is possible to ambush a deer while waiting in an anchored canoe or boat that has been hidden with brush. Remote rivers would likely be the best bets as hunting pressure on easily accessible lands contributes to making deer extra wary about showing themselves as well as following normal patterns of movement.

A few years ago I read in an outdoor magazine about a hunter who used a float tube to drift down Michigan rivers in quest of deer. He claimed he was able to get close enough to kill deer with a handgun. The method may have merit, but I have no personal experience with it.

I would bet too that wild turkeys could be hunted effectively during the spring season via a river float. Turkeys are often found in wet, lowland areas, and although rivers act as natural boundaries to them, it seems logical that a drifting hunter could at least pinpoint their whereabouts through the sounds of gobbling toms that he may hear en route. Again, access to adjacent lands is the key to setting up a bankside hide and then trying to talk a gobbler into shotgun range.

If you enjoy still-hunting and stalking game, then consider a float trip on a Michigan river. You will likely find that stops to wander lowland woods in quest of game or to decoy-hunt for ducks or crows won't be for long. The bubbling stream nearby will beckon you on to the next bend. There you may spot a muskrat or beaver arrowing across from bank to bank or witness a blue heron stalking the shallows on skinny crane legs. Most Michigan rivers are alive with animals and birds in early fall, which help make a rewarding contribution to a float trip.

But my memory says the biggest thrill is probing around a sharp bend to jump whatever wildlife happens to be there. The surprise is usually a mutual one.

Camping & Hunting

TO many sportsmen, fall hunting and camping in Michigan go together like pork and beans. But don't think for a minute that hunters who camp have to rely on such simple fare as pork and beans. Nor do they have to shiver in an unheated tent or an uninsulated sleeping bag. Not at all.

Space-age materials used in the construction of sleeping bags and tents now promise a warm, comfortable experience. Microwaves, toasters, and ovens in motorhomes and travel trailers go a long way toward preparing good meals at a moment's notice. No, sir, setting up a hunting camp can be smoothing it instead of roughing it.

Still, it is the primitive camp that many deer, bear, and small-game hunters remember with nostalgia and look forward to again each fall. And isn't it funny how the more miserable the experience, the longer it is apt to stay rooted in our memories? How well I know. A few years ago my dad and I hunted deer on Drummond Island at the far eastern tip of the Upper Peninsula. A 600-mile round-trip scouting excursion the week before the November 15 firearm opener had us excited about prospects. We had also picked a good campsite in the Lake Superior State Forest to pitch our canvas tent. When we pulled in at midnight on November 14, no one had bothered things, just as we had hoped.

But our plans for a good night's sleep were ill-founded. The temperature at nearby Sault Ste. Marie nose-dived to 12 degrees that night. Each of us had assumed the other was bringing a catalytic heater; consequently, neither did. By morning, the inside tent walls were frost-coated, and a gallon water jug had frozen solid.

Cold and tired, we dressed by lantern heat, and even though I was on the stand before daybreak, my optimism had flagged severely. A chilling ice storm at midday soured things further. We toughed it out one more night and then caught the 10 a.m. ferry for home. Ironically, on the drive en route we passed a well-built tent camp with smoke curling from a stovepipe...and two bucks on the meat pole.

The ideal hunting camp doesn't come about by chance. Just last fall three friends and I set up a tent camp in the Copper Country State Forest in Dickinson County. Careful planning, along with sharing equipment responsibilities and camp chores, helped make that experience a successful one.

Planning should begin well in advance of the hunting opener with a meeting of hunters and a discussion of who will bring what. Everyone should contribute a trip list or silently brainstorm for 15 minutes. Then lists can be shared and the essentials checked off.

Since that experience on Drummond Island, I have become a list maker for different types of camping. Although I don't always haul everything on these extensive lists (they keep growing!), the items are there for consideration. Depending upon when and where you are hunting in Michigan, here are what I figure are the essentials for a tent camp:

- Baled straw for ground cover.
- Tarp or plastic sheets (blaze-orange is a wise color).
- Heavy-duty tent with a ridge pole (to withstand snow).
- Tent poles and stakes.
- Extra rope.
- Sleeping bag, pillow, extra blanket(s).
- Water jugs.
- Campstove and fuel.
- Lantern, spare globe, mantles, and generator.
- Flashlight and extra batteries.
- Heater (consider a wood stove with pipe).
- Garbage bags.
- 10-quart pail.
- Axe.
- Shovel.
- Chain saw, fuel, oil, file, spare chain.
- Waterproofed wooden matches.
- Cooler.
- Camp stools.
- Portable table.
- Fire extinguisher.
- Camp permit (if camping on state or federal forest land outside of designated campground).
- Alarm clock.
- Topographic maps.
- Portable radio and extra batteries.
- Generator, extension cords, fuel.
- Broom, sponge, masking tape, duct tape.
- Tool kit.
- First aid kit.

Deer hunting in particular can be a rugged test of equipment. Some areas of the U.P. have snow on the ground by November 15, and by Thanksgiving hunters may need a 4WD with snowplow attached to get out to main roads. The same can be true during spring turkey-hunting season in northern Michigan. Therefore, each hunter should be certain that the items he is responsible for are in good condition. Those responsible for driving, for instance, should carry snow tires, spare fuses, bulbs, fan belts, a tow chain, extra keys, come-along, jumper cables, and a hydraulic jack.

A good idea is to make each hunter responsible for a day's supply of food, or simply pool money and let one person handle food-buying chores. In conjunction with menu planning and the actual cooking, consider the following items:

- One or more skillets.
- Dutch oven.
- Heavy-duty silverware.
- Plateware, cups, glasses.
- Saucepans.
- Cutlery.
- Coffee pot.
- Spatula, stirring spoons, tongs.
- Can opener.
- Condiments.
- Dish pan, soap, cloths, towels.
- Cutting block, sharpening stone.

Home cooking adds to the pleasures of camping. Facing page: Tent campers look on as deer is brought to camp buck pole.

Michigan DNR

More often than not, Upper Peninsula has snow on the ground for opening day of deer season. Below: Camping near hunting sites cuts down on driving time, increases hunting time.

•Pot holders.

Here is the personal checklist I use when planning to camp during deer season. Adjust it for your own needs and the quarry you are seeking.

•Deer rifle, case, cleaning kit.
•Shells.
•Scope covers.
•Silicone rag, lubricant.
•Compass.
•Waterproof matches.
•Belt or pocket knife.
•Rope.
•License tag, wire for deer tag.
•Small block and tackle.
•Sunglasses.
•Binoculars.
•Camera and film.
•Chocolate bars, dried fruit, granola.
•Hot seat.
•Hand warmer, fuel.
•Emergency phone numbers.
•Lightweight leather or rubber hunting boots.
•Wool socks of varying weights.
•Wool or flannel shirts.
•Lightweight hunting pants.
•Shooting cap.
•Felt Pac insulated boots.
•Long underwear, insulated.
•Fishnet underwear.

•Wool cap.
•Heavyweight hunting suit.
•Warm, lined gloves.
•Insulated vest.
•Blaze-orange clothing articles.
•Belt/suspenders.
•Rain jacket.
•Toiletries.
•Waterproof dressing for boots.
•Extra gloves, socks, underwear.
•Extra bootlaces.

A fair question is, "Why camp at all when hunters can enjoy the comfort and luxury of a motel?" Boy, do I have some answers for that one! First off, motels are in demand, often expensive, and not always available, especially during deer-hunting season. In addition to saving money, a camp in the woods cuts driving time involved with hunting. And it helps hunters tune into the environment, promotes camaraderie, and doesn't have to limit one to a 12- by 14-foot motel room.

Besides, many campgrounds have lower, off-season rates after Labor Day. Some don't charge at all. And hunters are rarely turned away by "Sorry, Campground Full" signs. There are no pesky bugs to contend with, and nights are cool and meant for sleeping.

Michigan ranks third nationally, behind Florida and California, in the number of campsites, and we

enjoy more than 33,000 private and 25,000 public places to pitch a tent or park a recreational vehicle (RV). For a free member's list of the Michigan Association of Private Campground Owners, write to MAPCO, 13480 Dunham Road, Milford, Mich. 48042. Also, the Michigan Association of RVs and Campgrounds will send its member directory if you write to them at 19045 Farmington Road, Livonia, Mich. 48152.

"Woodall's Michigan Campground Directory" is another good source of private campgrounds. It rates the campgrounds and lists opening and closing dates. You can buy the directory in most bookstores.

A free DNR publication called "Campground Directory" lists nearly 125 municipal, county, and township campgrounds scattered throughout the state. You can get a copy by contacting DNR Information Services Center, Box 30028, Lansing, Mich. 48909 (517/373-1220).

Fees for camping at Michigan's four national forests and two national lakeshores vary from $2 nightly to $10 for groups. The Hiawatha and Ottawa national forests and Pictured Rocks National Lakeshore in the U.P. offer more than 1,000 campsites. The Huron-Manistee National Forest and the Sleeping Bear Dunes National Lakeshore in the northern Lower Peninsula feature more than 1,500 campsites. For more information, refer to the special sections on those federal properties elsewhere in this book.

Michigan's six state forests contain 140 campgrounds with over 3,100 rustic sites open year-around. A nightly fee of $4 is charged. For more information, refer to the state forests discussed elsewhere in this book. Important point: state and federal forest lands in Michigan (about 3.8 and 2.6 million acres, respectively) are completely open to hunting.

There are a total of 72 state parks with camping facilities throughout Michigan too, with a campsite total nearing 1,400. In addition, many of the 225,000 acres of state-park land is open to hunting. Rustic sites start at $3 nightly; modern sites cost more. However, hunters should be aware that many state parks close their bathhouses in fall. Also, those entering park properties with vehicles must have a current state parks sticker affixed to the windshield. A daily permit is presently $2 and a season permit costs $10.

Hunters can get a free brochure by contacting DNR Parks Division, Box 30028, Lansing, Mich. 48909 (517/373-1270). Also, any state park with lands open to hunting is included in this publication.

Yes, hunting and camping for many sportsmen in Michigan go together like pork and beans. On second thought, make that bacon and eggs or chicken and dumplings or...

In addition to saving money, a camp in the woods helps hunters tune into the environment, promotes camaraderie, and doesn't limit sportsman to crowded confines of a motel room.

WHERE TO HUNT

Porcupine Mountains State Park

MICHIGAN'S largest state park, the 58,000-acre Porcupine Mountains State Park, located in northwestern Ontonagon and Gogebic counties (*both of which see*), is completely open to hunting. Sportsmen who wish a wilderness camping/hunting experience with the chance to bag a trophy buck or fat black bear should consider the "Porkies."

Black bear in particular are abundant, with some causing nuisance problems due to campers feeding them throughout the summer. Hardly a camping season goes by that someone doesn't encounter bruin trouble. Baiters can take advantage during the fall hunting seasons by putting out bait at remote interior places such as Mirror Lake and the Big Carp River. Low hunter pressure keeps competition light, unlike some other popular bear-hunting spots like the Dead Stream region near Houghton Lake in the Lower Peninsula.

Locker facilities in either Wakefield or Ontonagon, both about 17 miles from park ends, will protect your bear against spoilage.

The Porkies also house low to fair numbers of whitetails, including some bucks sporting trophy headgear. Hunters again exert light pressure, with most sticking to the 15 foot trails that wander for 80 miles throughout the park. Small parking lots are located at each trailhead. A good place to try for a late-season buck would be in deer yards along Lake Superior west of Union Bay. As snows deepen and temperatures drop, deer move along valleys to this area of heavy conifers for food and shelter.

Bobcats also frequent these lowland conifer areas, but few hunters are willing to tackle this tough winter sport with hounds. The Porkies with their steep hills, rocky outcroppings, and dense cover of northern hardwoods and hemlock offer a truly wilderness hunting experience. A few coyotes run the area and the lucky visitor is sometimes treated to a wolf track or howl from one of these shy, deep-woods animals. Wolves, however, are protected.

The state park hosts fair numbers of snowshoe hares and a few gray squirrels. Waterfowl hunting opportunities are good on inland lakes when migrating ducks and geese seek shelter and rest from Lake Superior. There are fair numbers of grouse and woodcock, with the latter offering good hunting potential.

Because Porcupine Mountains State Park is a wilderness area, it contains few roads. Hunters should therefore be prepared to hike. A visitor center near the junction of South Boundary Road and M-107 can provide hunters with information. Located at Union Bay is a modern campground with hot showers, flush toilets, electricity, and a sanitation station. Near the mouth of the Presque Isle River is a semimodern campground. There also are four rustic sites elsewhere. Trailside camping is also permitted.

Hunters might also be interested in renting a six-person trailside cabin for $20 nightly. Equipment includes bunks with springs and mattresses, wood stove, sink, cupboard, table and benches, cooking utensils, dishes, tableware, saw, and axe. Cabin users provide bedding, food, towels, lighting, and personal items. Reservation applications for deer season will be accepted until July 1 of each year.

There are also some Adirondack shelters available on a first-come, first-served basis. The only facilities, however, are bunks. These accommodations may be used until November 30. Roads are also plowed until that date each year.

Those entering the park with vehicles must have a valid state parks sticker affixed to the windshield. For more information about hunting opportunities, contact the Porcupine Mountains State Park Manager, Route 2, M-107, Ontonagon, Mich. 49953 (906/885-5798). You can also get information from the DNR Field Office in Ontonagon (906/885-5712).

McLain State Park

A total of 156 acres of 417-acre F. J. McLain State Park is open to hunting. The state park is located along Lake Superior at the end of the shipping canal in northern Houghton County (*which see*). The open-hunting area of gently-rolling hardwoods mixed with pine and lowland swamp conifers lies south of M-203.

Hunting opportunities exist but are quite limited for deer, hares, predators, waterfowl, grouse, and woodcock. However, there is a good population of gray and black-phase squirrels although few sportsmen take advantage of this.

Those entering with vehicles must have a valid state parks sticker affixed to the windshield. For more information regarding hunting opportunities, contact the McLain State Park Manager, M-203, Hancock, Mich. 49930 (906/482-0278).

Porcupine Mountains State Park

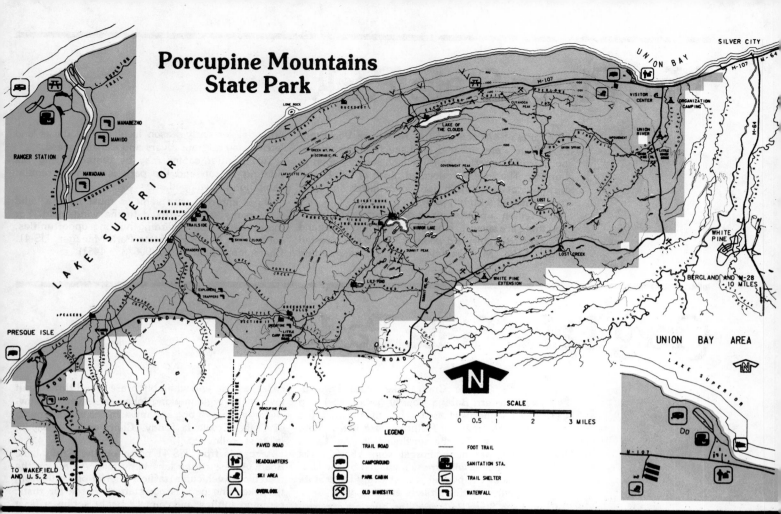

LEGEND

▬▬▬ PAVED ROAD	─── TRAIL ROAD	┄┄┄ FOOT TRAIL	
HEADQUARTERS	CAMPGROUND	SANITATION STA.	
SKI AREA	PARK CABIN	TRAIL SHELTER	
OVERLOOK	OLD MINESITE	WATERFALL	

SCALE
0 0.5 1 2 3 MILES

McLain State Park

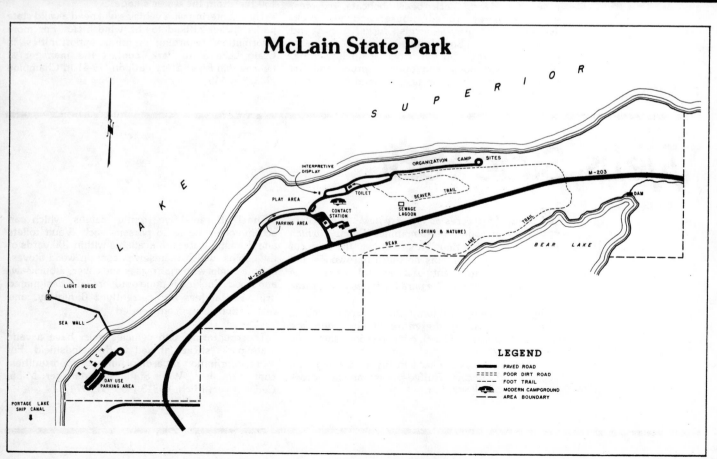

LEGEND

▬▬▬ PAVED ROAD
═══ POOR DIRT ROAD
┄┄┄ FOOT TRAIL
MODERN CAMPGROUND
──── AREA BOUNDARY

Van Riper State Park

A total of 870 acres of the 1,044-acre Van Riper State Park, located on Lake Michigamme in northern Marquette County (*which see*), is open to hunting. The lands are located north of US-41 and include mostly northern hardwoods (birch and hard maple) mixed with big pine.

The region supports fair to good numbers of deer and there are snowshoe hares in low-lying areas and a few ruffed grouse and woodcock along the forested edge. Lake Michigamme itself offers hunting potential for early-season local puddle ducks and late-season migrant divers and Canada geese.

Two frontier cabins may be rented during the hunting season and the park is open to regular camping in developed sites.

Those entering with vehicles must have a valid state parks sticker affixed to the windshield. For more information regarding hunting opportunities, contact the Van Riper State Park Manager, US-41, Champion, Mich. 49814 (906/339-4461).

Craig Lake State Park

THE 13,000-acre Craig Lake State Park in southeastern Baraga County (*which see*) is a designated wilderness area. That means that the ongoing development of facilities here will remain rather primitive. To the northeast is the Cyrus McCormick Experimental Forest, some 18,560 acres of Upper Peninsula wilderness managed by the U.S. Forest Service. The overall plan at Craig Lake State Park is to enhance this already-existing area.

Craig Lake State Park contains hunting opportunities for deer, black bear, bobcats, coyotes, snowshoe hares, ruffed grouse, and woodcock. There are also gray squirrels, ducks, geese, and raccoon within its boundaries.

Occupying dry, upland sites are white pine, northern hardwoods, and upland spruce and fir. Swamp conifers, black spruce, lowland hardwoods, cedar, aspen, and white birch are found throughout low, moist regions along lakes and streams. Low, swampy areas of bog and muskeg occur along much of Craig, Crooked, Teddy, Clair, and Keewaydin lakes shorelines.

Access is from US-41 north on the Craig Lake Road. Access to the lake is by foot. A gate on the road blocks vehicular traffic a quarter of a mile from the lake. The park is not staffed. A fee for rustic camping applies, and camps must be set up at least 150 feet from the water's edge.

Those entering with vehicles will need a valid state parks sticker affixed to the windshield. For more information regarding hunting opportunities in Craig Lake State Park, contact the manager at nearby Van Riper State Park on US-41 in Champion (906/339-4461).

Wells State Park

A total of 670 acres of 940-acre J. W. Wells State Park in southern Menominee County (*which see*) is open to hunting. This relatively flat area cut by a few ridges contains northern hardwoods and cedar and features plenty of additional nearby state land open to hunting. The park itself lies along three miles of Green Bay.

Biggest drawing card for hunters is large numbers of deer, indicative of the entire county. There are also good numbers of black bear, raccoon, snowshoe hares, gray/black squirrels, and waterfowl. Occasional wild turkeys are seen in the area along with coyotes and bobcats. Ruffed-grouse and woodcock hunting is rated only fair.

The DNR rents five frontier cabins, which can accommodate up to 18 persons each. Vault toilets and drinking water are available within 100 yards of the cabins, which themselves contain wood stoves, double bunks with mattresses and cover, a bucksaw, and wood. Cooking is done outdoors on a designated grill. Rental fees are currently $20 nightly, and reservations are recommended.

Those entering with vehicles must have a valid state parks sticker affixed to the windshield. For more information regarding hunting opportunities, contact the J. W. Wells State Park Manager, M-35, Cedar River, Mich. 49813 (906/863-9747).

Van Riper State Park

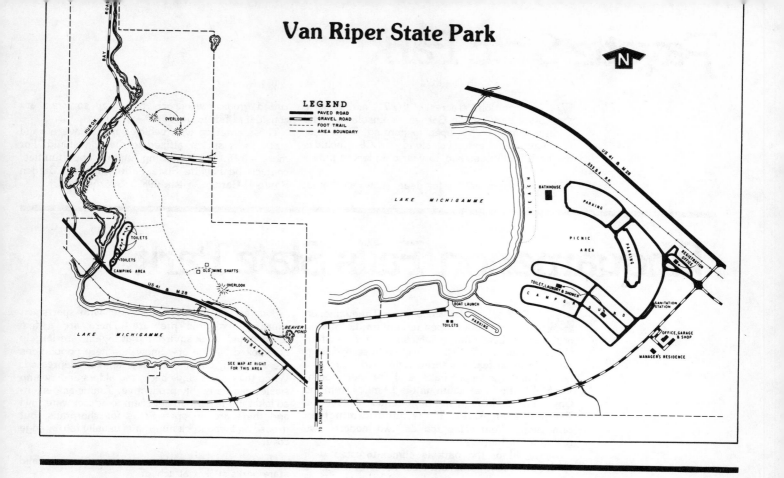

Craig Lake State Park

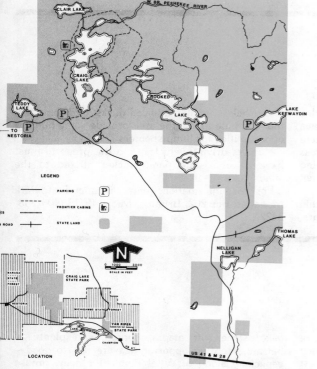

Wells State Park

Fayette State Park

A small portion (66 acres) of the 711-acre Fayette State Park on the Garden Peninsula in Delta County (*which see*) is open to hunting. This area, near the park entrance along CR-C8, includes northern hardwoods and 15-year-old planted pines.

Hunting opportunities for deer, snowshoe hares, ruffed grouse, woodcock, and gray squirrels are considered fair to good.

Those entering with vehicles must have a valid state parks sticker affixed to the windshield. For more information regarding hunting opportunities, contact the Fayette State Park Manager, Garden Route 1, Garden, Mich. 49835 (906/644-2603).

Tahquamenon Falls State Park

NEARLY all of the 35,800-acre Tahquamenon Falls State Park is open to hunters. Located in northeastern Luce County (*which see*) in the eastern U.P., Tahquamenon Falls (Michigan's second-largest state park) features three developed units: the Lower Falls, the Upper Falls, and the Rivermouth. Via M-123 the Rivermouth unit is 19 miles from the Upper Falls. Through the park center courses the Tahquamenon River. Three-hundred-nineteen campsites in four campgrounds (two modern, two rustic) await hunters.

Nearly all of the park is climax-forested with spruce and cedar dominant. Near the river are some hilly hardwoods of beech and maple. Deer production is rather poor, yet bear populations are as good as anywhere else in the five-county DNR district. In fact, there are usually more bear hunters here than deer hunters.

Coyotes are in excellent supply, with sportsmen exerting negligible pressure. There are a few raccoon and black squirrels that, again, are largely overlooked by hunters. Snowshoe hare populations are cyclical; currently, they appear depressed. When the cycle swings back, tag alders and swamp swales can be highly productive. Tannic-acid-stained lakes in the park do not seem to attract waterfowl and there are no open areas for sharptails, but grouse and woodcock hunting is usually fair in edge cover.

Hunters entering with vehicles must have a valid state parks sticker attached.

For more information regarding hunting opportunities, contact Tahquamenon Falls State Park Manager, Star Route 48, Box 225, Paradise, Mich. 49768 (906/492-3415).

Brimley State Park

A small parcel of state land adjoining Brimley State Park along Whitefish Bay in Chippewa County (*which see*) is open to hunting. The 40-acre parcel, an area of woods and swamp land, lies across Six-Mile Road. Snowshoe hares provide hunting potential as do a few grouse and deer. There is even an occasional report of a bear in the area.

The state park sewage lagoon used to lie within this tract but has been abandoned in recent years.

Nevertheless, mallards, wood ducks, and some teal that continue to use the area provide some hunting opportunities for jump-shooters.

Hunters driving vehicles onto the property must have a valid state parks sticker affixed to the windshield.

For more information, contact Brimley State Park Manager, Box 202, Brimley, Mich. 49715 (906/248-3422).

De Tour State Park

ALL but the campground safety area of 402-acre De Tour State Park in Chippewa County (*which see*) is open to hunting. The park is located just southwest of De Tour Village at the far eastern tip of the Upper Peninsula.

The park is completely forested with a mixture of oaks, some soft maple, spruce, and plenty of balsam. Hunting opportunities are fair to good—especially along St. Vital Point—for deer, grouse (currently in a down state, however), gray squirrels (with an occasional black squirrel), and waterfowl. Hunting pressure is quite low and limited to resident

Fayette State Park

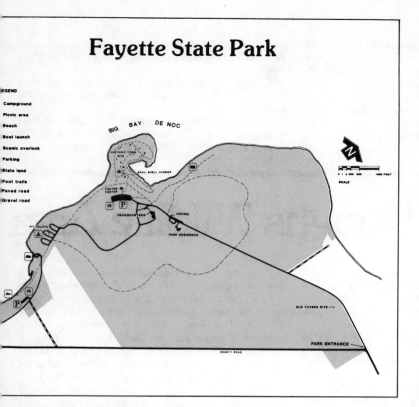

BIG BAY DE NOC

HISTORIC TOWN SITE
SNAIL SHELL HARBOR
VISITOR CENTER
HEADQUARTERS
PARK RESIDENCE
CONTROL
PIT TOILETS
OLD TAVERN SITE
PARK ENTRANCE
COUNTY ROAD

N

SCALE

Brimley State Park

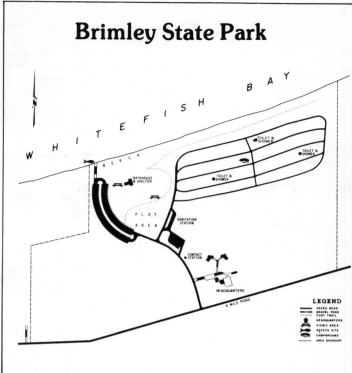

WHITEFISH BAY

BEACH

PLAY AREA

BATHHOUSE & SHELTER
TOILET & SHOWER
TOILET & SHOWER
TOILET & SHOWER
SANITATION STATION
CONTACT STATION
HEADQUARTERS
6 MILE ROAD

LEGEND
Paved road
Gravel road
Foot trail
Headquarters
Picnic area
Access site
Campground
Area boundary

Tahquamenon Falls State Park

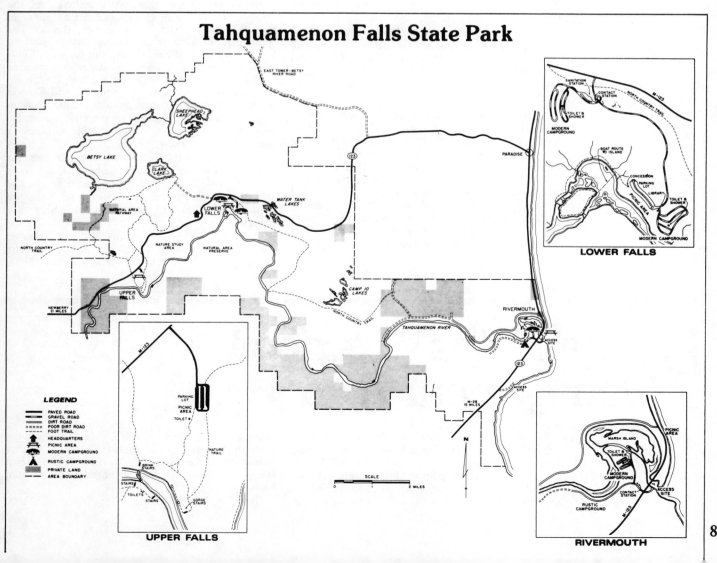

EAST TOWER - BETSY RIVER ROAD
SHEEPHEAD LAKE
BETSY LAKE
CLARK LAKE
NATURAL AREA PATHWAY
NORTH COUNTRY TRAIL
NATURE STUDY AREA
NATURAL AREA PRESERVE
UPPER FALLS
NEWBERRY 21 MILES
LOWER FALLS
WATER TANK LAKES
123
CAMP 10 LAKES
NORTH COUNTRY TRAIL
TAHQUAMENON RIVER
PARADISE
RIVERMOUTH
123
M-28 10 MILES
ACCESS SITE
ACCESS SITE

LEGEND
Paved road
Gravel road
Dirt road
Poor dirt road
Foot trail
Headquarters
Picnic area
Modern campground
Rustic campground
Private land
Area boundary

SCALE
0   1   2 MILES

N

LOWER FALLS

SANITATION STATION
CONTACT STATION
NORTH COUNTRY TRAIL
M-123
TOILET & SHOWER
MODERN CAMPGROUND
BOAT ROUTE TO ISLAND
CONCESSION
PARKING LOT
LIBRARY
PICNIC AREA
TOILET & SHOWER
MODERN CAMPGROUND

UPPER FALLS

M-123
PARKING LOT
PICNIC AREA
TOILET
NATURE TRAIL
BRINK STAIRS
STAIRS
TOILETS
STAIRS
GORGE STAIRS

RIVERMOUTH

MARSH ISLAND
PICNIC AREA
TOILET & SHOWER
MODERN CAMPGROUND
CONTACT STATION
ACCESS SITE
RUSTIC CAMPGROUND
M-123

sportsmen.

St. Vital Point should be excellent for duck hunting over decoys. A problem is that the state park does not contain a boat-launching site and the hike to the point is a long one. Waterfowlers would likely encounter early-season locals, but the best hunting would come in late October and November when flight ducks are down. Redheads, buffleheads, goldeneyes, old-squaws, scoters, scaup, and other diver species are then dominant in the eastern U.P.

The state park region gets an occasional visit by a black bear, and there are limited opportunities for raccoon and woodcock hunting. Coyotes are plentiful in the area.

Hunters driving vehicles onto the property must have a valid state parks sticker affixed to the windshield.

For more information, contact De Tour State Park Manager, De Tour Field Office, M-134 (Box 92), De Tour Village, Mich. 49725 (906/297-2581).

Sturgeon River Sloughs Wildlife Area

THE 32,000-acre project boundaries of the Sturgeon River Sloughs Wildlife Area are located in the lower Sturgeon River Valley between Otter and Portage lakes in Houghton and Keweenaw counties (*both of which see*). It is one of four Upper Peninsula areas selected by the DNR as best suited for the management of ducks and geese, partly because it lies along one of the nation's principal waterfowl migration corridors. Wisconsin's famed Horicon National Wildlife Refuge lies 250 miles south. The DNR's goal through intensive management at Sturgeon Sloughs is to attract a maximum of 25,000 Canada and blue (snow) geese and 30,000 diving and dabbling ducks to the area on an annual basis.

There are several reasons for this goal. First, holding migrating birds in this northern region will decrease crop damage in southern agricultural areas. Second, it will provide hunter recreation through dispersal of migrants. Third, it will increase local production of waterfowl.

After pine was logged off by the early 1900s, farmers began moving into the Sturgeon River Valley to attempt truck farming. Early efforts to drain the Arnheim Swamp to increase available land for cultivation failed, however. Peat farming which followed was another short-lived enterprise. Then, fires in the 20s and 30s burned over large portions of the lowlands. Sharp-tailed grouse grew numerous. By the 1950s aspen, willow, and mixed conifers were encroaching on the old burnings, causing a decline in both sharptails and waterfowl.

State-managed habitat improvement work began in the 60s with the construction of the first of 105 potholes, aerial herbicide application, mowings, and seeding of crops. In 1975 the DNR completed a dam and fish ladder on the Sturgeon River, which gave the department control over water levels in the sloughs. The next year saw completion of a seven-mile-long diversion ditch from the Sturgeon River west of Arnheim to the center slough at US-41 south of Chassell. The ditch would provide water for further impoundment and pothole development.

Topographically, the area is quite flat with the central portion poorly drained via organic soils underlain by alluvial deposits. About 60 percent of the project area is in marsh, lowland brush, and water cover. This is due to its inclusion of the Sturgeon River mouth as well as the floodplains of the Sturgeon, Otter, and Snake rivers. The remaining 40 percent is divided among conifer, aspen, and lowland hardwood cover types.

Local breeding species of waterfowl include mallards, black ducks, blue-winged teal, ringnecks, wood ducks, goldeneyes, mergansers, and Canada geese. Common migrants include scaup, buffleheads, redheads, baldpates, pintails, gadwalls, green-winged teal, shovelers, scoters, Canada geese, and blue (snow) geese.

There are additional hunting opportunities for ruffed grouse and woodcock (sharptails, although present, are currently off limits) on drier sites of aspen and alder. An occasional deer, black bear, red fox, coyote, bobcat, and snowshoe hare are reported.

The Sturgeon River Sloughs Wildlife Area is managed by the wildlife biologist at DNR District Headquarters, North US-41, Baraga, Mich. 49908 (906/353-6651).

Baraga Plains Waterfowl Management Area

THE 5,380-acre Baraga Plains Waterfowl Management Area is located about 10 miles south of Keweenaw Bay in Baraga County (*which see*). It is one of four Upper Peninsula areas selected by the DNR as best suited for the management of ducks and geese partly because it lies along a major waterfowl migration corridor. The DNR's goal through intensive management is to attract thousands of Canada and blue (snow) geese and many species of ducks to the area on an annual basis.

There are several reasons for this goal. First,

De Tour State Park

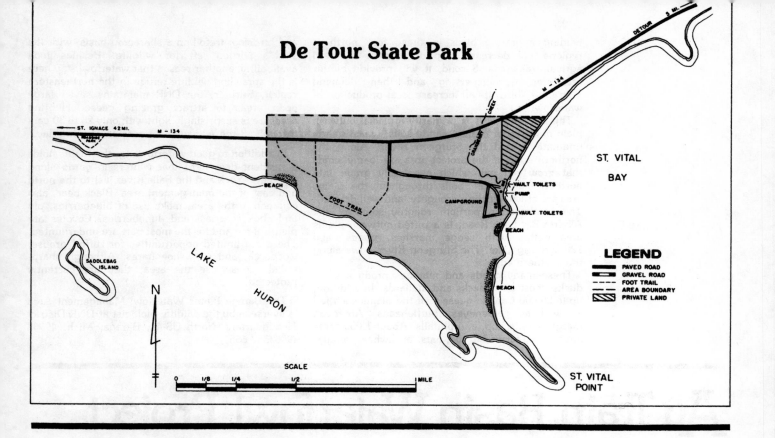

Sturgeon River Sloughs
Wildlife Area

Baraga Plains
Waterfowl
Management Area

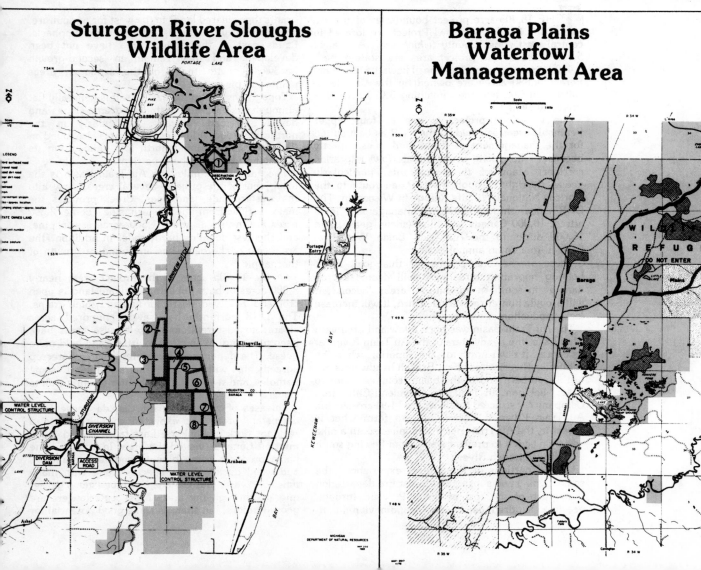

MICHIGAN
DEPARTMENT OF NATURAL RESOURCES

holding migrating birds in these four northern regions will decrease crop damage in southern agricultural areas. Second, it will provide hunter recreation by dispersing and then delaying migrants. Third, it will increase local production of waterfowl.

The Baraga Plains is primarily a glacial outwash plain made up of coarse, sandy soils, which gently undulate toward the Sturgeon River. Along the northern edge of the project area are loamy sands that grow red oak which eventually grade into northern hardwoods. Soils throughout the plains area are of low fertility, droughty, and well drained. The southeastern portion, roughly south of the Alberta-Big Lake Road, is a pitted outwash plains area dotted with sedge marshes, ponds, and 120-acre Big Lake. The Sturgeon River flows along the southern edge.

These many ponds and marshes produce some ducks, mostly ringnecks and mallards. In addition, up to 25,000 Canada geese visit the plains each fall as well as goldeneyes, buffleheads, American mergansers, scaup, and pintails. About 1,000 acres are actively farmed to rye, oats, buckwheat, alfalfa, and birdsfoot trefoil on a sharecrop basis, with the state's portion left for wildlife. Besides food availability, another reason that waterfowl stay here is the sprawling wildlife refuge in the northeastern region. Further, the DNR maintains seven large open areas to attract grazing geese. Hunting pressure is susprisingly light with only 25 to 30 cars throughout the management area on opening day.

In addition to good waterfowling, the Plains holds a resident deer herd that winters in yards along Ogemaw Creek and the Falls River just to the north and east of the management area. Black bear, also common in the area, make use of blueberries, pin and chokecherries, and Juneberries. Coyotes are plentiful too and for the most part are underhunted. There are limited opportunities for ruffed grouse, woodcock, and snowshoe hares. Although sharp-tailed grouse use the area, they are currently protected.

The Baraga Plains Waterfowl Management Area is overseen by the wildlife biologist at DNR District Headquarters, North US-41, Baraga, Mich. 49908 (906/353-6651).

Au Train Basin Waterfowl Project

THE 18,405-acre project boundaries of the Au Train Basin Waterfowl Project are located in central west Alger County (which see). A total of 5,065 acres in the project area are state-owned, 5,440 acres are part of the Hiawatha National Forest, 4,880 acres are owned by the Cleveland-Cliffs Iron Co., and the remaining 3,020 acres are privately owned.

The waterfowl project is one of four Upper Peninsula areas selected by the DNR as best suited for the management of ducks and geese, partly because it lies along a major waterfowl migration corridor. Many of these migrants, particularly geese, fly right through the U.P. en route to the Horicon National Wildlife Refuge in Wisconsin. The DNR's goal through intensive management is to attract 10,000 Canada and blue (snow) geese, and 15,000 ducks to the Au Train Basin Waterfowl Project area on an annual basis.

There are several reasons for this goal. First, holding migrating birds here will decrease crop damage in southern agricultural areas. Second, it will provide hunter recreation. Third, it will increase local production of waterfowl.

The Au Train Basin was once a lowland area with Mud Lake, the headwaters of the Au Train River, at its center. It flows north to Lake Superior, while the Whitefish River, whose East Branch headwaters are in the southern end of the basin, courses south to Lake Michigan. In 1930 the Cleveland-Cliffs Iron Company constructed a dam where M-94 crosses the Au Train River at Forest Lake to form what is presently the Au Train Basin. Six miles south a dike was then added to prevent water from flowing south into the Whitefish River.

Upland portions of the project experienced the same logging and subsequent forest fire devastation that much of the rest of the U.P. went through nearly a hundred years ago. Scandinavian immi-grants then cleared lands to the west for agriculture, of which dairy farming is still the main emphasis. Lands east of the project area have not been developed, and they remain in second-growth hardwoods, with many of the semiopen areas planted to pine.

Topography within the basin itself is generally flat although the east side contains extreme slopes and heavily forested hillsides, particularly in the northern portion. A long escarpment is also found on the west side, running north four miles from its beginning in the southern portion.

The narrow, six-mile-long Au Train Basin is the focal point of the project. Several creeks flow into the western side, and Joes' Creek provides the major inflow from the eastern side. Some 2,300 acres are in aspen, about 1,500 acres are in pine, and the rest contains hardwoods. In addition, the area west of the basin has an abundant growth of thornapple.

Of the 18,405 acres in the project area, nearly 3,000 acres of both public and private land is open cropland, reserved mostly for hay and some grains. The DNR currently has several hundred acres cleared to pasture (four goose-browse areas have been proposed) in an effort to attract and hold more geese. The department has entered into sharecrop agreements with local farmers, created some potholes, and seeded a single hunter walking trail to clover.

Releases of nuisance giant Canada geese from downstate areas are expected to help create a resident flock of honkers. Last fall a record 2,000 migrant Canadas visited the area. In addition, the basin produces some blue-winged teal, mallards, and wood ducks. These species along with many types of divers, plus Canada and blue (snow) geese, migrate through the area. Most waterfowlers are goose hunters, but there is some good potential for

Au Train Basin
Waterfowl Project

Scale
0   1/2   1 Mile

duck hunting on the lake as well as jump shooting along western-side streams. A wildlife refuge in the southern region is closed to hunting.

Migrating woodcock find the basin particularly attractive as do ruffed grouse. This is due to semiopen plains with scattered clumps of brush and aspen in the heart of the area, plus lowland hardwood sites to the east and upland aspen with hardwood timber and tag-alder swales bordering the plains. Sharptails also use the area but numbers fluctuate from year to year. Upland bird-hunting pressure is moderate. Deer frequent the region to provide fair hunting opportunities with medium pressure during the firearm season and light pressure during bow season. There is some underutilized potential for raccoon and coyote hunting. Area farm fields attract foraging black bears, with hunting pressure on the increase.

The Au Train Basin Waterfowl Project is managed by the wildlife biologist at DNR District Headquarters, 1126 North Lincoln Road, Escanaba, Mich. 49829 (906/786-2351).

Munuscong Waterfowl Management Area

THE 20,600-acre Munuscong Waterfowl Management Area is located at the far eastern end of the Upper Peninsula in Chippewa County (which see). It is one of four U.P. areas selected by the DNR as best suited for the management of ducks and geese. That is mainly because it lies along a major waterfowl migration corridor. The DNR's goal through intensive management is to attract 25,000 Canada, blue (snow) geese, and 75,000 ducks to the area on an annual basis.

There are several reasons for this goal. First, holding migrating birds in the U.P. will decrease crop damage in southern Michigan agricultural areas. Second, it will provide hunter recreation. Third, preservation of shorelands will help ensure resting and feeding places for diver species. Fourth, it will increase local production of waterfowl.

The Munuscong Bay area was recognized early as a tremendous region for waterfowl. In 1905 a group of wealthy sportsmen organized a private hunting club here, but by 1920 none was alive and so the land and a set of elaborate buildings were donated to the state. Parks, Wildlife, and Forestry divisions of the DNR have since managed the area by turn. Currently, it falls into the Lake Superior State Forest (which see) but is actually managed by the Wildlife Division, which began pothole, channel, and dike construction in the mid-60s. A state-forest campground and boat-launching site are located within the boundaries, and waterfowlers make use of both.

Cover types include marsh growth and open, grassland areas from abandoned farms along with some hardwoods. Soils are particularly well suited for flooding, pond construction, and impoundments. The far western, northeastern, and southeastern parts of the area are mostly muck, whereas greenwood and spalding peats occur in the northeastern region.

A wide variety of waterfowl use the area. Ringnecks, scaup, redheads, and buffleheads are most common among the divers. Mallards, blue-winged teal, and black ducks are puddlers attracted here. Coots are particularly abundant during fall migration. In addition, blue-winged teal, mallards, blacks, goldeneyes, mergansers, coots, and redheads nest in the one-square mile refuge (closed to hunting) on Munuscong Lake. A 14-year study showed an average of 21.5 local nesting waterfowl per lineal mile and 130 birds per square mile.

Fields adjacent to the refuge are used extensively by geese and dabbler species (goose hunting, however, has been closed in recent years to help build up a local flock of introduced giant Canada geese—check the current "Waterfowl Hunting Guide" for details). Overall, the area provides excellent waterfowling opportunities throughout the season. Some hunters employ field decoys while others use floating decoys and hunt from blinds or boats in Lake Munuscong. A few rely on layout boats and 100-block stools to sucker big flights of divers. The area falls into a steel-shot-only zone; again check the "Waterfowl Hunting Guide" for details.

Hunters also seek deer, snowshoe hares, grouse, and woodcock within the Munuscong Waterfowl Management Area. An occasional moose (no open season) visits the region too.

For more information, contact the wildlife habitat biologist at the DNR Sault Ste. Marie Field Office, Box 798, Sault Ste. Marie, Mich. 49783 (906/635-5281).

Drummond Island

DRUMMOND Island at the far eastern tip of the Upper Peninsula in Chippewa County (which see) has often been called the "Gem of the Huron." And for good reason. The 12-mile-by-24-mile island is scenic with rolling hills, huge dolomite boulders, bays dotted with islands, and remote wilderness areas. No wonder it has been popular with deer, waterfowl, grouse, woodcock, and snowshoe hare hunters for the past 100 years and with native hunters long before that.

Roughly 45,000 acres of the Lake Superior State Forest (which also see) is open to hunting on

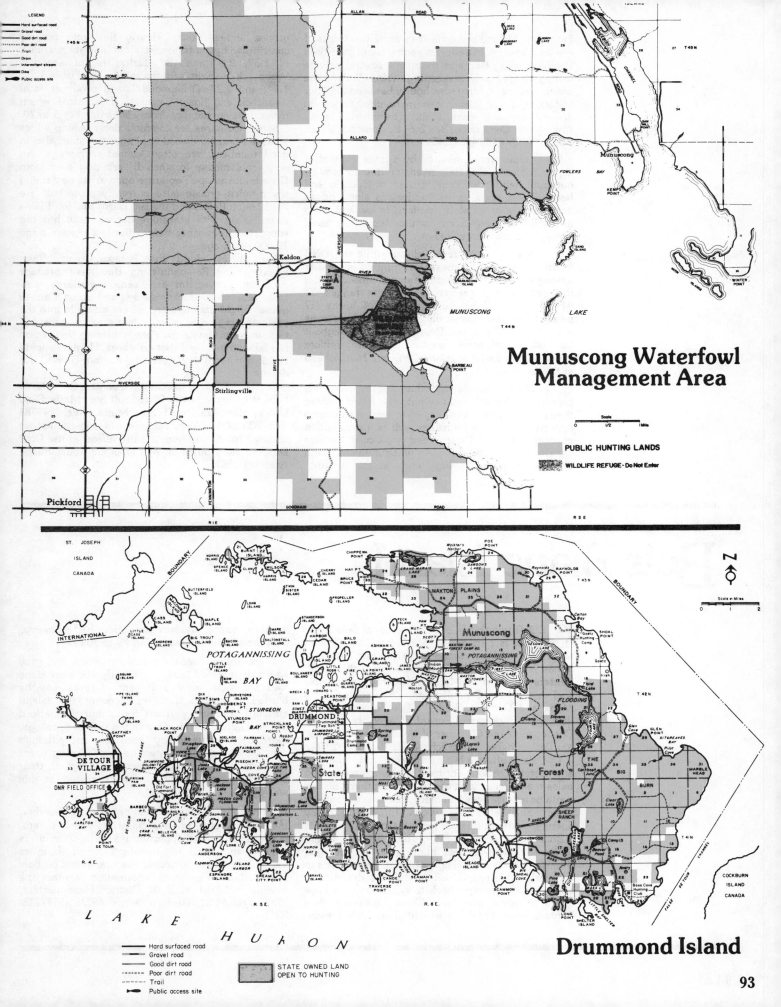

Munuscong Waterfowl Management Area

Scale
0   1/2   1 Mile

PUBLIC HUNTING LANDS

WILDLIFE REFUGE - Do Not Enter

Drummond Island

Hard surfaced road
Gravel road
Good dirt road
Poor dirt road
Trail
Public access site

STATE OWNED LAND
OPEN TO HUNTING

93

Drummond Island and comprises some two-thirds of the land base. A state-forest campground overlooks Potagannissing Bay and there are several private campgrounds and housekeeping cabins all along the western shore. A ferry runs hourly between De Tour Village and the island. For more information on accommodations, contact the Drummond Island Chamber of Commerce, Box 206, Drummond Island, Mich. 49726 (906/493-5245).

Cover types are dominated by a large amount of aspen, which desperately needs cutting to provide optimum habitat for deer, grouse, woodcock, and hares. There are also oak hardwoods along ridges and plenty of green stuff (conifers) in lowland areas as well as magnificent white birch scattered throughout the plains areas.

Bear hunting is currently closed while the DNR continues research studies. Deer hunting is popular among archers and firearm hunters alike. During the last hunting season 407 archers tagged 27 whitetails, and 1,306 hunters took 224 bucks (17 percent success). Generally, firearm success runs around 10 to 13 percent. Deer are found throughout the island. Hunters wanting a truly remote experience can hike or take a 4WD into Marblehead at the far eastern tip.

The DNR recently introduced gray squirrels captured at Houghton Lake onto the island, where they appear to be doing very well. Look for hunting opportunities in the future, as well as a resumption of bear hunting. Grouse and woodcock hunters experience fairly good success on Drummond Island although pressure is high and, at this writing,

grouse appear down. Hourly flush-rate records contributed by hunter-cooperators indicate averages of 1.37, 2.0, and .36 during recent seasons. Woodcock flush rates for the same period were 1.20, 1.44, and 2.23. Drummond Island produces local woodcock and hosts Canadian flight birds which make their appearance from about October 5 to 20.

Snowshoe hares are common along swamp edges in aspen and hardwood saplings. Coyotes, also in good numbers, are often hunted with dogs. An occasional moose (protected), crossing over from Canada, turns up. Two large open areas containing sharp-tailed grouse (also currently protected) are the Maxton Palins and the Big Burn. Maxton Plains is underlain with limestone deposits and has not supported trees since before the last glacier some 10,000 years ago.

Four lakes along the Potagannissing River Flooding and Potagannissing Bay itself produce excellent hunting for early-season mallards, pintails, teal, wood ducks, blacks, and some Canada geese. Flight dabblers and divers also pile into the protected region to provide late-season opportunities. In recent years the Potagannissing Bay region has fallen into a steel shot-only area. Hunters should check a current "Waterfowl Hunting Guide" for details.

For more hunting information, contact the wildlife habitat biologist at the DNR Sault Ste. Marie Field Office, Box 798, Sault Ste. Marie, Mich. 49783 (906/635-5281). Also, hunters can sometimes get updated conditions from the fire officer at the DNR De Tour field office on M-134 in De Tour Village (906/297-2581).

Bois Blanc Island

ABOUT two-thirds, or 8,000 acres, of Bois Blanc Island is part of the Mackinaw State Forest (*which see*) and therefore open to hunting. Although a map is not available for inclusion with this book, hunters can refer to Mackinac County (*which also see*) in the MUCC publication, "Michigan County Maps and Outdoor Guide." Two ferries operate daily from Cheboygan. For information, contact the Cheboygan Area Chamber of Commerce, Washington Park, Cheboygan, Mich. 49721 (616/627-2770).

The island offers a fair mixture of cover. Southern and eastern portions are mostly swamps containing balsam and cedar with aspen. The southern border contains mature oaks and there are mature stands of aspen and other hardwoods throughout. Few openings exist in this old-growth timber.

Bois Blanc (French for "white wood") Island offers fair to good deer hunting for archers and firearm hunters alike. High whitetail populations in the early 60s dropped off in the last decade but appear to be building back to good numbers once again. In recent years from 400 to 500 firearm deer hunters have shot 45 to 80 whitetails each season.

Archery hunting pressure runs about half as heavy, with the annual kill averaging 25 to 30 deer.

There are no bear on the island. Black and gray squirrels released here in the early 70s have done well and now, after a 10-year closure, may be hunted. Excellent numbers frequent the island although southern portions containing oaks afford the best opportunities. Due to the lack of openings, there are few grouse and woodcock, and although snowshoe-hare hunting can be good during years when the animals are experiencing a high in their population cycle, numbers are depressed at this writing.

A few red fox, coyotes, and bobcats are found on the island. Waterfowl, especially late-season divers, may offer additional opportunities for layout hunters between the island and mainland five or six miles away. About 40 to 50 people live year-round on Bois Blanc Island. For more information, contact the wildlife biologist at DNR District Headquarters, 1732 West M-32, Gaylord, Mich. 49735 (517/732-3541).

Pictured Rocks National Lakeshore

ABOUT 3,500 acres of northern Alger County (*which see*) is contained in the Pictured Rocks National Lakeshore. This is a narrow, 40-mile band of federally-owned land, administered by the National Park Service, on Lake Superior. The entire park is open to hunting; however, opportunities are limited for deer, bear, grouse, hares, and waterfowl.

Main reasons are the lack of openings in mature forest cover dominated by northern hardwoods (beech, maple, and birch) and the lack of aspen. Another 25 percent of the cover type includes red, white, and jack pine with the balance in lowland shrub wetlands. There are snowshoe hares in some of the conifer swamps as well as bear, which forage throughout the park. The Beaver Basin area in the central portion holds the most deer, although proximity to Lake Superior and consequent tough winters limit whitetail production. Beaver Lake offers the only potential for waterfowl hunting and that is considered poor.

Hunting pressure throughout the park is light, with most sportsmen trying for ruffed grouse and deer. Grouse hunting can be fair although populations are down at the moment. There is also some woodcock hunting potential, and although sharptails are legal in Alger County, none are found within park boundaries. For sharpies, consider the nearby Kingston Plains, a large, open area managed by the DNR.

There are no fees charged for camping at the three rustic campgrounds. They include the Hurricane River (15 sites), Little Lake (eight sites), and 12-Mile Beach (25 sites being expanded to 40 sites). Facilities include pit toilets, fire rings, tables, and a hand pump.

An overall map is not available for inclusion in this book. However, hunters can buy a one-inch-to-the-mile topographic map for $2 from Pictured Rocks National Lakeshore, Box 40 (end of Sand Point Road northeast of Munising), Munising, Mich. 49862 (906/387-2607). A free map of the park's trail system is also available. For more hunting information, contact the resources management specialist at headquarters. Hunters might also check with the ranger at the Grand Marais Ranger Station, 906/494-2611.

Seney National Wildlife Refuge

CARVED from string bogs and conifer swamps of the Great Manistique Swamp, the 95,000-acre Seney National Wildlife Refuge was dedicated in 1935. Habitat ranges from marshes and open water to hardwoods, spruce, and pine forests. There are 21 major managed impoundments totaling some 7,000 acres. In addition, over 25,000 acres in the western portion have been dedicated as a Wilderness Area. Contained within is the 9,000-acre Strangmoor Bog Registered Natural Landmark. Seney National Wildlife Refuge has no parallel.

This 153-square-mile area in central Schoolcraft County (*which see*) offers many unique hunting opportunities on that portion where sport is allowed. State hunting laws are in effect on the federal property but because special rules and regulations are somewhat complex and change annually, hunters should check with refuge personnel. Maps and regulations are free of charge at the interpretive center off M-77 between Germfask and Seney, or you can write/call the refuge manager at Seney 49883 (906/586-9851). The Germfask/Seney Lions Club sells a good map in area stores for 50 cents.

About 15,000 acres in the eastern region is closed to all hunting. However, the refuge attracts up to 15,000 geese in fall where the birds rest before migrating down the eastern edge of Lake Michigan. These geese nest in the James and Hudson Bay region and then winter in the Tennessee Valley. Seney is their first major stop. Local farmers rent blinds around the refuge perimeter to goose hunters. The DNR has recently sown portions of the Bullock Ranch (a sharp-tailed grouse management area along M-28) to rye. Hunter success varies, but altogether only 200 to 300 geese are shot each fall and the Seney Goose Management quota of 500 honkers has never been met.

The refuge produces only 100 or so geese each year, but since giant-strain Canadas were introduced from downstate areas, where they have grown to nuisance proportions, production is improving. Refuge personnel have a goal of raising 1,000 to 1,500 geese but admit that achievement is several years away. Sharecrop plantings of 400 acres of crops with local farmers serve to attract both local and passing waterfowl. Several thousand ducks also use the refuge. For example, refuge personnel have observed over 11,000 ringnecks here at one time.

Game species that may be hunted include deer and all small game, as well as coyotes, bobcats, and bear (no baiting or hunting with tracking dogs, however).

The refuge supports fair to good numbers of deer, which should increase fast during the next mild winter (Seney can get 125 inches of snow or more in a year) due to new browse from a devastating 1976 fire and, although none winter here, many move through the area heading south to Blaney, Gulliver, and Manistique yards. Internal roads within the refuge are closed until deer season, but hunters can get a special permit to scout (except in the Wilderness Area). Camping by permit is allowed west of the Driggs River (again, except in the Wilderness Area). During a recent season 42 camp permits were issued to 125 hunters.

Seney produces some huge deer as evidenced by the fact that the average buck carries eight points or more and is one-and-a-half to two-and-a-half years older than his downstate counterpart. Four recent seasons of records that we checked showed from 377 to 600 hunters on the refuge. They tagged from 40 to 75 bucks each year for a nine to 17 percent success ratio. Thus, low pressure equals a quality hunt.

A good early-season area is the Walsh Farm. Muzzleloader and December bow-season hunters (bowhunting is also allowed in October by permit) score well in low aspen mixed with conifers east of Holland Ditch in the northeastern region and again between the Chicago Farm and Manistique River Road in an area of heavy black spruce cover. Hunters can also intercept migrating whitetails along Marsh Creek and the Driggs River as well as in strings of cover running north and south.

Ruffed grouse are best hunted in young aspen and lowland brush. One good spot is along the Creighton River. Other patches of ideal habitat can be noted along M-28 as one drives west from Seney. These same areas produce woodcock, which sometimes concentrate during fall migrations. In fact, spring woodcock peenting counts (not a reliable indicator of fall populations but an indicator nevertheless) in the refuge are highest in the entire western flyway, which covers several states.

Estimates place the sharp-tailed grouse population at about 2,500 birds. At Seney hunters can roam for miles in quest of these prairie game birds. Good places are the eastern two-thirds of the Wilderness Area, in the southwestern portion east of the High Water Truck Trail, in the Bullock Ranch, and along Diversion Ditch. Pressure for grouse and woodcock is high except in the interior where most birds never face a dog's point and a hunter's gun.

Coyotes could accept far more hunting pressure. There are also raccoon, a few gray/black squirrels, and snowshoe hares. A good place for hares is between refuge headquarters and Seney on the west side of the road. Some hunters use field goose decoys in the sharptail management areas and then hide under tarps while waiting for a hungry flock of honkers to drop in. Other waterfowlers simply walk the drainage ditches to jump shoot both geese and ducks.

Hunting in the Seney National Wildlife Refuge has little impact on overall game populations because of its immense size and tough-to-access spots. Following the sport here amounts to a unique experience both for the unusual topography and the opportunity. You may see sandhill cranes, a bald eagle, even a timber wolf or moose (all protected species, incidentally). And the deeper you penetrate, the fewer hunters you will encounter.

Seney National Wildlife Refuge

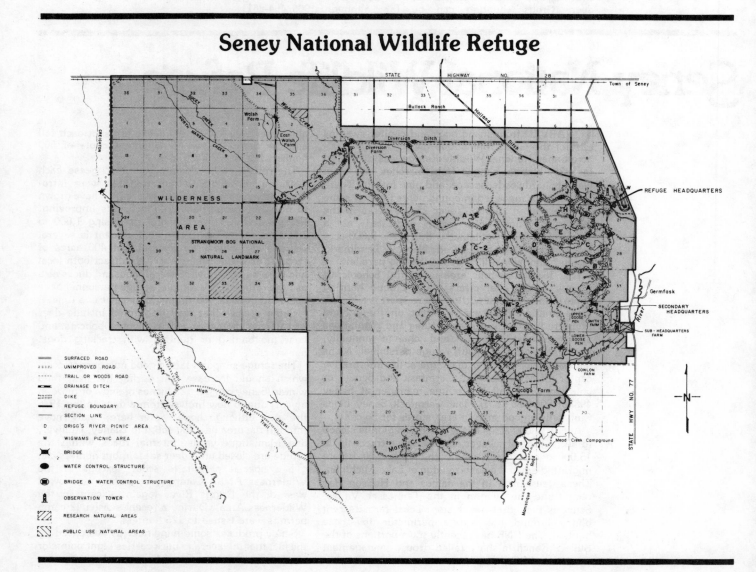

SURFACED ROAD
UNIMPROVED ROAD
TRAIL OR WOODS ROAD
DRAINAGE DITCH
DIKE
REFUGE BOUNDARY
SECTION LINE
D   DRIGG'S RIVER PICNIC AREA
W   WIGWAMS PICNIC AREA
     BRIDGE
     WATER CONTROL STRUCTURE
     BRIDGE & WATER CONTROL STRUCTURE
     OBSERVATION TOWER
     RESEARCH NATURAL AREAS
     PUBLIC USE NATURAL AREAS

Kenneth S. Lowe

Betsie River State Game Area

THE 697-acre Betsie River State Game Area is located one mile from Lake Michigan in Benzie County (*which see*). The village of Elberta lies along its western boundary, and M-22 runs from east to west on the northern side. The Betsie River winds the length of the game area.

About half (mostly in Section 35) is a dedicated waterfowl sanctuary closed to hunting, but the remaining portion is open. Game species found here include deer, snowshoe hares, grouse, woodcock, raccoon, ducks, and geese. Nesting ducks include mallards, blacks, blue-winged teal, and wood ducks. Large numbers of goldeneyes and buffleheads congregate during migrations late in the fall. Canada geese are both local and passage birds.

Sedge-cattail marsh occupies most of the river mouth area in Section 35 with lowland hardwoods and mixed conifers making up most of the remaining land in Sections 31 and 36. Tree species are largely black ash and scattered pockets of cedar and balsam. Topography is gently rolling with increasing hilliness as one approaches Lake Michigan.

For the most part, hunting pressure is light. Reasons include the closed-to-hunting sanctuary portion of the game area, the general swamp and tough-access nature of the open land, and the high number of hunting opportunities on surrounding areas. A few grouse and woodcock hunters use the open fringe areas. Deer-hunting pressure is moderate, there is very little interest in raccoon, and snowshoe hares receive moderate attention. The river is floatable among scenic surroundings and produces good duck-hunting potential for the few who take advantage.

For more information, contact DNR District Headquarters, 8015 South 131 Road, Cadillac, Mich. 49601 (616/775-9727).

Petobego State Game Area

LOCATED on the northern edge of Grand Traverse County (*which see*) adjacent to Lake Michigan is the 440-acre Petobego State Game Area. It lies directly in line with a well-recognized flyway corridor for ducks and geese which follow the eastern shore of Lake Michigan.

The game area consists of two medium-quality marsh areas which produce and attract fairly good numbers of waterfowl. The lower pond is less marshy, has a more-open water character, and offers less opportunity for management. Topography of the area is gently rolling and agricultural. The bulk falls into bulrush and cattail cover; however, there is a mixed stand of lowland hardwoods on the northern edge of the upper pond. Upland hardwoods, conifers, and aspen are also found.

Most hunters come to Petobego in moderate numbers to see mallards, blue-winged teal, black ducks, and wood ducks that both nest here and use the area as a migratory stopover. Small flocks of migrating geese also frequent the area in spring and fall, and coots are common visitors. Other game species include red fox, raccoon, squirrels (both fox and gray/blacks), woodchucks, ruffed grouse, snowshoe hares, woodcock, and deer.

The area produces an estimated 150 to 200 ducks each year. The other game species receive very light hunting pressure.

For more information, contact the wildlife biologist at the DNR Traverse City Field Office, 404 West 14th St., Traverse City, Mich. 49684 (616/946-4920).

Manistee River State Game Area

THE 3,613-acre Manistee River State Game Area, located along the Manistee River in Manistee County (*which see*), is entirely open to hunting. This floodplain region is nearly level, rising to bluffs in some areas. The river bottom itself is marshy with sedges, cattails, bulrushes, smartweed, bluejoint, and pondweed. Major lowland timber types include black ash, red maple, elm (mostly dead), northern white cedar, and birch. Shrubs include willow, red osier and silky dogwood, tag alder, spice bush, elderberry, and wild grape.

The river is deal for float waterfowl hunting, and bayous and potholes en route provide excellent opportunities to set up decoys and boat blinds. Common species include mallards, black ducks, blue- and green-winged teal, wood ducks, and Canada geese. Ruffed grouse frequent fruit-bearing shrubs between the floodplain and lowland hardwoods and they, along with woodcock, are found atop bluffs in aspen and young-growth hardwoods. Raccoon traverse the river bottomlands, and there are opportunities for cottontails and snowshoe hares. Fox and gray/black squirrels are found in oak forests mixed with pine.

Deer hunting is very good in this area, with big bucks coming from remote areas within. Some hunters walk in; for a quality experience in the wild, consider floating for deer.

For more information, contact the wildlife biologist at DNR District Headquarters, 8015 South 131 Road, Cadillac, Mich. 49601 (616/775-9727).

Petobego State Game Area

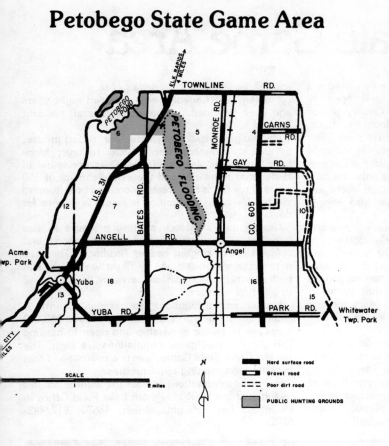

Legend:
- Hard surface road
- Gravel road
- Poor dirt road
- PUBLIC HUNTING GROUNDS

SCALE
1   2 miles

Betsie River State Game Area

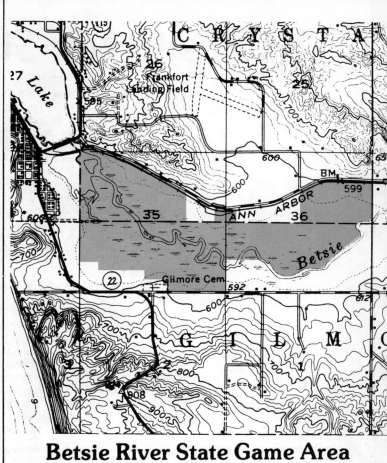

Manistee River State Game Area

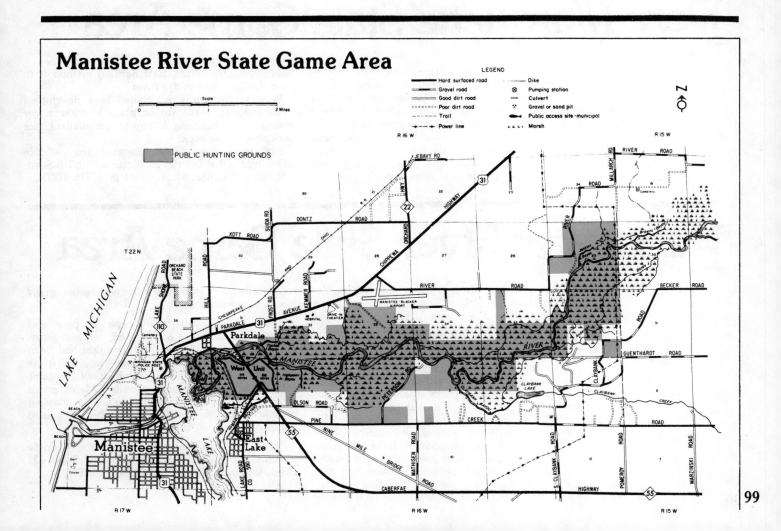

LEGEND
- Hard surfaced road
- Gravel road
- Good dirt road
- Poor dirt road
- Trail
- Power line
- Dike
- Pumping station
- Culvert
- Gravel or sand pit
- Public access site-municipal
- Marsh

Scale
0   1   2 Miles

PUBLIC HUNTING GROUNDS

Backus Creek State Game Area

THE Backus Creek State Game Area, a 3,406-acre parcel of public land open to hunting, is located in Roscommon County (*which see*) about three miles east of Houghton Lake. Highway I-75 runs along its eastern border. The watershed of the Backus Creek complex is about 14 square miles in size. The main water source is Backus Creek itself, which originates only one mile from Backus Creek Flooding, although there are numerous underground springs that also supply water to this system.

Three impoundments in the area average two feet in depth. They include Little Mud Lake (350 acres), Backus Creek Flooding No. 1 (520 acres), and Backus Creek Flooding No. 2 (550 acres). The area was formerly a large pine forest that was logged off before 1900. An aspen-oak stand that grew on upland areas was cut again about 30 years ago and has since regenerated. In addition, the area contains extensive swampy regions.

Hunters come to the Backus Creek State Game Area seeking many game species. Waterfowl living and nesting here include mallards, black ducks, wood ducks (especially), and lesser numbers of blue- and green-winged teal and ring-necked ducks. Other migrants include gadwalls, pintails, baldpates, shovellers, scaup, ruddy ducks, buffleheads, snow/blue geese, and Canada geese.

Further, 125 Canada geese released eight years ago have provided the basis for a small resident flock of honkers.

Upland game species include deer, ruffed grouse, woodcock, snowshoe hares, wild turkeys, black bear, and gray/black squirrels. Deer are found in fairly good numbers, and the establishment of 150 acres of rye fields has greatly increased bow-hunting efforts. Overall, gun hunting pressure is intense for deer.

Grouse and woodcock hunting pressure is also high, with sportsmen working aspen stands and lowland brush ringing beaver floodings. The area gets occasional visitation by flight woodcock, and both squirrels and snowshoe hares are usually found in plentiful numbers.

Hunter use throughout Roscommon County is among the highest in the state since over 200,000 acres are in public ownership and open to hunting and since overall game populations are high. The Backus Creek State Game Area is a reflection of that pressure and hunting opportunities.

For more information, contact the wildlife habitat biologist at the DNR Houghton Lake Field Office in Houghton Lake Heights, Mich. 48630 (517/442-5522).

Pere Marquette State Game Area

THE Pere Marquette State Game Area, located just south of Ludington in Mason County (*which see*), contains 178 acres on the Pere Marquette River. This is floodplain marshland containing waterfowl, and it is open to hunting. Main species are dabblers—mallards, blacks, teal, and wood ducks—but during the late season migrating ring-necked ducks, scaup, and golden-eyes also stop to rest and feed, providing further sporting opportunities. Best hunting method is to float the Pere Marquette River.

Because the entire watershed is a designated Natural River, there are no plans to make major changes. At this time a map is not available for inclusion in this book.

For more information, contact the wildlife biologist at DNR District Headquarters, 8015 South 131 Road, Cadillac, Mich. 49601 (616/775-9727).

Pentwater River State Game Area

LOCATED near Lake Michigan and the town of Pentwater in Oceana County (*which see*), the Pentwater River State Game Area contains 506 acres, all open to hunting. Topography is nearly level with both the North and South branches of the Pentwater River forming the marshland floodplain that characterizes this public-land region.

Waterfowl are the main attraction with mallards, blacks, teal, and wood ducks making up the major share. They are followed in numbers by Canada geese, scaup, and ring-necked ducks. Hunters either float the river or jump-shoot in the marsh. In upland portions flanking both sides of the river, hunters find ruffed grouse, woodcock, cottontails, and deer. Other game species include red fox, raccoon, squirrels (mostly fox, with some gray/black), and woodchucks.

When the original forest type of pine and hardwoods was logged and burned, oak and aspen took over on upland sites. Portions that had been cleared and farmed have given way to grass openings and pine. The marsh itself contains sedges, blue joint, and cattails. Management projects have thus far been limited to blasting potholes from the marsh, cutting aspen in upland areas, and planting shrubs.

For more information, contact the wildlife biologist at the DNR District Office, 8015 South 131 Road, Cadillac, Mich. 49601 (616/775-9727).

Backus Creek State Game Area

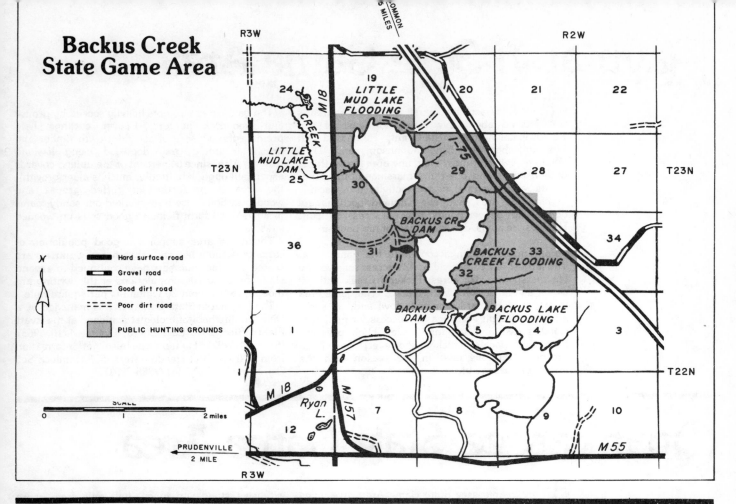

R3W   R2W

COMMON
5 MILES

19   LITTLE MUD LAKE FLOODING   20   21   22

24

81W CREEK

LITTLE MUD LAKE DAM   25

T23N   30   29   28   27   T23N

I-75

36   BACKUS CR DAM   31   BACKUS 33 CREEK FLOODING   34

32

Legend (key):
- Hard surface road
- Gravel road
- Good dirt road
- Poor dirt road
- PUBLIC HUNTING GROUNDS

N

BACKUS L. DAM   BACKUS LAKE FLOODING

1   6   5   4   3

T22N

SCALE

0   1   2 miles

M 18   Ryan L.   M 157   7   8   9   10

12

PRUDENVILLE 2 MILE   M 55

R3W

Pentwater River State Game Area

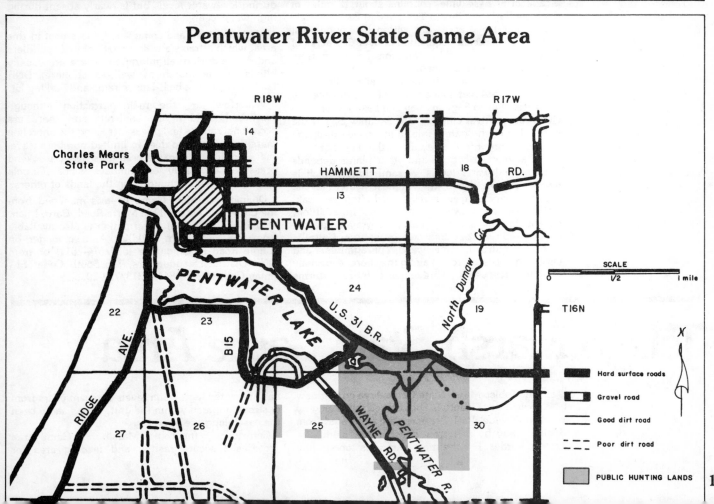

R18W   R17W

14

Charles Mears State Park

HAMMETT   18   RD.

13

PENTWATER

PENTWATER LAKE

22   23   24   North Dumaw Cr.   19   T16N

RIDGE AVE.   B15   U.S. 31 B.R.

SCALE

0   1/2   1 mile

N

27   26   25   WAYNE RD.   PENTWATER R.   30

Legend (key):
- Hard surface roads
- Gravel road
- Good dirt road
- Poor dirt road
- PUBLIC HUNTING LANDS

101

Haymarsh State Game Area

THE 6,287-acre Haymarsh State Game Area is located about five miles northeast of Big Rapids in northern Mecosta County. Purchased with Pittman-Robertson, Dingell-Johnson, and DNR Wildlife Division funds, the game area is two-thirds upland cover and one-third marshland, impoundments, and swamps. Beaver activity is especially high in the area, and even upland portions are dotted with beaver ponds, making access difficult. Hunters are advised to toss a pair of hip boots in the car.

Four major floodings constitute the game area. The largest is Featherbed at 425 acres, followed by Haymarsh with 375 acres, Pickerel Creek with 90 acres, and Little John with 70 acres. The game area is managed primarily for waterfowl and, as such, affords excellent early-season success for mallards, wood ducks, and sometimes teal. High pressure burns off locals quickly, however, and then prospects improve later in the season with the arrival of passage birds.

The game area also gets heavily socked by grouse and woodcock hunters. Beaver cuttings help promote the advance of second-growth timber and brush, including gray dogwood along lowland fringes. Also, since 64 percent of the upland cover is aspen (although, admittedly, much is older growth), the area is productive of ruffed grouse and woodcock. Soils vary from worked-out sandy loams in abandoned farm fields to good soils on wooded sites.

The game area supports a good population of cottontails and a few snowshoe hares. Squirrels are scarce, but deer numbers have continued to expand since the early 70s. Populations at this writing are thought to be about 20 whitetails per square mile.

The Haymarsh State Game Area is managed by a DNR wildlife habitat biologist stationed at the Evart Field Office, 2510 East US-10, Evart, Mich. 49631 (616/734-5492). Hunters can also get information from DNR District Headquarters, 501 Hemlock St., Clare, Mich. 48617 (517/386-7991).

Quanicassee State Game Area

THE Quanicassee State Game Area, five miles east of Essexville, contains about 12 miles of Saginaw Bay shoreline in Tuscola and Bay counties. More than 1,600 acres are within its boundaries, including the recent acquisition of over 300 acres of formerly leased land in Hampton Township from Consumers Power Company.

The shoreline, which is nearly level and lies at an elevation of 584 feet above sea level, is influenced by the water level in Saginaw Bay and Lake Huron. The Quanicassee River empties into Saginaw Bay at the north side of the game area, and various drainage ditches empty into the bay along the bay shore.

The amount of cattails and other plants depends upon annual water levels. A sand ridge, which is nearly always above the highest water levels, supports several tree species, including red oak, white ash, cottonwood, and willow. In addition, several brushy species, including gray dogwood, willow, and red ozier dogwood, grow here. Cattails, softstem bulrush, smartweed, phragmites, and various grasses are found along the shore, especially in low-water years. Three-square bulrush forms extensive stands up to one-half mile from shore during low-water levels but is nearly absent during high-water years.

Mallards, teal, and some wood ducks nest in this area, which attracts a wide variety of both puddlers and divers during fall migration. There are usually blinds in the marsh as well as offshore. DNR facilities include a boat-launch ramp and parking lot.

Waterfowl are the main attraction although hardwoods hold a few squirrels and there are occasional rabbits and pheasants along the shoreline marsh. Raccoon and deer in limited numbers travel the shoreline. The game area gets heavy weekend pressure, especially on Sundays since Tuscola County is closed to hunting on the lands of others.

Quanicassee State Game Area is managed from the Caro Field Office, 1123 Mertz Road, Caro, Mich. 48723 (517/673-3434). Information is also available from the Fish Point Wildlife Area manager on Ringle Road in Unionville (517/674-2511) or from DNR District Headquarters, 715 South Cedar St., Imlay City, Mich. 48444 (313/724-2015).

Tobico Marsh State Game Area

THE Tobico Marsh State Game Area on Saginaw Bay in Bay County is about three miles long by a half-mile wide. Its 1,791 acres are separated from Saginaw Bay by a narrow beach ridge along the eastern border. For the most part, this topography has prevented high-water levels of recent years from destroying marsh within the unit, as has sadly been the case along the open bay.

Consquently, the Tobico Marsh State Game Area provides a secure resting and feeding area for

Haymarsh State Game Area

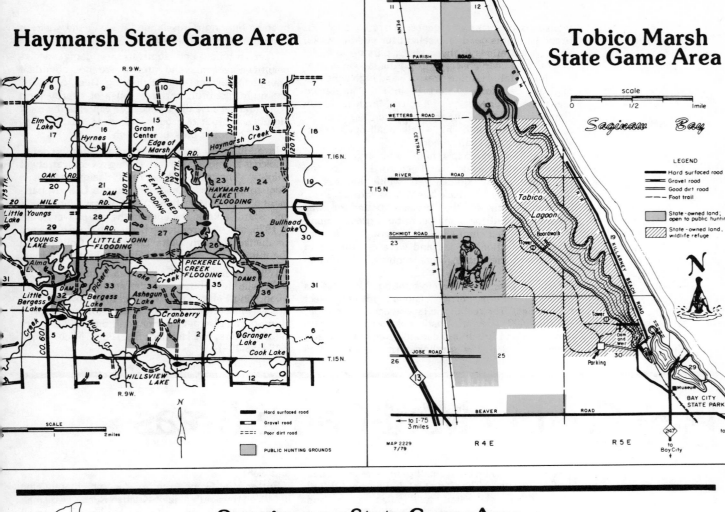

Tobico Marsh State Game Area

LEGEND

Hard surfaced road
Gravel road
Good dirt road
Foot trail

State-owned land; open to public hunting
State-owned land, wildlife refuge

Saginaw Bay

SCALE
Hard surfaced road
Gravel road
Poor dirt road
PUBLIC HUNTING GROUNDS

MAP 2229
7/79

Quanicassee State Game Area

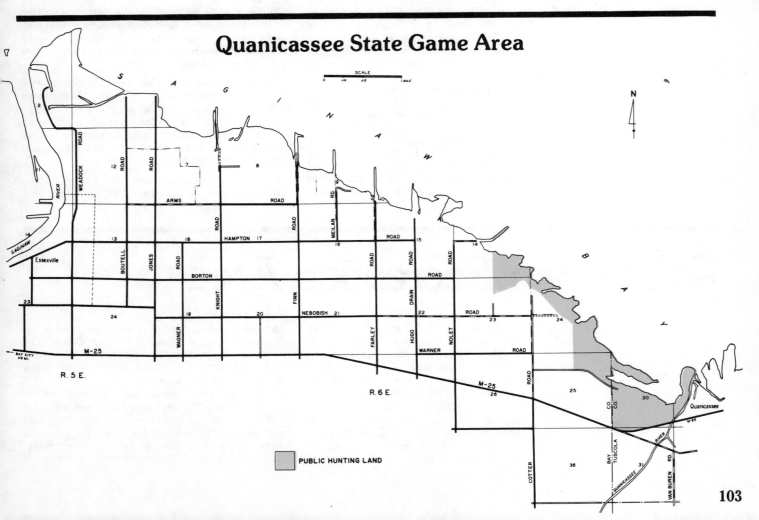

PUBLIC HUNTING LAND

thousands of ducks and geese in spring and fall. Brood habitat is good to excellent for puddle ducks, and concentrations of these birds, plus up to 8,000 divers, have been observed using the lagoon area at one time in fall. Hunting pressure and high winds on Saginaw Bay force waterfowl into the protected area. The lower portion of Tobico Marsh is mostly open water whereas the upper portion has a dense stand of cattails with only a few small open areas. Water levels are shallow here.

Tobico Marsh has a long hunting history, dating to Indians who traveled and camped along the shoreline. Indian guides led white hunters to memorable days of duck hunting as late as 1925. Further, much of the present boundary was privately owned for many years by a group calling itself the Tobico Hunt Club. Apparently, they were very conservation-minded and were careful not to overharvest the ducks. State acquisition began in 1955.

Today 782 acres are open to hunting. About half is in the northern portion (signs indicate exact boundaries). The rest of the lagoon acts as a refuge. Another 400 acres of mostly oak hardwoods with dense lowland brush and cattails (some of it nearly impenetrable) in the southwestern portion is also open to hunting. Grasslands lie along the western edge as one approaches M-13.

Deer, rabbits, and squirrels are game species sought. Pheasants and grouse are not abundant enough to warrant targeted hunting. Deer, however, are quite plentiful, partly because of nearby farm crops and because the Tobico area contains the most significant block of wooded cover in eastern Bay County. Hunting pressure is high.

In addition to its value as prime hunting land, Tobico is a unique area for viewing a wide variety of wildlife. The marsh has been designated as a Registered Natural Landmark by the U.S. Department of the Interior. Two 30-foot observation towers and boardwalks on the edge of the marsh were built in 1975, and prearranged scheduled nature hikes are conducted through Delta Community College and the interpretive program at Bay City State Park.

Tobico Marsh State Game Area is managed by a DNR wildlife habitat biologist stationed at nearby Nyanquing Point Wildlife Area, 1570 Tower Beach Road, Pinconning, Mich. 48650 (517/697-5101). Hunters can also get information from DNR District Headquarters, 501 Hemlock St., Clare, Mich. 48617 (517/386-7991).

Bay County Mini-Game Areas

BAY County has five small parcels of land open to hunting. The *Krystyniak Pheasant Mini-Game Area* is located two miles south and one-and-a-half miles east of Pinconning between Town Line and Almeda Beach roads. Its 80 acres contain pheasants and rabbits and serve as a corridor for deer.

The *Pinconning Mini-Game Area* is 50 acres in size and features a fenced five-acre pond and about 20 acres of sharecropped farming. Located along I-75 on the north side of Cody-Estey Road, the parcel holds rabbits and some pheasants.

Fraser Mini-Game Area No. 1 is 41 acres of mostly brushlands on the west side of I-75, south of Townline Road and west of Seven-Mile Road. There are no access restrictions to a shallow four-acre pond on the property; and the site offers deer, rabbits, and woodcock.

Fraser Mini-Game Area No. 2 is immediately east of I-75 on the south side of Kitchen Road. Two small ponds on the 32-acre site are off-limits. A small amount of sharecropping provides food for rabbits and some pheasants.

The *Quanicassee Mini-Game Area* is two 40-acre tracts located two miles south of the Quanicassee Wildlife Area and eight miles southeast of Bay City. School Drain cuts through the north boundary, while the Quanicassee River flows across the southwestern portion. Ducks along with some rabbits and occasional deer are featured.

Maps of the five mini-game areas in Bay County are not available; however, property boundaries are marked with signs.

Rifle River Recreation Area

NEARLY all of the 4,329-acre Rifle River Recreation Area in Ogemaw County (*which see*) is open to hunting for all game species except geese. The wilderness recreation area is a part of the Au Sable State Forest (*which also see*) and is located 15 miles northeast of West Branch and four-and-three-quarters miles east of Rose City.

Cover types include oak and aspen uplands surrounding Grebe Lake and evergreen swamps sprinkled throughout. Major ones occur in the northwestern portion just north of Oyster Creek, along the eastern portion of Skunk Creek, and in the southernmost region south of Clear Creek. The remainder of the area is a mixture of low aspen ridges and tag alder/balsam swamp with some stands of white-pine understory.

An 80-site modern campground is located on the northern shore of Grousehaven Lake, and there are 79 rustic campsites at Devoe Lake and two other locations on the Rifle River. Meandering throughout the recreation area are 12 miles of foot trails, popular with hunters. Also of interest to hunters is that several trailside cabins may be rented, but applications should be sent early as they fill fast.

Good populations of deer, raccoon, ducks (mostly dabblers), and woodcock are reported. Cottontails and hares, fox and gray/black squirrels, and ruffed grouse are found in moderate numbers. Also present are occasional wild turkeys, pheasants, fox, and coyotes. Hunting pressure for deer, grouse, and woodcock is heavy. The other game species receive light to moderate pressure.

Those entering with vehicles must have a valid state parks sticker affixed to the windshield.

For more information regarding hunting opportunities, contact the **Rifle River Recreation Area** manager in Lupton (517/473-2258).

Rifle River Recreation Area

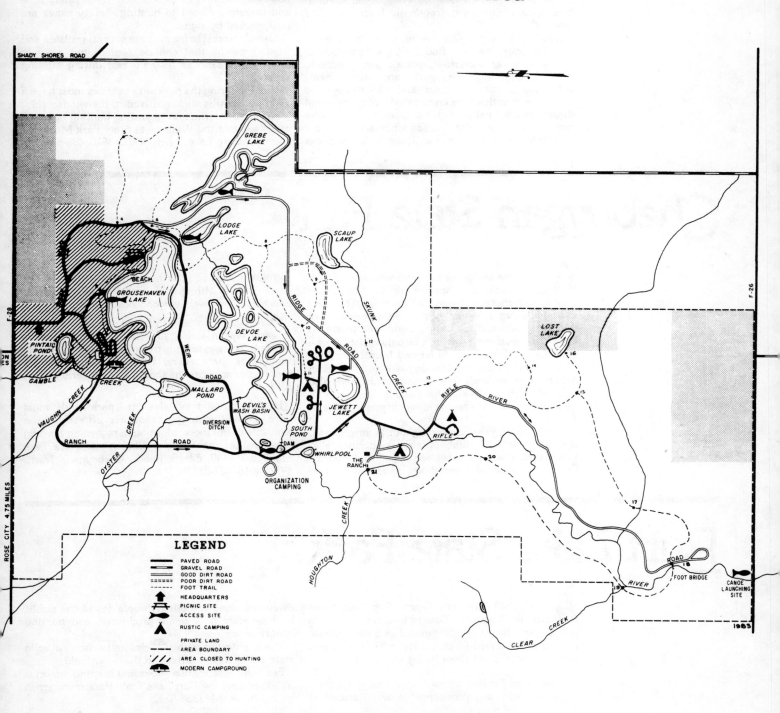

LEGEND

▬▬▬	PAVED ROAD
▭▭▭	GRAVEL ROAD
▬▬▬	GOOD DIRT ROAD
=====	POOR DIRT ROAD
- - -	FOOT TRAIL
⬆	HEADQUARTERS
🏕	PICNIC SITE
⚓	ACCESS SITE
⛺	RUSTIC CAMPING
	PRIVATE LAND
— — —	AREA BOUNDARY
///	AREA CLOSED TO HUNTING
	MODERN CAMPGROUND

Wilderness State Park

LOCATED at the extreme northern tip of the Lower Peninsula, Wilderness State Park in Emmet County (*which see*) contains vast evergreen forests (spruce, tamarack, white pine, balsam, hemlock, and red pine) interspersed with hardwoods (aspen, maple, beech, and white birch). Overall, the topography is one of swamps mixed with ridges. There is flat, barren land on Waugoshance Point. Beaver floodings occur frequently throughout the interior.

Nearly all of the 7,554-acre park is open to hunting. Sportsmen will find fairly good numbers of snowshoe hares, waterfowl, grouse, and woodcock. Also frequenting the park are deer, bear, cottontails, coyotes, raccoon, and wild turkeys (no open season at this time on turkeys). Deer are found throughout but not in high numbers. Hunters, who range mostly near main roads since access to the park interior is difficult, tag about a dozen bucks during each firearm season.

Waterfowlers jump mallards on the beaver ponds and along streams flowing either to Lake Michigan or Sturgeon Bay. Along Waugoshance Point they shoot migrating diving ducks, mergansers, and some Canada geese. There are also a few local-Canadas that nest on the pond near the park office; however, this may be located within the safety zone and therefore closed to hunting. Safety zones are well marked by signs.

Also of interest to hunters are several trailside and frontier cabins that can be rented, but send in applications early as they fill fast during hunting season.

Those entering the park with vehicles must have a valid state parks sticker affixed to the windshield.

For more information regarding hunting opportunities, contact the Wilderness State Park Manager, Box 380, Carp Lake, Mich. 49718 (616/436-5381).

Cheboygan State Park

ALL but the designated campground area of 932-acre Cheboygan State Park in Cheboygan County (*which see*) is open to hunting. The park evenly divides into two regions—the beach area (southern half) and the campground area (northern half). The southern portion is largely cedar swamp with plenty of small ponds formed from Little Billy Elliots Creek. Ridges containing oak and birch run next to these lowlands. The campground area is also wooded with pine and hardwoods but lacks a swampy nature. This region also contains some sand dunes.

Deer hunting pressure throughout is surprisingly light with whitetail numbers fairly good most falls. Visitors also see an occasional bear and bobcat. Good numbers of snowshoe hares and some cottontails receive little hunting pressure too. The same is true with grouse—most abundant in the beach area—as well as woodcock and squirrels.

Cheboygan Point affords fair to good duck hunting in early season and again later when migrants fly through. A few geese ply the area. Also of interest to hunters is that several trailside cabins may be rented, but applications should be sent early as they fill fast.

Hunters driving vehicles into park lands must have a valid state parks sticker affixed to the windshield. For more information regarding hunting opportunities, contact the Cheboygan State Park Manager, 4490 Beach Road, Cheboygan, Mich. 49721 (616/627-2811).

Burt Lake State Park

ABOUT 240 acres of 407-acre Burt Lake State Park in Cheboygan County (*which see*) is open to hunting. The parcel, designated as a nature area, lies across US-27/M-68 and is about 80 percent jack pine, the balance of cover being scrub oak.

Hunters might find a few fox and/or gray/black squirrels and an occasional deer. Residential dwellings along the other three sides of the public land severely limit game production and hunting opportunities.

Those entering with vehicles must have a valid state parks sticker affixed to the windshield.

For more information regarding hunting opportunities, contact the Burt Lake State Park manager in Indian River (616/238-9392).

Wilderness State Park

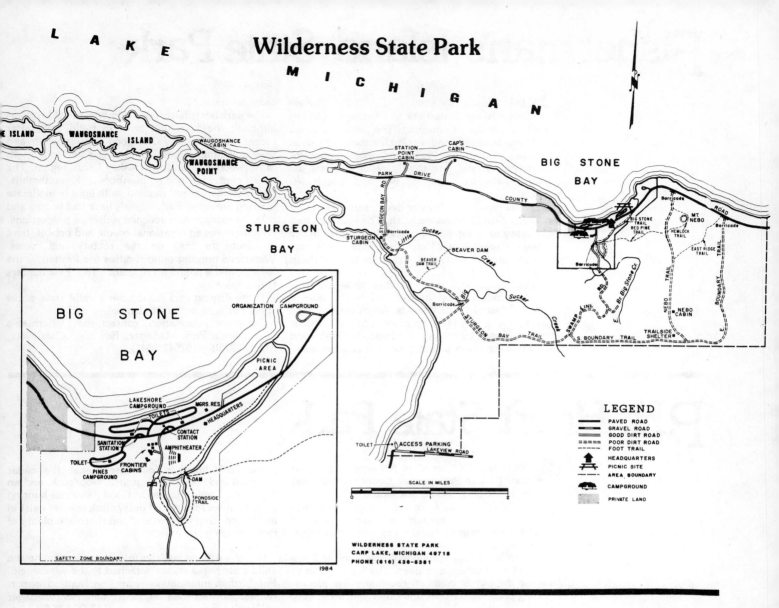

LAKE
MICHIGAN

WAUGOSHANCE ISLAND

WAUGOSHANCE POINT
WAUGOSHANCE CABIN

STATION POINT CABIN
CAP'S CABIN

BIG STONE BAY

PARK DRIVE
STURGEON BAY RD
COUNTY

STURGEON BAY

STURGEON CABIN
Barricade

Little
Sucker
Creek

BEAVER DAM
BEAVER DAM TRAIL

MT. NEBO
BIG STONE RED PINE TRAIL
HEMLOCK TRAIL
EAST RIDGE TRAIL
NEBO TRAIL
NEBO CABIN

Barricade

Big
Sucker
Creek

Barricade
STURGEON BAY TRAIL
SWAMP LINE RD
S. BOUNDARY TRAIL
TRAILSIDE SHELTER

BIG STONE BAY

ORGANIZATION CAMPGROUND

PICNIC AREA

LAKESHORE CAMPGROUND
MGRS. RES.
TOILETS
HEADQUARTERS
CONTACT STATION
SANITATION STATION
TOILET
PINES CAMPGROUND
FRONTIER CABINS
AMPHITHEATER
DAM
PONDSIDE TRAIL

SAFETY ZONE BOUNDARY

1984

TOILET
ACCESS PARKING
LAKEVIEW ROAD

SCALE IN MILES

0   1   2

LEGEND

PAVED ROAD
GRAVEL ROAD
GOOD DIRT ROAD
POOR DIRT ROAD
FOOT TRAIL
HEADQUARTERS
PICNIC SITE
AREA BOUNDARY
CAMPGROUND
PRIVATE LAND

WILDERNESS STATE PARK
CARP LAKE, MICHIGAN 49718
PHONE (616) 436-5381

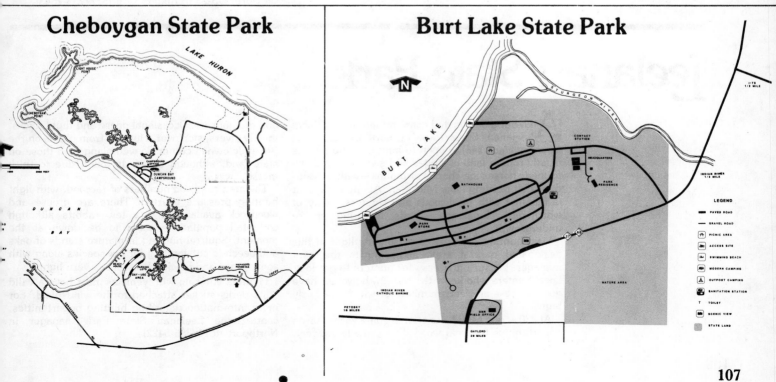

Cheboygan State Park

LAKE HURON

LIGHT HOUSE POINT
CHEBOYGAN POINT

DUNCAN BAY

TOILET
CAMPGROUND OFFICE
DUNCAN BAY CAMPGROUND

BEACH HOUSE
DAY-USE AREA
PARKING LOTS
LITTLE BILLY ELLIOTT
MANAGERS RESIDENCE
CONTACT STATION

Burt Lake State Park

N

STURGEON RIVER
I-75 1/2 MILE

BURT LAKE

CONTACT STATION
HEADQUARTERS
PARK RESIDENCE

BATHHOUSE
PARK STORE

INDIAN RIVER 1/2 MILE

PETOSKY 18 MILES
INDIAN RIVER CATHOLIC SHRINE

NATURE AREA

DNR FIELD OFFICE

GAYLORD 26 MILES

LEGEND

PAVED ROAD
GRAVEL ROAD
PICNIC AREA
ACCESS SITE
SWIMMING BEACH
MODERN CAMPING
OUTPOST CAMPING
SANITATION STATION
T TOILET
SCENIC VIEW
STATE LAND

Fisherman's Island State Park

ALL but about 25 acres of 2,822-acre Fisherman's Island State Park in Charlevoix County (*which see*) is open to hunting. The public lands lie along Lake Michigan and, except for about 150 acres of dunes along the mainland point opposite Fisherman's Island, are mostly cedar swamps (60 percent) between ridges of oak and beech (40 percent).

The area gets heavy firearm deer hunting pressure yet yields 20 to 25 bucks each fall. The southern half runs heavy to cedar swamps, and deer winter in the Whiskey Creek area. They also winter in cedar lowlands around McGeach Creek in the northern region.

Upland brush and small patches of aspen near swamps produce good grouse and fair woodcock hunting. Most of the hardwoods, which feature good hunting for fox and gray/black squirrels, occur along a ridge beginning at Inwood Creek and running northeasterly just past the southernmost campground.

The park hosts fairly good numbers of wild turkeys although the flock will have to build back after recent winter losses. One good area is south and west of Witmere Road. Another is a half-mile north of Norwood Road in the Whiskey Creek region. The park contains good numbers of cottontails, snowshoe hares, and raccoon, with light to moderate hunting pressure. Park officials have had to trap and relocate raccoon that reached nuisance proportions.

Hunters see an occasional coyote and bobcat, here no doubt to prey on the rabbits and hares. Waterfowl hunting opportunities are limited to the lee side of the island for migrant birds. Few hunters take advantage.

Those driving cars must have a valid state parks sticker affixed to the windshield.

For more information, contact the Fisherman's Island State Park Manager, Box 456, Charlevoix, Mich. 49720 (616/547-6641).

P.H. Hoeft State Park

ABOUT half (169 acres) of 307-acre P.H. Hoeft State Park in Presque Isle County (*which see*) is open to hunting. These are gently rolling lands fronting US-23 across from the designated campground area. They contain a mixed cover of hemlock, oak, maple, mature red and white pine, and swamp cedar.

Foot trails wander throughout the area and are used by both hunters and deer. The latter seem to traverse the public lands en route to other places. Hunting pressure for deer and other species is very light.

The park holds a few hares (near the cedar swamps) and cottontails, grouse, woodcock, and an occasional wild turkey. Good squirrel-hunting opportunities for fox and gray/black species exist in mast-producing hardwoods, and there are plenty of raccoon using the area.

Hunters driving vehicles into the park must have a valid state parks sticker attached to the windshield. For further information regarding hunting opportunities, contact the P.H. Hoeft State Park manager on North US-23 in Rogers City (517/734-2543).

Leelanau State Park

ALL but a designated campground in 1,307-acre Leelanau State Park in northern Leelanau County (*which see*) is open to hunting. The park is mostly rolling land of ridges and swamps—glacier-formed, horseshoe-shaped drumlins—with a sand-dune belt fronting Lake Michigan. About 80 percent is forested with hardwoods and conifers, many of which are climax-age stands featuring sparse undergrowth.

Deer-hunting pressure is reasonably light in this designated natural area, according to the park manager, because it is easy for hunters to get lost. Local hunters who know the terrain, however, have good success on deer, numbers of which are fairly high.

At 230 acres, Mud Lake affords some early-season opportunities for local wood ducks, mallards, teal, and mergansers. Occasional geese and flight ducks, mostly divers, stop over. Hunters from blinds on the privately-owned corner do well along with those on state land, although access is tough due to thick marsh cover.

The area has good numbers of raccoon, with light hunting pressure exerted. There are grouse and woodcock available and a few rabbits although cottontail populations seem to be down at the moment. Squirrel hunting in mature stands of oaks and beech is outstanding for fox species along with some grays and blacks. Pressure is very light.

Hunters entering with vehicles must have a valid state parks sticker attached to the windshield. For more information regarding hunting opportunities, contact the Leelanau State Park manager in Northport, (616/386-5422).

Fisherman's Island State Park

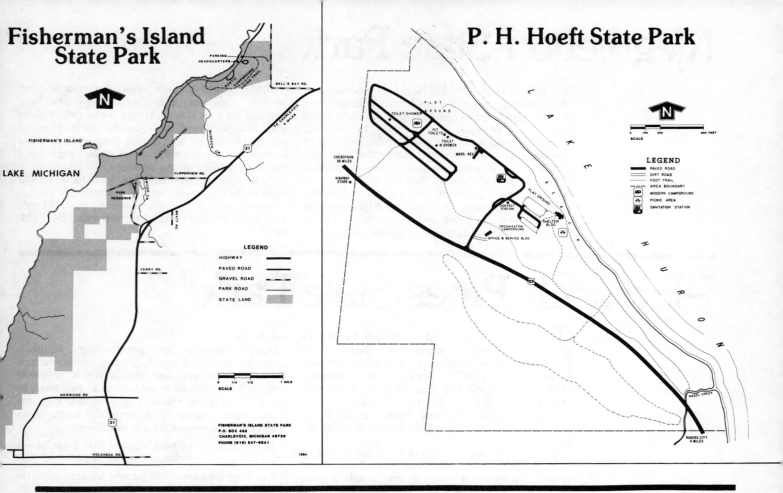

FISHERMAN'S ISLAND

LAKE MICHIGAN

N

PARKING
HEADQUARTERS
RUSTIC CAMPGROUND
HIKING TRAIL

BELL'S BAY RD.

MUSBACH CR.

31

TO CHARLEVOIX
5 MILES

CLIPPERVIEW RD.

WOOD CR.

PARK
RESIDENCE

BRATT RD.

FERRY RD.

NORWOOD RD.

31

HOLCHECK RD.

LEGEND
HIGHWAY	▬▬▬
PAVED ROAD	▬▬▬
GRAVEL ROAD	▭▭▭
PARK ROAD	───
STATE LAND	▨

0   1/4   1/2   1 MILE
SCALE

FISHERMAN'S ISLAND STATE PARK
P.O. BOX 456
CHARLEVOIX, MICHIGAN 49720
PHONE (616) 547-6641

1984

P. H. Hoeft State Park

PLAY GROUND
TOILET-SHOWER
PIT TOILETS
TOILET & SHOWER
MGRS. RES.
CHEBOYGAN 36 MILES
HIGHWAY STORE
CONTACT STATION
ORGANIZATION CAMPGROUND
OFFICE & SERVICE BLDG.
PLAY GROUND
SHELTER BLDG
23
NAGEL CREEK
ROGERS CITY 4 MILES

L A K E   H U R O N

LAKE BEACH

N

0 100 200   500 FEET
SCALE

LEGEND
▬▬▬	PAVED ROAD
───	DIRT ROAD
┄┄┄	FOOT TRAIL
▭▭▭	AREA BOUNDARY
	MODERN CAMPGROUND
	PICNIC AREA
	SANITATION STATION

Leelanau State Park

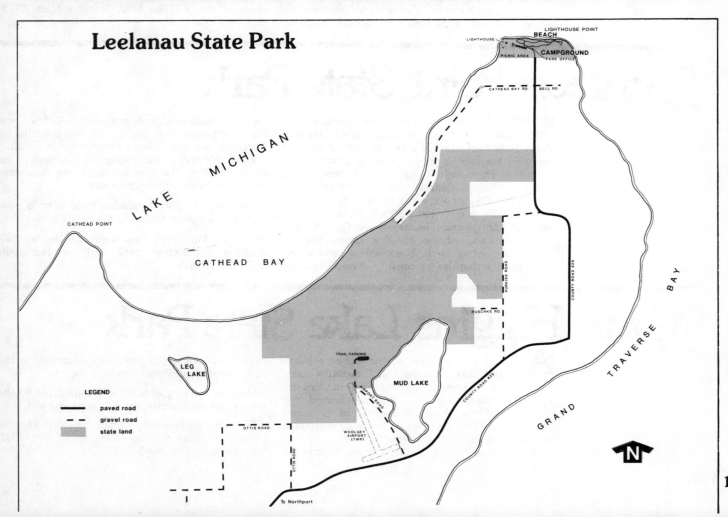

LIGHTHOUSE POINT
BEACH
LIGHTHOUSE
PICNIC AREA
CAMPGROUND
PARK OFFICE
CATHEAD BAY RD.   BELL RD.

L A K E   M I C H I G A N

CATHEAD POINT

CATHEAD BAY

PURKISS ROAD
COUNTY ROAD 629
RUSCHKE RD.

LEG LAKE

TRAIL PARKING

MUD LAKE

COUNTY ROAD 626

AIRPORT ROAD

OTTIS ROAD

WOOLSEY AIRPORT (TWP)

To Northport

G R A N D   T R A V E R S E   B A Y

N

LEGEND
▬▬▬	paved road
┅┅┅	gravel road
▨	state land

109

Negwegon State Park

LOCATED along Lake Huron in northeastern Alcona and southeastern Alpena counties (*both of which see*) is undeveloped Negwegon State Park. The 1,790-acre park site is open to hunting; however, a map is not yet available for inclusion in this book. To find the site, refer to the Michigan United Conservation Clubs publicaiton, "Michigan County Maps and Outdoor Guide."

Topography is quite flat, with a mixture of swamp lands and dry ground. The major cover types include cedar, white and red pine, hemlock, spruce, balsam, soft maple, white bich, black willow, and alder.

Hunting opportunities are considered good for deer, raccoon, squirrels, and predators. A few bear frequent the park site, and there is also potential for woodcock, waterfowl, and snowshoe hares. Hunting pressure for deer is high during the first week of the firearm season. The other game species experience low to moderate hunting pressure.

Those entering with vehicles must have a valid state parks sticker affixed to the windshield.

Negwegon State Park is managed by the DNR staff at Harrisville State Park in Harrisville (517/724-5126).

Hartwick Pines State Park

ABOUT 8,400 acres of 9,294-acre (nearly 14 square miles) Hartwick Pines State Park in Crawford County (*which see*) is open to hunting. Located on M-93, the park lies seven miles northeast of Grayling and only four miles off I-75. The largest state park in the Lower Peninsula, it features high rolling hills, built up by ancient glaciers; four lakes; and the broad valley of the East Branch of the Au Sable River.

In addition to virgin stands of jack pine and white pine, the park contains a broad mix of aspen and maple. Hunters will find oak and maple forests between Glory Lake and I-75 and again north and east of Camp Lehman. Dense cedar swamps lie along the Mertz Grade Trail and the East Branch of the Au Sable.

Hunters come for deer, bear, bobcats, squirrels (both fox and black/gray), grouse, woodcock, and raccoon. There are also coyotes and a few wild turkeys (no open season on turkeys at this time) in the park. Hunting pressure is generally high for deer, grouse, and woodcock, especially during years when these game species are abundant.

Those entering the park with vehicles must have a valid state parks sticker affixed to the windshield.

For more information regarding hunting opportunities, contact the Hartwick Pines State Park Manager, Route 3, Box 3840, Grayling, Mich. 49738 (517/348-7068).

Sturgeon Point State Park

LOCATED along Lake Huron in central Alcona County (*which see*) is undeveloped Sturgeon Point State Park. The 70-acre park site is open to hunting; however, a map is not yet available for inclusion in this book. To find the site, refer to the Michigan United Conservation Clubs publication, "Michigan County Maps and Outdoor Guide."

Topography is quite flat with a mixture of swamp lands and dry ground. The major cover types include cedar, white and red pine, hemlock, spruce, balsam, soft maple, white birch, black willow, and alder. Hunting opportunities are considered good for deer,

raccoon, squirrels, and predators. A few bear frequent the park site, and there is also potential for woodcock, waterfowl, and snowshoe hares. Hunting pressure for deer is high during the first week of the firearm season. The other game species experience low to moderate hunting pressure.

Those entering with vehicles must have a valid state parks sticker affixed to the windshield.

Sturgeon Point State Park is managed by the DNR staff at Harrisville State Park in Harrisville (517/724-5126).

North Higgins Lake State Park

ALTHOUGH 174 acres of the 428-acre North Higgins Lake State Park in Crawford County (*which see*) are open to hunting, opportunities are severely limited due to residences around the perimeter. Since about 70 percent of Crawford County is public land open to hunting, sportsmen may want to seek opportunities elsewhere.

Archery deer hunting is the only sport currently

being practiced in the park, and, according to the park manager, whitetail numbers are low.

Hunters entering with vehicles must have a valid state parks sticker attached to the windshield.

For more information, contact the North Higgins Lake State Park Manager, Route 1, Box 1252, Roscommon, Mich. 48653 (517/821-6125).

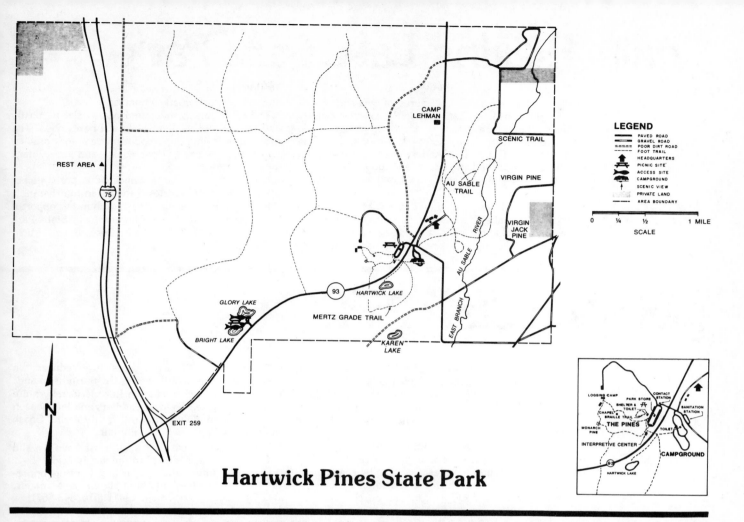

Hartwick Pines State Park

North Higgins Lake State Park

South Higgins Lake State Park

ONE-HUNDRED-TEN acres of 995-acre South Higgins Lake State Park in Roscommon County (*which see*) are open to hunting. These lands surround Marl Lake, across CR-100 and to the southeast of our map. At less than two feet deep throughout, Marl Lake offers fairly good hunting for local puddle ducks and geese and later passage birds of many species.

The Cut River that flows from Marl Lake to Houghton Lake is a natural corridor of cover and wildlife, including one of the state's largest stands of white birch. Portions along its route are state-owned and open to hunting.

The state park land around Marl Lake is mostly swampy and wooded with lowland hardwoods. The area affords hunting opportunities for grouse, woodcock, raccoon, deer, fox, and gray/black squirrels.

Hunters must have a valid state park sticker attached to their vehicles if they plan to drive in.

For more information regarding hunting opportunities, contact the South Higgins Lake State Park Manager, Route 2, Box 360, Roscommon, Mich. 48653 (517/821-6374).

Ludington State Park

NEARLY 3,400 acres of 4,515-acre Ludington State Park, located on Lake Michigan in central Mason County (*which see*), is open to deer hunting. Small-game hunting is prohibited although waterfowlers may try for ducks and geese on Hamlin Lake.

The park is located eight miles north of Ludington. An outstanding feature is eight separately marked foot trails totaling 18 miles. Deer can be seen on any of these trails, and they use the forested areas of pine, cedar, hemlock, oak, maple, beech, and ash.

Tough winters in recent years have reduced the park's deer herd significantly. On the other hand, waterfowl hunting on Hamlin Lake is usually quite good for early-season local puddlers and late-season divers and puddlers migrating through. Goose hunting for Canadas is usually fair.

Those entering with vehicles must have a valid state parks sticker affixed to the windshield.

For more information regarding hunting opportunities, contact the Ludington State Park Manager, Box 709, Ludington, Mich. 49431 (616/843-8671).

Silver Lake State Park

MOST of 2,765-acre Silver Lake State Park in Oceana County (*which see*) is open to hunting. The northern portion, a designated off-road vehicle area, is mostly sand dunes sparsely covered with vegetation. Hunting opportunities are poor here.

They improve somewhat throughout the rolling terrain of the rest of the park, mostly a mixture of mature oaks and beech. Hunters do fairly well on both fox and gray/black squirrels. There are a few raccoon, grouse, and woodcock, but sportsmen will have to work at getting game. An occasional fox or coyote is seen, and Silver Lake itself offers some duck and goose hunting both early and late in the season. High pressure, however, tends to burn off waterfowl early.

The assistant park manager rates deer hunting poor to fair, with high pressure during the firearm season.

Overall, the mature woods do not produce good numbers of game; however, there is some hunting potential.

Hunters entering with vehicles must have a current state parks sticker attached to the windshield. For more information regarding hunting opportunities, contact the Silver Lake State Park Manager, Route 1, Box 187, Mears, Mich. (616/873-3083).

Pinconning State Park

TWO miles east of Pinconning on Saginaw Bay in Bay County is a small parcel of state-owned land that provides limited hunting potential. Although referred to as Pinconning State Park, the 200-acre tract is undeveloped and currently administered by DNR Waterways Division. A total of 164 acres (marked by signs) is open to hunting.

Thick cattails are the norm along with bulrushes

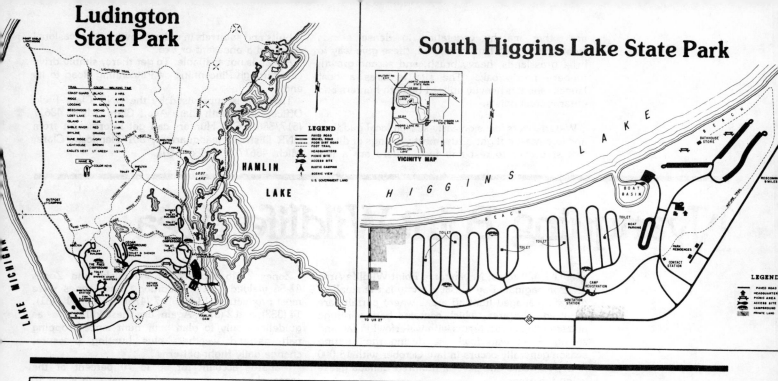

Ludington State Park

LEGEND

TRAIL	COLOR	WALKING TIME
COAST GUARD	BLACK	2 HRS.
RIDGE	MAROON	4 HRS.
LOGGING	DK. GREEN	4 HRS.
BEECHWOOD	ORCHID	4 HRS.
LOST LAKE	YELLOW	2 HRS.
ISLAND	BLUE	4 HRS.
SABLE RIVER	RED	
SKYLINE	ORANGE	1/2 HR.
DUNE RIDGE	IVORY	1 HR.
LIGHTHOUSE	GREEN	
EAGLE'S NEST	LT. GREEN	1/2 HR.

PAVED ROAD
GRAVEL ROAD
FOOT DIRT ROAD
FOOT TRAIL
HEADQUARTERS
PICNIC SITE
RUSTIC CAMPING
SCENIC VIEW
U.S. GOVERNMENT LAND

HAMLIN LAKE

LAKE MICHIGAN

South Higgins Lake State Park

VICINITY MAP

HIGGINS LAKE

BEACH

LEGEND

PAVED ROAD
HEADQUARTERS
PICNIC AREA
ACCESS SITE
CAMPGROUND
PRIVATE LAND

TO US 27

Silver Lake State Park

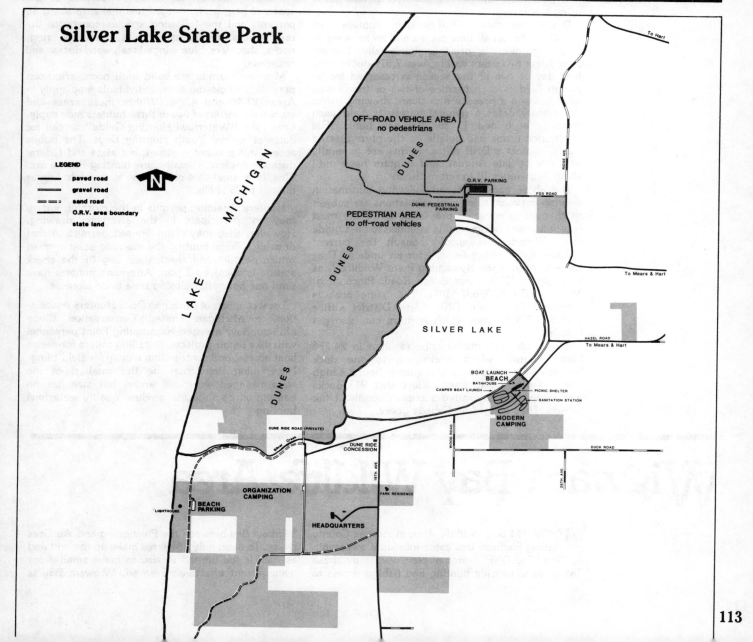

LEGEND

— paved road
— gravel road
— — sand road
— · — O.R.V. area boundary
state land

N

To Hart

OFF-ROAD VEHICLE AREA
no pedestrians

DUNES

O.R.V. PARKING

DUNE PEDESTRIAN PARKING

Fox Road

PEDESTRIAN AREA
no off-road vehicles

RIDGE AVE.

To Mears & Hart

LAKE MICHIGAN

DUNES

SILVER LAKE

HAZEL ROAD
To Mears & Hart

BOAT LAUNCH
BEACH
CAMPER BOAT LAUNCH
PICNIC SHELTER
SANITATION STATION

MODERN CAMPING

WOOD ROAD

DUCK ROAD

28TH AVE.

DUNE RIDE ROAD (PRIVATE)

Silver Creek

DUNE RIDE CONCESSION

18TH AVE.

PARK RESIDENCE

ORGANIZATION CAMPING

LIGHTHOUSE
BEACH PARKING

HEADQUARTERS

113

and other marshy vegetation in dense stands fronting the bay. Turning inland, these give way to brief grasslands, heavy brush, and second-growth timber—mostly oaks. The site features a boat launch, and it is heavily utilized by both hunters and other recreationists.

Waterfowlers focus on early-season local puddlers and late-season flight birds, mostly strings of divers that stop over to rest and feed. There are a few rabbits and squirrels in upland covers, an occasional deer and a pheasant or two.

A map is not available. To get there, simply drive east through Pinconning on Pinconning Road to its end.

The area is supervised by the DNR Clare Field Office, 8540 South Clare Ave., Clare, Mich. 48617 (517/386-4067). Hunters can get information from DNR District Headquarters, 501 Hemlock, Clare, Mich. 48617 (517/386-7991).

Nyanquing Point Wildlife Area

At 1,420 acres, Nayanquing Point Wildlife Area on Saginaw Bay in Bay County is the smallest of state-managed hunting areas where permits are required. The area, which contains both a refuge and standing crops, teems with waterfowl in fall and spring. Peak waterfowl use during the hunting season generally occurs in late October with 15,000 to 20,000 ducks and several hundred Canada geese using the area.

During the most recent season, hunters shot 10,272 ducks, an all-time record and an increase of 23 percent over the previous year's tally. The old record, set two years earlier, was 7,919 ducks. The first day or two of the season is reserved for 50 permit holders each (parties of two or three) who were lucky in a preseason postcard drawing. After those early dates a general lottery is held each morning at 6 and 11 for half-day hunts. For application forms and details on the preregistered hunts, contact a DNR office. Forms are generally available by late August, and hunters have until about September 10 to return them.

The above comments and following information relating to times, rules, and regulations are subject to change. Information presented is for the most recent hunting season and is intended to be a guide only. Waterfowlers should consult the current "Waterfowl Hunting Guide" for an update. They can also contact the Nyanquing Point Wildlife Area manager at 1570 Tower Beach Road, Pinconning, Mich. 48650 (517/697-5101). The game area is administered by the DNR Clare District Office (517/386-7991), from which hunters can also get details.

A total of 5,620 hunter trips resulted in 24,256 hours hunted, which works out to one duck harvested for every two-and-a-quarter hours, a high figure. Opening-day waterfowlers shot 943 ducks and enjoyed good hunting success throughout the season. They bagged 48 Canada geese.

Zones 27-46 produced 1,300 ducks and Zones 47-56 yielded 885. In addition, these zones were most productive: 13 (486), 7 (476), 6 (455), 4 (431), 14 (383), and 2 (374). Again, use these kill figures as guidelines only to plan your hunt since cropping patterns and weather, plus hunting pressure, change daily flight patterns.

Mallards account for 60 to 70 percent of the seasonal bag; green-winged teal make up about 10 percent; and the following species constitute the rest: blacks, baldpates, pintails, gadwalls, ring-necks, shovelers, blue-winged teal, wood ducks, and redheads.

Morning permits are valid until noon, afternoon permits until closing time. Individuals may apply in Areas 27-46 and 47-56. Within these areas and elsewhere parties of two or three hunters may apply. Check the "Waterfowl Hunting Guide" or call for dates of special Youth Hunting Days. The public access stamp is not required, but state and federal duck stamps and a small-game hunting license are. This is a steel-shot-only area, with each hunter limited to 25 shells.

Hunters obtaining permits in the morning lottery may not participate in the afternoon drawing. However, they may claim unused permits in that drawing. Those hunting the morning session must return permits and check their bag (if the check station is open) by 2 p.m. Afternoon hunters have until one hour after closing time to do likewise.

Local chapters of Michigan Duck Hunters Association, a Michigan United Conservation Clubs affiliate, have assisted Nayanquing Point personnel with dike repair projects, installing rollers for easier boat access, and contributing money for field tiling. Nayanquing Point may be the smallest of the state-managed waterfowl areas, but size has no bearing on its ability to produce quality waterfowl hunting.

Wigwam Bay Wildlife Area

Wigwam Bay Wildlife Area in Arenac County along Saginaw Bay came into state ownership in 1966. The DNR's original plan was to purchase 788 acres to provide hunting and fishing access to Saginaw Bay between the Pinconning and Au Gres rivers. To date, only 334 acres make up the unit and as such is too limited in size to make small-game management effective. Even so, Wigwam Bay is

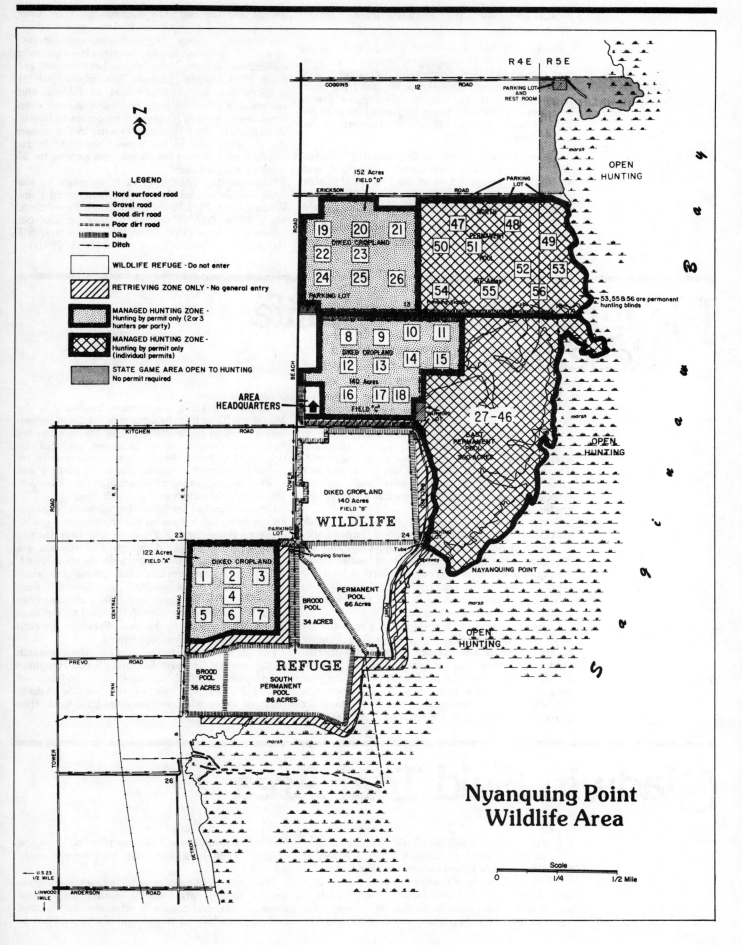

Nyanquing Point Wildlife Area

LEGEND

▬▬▬	Hard surfaced road
▬▬▬	Gravel road
▬▬▬	Good dirt road
▬▬▬	Poor dirt road
▬▬▬	Dike
▬▬▬	Ditch

WILDLIFE REFUGE - Do not enter

RETRIEVING ZONE ONLY - No general entry

MANAGED HUNTING ZONE - Hunting by permit only (2 or 3 hunters per party)

MANAGED HUNTING ZONE - Hunting by permit only (individual permits)

STATE GAME AREA OPEN TO HUNTING No permit required

N

COGGINS ROAD 12

PARKING LOT AND REST ROOM

R4E R5E

7

marsh

OPEN HUNTING

152 Acres FIELD "D"

ERICKSON ROAD

PARKING LOT

19 20 21

DIKED CROPLAND

22 23

24 25 26

PARKING LOT

NORTH PERMANENT POOL

47 48

50 51 49

52 53

54 55 56

53,55 & 56 are permanent hunting blinds

8 9 10 11

DIKED CROPLAND

12 13 14 15

140 Acres

16 17 18

FIELD "C"

AREA HEADQUARTERS

BEACH ROAD

27-46

EAST PERMANENT POOL 350 ACRES

marsh

OPEN HUNTING

NAYANQUING POINT

marsh

KITCHEN ROAD

R.R.

23

122 Acres FIELD "A"

DIKED CROPLAND

1 2 3

4

5 6 7

TOWER ROAD

PARKING LOT

Pumping Station

DIKED CROPLAND 140 Acres FIELD "B"

WILDLIFE

24

Tube

BROOD POOL

PERMANENT POOL 66 Acres

34 ACRES

Spillway

OPEN HUNTING

PREVO ROAD

PENN

CENTRAL

MACKINAC

ROAD

BROOD POOL 36 ACRES

REFUGE

SOUTH PERMANENT POOL 86 ACRES

Tube

marsh

TOWER

26

DETROIT

U.S. 23 1/2 MILE

LINWOOD 1 MILE

ANDERSON ROAD

Scale

0   1/4   1/2 Mile

115

popular with waterfowlers and a few deer and small-game hunters.

Indians named the area for a large wigwam or teepee they built along a shoreline trail used as a rest stop and shelter. Supposedly the wigwam was stocked with smoked muskrats for hungry Indian travelers. Further, surveys in 1839 suggest that a large portion of the Wigwam Bay area was once an Indian reserve. No doubt they hunted waterfowl and other game here.

Recent high-water levels on Saginaw Bay defeated DNR attempts to sharecrop corn for waterfowl, and so today no farming is done on the 33 acres of tillable land. The area is generally wet, brushy land that during exceptionally dry years is ideal for upland game birds and during wet years has good waterfowl-hunting potential.

Wigwam Bay is generally flat with a slight fall toward Saginaw Bay. The slow-moving Pine River empties into the bay among cattail and bulrush marshlands. Various stages of succession (grasslands to brushlands to woodlands—especially mature oaks and maples in the southern portion) are evident in upland covers. The mixed habitat supports fair to good numbers of rabbits and squirrels, a few pheasants and raccoon, and even some deer. Hunting pressure is moderate to heavy. Duck hunters score on puddlers early in the season and do quite well in late season on flight birds, mostly divers. A boat-launch site and parking for 28 vehicles are featured.

Wigwam Bay Wildlife Area is overseen by the DNR wildlife habitat biologist at Nayanquing Point Wildlife Area, 1570 Tower Beach Road, Pinconning, Mich. 48650 (517/697-5101). Hunters can also get information from DNR District Headquarters, 501 Hemlock St., Clare, Mich. 48617 (517/386-7991).

Houghton Lake Wildlife Research Area

THE Houghton Lake Wildlife Research Area, a 20- to 25-square-mile block of state land bordering M-55 in Roscommon and Missaukee counties (*both of which see*), is entirely open to hunting. The area is largely poor-quality cattail and sedge marsh in various stages of development. There is also a great deal of off-site aspen and jack pine. Local hunters and beaver and muskrat trappers often refer to the research areas as the Porter Ranch.

Water resources include the marsh, Bear Creek and Dead Horse Bridge floodings, and Barney Lake. A couple of ditches transect the property, and the Houghton Lake Sewer Authority runs treated water through the marsh (which helps to further filter the water). Someday the area could include a 1,000- to 1,500-acre impoundment with a water-control structure such as a lowhead dam.

Currently it receives intense hunting pressure for deer as hunters rely upon high surrounding pressure to drive animals into the protection of the marsh. Archery hunters take as many deer as firearm hunters, which can number 40 to 50 per square mile on opening day. The combined buck-kill success rate for both groups of sportsmen stands at about six percent, seemingly low until one considers the pressure involved.

Meandering along the western boundary is the Muskegon River from its origins in the Dead Stream Swamp farther north. Patient float hunters can tag deer, and there is some untapped potential for float-hunting for ducks. Early-season pressure for mallards, wood ducks, teal, and some pintails and black ducks falls off quickly both along the river and among jump-shooters in the marsh itself.

Limited hunting for fox and gray/black squirrels occurs along oak ridges on the southeastern corner of Dead Horse Bridge Flooding and near Barney Lake and Fox Ridge. Although wild turkeys are found on the area, hunting is currently not allowed. The research area supports a fair grouse population and good numbers of woodcock, augmented in mid- to late October by flight birds. Best opportunities occur on higher ground off Jeffs Road to the west and Nellsville Road to the east. Pressure for both grouse and woodcock is quite high.

For more information, contact the research biologist at the Research Station Office in Houghton Lake Heights on US-27 just south of the M-55 corner (517/422-5191). Or talk to the wildlife habitat biologist at the adjacent Houghton Lake field office (517/422-5522).

Gladwin Field Trial Area

THE 4,940-acre Gladwin Field Trial Area (also called the Gladwin Game Refuge) is a part of the Au Sable State Forest (*which see*). Located in the northwestern corner of Gladwin County (*which also see*), the area was first used for field trials in 1916. It still is today and, according to some, is the most ideal grouse trial area in the country. During spring and fall, pointing-breed owners from all over the country come here for trials held nearly every weekend.

The soils, topography, and forest-cover types (much aspen) are ideally suited to grouse management, and regularly scheduled commercial cuttings and habitat treatments are carried out to

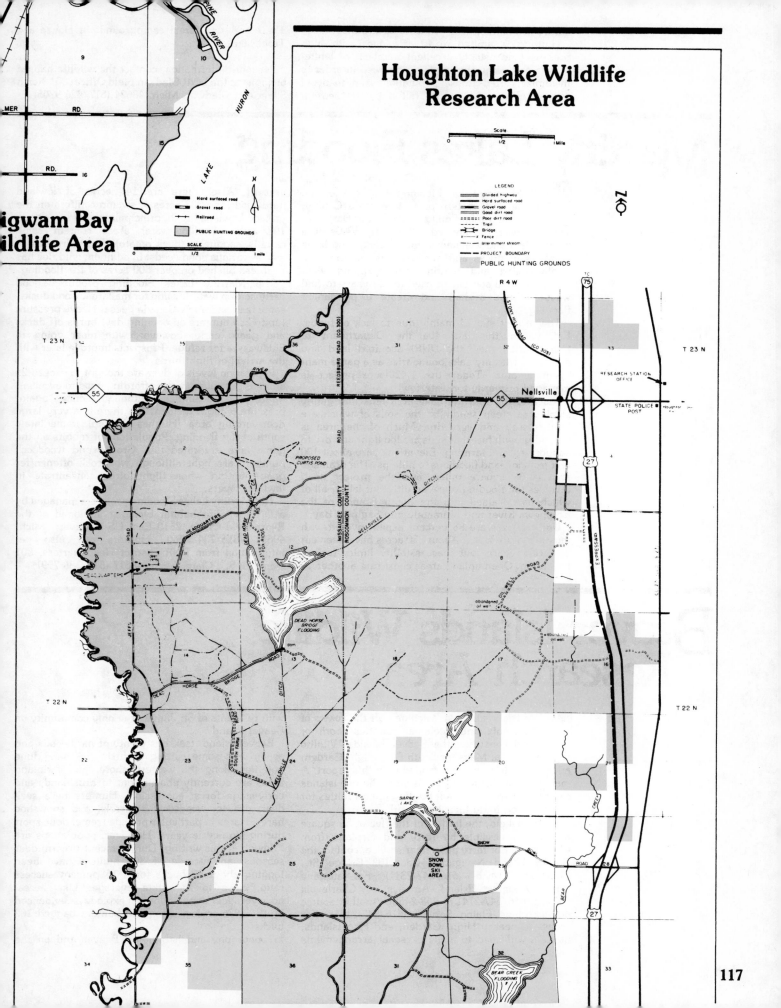

Houghton Lake Wildlife Research Area

Scale
0   1/2   1 Mile

LEGEND
Divided highway
Hard surfaced road
Gravel road
Good dirt road
Poor dirt road
Trail
Bridge
x — x Fence
Intermittent stream
PROJECT BOUNDARY
PUBLIC HUNTING GROUNDS

Wigwam Bay
Wildlife Area

Hard surfaced road
Gravel road
Railroad
PUBLIC HUNTING GROUNDS

SCALE
0   1/2   1 mile

PINE RIVER

LAKE HURON

MER   RD.

RD.

9

10

15

16

R 4 W

T 23 N   T 23 N

STONY HILL ROAD (CO. 301)

REEDSBURG ROAD (CO. 300)

36   31   32   33

RESEARCH STATION
OFFICE

Nellsville

55   55

STATE POLICE
POST

PROPOSED
CURTIS POND

MISSAUKEE COUNTY
ROSCOMMON COUNTY

DITCH

6   5   4

HEADQUARTERS

NELLSVILLE ROAD

DEAD HORSE ROAD

FOX RIDGE

abandoned
oil well

OIL WELL

abandoned
oil well

JEFFS ROAD

HEADQUARTERS

12

7   8

DEAD HORSE
BRIDGE
FLOODING

dam

14   13

ROAD

17   16

18

T 22 N   T 22 N

DEAD HORSE
BRIDGE

DITCH

SOUTH FARM ROAD

NELLSVILLE ROAD

22   23   24   19   20   21

BARNEY
LAKE

SNOW

SNOW BOWL
SKI AREA

ROAD

BEAR CREEK

27   26   25   30   29   28

34   35   36   31   32   33

BEAR CREEK
FLOODING

27

117

assure prime habitat is available at all times.

Hunting is limited to firearm deer with high pressure and usually excellent numbers of white-tails. Small-game hunting is not allowed in order to maximize ruffed-grouse populations and to avoid conflict of use during the fall field-trial season.

There are state forest campgrounds at House and Trout lakes.

For more information, contact the wildlife habitat biologist at the DNR Gladwin Field Office, 801 North Silverleaf, Gladwin, Mich. 48624 (517/426-9205).

Martiny Lakes Flooding

THE Martiny Lakes Flooding project is located in the northeastern part of Mecosta County, about three-and-a-half miles southwest of Barryton. The area was first flooded in the early 1900s by a beaver dam and was known for concentrating large numbers of ducks and muskrats. When the dam finally failed and hunting and trapping went downhill, local sportsmen tried for 20 years to find ways to build a dam and create a permanent flooding.

The project stalled mainly due to lack of funds. Finally, in the late 40s the Department of Conservation (now the DNR) acquired land and dedicated Martiny Lake boundaries as a game-management area. Today the 1,420-acre project is managed primarily for waterfowl.

Much of the Martiny Lake area falls into gently sloping to steep sandhills, the soils of which are light-colored and very dry. Much of the area is second-growth forest as soils are too light and dry to support general farming. Elevations vary about 100 feet from lowland floodings to hilltops. The drainage area is 38 square miles, and the project itself involves the flooding of seven different lakes, all of which had drained into the South Branch of the Chippewa River and ultimately into Saginaw Bay.

Upland areas are 88 percent aspen-covered with mostly mature trees. About 250 acres have been cut in recent years, but inaccessibility limits further timbering. Open upland areas constitute another 10 percent. Also, there are 141 acres of lowland hardwoods and 333 acres of swamp conifers on the project. Lowland brush, principally tag alder, covers 108 acres. Shalllow-water areas contain some cattails, saggitaria (duck potato), and bulrushes as well as various pondweeds. In addition, wild rice has been established on over 500 acres of the flooding.

The Martiny Lakes Flooding produces good early-season waterfowling for mallards, wood ducks, some teal, and a few Canada geese. Heavy pressure (up to 250 hunters on opening day) burns off ducks and geese early, however, with most going to Shiawassee for refuge. Prospects improve later with the arrival of flight birds.

Population levels of deer are thought to exceed 25 animals per square mile, affording good to excellent hunting opportunities, although, once again, pressure is high. Incidentally, there is a very large deer-yarding area (Hughes Swamp) immediately south of the flooding. Populations of rabbits on the game area are rated fair. Grouse and woodcock numbers are light although woodcock often offer good hunting when flight birds concentrate in lowland covers.

The Martiny Lakes Flooding project is managed by a DNR wildlife habitat biologist stationed at the Evart Field Office, 2510 East US-10, Evart, Mich. 49631 (616/734-5492). Hunters can also get information from DNR District Headquarters, 501 Hemlock St., Clare, Mich. 48617 (517/386-7991).

Beaver Islands Wildlife Research Area

FIVE islands in Lake Michigan off the coasts of Charlevoix and Leelanau counties (*both of which see*) constitute the Beaver Islands Wildlife Research Area. Maps for South Fox, High, Garden, and Beaver islands are included with this report. A map is not available for Hog Island. The five islands can furnish some unusual hunting opportunities for those willing to do their homework.

Beaver Island, the largest of the five at 55 square miles, is accessible by ferry and airplane from Charlevoix. For ferry passenger service, contact the Beaver Island Navigation Co., 102 Bridge St., Charlevoix, Mich. (616/547-2311). For airplane service, contact Island Airways at Charlevoix Airport (616/547-2141 or 448-2458). Another source is McPhillips Flying Service (616/547-2141). For access to nearby High, Garden, and Hog islands, hunters will need to make personal arrangements with residents of St. James, the only community on Beaver Island.

Beaver Island itself has plenty of hardwoods and aspen with some cutting occurring. A sand-dune belt lies along the western shore, and farmland areas are currently phasing out to brushlands and early-stage forest succession. Hunters here seek deer, grouse, woodcock, squirrels, and snowshoe hares. Hares in particular provide tremendous sport during high-cycle years. However, populations are "down" at this writing. During recent firearm deer seasons, an average of 300 hunters have been tagging about 50 bucks for a 16 percent success ratio, close to the state average. Like hares, however, deer populations can explode as evidenced by the 1976 season when 310 hunters bagged 102 bucks.

Topography and habitat on Beaver and on the

Gladwin Field Trial Area

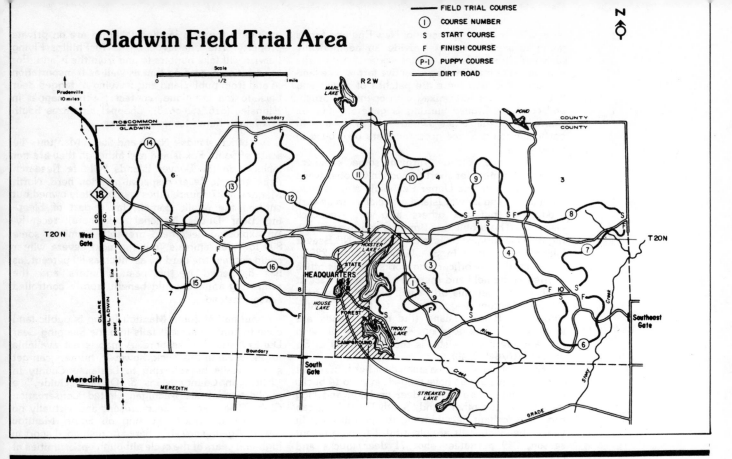

Martiny Lakes Flooding

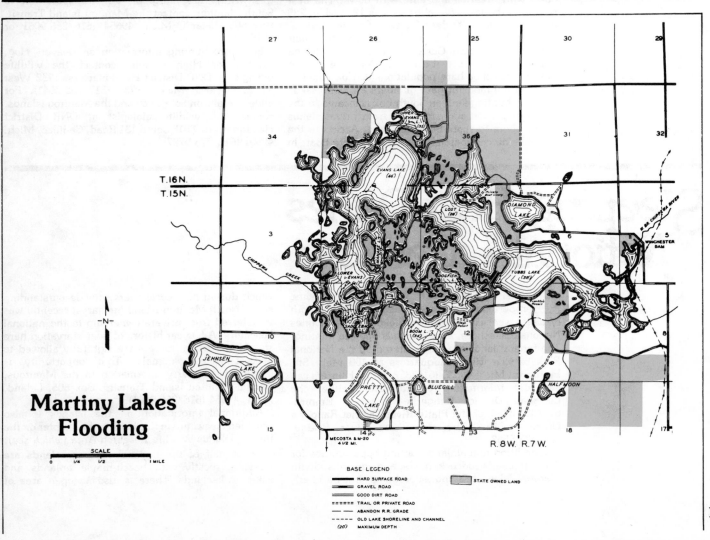

BASE LEGEND

HARD SURFACE ROAD
GRAVEL ROAD
GOOD DIRT ROAD
TRAIL OR PRIVATE ROAD
ABANDON R.R. GRADE
OLD LAKE SHORELINE AND CHANNEL
(20) MAXIMUM DEPTH

STATE OWNED LAND

other islands are reminiscent of New England farms going to seed and thus provide an aesthetically pleasing hunt. Stone fences often circle the abandoned or marginally productive farms. The land is mostly flat, and there are patches of aspen and hardwoods cover intermixed with openings, brush, and conifers. Grouse hunting is generally fair on Beaver and the other islands. High Island in particular can produce good numbers of grouse in some years.

Further, the islands furnish some excellent woodcock hunting for short periods in October when flight birds from the Upper Peninsula stop to rest. High Island and Beaver Island especially can be very productive, but the others also get woodcock visitation. The problem is timing a trip to catch the flights. One suggestion is to contact the DNR Beaver Island Field Office in St. James (616/448-2255). However, the fire officer who works from this office is often in the field and therefore hard to contact (it is likely too that this office will close in the near future). Another suggestion is to find a hunter contact on Beaver Island (the other islands are uninhabited). One good one—and a good place to hire a guide if you wish—is the Erin Motel in St. James (616/448-2240).

Garden Island also has a small deer herd. In recent years 30 to 40 hunters have tagged seven to 14 bucks each season. There are no deer on High and Hog islands. On the other hand, South Fox Island can produce excellent deer hunting (by permit only) in years when whitetails are plentiful. During a recent season, 249 permitees shot 71 deer (bucks and does) with firearms and nine with bows. The best season in the last several years was 1981 when 289 hunters tagged 190 deer for two-of-three success. Another 53 archers hunted that fall too, but their harvest is not known. Currently the South Fox Island deer herd appears to be stable. And like Beaver Island, snowshoe hare populations can be boom or bust. At the moment hare numbers are depressed.

Public-hunting land on South Fox is located in the northern portion and separated from private lands with a shore-to-shore boundary wire. Access to the island is by commercial aircraft or private boat; in each case the only landing facilities are on private property. The Charlevoix-based McPhillips Flying Service will take hunters to and from the island. For information regarding that as well as transportation to and from public land and ferrying of tagged deer back to the mainland, contact Keith Chappel in Kingsley (616/263-5613). Chappel organizes South Fox Island hunts for most visitors.

Two other islands—North and South Manitou—lie south of South Fox Island and although they are not included in the Beaver Islands Wildlife Research Area, they do deserve special mention here. North Manitou at 27 square miles was privately owned but entered the public domain (as a part of Sleeping Bear Dunes National Lakeshore) recently. An exploding deer herd presently numbers some 800 to 1,200 animals, but the next severe winter could depress the herd by as much as 80 percent, as has happened in the past. Hunters and the remaining animals could benefit from a controlled season instead.

About half of South Manitou Island is public land open to hunting since it falls into the Sleeping Bear Dunes National Lakeshore. A map is not available for inclusion in this book; however, hunters can get some details by referring to Leelanau County in "Michigan County Maps & Outdoor Guide," a publication of the Michigan United Conservation Clubs. There are no deer present and virtually no woodcock or grouse hunting on South Manitou Island. Again, snowshoe hares furnish good sport in high-end years of the cycle although opportunities at this writing are marginal. For transportation to South Manitou, contact the Manitou Island Transit, Box 605, Leland, Mich. 49654 (616/256-9061 or 9116).

For more hunting information on Beaver, Hog, Garden, or High islands, contact the wildlife biologist at DNR District Headquarters, 1732 West M-32, Gaylord, Mich. 49735 (517/732-3541). For added details on South Fox and the Manitou islands, contact the wildlife biologist at DNR District Headquarters, 8015 South 131 Road, Cadillac, Mich. 49601 (616/775-9727).

Sleeping Bear Dunes National Lakeshore

ABOUT 60,000 acres of Lake Michigan shoreline property in Benzie and Leelanau counties (*both of which see*) constitute the Sleeping Bear Dunes National Lakeshore, all of which is open to hunting. The federal lands are administered by the National Park Service with headquarters at 400 Main St., Frankfort, Mich. 49635 (616/352-9611). Hunters can also get information by contacting either the Leelanau District Ranger's Office in Empire, 616/334-3756, or the Platte River District Ranger's Office on M-22 by the Platte River Bridge, 616/325-5562.

In addition to mainland hunting opportunities for deer, grouse, woodcock, hares, and squirrels, South Manitou Island has snowshoe hares (but no deer), which during high-cycle years provide outstanding sport. North Manitou Island (no hares) recently was transferred from private ownership to the national lakeshore. A 50-year history of deer starvation here should end when hunters are rightfully allowed to harvest excess animals. That opportunity is imminent. For ferry information to the Manitous, contact Manitou Island Transit, Box 605, Leland, Mich. 49654 (616/256-9061).

Additional information on the islands is also provided elsewhere in this book in the chapter on the Beaver Islands Wildlife Research Area (*which see*).

About half of the national lakeshore lands are forested, mostly with beech-maple uplands and oak-pine lowlands. There is also an open area of

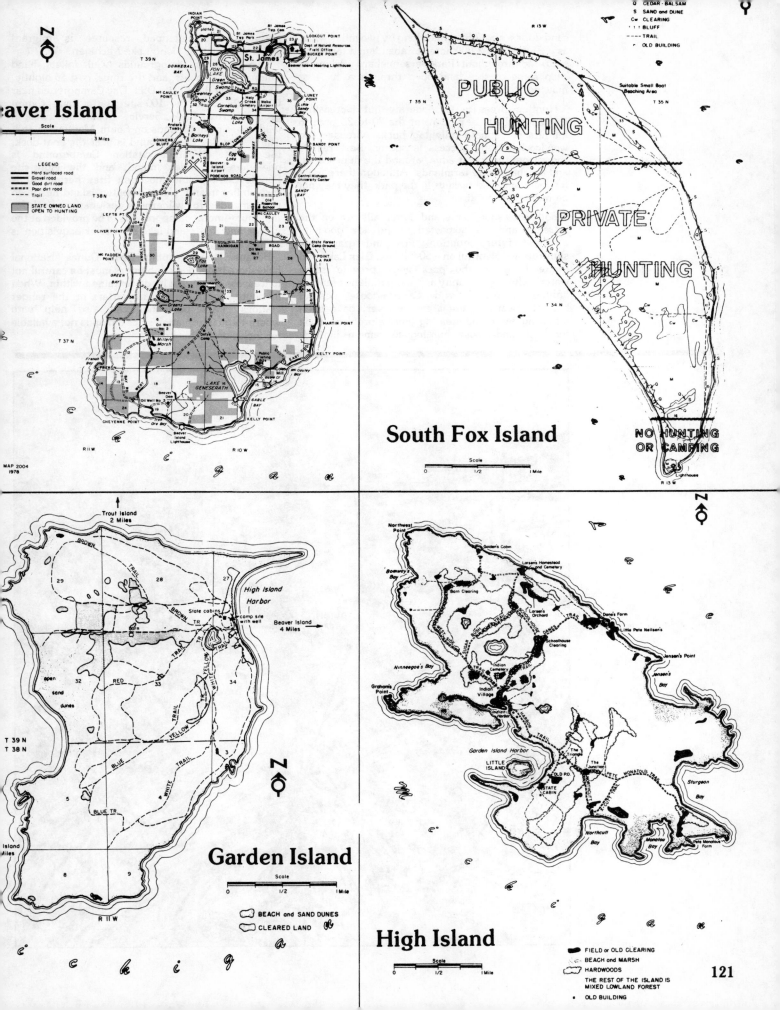

Beaver Island

South Fox Island

Garden Island

High Island

121

sand dunes, about five miles long by two miles wide, as well as some 2,000 acres of abandoned farmland scattered throughout. Park personnel are working to keep some of this land open through a cycle of mowing.

Hunting pressure is moderate but increasing. Currently about 10 percent of the 20 to 25 firearm hunters per square mile tag bucks. Grouse- and woodcock-hunting success is spotty. Best results come from the forest edge, around the dunes area, and on abandoned farmlands. Although there are a few bear and wild turkeys in the park, they may not be hunted at this time.

Both snowshoe hares and cottontails are on the increase and are expected to provide good to excellent future hunting. Fox and gray/black squirrels are plentiful on a 50/50 mix. Glen Lake and Platte Lake on the park edge provide some waterfowling opportunity and the park lands feature limited wood-duck and Canada-goose nesting habitat. Swans in the area, however, have been attacking geese and creating quite a problem. Look for duck and goose hunting to remain limited, although one untapped resource is migrant waterfowl hunting along Lake Michigan.

Two rustic-site campgrounds (vault toilets, hand pumps, picnic tables, and fire rings) cost $6 nightly. They include the 80-site D.H. Day Campground near Glen Arbor and the 100-site Platte River Campground. The Park Service maintains walk-in wilderness campgrounds on South Manitou Island. The 25-site Bay Campground is near the boat dock, the 36-site Weather Station Campground is one-and-a-half miles inland, and the eight-site Popple Campground (no open fires permitted) is three miles inland. North Manitou Island has been recommended for wilderness designation. Look for minimum-impact campgrounds to be provided at the village and the inland lake soon after acquisition is completed.

Because the Sleeping Bear Dunes National Lakeshore is not posted, hunters must be careful not to trespass on private lands contained within. When in doubt, check with headquarters or the ranger stations. Park personnel can also help with where-to-go information since a map is not available for inclusion in this book.

National Park Service

Muskegon State Game Area

THE Muskegon State Game Area is located in west-central Lower Michigan along a 10-mile stretch of the Muskegon River in central Muskegon County. The western boundary area is near the northeastern city limits of Muskegon. The game area totals over 8,500 acres and is adjacent to the Muskegon County Wastewater Management System (*which see*) where controlled waterfowl hunts are held. The game area offers good to excellent hunting for ducks, geese, deer, squirrels, rabbits, grouse, and raccoon.

It consists of delta land and floodplain, about 600 feet above sea level, with the exception of the eastern half, which is bordered by 60- to 80-foot bluffs. These bluffs were formed when the Muskegon River and its tributaries cut through the shores of a primitive lake here which rose and fell with the advance and retreat of glaciers thousands of years ago.

Portions of the game area, especially lowland areas are wilderness-like in appearance. Lowland hardwoods account for about 65 percent of the overall vegetative cover. Dominant species include red maple, willow, ash, cottonwood, and oak. Tag alder, elderberry, silky and gray dogwood, poison ivy (considerable amounts, by the way), and wild grapes are the primary shrub and vine species here. Ground cover consists of dense stands of nettles, ferns, perennial grasses, and associated weeds on better-drained sites. Aquatic plants such as pondweed, wild celery, yellow water lily, arrowhead, cattails, sedge, and cordgrass are also found.

The Muskegon River, its local tributaries, and their associated marshes represent the water resources in the area. The Maple River flows into the Muskegon from the south at the western end of the game area. Mosquito and Spring creeks feed into a large marsh on the southwestern end known as Mosquito Creek Marsh.

DNR management efforts center around waterfowl production and increased waterfowl use. Work projects include nest-box construction, dam repair, food plantings (rye, wheat, corn, millet, buckwheat, barley), and nesting and security cover development.

Waterfowl hunting is exclusively by boat, with the main point of access for both upstream and downstream hunts off Mill Iron Road. Many other two-track roads are closed, which forces hunters to walk in. The river-bottom area is pretty much flooded lowland hardwoods with some cattail openings. The easy-to-get-to spots go fast, but hunters willing to explore can get into remote areas where there is little or no competition.

Downstream from the access site, the area between the North and Middle channels is open marsh. A mile upstream from the site is the swing channel. Public access is also found just east of Island Road (county line boundary) on the north side of the river and again at the end of Holton/Duck Lake Road. A half-mile to the east of this site is a clearcut area, which eventually will fill in with cattails. Sharecrop farming occurs across from DNR headquarters off Maple Island Road and on the southeastern corner of Wolf Lake.

Waterfowlers throughout are likely to run into Canada geese, mallards, black ducks, wood ducks, and teal. Later in the season migrant birds replace locals, and diver species (scaup, goldeneyes, ring-necked ducks, bufflehead, and mergansers) begin to show up. Early season generally affords the best gunning as ducks become spotty through increased pressure. Again, hunters willing to paddle or motor into remote areas can be rewarded with good hunting anytime during the season.

Deer are abundant in the game area, and the shintangle cover produces trophy bucks for hunters willing to tackle it. Deer-hunting pressure is increasing, however. Raccoon are abundant throughout mature hardwood lowlands, and grouse frequent the transitional edge between upland and lowland covers. So do rabbits. Squirrels are plentiful in oak woods atop bluffs and near food plots.

For more information, contact the resident DNR wildlife biologist at the Muskegon State Game Area office, 7600 East Messinger, Twin Lake, Mich. 49457 (616/788-5055). The game area is administered through DNR District Headquarters, State Office Bldg., 350 Ottawa NW, Grand Rapids, Mich. 49503, (616/456-5071).

Langston State Game Area

THE Langston State Game Area is located nine miles north of Greenville in central Montcalm County. Grand Rapids lies 30 miles to the southwest. Hunters from this and other southern Michigan cities come to Langston seeking deer, grouse, woodcock, rabbits, ducks, squirrels, and raccoon. Hunting pressure on the 2,793-acre public area is high, especially for firearm deer.

Topography varies from nearly level to strongly sloping. A glacial moraine lies in the northern half where maximum elevation is 1,060 feet above sea level. The land encircling this moraine drops to 900

feet above sea level. The southern half of the game area consists of outwash plains and glacial channels with elevations fluctuating between 840 and 900 feet above sea level.

Three lakes lie within Langston's boundaries. Hunter Lake, on the southern end, has a surface area of about 43 acres and a maximum depth of 48 feet. The marshy upper end provides some duck-hunting possibilities. West and Tacoma lakes are part of a three-lake chain, the third of which (Spring Lake) is outside the game area. West Lake is 44 acres in size and Tacoma covers 21 acres. Both

Muskegon State Game Area

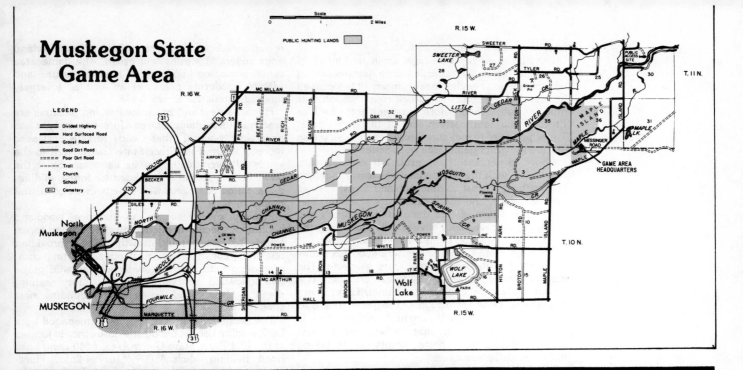

Langston State Game Area

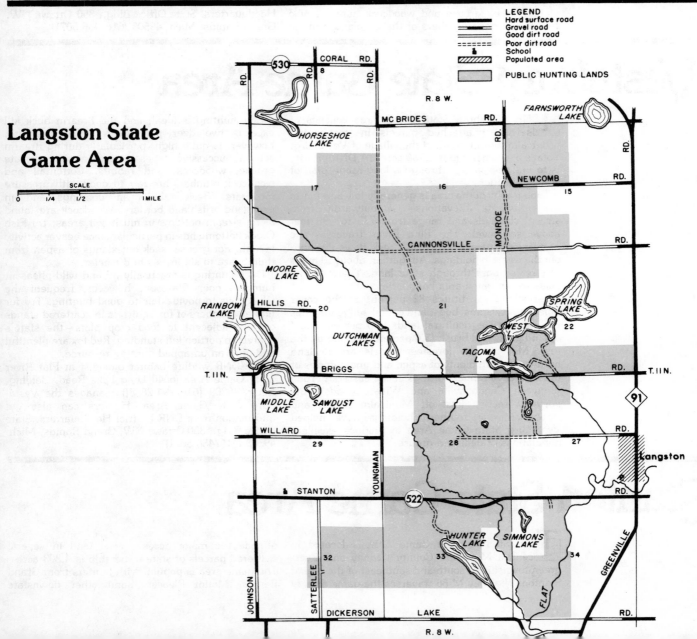

have maximum depths of 36 feet.

The Flat River flows through a mile and a half of the game area and affords some jump-shooting opportunities for wading duck hunters (it is too small for canoes). West Branch Creek runs through four miles of public land before emptying into the Flat River at the southeastern end of the game area. Three ponds of two or three acres each in size also are found within game area boundaries.

About 85 percent of the project is covered with forestland, with the rest divided between rangeland and wetlands. Most common upland forest species are red, white, and black oak; red and white pine; and aspen. Lowlands are dominated by brush and swamp conifer. Autumn-olive shrubs planted by the DNR constitute some eight miles of strip cover.

Langston State Game Area offers good fox-squirrel hunting with light to moderate pressure. The northern portion is largely oak forest, and there is a considerable stand of oaks near Hunter Lake. There is good deer hunting throughout the game area, but, as mentioned, pressure is very high. In fact, there is currently some concern that archers and firearm hunters with hunter's-choice permits may be taking too many antlerless deer.

In addition to deer and squirrels, the area gets visitations by grouse and woodcock hunters, who find fair to good numbers of these upland birds in mixed stands of aspen and along upland/lowland edge covers of shrubs and brush. The game area contains raccoon (moderate to heavy pressure) and rabbits (moderate pressure) as well as a largely ignored population of red fox.

Hunter-access and adequate parking facilities are scattered throughout. The oak forest cover type has observers hopeful that wild turkeys released recently at the Flat River State Game Area to the south will eventually populate Langston. Since the game area is primarily managed for forest wildlife, the addition of turkeys would be both welcome and practical.

Primary objectives are to improve woodland habitat for species mentioned by clear-cutting aspen stands to create multi-growth stages, providing openings, constructing brush piles, planting corn, promoting natural food growth such as wild grape and dogwood, creating meadows for nesting, planting shrubs and conifers, and building nest sites.

The Langston State Game Area is managed by a DNR wildlife habitat biologist whose office is located at the Flat River State Game Area, 6640 Long Lake Road, Belding, Mich. 48809 (616/794-2658). Hunters can also get information from DNR District Headquarters, State Office Bldg., 350 Ottawa NW, Grand Rapids, Mich. 49503 (616/456-5071).

Vestaburg State Game Area

THE Vestaburg State Game Area consists of several unattached parcels in east-central Montcalm County south of the village of Vestaburg. Total state ownership is 1,786 acres. A DNR priority is to link the parcels through a long-range plan of land acquisition.

Topography of the area is generally low and flat to gently rolling. Elevations rise outwardly from stream channels and range from 775 to 990 feet above sea level. The Pine River traverses the easternmost parcel, and Fish Creek flows throughout the western holdings. Altogether, about 10 miles of streams pass through state land. There are no lakes within game-area boundaries.

Forestland constitutes 82 percent of the cover type, with swamps, bogs, and cattail-sedge marshes (7.9 percent); agricultural lands (6.5 percent); and upland grass and brush (3.4 percent) making up the rest. Most of the forested parcels are lowland hardwoods with plenty of aspen and understories of brush. Heavy timber cuttings in the eastern portion (between Cannonsville and Willard roads), the northern section (just off Montcalm Road), and throughout the southern holdings have helped Vestaburg State Game Area to produce excellent populations of deer and grouse.

Bow hunting is ideal, and the firearm buck kill exceeds two deer per square mile. Pressure, however, is quite high, particularly during firearm season. Successive stages of aspen growth promote grouse, woodcock, and rabbits. Cottontail and woodcock numbers are fair to good with pressure moderate. Seek rabbits in openings and in grassland-brushland borders. Woodcock are found along stream bottoms in muck soil areas; try Fish Creek bottomlands in particular since beaver activity is high. For grouse, seek out stands of aspen from thumb-size to six inches in diameter.

Duck hunting is practically nil and wild-pheasant numbers poor. Raccoon, however, frequent the waterways to povide fair to good hunting. Try for limited numbers of fox squirrels in scattered stands of oaks adjacent to food crop plots—the state's sharecrop portion left standing. Red fox are plentiful and offer an untapped hunting resource.

The DNR wildlife habitat biologist at Flat River State Game Area (6640 Long Lake Road, Belding, Mich. 48809 [616/794-2658]) manages the Vestaburg State Game Area. Hunters can also get information from DNR District Headquarters, State Office Bldg., 350 Ottawa NW, Grand Rapids, Mich. 49503 (616/456-5071).

Stanton State Game Area

THE Stanton State Game Area is located in central Montcalm County (Sidney and Evergreen townships), south and southeast of the city of Stanton. Highway M-66 traverses the game area to provide the major access. Total land in several scattered parcels of state ownership is 4,303 acres. The game area is popular with hunters from Grand Rapids, Mount Pleasant, and other downstate

Vestaburg State Game Area

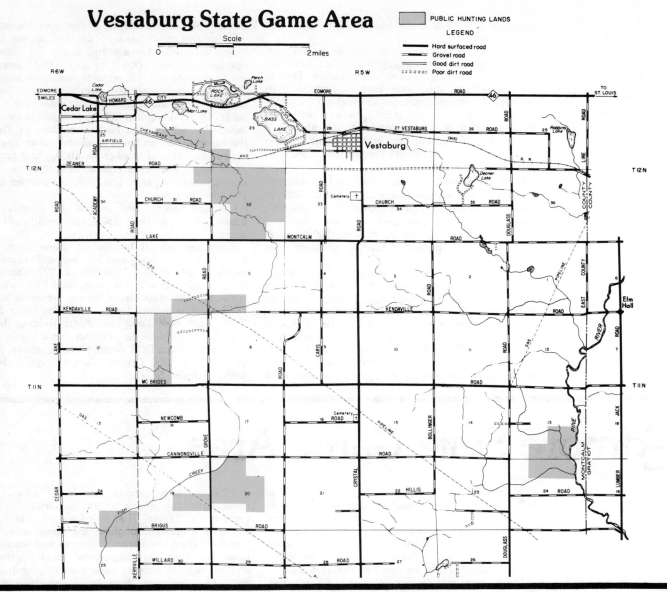

Scale

0 _____ 2 miles

Stanton State Game Area

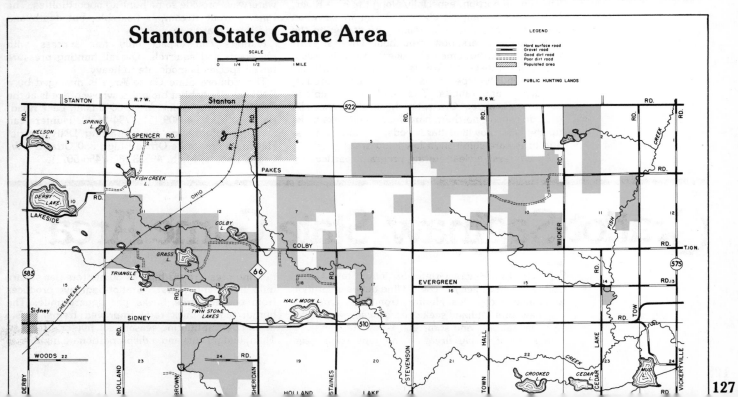

SCALE

0   1/4   1/2   1 MILE

127

communities. They come here seeking deer and small game.

Pressure overall is not as heavy as southern Michigan state game and recreation areas; however, it is intense during firearm deer season. That is largely because the game area supports a high number of deer and produces an excellent buck kill, which includes some trophy-racked animals. Grouse, rabbit, and woodcock hunting is also quite good; squirrel hunting fair; and pheasant hunting poor. A lack of water limits raccoon and waterfowl production and use.

State land borders four lakes in the western portion, which features some clear-cutting activity for grouse and deer habitat improvement. The dry, eastern section features open fields and farmland with some sharecrop farming of about 100 acres. A former put-take pheasant hunting program was centered here.

Topography ranges from nearly level to strongly sloping with altitudes varying from 850 to 950 feet above sea level. The most hilly terrain—a glacial morainic ridge—runs from a line west-southwest to the northeastern portion. About 15 miles of stream and 100 acres of lake surface occur within the Stanton State Game Area. Fish Creek, which passes through the easternmost portions, is a designated trout stream. The four lakes range in size from 12 to

38 acres and are each about 30 feet deep maximum.

Forestland constitutes 66 percent of the cover types, with upland grass and brush (20 percent), agricultural land (9.5 percent), and swamps, marshes, and bogs (4.2 percent) making up the rest. The dominant upland cover type is aspen, pure-stand pockets of which include nearly 900 acres. On an additional 300 acres aspen is found in association with oak or lowland hardwoods. Oak is the second-most prominent upland cover species, with some 700 total acres of stands. Upland grasses cover about 700 acres and occur mainly in large abandoned farm fields. The DNR has planted about 200 acres of pine.

Lowland cover types include hardwoods (750 acres), swamp conifers (150 acres), and brush (100 acres).

Estimated annual harvest of game birds and animals (made a few years ago but still reasonably valid) include 25 deer, 100 grouse, 200 rabbits, 75 fox squirrels, 25 wild pheasants, and 25 woodcock.

The Stanton State Game Area is managed by the DNR wildlife habitat biologist at Flat River State Game Area, 6640 Long Lake Road, Belding, Mich. 48809 (616/794-2658). Hunters can also get information from DNR District Headquarters, State Office Bldg., 350 Ottawa, Grand Rapids, Mich. 49503 (616/456-5071).

Edmore State Game Area

THE Edmore State Game Area is located in northeastern Montcalm County at the Isabella and Gratiot county lines. Three small parcels are within Isabella County itself. State ownership is in the form of scattered parcels totaling 2,400 acres. The game area is popular with hunters from Mount Pleasant and from as far away as Grand Rapids.

The western and eastern portions are nearly flat. The central portion, especially along the Pine River, is quite hilly, ranging about 150 feet in elevation difference. Six miles of streams, tributaries to the Pine and Flat rivers, flow throughout. These streams are mostly silt-bottomed and overhung with brush.

Edmore State Game Area is managed primarily for forest wildlife species such as deer, grouse, woodcock, and rabbits. The predominant upland cover type is aspen. Grass, brush, shrubs (especially gray dogwood), northern hardwoods, and oaks make up the rest. Lowland hardwoods, swamp conifers, and brush are common in low-lying areas.

An aggressive clear-cutting program, particularly

in the western parcels, involving aspen has encouraged the growth of this important tree in varying age classes. That is largely why deer and rabbits are found throughout the game area, and there is a good population of grouse and woodcock (especially during fall migrations). Duck hunting is limited to local woodies raised on impoundments and along streams. Raccoon frequenting these waterways provide some hunting opportunities. The Pine, a trout stream, is floatable, but depth and width are marginal.

Hunters can expect only fair success with pheasants and squirrels. Overall hunting pressure for all species is moderate to heavy.

The Edmore State Game Area is managed by a DNR wildlife habitat biologist, whose office is at the Flat River State Game Area, 6640 Long Lake Road, Belding, Mich. 48809 (616/794-2658). Hunters can also get information by contacting DNR District Headquarters, State Office Bldg., 350 Ottawa NW, Grand Rapids, Mich. 49503 (616/456-5071).

Gratiot-Saginaw State Game Area

THE 13,098-acre Gratiot-Saginaw State Game Area straddles the county line between Gratiot and Saginaw counties. Hunters from Flint, Lansing, Saginaw, and Midland seek deer, grouse, woodcock, raccoon, rabbits, and squirrels.

In spite of heavy firearm (shotguns only) deer

hunting pressure (as high as 60 hunters per square mile in recent years), Gratiot-Saginaw produces from one to three bucks per square mile. The hunter/tagged-buck ratio improved tremendously during permit hunting seasons for five or six years. Then, budget cuts and a disproportionate number of

Edmore State Game Area

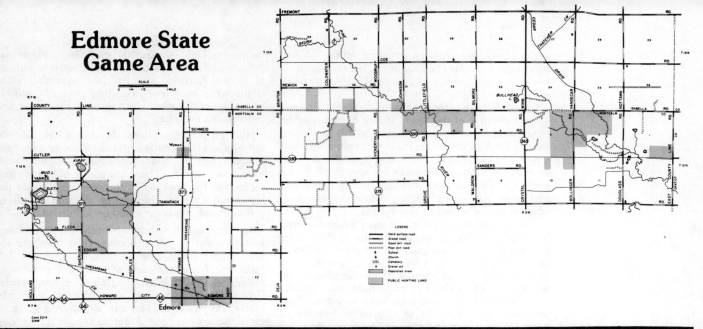

Gratiot-Saginaw State Game Area

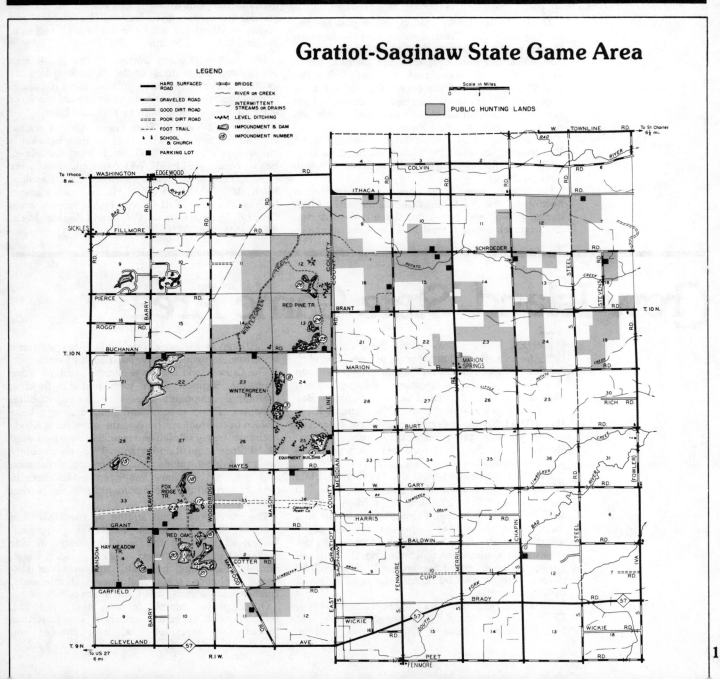

early- versus late-season hunters forced the DNR to return to noncontrolled hunting. Currently it is being managed again as a special hunter's-choice area.

Gratiot-Saginaw contains sandy, poorly drained soils, indicative of the heavy stands of virgin white pine that once covered the area. It is still 95 percent forested but mostly with lowland hardwoods—soft maple, black willow, black and green ash, and swamp oak. Cottonwood trees are also found in the lowlands. Upland areas contain mostly white oak and aspen. Red pine plantings and natural stands of white pine are scattered throughout.

Commercial use of the game area which benefits hunters includes sharecropping by a few local farmers and timber harvesting. The state's share of cropped fields is left as winter cover and food for birds and animals. A number of small timber sales, particularly of sawlogs in pure hardwood stands, have occurred over the past several years. This practice stems the tide of natural succession to climax forest types and provides more openings for wildlife.

The land is level, with a few gentle slopes. Ditches flowing into Potato Creek drain most of the Saginaw County portion. Water in the Gratiot County portion also flows into numerous drainage ditches, which empty either into Potato Creek, the south fork of the Bad River, or the Maple River. One of the most important of these is Limbecker Drain, which becomes Limbecker Creek, and eventually flows into the south fork of the Bad River.

It is interesting to note that water draining into the Bad River flows into Lake Huron via Saginaw Bay, while water flowing into the Maple River runs into Lake Michigan.

Predictably, some of the area is marshy, offering nesting habitat for Canada geese, mallards, black ducks, green- and blue-winged teal, wood ducks, and ringneck ducks. A total of 717 acres in impound-ments include some 300 potholes. Waterfowl hunting, however, is best in early season with an occasional flurry of action in late November when flight birds stop over. Gunning pressure quickly burns out local ducks, which move to Fish Point and Shiawassee for refuge.

Hunting pressure overall is quite high, particularly for deer and ruffed grouse. River-bottom oaks produce fair to good fox-squirrel hunting with moderate pressure. There are plenty of red fox and raccoon in the area too, with pressure high for the latter and light for the former. A good supply of cottontail rabbits is currently underhunted.

An increase in bow-hunting interest has translated into good early-season success. Deer numbers are fair at this time. The game area produces fair numbers of woodcock and at times in late October affords good to excellent hunting for migrant birds. Grouse-hunting fortunes run poor to good. In high-cycle years, hunters can experience three or more flushes per hour. Hunters should try wooded areas mixed with aspen (there are no pure aspen stands) that contain an understory of witch hazel and dogwood. Woodcock will be found here as well as in lowland stands of brush.

The Saginaw County portion of the game area offers easy access (most of the 21 parking lots are located here) and therefore gets the most pressure. Gratiot County, with limited access to solid blocks of state ownership, affords more secluded hunting.

The Gratiot-Saginaw State Game Area is staffed with a DNR biologist who splits his time between a game area office at 13350 South Meridian Road, Brant, Mich. 48614 (517/643-7000) and Rose Lake Field Office, 8562 East Stoll Road, East Lansing, Mich. 48823 (517/373-9358). Hunters can also get information from DNR District Headquarters, State Office Bldg., 350 Ottawa NW, Grand Rapids, Mich. 49503 (616/456-5071).

Crow Island State Game Area

THE 2,100-acre Crow Island State Game Area draws a tremendous amount of waterfowl each fall due to its location on the Saginaw River between Bay City and Zilwaukee (Saginaw and Bay counties). This area is ideally situated between Saginaw Bay and Shiawassee Flats from which the Saginaw River flows. The DNR supervises the planting of sharecrop grains on the game area with local farmers. Controlled flooding and food plots left standing attract waterfowl.

The area is managed from the St. Charles Field Office at the Shiawassee River State Game Area, 225 East Spruce St., St. Charles, Mich. 48655 (517/865-6211). It is open to hunting by permit only for parties of two or three during the early part of the waterfowl season (call for details). Hunters can get reservation applications by contacting DNR offices between August 26 and September 10. Normally 50 permits are issued by lottery for each day of controlled hunting.

After that, no permits are required; consequently, Crow Island eventually gets heavy pressure and reduced hunter success. Opportunities improve again later in the season as flight birds stop and waterfowlers turn to other game such as deer.

The Crow Island area is a natural overflow basin from the Saginaw River with periodic flooding limiting development other than for agricultural purposes. Flood control and land drainage have always been problems here as the game area floods both from heavy rainfall and from Saginaw Bay wind tides. Since acquisition began in 1953, an elaborate system of dikes, canals, ditches, control structures, and pumping stations has been established to permit agricultural development and to protect property.

The game area is not staffed by the DNR, and therefore hunter success is largely unknown. Waterfowl that use the area, however, include mallards (largely), wood ducks, blacks, teal, pintails, baldpates, gadwalls, ringnecks, canvasbacks, redheads, scaup, goldeneyes, buffleheads, ruddies, mergansers, and Canada geese.

Other game animals include deer, red fox, raccoon, woodchuck, and squirrels. The East Unit contains 40 acres of oak, ash, maple, and

Crow Island State Game Area

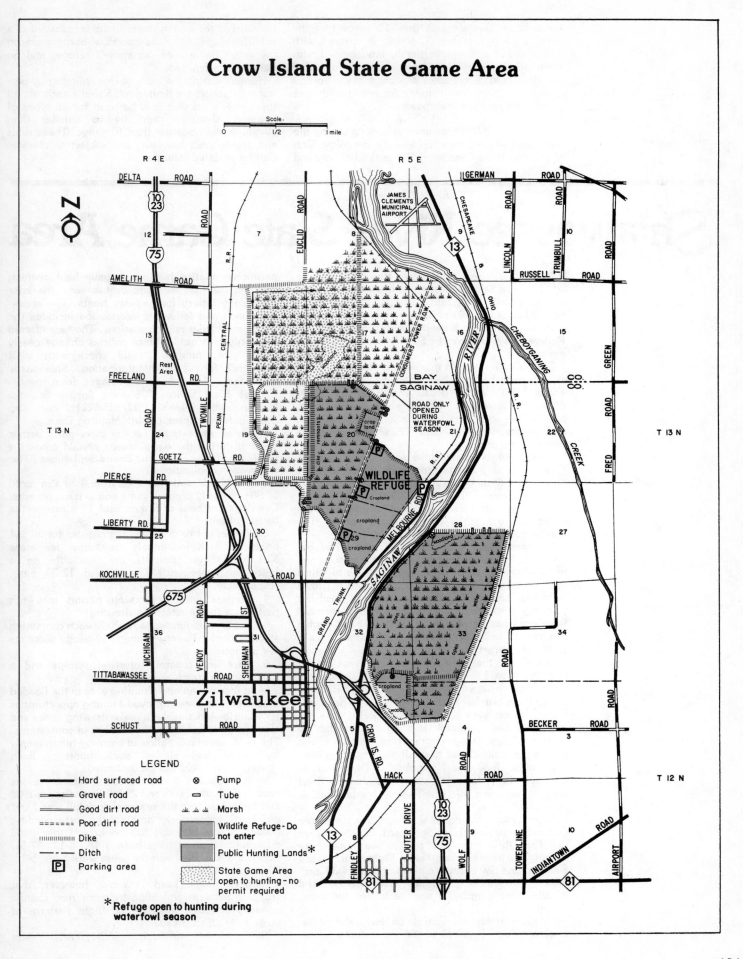

Scale:
0   1/2   1 mile

R 4 E   R 5 E

DELTA ROAD
GERMAN ROAD
JAMES CLEMENTS MUNICIPAL AIRPORT

AMELITH ROAD

Rest Area

FREELAND ROAD

BAY SAGINAW

ROAD ONLY OPENED DURING WATERFOWL SEASON

T 13 N

cropland

GOETZ RD.

PIERCE RD.

WILDLIFE REFUGE

Cropland

LIBERTY RD.

cropland

cropland

KOCHVILLE ROAD

TITTABAWASSEE ROAD

Zilwaukee

SCHUST ROAD

HACK ROAD

BECKER ROAD

T 12 N

LEGEND

———	Hard surfaced road
	Gravel road
	Good dirt road
=====	Poor dirt road
....	Dike
—·—·—	Ditch
P	Parking area
⊗	Pump
▱	Tube
↯↯	Marsh

Wildlife Refuge - Do not enter

Public Hunting Lands*

State Game Area open to hunting - no permit required

*Refuge open to hunting during waterfowl season

131

cottonwood. Overall, less than 10 percent of the game area is forested. The rest is covered with cattail sedge and willow marsh, interspersed with open ponds. The West Unit is largely a cattail marsh, although 352 acres are under water-control devices and therefore suitable for crop planting or permanent meadow maintenance.

The East Unit has been open to hunting during the waterfowl season since 1976 while the West Unit (lying east of the Consumers Power right-of-way and bounded on the east by the railroad) is managed as a wildlife refuge. After the waterfowl-hunting season the entire game area becomes a refuge, and no hunting is permitted.

Hunters during the early season, hunting-by-permit only period are limited to 25 shells each. At all times only steel shot may be used for all types of hunting. Shotguns must be no smaller than 20-gauge and no larger than 10 gauge. These rules and regulations, however, are subject to change. Call for updated information.

Shiawassee River State Game Area

THE 8,419-acre Shiawassee River State Game Area in Saginaw County is managed primarily for waterfowl. Peak fall usage by migrant birds occurs in late October or early November. Together with the adjacent Shiawassee National Wildlife Refuge, the totals may be 50,000 ducks and 25,000 geese.

Controlled hunting in this state game area during recent years has resulted in an annual harvest of about 2,000 Canada geese and 8,000 to 10,000 ducks, 80 percent or more of which are mallards. Most of the others are teal, blacks, other dabblers, and common mergansers. Few diving ducks frequent the area.

During the 1983 waterfowl season, the Saginaw County Goose Management Area, which includes Shiawassee State Game Area, saw its harvest quota of Canada geese lifted from 3,000 to 5,000. That liberal move has increased goose-hunting opportunities in the area by extending the season. The annual quota is set late each summer.

The state game area includes a wildlife refuge, about 1,700 acres in crop rotation (mostly rye, wheat, buckwheat, corn, soybeans), some of which is planted by the state and some of which is grown on a sharecrop basis with area farmers. Food left standing, the sanctuary's presence, and the general floodlands nature of the Shiawassee Flats region combine to make Shiawassee State Game Area a waterfowl attraction.

In addition, there are some cottontails on upland portions as well as squirrels although a shortage of mast trees makes for limited potential. Raccoon populations are fair with heavy hunting pressure. Pheasants are very scarce, a few local grouse are available, and woodcock hunting can be fair to occasionally good when migrant birds stop over. The area is generally closed to small-game hunting from September 15-30 and November 15-December 12 although these dates are subject to change. Steel shot is required of small-game hunters using shotguns.

Together with the national refuge, the game area currently supports a large deer herd. In recent years the first three days of regular-season archery hunting has been by permit only. Eighty hunters are awarded one-day permits determined in a 4:30 a.m. drawing that day. Shotgun (slugs only) and muzzleloader hunting is also permitted by reservation.

But most hunters concentrate on ducks and geese. In recent years 8,000 to 10,000 have shown up for permit reservation hunting (usually held opening day and the first weekend or two) and the later twice-daily lottery for half-day hunts. The above-mentioned and following information includes the most recent rules and regulations. They are offered here only as a guide. Since policies change nearly every year, hunters should check with DNR personnel for updated information. Shiawassee River State Game Area is managed from the St. Charles Field Office, 225 East Spruce St., St. Charles, Mich. 48655 (517/865-6211). Ask also about dates for special Youth Hunting Days.

1. Those interested in two- or three-party permit hunting during the early season should contact a DNR office between August 26 and September 10 for reservation applications.

2. The check station is open from 4:30 a.m. until 12:30 p.m. daily to check game and to issue permits. Drawings are held at 5 a.m. and 11 a.m. for the half-day hunts.

3. Parties of two or three may register for all 111 areas although individuals may draw for areas 57-111. Leftover permits are available on a first-come basis until 8 a.m. and 12:30 p.m., respectively.

4. Hunters with a morning permit may not participate in the afternoon drawing.

5. Hunters are limited to 25 shells each containing steel shot only. Twenty-gauge to 10-gauge shotguns are permitted.

6. State and federal waterfowl stamps and a public access stamp are required.

Most recently an open-hunting area in the flooded timber portion area improved hunting opportunities for waterfowlers unable to make drawing times and also served to cut down the number of contestants. The most recent rules allowed morning-hunting only for geese and all-day duck hunting. Such liberalization likely will be continued.

Most productive hunting areas in recent seasons have been Zones 21-28 and 29-38. Statistics for 1982 and 1983 show that the seasonal duck kill was 1,097 and 1,782, respectively, and that the corresponding goose kill was 308 and 535 honkers. Other good duck-hunting areas have been 1-4A, 5-12, 47-51, 52-56, and A-F. Best bets for geese were 1-4A, 5-12, 80-95, and A-F.

Hunters should keep in mind, however, that cropping patterns and blind locations may change annually and that weather and flight patterns of birds daily affect prospects.

The Tri-County and Saginaw Valley Waterfowlers

chapters of the Michigan Duck Hunters Association (both Michigan United Conservation Clubs affiliates) have assisted DNR personnel with various game-area improvement projects, including the construction and installation of rollers at boat pull-over sites here.

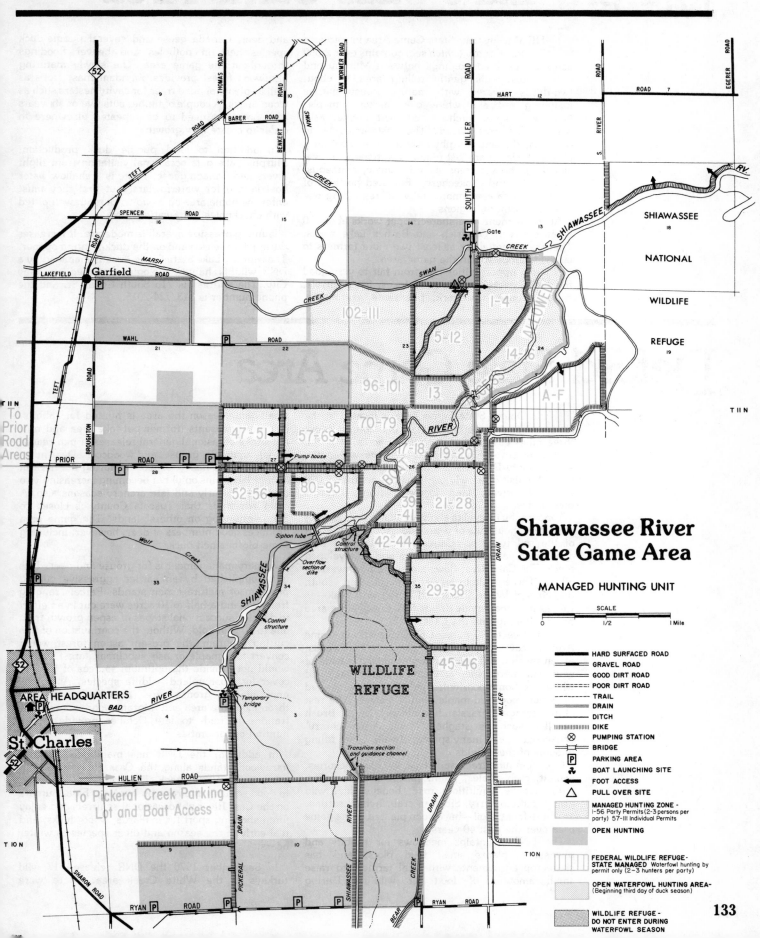

Shiawassee River State Game Area

MANAGED HUNTING UNIT

SCALE

0   1/2   1 Mile

▬▬▬	HARD SURFACED ROAD
	GRAVEL ROAD
	GOOD DIRT ROAD
	POOR DIRT ROAD
- - - -	TRAIL
	DRAIN
	DITCH
	DIKE
⊗	PUMPING STATION
	BRIDGE
P	PARKING AREA
	BOAT LAUNCHING SITE
◀	FOOT ACCESS
△	PULL OVER SITE
	MANAGED HUNTING ZONE - I-56 Party Permits (2-3 persons per party) 57-III Individual Permits
	OPEN HUNTING
	FEDERAL WILDLIFE REFUGE- STATE MANAGED Waterfowl hunting by permit only (2-3 hunters per party)
	OPEN WATERFOWL HUNTING AREA- (Beginning third day of duck season)
	WILDLIFE REFUGE- DO NOT ENTER DURING WATERFOWL SEASON

Murphy Lake State Game Area

THE Murphy Lake State Game Area in southern Tuscola County (*which see*) contains over 2,500 acres in scattered holdings between Murphy and Otter lakes. This gently rolling area is about two-thirds covered with mature forest species including red and white oak, hickory, maple, basswood, white birch, aspen, soft maple, ash, willow, and cottonwood. The rest amounts to potholes, 250-acre Murphy Lake itself, and old farm fields. The latter are fast filling in with early-successional shrubs and trees such as sumac, crataegus, wild apple, and chokecherry. Forested portions of the game area are remote and wild, reminding one of more northerly regions.

At the moment, one sharecropper works about 50 acres between Goodrich and Barnes Lake roads. There is potential for at least two more farmers to cultivate crops within the game area.

Hunting opportunities rate from fair to very good for ducks, geese, raccoon, red foxes, fox squirrels, ruffed grouse, woodcock, pheasants, cottontails, and deer. Canada geese and several puddle-duck species nest in potholes and beaver floodings throughout the game area. The slowly maturing hardwood forest provides abundant mast crops as well as plenty of dead trees for cavity nesters such as wood ducks. A couple of timber cuts five or six years ago, however, need to be repeated elsewhere in order to create new growth.

In addition to local puddle duck production, Murphy Lake gets occasional visitation from flight divers and Canada geese. There is a shallow-water boat launch for waterfowlers, but first they must enter the game area on a two-track road, well pitted with chuckholes, off Swaffer Road.

Hunting pressure overall is moderate. It increases during deer season and on the duck-hunting opener. The Murphy Lake State Game Area is managed by a DNR wildlife habitat biologist stationed at Imlay City. The address is 715 South Cedar St. and the phone number is 313/724-2015.

Deford State Game Area

THE Deford State Game Area is located in the east-central portion of Tuscola County about three miles east of Caro. At 9,607 acres, it is the largest of several public-land holdings within the seven-county DNR district headquartered at Imlay City. Acquisition slowly continues of another 9,000 acres of private land located within Deford's boundaries.

Topography is level to slightly rolling, the result of glaciation thousands of years ago. About 75 percent of the soil types is relatively infertile sand with another 25 percent in sandy loam and undeveloped muck. The Cass River flows along the northwestern edge. Three tributaries—the north and south branches of White Creek and Butternut Creek—as well as nine man-made drains flow through the area before running into the Cass.

Eighty-five to 90 percent of Deford State Game Area is covered with second-growth hardwoods, aspen mostly, but also containing mixed stands of white birch, red maple, white ash, red oak, and white oak. Some poorly-drained sites are dominated by cottonwood, red maple, and white ash. The rest of the acreage is grasslands or old farm fields. Brush species, such as staghorn sumac, pin cherry, chokecherry, and many species of willow, are filling in some of these fields.

Over a million trees and shrubs—oaks, hickories, walnut, crab apples, plum, pines, spruce, cedar, autumn olive, multiflora rose, honeysuckle, wild grape, buffalo berry, Siberian crab, hybrid sordan, and birdsfoot trefoil—have been planted in the game area over the past 40 years.

The DNR maintains meadows for rabbits and pheasants, plants small food plots, and has sharecrop agreements with local farmers to raise small amounts of food for wildlife. During small-game season the area is hunted for rabbits, raccoon, pheasants (former put-take area and now the site of occasional general releases of pen-reared birds), squirrels, grouse, and woodcock. Deer-hunting pressure is heavy, especially during the firearm opener (shotguns only) but becoming increasingly so during both early and late archery seasons also. A main reason is that Tuscola County is closed to Sunday hunting on others' lands. The game area produces good numbers of deer, however, including some big-beamed bucks.

Primary management is for grouse and deer. This is accomplished by an earlier aggressive cutting program of mature aspen stands. Parcels ranging from two-and-a-half to 10 acres were cut in an effort to develop successional stages of aspen growth from one to 40 years old. Without the continuation of this cutting program, the present aspen forest would convert to a maple or ash subclimax forest, which would not provide the optimum sources of food or cover for most upland wildlife species. As things now stand, grouse are reasonably plentiful throughout the area and migrant woodcock concentrations in mid- to late October provide bonus hunting opportunities.

In addition, the DNR has maintained mature hardwood stands along the Cass River and both branches of White Creek. These areas produce fair to good squirrel and raccoon hunting. Float hunters on the Cass River pot occasional squirrels and enjoy jump-shooting sport for mallards, wood ducks, and teal early in the season and diver species as winter nears.

In September 1970 the DNR released 17 wild turkeys in the White Creek area. There were

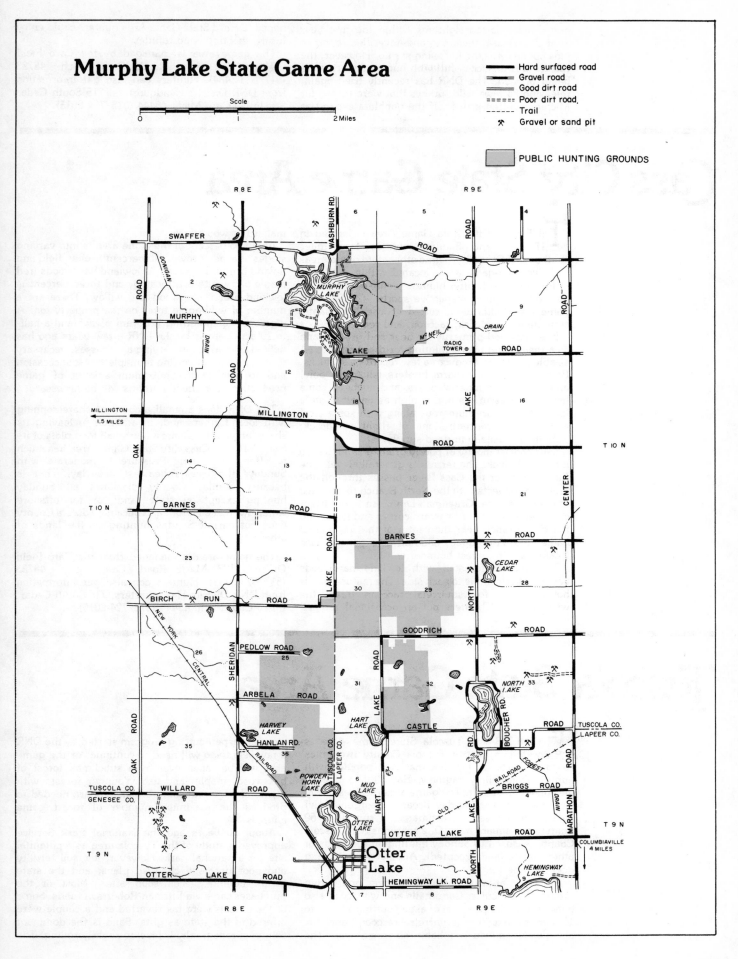

Murphy Lake State Game Area

Scale

0   1   2 Miles

Hard surfaced road	
Gravel road	
Good dirt road	
Poor dirt road	
Trail	
⚒ Gravel or sand pit	

PUBLIC HUNTING GROUNDS

numerous reported sightings within the first year after the release, including one unverified report of nine young birds the following spring. However, the release was unsuccessful, with human disturbances being blamed. The DNR has recently tried again, releasing 24 Iowa wild turkeys that were traded for Michigan ruffed grouse. If the gobblers expand as hoped, Deford State Game Area hunters could enjoy future shooting opportunities.

The game area is managed by the Caro Field Office, 1123 Mertz Road, Caro, Mich. 48723 (517/673-3434). Hunters can also get information from DNR District Headquarters, 715 South Cedar St., Imlay City, Mich. 48444 (313/724-2015).

Cass City State Game Area

THE Cass City State Game Area is located in Tuscola and Sanilac counties four miles southeast of Cass City. Three other state game areas and five mini-game areas located within a 10-mile radius collectively offer hunters plenty of opportunities to follow their respective sports. The 963-acre game area holds deer, ruffed grouse, pheasants, cottontails, woodcock, raccoon, and red fox.

It is managed primarily for deer and grouse, and as a result offers good hunting for these species. A sizable deer herd produces a few record-class bucks. Both archers and firearm hunters (shotguns only) and December muzzleloaders and archers come here, yet pressure is not as high as on other state lands. Grouse are numerous along with some local and periodic concentrations of flight woodcock. Rabbits are usually in good supply.

Soils consist mostly of poorly drained sand, sandy loam, and muck. The terrain is generally level. The East Branch of the Cass River passes through the area and connects with the North Branch to the west of the game area. Greenman Drain, an intermittent creek, enters the northeastern corner and flows into the East Branch near the center of the four-parcel game area. A dredged, one-half acre pond is also located within project boundaries.

The river is forested with lowland hardwoods about a quarter-mile to each side. The mature woods house a few fox squirrels, raccoon travel the waterway, and hunters pot an occasional jumped mallard or wood duck.

About 45 percent of the game area is into varying stages of aspen growth, 40 percent is open field and upland brush, 12 percent is lowland hardwoods (red maple and white ash mostly), and three percent is lowland brush—dogwood and willow. There are a number of wild-apple trees on the property too. A vigorous aspen-cutting program of two-and-a-half- to 10-acre parcels by the DNR a few years ago has helped keep aspen in varying age classes, necessary to stop it from converting to maple-forest succession and to provide the maximum amount of game production. Continued cuttings will be necessary.

The DNR does a small amount of sharecropping with local farmers and, in addition to leaving its share for wildlife, plants a few small food plots of its own. All in all, Cass City State Game Area has much to offer the hunter. Pressure is moderate with Sundays the week's heaviest use day. That is because Sanilac County disallows all Sunday hunting except on state lands or for offshore waterfowl (Lake Huron) and because Tuscola County does not permit Sunday hunting on the lands of others.

The game area is managed from the Caro Field Office, 1123 Mertz Road, Caro, Mich. 48723 (517/673-3434). Hunters can also get information from DNR District Headquarters, 715 South Cedar, Imlay City, Mich. 48444 (313/724-2015).

Tuscola State Game Area

THE 8,383-acre Tuscola State Game Area is located in central Tuscola County two miles south of Caro. Its location makes it popular with hunters from Flint, Saginaw, Bay City, and even metropolitan Detroit. The game area receives heavy weekend and opening-day firearm (shotguns only) deer-hunting pressure, estimated to run 40 to 50 hunters per square mile. One reason is that Tuscola County is closed to Sunday hunting on the lands of others (state land excepted). Another is a thriving deer herd here.

The game area is managed for deer and ruffed grouse in particular. Cottontails and woodcock also benefit from the program of aspen cutting in 2.5- to 10-acre chunks. Fox squirrels, raccoon, and fox along with some ducks inhabit the area as well. The vigorous aspen-cutting program started by the DNR a few years ago will need to continue, or the game area will be taken over by a subclimax forest of basswood, maple, and ash. Younger forests with plenty of edge and some brushlands are needed to produce the maximum number of forest game animals.

About 50 years ago the National Park Service approved a study of the Tuscola area as a potential site for a national park. However, low soil fertility and poor drainage changed plans, and the state began buying pieces soon after. Most of the purchases came via Pittman-Robertson funds. Some of the parcels were tax-reverted and a couple were offered to the state as gifts. Sand is the dominant soil type; topography is level to slightly rolling. The

Deford State Game Area

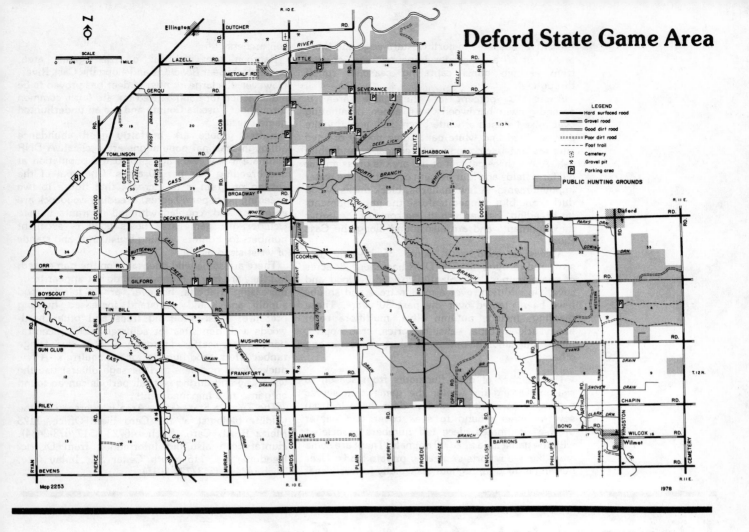

LEGEND

━━━━	Hard surfaced road
━━━	Gravel road
───	Good dirt road
┄┄┄	Poor dirt road
- - -	Foot trail
⊕	Cemetery
✕	Gravel pit
P	Parking area

PUBLIC HUNTING GROUNDS

Map 2253

1978

Cass City State Game Area

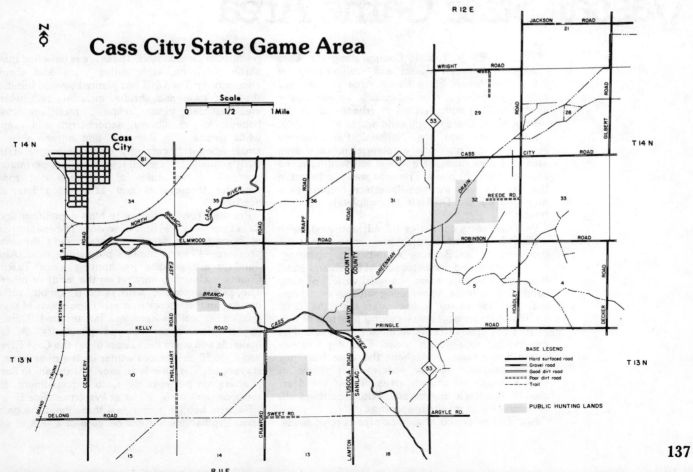

BASE LEGEND

━━━━	Hard surfaced road
━━━	Gravel road
───	Good dirt road
┄┄┄	Poor dirt road
- - -	Trail

PUBLIC HUNTING LANDS

137

Cass River borders the northwestern edge and there are about 60 small water impoundments created from earthen dams capturing seasonal runoff throughout.

About 92 percent of the game area is second-growth hardwoods with aspen dominating over mixed stands of white birch, red maple, white ash, and red and white oak. Some poorly drained sites are heavy to cottonwood, red maple, and white ash. About three percent of the area is grassland or old farm fields and four percent consists of the water impoundments. A few mallards, black ducks, wood ducks, and blue-winged teal use the impoundments for breeding. Beaver also utilize some of the larger impoundments and are also found along the Cass River.

Access is good, with some 35 parking lots scattered throughout. The DNR has about 20 acres of sharecropped land planted to wildlife food and cover. In addition, over a million trees and shrubs have been planted over the past 30 years. These plantings include autumn olive, multiflora rose, honeysuckle, grape, oaks, hickories, crab apples, plum, four kinds of pine, and white spruce among others.

The number of deer fluctuates from season to season. During the winter the game area serves somewhat as a winter yard as deer move in from several miles around to seek cover and winter browse. Estimates place fall numbers associated with the game area at 2,000 animals. There are some crop damage reports on nearby private lands. Deer hunting is good throughout, especially for early-season archers.

Raccoon are plentiful on the game area, particularly near floodings and along the Cass River. However, the large number of deer has proved to be a distraction for hounds. Red fox are fairly common throughout Tuscola County and are an underhunted game species.

Ruffed grouse are in fairly good abundance although seasonal populations are cyclical. A DNR estimate a few years ago placed the population at one breeding pair per 60 acres. One goal of the cutting program is to increase that figure to two breeding pairs per 40 acres. Breeding woodcock are abundant and, coupled with fall migrants in late October, the game area hosts good to excellent numbers for hunters working brushlands and stands of wrist-sized aspen.

There are some wild pheasants on the game area, but they are few in number and do not appear to be increasing. Rabbits, however, are in fair to good supply and could withstand increased hunting pressure. Mast-producing trees and other hardwoods with den sites for squirrels lack concentrations and are scattered throughout. Still, river fringe timber offers good hunting for fox squirrels. A few ducks (local puddlers and passage divers) use the waterway and during wet fall periods can be found on game-area impoundments.

The Tuscola State Game Area is overseen by the wildlife biologist at the Caro Field Office, 1123 Mertz Road, Caro, Mich. 48723 (517/673-3434). Hunters can also get information from District Headquarters, 715 South Cedar St., Imlay City, Mich. 48444 (313/724-2015).

Vassar State Game Area

LOCATED in Tuscola County along the Cass River between Vassar and Wahjamega, the 3,958-acre Vassar State Game Area is managed primarily for deer and ruffed grouse. Topography is slightly rolling with defined riverbanks along the waterway. Soils are mostly sand and of low fertility.

Fifty years ago the National Park Service considered this region as a potential national park area, but poor drainage and low soil fertility nixed any development plans. The area was purchased in the late 40s with Pittman-Robertson dollars. Now managed by the DNR, it is completely open to hunting.

Forested areas consist of mixed hardwoods with aspen, birch, red maple, and cottonwood the dominant species. Because of lumbering, pasturing, sand removal, and encroachment of brush and small trees into openings, there is a good variety of early successional forest types, along with an ever-present need for more. A few years ago the DNR embarked on an aggressive cutting program of 2.5- to 10-acre parcels to remove mature trees and thus provide for new-growth areas. Creating younger forest age classes throughout the area has thus helped promote wildlife species that thrive in early-successional growth areas. These are deer, grouse, woodcock, and rabbits. Future cuttings will be necessary to maintain openings.

About 15 percent of the game area is open fields, pasture, or cleared land. These areas have had many shrub plantings, with native trees and shrubs encroaching. The DNR has planted several hundred thousand trees and shrubs, including red, white, and Austrian pine; jackpine; multiflora rose; honeysuckle; coralberry; sandcherry; wild grape; white spruce; silky dogwood; and autumn olive. A small amount is currently sharecropped, and the DNR annually adds small food plots and permanent meadow. Three miles of two-track dirt roads meander throughout, and 12 parking lots are available.

Pressure runs moderate to high depending upon day of the week and time of season. The opening day of firearm deer season generally gets the most pressure—40 to 50 hunters per square mile. Also, Sundays are popular for hunting since Tuscola County is closed to hunting on the lands of others. The area is popular with raccoon, rabbit, ruffed grouse, and woodcock hunters. Populations of these species, as well as deer, are fair to good. Limited opportunities exist for wild pheasants. A few mallards and wood ducks nest along the Cass River, and 25 to 50 goldeneyes winter on the river when it stays open. The Cass is an excellent stream to float. Hunters can put in at the Caro Impoundment, the roadside park on M-46, or at Waterman Road.

Squirrel habitat is marginal throughout the game area. Populations are low because of a lack of den

Tuscola State Game Area

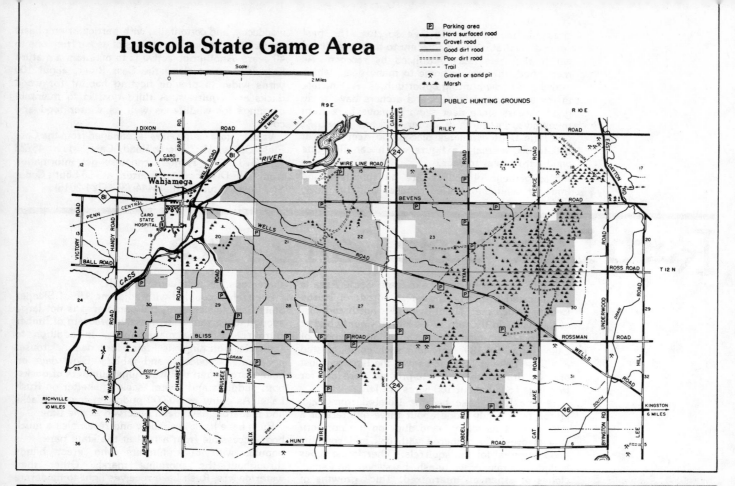

Vassar State Game Area

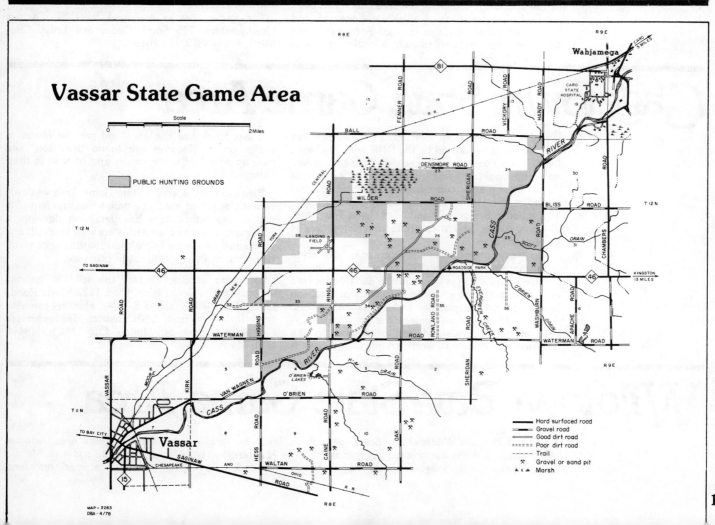

sites and mast-producing tree species. The best squirrel habitat is found adjacent to the Cass River, which also gets heavily utilized by raccoon. As mentioned, the area is home to many deer, which afford good bow-hunting opportunities. Again, late in the year, muzzleloaders and archers have fairly good success since deer seem to move here from miles away in search of winter food and cover. At one time DNR estimates placed the deer herd at 250 to 300 animals, a figure which can fluctuate widely from year to year.

Management objectives are to maintain and improve habitat for ruffed grouse, whitetail deer, woodcock, and cottontails, with particular emphasis on creating various age classes of aspen from one to 40 years. Another objective is to maintain a mature hardwood forest along the Cass River, about 100 yards wide, to provide nesting habitat for wood ducks and squirrels. A third goal is to maintain openings for wildlife as well as winter food and cover.

Vassar State Game Area is managed from the Caro Field Office, 1123 Mertz Road, Caro, Mich. 48723 (517/673-3434). Hunters can also get information from DNR District Headquarters at 715 South Cedar St., Imlay City, Mich. 48444 (313/724-2015).

Rush Lake State Game Area

THE 1,056-acre Rush Lake State Game Area is located in the northwestern corner of Huron County (which see), about five miles north and east of Caseville. In the late 1700s Huron County had at least 16 lagoon-type ponds, all originally part of Lake Huron. By 1897 only four such ponds existed and Rush Lake at 1,300 acres was the largest. Most of it was drained thereafter to provide more land for farming. Today about 100 acres are left.

In time Rush Lake became isolated from Lake Huron by a sandy ridge about three-quarters of a mile wide. This rolling sand dune on the northern side is presently timbered with oak and contains good potential for fox squirrels. Other forest types include red maple, white ash, basswood, and small clones of aspen all intermixed. Thick growths of cattail and sedge dominate the area which had been covered by water. Clumps of willow, dogwood, and other wetland shrubs also appear. Forty-two acres on the southern edge are tilled by a local farmer who

sharecrops his yield with the DNR.

Even when coupled with adjacent Albert Sleeper State Park (which see), the game area is not large enough to warrant an aggressive program of timber cutting and game management. In addition to squirrels, hunting is fair for deer, grouse, pheasants, woodcock, and rabbits. Blow days on Lake Huron often result in huge numbers of ducks, both puddlers and divers, seeking shelter on Rush Lake. As many as 10,000 puddlers, mostly blacks and mallards, have been observed at one time.

Rush Lake itself is shallow and resembles a muck bog. Accessible from a trail at the state park, it is popular with duck hunters who erect blinds throughout the shoreline marsh. Other than waterfowlers, Rush Lake receives light to moderate hunting pressure.

The game area is managed by DNR District Headquarters, 715 South Cedar St., Imlay City, Mich. 48444 (313/724-2015).

Gagetown State Game Area

THE 480-acre Gagetown State Game Area was recently purchased by the DNR with Michigan Land Trust Fund money. Located between Owendale and Gagetown and about three miles east of those Thumb-area communities, the public land straddles the Huron-Tuscola county line. Specifically, it lies in Sections 29 and 32 of Grant Township. The only access is by Maxwell Road, which serves as its western boundary.

The area contains swamp conifers of mostly white cedar that ring a shallow, 20-acre lake in the center. Hunting acquisition is tough in the densely-covered area. However, the rewards are good early-season jump-shooting for puddle ducks (mallards, wood ducks, and blue-winged teal) on the bog-like lake. A field of mixed grassland and brushland on the northwestern corner is worth trying for grouse. A

few woodcock use the area and can be found in fringe cover. Raccoon are found here too, and yarding deer find winter cover and browse to their liking.

Because the Gagetown State Game Area was only recently acquired, neither a game-management plan nor a map for hunters has yet been developed. However, property boundaries are well marked, and sportsmen can enjoy fairly good hunting opportunities with, at this writing, little pressure.

For more details, contact the wildlife habitat biologist at the Caro Field Office, 1123 Mertz Road, Caro, Mich. 48723 (517/673-3434). Hunters can also get information from DNR District Headquarters, 715 South Cedar St., Imlay City, Mich. 48444 (313/724-2015).

Wildfowl Bay State Game Area

THE 1,790-acre Wildfowl Bay State Game Area is located in the northwestern corner of Huron County (which see) along Saginaw Bay between Sebewaing and Bay Port. The game area includes Heisterman, Lone Tree, Maisou, and the Middle Grounds islands as well as scattered mainland

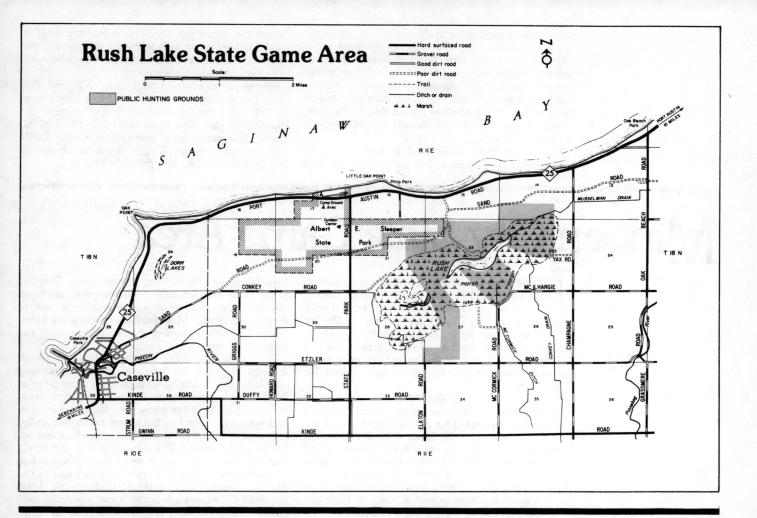

Rush Lake State Game Area

Scale:
0   1   2 Miles

PUBLIC HUNTING GROUNDS

Hard surfaced road
Gravel road
Good dirt road
Poor dirt road
Trail
Ditch or drain
Marsh

parcels. From 1965-73, a square-mile area was designated as a waterfowl refuge, mainly to protect migrant flocks of diving ducks. The refuge was abandoned when diver populations dipped due to high water and turbidities and the subsequent loss of both submergent and emergent vegetation.

The Wildfowl Bay area has long been a traditional feeding, breeding, and resting area for both diving ducks and puddle ducks. Redheads, canvasbacks, shovelers, green-winged and blue-winged teal, wood ducks, mallards, black ducks, coots, and gallinules have all used the marsh area for brood production. In spring and fall migrating waterfowl stop to rest and make foraging raids on Huron County croplands. Fall peak populations have been estimated at several thousand ducks and up to 4,000 geese.

At one time more than half the game area was mixed hardwood forest, another 29 percent was marsh, 11 percent was mixed grasslands and agricultural lands, and six percent was in brush. Although 280 mainland acres in Sections 2, 11, and 14 still contain forests (some of which need selective cutting), most of the offshore marsh and brush areas have disappeared. Recent scientific studies, funded by the Saginaw Valley Waterfowlers Chapter of the Michigan Duck Hunters Association, suggest that high water levels, combined with winds, create a whirlpool effect to drive heavily-silted water through Dynamite Cut in the Middle Grounds. When turbidities settle out, cattail suffocation is the result. To save the marsh, the waterfowlers hope to dam this cut and to provide other incentives for marsh

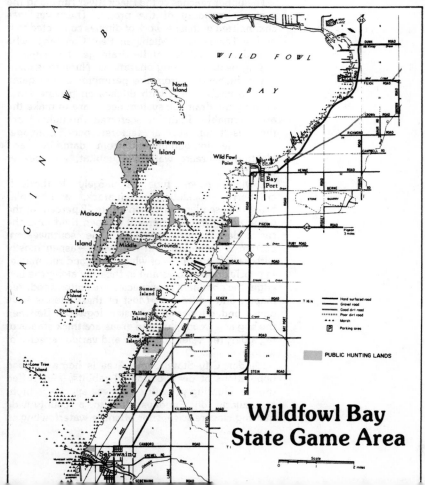

Hard surfaced road
Gravel road
Good dirt road
Poor dirt road
Marsh
P Parking area

PUBLIC HUNTING LANDS

Wildfowl Bay State Game Area

141

vegetation to grow once again.

Waterfowl hunting, although not as good as in former years, is still attractive to hunters who exert heavy weekend pressure. In addition to state access sites at Pigeon Road, Sumac Island (Geiger Road), and Mud Creek (Filion Road), hunters can launch boats at Pop's (just south of Geiger Road), Bud's or Charlie's (at Kilmanagh Road), or Wienecke's marinas (Sebewaing).

The islands themselves used to yield 20 to 25 bucks each hunting season, but the lack of cover has driven deer to the mainland. Here they are found in good numbers along with rabbits, fox squirrels, and raccoon. Hunters also bag an occasional pheasant, ruffed grouse, and woodcock.

For more information regarding Wildfowl Bay State Game Area, contact the wildlife biologist at DNR District Headquarters, 715 South Cedar St., (Box 218), Imlay City, Mich. 48444 (313/724-2015). The wildlife technician at nearby Fish Point Wildlife Area (*which see*) on Ringle Road in Unionville (517/674-2511), may also prove helpful.

Minden City State Game Area

THE Minden City State Game Area is located in the north-central portion of Sanilac County about 10 miles north of Sandusky. It is popular with Flint, Saginaw, Bay City, and metropolitan Detroit hunters who seek deer, grouse, woodcock, rabbit, raccoon, and waterfowl on its 6,422 acres. Plans to link another 5,000 acres in the project area move forward whenever private parcels are offered for sale or gift.

Land in Sections 20 and 29 of the game area consists partly of Greenwood peat, which has been commercially extracted for a long time. Most of the soils throughout are bog types of peat and muck. Upland areas are largely sand that once supported blueberry cultivation. About 65 percent of the game area is nonagricultural peat, 30 percent undeveloped agricultural peat, and five percent good mineral soil. Land here is mostly level, with upland areas featuring seven- to 14-degree slopes.

The upper reaches of the Black River run along the eastern boundary of the projet. The river was channelized with a network of ditches connected to it by the Texas-based Michigan Peat Company, who owned the land, to handle drainage of the marsh during peat-harvesting operations. Numerous man-made ditches run from the perimeter of the game area to interconnect with ditches on private land, forming the drainage system necessary to make the area farmable. Potholes scattered throughout are the result of several factors: poor drainage, man-made impoundments from damming and blasting to create waterfowl habitat, and beaver activity.

Lowland cover type is largely leatherleaf, cranberry, huckleberry, tamarack, and poplar brush. These plant types constitute 42 percent of the game area. Only 2.5 percent is open field, and the remainder is forested land. The southwestern portion is second-growth hardwood—aspen mostly with various mixtures of white birch and red maple. In poorly drained sites and in the area along the bog edge, the dominant tree species are cottonwood, red maple, and white ash. Most of these stands have dense understories of red-osier dogwood. Between the bog and wooded upland areas are thick stands of tag alder, red-osier dogwood, and various species of willow.

Minden City State Game Area is home to good populations of deer, cottontail rabbits, and ruffed grouse. Hunting pressure for these species is high, particularly on Sundays due to a county-wide hunting closure except for offshore waterfowling in Lake Huron and for hunting on state lands. Portions of the game area are nearly impenetrable due to an intricate system of bogs and marshlands and to dense understory. Most hunters concentrate along perimeter areas; hardier types plunge into the interior. Be sure to carry a compass.

Deer take the most hunting pressure, which appears to be on the increase. December hunting with bow and muzzleloader is perhaps more popular here than elsewhere in southern Michigan because deer congregate in the game area for winter browse and security. Some fine bucks are taken each fall.

Grouse numbers fluctuate, but generally there are fair to good numbers. The same is true of cottontails and there is even a small population of snowshoe hares that were released here a few years ago by the Sanilac County Sportsmen's Club, with DNR approval. The area produces some woodcock and receives late-October migrant longbills in edge cover between upland and lowland habitats. A few mallards, black ducks, wood ducks, blue-winged teal, and an occasional ringneck duck or goldeneye have been observed on potholes throughout the area. Duck-hunting opportunities are best in early season.

Many roads and trails in the game area are impassable in wet weather. Hunters are advised to wear hip boots or at least rubber-bottom footwear. In fact, much of Minden City State Game Area rivals a northern Michigan swamp for both remoteness and dense cover. All parking areas consist of natural openings along roads and trails. Rather than sharecrop fields or food patches, the DNR has planted a wide variety of plants and shrubs, including autumn olive, hawthorn, wild grape, multiflora rose, and highbush cranberry. An aggressive timber-cutting program a few years ago has helped with multistage growths of aspen, which in turn has promoted an increase in the numbers of deer, grouse, and rabbits. Continued cutting will ensure good game populations.

There are very few squirrels in the game area. A few wild pheasants inhabit the fringe. Raccoon numbers are fairly good throughout and red fox are occasionally seen. Hunting pressure overall is moderate to high.

The game area is managed by a wildlife habitat biologist who works out of the Caro Field Office, 1123 Mertz Road, Caro, Mich. 48723 (517/673-3434). Hunters can also get information from DNR District Headquarters, 715 South Cedar St., Imlay City, Mich. 48444 (313/724-2015).

Minden City State Game Area

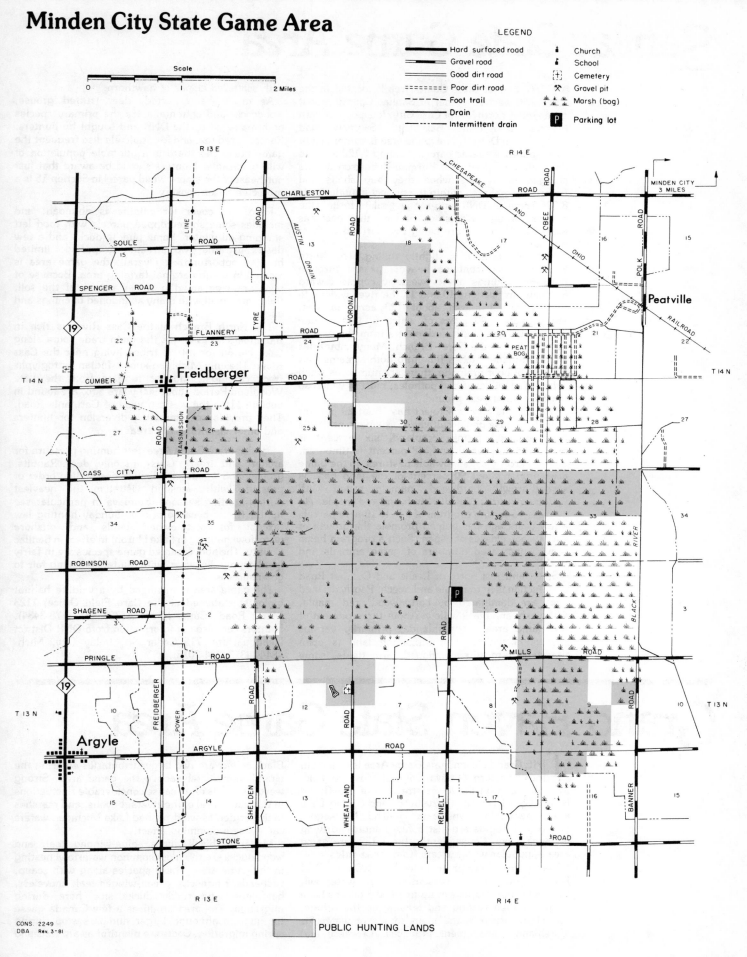

LEGEND

Hard surfaced road	Church
Gravel road	School
Good dirt road	Cemetery
Poor dirt road	Gravel pit
Foot trail	Marsh (bog)
Drain	Parking lot
Intermittent drain	

Scale

0   1   2 Miles

PUBLIC HUNTING LANDS

CONS. 2249
DBA   Rev. 3-81

Sanilac State Game Area

THE Sanilac State Game Area is located in the northwestern corner of Sanilac County, about seven miles northeast of Cass City. It is popular with hunters from Flint, Bay City, Saginaw, and metropolitan Detroit. The game area is comprised of a half-dozen scattered parcels totaling 1,120 acres to date, all purchased with Pittman-Robertson dollars charged to hunters when they buy shells and firearms. Total area within the project boundaries is 8,320 acres. A DNR long-range goal is to link the parcels through acquisition of land that becomes available. Priorities are along the North Branch of the Cass River.

Most of the area is slightly rolling. The North Branch, which contains beaver, passes through northern holdings on its westerly course toward Saginaw. In Sections 10 and 11 the river widens to form a cattail marsh about 120 acres in size, approximately 40 acres of which is under state ownership. The South Fork enters from the east to eventually join the North Branch. Many tributaries and man-made ditches flow into both streams; but because of poor drainage, there are numerous small cattail- and willlow-filled potholes, most of which do not hold water year around.

Overall, the Sanilac Project has about 29 percent of its land base under cultivation, six percent is idle or abandoned former cropland, six percent is brushland and marshland, 48 percent is timbered, and 11 percent is nonplowable pastures. In the game area proper about 90 percent of the land base is second-growth hardwood, namely aspen with various mixtures of white birch and red maple. An aggressive cutting program of 2.5- to 10-acre parcels a few years ago has helped promote the growth of various age classes of aspen. Such a program helps provide increased numbers of game animals and birds.

State land just north of Leslie and Cumber Road intersection is hard maple and beech. Poorly drained sites are dominated by cottonwood, red maple, white ash, and black willow. About three percent of the game area is brushlands, primarily various species of willow. The remaining land is open grasslands—mostly abandoned farm fields, some with scattered clones of hawthorn.

As might be expected, deer, ruffed grouse, woodcock, and cottontails are the primary species both managed by the DNR and sought by hunters. Raccoon, red fox, and fox squirrels also frequent the game area, and there is a huntable population of wild pheasants. Hunters should be aware that just northeast of the state-owned parcel in Section 15 is a protected heron rookery.

Food and cover for wildlife is abundant and includes some sharecropped parcels with food left standing all winter. Some puddle ducks and a few divers use the two streams to provide limited hunting opportunities. Overall, the game area is located in a submarginal farming area. Because of poor drainage and the stoney nature of the soil, fields are small with many abandoned openings and edges.

The North Branch of the Cass River is rich in Indian legend as it was the main trade route along Lake Huron for inland tribes living near the Cass River. The only Michigan-known Indian petroglyphs (rock carvings), thought to date from the Late Woodland Period about 900 years ago, are found in Section 11 on the western wide of Germania Road. They provide an interesting diversion for hunters and other visitors to the area.

Sanilac State Game Area gets hunting pressure for archery and firearm (shotguns only) deer. Rabbits, grouse, and woodcock follow in descending order of pressure with weekend visitation the heaviest during hunting seasons. Sundays in particular see hunter traffic because of a no-Sunday hunting law (except for state-owned lands and offshore waterfowl hunting in Lake Huron) in effect in Sanilac County. The above-named game species are in fairly good supply, however, with hunters enjoying fair to good success.

The game area is managed by a wildlife habitat biologist stationed at the Caro Field Office, 1123 Mertz Road, Caro, Mich. 48723 (517/673-3434). Hunters can also get information from DNR District Headquarters, 715 Cedar St., Imlay City, Mich. 48444 (313/724-2015).

Grand Haven State Game Area

THE Grand Haven State Game Area is located in northwestern Ottawa County, close to Lake Michigan and on the lower stretches of the Grand River. Grand Haven, Ferrysburg, and Spring Lake are immediately downstream. Holland, Muskegon, and Grand Rapids are just a few minutes' driving distance away. Consequently, the 1,139-acre game area is popular with hunters from those cities.

Management, which includes the 300-acre Poel Island Sanctuary, is essentially for waterfowl. Migrant concentrations of up to 1,000 mallards have been observed resting and feeding on the refuge. The Grand River is the main source of water for marshland management practices. Crockery and Black creeks are two larger tributaries entering the Grand immediately above the game area. Strong westerly winds often cause considerable fluctuations in the water level of the rivers, bayous, and marshes in this region as wind-pushed Lake Michigan waters can cause a damming effect.

Mallards, black ducks, blue-winged teal, and wood ducks are the most common waterfowl nesting in the game area. These species along with scaup, redheads, ringnecks, green-winged teal, shovelers, baldpates, and ruddy ducks stop here during migration. The area produces a few Canada geese for hunters although larger numbers stop during spring migration. Coots are plentiful as are rails and

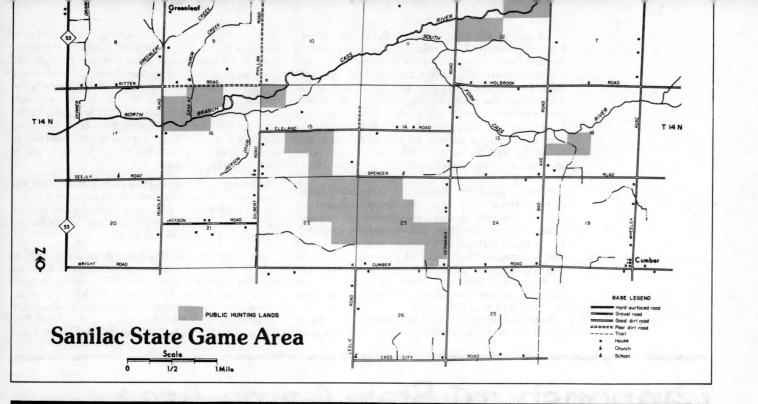

Sanilac State Game Area

Scale

0   1/2   1 Mile

PUBLIC HUNTING LANDS

BASE LEGEND
- Hard-surfaced road
- Gravel road
- Good dirt road
- Poor dirt road
- Trail
- House
- Church
- School

Grand Haven State Game Area

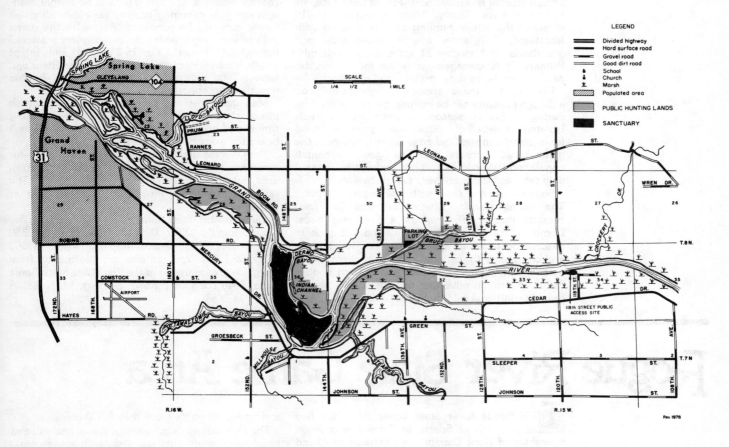

LEGEND
- Divided highway
- Hard surface road
- Gravel road
- Good dirt road
- School
- Church
- Marsh
- Populated area
- PUBLIC HUNTING LANDS
- SANCTUARY

SCALE

0   1/4   1/2   1 MILE

Rev. 1978

snipe during low-water periods. Permanent blinds are not permitted in order to discourage some hunters from monopolizing the resource.

Waterfowlers will need a boat to hunt successfully. Foot access to the river is availble in a couple places, but the going is tough. Best boat access occurs at four sites: (1) at the end of 118th Street, (2) at the tip of 132nd Avenue in the Bruce Bayou region, (3) from a parking lot just to the west and below the trail dogleg off 138th Avenue, and (4) at the end of 144th Street north of the Poel Island Sanctuary.

About 75 percent of the game area includes marsh or river-fringe cover. Most common plant types are cattails, bulrush, sedges, smartweed, arrowhead, water willow, water lilies, and duckweeds. Lowland-brush types include cottonwood, box elder, silver and red maple, basswood, ash, swamp white oak, and dogwood. An old apple orchard is located north of the river. Black oak, white oak, aspen, sugar maple, sassafras, sumac, witch hazel, and ragweed can be found in upland areas.

There is a limited amount of sharecrop farming at Grand Haven State Game Area. A particularly good region of northern hardwoods that produces fox-squirrel hunting is located south of the river, north and a little east of 138th Avenue. Hunters will likely need a boat for access. Deer are reasonably abundant and appear to winter in the game area. Grouse, woodcock, and pheasants are severely limited in numbers; however, there are some rabbit hunting opportunities along edges of farm fields and marshland cover. Raccoon traverse the waterway in good numbers and are the target for moderate to heavy hunting pressure.

But waterfowl, particularly puddle ducks, are the main draw. Pressure is intense on opening day and during weekends. A mid-week hunt, if possible, can be more productive. Also, consider a late-season visit when flight birds are down.

The Grand Haven State Game Area is managed by a DNR wildlife habitat biologist stationed at the Muskegon State Game Area, 7600 East Messinger, Twin Lake, Mich. 49457 (616/788-5055). Hunters can also get information by contacting DNR District Headquarters, State Office Bldg., 350 Ottawa NW, Grand Rapids, Mich. 49503 (616/456-5071).

Cannonsburg State Game Area

THE 1,331-acre Cannonsburg State Game Area is located five miles northeast of Grand Rapids in central Kent County. About 80 percent (1,016 acres) of the public hunting area is covered with forestland, 287 acres are in brushlands and grasslands, and another 21 acres are in wetlands. Primary DNR management is for forest wildlife: deer, squirrels, rabbits, grouse, and woodcock.

Hunting for these species is generally good although pressure can be intense, especially for deer during the firearm season (shotguns only allowed). Isolated stands of pure oak produce good fox-squirrel hunting, and edge cover throughout the game area harbors fair to good cottontail populations. Woodcock and grouse hunting is rated only fair, and there are very few pheasants.

Soils are mostly sand with low natural fertility. The rolling terrain, which fluctuates 150 feet, consists mostly of moraines and stream beds. Dominant trees are oak, aspen, and red pine in descending order of appearance. Low-lying areas are covered with cattails and other hardwoods, notably ash, elm, red maple, and balsam poplar. Strips of autumn olive and multiflora rose shrubs provide additional wildlife habitat along field edges.

The DNR also plants small food plots but does no sharecropping at present. There is no timber-management plan currently in progress either although future cuts will be proposed. Access to the game area is very good, with nine parking lots scattered throughout. Hyser Lake (5.2 acres) and Egypt Creek, a cold-water tributary to the Grand River and former site of trout releases, offer limited waterfowling opportunity.

Management plans include establishing brush piles, creating and maintaining meadows, cutting timber and brush, planting trees, and building nest boxes for wood ducks and squirrels.

The DNR maintains three outdoor stations each for centerfire and rimfire rifle and a shotgun handtrap area, all open to public use without charge. The range is located on Five-Mile Road just east of Dursam Avenue.

Cannonsburg State Game Area is managed by Grand Rapids DNR District Headquarters, 350 Ottawa St. NW, Grand Rapids, Mich. 49503 (616/456-5071). You can also get information from the game area manager at the Flat River State Game Area, 6640 Long Lake Road, Belding, Mich. 48809 (616/794-2658).

Rogue River State Game Area

THE Rogue River State Game Area lies five miles north of Sparta in Tyrone and Solon townships of Kent County. Its nearness to Grand Rapids makes it popular with hunters from that city as well as throughout southwestern lower Michigan. They seek deer, rabbits, squirrels, raccoon, grouse, and woodcock on its more than 5,500 acres.

The game area lies in a former glacial channel and is largely smooth outwash plain with some gently rolling terrain. Lowland depressions contain a few small lakes and wetlands. Elevation differences vary by about 50 feet. Flowing through the western side

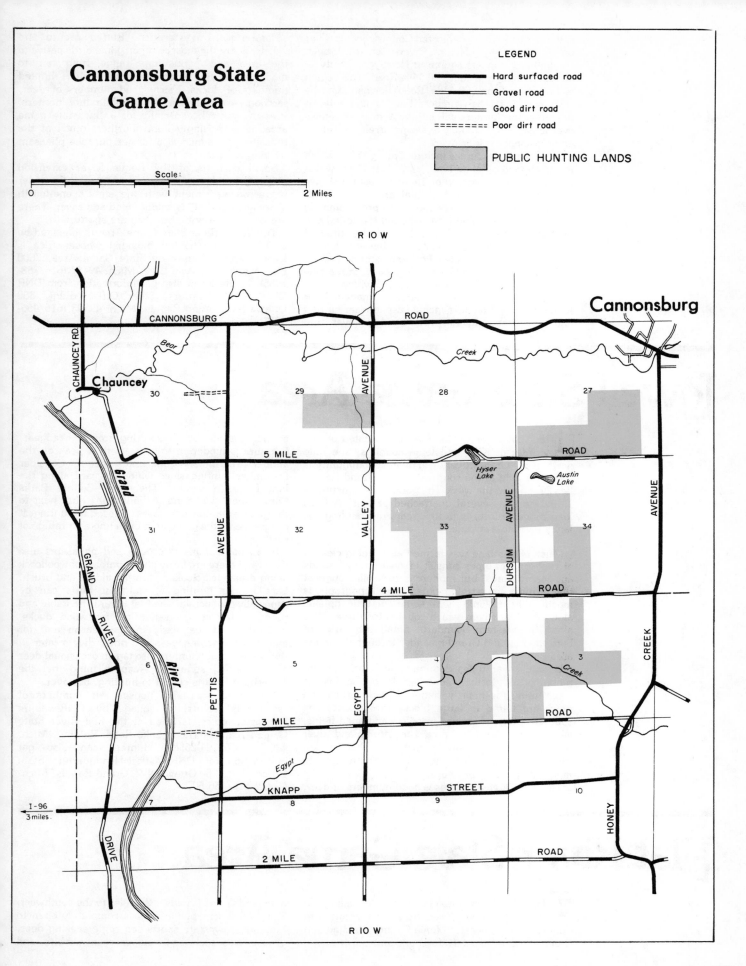

Cannonsburg State Game Area

LEGEND

━━━━━ Hard surfaced road
━━━━━ Gravel road
───── Good dirt road
======= Poor dirt road

▨ PUBLIC HUNTING LANDS

Scale:
0   1   2 Miles

R 10 W

Cannonsburg

CANNONSBURG ROAD

Bear Creek

Chauncey

CHAUNCEY RD

30

29

28

27

5 MILE ROAD

Grand River

Hyser Lake

Austin Lake

VALLEY AVENUE

DURSUM AVENUE

CREEK AVENUE

31

32

33

34

4 MILE ROAD

PETTIS AVENUE

GRAND RIVER DRIVE

6

5

4

3

Creek

EGYPT

3 MILE ROAD

Egypt

I-96
3 miles

7

KNAPP STREET

8

9

10

HONEY CREEK

2 MILE ROAD

R 10 W

147

is the Rogue River, a dedicated Country Scenic River under the Michigan Natural Rivers Act. It has been channelized from its source in Newaygo County to about one-half mile above 20-Mile Road. This region is floatable. From 20-Mile Road downstream the river contains fallen timber. Fall rains render it passable, but hunters will still have to drag canoes over logs. They are likely to see squirrels as well as an occasional duck or deer.

Other water resources include Spring Lake, which is surrounded by state land, and Clear Lake, which features state ownership on its northeastern shore.

About 80 percent of the total area is forested. Upland forest types of oak and aspen predominately include red, black, and white oak and trembling and big-toothed aspen. Lowland hardwoods, situated mostly along streams, include ash, basswood, elm, willow, and red maple. Lowland shrub species include red-osier and gray dogwood, tag alder, nannyberry, highbush cranberry, and willow.

Rogue River State Game Area is managed for forest wildlife. Practices include aspen clear-cutting and oak timbering to provide edge cover and second-growth regeneration. Ruffed grouse and woodcock are the most common game birds native to the area and populations range from fair to moderate. A few impoundments produce limited numbers of ducks. Fairly good numbers of deer, raccoon, fox squirrels, and rabbits lure hunters. Pressure overall, especially for a downstate game area, is surprisingly light. Further, much of the pressure was aimed at a former put-take pheasant hunting program.

Small portions of the Rogue River extension property in Algoma Township are presently under sharecrop agreement with the state's one-fourth share left standing as wildlife food and cover. There are a few pheasants, but they are spotty.

The Rogue River State Game Area is managed by a DNR wildlife habitat biologist whose office is located at the Muskegon State Game Area, 7600 East Messinger, Twin Lake, Mich. 49457 (616/788-5055). Hunters can also get information from DNR District Headquarters, State Office Bldg., 350 Ottawa NW, Grand Rapids, Mich. 49503 (616/456-5071).

Lowell State Game Area

THE Lowell State Game Area is located on the border of Kent and Ionia counties, one mile north of the Grand River. The nearest community is Lowell, a mile to the southwest, and Grand Rapids lies 20 miles to the west. The game area constitutes 1,800 acres in several unattached parcels. A DNR long-range priority is to link scattered holdings as lands become available.

Much of this land was farmed after being cleared of timber. Soil types consist of well-drained sands and loamy sands, but numerous rock piles suggest that farming was a trying experience. Topography is mostly hilly or sloping with some small floodplains along the Flat River, which courses for three miles along the western boundary. Small tributaries of both the Flat and Grand meander through the game area.

Upland cover types dominate, with oak, aspen, pine, black locust, and northern hardwoods constituting the main varieties. Upland brush and grass are found in large blocks throughout. The southern portion is mixed woodlots and open fields, whereas the northern area runs to upland river habitat with oak predominating. This is an exceptionally good fox-squirrel area with light to moderate hunting pressure.

The game area also houses good numbers of deer, including some bucks sporting trophy headgear. Pressure is moderate to heavy with a peak on the annual firearm (shotguns only) opener. Consider December hunting since whitetails yard along the Flat River in winter. The Kent County Parks Commission owns land in Fallasburg Park next to the game area. Since the park is closed to hunting, it complements the game area by acting as a refuge of sorts.

Small populations of grouse and pheasants also exist, and there are fairly good numbers of woodcock along drainages cloaked with tag alders and brush. Late-October hunting for migrant birds can be especially productive. The Flat River is floatable and produces fair to good hunting for wood ducks, mallards, and teal early in the season and for mergansers, goldeneyes, and other divers later in the season. Float hunters also tag an occasional deer and some fox squirrels. Keep in mind that the Fallasburg Park is closed to hunting, however.

The game area also houses fair numbers of raccoon and rabbits. It is managed by a DNR wildlife habitat biologist stationed at the Flat River State Game Area, 6640 Long Lake Road, Belding, Mich. 48809 (616/794-2658). Hunters can also get information from DNR District Headquarters, State Office Bldg., 350 Ottawa NW, Grand Rapids, Mich. 49503 (616/456-5071).

Flat River State Game Area

THE Flat River State Game Area lies along the border between southwestern Montcalm County and northwestern Ionia County. Belding and Greenville are respectively south and north of the area, and Grand Rapids is 25 miles to the southwest. The 10,603-acre public area is completely open to hunting. Downstate sportsmen come seeking deer, grouse, woodcock, squirrels, raccoon, rabbits, and

Rogue River State Game Area

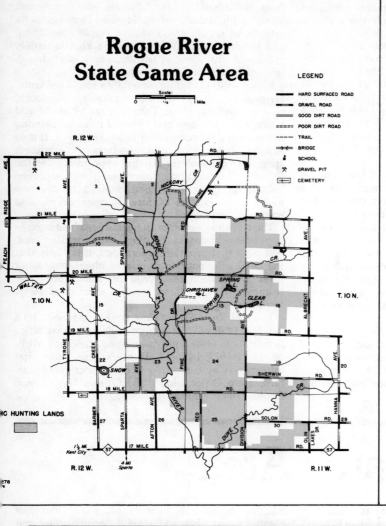

LEGEND

HARD SURFACED ROAD
GRAVEL ROAD
GOOD DIRT ROAD
POOR DIRT ROAD
TRAIL
BRIDGE
SCHOOL
GRAVEL PIT
CEMETERY

PUBLIC HUNTING LANDS

Lowell State Game Area

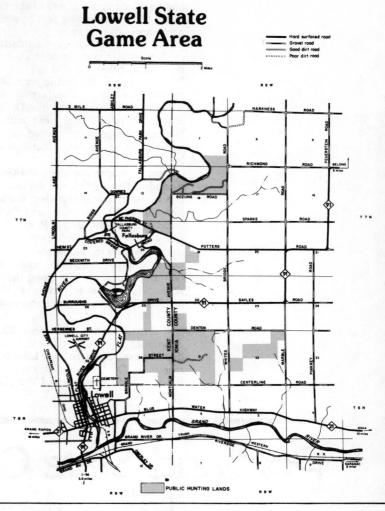

Hard surfaced road
Gravel road
Good dirt road
Poor dirt road

PUBLIC HUNTING LANDS

Flat River State Game Area

PUBLIC HUNTING LANDS

Hard surfaced road
Gravel road
Good dirt road
Poor dirt road
Trail
Cemetery
Public Access Site

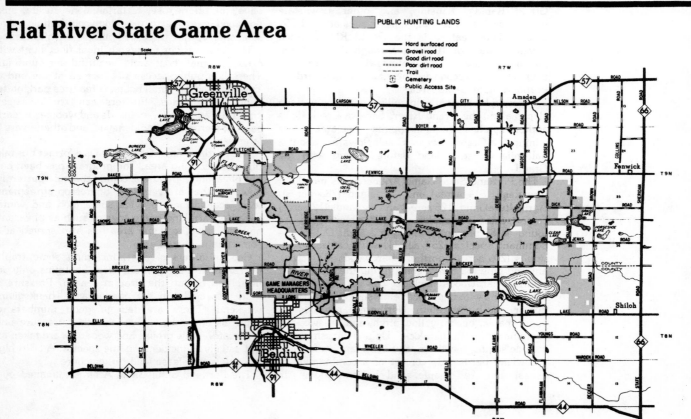

waterfowl. Hunting pressure is moderate to high and peaks on opening day of the firearm (shotguns only—the dividing line is just a mile north of the game area) deer season.

Soils in the game area are relatively unfertile, as evidenced by the number of abandoned farms and the very fact that the land fell into state hands some 35 years ago. Land that is somewhat productive is sharecropped with area farmers and grows small food patches put in by the DNR. Lowland soils consist of mucks and peat with poor drainage. Sloping topography, caused by glaciation and subsequent weathering, features variations to 150 feet.

Steepest slopes are along the Grand River, which meanders its way through the western portion. This is a first-rate stream for float hunters interested in jumping ducks, squirrels, and the occasional deer. Good access sites are off Bricker and Baker roads, just east of M-91. Dickerson and Wabasis creeks drain the eastern and western regions respectively before emptying into the Grand. Non-navigable and featuring dense habitat along the fringe (including some lowland-timber floodings), they nevertheless produce jump-shooting opportunities for wood ducks and other puddlers.

A dozen small lakes, some 30 impoundments, dozens of potholes, thousands of feet of level ditching, and 356-acre Long Lake contribute to water resources. Duck hunting throughout is fair to good (best in early season), and the game area hosts a good raccoon population.

About 70 percent of the Flat River State Game Area is forested. Upland forests are mostly oak mixed with aspen, while lowland woods are a mixture of aspen, ash, elm, red maple, basswood, and balsam poplar. The rest of the area is largely grassland with some brush, including witch hazel, gray dogwood, and thornapple.

Management is for forest wildlife species—namely deer, grouse, rabbits, squirrels, woodcock, raccoon, and waterfowl. Twenty-three Missouri wild turkeys (six gobblers and 17 hens) released recently in the central portion appear to be doing well. If they expand their range and numbers as expected, sportsmen can look for hunting opportunities in the future. Clear-cutting throughout has improved habitat for game birds and animals by creating multi-growth stages of forests, open areas, and increased edge cover.

The western portion of the game area was used as a put-take pheasant hunting zone for 10 years. Although that program is scrapped, it is likely that the DNR will continue to release pheasants two or three times each fall. Wild pheasants are rare. Numbers of other game species mentioned range from fair to good.

The Flat River State Game Area is managed by a resident DNR wildlife habitat biologist whose office is located at 6640 Long Lake Road, Belding, Mich. 48809 (616/794-2658). Hunters can also get information by contacting DNR District Headquarters, State Office Bldg., 350 Ottawa NW, Grand Rapids, Mich. 49503 (616/456-5071).

Portland State Game Area

THE Portland State Game Area is located in Danby Township in southeastern Ionia County. Grand Rapids, Lansing, and other downstate hunters seek a variety of game species on its 1,759 acres. Major feature is the Grand River, which twists its way for 10 miles through the scattered parcels of state land. Waterfowl, deer, rabbits, squirrels, and raccoon are the main drawing cards at Portland State Game Area.

Topography is gentle to rolling with some steep slopes along the Grand River. Sebewa Creek flows approximately one mile inside the game area before joining the Grand. Frayer Creek flows for about a half-mile on state land before linking with the Grand.

The Portland State Game Area consists mostly of forestland (814 acres) and rangeland (785 acres). Agricultural land (126 acres) and wetlands (12 acres) comprise the remainder. Upland cover types are found on 85 percent of the game area. Oak is the dominant species (257 acres), with central hardwoods (206 acres), northern hardwoods (87 acres), and red pine (32 acres) constituting the remainder. Central hardwoods include oak or hickory in combination with basswood, elm, sugar maple, tulip poplar, and black walnut. Northern hardwoods are sugar maple, beech, yellow birch, and basswood in combination with hemlock. Upland brush areas include sumac, hawthorn, dogwood, and wafer ash. Lowland hardwoods consist of a combination of ashes, elm, red maple, and balsam poplar. In addition to natural cover types, the DNR has planted many trees and shrubs, including autumn olive, multiflora rose, tartarian honeysuckle, silky dogwood, nannyberry, gray dogwood, buffalo berry, sand cherry, wild grape, red pine, and white spruce.

The Grand River makes an ideal float hunt with canoe or small boat amid beautiful surroundings. There is a public-access site located at the end of Towner Road for small boats. It features parking for about 20 vehicles. Floaters can try for deer, squirrels, and ducks—mallards and woodies in early season; mergansers, goldeneyes, and other divers in later season.

The Portland State Game Area is a former put-take pheasant hunting area. The program has been cut, but pheasant populations could rebound. Currently, however, they are very low. Sharecrop agreements with local farmers provide some food and winter cover for farmland game species such as pheasants and rabbits. The game area has also served as a sometime field-trial area.

Good numbers of deer, including some trophy bucks, inhabit the general area. Shotguns only are permitted during the firearm season. Pressure is high, especially on the opener and Thanksgiving weekend. There are fair to good numbers of squirrels and rabbits, with hunting pressure only moderate. A few grouse and woodcock are taken too but usually as incidental game species. A DNR high priority is to release wild turkeys here.

The Portland State Game Area is managed by a

DNR wildlife habitat biologist at Flat River State Game Area, 6640 Long Lake Road, Belding, Mich. 48809 (616/794-2658). Hunters can also get information from DNR District Headquarters, State Office Bldg., 350 Ottawa NW, Grand Rapids, Mich. 49503 (616/456-5071).

Portland State Game Area

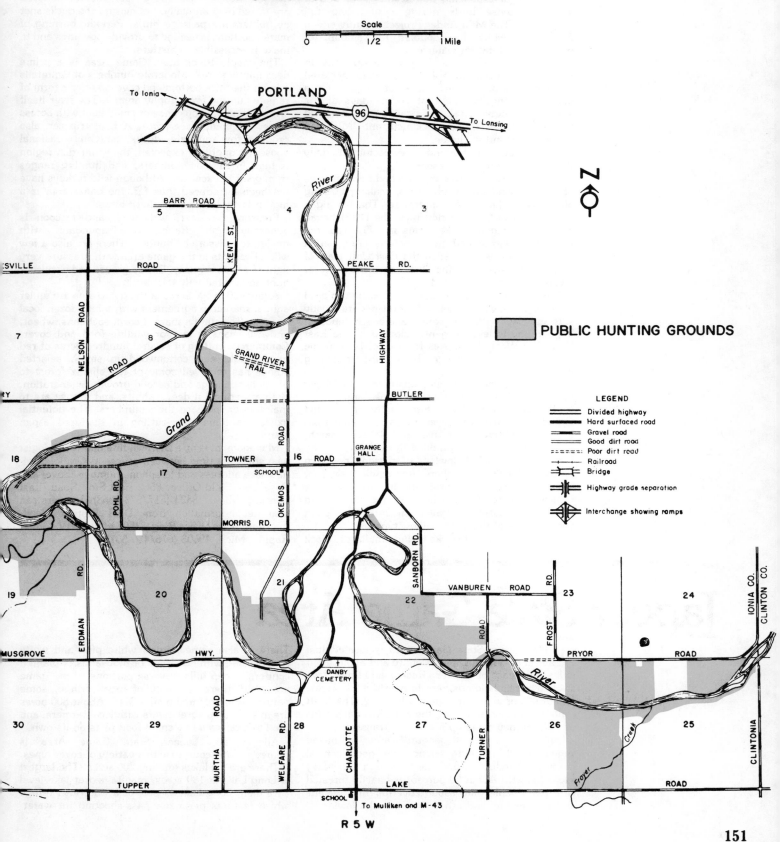

Scale
0   1/2   1 Mile

PUBLIC HUNTING GROUNDS

LEGEND
Divided highway
Hard surfaced road
Gravel road
Good dirt road
Poor dirt road
Railroad
Bridge
Highway grade separation
Interchange showing ramps

R 5 W

Maple River State Game Area

THE Maple River State Game Area is located in portions of Clinton, Gratiot, and Ionia counties. The 6,415-acre project is a wetlands management unit aimed at producing ducks and geese and at attracting these birds during spring and fall migrations. The Milli-Ander Project recently added 200 acres, which has doubled the amount of marshland habitat for waterfowl.

The marsh is open to hunting with restrictions. In recent years even-numbered days were declared hunting days and waterfowlers could apply for a permit drawing for the first couple days of the season. For details, call the Gratiot-Saginaw Field Office (517/643-7000) or check a current "Michigan Waterfowl Hunting Guide."

Other types of hunting are permitted daily throughout respective seasons.

The Maple River in this area has had a long history of flooding and diking problems, making farming along its banks a risky enterprise. The Michigan Department of Conservation (now the DNR) began acquisition of gone-broke farms in 1951, repaired the dikes, and added new controls. Acquisition began in what is now called the East Unit (east of Maple Rapids). Today the DNR can manage water levels in the marsh created.

The area lies upon the lake bed of ancient glacial Lake Saginaw, whose lake-bed sediments are mostly silts and clays with sandy areas and beach deposits. Topography is level to gently sloping in the East Unit. The West Unit varies from level land in the floodplain to rolling topography in the surrounding area.

Originating about 30 miles upstream, the Maple River flows throughout the game area in a southwesterly direction before emptying into the Grand River at Muir, seven miles upstream from Ionia. In addition to the river and 400-acre marsh, some 60 potholes are sprinkled throughout.

Forest types include lowland hardwoods, northern hardwoods, oak, and hickory. Red maple, oak, ash, maple, hickory, cottonwood, and basswood are the principal species. Some willow, walnut, cherry, and beech are present in smaller amounts. Floodplain vegetation is of the sedge-willow type.

Common species of ducks include mallards, black ducks, blue-winged teal, wood ducks, pintails, baldpates, gadwalls, ringnecks, canvasbacks, redheads, scaup, goldeneyes, buffleheads, ruddy ducks, mergansers, and Canada geese. Several hundred are raised here annually, but most of the ducks shot by hunters are passage birds. Periodic burning of marsh portions is needed to provide openings and to make it accessible to hunters.

The Maple River State Game Area is a prime deer-hunting area. Moderate numbers of whitetails inhabit the thick bottomland cover to offer a form of remote hunting for a trophy animal. The river itself is easily floatable by canoe or small boat with access at several points (see map). A float trip can also produce fox squirrels, ducks, and an occasional goose. As might be expected, the water-rich region is high in raccoon numbers, and hunting ranges from good to excellent. Although wild turkeys have not been introduced thus far, the game area is a high-priority location for these birds.

Pressure for deer, waterfowl, and raccoon is generally high. Rabbits are abundant, with moderate pressure by hunters. There are also a few wild pheasants in the game area with pressure very light after opening day. Ruffed grouse and woodcock hunting is rated only fair.

About 400 to 500 acres of the game area are under annual sharecrop agreement with a half-dozen local farmers. The state's share of corn, soybeans, wheat, and dry beans is left for wildlife food and cover. Commercial cutting of several hundred acres of red maple, oak, and cottonwood in small, selected stands has removed some of the climax forest to promote openings and second-growth regeneration. Both are critical if deer, rabbits, and grouse are to maintain or increase their numbers. The potential exists for some clear-cutting in scattered aspen stands.

Management is by a DNR wildlife habitat biologist who splits his time between offices at Gratiot-Saginaw (see address and telephone number above) and Rose Lake Field Office, 8562 East Stoll Road, East Lansing, Mich. 48823 (517/373-9358). Hunters can also get information from DNR District Headquarters, State Office Bldg., 350 Ottawa NW, Grand Rapids, Mich. 49503 (616/456-5071).

Lapeer State Game Area

THE Lapeer State Game Area is located just west of central Lapeer County and about eight miles northeast of Lapeer. Recent additions have swollen public holdings here to nearly 8,000 acres, all but 400 of which are open to hunting. The DNR continues to eye land along the Flint River and adds parcels as they come up for sale or transfer.

Lapeer is a true "general" area of mixed vegetation. It is south enough for good central hardwood production and north enough for heavy aspen growth. About 60 percent is heavily forested with oak, maple, and aspen covering the uplands and elm, maple, and ash dominating the lowlands.

There is also some natural white pine and white cedar, along with hundreds of thousands of planted conifers. Steep hills traverse portions of the game area, and there is plenty of brush fringe, some natural, some planted by the DNR. About 300 acres are in sharecrop agreements with local farmers, and the DNR raises a few small food plots on its own.

All in all, Lapeer State Game Area is gamey-looking country with a variety of cover types.

There are six lakes totaling 200 acres. The largest is Long Lake at 180 acres, maintained at lake level by a dam. Long Lake is part of a waterfowl refuge which features perimeter pass-shooting for water-

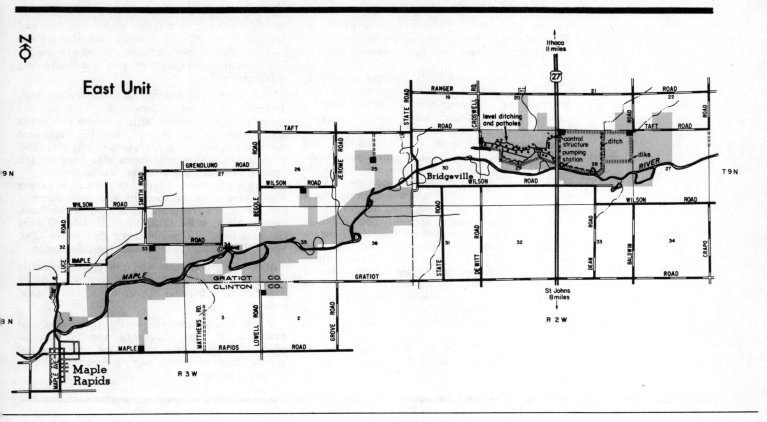

East Unit

West Unit

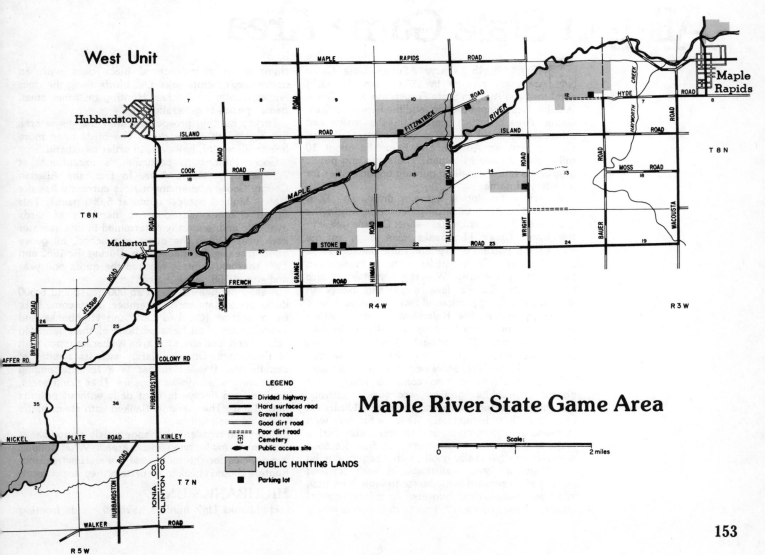

LEGEND

- Divided highway
- Hard surfaced road
- Gravel road
- Good dirt road
- Poor dirt road
- Cemetery
- Public access site

PUBLIC HUNTING LANDS

■ Parking lot

Maple River State Game Area

Scale:

0   1   2 miles

fowl, especially geese. The DNR has also developed 30 water impoundments varying from one-half acre to 190 acres. Trappers have been removing about 50 beaver annually.

Lapeer State Game Area is managed intensively for ruffed grouse and cottontail rabbits. The DNR maintains open areas, clearcuts other sections through selected timber sales, and encourages second-growth aspen in varying stages. Cottontails have been plentiful in recent years; hunters seek them in lowland brush and along edge cover. Grouse populations are stable. Birds are best hunted in lowland areas containing gray dogwood thickets and aspen stands. Local and flight woodcock use these same areas as well as wet tag-alder tangles.

Fox-squirrel populations are fairly good although hunting pressure keeps numbers in check. There are plenty of oak ridges for hunters to post. Although wild pheasants have slipped in recent years, there are still scattered pockets of good habitat. Some of the best are in Sections 9, 23, and 24. A portion of the game area was a designated put-take pheasant hunting area, and the DNR will likely continue some type of farm-bred bird release at least for a few years.

Deer hunting, although not as good as in Tuscola County state game areas (*all of which see*), is nevertheless rated fair. The DNR area manager usually checks up to a dozen bucks each fall, and probably that number or more are harvested without his knowledge. There are some big bucks produced. The game area also affords raccoon- and fox-hunting opportunities.

Good hunting is availble for blue-winged teal, mallards, and wood ducks. The refuge and surrounding area attract large numbers of Canada geese. About 200 are raised locally, but flight bird numbers can swell to 5,000. Hunters bag about 200 annually. At present, the game area does not fall into the extended goose-season boundaries.

There is a designated field-dog trial area in Lapeer State Game Area. For permits and other information, contact the area manager at 3116 Vernor Road, Lapeer, Mich. 48452 (313/664-8355). DNR District Headquarters, 715 South Cedar St., Imlay City, Mich. 48444 (313/724-2015) also has information.

About 20 Pennsylvania wild turkeys were recently released west of M-24. If the flock expands as hoped, future hunting opportunities are a good possibility.

Overall hunting pressure on this game area runs moderate to high. Weekends and the firearm (shotguns only) deer opener get the heaviest pressure from sportsmen living in Flint, Port Huron, Detroit, and suburbs.

Allegan State Game Area

THE nearly 45,000-acre Allegan State Game Area was created in 1964 when the DNR combined the Allegan State Forest, the Swan Creek Wildlife Experiment Station, and the Fennville State Game Area. It is located in the oak- and pine-covered sand plains of west-central Allegan County between Allegan and Fennville about 10 miles east of Lake Michigan. The sprawling public area offers fair to excellent hunting opportunities for a variety of game.

Waterfowl hunting is a major draw. The DNR operates two permit-controlled sections within the game area: hunters may pass-shoot Canada geese at the Swan Creek Highbanks (*see map*) in the east-central portion or dry-land hunt Canada geese at the Fennville Farm Unit (*see map*) in the western part of the game area. Waterfowl hunting is also open in the Ottawa (*see map*) and Koopman marshes and along portions of Swan, Bear, and Sand creeks as well as the Kalamazoo River. Another good spot, for fringe hunting at least, is Crooked Lake (which in itself is a refuge). Many waterfowlers turn here when they draw poorly at the two controlled-hunt units. More on those in a moment.

Small-game hunters also come to Allegan for pheasants, rabbits, grouse, woodcock, squirrels, and raccoon during fall seasons and for wild turkeys in spring. There is moderate pressure for deer with bow and arrow, shotgun, and muzzleloader during respective seasons. Success is rated fair. Raccoon numbers are generally good in this region cut by many streams and well-timbered with lowland hardwoods. Pressure is moderate to high from both state and nonresident hunters. Excellent squirrel hunting shapes up each fall south of the river where there is an abundance of black oaks with an understory of white oaks. Oak bluffs along the river are especially productive. Hunting for other small game species is generally fair.

Turkey hunting prospects within the game area are best north of the river. The birds need more habitat diversity, however, in order to expand.

Goose hunting in particular is exceptional at Allegan State Game Area. In fact, the Allegan County Goose Management Area currently has the state's highest harvest quota at 6,000 geese. This figure changes according to numbers of birds available and is usually determined in late summer each year. When the quota is reached, all goose hunting ceases for that season. During the 1982 and 1983 seasons, hunters reached the quota one year and shot 4,158 geese the next.

A seasonal peak of about 25,000 geese and 6,500 ducks occurs late each November. They come here for protection (Crooked Lake and Highbanks and Fennville units all have portions of their lands in refuge) and food since the area is sharecropped with local farmers. Ottawa Marsh with its habitat of cattails and flooded timber is a favorite among waterfowlers in high-water years. They bring boats, waders, and decoys to hunt daily without permits until 3 p.m. The marsh is flanked with steep bluffs containing oak woods.

Rules and regulations change nearly every year at state waterfowl-management areas. What follows are policies for the most recent waterfowl season; hunters should check to be certain they are current.

HIGHBANKS UNIT

Highbanks Unit hunters have 80 blinds fronting

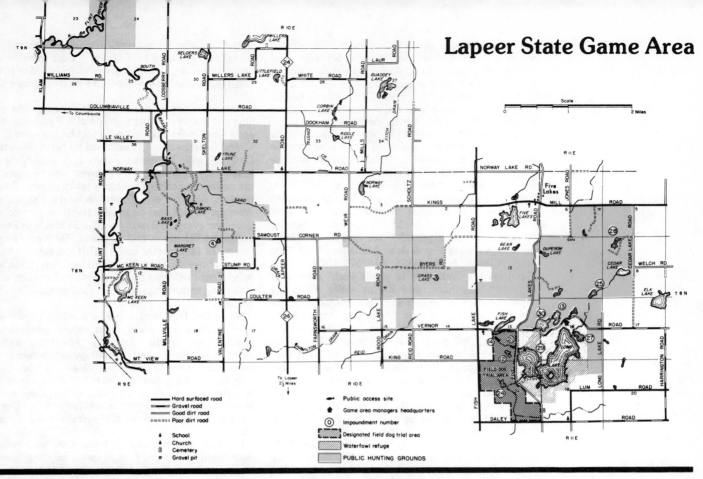

Lapeer State Game Area

Scale
0 — 1 — 2 Miles

Legend
— Hard surfaced road
— Gravel road
— Good dirt road
--- Poor dirt road

🏫 School
⛪ Church
🏛 Cemetery
✴ Gravel pit

🛥 Public access site
🏠 Game area managers headquarters
Ⓞ Impoundment number
░ Designated field dog trial area
▓ Waterfowl refuge
▒ PUBLIC HUNTING GROUNDS

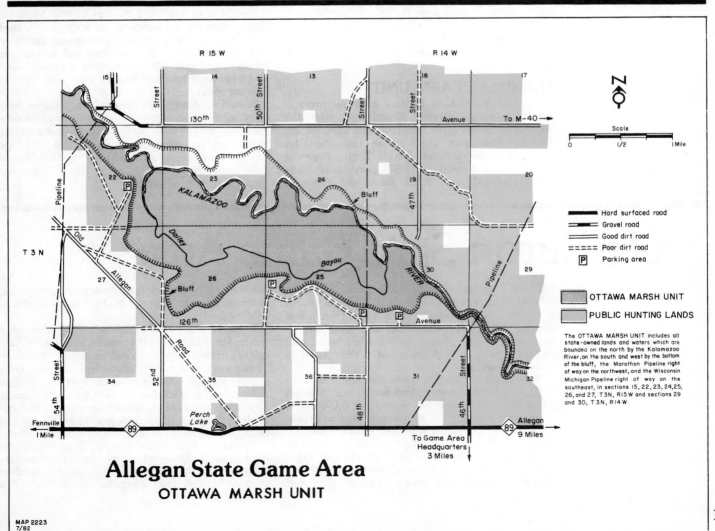

Scale
0 — 1/2 — 1 Mile

Legend
— Hard surfaced road
— Gravel road
— Good dirt road
--- Poor dirt road
Ⓟ Parking area

▓ OTTAWA MARSH UNIT
▒ PUBLIC HUNTING LANDS

The OTTAWA MARSH UNIT includes all state-owned lands and waters which are bounded on the north by the Kalamazoo River, on the south and west by the bottom of the bluff, the Marathon Pipeline right of way on the northwest, and the Wisconsin Michigan Pipeline right of way on the southeast, in sections 15, 22, 23, 24, 25, 26, and 27, T3N, R15W and sections 29 and 30, T3N, R14W.

Allegan State Game Area
OTTAWA MARSH UNIT

MAP 2223
7/82

the refuge from which to choose. Generally, pre-season applications for permits for two- and three-party groups (30 total) during the first month of the hunting season are required. Application forms are available from most DNR offices in late August, and hunters usually have until about September 10 to submit their date preferences.

Until the most recent hunting season, daily Highbanks lotteries were held at the respective unit office (616/673-2430). Budget cuts moved the lottery to the Fennville Farm Unit on 118th Ave. (616/561-2258), where it was held at 5:30 a.m. during the first month and 5 a.m. thereafter. Both times were 30 minutes before the Farm Unit drawing. Hunters should check the current "Waterfowl Hunting Guide" for details or contact the Allegan State Game Area Manager, 4120 Dam Road, Allegan, Mich. 49010 (616/673-4747).

Hunters are limited to 12 shells each (steel shot only) and may hunt until 2 p.m. daily. They are required to return permits and check all game (if the station is open) by 4 p.m. During the most recent season, 5,995 Highbanks hunters (an average of 126 daily) shot 1,392 geese. Best posts were 41 with 78 geese for the season and post 42 with 73 geese. Posts 31 through 46 averaged 50 geese or more each. Daily kill totals are surprisingly uniform throughout the season.

Six blinds (A-F) in the Upper Pool of the Highbanks refuge are open in the daily general drawing to duck hunters with boats. Motors are not permitted; dogs are. Hunters are limited to 25 shells each (steel shot only). To minimize the disturbance of waterfowl, hunters must wait 30 minutes after legal shooting time to enter the refuge, but they may hunt daily until 3 p.m. During the most recent season a total of 347 permits were issued and 234 ducks harvested. Best spot was Blind A with 100 ducks killed.

FENNVILLE FARM UNIT

Fennville Farm Unit hunters have no preregistered drawing. Instead, 30 minutes after the Highbanks drawing (6 a.m. through October 29, 5:30 a.m. thereafter—check current regulations for changes), a general lottery is held. During the most recent season a total of 12,574 permittees (daily average of 251) shot 2,766 geese and 269 a.m.

ducks. Highest weekday pressure occurred on Fridays, the lowest on Tuesdays. Best hunting day was the opener with 149 geese checked. Worst day occurred toward the season end when hunters shot 15 geese.

Zones 2-7 border the refuge and require permits. One goose was shot per average of 3.9 permits. Best zone was No. 5 with 556 geese (hot blinds were B, D, C, and E, respectively), followed by No. 4 (Blinds F, D, E, C), with 389 geese. Zones 1, 9, and 10 do not touch the refuge, dogs are allowed, and permits are not required. Zone 10 hunters shot 29 geese, Zone 9 hunters shot 25, and Zone 1 hunters bagged six. Average in this three-zone section dropped to one goose for every 16.3 permits. The 38 blinds in Zone 8 produced 921 geese and 92 ducks. Best spots were Blinds 12 (122 geese) and 11 (101 geese).

The above figures are mentioned as guidelines only. Flight patterns for waterfowl can change daily according to hunting pressure, food availability, and weather.

As at the Highbanks, goose hunting closes at 2 p.m. daily and hunters must return permits and check game (if the station is open) by 3 p.m. Afternoon duck and small-game hunting is permitted from 3 p.m. and closes at the listed migratory bird shooting hours. A drawing is not required but seasonal permits are, and they will be issued by the DNR to any interested hunter. During the most recent season 924 permits were handed out.

Hunters are required to have state and federal duck hunting stamps, a small-game hunting license, and a public access stamp.

Members of the local chapter of the Michigan Duck Hunters Association, a Michigan United Conservation Clubs affiliate, contributed considerable time and materials in erecting and maintaining blinds, clearing brush from nesting sites and brush and trees from potential nesting sites, and erecting nesting boxes.

Waterfowl hunting at Allegan Stage Game Area involves a complicated set of rules and regulations. However, for the most part, hunters enjoy a quality experience as compensation. One final note: the DNR has one or more special Youth Hunting Days at both managed areas. Check the "Waterfowl Hunting Guide" for details.

Port Huron State Game Area

THE Port Huron State Game Area, located in northeastern St. Clair County, is 50 miles north of Detroit and 10 miles northwest of Port Huron. It is popular with both metropolitan and local hunters who seek deer, pheasants, grouse, woodcock, squirrels, rabbits, and waterfowl within its more than 6,500 acres.

Established in 1942, the game area features seven DNR-established water impoundments totaling about 100 acres. Around 80 percent, or 5,000 acres, is forested, and another 10 percent contains brush. Prior to 1977 the game area had received 632,000 trees and shrubs. Since then annual plantings of autumn olive, silky dogwood, honeysuckle, highbush cranberry, and Austrian pine have been made. Two-and-one-half- to 10-acre prescribed cuttings of

mature forest each year contribute to varying stages of timber growth—a practice which helps maximize wildlife production.

These efforts have helped to bring about good hunting prospects. The Port Huron State Game Area offers a variety of game as well as habitat. Although 75 percent of the terrain is characterized as gently sloping or level, 100-foot relief changes occur within a distance of only 500 feet, making for tough terrain. The turbid waters of the Black River flow throughout its length. Main tributaries are Plum Creek and clear-running Mill Creek.

The game area nicely breaks down into three hunting areas. Pheasant hunters should concentrate on the northern third. Seventy acres of sharecrop land and small food plots put in by the DNR

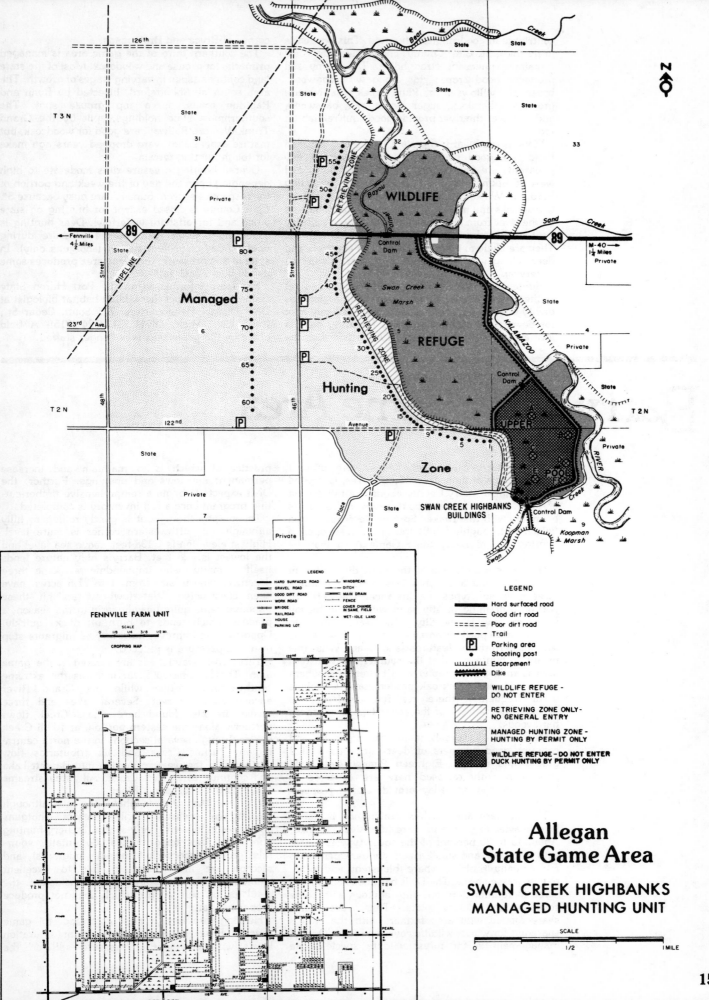

LEGEND

Hard surfaced road	Windbreak
Gravel road	Ditch
Good dirt road	Main drain
Work road	Fence
Bridge	Cover change in same field
Railroad	
House	
Parking lot	

FENNVILLE FARM UNIT

SCALE
0   1/8   1/4   3/8   1/2 MI.

CROPPING MAP

LEGEND

Hard surfaced road
Good dirt road
Poor dirt road
Trail
P   Parking area
•   Shooting post
Escarpment
Dike

WILDLIFE REFUGE -
DO NOT ENTER

RETRIEVING ZONE ONLY -
NO GENERAL ENTRY

MANAGED HUNTING ZONE -
HUNTING BY PERMIT ONLY

WILDLIFE REFUGE - DO NOT ENTER
DUCK HUNTING BY PERMIT ONLY

Allegan
State Game Area

SWAN CREEK HIGHBANKS
MANAGED HUNTING UNIT

SCALE
0   1/2   1 MILE

contribute to good ringneck hunting. This portion is in northern St. Clair County, one of the state's few remaining pheasant strongholds. The loamy soil produces good crop yields along with dogwood, brush, and willows in the Plum Creek area. Mature growths of hemlock, sugar maple, ash, basswood, and elm near the river provide good squirrel habitat too.

Moving southward, the state land along Norman Road is a good place to try for grouse. A few pheasants are found along Gibson Road north and west of Atkins, but the central portion, including Ford and Walker Flats impoundments, is noted for wood ducks and mallards. Hunters can launch boats on the river from Highway 136 and enjoy a half-day float to the takeout at Wadhams on Highway 21. They are likely to jump ducks and see squirrels and deer, along with an occasional beaver, along the waterway.

Hunters hiking in on Fieck Road at Atkins can get to the dam on Ford Impoundment. This region has plenty of second-growth timber and is a likely spot for deer. A good squirrel stand featuring oaks is located a mile and a half east of Abbottsford on the corner of Bryce and Brott roads.

The southern third of the game area is managed primarily for grouse and woodcock. Most of the state land contains aspen in varying stages of growth. The area south of Abbottsford, bisected by Rynn and Rabidue roads, is a top grouse spot. The southernmost state holdings, split by the Grand Trunk Western Railway, are good for woodcock, but mature aspens that were dropped years ago make for tough hunting terrain.

Overall hunting pressure runs moderate to high depending upon the day of the week and portion of the respective season. Sundays are busy because St. Clair County is closed except for hunting on state lands and for offshore waterfowl. Deer hunting is especially popular with intense pressure during opening day of firearm season (shotguns only). In spite of that pressure, the game area produces some dandy bucks each fall.

For more information on the Port Huron State Game Area, contact the wildlife habitat biologist at DNR District Headquarters, 715 South Cedar St., Imlay City, Mich. 48444 (313/724-2015). A field office on the game area is no longer staffed.

Barry State Game Area

THE Barry State Game Area, with present holdings of more than 15,000 acres, is located in west-central Barry County about five miles west of Hastings. It shares about seven miles of its boundary with the Yankee Springs Recreation Area (*which see*), roughly 3,500 acres of which are open to hunting. All of Barry State Game Area may be hunted.

The game area is one of the most diversified in terms of habitat and huntable species. It features three main soil types, for instance. The northern portion containing mostly sand with a thin topsoil layer is low in fertility. The east-central to southwestern portion contains loamy sand, while the southeastern region features sandy loam. What this means to hunters is that the southern and eastern area is rolling topography with better soils where white, red, and black oak predominate. Openings occur frequently, there are few conifers, and perhaps five percent of the cover type is northern hardwoods.

This region is excellent for fox squirrels and contains good numbers of deer and some ruffed grouse and rabbits. Eighteen Pennsylvania wild turkeys recently released here are expected to thrive and may someday provide hunting opportunity.

The northern and north-central region is flatter land heavier to sand and more intensively farmed. About 15 to 20 percent of the cover type is pines, with scrub oak and small aspen stands. Open areas are actually prairies where bluestem and other native grasses grow. The DNR has about 500 to 600 acres in rotation for corn and legumes with some soybean and celery plots. These are lands sharecropped with area farmers with the state's share left for winter wildlife cover and food. Overall management is for forest wildlife species, one practice of which is to maintain and increase permanent meadows and openings. Further, the DNR expects to begin a comprehensive timber-cutting program once a full inventory is completed.

Topography throughout is gently rolling to hilly although the northwestern corner is quite level. Highest elevation is 1,138 feet above sea level and the lowest is 728 feet. Barry's hilly nature lends itself to many water impoundments. Some three dozen, varying in size from .1 to 21.5 acres, have been constructed. Waterfowl hunters hit these impoundments quite heavily early in the season, a practice which tends to burn off ducks quickly. Opportunities improve, however, as migrants stop over and pressure is reduced.

Three river watersheds are located in the game area. The Kalamazoo River includes the extreme southwestern portion while the Grand River encompasses the rest. Several lakes and three creeks are also found here. Glass Creek flows northerly along the eastern portion, and Hill Creek moves through several sections in the north-central region. Turner Creek and its tributaries flow northerly on the western portion into Bassett Lake and continue as Bassett Creek. All three streams flow into the Thornapple River.

High numbers of deer inhabit the area although opening-day pressure during firearm (shotguns only) season is keen. Early-season archery hunting affords the best opportunities. Cottontails, squirrels, grouse, woodcock (especially migrants), and raccoon are also found in fair to excellent abundance. Pheasants are nearly nonexistent, the result of low soil fertility which does not produce proper habitat.

Hunting pressure varies according to game species. Firearm deer hunters are at saturation levels with bow-hunting pressure still on the

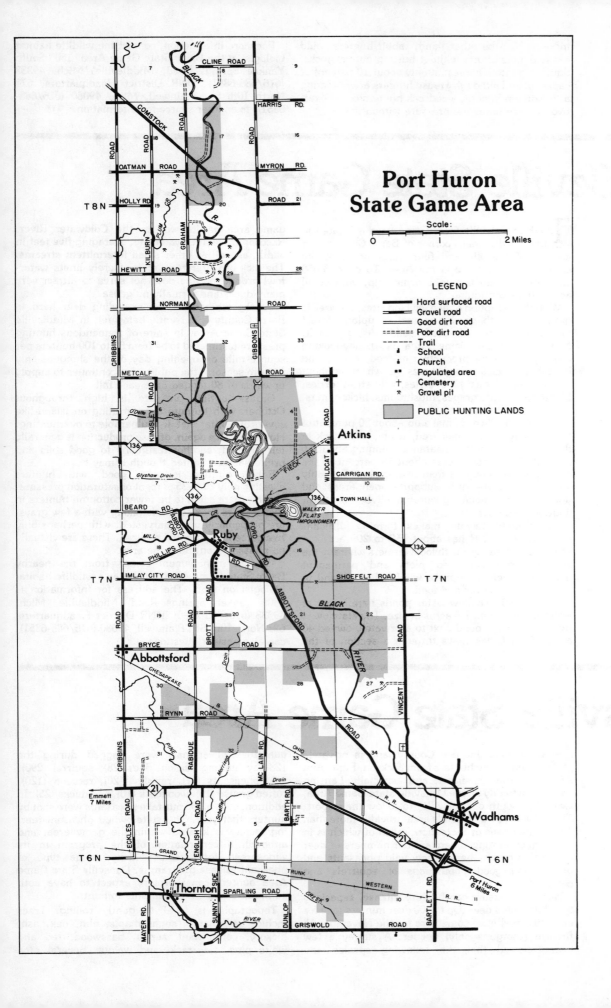

Port Huron
State Game Area

Scale:

0   1   2 Miles

LEGEND

▬▬▬	Hard surfaced road
══	Gravel road
═	Good dirt road
======	Poor dirt road
-----	Trail
⌂	School
⌂	Church
▪▪	Populated area
+	Cemetery
⚲	Gravel pit
▨	PUBLIC HUNTING LANDS

increase. On the other hand, rabbit hunters could easily double efforts without hurting native stocks. Squirrel hunters harvest at only about 10 percent of capacity, and although grouse hunters are operating at maximum benefit, woodcock hunters could exert two to three times the pressure without harm.

For more information, contact the wildlife habitat biologist at the Barry State Game Area, 1805 South Yankee Springs Road, Middleville, Mich. 49333 (616/685-6851). DNR District Headquarters, 621 North 10th St., Plainwell, Mich. 49080 (616/685-6851), is another source for information.

Middleville State Game Area

THE Middleville State Game Area is located in the northwestern corner of Barry County, just east of Middleville and four miles north of the sprawling Barry State Game Area. To date, 3,450 acres of land are in public ownership, with small acquisitions continuing.

With the exception of two lowland sites, the area is quite hilly, with good dispersal of upland forest types, indicative of good soils. As a result, Middleville State Game Area is gamey-looking country and quite productive of food, cover, and huntable species. Food types grown throughout include raspberries, blueberries, wild strawberries, blackberries, wild grapes, mushrooms, hickory nuts, walnuts, and butternuts.

Northern hardwoods make up about 20 percent of the cover type, with oak (red, white, and black in descending order of appearance) running about 15 percent. Aspen constitutes about 15 percent of the cover growth, pine less than five percent. Probably 40 percent of the area supports open areas and upland brush, including autumn olive, hawthorn, dogwood, and sumac.

The rugged terrain makes farming difficult. Currently the DNR has about 150 to 200 acres in sharecrop agreement with local farmers whereby the state's portion of food plots and permanent meadows is left to improve wildlife habitat and to provide winter cover and food.

There are 14 shallow-water ponds here, most of which are less than 1.5 acres in size. The state owns five acres on one pond next to a privately-owned 40 acres. Cain Creek flows through a section of the game area on its way to the Coldwater River. Raccoon travel this waterway, averaging five feet in width, as well as other small intermittent streams. The lack of water resources severely limits waterfowl production and does not serve to attract very many ducks and virtually no geese.

On the other hand, an exploding deer herd in Barry County is currently being felt in Middleville State Game Area. In spite of tremendous hunting pressure (estimated to be from 80 to 100 hunters per square mile on opening day of the shotguns-only firearm season), the public area continues to supply upwards of 80 tagged deer each fall.

Grouse-hunting pressure is high throughout October, with hunters concentrating on island-like covers of habitat that are vulnerable to overhunting. However, once again, grouse production is generally fair to good, another testimony to good soils and prime habitat, limited though it may be.

Rabbit hunting is quite good, with hunters exerting only 20 to 25 percent of saturation pressure. In fact, there seem to be fewer cottontail hunters in recent years. Fox squirrels (along with a few grays) are particularly underharvested, with perhaps only five percent of potential realized. There are virtually no pheasants on the game area.

Wildlife management comes from the nearby Barry State Game Area which has a wildlife habitat biologist on staff. The address for information is 1805 Yankee Springs Road, Middleville, Mich. 49333 (616/795-3280). DNR District Headquarters, 621 North 10th St., Plainwell, 49080 (616/685-6851), can also answer questions.

Dansville State Game Area

SINCE most Ingham County land is privately owned, many hunters from Jackson, Flint, Ann Arbor, Detroit, Ypsilanti, and especially Lansing have come to rely on the Dansville State Game Area, two miles south of Dansville, to follow their sport. The 4,200-acre public lands area provides more than 20,000 man-days of recreation, much of which is in the form of hunting. There are fair numbers of deer and ruffed grouse here, a few wild pheasants and ducks, and good populations of squirrels and cottontails.

Hunting pressure can be very intense, especially for white-tailed deer. Up to 400 deer hunters (one for each 10 acres) have come here for the November 15 firearm (shotguns only) opener. A survey a few years showed that the following species and quantities of animals were bagged during the 128-day hunting season: deer (28), squirrel (290), wild pheasants (67), rabbits (420), raccoon (120), ruffed grouse (15), woodcock (10), and ducks (25). In addition, over 6,000 put-take pheasants were shot by hunters that year. The state-owned pheasant-rearing facility is located within the game area, and although a continuation of the program in its widespread form is not likely, some type of pheasant-release program is. Dansville State Game Area hunters can therefore expect to have both pen-reared and wild pheasants to hunt.

Topography is level to gently rolling. Trees include red maple, sugar maple, elm, oak, ash, hickory, cottonwood, aspen, basswood, red and white pine, tamarack, and walnut. Several pine

Barry State Game Area

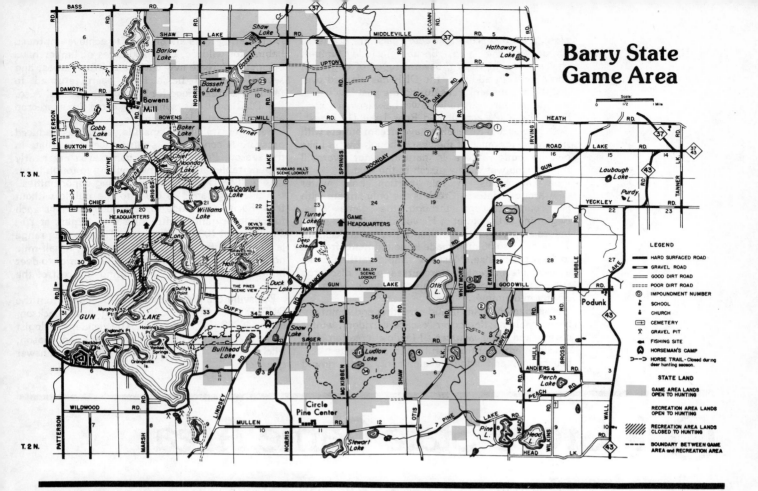

LEGEND
- ━━━ HARD SURFACED ROAD
- GRAVEL ROAD
- GOOD DIRT ROAD
- POOR DIRT ROAD
- ⊙ IMPOUNDMENT NUMBER
- 🏫 SCHOOL
- ⛪ CHURCH
- ⊞ CEMETERY
- ✕ GRAVEL PIT
- 🎣 FISHING SITE
- ⛺ HORSEMAN'S CAMP
- ⊳--⊳ HORSE TRAIL - Closed during deer hunting season.

STATE LAND
- GAME AREA LANDS OPEN TO HUNTING
- RECREATION AREA LANDS OPEN TO HUNTING
- RECREATION AREA LANDS CLOSED TO HUNTING
- BOUNDARY BETWEEN GAME AREA and RECREATION AREA

Middleville State Game Area

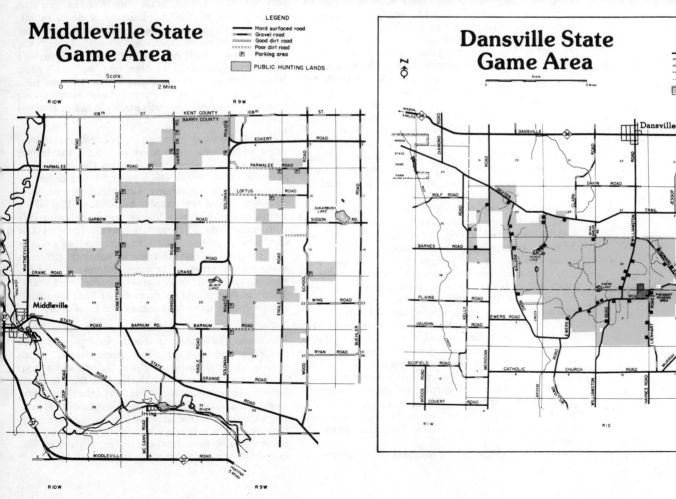

LEGEND
- ━━━ Hard surfaced road
- Gravel road
- Good dirt road
- Poor dirt road
- Ⓟ Parking area
- PUBLIC HUNTING LANDS

Dansville State Game Area

LEGEND
- ━━━ Hard surfaced road
- Gravel road
- Good dirt road
- Poor dirt road
- Foot trail
- PUBLIC HUNTING GROUNDS
- ■ Parking area

plantations of up to eight acres each are scattered throughout the area. Shrubs include juniper, chokecherry, hawthorn, several types of dogwood, and others. In addition, the DNR has planted over 400,000 shrubs and trees during the past few years.

Water resources include Hewes Lake (seven acres), Ewers Lake (24 acres), and Rose Lake (18 acres). Both Hewes and Rose lakes have stream outlets with flowing water much of the year. Though Ewers Lake has no outlet, there is natural water overspill through the wet willow marsh to the east.

Several ponds in this portion hold water year-around. Bateese Creek is the only stream with year-round flowage through the game area. Beginning at the outlet of Hewes Lake, it runs south before emptying into the Grand River near Jackson. There are also 36 man-made impoundments from .2 to 18 acres in size. Most are simple earthen dams across intermittent watercourses with discharge culverts to control maximum water levels. Most are dry by midsummer.

Management plans include creating and maintaining suitable nesting cover, escape corridors, winter cover, and food sources. Meadow creation and development, planting shrubs and coniferous trees, brushpiles, and edge development, and pruning

fruit-bearing trees are all ways to achieve improved habitat for wildlife. Over 200 acres of timber have been cut to create new cover and brush areas, and several reverted fields have been returned to farming to create food for farm-game species. Also, the DNR now has some 400 acres in sharecrop agreements with local farmers.

Best time to hunt Dansville, as far as reduced pressure is concerned, is during week days late in the season. Portions of the game area are nearly impenetrable, and the hunter willing to tough it out may well be rewarded with sporting opportunities.

A shooting range is open to the public without fees. Facilities include three outdoor stations each for centerfire and rimfire rifle with targets at 25-, 50-, 75-, and 100-yard intervals. The shooting range is located at the dogleg on Kelly Road, a half-mile north of Barnes Road. Usage is intense prior to deer hunting season but is light during the rest of the year.

Dansville State Game Area is managed from the DNR District Office, 3335 Lansing Ave., Jackson, Mich. 49202 (517/784-3188). The resident biologist at the State Game Farm, 1219 Hawley Road, Mason, Mich. 48854 (517/676-4600), can also answer questions.

Oak Grove State Game Area

THE Oak Grove State Game Area is located in Cohoctah and Deerfield townships in Livingston County. The 2,007-acre public lands area is popular with hunters from Flint and metropolitan Detroit who come to hunt deer, rabbits, waterfowl, squirrels, grouse, woodcock, and raccoon. Continued state acquisition is aimed at linking scattered parcels to provide more recreational opportunity, including hunting.

Upland areas are rolling hills and lowland types are level marshy areas that contain several small lakes along the Shiawassee River watershed. Most of the area is third-rate mineral soils or undeveloped muck along the drainages. Major soils are poorly drained, low-lying types with black muck surface layers.

General timber types include lowland swamp, pine, lowland hardwoods, northern hardwoods, and oak-hickory. Red maple, elm, ash, sugar maple, hickory, cottonwood, aspen, basswood, red and white pine, tamarack, walnut, and red, white, and black oak are the major species. Most large elm have been killed by Dutch elm disease over the past several years. Small pine plantations of up to eight acres each in size are scattered throughout.

Major thinning projects of mature hardwoods are needed to produce openings and to encourage second-growth succession that helps produce more game. Pine stands also need thinning and many open areas that converted to brush years ago are quickly progressing to shrub-tree stage. Currently about 25 percent of the game area is open fields, 29 percent is woods, 28 percent is brush, and seven percent is marsh. Lakes constitute the other 11 percent.

These comments do not suggest that hunting is

poor at Oak Grove State Game Area. To the contrary, fair to good populations of deer, rabbit, squirrels, raccoon, grouse, and waterfowl lure hunters. Two major river systems pass through the area. Bogue Creek and the Shiawassee River are major flowages on the western side, and the Yellow River along with its numerous feeder streams runs through the eastern portion. These slow-moving streams are associated with marsh areas of lowland cover.

Overall hunting pressure is medium to heavy. Some of the best deer cover is around the Indian Lake chain, the shoreline of which the state owns about 90 percent. The lakes were the site of former marl extraction operations. Good numbers of deer, including some fine trophy bucks, use the lake's fringe cover, which is largely lowland hardwoods with some oak. The eastern portion contains fair numbers of grouse. The lakes themselves provide fair to good goose and duck hunting although early-season pressure is often intense. Mallards, blue-winged teal, and Canada geese nest here. There is one primitive carry-down boat-launching site on Indian Lake for hunters and fishermen.

The northernmost portion containing the old Ball Farm and Ball Pond is mostly loamy sand with muck-wetland pockets. The pond itself, which outlets to the Shiawassee River, is actually a bog. The area produces wood ducks and affords some hunting opportunity for these and other puddlers, namely mallards and teal. Main forest-cover type is black locust. About 40 acres of land is sharecropped, with the state's portion left for wildlife food and cover. Again, deer hunting is fairly good in this portion of the game area.

The southernmost section is a good rabbit and grouse hunting area with opportunities for fox squirrels. Much of the cover type is lowland edge containing aspen, especially toward the western boundary along Bogue Creek. Deer hunting opportunities are fair. Hunters also bag ring-necked pheasants and woodcock.

The Oak Grove State Game Area is a relatively unspoiled piece of state-owned land located near a large urban population. Overall, it affords excellent raccoon, squirrel, and rabbit hunting. Deer-hunting pressure is heavy during both archery and firearm (shotguns only) seasons, with prospects fair. Pockets of pheasants, woodcock, and ruffed grouse provide good hunting opportunities for hunters operating in proper habitat and using dogs.

The game area is overseen by a DNR wildlife habitat biologist stationed at the State Game Farm, 1219 Hawley Road, Mason, Mich. 48854 (517/676-4600). Hunters can also get information from DNR District Headquarters, 3335 Lansing Ave., Jackson, Mich. 49202 (517/784-3188).

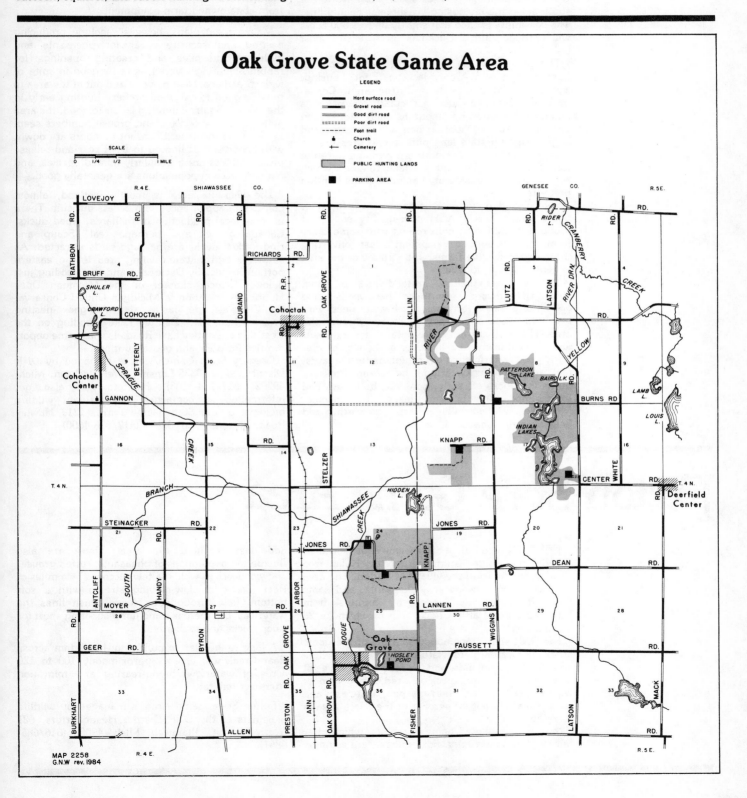

Oak Grove State Game Area

LEGEND

Hard surface road
Gravel road
Good dirt road
Poor dirt road
Foot trail
Church
Cemetery
PUBLIC HUNTING LANDS
PARKING AREA

SCALE
0 1/4 1/2 1 MILE

MAP 2258
G.N.W rev. 1984

Gregory State Game Area

THE Gregory State Game Area is located in southwestern Livingston County a couple miles north and west of Pinckney. The 3,474-acre public area consists of three separate units of land. Two blocks are north of M-36, while the third—the Unadilla Wildlife Area—lies about 3.5 miles to the south along the Livingston-Washtenaw county line. The possibility is good that shortly up to 1,500 acres will be added south of Duck Lake in the easternmost unit.

The area is within a short driving distance of hunters from Ann Arbor, Jackson, Flint, Lansing, Ypsilanti, and the western Detroit area. Consequently, it gets heavy use, particularly on weekends and during the firearm (shotguns only) deer season opener. A Sunday hunting ban with firearms and dogs except on state land puts undue pressure on this game area. The two northern portions were the former sites of pheasant put-take releases which accounted for a considerable amount of the hunting pressure.

Typical land use around the game area is farming, but a closer look reveals poor-quality soils that produce limited cash crop grains with some dairy farming. Residential development is fast converting these nonproductive farms. Topography of the area is gently sloping to level.

Timber types include lowland swamp, pine, lowland hardwoods, northern hardwoods, and oak-hickory mixes. Streams are heavily lined with brush. Livernois and Honey creeks run through the area. The northeastern unit contains several lakes and impoundments to 40 acres each, which offer fairly good waterfowling opportunities for mallards, teal, and wood ducks early in the season. Pressure burns the ducks off early, however, both here and from impoundments and lakes (McConachie, McIntyre, Williamsville, Sharp, Illsworth, and Sheets) in the Unadilla Unit.

The DNR currently has sharecrop agreements with local farmers whereby about 100 acres are in crop production. This is mostly in the central unit but also includes some food plots (the state's share left standing) in the Unadilla Unit. The DNR does not maintain its own food plots because of the distance from state-owned farm equipment.

Management plans, however, include producing nesting and security cover for pheasants and building brushpiles and creating openings for rabbits. Hunting, overall, is fairly good in spite of widespread use. Deer move in and out of the area to provide good to excellent archery hunting early in the season. Squirrel hunting is fair to good, the area gets migrant woodcock, and grouse numbers seem to be on the increase. Pheasant numbers are down, with opportunities limited to DNR rear-and-release birds. Rabbits are a popularly-hunted species, and fox and raccoon populations are generally good.

The Unadilla area is mostly wetland, almost bog-like in appearance, with access difficult. There is some local production of mallards, wood ducks, Canada geese, and perhaps teal. Scaup and ring-necked ducks are passage birds attracted. As stated, a better waterfowling area is the eastern portion, especially Duck Lake and the flooding just below. A local chapter of the Michigan Duck Hunters Association, a Michigan United Conservation Clubs affiliate, has assisted with goose-nesting projects here. The Bentley Lake Flooding on the west side of Bentley Lake Road also has some opportunities for duck and goose hunting.

Gregory State Game Area is managed by DNR District Office, 3335 Lansing Ave., Jackson, Mich. 49202 (517/784-3188). Hunters can also get information by contacting the resident wildlife biologist at the State Game Farm, 1219 Hawley Road, Mason, Mich. 48854 (517/676-4600).

Fulton State Game Area

THE 671-acre Fulton State Game Area is located in the southeastern corner of Kalamazoo County, southeast of the village of Fulton. The area produces grouse, woodcock, pheasants, and some deer. It is heavily visited by hunters from Kalamazoo and Battle Creek, both of which lie 20 miles away.

The DNR sharecrops about 80 acres of the game area with local farmers. Natural cover types include grasslands, brushlands, and the following species of trees: red, white, and black oak; red elm; dogwood; willow; hickory; black cherry; aspen; white ash; and tulip poplar. About 60 percent of the game area is forested.

Most widely-hunted game is rabbits, which offer fair to good opportunity. Fox squirrels are common and deer frequent the area. There are also fluctuating populations of pheasants, ruffed grouse, and woodcock as well as a few raccoon. Two miles of Bear Creek, a slow-moving stream with a soft bottom, flow throughout. Heavy brush lines the waterway, but there is some jump-shooting sport for wood ducks and mallards.

A long-range plan to build a lowhead dam across Bear Creek will create approximately 100 to 120 acres of waterfowl brood-rearing and migration stop-over habitat.

Fulton State Game Area is managed by wildlife biologists at the DNR District Headquarters, 621 North 10th St., Plainwell, Mich. 49080 (616/685-6851).

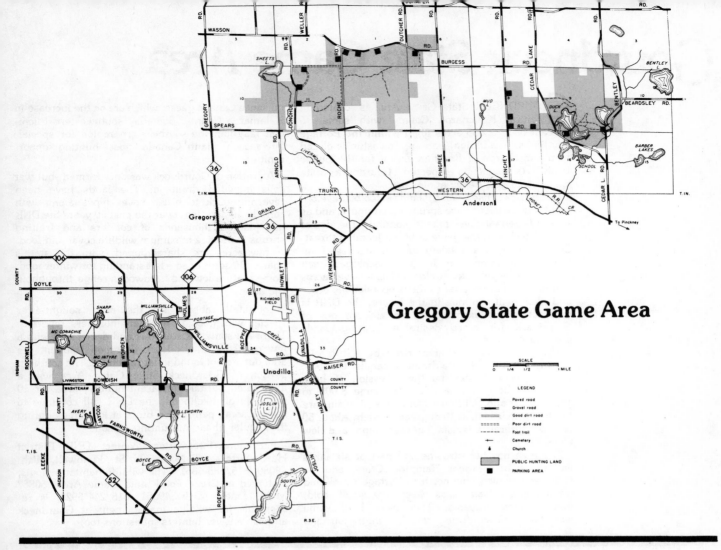

Gregory State Game Area

SCALE
0   1/4   1/2   1 MILE

LEGEND

▬▬▬	Paved road
▭▭▭	Gravel road
═══	Good dirt road
======	Poor dirt road
- - -	Foot trail
+	Cemetery
♠	Church
▨	PUBLIC HUNTING LAND
■	PARKING AREA

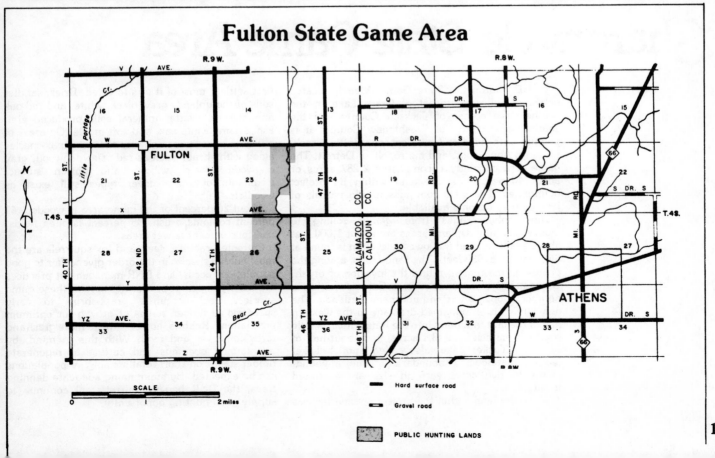

Fulton State Game Area

SCALE
0   1   2 miles

▬	Hard surface road
▭	Gravel road
▨	PUBLIC HUNTING LANDS

165

Gourdneck State Game Area

GOURDNECK State Game Area is located in central Kalamazoo County with some 75 percent of its 2,035 acres lying within the Portage city limits. In addition, Portage Township is closed to the discharge of firearms except for the public lands. As might be expected, Gourdneck State Game Area gets heavy hunter use.

Gourdneck is like a wood island ringed by development. Subdivisions have sprung up around it, and as these residential developments continue, the idea of some day closing the game area is a looming threat. State law requires a safety zone of 450 feet from occupied buildings for firearm discharge. Each safety zone can effectively close off up to seven acres of hunting land. Because conflicts occasionally occur and likely will continue in the future, the DNR is considering the exchange of certain portions of Gourdneck for more desirable hunting lands elsewhere.

The game area is characterized by flat glacial outwash plains and wide drainage canals. Geologic features were created by the recession of Lake Michigan during the last ice age some 8,000 to 12,000 years ago. All slopes from outwash plains are gradual with less than 10 degrees of pitch. About 50 feet of difference exists between high and low elevations.

The area has two streams and part of six lakes within its boundaries. Hampton Creek and its tributaries, which flow north to Portage Creek and ultimately the Kalamazoo River, are small, cold, quick-running streams. The lakes hold some waterfowl—ducks during the fall migration and nuisance Canada geese, which are on the increase in Kalamazoo County. Someday southwestern Michigan may join the southeastern region for special, late-season giant Canada goose-hunting opportunities.

A portion of Gourdneck was once farmed, but wet soils impeded drainage. The lands have been reverting back to brush cover types along with cattails. In addition, over the past 30 years the DNR has planted thousands of conifers and fruiting shrubs to provide maximum wildlife cover and food. A few acres are sharecropped, with the state's share—10 acres or so—left standing for winter food. Some mature lowland hardwoods range throughout the area.

Cottontail rabbits are the most sought-after species with good to excellent numbers reported. There are some fox squirrels and deer along with a few grouse and woodcock. Raccoon frequent the area but are not found in large supply. The southern portion of Gourdneck State Game Area was a designated put-take pheasant hunting area for 10 years. In all likelihood, the DNR will continue to release some pen-reared birds at key times during the regular pheasant hunting season.

For more information, contact DNR District Headquarters, 621 North 10th St., Plainwell, Mich. 49080 (616/685-6851). The wildlife habitat biologist stationed at Crane Pond State Game Area, 60887 M-40, Jones, Mich. 49061 (616/244-5928) is responsible for wildlife management at Gourdneck and can answer hunters' questions too.

Sharonville State Game Area

THE Sharonville State Game Area is located four miles southeast of Grass Lake in the southeastern corner of Jackson County and the southwestern corner of Washtenaw County. It is popular with hunters from Jackson, Battle Creek, Lansing, Ann Arbor, and metropolitan Detroit. The game area currently encompasses 2,287 acres or about 40 percent of the land within its project boundaries. The state continues to add parcels of land as they become available.

Topography ranges from gently rolling to moderately hilly. Upland areas are about 1,000 feet above sea level, and the lowest elevation is found at Sweezey Lake (930 feet). The sandy soils, among the poorest in the region, retard the invasion of brush. Consequently, Sharonville State Game Area has a number of open areas and not many wetlands. The only stream is an unnamed drainage in the western half of the unit that flows into the Raisin River a mile south. Tamarack Lake (3.1 acres) and about half of 11.2-acre Tucker Lake (also called Sunfish Lake) feature state-owned boundaries. Nine impoundments to five acres each in size are scattered throughout.

When the land within the project boundaries was first settled, most of it was forested. Drier, sandier soils of the uplands grew black, white, and red oak and hickory. Wetter mineral soils produced elm, ash, swamp white oak, and soft maple. On areas of muck or peat, tamarack was the principal species along with shrubs such as red-osier dogwood, gray dogwood, dwarf willow, and poison sumac. Remnants of these cover types still exist as woodlots.

About 20 percent of the game area is wooded, 41 percent contains brush, 35 percent is open fields, and four percent is wet areas.

Cottontail rabbits, deer, and fox squirrels are the most hunted species in the order given. Fair to good populations occur, and DNR management practices are mostly aimed at producing more of these game species. Each requires grass-shrub to early successional timber stages of growth for optimum populations. Rabbits, however, need more grass and forbs for cover and food. With this in mind, by maintaining openings and cutting to regenerate timber stands on short rotations, higher populations can be expected. By maintaining adequate denning trees, the DNR hopes squirrels will continue to supply good hunting opportunity.

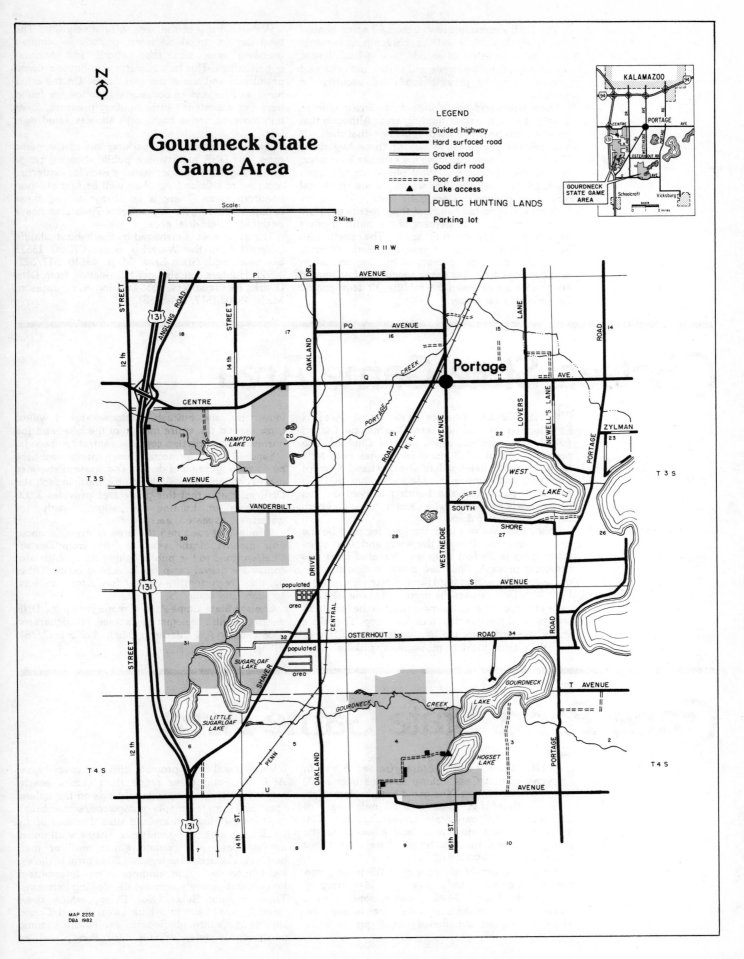

Gourdneck State Game Area

LEGEND

▬▬▬	Divided highway
▬▬▬	Hard surfaced road
═══	Gravel road
─────	Good dirt road
=======	Poor dirt road
▲	Lake access
▓▓▓	PUBLIC HUNTING LANDS
■	Parking lot

Scale:
0   1   2 Miles

KALAMAZOO

Portage

Schoolcraft   Vicksburg

GOURDNECK STATE GAME AREA

scale

2 miles

R II W

N

HAMPTON LAKE

WEST LAKE

SUGARLOAF LAKE

LITTLE SUGARLOAF LAKE

GOURDNECK LAKE

HOGSET LAKE

GOURDNECK CREEK

PORTAGE CREEK

Portage

populated area

populated area

AVENUE

PQ AVENUE

P AVENUE

CENTRE

R AVENUE

VANDERBILT

OSTERHOUT 33   ROAD   34

S AVENUE

SOUTH SHORE

T AVENUE

ZYLMAN

LOVERS LANE

NEWELL'S LANE

PORTAGE

WESTNEDGE

CENTRAL

OAKLAND

SHAVER DRIVE

ANGLING ROAD

12 th STREET

14 th STREET

14 th ST.

16 th ST.

PENN ST.

PORTAGE

131

T 3 S

T 4 S

T 3 S

T 4 S

18   17   16   15   14

19   20   21   22   23

30   29   28   27   26

31   32   33   34

6   5   4   3   2

7   8   9   10

U

Q

R

S

MAP 2252
DBA 1982

167

The DNR currently grows about 40 acres of food that is left for wildlife and has sharecrop agreements with two area farmers. In addition, it has planted close to a half-million trees and shrubs over the past several years to provide food and security for wildlife.

Open fields and brushlands made Sharonville an ideal put-take pheasant hunting area. Although that program has been canceled, it is likely that the DNR will release pheasants at two or three key times during the season, including the October 20 opener, for the next few years. Wild pheasants are quite rare. Likewise, grouse and woodcock are incidental species as populations are quite low.

A study during the height of the put-take program showed that about 85 percent of the hunting effort was directed toward that sport. The study also revealed that about 2,125 man-days (one or more hours of hunting per person) of hunting recreation was provided for other game species and estimated that hunters took about 200 rabbits, 12 deer, and 50 fox squirrels each year.

Waterfowl use of the area is relatively low. The two largest impounds provide a limited breeding area and thus afford low hunting opportunities. This lack of water also limits raccoon production and use of the game area. On the other hand, red fox and an occasional gray fox are found here but experience little hunting pressure. Deer hunting pressure is high, with success rated only fair.

There are a total of 22 parking lots in the game area. The DNR maintains a public shooting range containing three outdoor stations each for centerfire and rimfire rifle and pistol as well as four shotgun handtrap areas. There is no charge to use these facilities. Sharonville State Game Area also has a designated field-trial area.

The game area is managed by the habitat wildlife biologist from the Waterloo Game Office, 13578 Seymour Road, Grass Lake, Mich. 49240 (517/522-4097). Hunters can also get information from DNR District Headquarters, 3335 Lansing Ave., Jackson, Mich. 49202 (517/784-3188).

Chelsea State Game Area

THE 652-acre Chelsea State Game Area is located in northwestern Washtenaw County (*which see*), just two miles west of Chelsea. The property, of which 200 acres constitutes Four-Mile Lake, formerly belonged to the Portland Cement Company and came into state ownership in 1940. About 95 percent of the hunting activity on this game area is for waterfowl—Canada geese and both diver and puddler ducks.

Four-Mile Lake was once dredged for marl by the cement company. Pits on the north and west sides ranging up to 25 feet deep were created from this dredging process. Soils are muck and loam. The game area lies within the Huron River watershed— Four-Mile Drain enters the north end of the lake and exits at the south end. Deepest point in the lake is 18 feet; most of it is less than four feet deep. The lake's entire western shoreline is a cattail marsh. Other aquatic plants include muskgrass, pickerelweed,

loosestrife, and bulrush. Cottonwood and willow grow around the entire margin of the lake, and the narrow eastern portion contains central hardwoods.

Sandhill cranes (protected from hunting) nest here as do some geese and ducks. The western shore of marsh contains about 15 hunting blinds. In fact, the DNR estimates that this game area provides 3,000 man-hours of hunting recreation, mostly for waterfowl, as stated, each year.

A mile-long road into the area is drivable about nine months of the year. It runs from Dexter-Chelsea Road to the public fishing site, which also contains a gravel ramp for launching boats. Other hunting opportunities exist for deer, rabbits, raccoon, and squirrels.

Chelsea State Game Area is managed by the DNR district wildlife biologist at Jackson Headquarters, 3335 Lansing Ave., Jackson, Mich. 49202 (517/784-3188).

Crane Pond State Game Area

THE Crane Pond State Game Area in east-central Cass County contains over 3,700 acres open to hunting. The game area is located six miles south of Marcellus and 10 miles east of Cassopolis. Michigan State University owns 200 acres of forest-management land adjacent to the game area, and the two tracts share almost two miles of common boundary.

Steep hills, gently-rolling glacial till plains, and flat, muck-bottom lands give a wide variety of topographic change. Mucks, loams, sandy loams, and loamy sands make up the soil types found here. There is also an abandoned gravel pit on state property.

Varying soil types promote differing cover types. At Crane Pond these range from climax beech-maple forest to semiopen brushlands on the upland areas and from red maple or dogwood/sumac brush to sedge meadows on lowland sites. Portions of six small lakes enter the game area. They are all under 20 feet deep and contain either mud or marl bottoms. The area also features 23 natural potholes, eight man-made impoundments on intermittent flows, and three permanently-flowing streams. These include Belas Lake Drain, which flows through Belas Lake into Kirk Lake; Bogart Creek, which passes through Bogart Lake before running northeasterly into Streeter Mill Pond; and an

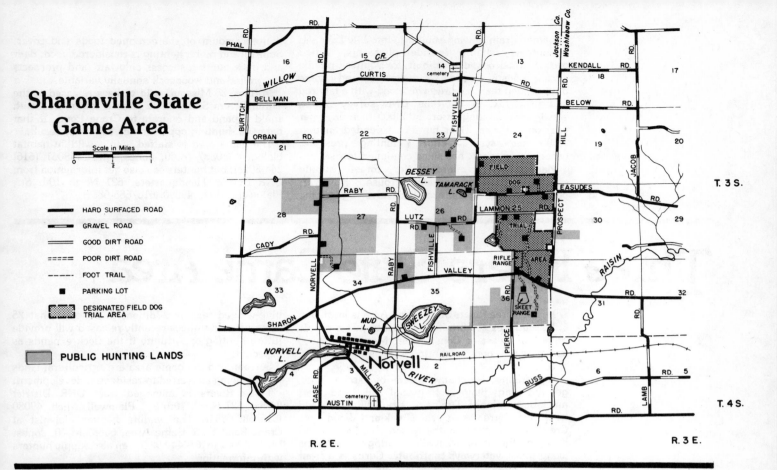

Sharonville State Game Area

Scale in Miles

0   1/2   1

- ▬▬ HARD SURFACED ROAD
- ▭▭ GRAVEL ROAD
- ═══ GOOD DIRT ROAD
- ===== POOR DIRT ROAD
- ----- FOOT TRAIL
- ■ PARKING LOT
- ▨ DESIGNATED FIELD DOG TRIAL AREA
- ▨ PUBLIC HUNTING LANDS

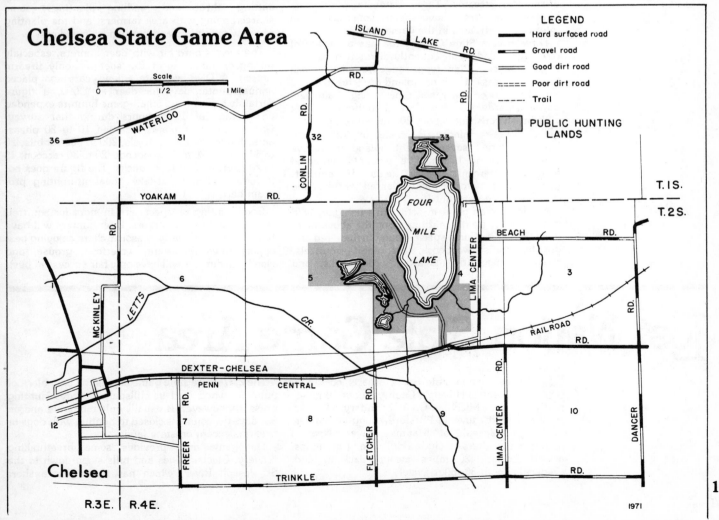

Chelsea State Game Area

Scale

0   1/2   1 Mile

LEGEND
- ▬▬ Hard surfaced road
- ▭▭ Gravel road
- ═══ Good dirt road
- ===== Poor dirt road
- ----- Trail
- ▨ PUBLIC HUNTING LANDS

Chelsea

R.3E. | R.4E.

169

1971

MAP 2286

unnamed drain flowing southerly into Lily Lake.

Huntable wildlife include pheasants, ruffed grouse, woodcock, deer, rabbit, fox squirrel, puddle ducks (mostly woodies, mallards, and some blue-winged teal), and raccoon along with a few red and grey fox. A one-time DNR survey placed small-game hunting effort at 2,000 man-days per year on the area. Deer hunters expended another 1,500 man-days of effort. Hunting pressure, especially for deer, has since continued to rise.

Management is largely for forest wildlife species—namely deer and grouse. However, pheasants utilizing the area take advantage of the limited amount of sharecropped foods and cover. Squirrel and rabbit hunting is considered good, deer and duck hunting success only fair, and prospects for grouse and woodcock annually variable.

In time, 25 Missouri wild turkeys released at the Three Rivers State Game Area a few miles south could expand and migrate to Crane Pond. If that happens, hunting opportunities will likely result.

The game area is staffed with a wildlife habitat biologist (60887 M-40, Jones, Mich. 49061 [616] 244-5928), but hunters can also get information from DNR District Headquarters, 621 North 10th St., Plainwell, Mich. 49080 (616/685-6851).

Three Rivers State Game Area

THE Three Rivers State Game Area is located in southwestern St. Joseph County just a couple miles northwest of Constantine. More than 2,000 acres are now open to hunting for a variety of game species.

Topography is characterized by steep hills, gently-rolling plains of glacial till, and flat, muck-bottom lands. Drainage is by Mill Creek and its tributary streams—Curtis Creek and Wood Lake Creek—which flow southerly into the St. Joseph River northeast of Mottville. Springs and seeps along these waterways contribute. Curtis is a trout stream, and the other two are good-quality warmwater streams. Three water impoundments totaling 18 acres have been constructed on intermittent streams in the game area.

Three Rivers State Game Area has a variety of cover types and a consequently diversified number of game species. Plant types range from mature oak forest and grassy fields on upland dry sites to sedge cattail marsh on muck soil types along drainages. Lowland hardwoods and lowland coniferous forest with brush constitute about 20 percent of the cover types. The remainder is made up of upland hardwood forest, seven percent; upland brush, five percent; lowland brush, five percent; cultivated fields, 20 percent; grassy fields, 10 percent; marshes, 10 percent; and planted shrubs and conifers, three percent.

A seldom-seen plant in southern Michigan, wild rice, grows in great quantities along the above-mentioned streams. Game species found include red and gray fox, grouse, woodcock, deer, rabbits, squirrels, raccoon, pheasants, mallards, wood ducks, and blue-winged teal. In addition, it is hoped that 25 Missouri wild turkeys recently released will provide future hunting opportunity if the flock expands as expected.

Surrounding the game area are agricultural lands rapidly being converted to residential development.

Three Rivers is managed from DNR District Office, 621 North 10th St., Plainwell, Mich. 49080 (616/685-6851). The wildlife habitat biologist at Crane Pond State Game Area, 60887 M-40, Jones, Mich. 49061 (616/244-5928), can also supply hunters with information.

Management practices include some timber cutting, shrub and seedling plantings, some sharecropping with area farmers, and the planting of a few food plots and permanent meadows.

The area is hard hit with deer hunters, especialy during opening day of the shotguns-only firearm season. A DNR estimate a few years ago placed annual hunter days for deer at 1,000, a figure certainly higher now. Small-game hunters expended an average of 1,300 hours during that survey. Game-harvest estimates included 10 to 20 pheasants, 100 to 125 fox squirrels, 200 to 300 rabbits, 20 to 30 grouse, 20 to 30 woodcock, 20 to 30 raccoon, 15 to 20 deer, and 30 to 40 ducks. The figure does not include a former put-take pheasant-hunting program here.

Good hunting prospects are in store for squirrel, raccoon, and rabbit hunters. Deer hunters will have fair success, with early-season archers enjoying best opportunities. Pheasant, waterfowl, grouse, and woodcock hunters will have only fair success at best.

Lost Nation State Game Area

THE Lost Nation State Game Area is located in south-central Hillsdale County, about 10 miles north of the Michigan-Ohio boundary. It lies southwest of the town of Pittsford, along both sides of the St. Joseph of Maumee River. Nearby population centers include Hillsdale (six miles away), Adrian (20 miles away), Jackson and Coldwater (both 30 miles away).

The 2,374-acre state game area is the only block of publicly-owned land in Hillsdale County. Hunting pressure, however, is usually only moderate and on Sundays the county is closed to hunting with dogs or firearms except on state land.

The game area provides some breathtaking scenery. Glacial ridges and hills slope down to the St. Joseph River, which has its origins a short

Crane Pond State Game Area

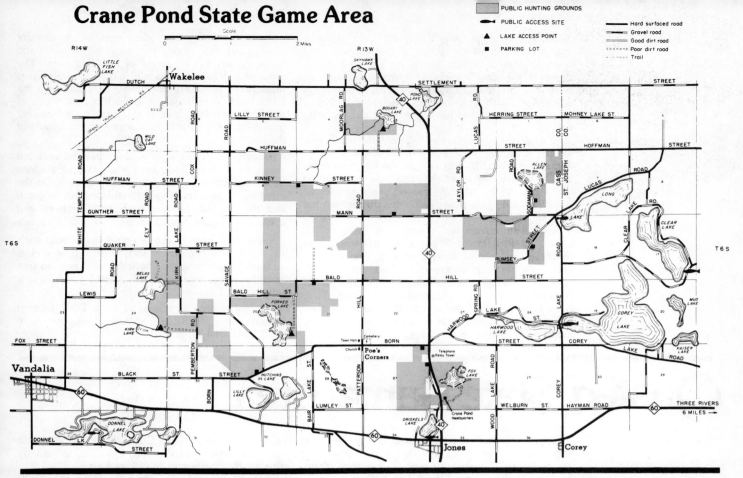

Three Rivers
State Game Area

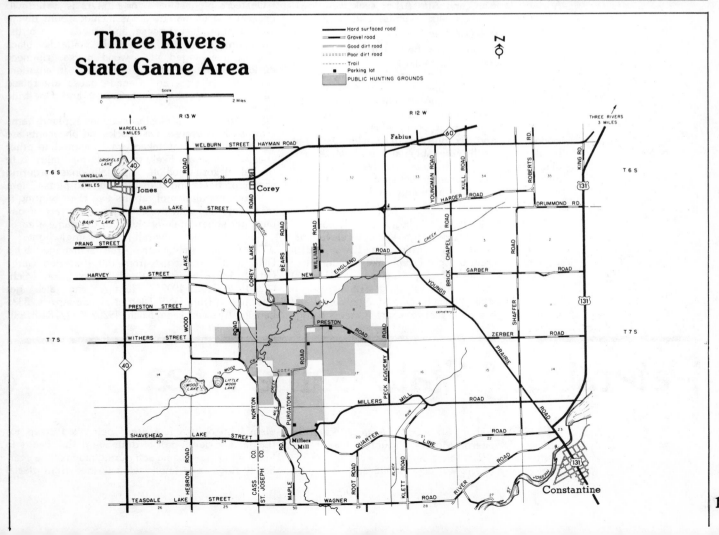

distance to the north, with an elevation difference of over 200 feet. Soils are generally fine-textured and strongly sloping. The steepness of the slope prevents the development of commercial agriculture; still, the DNR has about 200 acres in sharecrop agreements with local farmers. The state's third or quarter portion is left for winter food and security cover.

Most of the game area is heavy to brush and woods. Common shrubs and trees include thornapple, tamarack, hickory, sugar maple, sycamore, aspen, cherry, some walnut, red oak, and swamp white oak. A DNR planting project years ago added small red and white pine plantations throughout the area.

Besides the river, water resources include Bell Lake, the Pittsford mill pond, an unnamed lake touching the northwestern boundary, and a dozen shallow-water impoundments. Wood ducks, mallards, blue-winged teal, and other puddle ducks occasionally use the impoundments and lakes. They provide some early-season shooting opportunities, but gunning pressure quickly drives them off. The same is true along the St. Joseph River.

Squirrel hunting is good to excellent in mature mast-producing woodlots, especially oaks and hickories adjacent to strips of standing corn. The area is too grown up, though, to be a solid pheasant producer. Grouse are not native here although the DNR wants to release up to 40 birds in hopes of building to a huntable surplus if it can get a five-year grouse-hunting moratorium agreement throughout the county.

Rabbits are in fair supply. Quail use the area too although since 1977 southern Michigan populations have been too low to allow a hunting season. On the other hand, deer hunting is considered fair to good, and the area is popular with both archers and firearm (shotguns only) hunters.

A shooting range offers two outdoor stations each for pistol and centerfire and rimfire rifle and a shotgun handtrap area. There is no charge to use these facilities, located on Way Road a mile and a half west of Pittsford.

The game area is managed from DNR District Headquarters, 3335 Lansing Ave., Jackson, Mich. 49202 (517/784-3188).

Onsted State Game Area

THE 650-acre Onsted State Game Area is located five miles northwest of Onsted in northwestern Lenawee County. Hunters from Adrian, Jackson, and Ann Arbor seek waterfowl, deer, raccoon, squirrels, rabbits, and occasional woodcock, grouse, and pheasants.

The game area can best be classified as hip-boot country. About three-fourths is comprised of wetlands—sedge meadows, creeks, brushy edges, one man-made impoundment, and four natural lakes. An inventory taken 10 years ago showed 29 percent of the area to be surface water, 39 percent in wet areas, 16 percent in open fields, 10 percent in woodlands, and six percent in brushlands. That breakdown is still reasonably valid. Red, white, and black oaks along with sugar maples, beech, and hickory are the dominant forest species. In addition, the DNR has planted autumn-olive hedgerows and red pine.

Topography is slightly rolling, with only some 40 feet difference between high and low elevations. The game area lies within the River Raisin watershed. From 65-acre Deep Lake, an unnamed creek flows northerly through Grassy Lake (54 acres) and the Grassy Lake Flooding (12 acres). It continues northerly through One-Mile (29 acres) and Cleveland lakes (14 acres) to where it meets Briggs

Lake Creek. Briggs Lake Creek flows northerly into Jackson County into Vineyard Lake and eventually runs southeasterly into the River Raisin.

Onsted's biggest card for hunters is waterfowl. Present use of marshy areas includes both diving and dabbling ducks, geese, and other marsh birds. Common species in fall include mallards, black ducks, blue-winged teal, wood ducks, ringneck ducks, goldeneyes, and Canada geese. In addition, woodies, mallards, and Canada geese are raised here. Hunters' blinds dot Grassy and One-Mile lakes.

Since the area is mostly wetlands, upland game birds such as grouse, woodcock, and pheasants are not abundant. Most taken are incidental to other species. Those are likely to include fox squirrels in the oak-hickory woodlots, especially ones bordering sharecrop fields and DNR-planted food plots. There is a good population of rabbits too. Deer hunting is rated only fair with the county harvest rate of one buck per square mile applying to the game area.

Hunting pressure overall is surprisingly light.

The Onsted State Game Area is managed by a DNR wildlife biologist from the Waterloo Game Office, 13578 Seymour Road, Grass Lake, Mich. 49240 (517/522-4097). Hunters can also get information from DNR District Headquarters, 3335 Lansing Ave., Jackson, Mich. 49202 (517/784-3188).

Petersburg State Game Area

THE Petersburg State Game Area is located in southwestern Monroe County, two miles southeast of Petersburg and just west of US-23. Topography of the 441-acre public area is rolling

plain with only a few areas being too steep for tillage. The gentle fall of drainage paths results in lower lying areas being soft during much of the year. Sandy ridges and knolls were formed from glacial

Lost Nation State Game Area

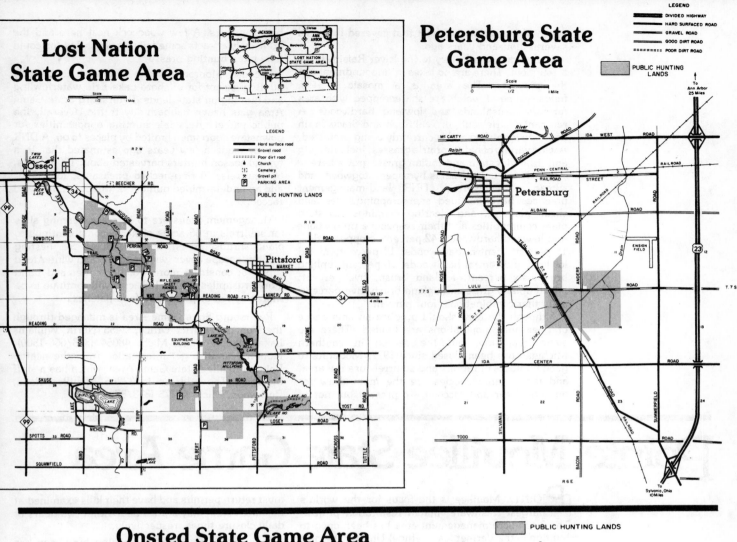

LEGEND
- Hard surface road
- Gravel road
- Poor dirt road
- Church
- Cemetery
- Gravel pit
- Parking area
- PUBLIC HUNTING LANDS

Petersburg State Game Area

LEGEND
- DIVIDED HIGHWAY
- HARD SURFACED ROAD
- GRAVEL ROAD
- GOOD DIRT ROAD
- POOR DIRT ROAD
- PUBLIC HUNTING LANDS

Onsted State Game Area

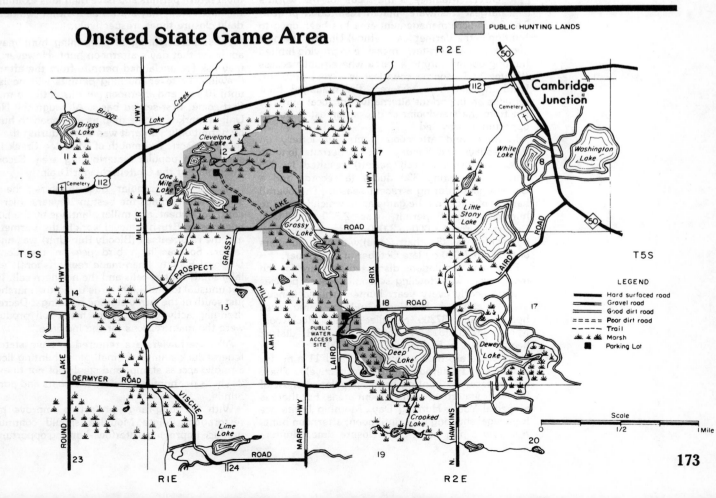

PUBLIC HUNTING LANDS

LEGEND
- Hard surfaced road
- Gravel road
- Good dirt road
- Poor dirt road
- Trail
- Marsh
- Parking Lot

action of a massive ice sheet that covered this area several thousand years ago.

Stacy Drain, a tributary to the River Raisin, flows throughout. There are no lakes or impoundments on the property. The area is a mosaic of idle fields—some of which are sharecropped with area farmers—brushlands and lowland hardwoods. A remnant prairie south of Teal Road and Stacy Drain has been identified and is currently being protected. A wide variety of native prairie grasses, including big and little bluestem and Indian grass, grows here.

Invasion of upland fields by aspen, dogwood, and sumac is widespread. DNR land-management practices have included sharecropping, tree and shrub planting, and clearing openings. Existing plant communities and their respective proportions are: lowland hardwoods, 42 percent; cropped fields, 16 percent; central hardwoods, 12 percent; mixed lowland and central hardwoods, 10 percent; upland brush, six percent; lowland brush, five percent; mixed upland grass and upland brush, five percent; and other combinations, four percent.

Although the area should produce an abundance of pheasants, populations are limited. There are some quail too, but the season in southern Michigan has been closed since 1977. Moderate to good numbers of rabbits and squirrels use the area, and these game species are the main draw for hunters. Deer and raccoon are present but not in high numbers. A few woodcock nest here and the area likely attracts some fall migrants. Red fox could take more hunting pressure.

Because Monroe County is closed to Sunday hunting except for offshore Lake Erie waterfowling and hunting on state lands, Petersburg State Game Area gets heavy Sabbath-day traffic. Overall, the public parcel offers fair hunting opportunities for downstate sportsmen limited by places to go. A DNR survey made a few years ago estimated that in a typical season hunters harvested about 100 rabbits, 60 squirrels, 26 ring-necked pheasants, four deer, and an undetermined number of woodcock, fox, and raccoon.

Management plans are to increase denning sites for squirrels in 45 acres of hardwoods; continue to plant shrubs, trees, and meadows for nesting habitat, escape cover, winter cover, and winter food supplies; construct more woodlot edge; and build more brushpiles. About 100 acres will continue to be sharecropped or planted to food patches.

Petersburg State Game Area is managed through the Pontiac District Office, 2455 North Williams Lake Road, Pontiac, Mich. 48054 (313/666-1500). Hunters can also get information from the nearby Pointe Mouillee State Game Area, which has a staff biologist. The address is 37205 Mouillee Road, Rockwood, Mich. 48173 (313/379-9692).

Pointe Mouillee State Game Area

POINTE Mouillee is the focus for the world's largest freshwater marsh restoration project. The 3,614-acre management area has been open to hunting in the Vermet (east refuge) Unit for the past six years as a short-term measure to provide limited hunting opportunity in an area where public access (Wayne and Monroe counties) is a real problem. Until the marsh is restored, the managed hunt remains an important alternative for local hunters, not from the standpoint of ducks harvested but as opportunity provided.

Morning and afternoon hunts by lottery on Wednesdays and Sundays for 30 permits (one to three hunters for each permit) resulted in 396 hunters harvesting 330 ducks (a record) and a Canada goose during a recent season. The overall harvest of ducks on the game area, which is open to hunting without permit, was 2,500 to 3,000. Generally, about 2,000 to 3,000 birds are in the area by opening day (Southern Zone) with peak numbers of 6,000 to 7,000 by late October or November.

Rules and regulations discussed here are for the most recent waterfowling season. Because policies change nearly every year, hunters should consult the "Waterfowl Hunting Guide"; game area headquarters (37205 Mouillee Road, Rockwood, Mich. 48713 [313/379-9692]); or DNR district headquarters in Pontiac (313/666-1500).

Drawings are held at 5:30 a.m. and 11 a.m. for morning and afternoon hunts, respectively. There are no reserved hunting dates, popular at most of the other waterfowl-management areas, but there is a special Youth Hunting Day. Morning hunts are from legal shooting time until noon; afternoon hunts run from 1 p.m. until daily closure time. Hunters must return permits and have their kills examined at the check station by 2 p.m. and within two hours of daily closure times, respectively.

Those participating in a morning hunt may not apply for that day's afternoon hunt. However, they may ask for unclaimed permits from the afternoon drawing. Leftover morning permits will be issued until 10 a.m. and afternoon permits until 1 p.m. on a first-come, first-served basis. Although the Nelson Unit is marked on the map as an "open to hunting by permit only" area, it was closed during the most recent season. The mouth of Mouillee Creek is the single most popular waterfowling area. Second is the mouth of the Lautenschlager Drain.

According to regular duck hunters, the 1983 season was perhaps the best in 10 years. Increased corn, buckwheat, and millet plantings by the DNR is one reason. Brush removal work in the Vermet Unit and the refuge itself (Bloody Run Unit) was another factor. So was high bird use on the Confined Disposal Facility (man-made reef offshore), especially south-central cells and the northern cell. It was not unusual to find 3,000 birds using the marshy cell just south of the Army storage buildings. Decreased dredging activity and better moist-soil production were the main reasons for the increase.

All waterfowlers are required to have state and federal duck stamps, a small-game hunting license, a public access stamp, and steel shot not to exceed 25 shells per hunter. Hunters use boats and portable blinds.

With the long-range project to improve marsh restoration, Pointe Mouillee should continue to produce improving waterfowl-hunting opportunities.

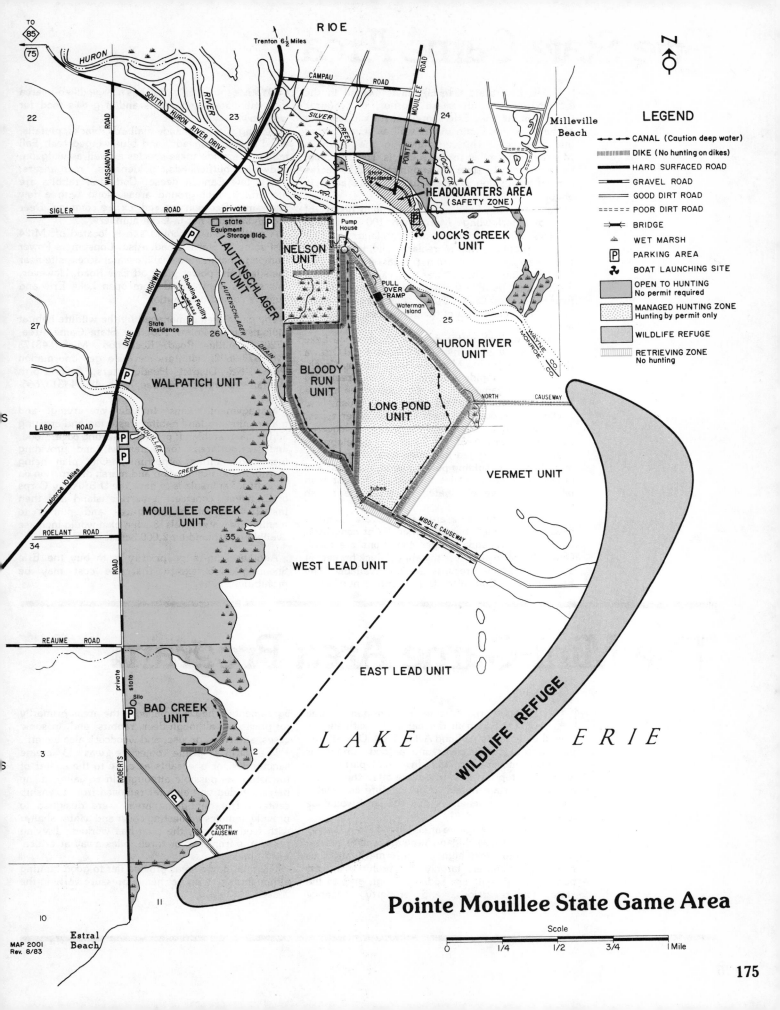

Pointe Mouillee State Game Area

TO 85 75

R 10 E

Trenton 6½ Miles

CAMPAU ROAD

POINTE MOUILLEE ROAD

JOCKS CR

Milleville Beach

N

LEGEND

—◄——► CANAL (Caution deep water)
|||||||||| DIKE (No hunting on dikes)
———— HARD SURFACED ROAD
———— GRAVEL ROAD
———— GOOD DIRT ROAD
====== POOR DIRT ROAD
—⋈— BRIDGE
⋏⋏ WET MARSH
P PARKING AREA
⚓ BOAT LAUNCHING SITE

OPEN TO HUNTING
No permit required

MANAGED HUNTING ZONE
Hunting by permit only

WILDLIFE REFUGE

RETRIEVING ZONE
No hunting

HURON RIVER

SOUTH HURON RIVER DRIVE

SILVER CREEK

22

23

24

WASSANOVA ROAD

SIGLER ROAD   private

state
Equipment Storage Bldg.

Pump House

State Residence

HEADQUARTERS AREA
(SAFETY ZONE)

JOCK'S CREEK UNIT

LAUTENSCHLAGER UNIT

P

NELSON UNIT

PULL OVER RAMP

Waterman Island

DIXIE HIGHWAY

Shooting Facility

State Residence

LAUTENSCHLAGER DRAIN

27

26

HURON RIVER UNIT

25

WAYNE MONROE CO.

WALPATICH UNIT

BLOODY RUN UNIT

LONG POND UNIT

NORTH   CAUSEWAY

LABO ROAD

MOUILLEE CREEK

P
P

VERMET UNIT

Monroe 10 Miles

MOUILLEE CREEK UNIT

tubes

ROELANT ROAD

34

35

MIDDLE CAUSEWAY

WEST LEAD UNIT

REAUME ROAD

EAST LEAD UNIT

private   state

ROBERTS ROAD

P   Silo

BAD CREEK UNIT

2

P

LAKE   ERIE

WILDLIFE REFUGE

SOUTH CAUSEWAY

3

11

10

Estral Beach

MAP 2001
Rev. 8/83

Scale

0   1/4   1/2   3/4   1 Mile

175

Erie State Game Area

THE Erie State Game Area is located in the extreme southeastern corner of Monroe County on the Lake Erie shoreline. It includes most of the Woodtick Peninsula as well as several other inland parcels. Thirteen miles to the north is Monroe; nine miles to the south is Toledo, Ohio. Land currently in state ownership totals 2,100 acres and an acquisition program to add more acres is ongoing.

Marshes along Lake Erie have a long history of superb waterfowling. More than 100 years ago farmers and sportsmen owning land in Erie Township put all their marshland holdings into one preserve to protect it from trespassers. The Bay Point Shooting Club, as it was then called, controlled 4,000 acres. In 1889 the name was changed to the Erie Shooting Club. Today club-owned lands, located north and west of the game area, total 1,800 acres.

Periods of high water destroy marsh since Lake Erie is shallow. In addition, the Maumee and Ottawa rivers discharge into Maumee Bay. Halfway Creek, Morin Creek, Rapideau Drain, and Flat Creek also flow into the game area. Topography of the area is flat with cattails, upland grass and brush, and lowland hardwoods the most common cover types. Although dense forests and marshes once covered the area, clearing of the land for development purposes has changed its appearance. Farm fields and filled lands holding power plants, marinas, and other structures now dot the region. Recent high lake levels have eliminated much of the marsh vegetation.

Still, the state game area and private holdings produce good duck hunting when flight concentrations are down and weather conditions are ideal. One DNR estimate places the annual duck harvest at 1,000, but precise records are not available. The Erie Shooting Club attracts the largest number of birds since the organization has a large diked-in area to manipulate water levels and it grows food for waterfowl.

Nesting species include mallards, blacks, pintails, wood ducks, redheads, and blue-winged teal. Fall migrants include these species as well as widgeon, gadwalls, buffleheads, goldeneyes, mergansers, and a few Canada geese. Cottontail rabbits are plentiful in high-ground areas along with a few pheasants. Raccoon and red fox are common. Deer are present but not in large numbers.

A public boat-launching site is located off M-24 just south of Sterns Road. Also, Consumers Power Company maintains a shallow-water access site near the site of the power plant off Erie Road. However, this site is unprotected from open Lake Erie and hunters should use caution.

The game area is managed by the wildlife habitat biologist from Pointe Mouillee State Game Area, 37205 Mouillee Road, Rockwood, Mich. 48173 (313/379-9692). Hunters can also get information from DNR District Headquarters, 2455 North Williams Lake Road, Pontiac, Mich. 48054 (313/666-1500).

Management plans include preserving and maintaining wetland habitat; restoring and creating additional marshland; providing nesting cover, food, and resting areas for waterfowl; and providing increased hunting opportunity. One plan being considered to stop erosion and marsh destruction on Woodtick Peninsula is to have the U.S. Army Corps of Engineers construct a barrier island and then install water-control structures and pumps to manipulate water levels. Such a plan would increase availble marshland by 2,000 acres.

Another long-range priority is to buy the Erie Shooting Club except that the cost may be prohibitive.

The Mini-Game Area Program

THE southern Michigan mini-game area program began in the early 70s with money from the Recreational Bond Act of 1968. Overall, the plan was to create cover and a food supply for wildlife from bare cropland. In a joint partnership with sharecrop farmers, who were often the former owners, the state hoped to get wildlife cover at a low cost. A side benefit is that the land would be open to hunting.

There are 35 mini-game areas from 40 to 320 acres each in southern Michigan. Although land prices are three and four times higher than formerly and thus new acquisitions are largely cost prohibitive, new parcels occasionally are added through gifts to the state, tax reversions, and property exchange agreements. The DNR manages the areas primarily for pheasants although deer, rabbits, and, in some cases, squirrels, grouse, and woodcock also benefit.

The DNR's prime objective was to create sanctuaries for pheasants as close to the center of townships as possible although, in actuality, many parcels ended up being far removed from township centers. The mini-game areas were designed to provide unmolested nesting cover and winter shelter with food. Overall, the plan has worked, drawing pheasants from two or three miles away at critical need times.

The mini-game areas provide fair to good hunting although they often get heavy pressure early in the season.

Erie State Game Area

Scale

0   1   2 miles

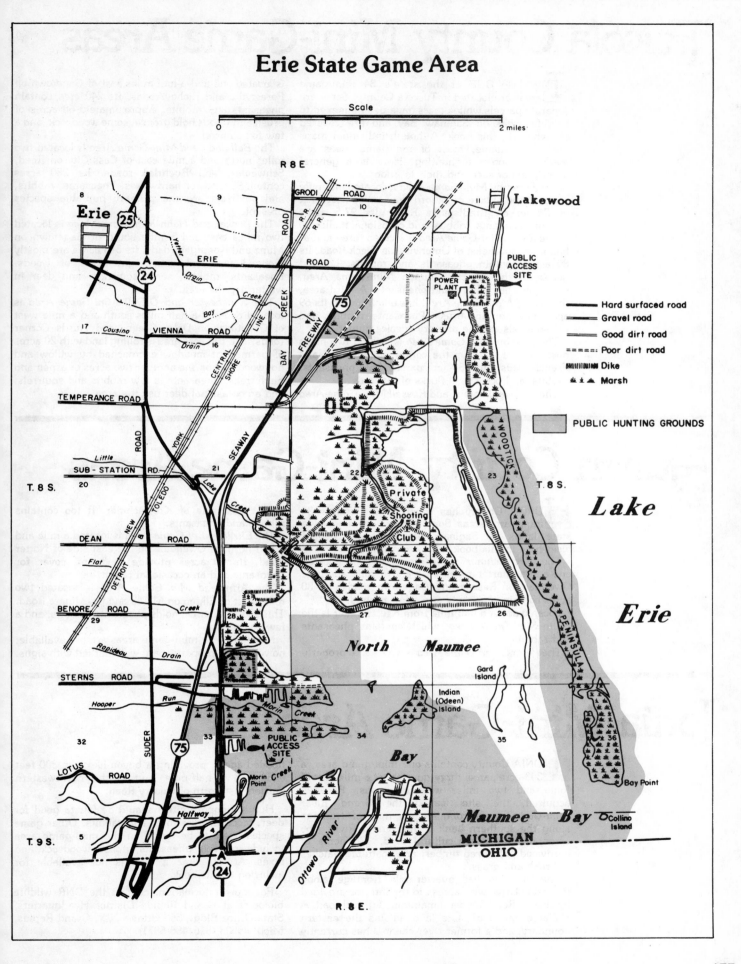

▬▬▬▬	Hard surfaced road
═══	Gravel road
───	Good dirt road
=====	Poor dirt road
▥▥▥	Dike
⚘⚘⚘	Marsh

▨ PUBLIC HUNTING GROUNDS

Tuscola County Mini-Game Areas

TWENTY-ONE of the state's 34 mini-game areas are located in Tuscola County. Some are separate parcels while others have been annexed to wildlife areas on Saginaw Bay and are covered elsewhere in this book. Although individual maps are not available, most of the game areas are marked as open to hunting. Here is a general description of each and their location:

The *Pomeroy Mini-Game Area* is located one mile south of the village of Gilford (four miles northeast of Reese) on Bradleyville Road. Its 97.5 acres contain pheasants, rabbits, and occasional mallards.

The *Rieck Mini-Game Area* is located three-and-a-half miles southeast of Unionville on Rieck Road. Its 80 acres contain pheasants and rabbits. Located nearby is the 52-acre *Lehman Mini-Game Area*, which also has rabbits and pheasants. A third area, the *Scharf Mini-Game Area*, has about half of its 69 acres in aspen and brush. Pheasants, rabbits, and fox squirrels are the primary species hunted.

The *Findlay Mini-Game Area* is located two miles northwest of Caro on the corner of Fairgrove and French roads. Twin 80-acre parcels hold pheasants, rabbits, and occasional flocks of mallards.

The *LaFave, Loomis,* and *Russell Mini-Game Area* is located one-and-a-half miles east of Gagetown on Forestville and Richey roads. Its 240 cres contain pheasants and rabbits. Approximately 68 acres of brush and woods hold grouse, some woodcock, and a few fox squirrels.

The *Bell and Seed Mini-Game Area* is located two miles north and a mile east of Cass City on Reed, Schwegler, and Buehrley roads. Its 280 acres contain 95 acres of hardwoods. Pheasants, rabbits, and squirrels are the primary huntable species present.

The *Becker* and *Hahn Mini-Game Area* is located two miles east and a mile south of Gagetown on Munz and Koepfgen roads. Its 315 acres are mostly cropped farmland with eight acres of woods. Pheasants, rabbits, some squirrels, and deer in winter use the area.

The *Winchester and O'Dell Mini-Game Area* is located two-and-a-half miles south and a mile west of Gagetown on Dale, Green, and Hurds Corner roads. The 190-acre area is rolling land with 20 acres of permanent meadow encroached by willow and dogwood shrubs and another two acres of aspen and birch trees. Pheasants, a few rabbits and squirrels, and an occasional deer use the area.

Huron County Mini-Game Areas

HURON County has seven of the state's 34 mini-game areas. Some of these are annexed to state lands on Saginaw Bay and are covered elsewhere in this book. Five are distinct.

The *Kretzschmer Mini-Game Area* is located one-and-a-quarter miles east and a mile south of Owendale on Rescue and Gagetown roads. Its 80 acres contain pheasants and a few rabbits.

Located about a half mile from Kretzschmer is the *Kelin Mini-Game Area*, which contains pheasants and rabbits.

The *Peters Mini-Game Area* is a 123-acre property on the east side of Kretzschmer. It too contains rabbits and pheasants.

The *Ehrlich Mini-Game Area* is located a mile and a half north of Owendale on the east side of Notter Road. Its 40 acres provide food and cover for pheasants and an occasional rabbit.

The *Armstead Mini-Game Area* is located two miles east of Elkton on M-142 and Grassmere Road. This 130-acre parcel holds pheasants, rabbits, and a few squirrels.

Maps of these mini-game areas are not available; however, the properties are well marked with signs.

Ionia Mini-Game Area

IONIA County contains one mini-game area, a 343-acre parcel three-quarters of a mile east of Ionia and two miles west of Lyons. Recently acquired, the site (called the *Grand River Mini-Game Area*) contains one mile of frontage along the southern bank of the Grand River, 166 acres of tillable agricultural land, 176 acres of hardwood pole-sized timber, and scattered patches of brush and grass.

The property has quarter-mile frontage along Riverside Drive with access to the interior provided by Quarry Road, a poorly maintained gravel road. A 102-acre parcel of state land adjoins the eastern boundary, and a former river channel has currently flooded again, providing a bayou-like lake 300 feet wide and a half-mile long in the northwestern portion just north of Quarry Road.

Hunting opportunities should be fair to good for deer, raccoon, waterfowl, and rabbits. Other game species likely to be found on the mini-game area include squirrels, pheasants, grouse, woodcock, and foxes. At this time a map is not available for inclusion in this book.

For more information, contact the DNR wildlife biologist at Grand Rapids District Headquarters, State Office Bldg., 350 Ottawa NW, Grand Rapids, Mich. 49503 (616/456-5071).

Sanilac County Mini-Game Area

SANILAC County has the *Buskirk Mini-Game Area*, located eight miles southeast of Marlette on Montgomery Road with an unattached parcel between Willis and Stilson roads. The 264-acre mini-game area is mostly woodland and marshland with about 25 acres in sharecropped grains. The parcel contains food and cover for pheasants, rabbits, and squirrels as well as some grouse, woodcock, and deer. Sometimes mallards and wood ducks use drainage ditches.

Although a map of the mini-game area is not available, the property boundaries are well-marked with signs.

Ottawa Mini-Game Area

OTTAWA County has seven parcels of land totaling 427 acres that are singly managed as one mini-game area. They are located in Blendon and Olive townships, about four miles north of Zeeland and one to two miles both west and east of 96th Avenue.

About 60 percent of the parcels consists of old agricultural fields. Wooded areas include small, mixed hardwood stands and conifer plantings. Other cover types include wetland grasses and lowland brush. About 80 acres are designated cropland, which is being farmed on a sharecrop agreement with local farmers.

Hunting for pheasants, rabbits, a few squirrels, woodcock, and grouse is very intense, especially early in the season. Hunting pressure tends to disseminate game to nearby private properties. Later in the season opportunities improve. Although a map is not available, property boundaries are marked with signs.

St. Clair Mini-Game Area

ST. Clair County has the 90-acre *St. Clair County Mini-Game Area*. It is located two miles northwest of the city of St. Clair and is bounded by Kennedy and Vine roads. The sharecropped area contains pheasants and rabbits along with an occasional woodcock, grouse, and deer. Although a map is not availble, the public land is marked with signs.

Livingston Mini-Game Area

LIVINGSTON County is the site of the 253-acre *Hill Crest Mini-Game Area* located two miles west and a mile south of Howell on Crofoot and Cedar Lake roads. The Cedar River flows through it. Since this property has only recently been transferred to the DNR Wildlife Division from the State Mental Health Department, a management plan is just now being formulated. Deer- and grouse-hunting opportunities are currently fairly good; and rabbit, pheasant, and squirrel hunters should benefit over the next several years as well. The game area is nearly all wooded with oaks and conifers predominating. A large marsh area has some duck-hunting possibilities.

Hillsdale Mini-Game Area

HILLSDALE County has the *Adams Township Mini-Game Area*, which recently came into state ownership. Location of the 180-acre tract is eight miles northeast of Hillsdale in the central portion of the county. The level, well-drained parcel is composed of 110 acres of agricultural croplands; 33 acres of forestland containing second-growth hickory, maple, cherry, and beech; with the rest holding upland brush, sedge meadows, and some grassland. Access is provided by Holcomb and Mauck roads, both county-maintained gravel roads.

The game area has pheasants, rabbits, squirrels, and deer. Although a map is not available, the property is marked by boundary signs.

Oakland Mini-Game Area

OAKLAND County has the *Davisburg Trout Pond Mini-Game Area,* located a mile east of Davisburg. It is bounded by Davisburg and Dilley roads. The 109-acre parcel features rolling terrain that is 60 percent marshland and lowland brush, 23 percent upland grass and brush, and 17 percent central hardwoods. The area is popular with local and migrant waterfowl, most notably mallards, wood ducks, blue-winged teal, ring-necked ducks, and Canada geese.

In addition to ducks and geese, the area contains rabbits and squirrels. Although the parcel has been in state ownership since 1948, it has only recently been declared a mini-game area under DNR Wildlife Division responsibility. Prime management for wildlife has thus become only a recent concern. Although limited in size, the area has the potential to offer good to excellent sport for a small number of hunters. Although a map is not available, the public property is well marked with signs.

Van Buren Mini-Game Areas

VAN Buren County has three mini-game areas totaling 410 acres. One is located two-and-a-half miles south of I-94 on 64th Street in *Keeler Township.* Another is two miles farther to the southwest at 68th and 84th streets. The first area contains upland grass and brush, cultivated fields, and lowland forest and brush. The second area features stands of hardwood forest along with an old orchard and grasslands, cultivated fields, upland grass and brush, aspen, marshland, and lowland forest and brush.

A third parcel is called the *Kinney Waterfowl Production Area.* It is located in Porter Township, four miles southeast of Lawton with access provided from the end of 20th Street. The area is managed for ducks, a few of which—namely mallards, some teal, and ringneck ducks—nest here. (The ringneck's southernmost nesting grounds in Michigan previously were thought to be in the Upper Peninsula.) Passage birds also use the area, which features several lakes.

The mini-game areas provide food and cover for pheasants, squirrels, rabbits, raccoon, ruffed grouse, woodcock, deer, and a few ducks. Hunting pressure is heavy. Although maps are not availble, the public lands are well marked with signs.

Metamora-Hadley Recreation Area

METAMORA-HADLEY Recreation Area is located in Lapeer County two miles west of the village of Metamora. Nearly 500 of its 683 acres are open to hunting for those driving vehicles with current state park stickers. Day-long or seasonal permits are available from area headquarters at 3871 Hurd Road, Metamora, Mich. 48455 (313/797-4439), or from any other DNR office.

Topography is mostly rolling hills, underlain by morainic gravel deposits and covered by dense stands of mature oaks. The area falls into what is locally called the Hadley Hills. Deer are plentiful and the recreation area gets fairly high pressure during the firearm season (shotguns only) and on weekends during bow season.

Metamora-Hadley Recreation Area centers around Lake Winnewanna, which gets occasional visitation by migrant ducks and Canada geese to offer some hunting opportunities. Restricted areas that are off-limits to hunting are marked as such with signs. The area is popular with squirrel and rabbit hunters. A few raccoon, an occasional red fox, and very limited numbers of pheasants frequent the area. Early successional stages of brush and second-growth timber produce some ruffed grouse and woodcock, the latter especially during the peak of the migrating season, usually in late October.

Wildlife species are managed by DNR District Office, 2455 North Williams Lake Road, Pontiac, Mich. 48054 (313/666-1500).

Ionia Recreation Area

ALL 3,977 acres of the Ionia Recreation Area, located in central Ionia County southwest of Ionia, are open to hunting. Hunters entering with vehicles, however, must have a current state parks vehicle sticker. Day-long and seasonal permits are available at any DNR office or at the Ionia Recreation Area itself, 2132 West Riverside Drive, Ionia, Mich. 48846 (616/527-3750).

Metamora-Hadley Recreation Area

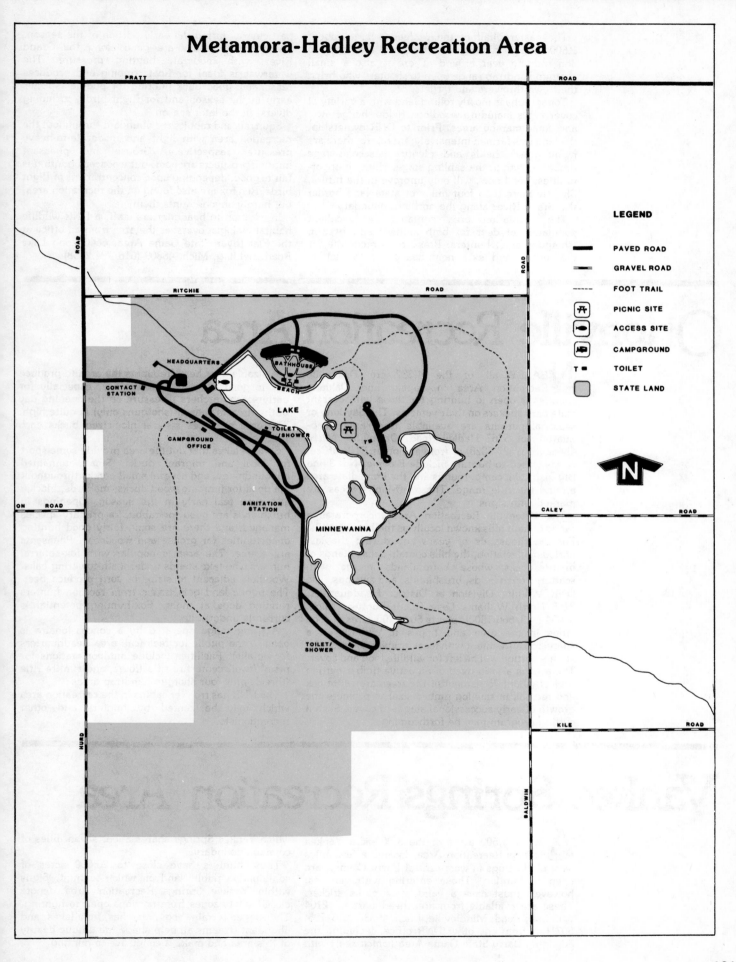

LEGEND

▬▬▬ PAVED ROAD

══ GRAVEL ROAD

---- FOOT TRAIL

⊞ PICNIC SITE

🐟 ACCESS SITE

🚐 CAMPGROUND

T ■ TOILET

▨ STATE LAND

N

PRATT ROAD

RITCHIE ROAD

HEADQUARTERS

CONTACT STATION

BATHHOUSE

BEACH

LAKE

TOILET/SHOWER

CAMPGROUND OFFICE

MINNEWANNA

SANITATION STATION

TOILET/SHOWER

ON ROAD

CALEY ROAD

KILE ROAD

HURD

BALDWIN

ROAD

The eastern half of the recreation area, about 1,500 acres, is a designated field-trial area open to dog training year around. There is also a small shotgun handtrap range open to shooters who bring their own throwers and targets.

Topography is mostly rolling land with a variety of cover types including woodlots, fields, hedgerows, and some marshy areas. Prior to DNR ownership, the land was farmed intensively; therefore, there are many grassy fields and plenty of second-stage timber growth in the sapling stage. Hunting opportunities, good now, will only improve in the future. Slightly more than four miles of state land border the Grand River along the northern boundary.

The recreation area contains an excellent population of deer for both archery and firearm (shotguns only) hunters. Pressure is moderate for the former and extremely heavy for the latter,

particularly during the early portion of the season. Raccoon populations are good along the Grand River, with moderate hunting pressure. The waterway is ideal for float tripping and produces reasonably good duck hunting for puddler species early in the season and for flight birds, including divers, in the later season.

Squirrels and rabbits are abundant throughout the recreation area with light and moderate-to-heavy pressure, respectively. Grouse and pheasant hunting prospects are poor, but woodcock hunting is fair to good, depending upon concentrations of flight birds. Red fox are also found on the recreation area, but hardly anyone hunts them.

In addition to headquarters staff, a DNR wildlife habitat biologist oversees the area from an office at the Flat River State Game Area, 6640 Long Lake Road, Belding, Mich. 48809 (616/794-2658).

Ortonville Recreation Area

NEARLY all of the 4,232-acre Ortonville Recreation Area in Lapeer and Oakland counties is open to hunting for those with current state park stickers on their vehicles. The day-long or seasonal permits are available from area headquarters at 5767 Hadley Road, Ortonville, Mich. 48462 (313/627-3828) or from any other DNR office. Areas closed to hunting include Bloomer No. 3 and Big Fish Lake campgrounds and the immediate area around the rifle range. These off-limits areas are marked with signs.

The Ortonville Recreation Area incorporates a range of high hills known locally as the Hadley Hills. Formed thousands of years ago during the last period of glaciation, the hills contain dense stands of mature oaks whose bottomlands merge with scattered open fields, brushlands, and swamps. The DNR Wildlife Division at District Headquarters, 2455 North Williams Lake Road, Pontiac, Mich. 48054 (313/666-1500), plants 50 to 100 acres of food crops in the area and hopes to embark on a sharecrop agreement with local farmers whereby the state's portion will be left for wildlife food and cover. The area is also in need of an active timber-cutting project (about 75 percent of the trees are white oak and red oak in saw-log timber size) to promote the growth of early successional stages of cover. Such a cutting program may be forthcoming.

A sizable deer herd frequents the area to produce fair to good hunting opportunities, especially for early-season archers. Pressure on the opening day of the firearm season (shotguns only) is quite high. The area produces several nice-sized bucks each fall.

Sixteen lakes that dot the area provide some sport for local and migrant ducks. Small, unnamed impoundments and several small creeks throughout are good for jumping wood ducks, mallards, blacks, and even teal early in the season. Openings in brushlands are good for rabbits, a primary species managed, and there are some fairly good hunting opportunities for grouse and woodcock. Pheasants are scarce. The area is popular with fox-squirrel hunters who take stands underneath towering oaks. Woodlots adjacent to strips of corn produce best. The public land gets traffic from raccoon hunters running dogs at night. Fox-hunting potential is currently underutilized.

A firing range operated by a concessionaire is open to the public for fees (call area headquarters for details). Facilities include outdoor stations for pistol (two), centerfire rifle (four), and rimfire rifle (three), plus four shotgun handtrap areas.

The DNR has frontier cabins in the recreation area which may be rented by hunters and other recreationists.

Yankee Springs Recreation Area

ABOUT 3,500 acres of the 5,000-acre Yankee Springs Recreation Area, located a few miles west of Hastings in west-central Barry County, are open to hunting. Those entering with vehicles, however, must have a valid state parks sticker. These are available from area headquarters, 2104 Gun Lake Road, Middleville, Mich. 49333 (616/795-5071) or from any other DNR office, including the adjoining Barry State Game Area (*which see*), with

which Yankee Springs shares about seven miles of common boundary.

Thus, hunters have close to 20,000 acres of combination public land on which to hunt. Signs within Yankee Springs Recreation Area denote closed safety zones from portions open to hunting. The rugged terrain, bogs, marshes, nine lakes, and abundant streams all help shape the unique beauty of this area and make it conducive to hunting.

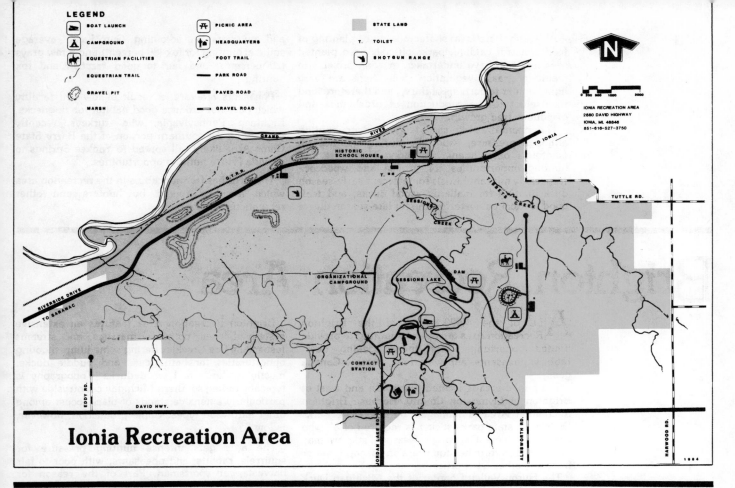

LEGEND

- 🛥 BOAT LAUNCH
- ⛺ CAMPGROUND
- 🐎 EQUESTRIAN FACILITIES
- EQUESTRIAN TRAIL
- GRAVEL PIT
- MARSH
- 🏕 PICNIC AREA
- HEADQUARTERS
- FOOT TRAIL
- PARK ROAD
- PAVED ROAD
- GRAVEL ROAD
- STATE LAND
- T. TOILET
- SHOTGUN RANGE

N

IONIA RECREATION AREA
2880 DAVID HIGHWAY
IONIA, MI 48846
851-616-527-3750

Ionia Recreation Area

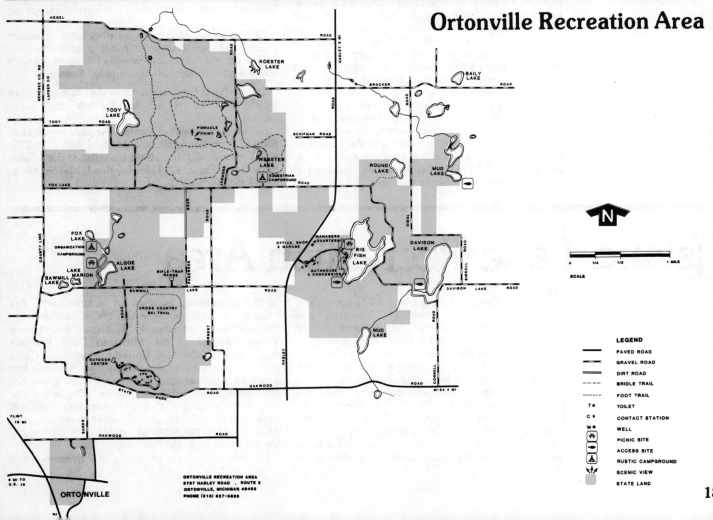

Ortonville Recreation Area

N

SCALE

LEGEND

- PAVED ROAD
- GRAVEL ROAD
- DIRT ROAD
- BRIDLE TRAIL
- FOOT TRAIL
- T = TOILET
- C = CONTACT STATION
- W ● WELL
- 🏕 PICNIC SITE
- ACCESS SITE
- ⛺ RUSTIC CAMPGROUND
- SCENIC VIEW
- STATE LAND

ORTONVILLE RECREATION AREA
5767 HADLEY ROAD , ROUTE 2
ORTONVILLE, MICHIGAN 48462
PHONE (313) 627-3828

183

Although there is no sharecropping or planting of food plots for wildlife, parks officials have planted seedlings and have undertaken mowing projects to maintain grassy vegetation. Soils here are very light, similar to portions of Barry, and therefore lend themselves to the production of brushlands and deciduous tree growth.

The main drawing card is good deer hunting although pressure, especially during the firearm (shotguns only) opener, is high. There are fair hunting opportunities for grouse and woodcock (especially migrant birds); some decent early-season duck hunting for mallards, wood ducks, and teal; good to excellent waterfowling for late-season divers and puddlers on adjoining Gun Lake; average squirrel hunting for fox (80 percent) and a few grays (20 percent); and fair to good raccoon and fox hunting.

Pheasants are rare, a result of low soil fertility which does not produce good habitat for ringnecks. Eighteen Pennsylvania wild turkeys recently released in the southern portion of the Barry State Game Area likely will spread to Yankee Springs to provide future hunting opportunities.

The DNR has frontier cabins in the recreation area which may be rented by hunters and other recreationists.

Brighton Recreation Area

ALL of the 4,900 acres of the Brighton Recreation Area are open to hunting to provide limited opportunities for those seeking deer, rabbits, pheasants, and waterfowl, notably Canada geese.

The public area is located just south and west of Brighton in Livingston County. Because Brighton Recreation Area is managed by the DNR Parks Division, a state parks sticker is required of all who enter via vehicle. Day-long or seasonal stickers may be purchased from headquarters on Bishop Road or from any other DNR office.

The Huron Valley Chapter of the Michigan Duck Hunters Association, a Michigan United Conservation Clubs affiliate, has annually planted food patches of five acres each to attract area geese. In an agreement with the DNR Wildlife Division, the sportsman's group supplied equipment and labor needed to plant DNR-donated corn, fertilizer, and herbicide. These efforts have resulted in improved hunting opportunities.

Nuisance giant Canada geese frequent this region of southern Michigan and provide late-season sport during a special extended season. In winter the geese typically roost on Ore Lake and then disperse twice daily over the recreation area in search of food. Incidentally, the DNR recently signed a sharecrop agreement with a farmer in this area.

Brighton Recreation Area features an extensive system of lakes, potholes, marshes, and streams (especially Ore Creek), offering some jump-shooting opportunities for both geese and puddle ducks, mostly mallards and wood ducks. Topography is typically rolling southern Michigan countryside with particularly extensive stands of black locust among other hardwood types. Game production, however, is low.

The area gets intense hunting pressure for squirrels, rabbits, and pheasants, with poor to fair harvests per sportsman. Part of the reason for crowding is because Livingston County is closed to Sunday hunting with dogs or firearms except on state lands.

DNR releases of pen-reared pheasants in recent years have contributed to hunting opportunities. Deer frequent the area to provide fair sport for both archers and firearm (shotguns only) hunters.

The DNR has frontier cabins in the recreation area which may be rented by hunters and other recreationists.

For more information, contact the park manager at 6360 Chilson Road, Howell, Mich. 48843 (313/229-6566), or the wildlife habitat biologist at the Mason State Game Farm, 1219 Hawley Road, Mason, Mich. 48854 (517/676-4600).

Island Lake Recreation Area

ALL but about 130 acres of the 3,724-acre Island Lake Recreation Area in Livingston and Oakland counties, just east of Brighton and south of I-96, is open to hunting for those driving vehicles with current state park stickers. Day-long or seasonal permits are available at recreation area headquarters or from any other DNR office.

Much of the public land is reclaimed farm pastures with a mixture of grasslands, brushlands, and forests, and includes lowland hardwoods along the Huron River which meanders throughout.

Kent Lake is a roosting/staging area for a huge flock of giant Canada geese. That lake portion south of the expressway is open to hunting, with the balance closed because it falls within the Huron-Clinton Metropark System. The Huron Valley Chapter of the Michigan Duck Hunters Association, a Michigan United Conservation Clubs affiliate, planted corn donated by the DNR for a few years as a goose attraction, but the club has not continued that service recently. There is no sharecrop farming at this time, nor does the DNR grow food for wildlife. One objective, however, is to develop sharecrop farming agreements on the old Gauge Farm on south Kensington Road.

In spite of the lack of food plots, goose-hunting

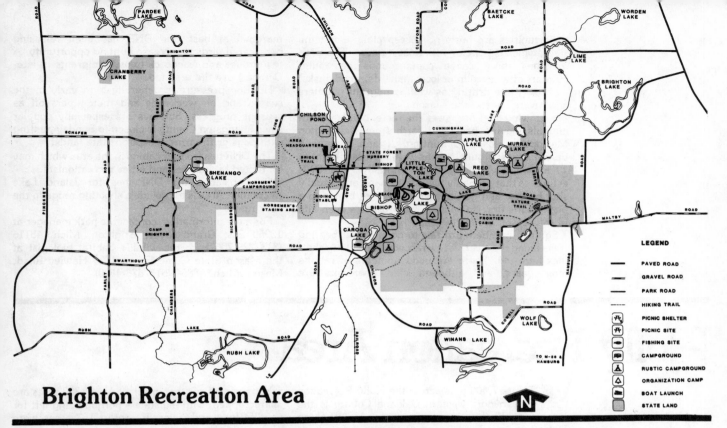

Brighton Recreation Area

LEGEND

———	PAVED ROAD
– – –	GRAVEL ROAD
········	PARK ROAD
- - - -	HIKING TRAIL
🏕	PICNIC SHELTER
🏕	PICNIC SITE
	FISHING SITE
	CAMPGROUND
🏕	RUSTIC CAMPGROUND
🏕	ORGANIZATION CAMP
	BOAT LAUNCH
▓	STATE LAND

N

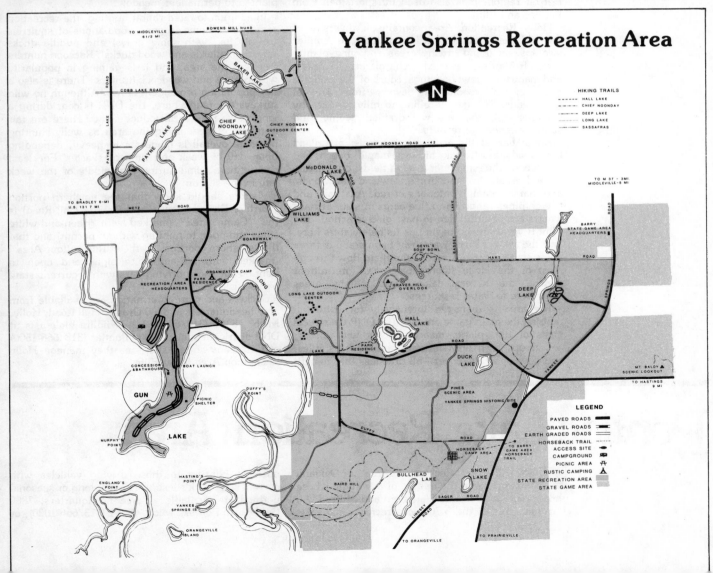

Yankee Springs Recreation Area

N

HIKING TRAILS

-·-·-·	HALL LAKE
-··-··-	CHIEF NOONDAY
-o-o-o-	DEEP LAKE
-···-···	LONG LAKE
·······	SASSAFRAS

LEGEND

━━━	PAVED ROADS
▬▬▬	GRAVEL ROADS
════	EARTH GRADED ROADS
	HORSEBACK TRAIL
	ACCESS SITE
	CAMPGROUND
🏕	PICNIC AREA
🏕	RUSTIC CAMPING
▓	STATE RECREATION AREA
▒	STATE GAME AREA

185

opportunities are fairly good, especially along the river, which is popular with float hunters. The DNR manages three canoe campgrounds en route. Hunters often encounter local mallards, wood ducks, and teal while drifting as well as migrant puddlers and divers later in the season.

A growing deer herd uses the recreation area with animals moving back and forth from Kensington Metropark (closed to hunting). Island Lake is a bucks-only (shotguns-only as well) area with eight to 10 known deer being taken annually. The DNR estimates that probably twice that many are actually shot by bow and gun hunters. Pressure builds to a peak on the firearm opener, but prospects even late in the season are fairly good.

Squirrel numbers are fair to good in nut-bearing trees along the river. A few raccoon hunters try their luck here too. There are good numbers of rabbits most years, and although wild pheasants are marginal at best, the DNR has been releasing pen-reared birds to increase hunting opportunity. A few grouse and woodcock (mostly migrants in late-October) use the area too.

Hunting pressure is generally high early in the season and on weekends and then tapers off as seasons progress. Sundays are especially popular since Livingston County is closed to Sunday hunting with dogs or firearms except on state lands.

The DNR has frontier cabins in the area which may be rented by hunters and other recreationists.

One objective the DNR has for Island Lake Recreation Area is to provide a shooting range in the near future.

For more information, contact the park manager at 12950 East Grand River, Brighton, Mich. 48116 (313/229-7067), or the wildlife habitat biologist at the Mason State Game Farm, 1219 Hawley Road, Mason, Mich. 48854 (517/676-4600).

Holly Recreation Area

WITH its 7,400-plus acres, the Holly Recreation Area in northwestern Oakland County is the largest public hunting area in the metropolitan Detroit region. It is also used by sportsmen from Pontiac and Flint.

Holly Recreation Area contains a diversity of habitat from rolling hardwood hills to conifer swamps, including brushy areas and pine plantations. It features reverted orchardlands, 17 lakes, and many waterfowl floodings. Much of the land has been left in woodlot or pasture from original farmsteads. The gently-rolling to hilly topography contains soils that are well-drained, loamy, and sandy of moderate fertility.

About half of the cover types consist of upland hardwoods, mostly oak, hickory, maple, beech, and basswood. The remainder is open fields, crop fields, upland brush, lowland brush, lowland hardwoods, and marsh. Small plantations of red, Austrian, and Scotch pines range up to five acres in size. Surface waters are plentiful due to past glacier action. The Flint River drainage basin has its headwaters here, and the Huron River waterway begins about three miles south. Thread Creek is the main flow through most of the Holly Recreation Area. Intermittent creeks, the several lakes, and marshy areas contribute to water resources.

The area is managed intensively for cottontail rabbits, the main game animal. The DNR constructs nests of tile, plants meadow areas with clover, sharecrops with area farmers, builds brushpiles, and develops edge cover—all practices that benefit rabbits as well as other species. About 300 acres are sharecropped, with the state's portion being left for wildlife food and cover. Recently, 153 acres were planted to permanent meadow.

In addition to rated rabbit hunting, the recreation area is also home to good populations of squirrels (mostly fox, with some grays) and puddle ducks (mostly mallards and wood ducks). Raccoon hunters frequent the area, and it is gaining in popularity with grouse and woodcock hunters. There is also a fair population of resident crows. Although no wild turkeys are found here, the DNR is considering a long-range plan to introduce some. There are fair numbers of deer using the area as well. Hunting pressure overall is moderate to heavy, depending upon day of week and time of season. For least competition, come during the middle of the week late in the season.

Visitors should know that the northern portion (north of Dixie Highway and Grange Hall Road) is the "Game Area" (marked with green-and-white signs and open to hunting without permit) and that the southern portion is the "Recreation Area" (marked with red-and-white signs and open to hunting for those driving cars with a current state parks sticker).

Stickers and more information are available from area headquarters at 8100 Grange Hall Road, Holly, Mich. 48442 (313/634-8811). Wildlife biologists at DNR district headquarters in Pontiac (313/666-1500) can also answer questions as they manage Holly Recreation Area for wildlife.

Pontiac Lake Recreation Area

PONTIAC Lake Recreation Area in Oakland County falls in the middle of a triangle whose three points are Pontiac, Clarkston, and Milford. All but 406 acres of the 3,708-acre recreation area is open to hunting to those driving vehicles with current state park stickers. The day-long or seasonal permits are available at area headquarters, 7800 Gale Road, Pontiac, Mich. 48054 (313/666-1020), or

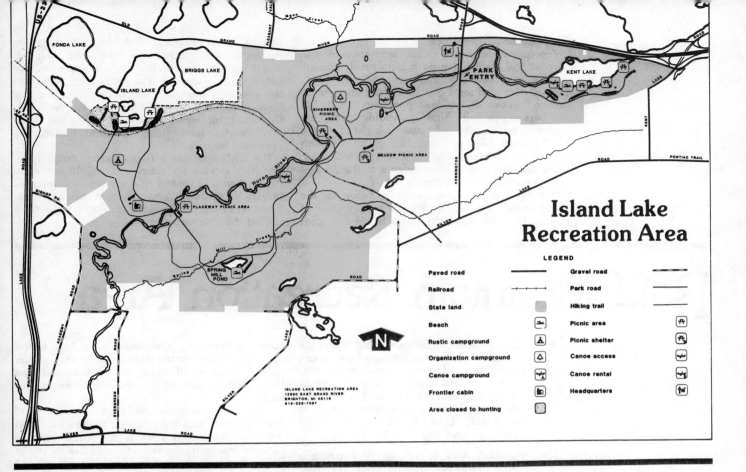

Island Lake Recreation Area

LEGEND

Paved road		Gravel road	
Railroad		Park road	
State land		Hiking trail	
Beach		Picnic area	
Rustic campground		Picnic shelter	
Organization campground		Canoe access	
Canoe campground		Canoe rental	
Frontier cabin		Headquarters	
Area closed to hunting			

ISLAND LAKE RECREATION AREA
12950 EAST GRAND RIVER
BRIGHTON, MI 48116
313-229-7067

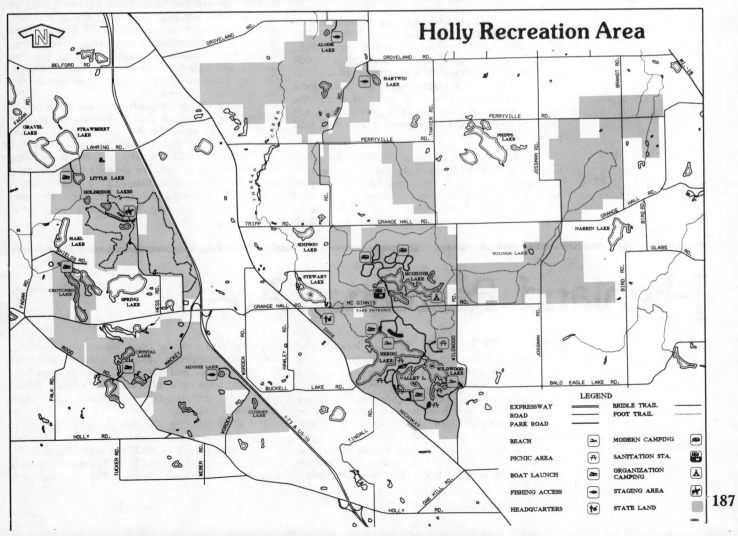

Holly Recreation Area

LEGEND

EXPRESSWAY		BRIDLE TRAIL	
ROAD		FOOT TRAIL	
PARK ROAD			
BEACH		MODERN CAMPING	
PICNIC AREA		SANITATION STA.	
BOAT LAUNCH		ORGANIZATION CAMPING	
FISHING ACCESS		STAGING AREA	
HEADQUARTERS		STATE LAND	

from any other DNR office.

Topography is largely rolling land covered with successional stages of growth from brush through mature oak. Lowland drainages hold woodcock, rabbits, deer, and some grouse. Upland areas house grouse, woodcock, a few pheasants, and fair numbers of squirrels. Although wildlife species are managed by the wildlife habitat biologist at nearby DNR District Headquarters, 2455 North Williams Lake Road, Pontiac, Mich. 48054 (313/666-1500), there are no sharecrop agreements at the present and no state-planted food plots.

Hunting pressure is moderate to heavy for the above-named species. Perhaps the biggest draw of Pontiac Lake Recreation Area for hunters is giant Canada geese hunting and duck hunting for mallards, wood ducks, teal, and some migrant divers such as scaup, ring-necked ducks, buffleheads, and goldeneyes. The entire area is open to late-season Canada goose hunting, and a fair number of birds generally stage on Pontiac Lake. Dispersing birds can be pass-shot or talked down into nearby feed fields (privately-owned) by persistent hunters.

The DNR operates a free shooting range here. Facilities include six pistol stations, 12 centerfire rifle stations, 18 rimfire rifle stations, four archery targets (all outdoors), and a shotgun handtrap area. Shooting instruction is featured. For more details, contact the area manager.

Bald Mountain Recreation Area

NEARLY all of the 4,580-acre Bald Mountain Recreation Area, located between Pontiac and Lake Orion in Oakland County, is open to hunting. Hunters, however, must have a current state parks sticker to enter with vehicles. Day-long or seasonal permits are available from area headquarters at 1350 Greenshield, Lake Orion, Mich. 48035 (313/693-6767), or from any other DNR office.

The recreation area is rolling land partially forested with hardwood species and featuring scattered openings throughout. Game species available include deer, squirrel, rabbits, pheasants, grouse, woodcock, ducks, and geese. DNR Wildlife Division personnel at Pontiac District Office (2455 North Williams Lake Road, Pontiac, Mich. 48054 [313] 66-1500]) oversee the management of wildlife. One key practice is sharecrop agreements with local farmers to produce about 500 acres of crops, the state's portion of which is left to provide food and cover. In addition, the state grows a few small food plots.

The area has tremendous potential for giant Canada goose hunting since the Lake Orion area is one hotbed of nuisance problems. Lake Orion itself as well as numerous lakes throughout Oakland County get heavy traffic from the birds. When flocks disperse to feed and loaf on recreation-area lakes, goose hunters take advantage. As a bonus, the entire area falls into the boundaries for late-season sport. Further, small impoundments as well as area lakes produce both decoy- and jump-shooting for ducks.

Open fields west of M-24 provide an ideal demonstration area for pheasant restoration. Bald Mountain Recreation Area is the former site of put-take pheasant releases, and in all likelihood the DNR will continue to operate some type of farm-bred bird release program here. There are some quail on state land too, although there has been no southern Michigan bobwhite season since 1977. Fox squirrels are reasonably abundant in mature oaks next to crop fields. Brushlands and woods openings produce rabbits, and a sizable deer herd frequents the area. Grouse and woodcock utilize brushlands and second-growth timberlands.

Hunting pressure ranges from moderate to heavy.

The state leases its public shooting range to a concessionaire who operates it for fees. Facilities include 20 outdoor stations each for pistol, centerfire and rimfire rifle, 12 archery targets, and three fields each for skeet and trap. For fee schedule, operating times, and other information, call the area manager.

The DNR has frontier cabins in the recreation area which may be rented by hunters and other recreationists.

Highland Recreation Area

HIGHLAND Recreation Area is located just north of Milford in Oakland County. About 60 percent (4,017 acres) of its 5,552 acres is open to hunting for sportsmen driving vehicles with day-long or seasonal state park stickers. These are available from area headquarters at 5200 East Highland Road, Milford, Mich. 48042 (313/887-5135), or from any other DNR office.

Topography is largely rolling ridges containing morainic gravel deposits and covered by mature oaks and black-locust trees. Portions are heavily timbered and provide good fox-squirrel hunting. Brushy areas throughout hold huntable populations of ruffed grouse and woodcock, and openings here and along edge cover of open fields support fair to good numbers of rabbits. Deer are found throughout the area in moderate numbers.

The DNR Wildlife Division through its Pontiac office (2455 North Williams Lake Road, Pontiac, Mich. 48054 [313/666-1500]) manages the area for wildlife. Practices include 50 to 100 acres annually sharecropped with area farmers. The state's share is

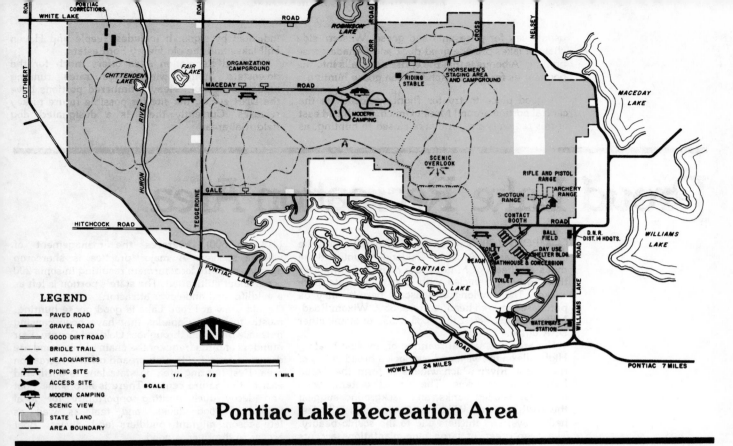

Pontiac Lake Recreation Area

LEGEND

— PAVED ROAD
— GRAVEL ROAD
— GOOD DIRT ROAD
- - - BRIDLE TRAIL
↑ HEADQUARTERS
🏕 PICNIC SITE
🐟 ACCESS SITE
MODERN CAMPING
SCENIC VIEW
STATE LAND
- - AREA BOUNDARY

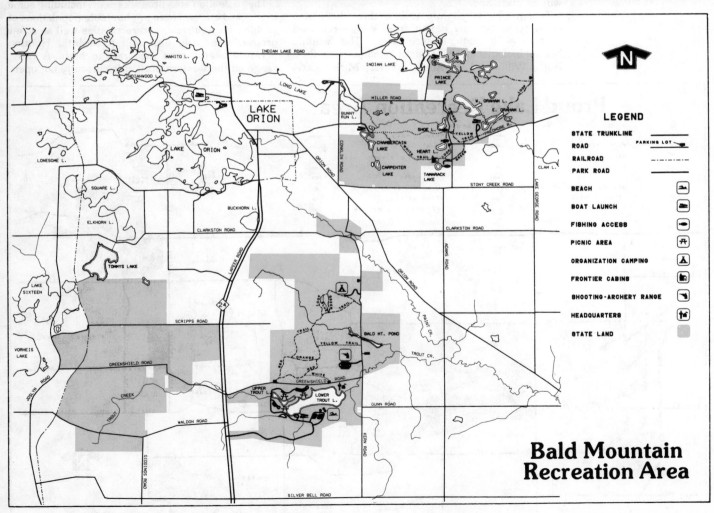

Bald Mountain Recreation Area

LEGEND

STATE TRUNKLINE
ROAD   PARKING LOT
RAILROAD
PARK ROAD
BEACH
BOAT LAUNCH
FISHING ACCESS
PICNIC AREA
ORGANIZATION CAMPING
FRONTIER CABINS
SHOOTING-ARCHERY RANGE
HEADQUARTERS
STATE LAND

usually left for pheasants and geese. Western-side chain of lakes provide good duck and Canada goose hunting. A bonus is that the entire area falls into the boundaries for late-season Canada goose hunting.

A good place to try for flight woodcock is the central portion around Mount Omich. North and east of this region is a natural area closed to hunting, as indicated by signs. It includes Teeple and Haven Hill lakes and the old Henry Ford estate.

Highland Recreation Area offers much for the downstate hunter with usage rates running moderate to high. Heavily-timbered portions have the DNR eyeing the site for possible future turkey releases. Currently there is a designated dog field-trial area.

Proud Lake Recreation Area

ABOUT 2,300 acres of the 3,727-acre Proud Lake Recreation Area in Oakland County, three miles southeast of Milford, are open to hunting for those driving vehicles with a current state park sticker. The day-long or seasonal permits may be purchased at area headquarters, 3500 Wixom Road, Milford, Mich. 48042 (313/685-2433), or at any other DNR office.

The area has natural features of unusual beauty. High hills on the west end overlook a broad valley of the Huron River which widens to form the Proud Lake chain of lakes. The varied waters, wide marshes, wooded banks, and background suggest the north country. Wild meadows, rough hillsides, hedgerows, and thickets add to the scenic beauty. The deep green of large pine plantations accents winter landscape.

Topography is slightly rolling throughout and cover types run the gamut from early brushland succession through mature oaks. The wildlife habitat biologist at DNR District Headquarters, 2455 North Williams Lake Road, Pontiac, Mich. 48054 (313/666-1500), oversees the management of wildlife species. A major practice is sharecrop agreements with local farmers resulting in some 200 acres under cultivation. The state's portion is left as a wildlife food and cover attractor.

Main draw at Proud Lake is good goose hunting, mostly for giant Canadas that have been causing nuisance problems throughout Oakland County. Fair numbers of birds frequent the chain of lakes and are drawn to farm fields both on and off the recreation area. Best hunting area on state land is north and east of the nature center. There is also some float and decoy duck hunting opportunity for local mallards, wood ducks, and teal as well as late-season migrant puddlers and divers. Boat access to the river is good.

The recreation area produces deer, including some big-racked bucks. There are huntable populations of rabbits, fox squirrels, and raccoon as well as a few grouse, woodcock, and wild pheasants. Hunting pressure overall runs moderate to high. A firing range on the western portion is currently not open.

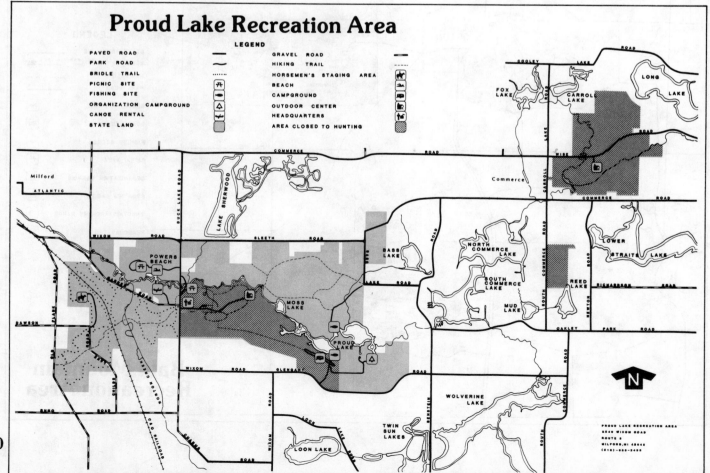

Highland Recreation Area

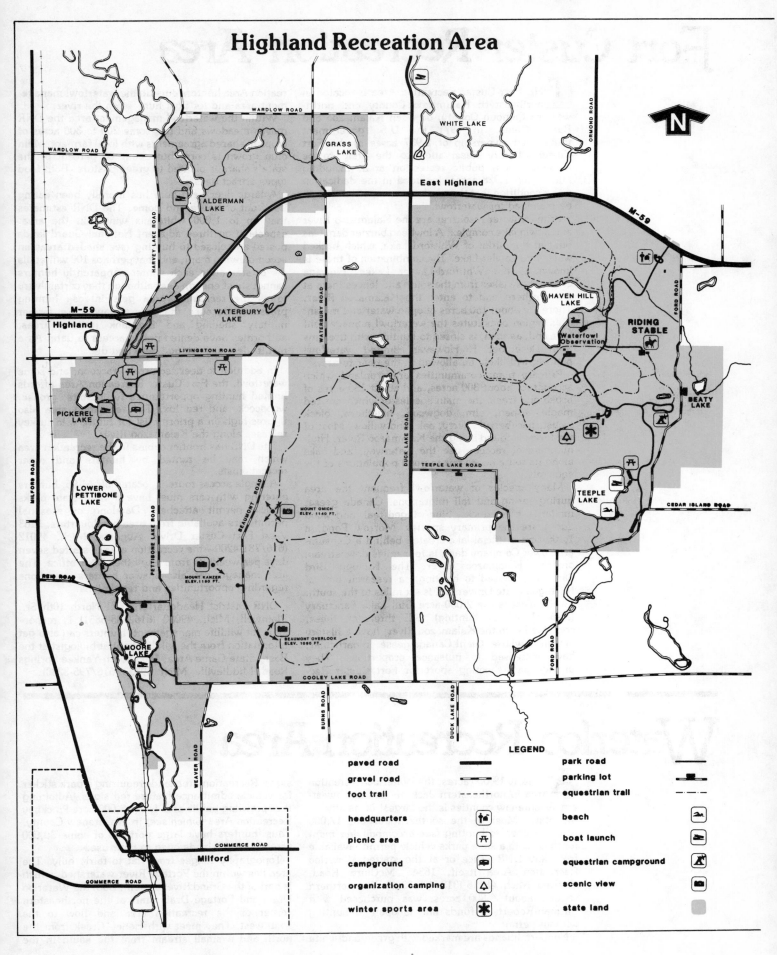

WARDLOW ROAD

WHITE LAKE

GRASS LAKE

East Highland

M-59

WARDLOW ROAD

ALDERMAN LAKE

HARVEY LAKE ROAD

WATERBURY LAKE

M-59

Highland

WATERBURY ROAD

LIVINGSTON ROAD

HAVEN HILL LAKE

Waterfowl Observation

RIDING STABLE

BEATY LAKE

PICKEREL LAKE

DUCK LAKE ROAD

LOWER PETTIBONE LAKE

PETTIBONE LAKE ROAD

TEEPLE LAKE ROAD

TEEPLE LAKE

CEDAR ISLAND ROAD

MILFORD ROAD

MOUNT OMICH ELEV. 1140 FT.

BEAUMONT ROAD

MOUNT KANZER ELEV. 1160 FT.

FORD ROAD

REHD ROAD

MOORE LAKE

BEAUMONT OVERLOOK ELEV. 1080 FT.

WEAVER ROAD

COOLEY LAKE ROAD

BURNS ROAD

DUCK LAKE ROAD

FORD ROAD

ORMOND ROAD

COMMERCE ROAD

Milford

COMMERCE ROAD

LEGEND

paved road	park road	
gravel road	parking lot	
foot trail	equestrian trail	
headquarters	beach	
picnic area	boat launch	
campground	equestrian campground	
organization camping	scenic view	
winter sports area	state land	

Fort Custer Recreation Area

THE Fort Custer Recreation Area is located in northeastern Kalamazoo County and northwestern Calhoun County, between Kalamazoo and Battle Creek. In 1971 the U.S. government transferred ownership of 2,937 acres of the Fort Custer Military Reservation to the state to be managed as a public recreation area, including hunting on 1,928 acres. Included in the dedication was a condition that the southwestern portion was to be managed for waterfowl.

Primary water resources are the Kalamazoo River and a twin lake complex. A lowhead barrier dam was built at the outlet of Whitford Lake, which backed water into Lawler Lake. The combination of these is known as the Whitford-Lawler Lakes. Flowage enters these lakes from the south and leaves them at the northern end to enter the Kalamazoo River. There are about 150 acres of open water and marsh. This region constitutes the waterfowl management area and, as such, is closed to hunting with firearms until December 1. However, limited waterfowl hunting will likely be allowed in the near future.

Primary plant communities are cropland which account for about 300 acres, and about 150 acres of brush and trees, the main species of which are red maple, aspen, elm, dogwood, hawthorn, black locust, hackberry, cherry, oak, and willow. Most of the forest is found along the Kalamazoo River. High numbers of raccoon use the waterway, and oaks along its route house fair to good populations of fox squirrels.

Many species of waterfowl frequent the area during spring and fall migrations. Canada geese, mallards, black ducks, blue-winged teal, and wood ducks are the primary species. Morrow Pond, a 1,100-acre artificial lake created behind a Consumers Power Company dam, is four miles downstream on the Kalamazoo River. The Kellogg Bird Sanctuary (closed to hunting), a research unit of Michigan State University, is six miles to the south. To the west is the 2,030-acre Gull Lake Sanctuary (also closed to hunting). All three of these, combined with the Kalamazoo River, have a history of waterfowl use. Giant Canada geese, in particular, have increased to nuisance proportions. They provide pass-shooting sport for Fort Custer Recreation Area hunters outside the waterfowl management area and for float hunters on the river.

Within the waterfowl management area the DNR moves meadows and has some 200 to 300 acres of crops in shared agreements with local farmers. Main crop grown is corn, but about 20 percent of the state's share is planted to green pasture. Both food types attract geese.

A large deer herd here has literally been eating itself out of house and home. The DNR estimates that up to 1,000 whitetails winter in the area, especially on three adjacent National Guard lands posted and closed to hunting (see shaded areas on accompanying map), and that perhaps 100 whitetails die of starvation each winter. Apparently hunters cannot shoot enough deer although they certainly try to as the recreation area gets intense hunting pressure. Because the federal lands are former military shelling and fuel-tank jettison areas, authorities have denied public access to date. As a result, deer seek refuge here and die.

In addition to deer, squirrels, raccoon, and some waterfowl, the Fort Custer Recreation Area affords limited hunting opportunities for rabbits, grouse, woodcock, and red fox. The recreation area also figures high on a priority list for future wild turkey releases along the Kalamazoo River.

The DNR has frontier cabins in the recreation area which may be rented by hunters and other recreationists.

A single access route is located off M-96; hunters entering with cars must have a valid state parks vehicle permit attached. Day-long or seasonal permits are available from area headquarters, 5163 West Fort Custer Drive, Augusta, Mich. 49012 (616/731-4200—the recreation area is staffed seven days per week) or from any other DNR office. The area manager can also answer hunters' questions regarding opportunities and regulations.

DNR District Headquarters, 621 North 10th St., Plainwell, Mich. 49080 (616/685-6851) is responsible for wildlife management. Hunters can also get information from the wildlife habitat biologist at the Barry State Game Area, 1805 South Yankee Springs Road, Middleville, Mich. 49333 (616/795-3280).

Waterloo Recreation Area

AT nearly 19,000 acres, the Waterloo Recreation Area in northeastern Jackson and northwestern Washtenaw counties is the largest of its kind in the state. Most of the southern portion, 17,000 acres, is open to hunting (see accompanying map) for those with a state parks vehicle permit, available from any DNR office or at the staffed Waterloo Recreation Area itself, 16345 McClure Road, Chelsea, Mich. 48118 (313/475-8307). The northern region, about 4,800 acres, was purchased with Pittman-Robertson funds and is open to hunting without permit.

Nonpermit lands are marked with green-and-white signs. Recreation-area lands requiring a park sticker for vehicle admittance feature red signs. Adjoining the sprawling public area is the 8,000-acre Pinckney Recreation Area (which see) in Washtenaw County. Thus, hunters have large portions of some 30,000 acres of public lands open to their use.

Topography ranges from flat to fairly hilly. The area lies within the Portage River watershed, which is part of the Grand River system. Both the Waterloo Drain and Portage Drain start at the northeastern corner of the recreation area and flow to the southwest. They meet with Honey Creek from the north and a small stream from the south in the

Fort Custer Recreation Area

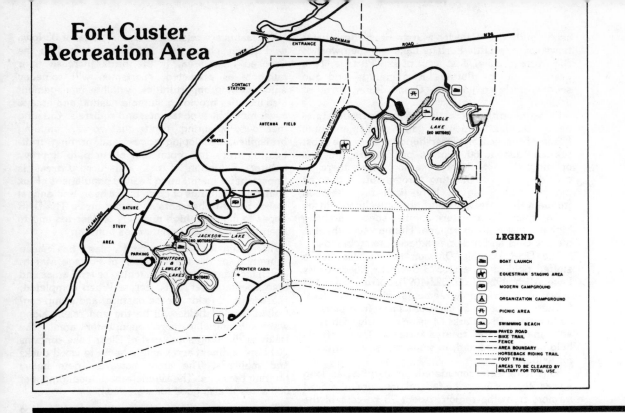

LEGEND
- 🚤 BOAT LAUNCH
- 🐎 EQUESTRIAN STAGING AREA
- 🏕 MODERN CAMPGROUND
- ⛺ ORGANIZATION CAMPGROUND
- 🏕 PICNIC AREA
- 🏊 SWIMMING BEACH
- ▬▬▬ PAVED ROAD
- ─── BIKE TRAIL
- ─ ─ ─ FENCE
- ──── AREA BOUNDARY
- ········· HORSEBACK RIDING TRAIL
- ········· FOOT TRAIL
- ☐ AREAS TO BE CLEARED BY MILITARY FOR TOTAL USE.

Waterloo Recreation Area

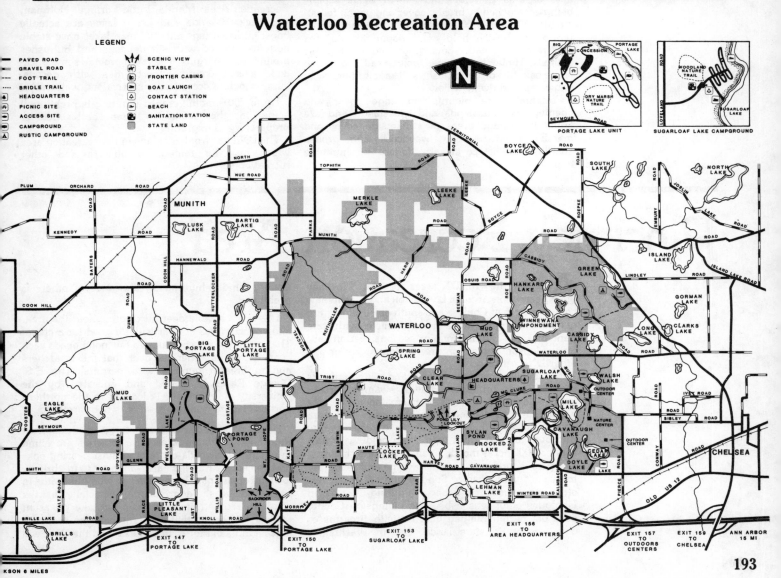

LEGEND
- ▬▬▬ PAVED ROAD
- ══════ GRAVEL ROAD
- ········· FOOT TRAIL
- ─ ─ ─ BRIDLE TRAIL
- 🏠 HEADQUARTERS
- 🏕 PICNIC SITE
- 🚗 ACCESS SITE
- ⛺ CAMPGROUND
- ⛺ RUSTIC CAMPGROUND
- 🔱 SCENIC VIEW
- 🐎 STABLE
- 🏠 FRONTIER CABINS
- 🚤 BOAT LAUNCH
- 🏠 CONTACT STATION
- 🏊 BEACH
- 🚻 SANITATION STATION
- ▨ STATE LAND

PORTAGE LAKE UNIT

SUGARLOAF LAKE CAMPGROUND

KSON 6 MILES

center portion of Waterloo Marsh. From there water flows south to Little Portage Lake and then west to Big Portage Lake. Just west of Big Portage, twin branches of the Portage River merge and run southwesterly to join the Grand River north of Jackson.

Pressure on the recreation area runs moderate to heavy, depending upon the game species and time frame of the season. Deer hunters exert the most pressure (about 60 hunters per square mile on opening day of firearm season), yet there is considerably good hunting throughout, and some big bucks are tagged here each fall. Raccoon frequent the waterways and are actively sought by hound men. Squirrels are another species drawing high interest from sportsmen. Hunters seek them in mature oaks and hickories adjacent to croplands.

The DNR Wildlife Division (which also has a staffed field office at 13573 Seymour Road, Grass Lake, Mich. 49240 [517/522-4097]) currently has 157 acres in sharecrop agreements with seven local farmers, plus about 50 acres of its own food plots. In addition, the DNR Parks Division recently cash-rented some 350 acres to area farmers. These efforts help produce food and, in some cases, winter cover for wildlife.

Soils here were considered submarginal as long ago as 50 years when the federal government moved farmers from the region. About 75 percent of the land base is therefore old-growth fields rapidly being encroached by brushy cover and young forest. Around 3,000 to 4,000 acres are in mature woods, portions of which hold good populations of fox squirrels along with some grays and black-phase animals. Timber cover types include red, black, and white oak; hickory; elm; ash; soft maple; tamarack; dogwood; and dwarf willow.

Cottontails are plentiful in edge cover and openings of brushlands and grasslands and are found in lowland areas of streamside cover and marshy growths. Some woodcock and grouse sharing similar cover are found in huntable numbers.

Pheasants are relatively scarce. A total of 35 Iowa wild turkeys have thus far been released in the Crooked Lake area. If the birds increase their numbers as predicted, sportsmen will someday enjoy hunting opportunities. Wildlife management also includes providing suitable nesting and escape cover for rabbits, pheasants, and squirrels. Creating meadows, planting coniferous cover, building brushpiles, developing edges, and pruning fruit-bearing trees for production all help to improve habitat. Retention of oak and hickory trees is important for maintaining healthy populations of fox squirrels. Plantings of corn, buckwheat, and annual weeds benefit pheasants and other birds. The DNR hopes to maintain high numbers of deer too and to keep the area open to antlerless hunting.

An extensive development plan has been submitted for the main portion of Portage Marsh, which includes diking and ditching several areas and then flooding over 1,700 acres. When completed, sharecropped fields, goose pasture, and pump-controlled flooded fields will be the end result along with substantially more open-water area. The Baldwin Flooding southwest of Clear Lake contains 200 impoundment acres and is home to wood ducks and mallards. The area, however, gets heavy hunting pressure. The Winnewana Impoundment at 600 acres is also good for waterfowl.

There are currently four lakes within the Waterloo Recreation Area: Markla, Little Portage, Hoffman, and Leeke. Markla and Leeke lakes are actually bogs; Little Portage and Hoffman lakes have stable bottoms covered with silt deposits and bulrushes around their margins. The lakes provide some duck- and goose-shooting opportunities with decoys. Jump-shooters occasionally score along waterways.

Up to 700 sandhill cranes (hunting is prohibited) stage in the recreation area each October preparatory to migrating.

The DNR has frontier cabins in the recreation area which may be rented by hunters and other recreationists.

Pinckney Recreation Area

ALL of the 10,200 acres of the Pinckney Recreation Area, in Livingston and Washtenaw counties north of Chelsea and south of Pinckney, are open to hunting for those driving vehicles with state park stickers. The day-long or seasonal permits are available from recreation area headquarters or any other DNR office.

Pinckney is a vast area of lakes and rolling uplands of hardwoods interspersed with swamps, brushlands, and farmland fields. Portions include remote wildland a long distance from any roads. The area adjoins the Waterloo Recreation Area (which see) to the south and, together with those holdings, totals some 30,000 acres mostly open to hunters. Hunting pressure is moderate for small game and moderate to heavy for big game. Sunday hunters, however, often appear in force, especially during the firearm (shotguns only) season because Livingston County does not permit Sunday hunting with firearms or dogs except on state lands, and in Washtenaw County Sunday hunting on the lands of others is prohibited.

There is a sizable deer herd throughout the area, and opportunities are particularly good for archers. The recreation area produces a few good heads each year as well as antlerless deer that fall to archers and to firearm hunters with permits. The E.S. George Reserve, owned and operated by the University of Michigan, is located in the northern portion. Hunting in the reserve is not permitted.

Game populations are fair to good throughout Pinckney Recreation Area. Fox squirrels are found in upland hardwoods containing mast-bearing oaks and hickory. Rabbits are abundant in brushy lowland openings. There are a few wild pheasants in field and brush-edge covers, especially in the southern region, site of former put-take pheasant releases. Although that program has been dropped, at least in its old form, in all likelihood the DNR will continue to release farm-bred birds at key times throughout the general pheasant-hunting season.

Most area lakes hold a few geese, and the region is open during the late season for nuisance Canada geese. Local ducks produced include mallards, teal, and woodies. They and migrant puddlers and divers provide hunting opportunity. Wild turkeys released in the Waterloo Recreation Area are expected to expand their range to the Pinckney Recreation Area and may some day produce hunting potential. In addition, there are some untapped raccoon and fox populations.

For more information, contact the area manager at 8555 Silver Hill Road, Pinckney, Mich. (313/426-4913). Hunters can also get information from the wildlife habitat biologist at DNR District Headquarters, 3335 Lansing Ave., Jackson, Mich. 49202 (517/784-3188).

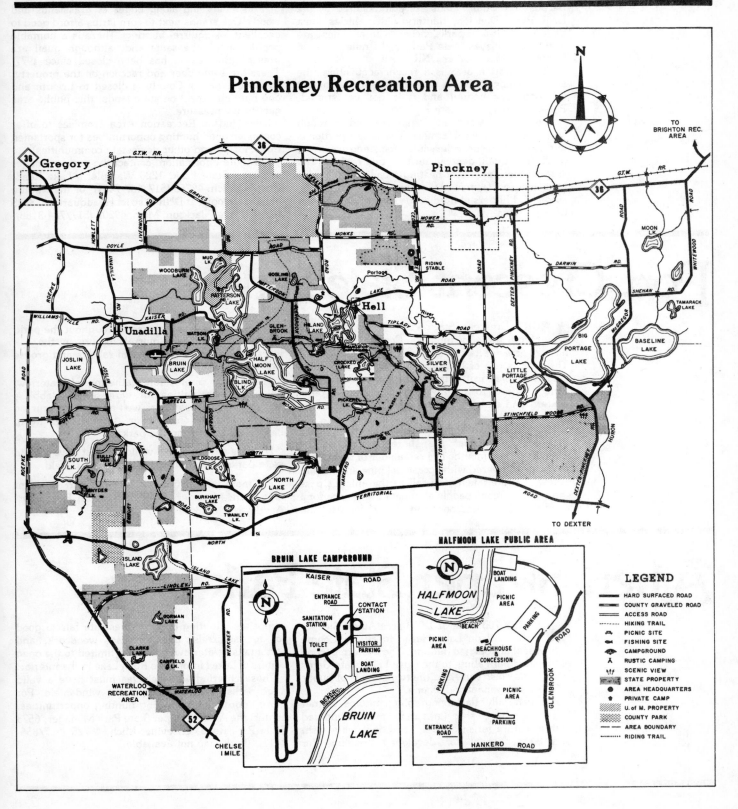

Pinckney Recreation Area

Lake Hudson Recreation Area

THE Lake Hudson Recreation Area, located about 10 miles southwest of Adrian in Lenawee County, is all open to hunting except for safety zones around picnic areas. Currently, 2,690 acres constitute this largely-open area in farm country. Because the public lands are administered by the DNR Parks Division, hunters with vehicles must have a current-year parks sticker to enter. These are available at Hayes State Park, eight miles west of Clinton, or at any other DNR office.

The recreation area is a recent acquisition (the accompanying map is a master plan—development has only just begun) and it is not yet staffed. Personnel at Hayes State Park oversee operations.

About 600 acres are sharecropped through agreements with local farmers. The state's portion is left standing to provide winter food and cover for pheasants, quail, deer, waterfowl, and rabbits. The area features plenty of nesting meadows, 500-acre Lake Hudson (a man-made impoundment), brushlands, and fingers of hardwoods atop rolling hills in back portions.

Waterfowl hunting on Lake Hudon is fairly good for mallards and teal early in the season as well as for migrant puddlers, scaup, and ring-necked ducks later. The meandering lake has potential for Canada-goose hunting as well. Rabbits are plentiful in brushlands and along edges of grasslands and woods. Oak stands next to corn strips afford good to excellent fox-squirrel hunting. There is a huntable population of pheasants and, although quail are present, the season has been closed since 1977. There are some deer and raccoon on the property. Because Lenawee County is closed to firearm and dog hunting except on state lands, this public area gets heavy pressure.

Lake Hudson Recreation Area promises to offer continued good hunting opportunities for sportsmen from Adrian and other downstate communities.

For more information, contact the parks manager at Hayes State Park, 1220 Wampler's Lake Road, Onsted, Mich. 49265 (517/467-7401), or the wildlife habitat biologist at DNR District Headquarters, 3335 Lansing Ave., Jackson, Mich. 49202 (517/784-3188).

Port Crescent State Park

PORT Crescent State Park, along the Lake Huron shoreline in Huron County (*which see*), has 473 acres of its 569 total acres open to hunting. The park is one of Michigan's most popular, however, and even in the fall attracts campers. Safety zones (closed to hunting) include the extreme eastern end and the area around the organization campground.

Jack pine mixed with oaks occur in the western half and again near the shoreline east of the Pinnebog River mouth. The remainder of the park is mostly oak-covered with occasional pine and maple. A few deer are taken each fall as the animals pass through (too many people eliminate the chance for a resident herd). Raccoon and waterfowl use the Pinnebog River which courses throughout the park. Fair hunting for fox squirrels occurs in the oak forest, and there are occasional rabbits and grouse sighted.

There is no appreciable gathering of waterfowl although opportunities for early-season dabblers and late-season divers, as well as geese, occur on the open lake and on the river. A canoe rental livery lies across M-25 from the park.

Hunters entering with vehicles must have a valid state parks sticker attached to the windshield.

For more information, contact the Port Crescent State Park Manager, 1775 Port Austin Road, Port Austin, Mich. 48467 (517/738-8663).

Albert Sleeper State Park

NEARLY 700 acres of 1,003-acre Albert Sleeper State Park on Lake Huron in Huron County (*which see*) are open to hunting. The eastern portion of the state park abuts to the Rush Lake State Game Area (*which also see*), and the two parcels of public land are often managed as one.

The generally flat topography contains former Lake Huron beach shorelines and is mostly timbered with a mature forest of oak, basswood, white ash, and birch, except for developed openings for campsites. Hunting opportunities rate fair to good for fox squirrels, deer, grouse, woodcock, and cottontails. Waterfowl hunting is limited to the open waters of Lake Huron or to Rush Lake in the interior.

Those entering with vehicles must have a valid state parks sticker affixed to the windshield. For more information regarding hunting opportunities, contact the Albert Sleeper State Park Manager, 6573 State Park Road, Caseville, Mich. 48725 (517/856-4411). (Park map not available.)

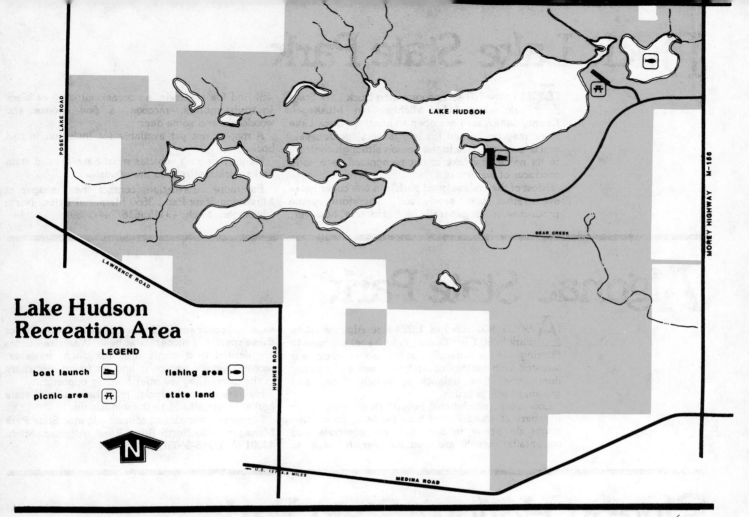

Lake Hudson
Recreation Area

LAKE HUDSON

POSEY LAKE ROAD

LAWRENCE ROAD

HUGHES ROAD

MEDINA ROAD

MOREY HIGHWAY M-156

DEAR CREEK

← U.S. 127 9.6 MILES

LEGEND

boat launch		fishing area	
picnic area		state land	

N

Port Crescent State Park

S A G I N A W   B A Y

CASEVILLE 16 MILES

SAND ROAD

PINNEBOG RIVER

M-25

SCHRAM DRAIN

PORT AUSTIN 8 MILES

CHIMNEY MONUMENT

OLD PINNEBOG RIVER

PINNEBOG RIVER

PORT CRESCENT ROAD   M-53 2 MILES →

KENNEDY ROAD

LEGEND

	PAVED ROAD
	GRAVEL ROAD
	DIRT ROAD
	FOOTTRAIL
	HEADQUARTERS
	PICNIC SITE
	ACCESS SITE
	CAMPGROUND
	SANITATION STATION
	ORGANIZATION CAMPGROUND
	SWIMMING BEACH
	SHELTER, TOILET, CHANGECOURT
C	CONTROL
	OVERLOOK
T	TOILET
	STATE LAND

N

SCALE IN FEET
0   500   1000

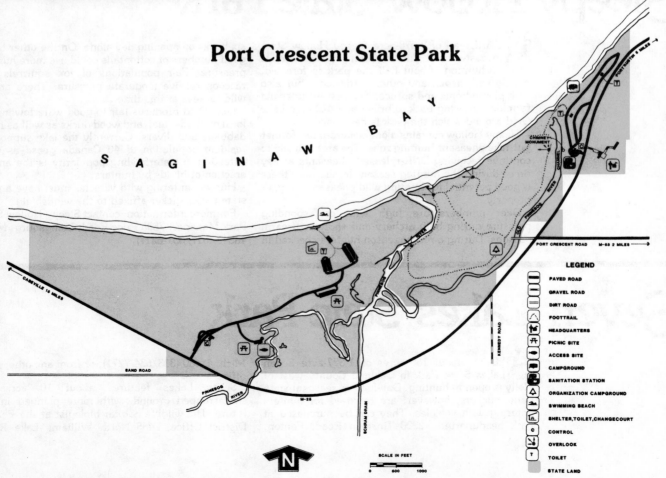

Duck Lake State Park

ALL of the 707 acres comprising Duck Lake State Park along Lake Michigan in Muskegon County (*which see*) are open to hunting. Duck Lake itself may be hunted for mergansers, goldeneyes, and a few scaup late in the season although contrary to its name, the lake is not recognized as a solid producer of waterfowl.

Most of the undeveloped park is in oak cover types over rather poor sandy soil. Therefore, game production is not generally high. Hunters, however, will find fox squirrels, an occasional gray or black squirrel, rabbits, raccoon, a few grouse and woodcock, and some deer.

A map is not yet available for inclusion in this book.

Hunters driving vehicles must have a valid state parks sticker affixed to the windshield.

For more information, contact the manager at Muskegon State Park, 3560 Memorial Drive, North Muskegon, Mich. 49445 (616/744-3480).

Algonac State Park

ABOUT 900 acres of 1,023-acre Algonac State Park in St. Clair County (*which see*) are open to hunting. This is generally flat land about 40 percent forested with various cover types, oak and hickory dominating. The balance is mostly farm land growing back to brush.

Low deer populations nevertheless draw large numbers of shotgun and bow hunters. Sportsmen might do better to seek out fox squirrels and cottontails, which are usually plentiful due to excellent cover and food types. Hunting pressure for these species is moderate at best. Water resources are limited to a single drainage ditch; however, raccoon use the waterway and are found elsewhere in the park. They too offer hunting opportunity.

Hunters driving vehicles must have a valid state parks sticker affixed to the windshield.

For more information, contact Algonac State Park Manager, 8730 North River Road, Algonac, Mich. 48001 (313/765-5605).

Sleepy Hollow State Park

NEARLY all of 2,678-acre Sleepy Hollow State in east-central Clinton County (*which see*) is open to hunting. About half the park is forested, mostly with aspen and other hardwoods, but also with planted pine and spruce. The rest includes old farmland growing back to brush and 420-acre Lake Ovid around which the park is developed.

Sleepy Hollow contains a one-square-mile, former put-take pheasant-hunting zone. The area is likely to continue receiving DNR-released pheasants at key times during the hunting season. In addition, there is good potential for hunting wild pheasants on park property.

Deer numbers are high with corresponding pressure during both archery and shotgun firearm seasons. During a recent season hunters checked in six bucks on opening day alone. On the other hand, good numbers of cottontails could use more hunting pressure. Fair populations of fox squirrels and raccoon receive moderate pressure. There are no wild turkeys at this time.

Lake Ovid produces fair to good waterfowling for local mallards, teal, and wood ducks as well as flight dabblers and divers. Currently the lake supports a resident population of 40 Canada geese as well. Attesting to waterfowling popularity is the annual erection of blinds by hunters.

Hunters entering with vehicles must have a valid state parks sticker affixed to the windshield.

For more information, contact Sleepy Hollow State Park Manager, 7835 Price Road, Laingsburg, Mich. 48848 (517/651-6217).

Seven Lakes State Park

ALL but about 160 acres of 1,377-acre Seven Lakes State Park in Oakland County west of Holly is open to hunting. Day-long or seasonal state parks stickers, however, are required for hunters entering with vehicles. They can be purchased at park headquarters, 2220 Tinsman Road, Fenton, Mich. 48430 (313/634-7271), or from any other DNR office.

Seven Lakes features about 10 acres of sharecropped ground, with more planned in the future. The wildlife habitat biologist at the Pontiac District Office, 2455 North Williams Lake Road,

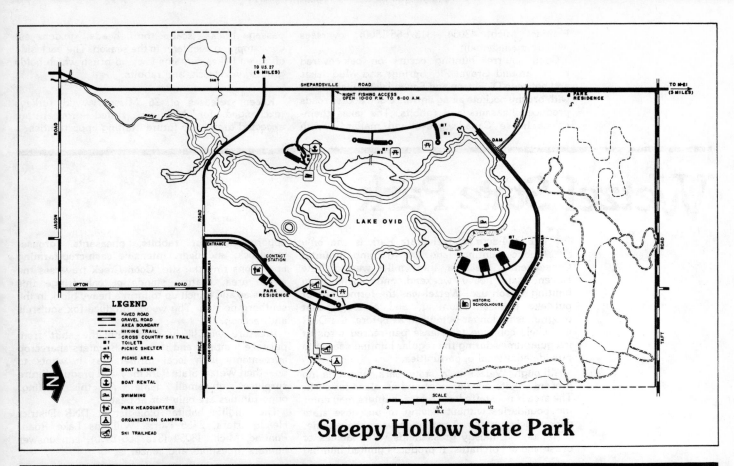

LEGEND
PAVED ROAD
GRAVEL ROAD
AREA BOUNDARY
HIKING TRAIL
CROSS COUNTRY SKI TRAIL
TOILETS
PICNIC SHELTER
PICNIC AREA
BOAT LAUNCH
BOAT RENTAL
SWIMMING
PARK HEADQUARTERS
ORGANIZATION CAMPING
SKI TRAILHEAD

Sleepy Hollow State Park

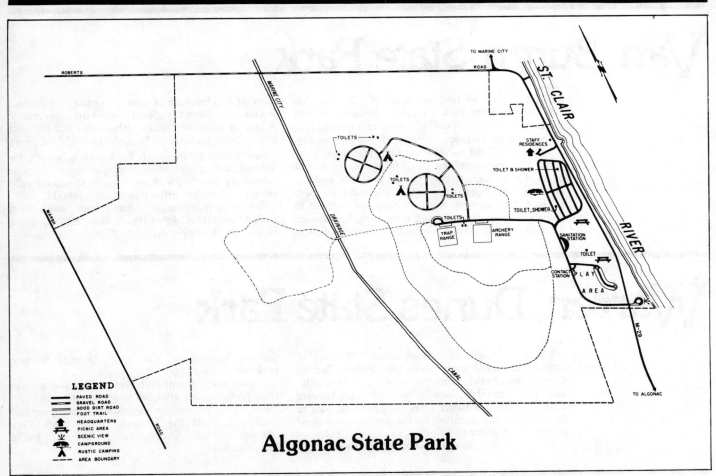

LEGEND
PAVED ROAD
GRAVEL ROAD
GOOD DIRT ROAD
FOOT TRAIL
HEADQUARTERS
PICNIC AREA
SCENIC VIEW
CAMPGROUND
RUSTIC CAMPING
AREA BOUNDARY

Algonac State Park

Pontiac, Mich. 48054 (313/666-1500), oversees wildlife management.

Good squirrel hunting occurs on oak-covered ridges around Gravel Pit, Spring, and Mud lakes and between Dickinson and Seven lakes. Field areas with brushy pockets along entrance and access roads produce pheasants and rabbits. The lakes themselves house Canada geese and mallards, with passage ducks (scaup, buffleheads, goldeneyes, etc.) stopping over later in the season. The back side of Seven Lakes contains lowland brush which holds grouse, woodcock, and rabbits.

Recent releases of 26 Missouri wild turkeys (exchanged for Michigan ruffed grouse) are expected to provide future hunting opportunities.

Wetzel State Park

THE 844-acre Wetzel State Park is the only public hunting land in Macomb County. Consequently, the area, three miles west of New Haven, gets heavy weekend and opening-day hunting season use. Wetzel was the former site of put-take pheasant hunting, and although that program is no longer being run as before, the DNR will likely continue to release pen-reared birds at irregular times during the regular hunting season to provide additional opportunities.

Although Wetzel is a state park, there is no present on-site development and no plans for such. The area is not staffed; therefore, hunters may enter the boundaries without having to purchase state park vehicle permits. A park map was not available.

The unit is mostly grass fields with patches of brush and old orchards. It produces limited hunting opportunities for rabbits, pheasants, grouse, woodcock, and deer. Intensive cash-crop-farming operations ring the site. Coon Creek traverses the entire area. Mature stands of oak fringe this waterway and bunch up to form a heavy block in the southern portion. The woods produce fox squirrels and raccoon.

Pressure will likely drop with the shift from put-take hunting, and if the DNR enters sharecrop agreements with local farmers—as it wants to do—then Wetzel State Park may well produce future surpluses of small game. At this writing, opportunities are only fair at best.

The wildlife habitat biologist at DNR District Headquarters, 2455 North Williams Lake Road, Pontiac, Mich. 48054 (313/666-1500), can answer hunters' questions and concerns.

Van Buren State Park

TWO hundred fifty-one acres of 326-acre Van Buren State Park on Lake Michigan in Van Buren County (which see) are open to hunting. This is rolling land, heavily covered with beech, oak, and a few pines. Sand dunes front Lake Michigan.

Hunting opportunities have fallen off in recent years due perhaps to both people pressure and the climax forest. There used to be fairly good numbers of deer, for example, but now they are reduced to transient animals pressured here from hunters on adjoining private land. Cottontails are also few in number and because of heavy day use in summer, the park is unable to support game-bird populations. A lack of water resources, other than the big lake itself, limits park usage by waterfowl and raccoon.

Best hunting potential is for squirrels, mostly fox species, with a sprinkling of grays/blacks.

Hunters entering with vehicles must have a valid state parks sticker affixed to the windshield.

For more information, contact Van Buren State Park Manager, Ruggles Roads (Box 122-B), South Haven, Mich. 49090 (616/637-2788).

Warren Dunes State Park

THE northern portion, or about 590 acres of 1,052-acre Warren Dunes State Park in Berrien County (which see), is open to hunting. This is hilly, sand-dune country, largely wooded with mature oaks. The park manager rates deer hunting poor to fair with fair opportunities for fox squirrels and good potential for cottontails.

There is also limited woodcock, grouse, and raccoon hunting in the area. Overall hunting pressure is very light.

Those entering with vehicles must have a valid state parks sticker attached to the windshield.

For more information regarding hunting opportunities, contact the Warren Dunes State Park Manager, Red Arrow Hwy., Sawyer, Mich. (616/426-4013).

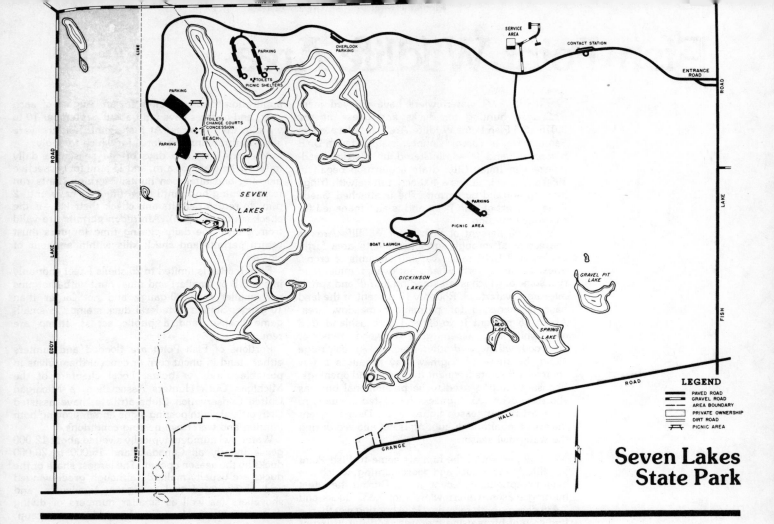

Seven Lakes
State Park

LEGEND
- PAVED ROAD
- GRAVEL ROAD
- AREA BOUNDARY
- PRIVATE OWNERSHIP
- DIRT ROAD
- PICNIC AREA

Van Buren State Park

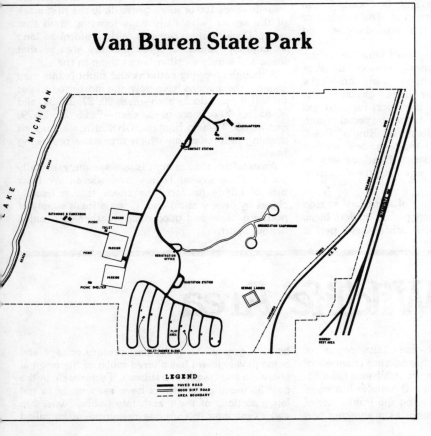

LEGEND
- PAVED ROAD
- GOOD DIRT ROAD
- AREA BOUNDARY

Warren Dunes
State Park

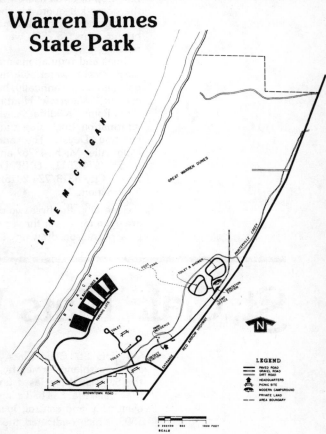

LEGEND
- PAVED ROAD
- GRAVEL ROAD
- DIRT ROAD
- HEADQUARTERS
- PICNIC SITE
- MODERN CAMPGROUND
- PRIVATE LAND
- AREA BOUNDARY

SCALE

Fish Point Wildlife Area

SINCE 1971 waterfowlers have enjoyed managed hunting for ducks and geese at the 3,076-acre Fish Point Wildlife Area. It is located on Saginaw Bay in Tuscola County, is staffed with DNR personnel, and is administered by district headquarters in Imlay City. State acquisition began in 1950 and now includes a 400-acre refuge with fringe hunting allowed by permit. The unattached Gaede Area is a part of Fish Point and is also managed for controlled hunting.

About 60 percent of Fish Point Wildlife Area is sharecropped through agreements with area farmers and the DNR raises varying amounts of crops. These consist of corn, wheat, buckwheat, millet, and rye, some of which is left standing for fall and spring migratory waterfowl. Roughly 10 percent of the land base is managed for permanent meadow area. About 16 percent is forestland or brushland (red oak, white oak, aspen, gray dogwood, red-osier dogwood, willow, and other species). An oak ridge along the shore of Saginaw Bay produces a few squirrels. Rabbits frequent the brushland openings. Pheasant hunting used to be phenomenal but has slid from over 400 ringnecks harvested annually to the most recent season figure of 17. Deer frequent the area too, although hunting is not allowed during the waterfowl season.

But 99 percent of the hunters come to Fish Point Wildlife Area for duck and goose hunting, which has been exceptional in recent years. During the latest hunting season, waterfowlers shot 9,337 ducks and 2,435 geese—both records. Good hunting weather, a fine crop of birds using the area, and the lifting of the goose-kill quota for the Tuscola County Goose Management Area all contributed. The number of hunter trips (8,285) was the second-highest on record.

Rules and regulations mentioned here are for the most recent waterfowl hunting season. Because policies change annually, hunters should consult the current "Waterfowl Hunting Guide" or contact the Fish Point Wildlife Area manager for updated information (including the dates of special Youth Hunting Days). The address is Ringle Road, Unionville, Mich. 48767 and the telephone number is 517/674-2511. DNR District Headquarters in Imlay City (313/724-2015) will also have current information.

Generally, the first two days of waterfowl season are open to two- or three-party permit holders lucky in a preseason drawing. DNR offices have permit application forms available in late August of each year, and hunters have until about September 10 to write in their choices. At Fish Point, hunters were allowed three hunting dates for which to apply.

After the first two days of the season, a daily lottery is held at 5:30 a.m. and 11 a.m. for respective morning and afternoon hunts. Morning hunts run from opening hour until noon (hunters have until 2 p.m. to return permits and check their kill—if the check station is open). Afternoon permits are valid from 1 until the daily closing time (hunters must return permits and check kills within an hour of closure).

Each hunter is limited to 25 shells (steel shot only in size BB or smaller) and must hunt with shotguns not smaller than 20-gauge and not larger than 10-gauge. State and federal duck stamps, a small-game license, and a public access stamp are required.

Portions of Fish Point are flooded and hunters either stand in uncut corn or conceal themselves in portable blinds or boats. Local chapters of the Michigan Duck Hunters Association, a Michigan United Conservation Clubs affiliate, have assisted DNR officials with posting signs and improving both hunting and waterfowl-nesting conditions.

Waterfowl numbers typically swell to about 12,000 geese (nearly all Canadas) and 15,000 to 20,000 ducks by the season opener. The largest share of the ducks are usually mallards although green-winged and blue-winged teal, widgeons, gadwalls, and shovellers (as well as smaller numbers of diving ducks—redheads, buffleheads, goldeneyes, scaup, canvasbacks) also frequent the area. Hunters usually shoot 100 or more geese daily the first week of the season with daily bags tapering from that point. Duck hunting remains fairly uniform so long as migrants replenish birds that are shot or that leave and windy weather keeps them in the air.

Although cropping patterns and flight habits may change, these zones have been the most productive: for 300 or more ducks each—8, 9, 20, 27, 30, 34, and 80-85; for 90 or more geese each—9, 26, 27, 74-79, and 80-85. To help hunters, DNR officials keep an ongoing tally chart on which areas are producing best.

An excellent time to hunt is late season, especially the final two weeks. Then waterfowlers have their pick of blinds (in fact, the check station usually closes by deer season) and, given a fresh supply of northern birds and good duck weather, can enjoy banner sport.

St. Clair Flats Wildlife Area

THE St. Clair Flats is the delta region of marshland formed by meandering channels of the St. Clair River as it fingers itself into Lake St. Clair. The Flat has had a long and complex history of ownership and control, including the Public Act of 1899, which dedicated the area as a shooting and hunting ground. Over the past century cottage and home development has altered much of the original shoreline and fragile marshlands. Fortunately in the past 35 years great efforts have been made to get large portions of the marsh into public ownership and to manage this unique resource—often called

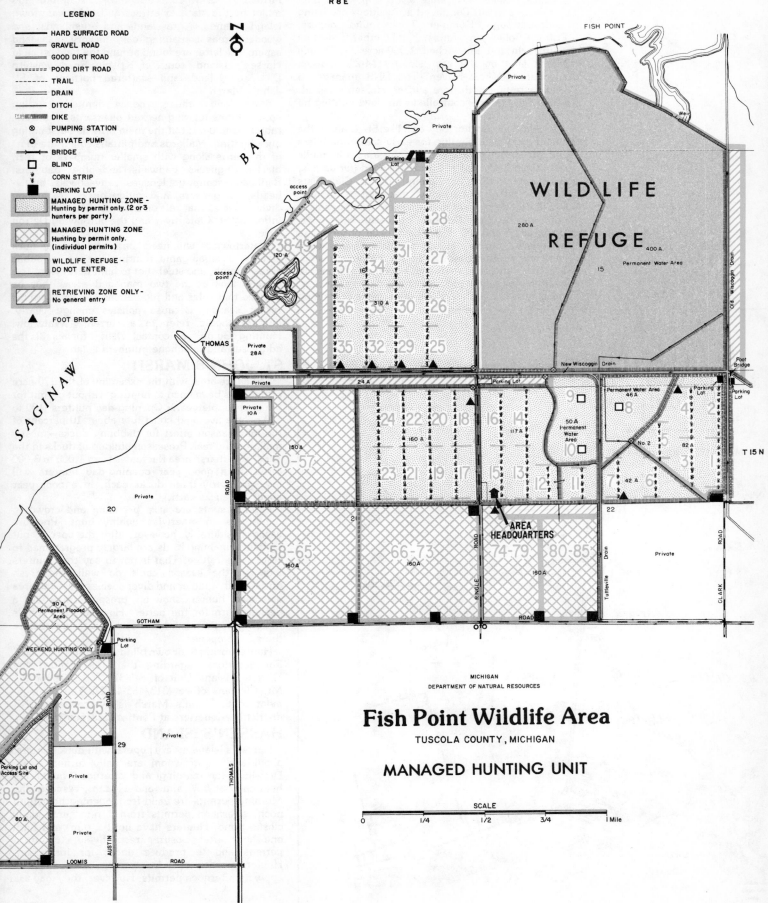

LEGEND

———— HARD SURFACED ROAD
———— GRAVEL ROAD
———— GOOD DIRT ROAD
-------- POOR DIRT ROAD
— — — TRAIL
———— DRAIN
———— DITCH
▨▨▨▨ DIKE
⊗ PUMPING STATION
⊙ PRIVATE PUMP
⊢⊶ BRIDGE
▢ BLIND
↓ CORN STRIP
■ PARKING LOT

MANAGED HUNTING ZONE –
Hunting by permit only. (2 or 3 hunters per party)

MANAGED HUNTING ZONE
Hunting by permit only. (individual permits)

WILDLIFE REFUGE –
DO NOT ENTER

RETRIEVING ZONE ONLY–
No general entry

▲ FOOT BRIDGE

R 8 E

FISH POINT

WILDLIFE REFUGE

280 A

400 A

Permanent Water Area

15

BAY

SAGINAW

THOMAS

Private 28 A

Private

Private 10 A

150 A

50–57

58–65
160 A

66–73
160 A

74–79

80–85
160 A

90 A Permanent Flooded Area

WEEKEND HUNTING ONLY

96–104

93–95

Parking Lot and Access Site

86–92

80 A

GOTHAM

LOOMIS ROAD

AUSTIN

THOMAS ROAD

120 A

38–49

37 34

36

35 32 29 25

31 27

30 26

28

24 22 20 18 16 14

23 21 19 17 15 13

12 11

9

10

50 A Permanent Water Area

7

42 A 6

8

46 A Permanent Water Area

4 2

5

82 A

3

Parking Lot

New Wiscoggin Drain

Old Wiscoggin Drain

Foot Bridge

Weir

No. 2

Tuttleville Drain

Private

Private

CLARK ROAD

RINGLE ROAD

AREA HEADQUARTERS

310 A

160 A

117 A

access point

access point

Parking Lot

Parking Lot

T 15 N

MICHIGAN
DEPARTMENT OF NATURAL RESOURCES

Fish Point Wildlife Area

TUSCOLA COUNTY, MICHIGAN

MANAGED HUNTING UNIT

SCALE

0   1/4   1/2   3/4   1 Mile

the Michigan Everglades—as wisely as possible.

Today about half of Harsen's Island and most of Dickinson Island is in state ownership, more than 6,600 acres in all. Continued acquisitions are being made through Kammer Trust Fund dollars, Pittman-Robertson funds, and other revenue sources in the unattached 1,900-acre St. John's Marsh Unit on the east side of M-29 between Algonac and Fair Haven. The DNR manages a wildlife refuge both here and on Harsen's Island, which also features controlled waterfowl hunting by permit.

In addition, Anchor Bay on Lake St. Clair is the site of good duck hunting for early-season puddlers and late-season divers. Much of this area is in public ownership (*see map*) and access is good (*for details, see chapter on St. Clair County*). The St. Clair Flats Wildlife Area is currently managed to handle 40,000-60,000 migrant ducks, which usually peak in numbers by late October or early November. Upwards of 150,000 ducks have been observed to use this staging area in high-population years when wind and weather conditions force migrants to stop. Sanctuary and food resources are other reasons. In addition, the region produces many ducks each year.

The area is a unique blend of marshes containing bulrushes, cattails, phragmites, and sedge meadows; croplands—about 400 to 800 acres mostly farmed to buckwheat, corn, barley, sorghum, and millet by the state to attract and hold waterfowl; island uplands of grasslands and brushlands; and wooded areas containing oak, hickory, ash, and aspen. The latter are found around the field office at Harsen's Island, south of Krispin Road, eastern Dickinson Island, and scattered portions of St. John's Marsh.

State lands thus produce limited hunting opportunities for ring-necked pheasants, squirrels, rabbits, and deer; but the main draw is outstanding duck hunting. Mallards and pintails constitute most of the birds along with smaller numbers of teal, blacks, ringnecks, gadwalls, and other dabblers. Redheads, scaup, goldeneyes, canvasbacks, buffleheads, mergansers, and ruddy ducks are among diving species that raft on Lake St. Clair, along the inflowing St. Clair River and the outflowing Detroit River.

Waterfowlers will need state and federal duck stamps, a small-game hunting license, a public access stamp, and steel shot to hunt here. Here is a closeup look at the two managed areas, but be advised that rules and regulations are for the most recent season. Because policies change yearly, hunters should refer to a current ''Waterfowl Hunting Guide'' or contact DNR officials at the addresses and telephone numbers listed.

ST. JOHN'S MARSH

The entire area, with the exception of the 170-acre refuge, has been open to hunting without permit for the past couple years. Opening-day hunters (100 to 140 people average) constitute about 10 percent of the total season effort for dabbling ducks—mostly mallards and teal. Preseason buildup of ducks in the 1,900-acre marsh area fluctuates from 1,000 to 3,000 birds. In a good year opening-day hunters will average nearly three ducks each, in a poor year about 1.5 ducks each.

Parking spots are at a premium and crowding diminishes an otherwise quality hunt. Pressure eases considerably, however, after the opener, but by then remaining birds are largely programmed to stay in the refuge. That is not to say that hunters later in the season can't do well. As fresh birds—both puddler and diver species—use the area and fewer hunters show up, prospects may take a decided turn for the better. However, St. John's Marsh gets its maximum use by waterfowl before the season opener.

Hunters bring their own blinds or hunt from boats. For questions regarding the area, contact the Harsen's Island Unit office (313/748-9504) or the Mt. Clemens office (313/465-4771). The management of St. John's Marsh is overseen by DNR district headquarters at Pontiac (313/666-1500).

HARSEN'S ISLAND

Harsen's Island is very popular with duck hunters, about a third of whom are daily turned away. Drawings for morning and afternoon hunts are held daily at 5:30 a.m. and 11 a.m., respectively. Morning permits are valid from opening hour until noon, afternoon permits from 1 p.m. until daily closure time. Hunters have until 2 p.m. and until one hour after closure, respectively, to return permits and to produce ducks for inspection. Hunters participating in morning hunts may not apply for afternoon permits. However, they may ask

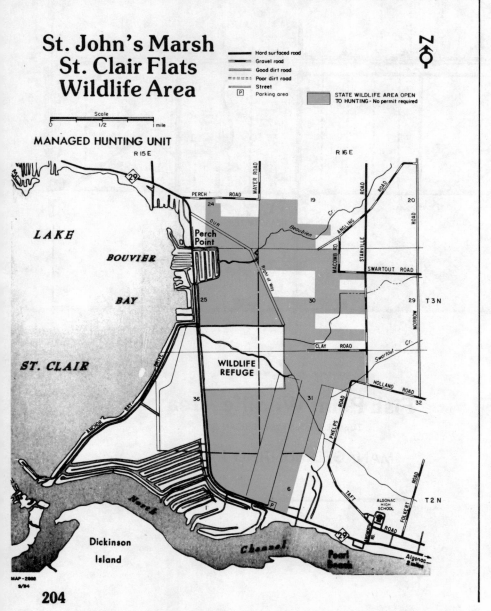

St. John's Marsh
St. Clair Flats
Wildlife Area

Hard surfaced road
Gravel road
Good dirt road
Poor dirt road
Street
P Parking area

STATE WILDLIFE AREA OPEN TO HUNTING - No permit required

N

Scale
0   1/2   1 mile

MANAGED HUNTING UNIT

LAKE

BOUVIER

BAY

ST. CLAIR

Perch Point

WILDLIFE REFUGE

Dickinson Island

St. Clair Flats Wildlife Area

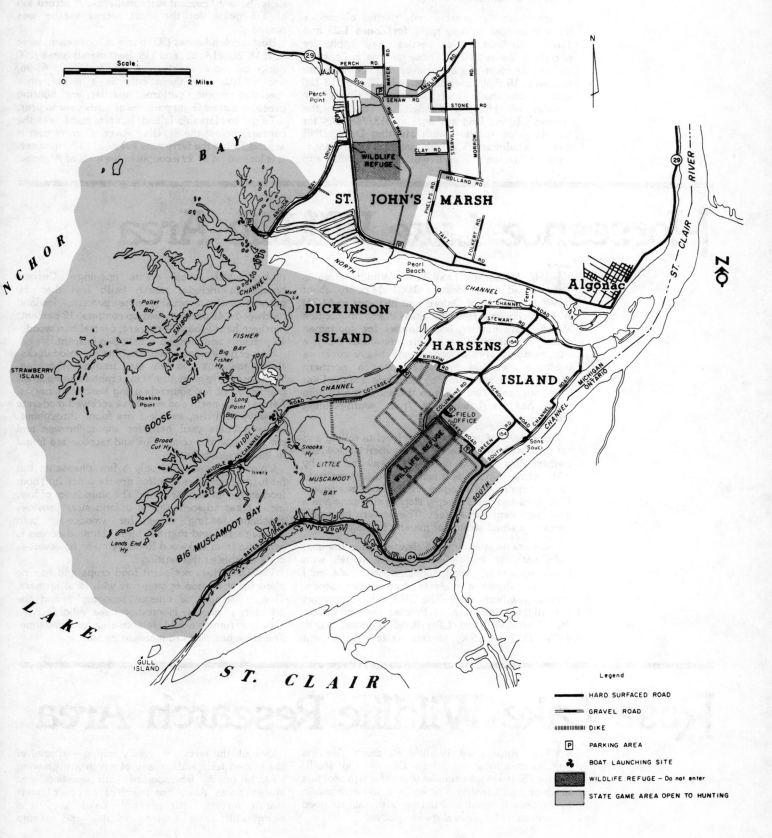

Scale:
0   1   2 Miles

Legend

▬▬▬	HARD SURFACED ROAD
▭▭▭	GRAVEL ROAD
▨▨▨	DIKE
P	PARKING AREA
⚓	BOAT LAUNCHING SITE
▓▓▓	WILDLIFE REFUGE – Do not enter
░░░	STATE GAME AREA OPEN TO HUNTING

Map labels: ANCHOR BAY, PERCH RD, MAYER RD, ANGLING RD, STONE RD, CLAY RD, MORROW RD, STARVILLE RD, HOLLAND RD, PHELPS RD, FOLKERT RD, TAFT RD, Perch Point, Genaw Rd, WILDLIFE REFUGE, ST. JOHN'S MARSH, Pearl Beach, Algonac, ST. CLAIR RIVER, DICKINSON ISLAND, North Channel, Old Channel, Mud I., Pollet Bay, Shibora, FISHER BAY, Big Fisher Hy, Strawberry Island, Hawkins Point, GOOSE BAY, Long Point Bay, Broad Cut Hy, MIDDLE CHANNEL, livery, Snooks Hy, LITTLE MUSCAMOOT BAY, Lands End Hy, BIG MUSCAMOOT BAY, Gull Island, LAKE ST. CLAIR, HARSENS ISLAND, N. Channel Rd, Stewart Rd, Ferry, Krispin Rd, FIELD OFFICE, LaCroix Rd, Columbine Rd, Yokel Road, Green Rd, South Rd, Sans Souci, MICHIGAN ONTARIO, SOUTH CHANNEL, Middle Channel, Cottage Road.

for unclaimed permits.

On the first day of the duck season all hunting is limited to groups of two or three persons holding a hunting reservation. DNR offices have permit applications available by late August each year, and hunters have until about September 10 to return them for the annual drawing.

Throughout the season, only parties of two or three waterfowlers may apply for Zones 1-23 and 118-120. Individuals or parties may apply for permits in Zones 24-117. Those hunting in Zones 7, 18, and 22 must use a retriever dog. Hunters are limited to 15 shells each in Zones 17-22 and 118-120 and to 25 shells each elsewhere. Check the "Waterfowl Hunting Guide" or contact the Harsen's Island Unit manager at 313/748-9504 for the dates of special Youth Hunting Days. DNR district headquarters, which oversees the management of Harsen's Island, will also have that and other information. Call 313/666-1500.

Hunters bring their own blinds or hunt from boats and in standing corn. Waterfowl numbers vary annually from about 7,000 to 8,800. The record duck harvest was set a few years ago with 12,033 birds shot; in the most recent season the figure was 8,846, or an average of 159 hunters who shot 177 ducks daily. Seventy percent were mallards. A record kill of 116 geese for the most recent season was posted.

Best cropland zones (300 ducks or more each) were 3, 7, 18, 20, 21A, 22, and 119. Best marsh zones (200 ducks or more each) were 34-37, 79-82, 63-86, and 99-102. Use these only as a guide since changing cropping patterns, weather, and hunting pressure dictate flight patterns of birds year to year.

To get to Harsen's Island, hunters must take the car ferry across the St. Clair River. Current cost is around $3 and the ferry runs every 20 to 30 minutes. It is located on M-29 a couple miles west of Algonac.

Horseshoe Lake Wildlife Area

THE Horseshoe Lake State Wildlife Area is located in northeastern Oakland County, about three miles north of Oxford and just east of M-24. Although currently only 237 acres in size, this region affords good hunting opportunities for sportsmen willing to walk in. Hip boots are advised as this is a wet, swampy area of cedars and heavy cover—a wildland area not unlike regions in northern Michigan. The north-flowing headwaters of the Flint River are here. Two miles to the south the Clinton River has its headwaters from south-running streams.

Topography of upland areas is level to rolling and covered with brush and noncommercial lowland timber. Most of the wildlife area is low and marshy with some small permanent and intermittent streams draining the region. Horseshoe Lake covers 15.4 acres and has a steeply sloping shoreline and a maximum depth of 47 feet. The eastern boundary contains a small stretch of marshy frontage.

There are no open, upland clearings, and the land lacks early to middle successional stages with brush (such as dogwood, sumac, honeysuckle, etc.) or sapling stages of intolerant tree species (aspen, cherry, hawthorn, etc.). The DNR, which manages the wildlife area from its Pontiac District Office, 2455 North Williams Lake Road, Pontiac, Mich. 48054 (313/666-1500), hopes selectively to cut timber which would create openings. Current breakdown includes marsh (with less than 50 percent lowland brush), nine percent; lowland hardwoods, 42 percent; swamp conifers, 12 percent; northern hardwoods, 29 percent; central hardwoods, 15 percent; and lowland brush, two percent.

Beaver have created some habitat for wood ducks. A few mallards and teal also frequent the area. There are fairly good numbers of rabbits and a small population of fox squirrels using hardwood ridges. Farms to the north and east have received moderate to heavy deer use, and deer are found throughout. Some animals yard here for winter browse and coniferous winter cover. Fox and raccoon are found in limited numbers.

Upland birds include only a few pheasants but fairly good numbers of ruffed grouse which find both food and cover to their liking. The abundance of low, moist areas adjacent to the upland sites provides excellent feeding areas for woodcock, both locally-reared and migrant birds. Limited access is available from Oakwood Road. A map, however, is not available at this writing.

The DNR does not plant food crops and has no plans for sharecrop agreements with local farmers. That is because of uneven topography and the difficulty of access. Horseshoe Lake Wildlife Area will likely remain a wild, remote area for some time. The state has plans to increase its size.

Rose Lake Wildlife Research Area

THE Rose Lake Wildlife Research Area is located in southeastern Clinton and southwestern Shiawassee counties (*both of which see*) just north of East Lansing. The entire 3,450-acre public lands area is open to hunting with fair to good opportunities for several game species.

Overall, the terrain is gently rolling—an area of abandoned farmlands, many of which are growing back to brush, interspersed with woodlots and lowland areas. About one-fourth of the cover type is mature forests, with primarily oak-hickory type along with some lowland maples and swamp

Harsen's Island
St. Clair Flats
Wildlife Area

MANAGED HUNTING UNIT

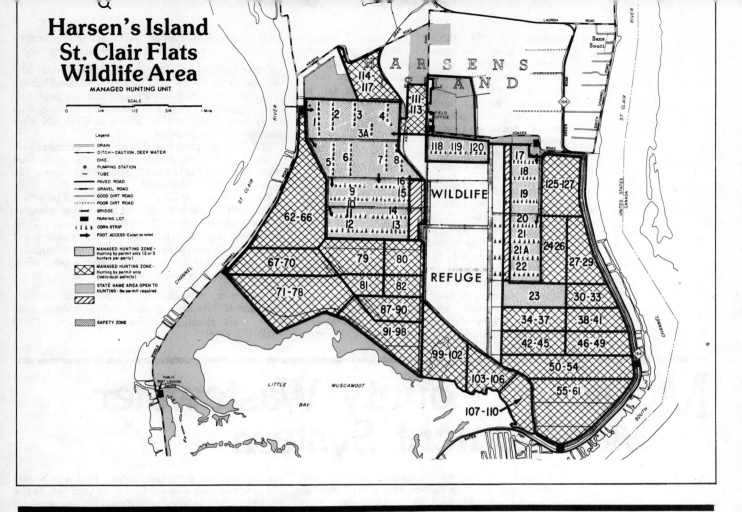

Rose Lake Wildlife Research Area

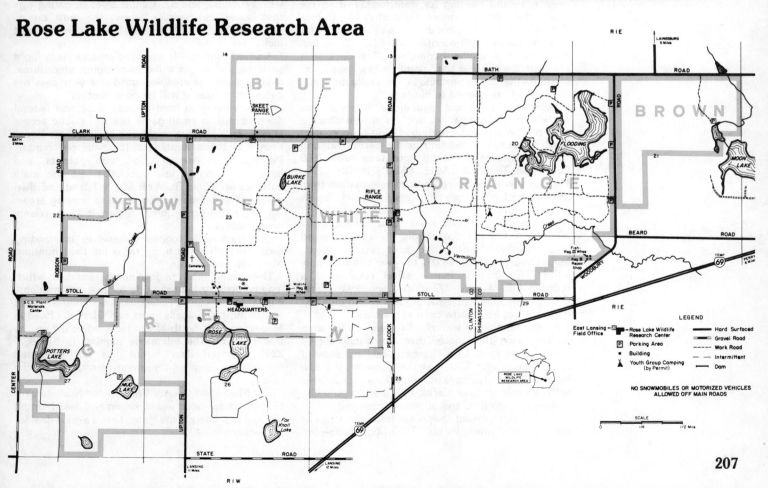

tamaracks. Another third of the research area is brushlands, with the remainder in open grasslands.

Deer hunting here is as good as on surrounding private land. Biologists estimate that the public lands produce 20 to 25 whitetails each fall for archers and shotgun hunters. Deer populations are stable, perhaps increasing slightly. However, high hunting pressure tends to crowd deer off the property.

Fox squirrels and cottontails, usually in good supply, attract the interest of numerous sportsmen. The five lakes and waterfowl flooding produce some early-season sport for local wood ducks, mallards, and teal, but heavy pressure tends to burn off ducks quickly. About 20 to 25 pairs of Canada geese nest here but provide only limited hunting opportunities (mostly on Rose Lake itself) due in part to nearby Lake Lansing, which is closed to hunting.

Very low populations of wild pheasants are frequently augmented by DNR hatchery-reared roosters released a couple of times during the regular three-week pheasant hunting season. Hunters probably shoot more grouse, available in fair to good numbers most falls. There is also some local woodcock production and the game area hosts a few flight birds in mid- to late October each year.

Other hunting opportunities include raccoon and red fox. In the future, wild turkeys—released here in both 1983 and 1984—may provide hunting potential. The original releases of 27 Iowa and Pennsylvania birds have grown at this writing to 75 to 100 after just two nesting seasons.

The DNR currently has sharecrop agreements with three local farmers and plants several small food plots of several acres each. Altogether, some 150 acres are under cultivation.

A rifle range with 25-, 50-, and 100-yard targets is located off Peacock Road, and a handtrap shotgun range is found north of Clark Road (see map). DNR personnel supervise the free ranges, passing out targets on Wednesday through Friday throughout the year, except during the hunting season when they are available seven days per week.

For more information, contact the wildlife biologist at Rose Lake Wildlife Research Area, 8562 East Stoll Road, East Lansing, Mich. 48823 (517/373-9358).

Muskegon County Wastewater Management System

A Muskegon County wastewater program that features 5,500 acres of crops fertilized by wastewater nutrients in 1,700 acres of lagoons is open to permit hunting for waterfowl. During the most recent season parties numbering two to four hunters could participate in 5:30 a.m. drawings for half-day hunts (until noon) on Tuesday, Thursday, Saturday, and Sunday beginning a few days after the waterfowl opener until within a few days of its close. As the season progresses, generally more and more areas are opened to hunting.

Because all rules and regulations mentioned are subject to annual change, hunters should check a current "Waterfowl Hunting Guide" or contact DNR officials, who administer the permit hunting from the adjacent Muskegon State Game Area, 7600 Messinger, Twin Lake, Mich. 49457 (616/788-5055). Hunters can also secure updated information from DNR district office headquarters in Grand Rapids (616/456-5071).

Waterfowlers generally shoot about 500 ducks and 300 to 400 Canada geese from the county-owned area. However, during the most recent season, hunter hours fell from 10,051 the year before to only 3,814. This drop in hunter effort resulted in a reduced kill of only 277 ducks and 293 geese. Changed cropping patterns, dry fields, and bluebird days without wind were cited as reasons.

A high number of waterfowl depend on the area for sanctuary (the lagoons themselves may not be hunted) and food. Late October peak use showed 30,000 ducks and 4,000 Canada geese on the two lagoons. Over 80 percent of the ducks were mallards with concentrations of blacks, ruddy ducks, pintails, gadwalls, shovelers, and others also present.

Most of the hunting took place from cornstrips in the "triangle" area, Fields 27, 28, 29, 34, 35—immediately north of the last lagoon. That was largely because this area was the first to be cropped. In the past Field 36 has been exceptional for geese, along with 27-29, 30, and 32. Center-pivot irrigating rigs that leave field puddles attract the most ducks. Traditionally 19, 24, and 40 have been the best picks.

A smart hunter will scout the area to learn flight patterns and to get a fix on cropping procedures. Just because one area was good one year does not necessarily mean it will be good another.

Requirements to hunt include state and federal duck stamps, a small-game license, public access stamp, daily lottery permit, and steel shot no larger than No. 1 and limited to 15 shells per hunter. Parking areas are assigned with permits, and hunters driving in and out must use the main entrance on White Road off Maple Island and then must follow the most direct route to hunting areas. All other driving requires a permit from county headquarters.

Hunters usually conceal themselves in standing corn although some bring tarps for field hunting. Most use field decoys.

The area holds fair to good numbers of deer, which may be archery hunted by special permit available only through county headquarters. Hunters must stop in during business hours at 8301 White Road in Muskegon (just north of the lagoons) to obtain the free permits. The telephone number is 616/853-2291. Shotgun deer hunting is not permitted because of ongoing cropping practices by the county.

The Muskegon County Wastewater Management System affords good waterfowling and deer hunting at a low-cost basis to the state. That's a good deal for hunters too.

Muskegon County Wastewater Management System

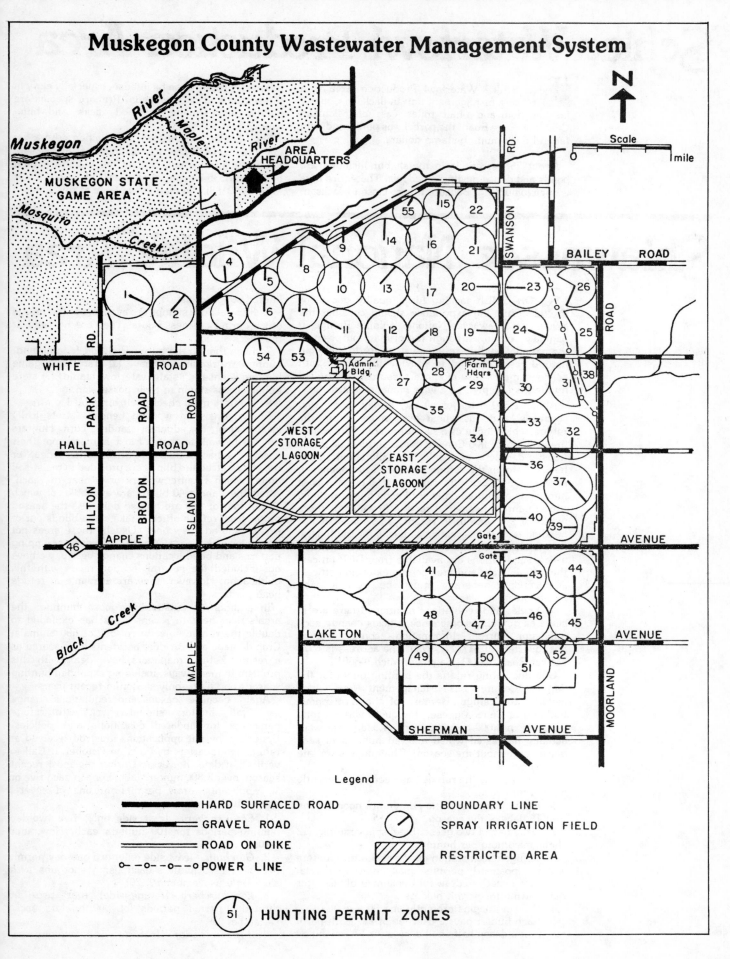

Legend

HARD SURFACED ROAD — — — BOUNDARY LINE

GRAVEL ROAD — SPRAY IRRIGATION FIELD

ROAD ON DIKE — RESTRICTED AREA

o—o—o—o POWER LINE

51 HUNTING PERMIT ZONES

Schlee Waterfowl Production Area

THE Schlee Waterfowl Production Area is a 160-acre management unit in Jackson County. Located four-and-a-half miles east of Michigan Center on Page Road, the parcel was purchased with federal duck-hunting-stamp dollars.

About 25 percent is in marsh but included are ponds and dense nesting meadows. The entire area is open to hunting. Because it is so close to Jackson,

however, pressure can be intense, especially early in the season and on weekends. Primary species are puddle ducks—mallards, wood ducks, and blue-winged teal.

The Schlee Waterfowl Production Area is managed by DNR District Headquarters at Jackson. For more information, contact the wildlife habitat biologist, 3335 Lansing Ave., Jackson, Mich. 49202 (517/784-3188). No map is available at this time.

Shiawassee National Wildlife Area

SPORTSMEN looking for a quality goose- or deer-hunting experience should consider the 8,900-acre Shiawassee National Wildlife Refuge in Saginaw County. Although the primary purposes of the national wildlife refuge system are to maintain natural resources and to provide the public with nonconsumptive use of those resources, controlled hunting is accepted as a wise management tool.

About 1,500 acres of wheat, barley, corn, rye, soybeans, and buckwheat are grown within the refuge, which includes a sanctuary area. The refuge draws up to 25,000 Canada geese and 50,000 ducks (mostly dabblers) each fall. Normally about 15,000 honkers are on the refuge by the season opener in early October. Duck hunting is not allowed. Goose hunting is permitted daily until noon by permit only (three hunters per party) for the first two or three weeks of the season. In recent years the DNR has handled permit reservation requests for the federal refuge along with the state waterfowl-management areas. Applications are available from DNR offices, the refuge itself, and area county extension offices. Applications generally must be returned by mid-September.

Any rules and regulations mentioned here are to serve as guidelines only since policies change each fall. For current information, contact refuge headquarters at 517/777-5930. The address is 6975 Mower Road, RR #1, Saginaw, Mich. 48601.

One fluctuating rule is the hunting quota for the Saginaw County Goose Management Area, which includes the refuge. Because of the tremendous build-up of Canada geese, this quota was recently raised from 3,000 to 5,000 birds (4,323 geese were actually harvested which allowed hunters to seek geese throughout the season). The quota is set late each summer.

This is the way the refuge has been most recently hunted for geese:

1. Hunting by reservation only until noon for the first 16 days of the season.

2. Daily bag of two geese. Steel shot required (12 shells maximum per hunter).

3. Refuge check station opens at 5 a.m. Hunters without postcard permits may sign a special "standby sheet" to draw for unclaimed blinds after the drawing for permit holders.

4. Drawing begins promptly at 5:30 a.m.

5. Each hunter pays a user fee of $2. Each party may rent a dozen half-shell decoys for $1 as long as

limited supplies last.

6. Federal duck stamps are available at the refuge office during business hours. They are not sold at the check station.

7. Even though the hunt is held on federal land, hunters are required to have (1) state small-game hunting license, (2) state waterfowl stamp, (3) state public-access stamp in their possession.

8. Hunters must check their birds by 1 p.m.

Blinds consist of wooden benches strategically located along the edges of standing corn. Hunters can easily walk to them. Most hunters spot their decoys in adjacent fields of barley, winter wheat, or rye. A few structure blinds are provided in moist-soil units, which require waders or a boat to reach. Altogether, about 40 blinds are available, of which all but four or five are hunted daily. As the season progresses, refuge officials take some blinds out of service and add new ones. Usually those areas not producing well are closed. Because cropping patterns and blind locations change yearly, we have not included the several location maps with this publication. However, they are available at refuge headquarters.

In addition to outstanding goose hunting, the area's deer herd in recent years has exploded to double the refuge objective of 500 or 600 animals. Crop damage and car-deer accidents have soared as a result. Refuge managers have dealt with this problem in many ways, including expanded hunting seasons and a doe-only season in recent years.

Again, because seasons and regulations change each fall, hunters should check with refuge personnel for updated conditions and policies. Generally, permit applications must be received at refuge headquarters by noon on October 1. Call to verify that date, however. During the most recent season, over 2,300 hunters (about one in each five or six applicants) drew permits for one of several special hunts:

1. *Early archery*—(east side only) five two-day hunting periods for 100 hunters each. November 1-10.

2. *Gun hunt*—(east side only) two one-day permit periods for 75 hunters each using shotguns *with slugs only* (November 19, 20).

3. *Late archery*—(refuge-wide) four two- or three-day permit periods for 300 hunters each, December 1-9.

4. *Muzzleloader*—(refuge-wide) two one-day

hunting periods for 250 hunters each, December 10, 11.

5. *Open archery*—no permit required from December 12 to January 1.

Deer hunters may apply individually or in groups of two or three. They may apply once each for firearm and archery hunting periods if they use a separate card for each. Refuge personnel will mail application cards to hunters if they (1) send a stamped, self-addressed envelope, (2) specify how many cards they need, (3) indicate whether the cards are for goose or deer hunting.

Although the chances of getting a permit for deer or during the early days of the goose season are slim, those that do are treated to quality hunting. Deer hunters overall score 25 to 30 percent success (double the state average), but, depending upon the type of hunt, this figure can go to 60 percent. Early-season goose hunters score at a 90 percent rate, but this figure drops rapidly as geese wise up.

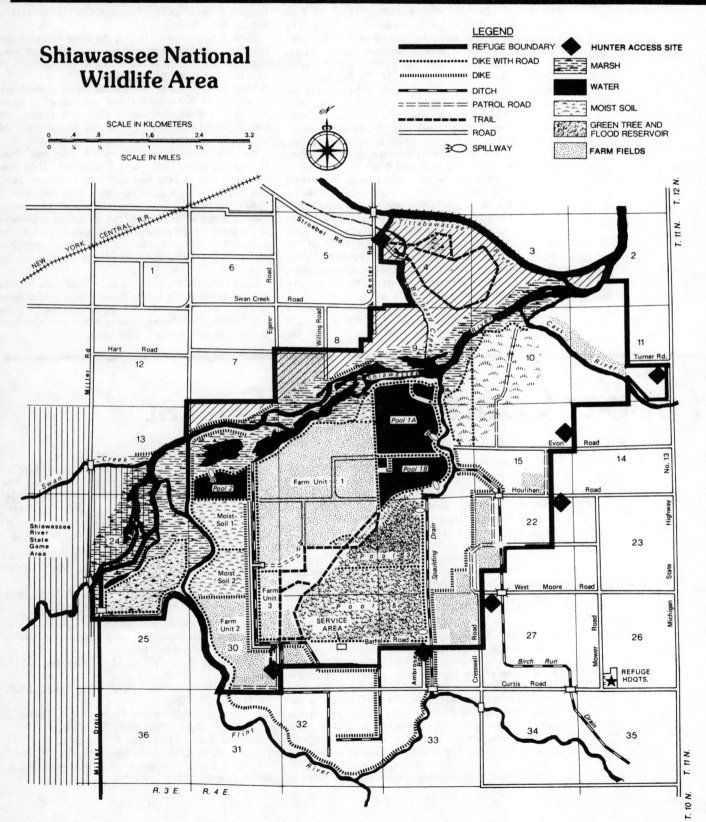

Shiawassee National Wildlife Area

LEGEND

▬▬▬▬ REFUGE BOUNDARY	◆ HUNTER ACCESS SITE
•••••••• DIKE WITH ROAD	MARSH
∎∎∎∎∎∎ DIKE	WATER
▪▪▪▪▪▪ DITCH	MOIST SOIL
═══════ PATROL ROAD	GREEN TREE AND FLOOD RESERVOIR
▬ ▬ ▬ TRAIL	FARM FIELDS
══════ ROAD	
⊙ SPILLWAY	

SCALE IN KILOMETERS
0 .4 .8 1.6 2.4 3.2
0 ¼ ½ 1 1½ 2
SCALE IN MILES

Michigan State Forests

THE last glacier that visited northern Michigan some 10,000 years ago scoured the land and, upon its retreat, left a wide variety of soil types. These varying soils produce many different types of trees and other vegetative cover, which in turn harbor a mixture of game animals and birds. For instance, sandy soils in glacial outwash areas produce jack pine and scrub oak (deer, hares, coyotes). Soils of moderate fertility yield aspen (deer, grouse, hares, woodcock). Richer morainic soils contain northern hardwoods of beech, maple, oak, birch, and ash (squirrels, turkeys, deer). Wet, poorly drained areas are often timbered with lowland hardwoods (black oak, basswood, cottonwood) and conifer types (spruce, balsam, cedar). These in turn yield bear, coyotes, bobcats, deer, snowshoe hares, and gray and black squirrels.

After loggers cut the pine and hardwoods, forest fires burned through leftover slashings so that by 1920 much of the original cover was gone, thus leaving a wasteland. Thousands of acres then came into public ownership through tax reversions during the Great Depression, accounting for much of the land in Michigan's state forest system today. Aggressive fire protection and Civilian Conservation Corps plantings helped the forests to once more thrive and to produce huntable game.

The DNR Forest Management Division is in the process of inventorying 1,500- to 2,500-acre units (called compartments) in the state forests for 10-year prescriptive management plans. These may include timber harvesting, wildlife planting, reforestation, or development of openings. Timber cutting, which provides openings, edge cover, and regeneration of young forest types, is especially helpful for wildlife.

Thus, when done correctly, the state can produce wildlife habitat at a monetary gain. Another way that hunters benefit is through the construction of access roads made by loggers.

Most campgrounds in the state forest system are small (five to 50 campsites) and are located on lakes or rivers. Facilities include tables, fire circles, pit toilets, and hand pumps. The fee is currently $4 daily.

Hunters simply select a vacant site and then register by filling out a form and permit. They tear off the permit, put the payment in an envelope, seal, and deposit it in a collection pipe and then attach their ''paid-for'' camp permit to the marker post. Camping is also permitted free of charge anywhere in the state forest, providing that hunters fill out the permit first. These are available at most campsites and at DNR district and field offices throughout the state.

Unfortunately, maps of the individual state forests are not availble. To locate these public lands, refer to the Michigan United Conservation Clubs publication, ''Michigan County Maps and Outdoor Guide,'' or use a county plat book.

Copper Country State Forest

LOCATED in the far western Upper Peninsula, the Copper Country State Forest headquartered at Baraga contains some 440,000 acres, all open to hunting. Counties with state forest land include Baraga, Houghton, Keweenaw, Gogebic, Ontonagon, Iron, and Dickinson (all of which see).

The Copper Country State Forest has good populations of deer, snowshoe hares, ruffed grouse, and woodcock. Other game species include squirrels, black bear, bobcats, raccoon, coyotes, and waterfowl.

The Copper Country State Forest contains some of the best sugar-maple timber lands in the Upper Peninsula. In addition, excellent stands of aspen, pine, spruce, and balsam have been managed for pulpwood and sawlogs. Iron and Dickinson counties have some of the highest deer populations in the state and provide good opportunities for grouse and woodcock hunters. Also of interest to hunters is the variable climate within the state forest. Along the Lake Superior snow belt, 250 inches or more of snow is not unusual each winter whereas in southern Dickinson County the norm is about 50 inches per winter.

The Copper Country State Forest has 218 miles of roads and many other miles of two-tracks and trails.

The Copper Country State Forest is divided into three geographical areas with staff personnel available at each:

1. Baraga Forest Area (Baraga District Office), North US-41, Baraga, Mich. 49908 (906/353-6654).

2. Crystal Falls Forest Area (Crystal Falls District Office), US-2 West, Crystal Falls, Mich. 49920 (906/875-6622).

3. Norway Forest Area (Norway Field Office), US-2, Norway, Mich. 49870 (906/563-9247).

Hunters can sometimes get further information by contacting DNR personnel at these locations (they may not be staffed full time):

1. Calumet Field Office, M-26, Calumet, Mich. 49913 (906/377-1700).

2. Felch Field Office, Hwy. 569, Felch, Mich. 49831 (906/246-3245).

3. Porcupine Mountains Field Office, Route 1, Ontonagon, Mich. 49953 (906/885-5712).

4. Twin Lakes Field Office, Route 1, Box 234, Toivola, Mich. 49965 (906/288-3321).

5. Wakefield Field Office, US-2, Wakefield, Mich. 49968 (906/224-2771).

Michigan DNR

213

Escanaba State Forest

LOCATED in the central Upper Peninsula, the Escanaba River State Forest headquartered at Escanaba contains over 400,000 acres, all open to hunting. Counties with state forest land include Marquette, Alger, Delta, and Menominee (all of which see).

The Escanaba River State Forest has good populations of deer, snowshoe hares, and ruffed grouse. Other game species include woodcock, black bear, bobcats, squirrels, raccoon, wild turkeys, coyotes, and waterfowl.

The forest climate varies from mild winters in southern Menominee County to rugged winter conditions along the Lake Superior shore. Partly due to mild winters, southern Menominee County contains excellent central hardwoods of white oak, butternut, and hickory and good numbers of deer, turkeys, and squirrels. The largest deer population in the Upper Peninsula is found here, attracted to both the hardwoods food and cover and the many stands of white cedar.

Cover types throughout the Escanaba River State Forest include aspen (29 percent), swamp conifers (14 percent), northern hardwoods (13 percent), black spruce (seven percent), lowland brush (six percent), and smaller amounts of jack pine, lowland hardwoods, cedar, red pine, and spruce.

During a recent year the Escanaba River State Forest yielded a record $570,000 paid for 100,000 cords of sawlogs, pulpwood, and miscellaneous products.

The forest contains 266 miles of permanent roads and 27 bridges as well as countless miles of trails and two-tracks.

Hunters should know that the Escanaba River State Forest contains 11 rustic-type campgrounds with about 170 campsites.

Of special interest to hunters is the recent addition of a 5,000-acre block of rolling hills with varying forest types just north of Escanaba. It is called the Days River Ski Pathway. Also, just north of Marquette is the 3,000-acre Little Presque Isle tract. Lying along the eastern base of the Huron Mountains and including some Lake Superior shoreline, the region contains heavy stands of hemlock, pine, and birch.

The Escanaba River State Forest is divided into three geographical areas with staff personnel available at each:

1. Ishpeming Forest Area (Ishpeming Field Office), 632 Teal Lake Road, Ishpeming, Mich. 49849 (906/485-4193).

2. Gwinn Forest Area (Gwinn Field Office), M-35, Box 800, Gwinn, Mich. 49841 (906/346-9201).

3. Escanaba Forest Area (Escanaba Field Office), 1126 North Lincoln Road, Escanaba, Mich. 49829 (906/786-2353).

Hunters can sometimes get further information by contacting DNR personnel at these locations (they may not be staffed full time):

1. Champion Field Office, Box 163, Champion, Mich. 49814 (906/339-2251).

2. Marquette Field Office, 110 Ford Road, Marquette, Mich. 49855 (906/249-1497).

3. Stephenson Field Office, Box 308, Stephenson, Mich. 49887 (906/753-6317).

Lake Superior State Forest

LOCATED in the eastern Upper Peninsula, the Lake Superior State Forest headquartered at Newberry contains over one million acres of land open to hunting. It is the largest state-owned forest in Michigan and includes nearly 105 miles of shoreline on Lakes Superior, Michigan, and Huron. Counties with state forest land include Alger, Schoolcraft, Luce, Mackinac, and Chippewa (all of which see). Most of Drummond Island (which also see) at the far eastern tip of the Upper Peninsula also falls into Lake Superior State Forest ownership.

The Lake Superior State Forest has good populations of deer, snowshoe hares, ruffed grouse, sharp-tailed grouse, woodcock, and waterfowl. Other game species include black bear, bobcats, raccoon, squirrels, coyotes, and fox. Occasionally a moose or lynx (both protected) is seen.

Over the past five years average harvests of 18,000 cords and 2.4 million board feet of hardwood and 39,000 cords and 1.5 million board feet of softwood have generated an average yearly income to the state of $575,000. If markets were available for all scheduled harvests, these figures would likely be five times higher.

The Lake Superior State Forest contains 45 rustic-type campgrounds with 780 campsites.

The Lake Superior State Forest is divided into four geographical areas with staff personnel available at each:

1. Shingleton Forest Area (Shingleton Field Office), M-28, Shingleton, Mich. 49884 (906/452-6226).

2. Newberry Forest Area (Newberry Field Office), M-123 South, Newberry, Mich. 49868 (906/293-8791).

3. Naubinway Forest Area (Naubinway Field Office), US-2, Naubinway, Mich. 49762 (906/477-6262).

4. Sault Ste. Marie Forest Area (Sault Ste. Marie Field Office), Box 798, Sault Ste. Marie, Mich. 49738 (906/635-5281).

Hunters can sometimes get further information by contacting DNR personnel at these locations (they may not be staffed full time):

1. De Tour Field Office, M-134, De Tour Village, Mich. 49725 (906/297-2581).

2. Seney Field Office, M-28, Seney, Mich. 49883 (906/499-3346).

3. Thompson Field Office, Route 2, Box 2555, Manistique, Mich. 49854 (906/341-6917).

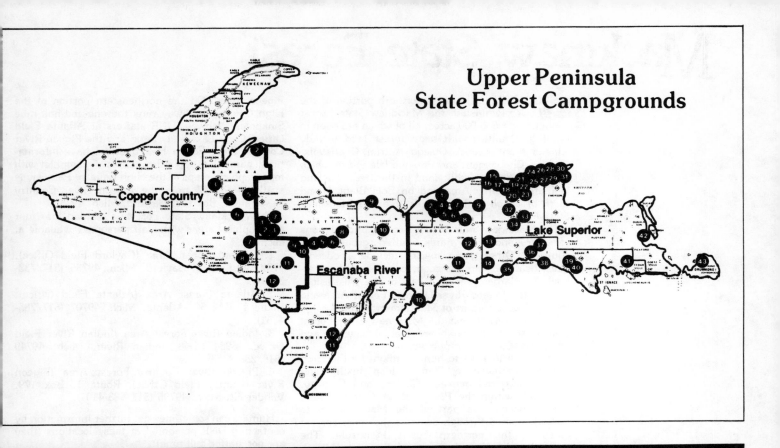

Upper Peninsula State Forest Campgrounds

Copper Country State Forest
430,291 acres

Baraga
906-353-6651

Map Number	Name and Location of Campground	No. of Sites	Boating/Canoeing	Swimming	Fishing *	Special Attractions Pathways
1	EMILY LAKE—2.5 Mi. S. of Twin Lake St. Park via M-26 & Pike Lake Co. Rd.	9	B	2	C W	Good trout and bass fishing
2	BIG ERIC'S BRIDGE 6 Mi. E of Skanee	19		2	6	Huron River Pathway
3	BIG LAKE—9 Mi. NW of Covington Via US-141 & Co. Rd.	15	B	1	W	Good swimming beach
4	KING LAKE—15 Mi. E of Covington Via M-28, U.S. 41 & Co. Rd.	5	B	3	W	Very scenic lake
5	BEAUFORT LAKE—1.5 Mi. SE of Three Lakes via US-41 & Co. Rd.	15	B	1	W	Good walleye fishing
6	DEER LAKE—17 Mi. N of Crystal Falls Via US-141 & Deer Lake Rd.	12	B	1	W	Secluded Area
7	LAKE ELLEN—4 mi. W of Channing Via Campground Rd.	10	B	3	C W	Good trout fishing
8	GLIDDEN LAKE—8 Mi. SE of Crystal Falls Via M-69 & Lake Mary Rd.	23	B		W	Pathway available
9	WEST BRANCH—7 Mi. N of Ralph Via Co. Rd. 581	24	C	3	C	Big West Branch Escanaba River, Pathway
10	LOWER DAM—11 Mi. NE of Ralph Via Co. Rd. 581	5	C	3	C	Big West Branch Escanaba River
11	GENE'S POND—6.5 Mi. NW of Theodore Via Co. Rd. 581 (G-67). Co. Rd. 422 & Campground Rd.	14	B	3	W	Scenic area around the flooding
12	CARNEY LAKE—11 Mi. NE of Iron Mountain Via M-95 & Merriman Truck Trail	11	B	2	W	Very scenic area, Pathway

Escanaba River State Forest
402,696 acres

Escanaba
906-786-2351

Map Number	Name and Location of Campground	No. of Sites	Boating/Canoeing	Swimming	Fishing *	Special Attractions Pathways
1	SQUAW LAKE—4 Mi. NW of Witch Lake Via Fence River Rd & Squaw Lake Rd.	15	B	2	C W	Lake contains some large splake
2	HORSESHOE LAKE (NORTH UNIT)— 1.25 Mi. W of Witch Lake Via Fence River Rd.	11	B	1	W	Walk-in tent sites available
3	HORSESHOE LAKE (SOUTH UNIT)— 1 Mi. W of Witch Lake Via Fence River Rd.	13	B	1	W	Generally good bass fishing
4	BASS LAKE—12 Mi. SW of Gwinn	21	B	1	C W	Good rainbow fishing
5	PIKE LAKE—9 Mi. SW of Gwinn	10	B	3	W	Secluded camping area, Two walk-in sites
6	ANDERSON LAKE WEST—7 Mi. SW of Gwinn Via Co. Rd. 577	19	B	1	W	Good swimming, Pathway
7	WITBECK RAPIDS—2.25 Mi. N of Witch Lake Via M-95 and Campground Rd.	19	C	3	C	14 drive-in and 5 walk in sites
8	LITTLE LAKE—1 Mi. SE of Little Lake Via M-35	26	B	1	W	Good swimming & walleye fishing
9	LAUGHING WHITEFISH—12 Mi. W of Au Train via M-28 then 2 Miles N on Campground Rd.	15		3		Good spring & fall steelhead fishing

Lake Superior State Forest
1,026,058 acres

Newberry
906-293-5131

Map Number	Name and Location of Campground	No. of Sites	Boating/Camping	Swimming	Fishing *	Special Attractions Pathways
10	FOREST LAKE—2.5 Mi. SW of Forest Via M-94 & Campground Rd.	23	B	2	W	Good pike fishing, 3 walk-in sites
11	CEDAR RIVER—5 Mi NW of Cedar River Via M-35 and River Rd.	8	C	2	C W	Pathway available
12	CEDAR RIVER NORTH—6 Mi. NW of Cedar River Via M-35 and River Road	15	C		C W	Pathway
1	KINGSTON LAKE—16 Mi NE of Melstrand Via Au Sable Pt. Rd.	14	B	2	W	Near pictured rocks, Pathway
2	NORTH GEMINI LAKE—10 Mi NE of Melstrand Via Co. R. M-58 & Twin Lakes Truck Trail	17	B	2	W	Pathway
3	SOUTH GEMINI LAKE—12 Mi. NE of Melstrand Via Co. Rd. M-58 and Twin Lakes Truck Trail	8	B	2	W	Secluded campground Pathway
4	ROSS LAKE—14 Mi. NE of Melstrand Via Co. Rd. M-58 & Crooked Lake Rd.	10	B	2	W	Large hardwood area
5	CANOE LAKE—9 Mi. E of Melstrand Via Co. Rd. H-528 & 450 & Wolf Lake Rd.	4		3	W	Small secluded lake
6	CUSINO LAKE—11 Mi. E. of Melstrand Via Co. Rds. H-52 & 450	6	B	1	W	Good swimming beach, bass fishing
7	STANLEY LAKE—15 Mi. NW of Seney Via Co. Rd. 450 & Mahoney Lake Rd.	10	B	3	W	Good fishing, Pathway
8	FOX LAKE—5 Mi. NW of Seney Via Co. Rd. 450	6	C	3	C	Good trout fishing, Pathway
9	EAST BRANCH OF FOX RIVER—8 Mi. N of Seney Via M-77	16		3	C	Good trout fishing
10	PORTAGE BAY—10 Mi. S of Garden Via Co. Rd. 483 & Portage Bay Rd.	18	B	1	W	On Lake Michigan. Interpretive pathway
11	MERWIN CREEK—9 Mi. NW of Gulliver Via US-2, Co. Rds. 438 and 433.	11	C	3	W	Manistique River 4 miles west off US-2
12	MEAD CREEK—6 Mi. SW of Germfask Via M-77 and Co. Rd. 436	10	C	3		Located south of the Seney National Wildlife Refuge
13	SOUTH MANISTIQUE LAKE—6 Mi. SW of Curtis Via S. Curtis Rd. & Long Point Rd.	29	B	2	W	Good walleye fishing
14	MILAKOKIA LAKE—7 Mi. SW of Gould City Via US-2 & Pike Lake Grade	36	B	2	W	Northern pike fishing
15	LAKE SUPERIOR—15 Mi. E of Grand Marais Via Grand Marais Truck Trail	18		1	C	Agate hunting on beach, Pathway
16	BLIND SUCKER NO. 1—14 Mi. E of Grand Marais Via Grand Marais Truck Trail	13	B	1	W	Good pike fishing
17	BLIND SUCKER NO. 2—16 Mi. E of Grand Marais Via Grand Marais Truck Trail	36	B	2	W	Duck hunting
18	PRATT LAKE—28 Mi. NW of Newberry Via M-123 & Co. Rds. 407 & 416	6		2	C	Small secluded campground
19	HOLLAND LAKE—26 Mi. NW of Newberry Via M-123 & Co. Rds. 407 & 416	15		2	W	Good trout fishing

Map Number	Name and Location of Campground	No. of Sites	Boating/Canoeing	Swimming	Fishing *	Special Attractions Pathways
20	PRETTY LAKE—27 Mi. NW of Newberry Via M-123, Co. Rd. 407, 416 & Campground Rd.	18	B	1	C	No boat motors. Canoe or walk-in. Pathway.
21	PERCH LAKE—25 Mi. N of Newberry Via M-123 & Co. Rd. 407	35	B	1	W	Good bass fishing
22	HEADQUARTERS LAKE—24 Mi. N of Newberry Via M-123 & Co. Rd. 407	8		3		Quiet Pine Area
23	HIGH BRIDGE—23 Mi. N of Newberry Via M-123 & Co. Rd. 407	7	C	3	C	Good steelhead fishing & canoeing
24	REED & GREEN BRIDGE—31 Mi. N of Newberry Via M-122 & Co. Rds. 401 & 410	4	C	1	C	Two Hearted River
25	TWO HEARTED RIVER CANOE CAMP 28 Mi. N of Newberry	4	C	3	C	Two Hearted River, canoe access only
26	MOUTH OF TWO HEARTED RIVER— 35 Mi. NE of Newberry Via M-123. Co. Rds. 500, 414, 412, & 423	45	B	1	C	Agate hunting along Lake Superior
27	PIKE LAKE—29 Mi. NE of Newberry Via M-123, Co. Rds. 500 & 437	23	B	2	W	Blueberry Country
28	BODI LAKE—32 Mi. NE of Newberry Via M-123, Co. Rds. 500 & 437	20	B	1	W	Excellent swimming beach
29	CULHANE LAKE—30 Mi. NE of Newberry Via M-123 & Co. Rd. 500	22	B	2	W	Secluded campground in big pines
30	ANDRUS LAKE—6 Mi. N of Paradise Via Wire Rd. & Vermillion Rd.	25	B	1	C	Good swimming
31	SHELLDRAKE DAM—8 Mi. N of Paradise Via Wire Rd. & Vermillion Rd.	17	B	3	W	Good pike fishing
32	BASS LAKE—9.5 Mi. N of McMillan Via Co. Rds. 415 & 421	18	B	3	C W	isolated hardwood country
33	SIXTEEN CREEK—16 Mi. N of Newberry Via M-123 & Charcoal Grade	12	B	3	C	Tahquamenon River, secluded campground
34	NATALIE—4.5 Mi. W of Newberry Via Co. Rds. 405 & 43A	12	B	3	W	Dollarville flooding backwaters
35	BIG KNOB—14 Mi. SW of Naubinway Via US-2 & Big Knob Rd.	23		1		Lake Michigan beach, sand dunes, Pathway
36	BLACK RIVER—7 Mi. NE of Naubinway Via US-2 & Black River Rd.	12		3		Secluded campground with good trout fishing
37	GARNET LAKE—1 Mi. SE of Garnet	8	B	2	W	Northern pike and perch fishing
38	HOG ISLAND POINT—7 Mi. E of Naubinway Via US-2	58	B	1	C	On Lake Michigan, Good beach
39	LITTLE BREVOORT LAKE (NORTH UNIT)—2 Mi. NE of Brevort Via Carp River Rd. & Worth Rd.	20	B	2	W	Pathway
40	LITTLE BREVOORT LAKE (SOUTH UNIT)—1.5 Mi. SE of Brevort Via US-2	12	B	2	W	Pathway on sand dune ridges
41	BAY CITY LAKE—3 Mi. NW of Hessel Via 3 Mile Road	19	B	2	W	Les Cheneaux Islands
42	MUNUSCONG RIVER—8 Mi. NE of Pickford Via M-48 & Sterlingville Rd.	50	B	3	C	Group camping, Good fishing & duck hunting
43	MAXTON BAY—4.5 Mi. NE of Drummond Via Maxton Plains Rd.	18	B	3	W	Drummond Island, perch and walleye fishing

*C stands for coldwater fish species, W for warmwater species

Mackinaw State Forest

LOCATED in the most northern portion of the Lower Peninsula, the Mackinaw State Forest contains over 660,000 acres, all of which are open to hunting. Counties with state forest land include Alpena, Montmorency, Otsego, Antrim, Charlevoix, Emmet, Cheboygan, and Presque Isle (*all of which see*). In addition, public land in the Beaver Island Wildlife Research Area and on Bois Blanc Island (*both of which see*) also falls into the Mackinaw State Forest.

The Mackinaw State Forest has good populations of deer, snowshoe hares, ruffed grouse, and squirrels. Other game species include woodcock, black bear, bobcats, raccoon, coyotes, and waterfowl. The largest elk herd east of the Mississippi lives in the Pigeon River Country Forest Area and the northwestern part of Montmorency County.

During a recent year the Mackinaw State Forest yielded seven million board feet of sawlogs and nearly 58,000 cords of pulpwood.

Of special interest to hunters might be the High Country Pathway, a 70-mile loop hiking and backpacking trail between Gaylord and Onaway. The trail, within the Pigeon River Country State Forest (which is a part of the Mackinaw State Forest), passes through some of the most remote areas in the northern Lower Peninsula. The well-marked trail winds across the Pigeon and Black rivers and Canada Creek as well as many small streams. Ten lakes and two wildlife floodings are close to the trail.

Hunters will see old-growth virgin white and red pine along with well-managed stands of beech, ash, and sugar maple. Interspersed throughout are dense swamps containing cedar, spruce, and tamarack and upland jack-pine areas. Deer, hares, grouse, squirrels, and occasional bobcats, bear, and elk may be seen.

Also, the Shingle Mill Pathway, a series of loop trails which form part of the western side of the High Country Pathway, offers an 11.5-mile hike for hunters. Much of it runs along the banks of the Pigeon River. On the northeastern portion of the High Country Pathway runs the one-and-half-mile Sinkholes Pathway. DNR staffers at Atlanta Field Office, Clear Lake State Park, and the Pigeon River Country State Forest Headquarters have informational pamphlets about these trails. A pamphlet with topographical maps of the High Country Pathway is available for $2 from the Pigeon River Country Association, Box 122, Gaylord, Mich. 49735.

The Mackinaw State Forest is divided into four geographical areas with staff personnel available at each:

1. Gaylord Forest Area (Gaylord Field Office), 1732 West M-32, Gaylord, Mich. 49735 (517/732-3541).

2. Atlanta Forest Area (Atlanta Field Office), Route 1, Box 30, Atlanta, Mich. 49707 (517/785-4251).

3. Indian River Forest Area (Indian River Field Office), 6984 M-68, Indian River, Mich. 49749 (616/238-9313).

4. Pigeon River Country Forest Area (Pigeon River Country Field Office), Route 1, Box 179, Vanderbilt, Mich. 49795 (517/983-4101).

Hunters can sometimes get further information by contacting DNR personnel at these locations (they are not staffed full time):

1. Alpena Field Office, 4343 M-32, Alpena, Mich. 49707 (517/354-2209).

2. Beaver Island Field Office, St. James, Mich. 49782 (616/448-2255).

3. Bellaire Field Office, 701 Cayuga St., Bellaire, Mich. 49615 (616/533-8341).

4. Boyne City Field Office, 303 North Street, Boyne City, Mich. 49712 (616/582-6681).

5. Cheboygan Field Office, 120 A Street, Cheboygan, Mich. 49721 (616/627-9011).

6. Onaway Field Office, Route 1, Box 32, Hwy. M-211, Onaway, Mich. 49765 (517/733-8775).

7. Pellston Field Office, 304 Stimson, Pellston, Mich. 49769 (616/539-8564).

Pere Marquette State Forest

LOCATED in the northwestern Lower Peninsula, the Pere Marquette State Forest contains over 620,000 acres, all open to hunting. Counties with state forest land include Mecosta, Oceana, Osceola, Lake, Missaukee, Wexford, Manistee, Benzie, Grand Traverse, Leelanau, and Kalkaska (*all of which see*).

The Pere Marquette State Forest has good populations of deer, snowshoe hares, ruffed grouse, and squirrels. Other game species include woodcock, black bear, bobcats, raccoon, coyotes, and waterfowl.

During a recent year the Pere Marquete State Forest yielded $800,000 in revenue from the sale of timber.

The forest contains some 30 rustic-type campgrounds with about 700 campsites.

The Pere Marquette State Forest is divided into three geographical areas with staff personnel available at each:

1. Baldwin Forest Area (Baldwin Field Office), Route 2, Box 2810, Baldwin, Mich. 49304 (616/745-4651).

2. Kalkaska Forest Area (Kalkaska Area Office), 605 North Birch, Kalkaska, Mich. 49646 (616/258-9471).

3. Traverse City Forest Area (Traverse City Field Office), 404 West 14th St., Traverse City, Mich. 49684 (616/946-4920).

Hunters can sometimes get further information by

Lower Peninsula State Forest Campgrounds

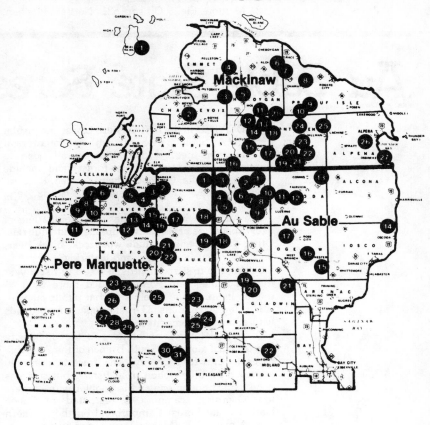

Mackinaw State Forest
663,843 acres — Gaylord — 517-732-3541

Map Number	Name and Location of Campground	No. of Sites	Boating/Canoeing	Swimming	Fishing*	Special Attractions Pathways
1	BEAVER ISLAND—7 Mi. S of St. James Via East Side Rd.	25	B		C	On Beaver Island, Pathway
2	GRAVES CROSSING—10 Mi. N. of Mancelona Via US-131 & M-66.	10	C	3	C	In Jordan Valley Pathway, fishing in Jordan River
3	WEBER LAKE—7.5 Mi. NW of Wolverine Via Wolverine Rd. & Prue Rd.	18		3	C	Lost Tamarack Pathway Special Fishing Regulations
4	MAPLE BAY—3.5 Mi. E of Brutus Via Brutus Rd.	36	B	1	W	On Burt Lake, Swimming beach
5	HAAKWOOD—2 Mi. N of Wolverine Via Old 27, then E on Campground Rd.	18	C	3	C	On Sturgeon River, good trout fishing
6	TWIN LAKES—6 Mi. SE of Alverno Via Black River Rd. & Twin Lakes Rd.	19			C	Good pan fishing
7	BLACK LAKE—11 Mi. NE of Onaway Via M-211, Co. Rd. 489, Black Mt. Rd. & Donva Road.	50	B	1	W	Sand swimming beach Pathway
8	OCQUEOC FALLS—10 Mi. NE of Onaway Via M-68 & Millersburg.	14		3	C	At Ocqueoc River Falls Scenic Site
9	SHOEPAC LAKE—12 Mi. SE of Onaway Via M-33 & Tomahawk Lake Hwy.	50	B	3	W	Natural limestone sink holes. Pathway. Motor size limited
10	TOMAHAWK LAKE—11 Mi. SE of Onaway Via M-33 & Tomahawk Lake Hwy.	42	B	2	W	Good pan fishing, Pathway
11	PINE GROVE—2 Mi. SE of Wolverine Via Wolverine Rd. & Webb Rd.	8			C	Secluded campground on Pigeon River, Pathway
12	PICKEREL LAKE—10 Mi. E of Vanderbilt Via Sturgeon Valley Rd. & Pickerel Lake Rd.	39	B	1	C	Old CCC historic site, Pathway
13	PIGEON RIVER—13 Mi. E. of Vanderbilt Via Sturgeon Valley Rd. & Osmund Rd.	19		3	C	On Pigeon River, Pathway
14	PIGEON BRIDGE—11 Mi. E of Vanderbilt Via Sturgeon Valley Rd.	10		3	C	11 mile pathway connects 2 campgrounds
15	ROUND LAKE—14 Mi. SE of Vanderbilt Via Sturgeon Valley Rd. & Round Lake Rd.	6		3	W	High Country Pathway
16	LAKE MARJORY—1.25 Mi. SE of Waters Via Old US-27.	10	B	3	W	Near Gaylord
17	BIG BEAR LAKE—1.5 Mi. SW of Vienna Via Principal Meridian Rd. & Little Bear Lake Rd.	43	B	1	W	Pathway, good beach and walleye fishing
18	TOWN CORNER—Inquire at District Headquarters Gaylord. Phone 517-732-3541	12	B	2	W	Secluded campground, Pathway
19	LITTLE WOLF LAKE—3 Mi. SE of Lewiston Via Co. Rd. 489 & Wolf Lake Rd.	28		1	C/W	Pan fishing
20	McCORMICK LAKE—10 Mi. SW of Atlanta Via M-32 & Camp 8 Rd.	10	C	3	C	Trout fishing, very deep lake
21	BIG OAKS—10 Mi. SW of Atlanta Via Co. Rd. 487 & Avery Lake Rd.	29	B	3	C/W	On Avery Lake, Boat ramp, Campground
22	AVERY LAKE—9 Mi. SW of Atlanta Via Co. Rd. 487 & Avery Lake Rd.	14	B	3	C	Secluded lake, Drive in and walk in sites
23	LAKE 15—3 Mi. SW of Atlanta.	12		3	C	Pike & Trout fishing
24	JACKSON LAKE—6 Mi. N of Atlanta Via M-33.	24	B	2	W	Pan fishing, Pathway
25	ESS LAKE—16 Mi. NE of Atlanta Via M-33 M-33 & Co. Rd. 624.	29	B	1	C	Good swimming beach
26	THUNDER BAY RIVER—9 Mi. SW of Alpena Via M-32 & Indian Reserve Rd.	17	B	3	W	On Thunder Bay River, Bass & Pike, Pathway
27	OSSINEKE—1 Mi. E. of Ossineke.	42	B	1	C	On Lake Huron, Pathway
28	ELK HILL—13.5 Mi. E of Vanderbilt Via Sturgeon Valley Rd and Osmund Rd.	5	C	3	C	End of N-S Spur of Shore to Shore trail

Pere Marquette State Forest
621,052 acres — Cadillac — 616-775-9727

Map Number	Name and Location of Campground	No. of Sites	Boating/Canoeing	Swimming	Fishing*	Special Attractions Pathways
1	PICKEREL LAKE—13.5 Mi. NE of Kalkaska Via Co. Rd. 612 & Sunset Trail Rd.	12	B	2	W	
2	GUERNSEY LAKE—8 Mi. W. of Kalkaska Via Island Lake Rd. & Campground Rd.	26	B	2	C	In Sand Lakes area, pathway, walk-in campsites
3	FORKS—7 Mi. S of Williamsburg Via Williamsburg Rd., Supply Rd. & River Rd.	8	C	3	C	Boardman River, Good trout fishing
4	SCHECK'S PLACE—7 Mi. S of Williamsburg Via Williamsburg Rd., Supply Rd. & Brown Bridge Rd.	31	C	3	C	Boardman River, Pathway
5	ARBUTUS NO. 4—10 Mi. SE of Traverse City Via Garfield Rd., Potter Rd., 4 Mi. Rd & N. Arbutus Lake Rd.	50	B	1	W	Pathway, string of lakes, good swimming
6	LAKE DUBONNET—5 Mi. NW of Interlochen State Park Via M-137, US-31 & Wildwood Rd.	50	B	3	W	Interpretive pathway
7	LAKE ANN—2 Mi. SW of Lake Ann Via Almira Rd. & Reynolds Rd.	30	B	1	W	Interpretive pathway
8	VETERANS MEMORIAL—3.5 Mi. E of Honor Via US-31.	24	C	3	C	Near Platte River Hatchery, Interpretive pathway
9	PLATTE RIVER—2.5 Mi. SE of Honor Via US-31 & Goose Rd.	26	C	3	C	On Platte River, Interpretive pathway
10	GRASS LAKE—10 Mi. SE of Thompsonville Via Co. Rd. 669 & Wallin Rd.	15	B/C		W	Pathway, duck hunting
11	HEALY LAKE—7.5 Mi. SW of Copemish Via Co. Rd. 669 & Piagany Rd. & entrance Rd.	24	B	1	W	Pathway
12	INDIAN CROSSING—6.5 Mi. NE of Sherman Via Rd. No. 14 & Campground Rd.	19	C	3	C	On Manistee River, Poor access to site
13	BAXTER BRIDGE—12 Mi. NW of Manton Via M-42 & Rd. No. 31.	15	C	3	C	On Manistee River, Canoe group campsites
14	OLD US-131—6 Mi. N of Manton on US-131.	19	C	3	C	On Manistee River, Canoe group campsites
15	SPRING LAKE—1.5 Mi. SW of Fife Lake Via US-131.	32		2	W	Access canal to Fife Lake
16	CHASE CREEK—7.5 Mi. NE of Manton Via M-42 & Rd. No. 45½.	6	C	3	C	On Manistee River, Canoe group campsites
17	SMITHVILLE—.5 Mi. NW of Smithville Via M-66.	15	C	3	C	On Manistee River, Canoe group campsites
18	C.C.C. BRIDGE—20 Mi. SE of Kalkaska Via M-72 & Sunset Trail Rd.	23	C	3	C	On Manistee River, Canoe group campsites
19	REEDSBURG DAM—5 Mi. NW of Houghton Lake Via M-55 & Co. Rd. 300.	42	B	3	W	Good fishing, Boat rental, Near Dead Stream Swamp

Map Number	Name and Location of Campground	No. of Sites	Boating/Canoeing	Swimming	Fishing*	Special Attractions Pathways
20	LONG LAKE—8 Mi. NE of Cadillac Via US-131 & Campground Rd.	5	B	3	W	Nestled in hilly hardwoods
21	GOOSE LAKE—2.5 Mi. NW of Lake City Via M-66 & Goose Lake Rd.	54	B	1	W	Good swimming beach
22	LONG LAKE—3.5 Mi. NW of Lake City Via M-66 & Goose Lake Rd.	16	B	1	W	One way access road, Hilly and scenic
23	LINCOLN BRIDGE—7 Mi. N of Luther Via State Rd. & 10 Mile Rd.	9	C	3	C	On Pine River, Pathway and walk-in campsites
24	SILVER CREEK—5.5 Mi. N of Luther Via State Rd.	29	C	3	C	On Pine River, Pathway
25	SUNRISE LAKE—6 Mi. E of LeRoy Via Sunset Lake Rd. & 15 Mile Rd.	17	B	2	C/W	Good trout fishing
26	CARRIEVILLE—3 Mi. W of Luther Via Old M-63 & Kings Hwy.	26		3		On Little Manistee River
27	BRAY CREEK—1.5 Mi. NE of Baldwin Via M-37, North St., Maryville Rd. & 40th St.	10		3	C	On Baldwin River Pathway
28	LITTLE LEVERENTZ—2 Mi. NE of Baldwin Via Campground Rd.	7		1		Special boat motor regulations, Pathway
29	BIG LEVERENTZ—2 Mi. NE of Baldwin Via Campground Rd.	10		1		Special boat motor regulations, Pathway
30	TUBBS ISLAND—7 Mi. SW of Barryton Via M-66, 17 Mile Rd. & 45 Ave.	9	B	1	W	Good pan fishing
31	TUBBS LAKE—6.5 Mi. SW of Barryton Via M-66, 17 Mile Rd. & 45 Ave.	21	B	3	W	Good pan fishing

Au Sable State Forest
748,458 acres — Mio — 517-826-3211

Map Number	Name and Location of Campground	No. of Sites	Boating/Canoeing	Swimming	Fishing*	Special Attractions Pathways
1	SHUPAC LAKE—2 Mi. N of Lovells Via Twin Bridge Rd.	30	B	1	W	Special regulation on boat motors
2	JONES LAKE—9 Mi. E of Frederic Via Co. Rd. 612.	42	B	2	W	Ramp for small boats
3	UPPER MANISTEE RIVER—6.5 Mi. W of Frederic Via Co. Rd. 612.	30	C	3	C	Group camping for canoeists
4	MANISTEE RIVER BRIDGE—8 Mi. W of Grayling Via M-72.	23	C	3	C	Good trout fishing, canoe access
5	LAKE MARGRETHE—5 Mi. W of Grayling Via M-72.	40		1	W	Good swimming
6	AU SABLE RIVER CANOE CAMP—7 Mi. E of Grayling Via North Down River Rd. & Headquarter's Rd.	15	C	3	C	20 campsites for canoe group, canoe access
7	BURTON'S LANDING—4.5 Mi. E of Grayling Via M-72 & Burton's Landing Rd.	12	C	3	C	On the Au Sable River, canoe access
8	KEYSTONE LANDING—6 Mi. E of Grayling Via M-72 & Keystone Landing Rd.	18	C	3	C	On the Au Sable River, canoe access
9	CANOE HARBOR—14 Mi. SE of Grayling Via M-72.	45	C	3	C	On Au Sable S Branch, Canoe access
10	WHITE PINE CANOE CAMP—12 Mi. E of Grayling Via M-72 & McMaster's Bridge Rd.		C	3	C	On Au Sable, 25 canoe group campsites
11	PARMALEE BRIDGE—5 Mi. N of Luzerne Via Co. Rd. 489.	7	C	3	C	On Au Sable, canoe access, canoe group campsites
12	MIO POND—3 Mi. NW of Mio Via M-33 & Popps Rd.	24	C	2	W	On Au Sable, canoe access, canoe group campsites
13	McCOLLUM LAKE—8.5 Mi. NW of Curran Via M-65 & McCollum Rd.	32	B	2	W	Good pan fishing
14	VAN ETTEN LAKE—4.5 Mi. NW of Oscoda Via US-23 & F-41 (Old M-171).	62	B	2	W	Located near Wurtsmith Air Force Base
15	HARDWOOD LAKE—13.5 Mi. SE of West Branch Via M-55 & Co. Rd. 21	22	B	2	W	
16	RIFLE RIVER—11 Mi. SE of Rose City Via M-33 & Peters Rd.	40	C		C	Good trout fishing and canoeing
17	AMBROSE LAKE—11 Mi. N of West Branch Via Co. Rd. 15 & Co. Rd. 20.	30	B	2	W	On MCC Cycle Trail
18	HOUGHTON LAKE—6 Mi. NW of Houghton Lake Hgts. Via W Shore Drive.	50	B	2	W	On the north shore of Houghton Lake
19	HOUSE LAKE—2.5 Mi. NE of Meredith Via Meredith Grade.	41		1	W	Offers a 2.7 mile pathway
20	TROUT LAKE—3 Mi. NE of Meredith Via Meredith Grade.	35	B	2	C	Good trout fishing Pathway
21	WILDWOOD—13 Mi. S of West Branch Via M-30 & Wildwood Shores Rd.	18		3	W	On backwaters of Tittabawassee River
22	BLACK CREEK—3 Mi. NW of Sanford Via Saginaw Rd. & W River Rd.	22		3	W	Good panfish fishing
23	TEMPLE—10.5 Mi. W of Harrison Via M-61.	25	C	3	W	On the Muskegon River
24	PIKE LAKE—9.5 Mi. NW of Farwell Via M-115.	32		3	W	Pathway to campground and to Mud & Green Pine Lakes
25	MUD LAKE—11 Mi. E of Evart Via US-10, M-66, Grand Rd & Brown Rd.	8	B	3	W	Offers a pathway to Pike Lake

*C stands for coldwater fish species, W for warmwater species

contacting DNR personnel at these locations (they are not staffed full time):

1. Evart Field Office, 2510 East US-10, Evart, Mich. 49631 (616/734-5492).

2. Manton Field Office, 521 North Michigan, Manton, Mich. 49663 (616/824-3591).

3. Platte River Field Office, 15200 Honor Hwy., Beulah, Mich. 49617 (616/325-4611).

4. Silver Lake Field Office, Box 67, Mears, Mich. 49436 (616/873-3082).

Au Sable State Forest

LOCATED in the northeastern Lower Peninsula, the Au Sable State Forest with headquarters at Mio contains nearly 750,000 acres, all open to hunting. Counties with state forest land include Midland, Isabella, Clare, Gladwin, Arenac, Roscommon, Ogemaw, Iosco, Crawford, Oscoda, and Alcona.

The Au Sable State Forest has good populations of deer, snowshoe hares, ruffed grouse, and squirrels. Other game species include woodcock, black bear, bobcats, raccoon, coyotes, and waterfowl.

During the first six months of a recent fiscal year the Au Sable State Forest yielded more than $1 million in stumpage receipts sold at public auction.

The forest contains 33 rustic-type campgrounds with about 745 campsites.

Of special interest to hunters is the 3,000-acre Mason Tract along the South Branch of the Au Sable River in Crawford County. The tract is primarily managed for blue-ribbon trout fishing but contains good game populations and is popular with hunters too. Overnight camping is restricted to Canoe Harbor State Forest Campground on the northern end. A map of the Mason Tract is not available.

Another special area of significance is the Gladwin Field Trial Area (which see), located in the northwestern corner of Gladwin County. State forest campgrounds are located at House and Trout lakes.

The Au Sable State Forest is divided into three geographical areas with staff personnel available at each:

1. Gladwin Forest Area (Gladwin Field Office), 801 North Silverleaf, Gladwin, Mich. 48624 (517/426-9205).

2. Mio Forest Area (Mio Field Office), 191 South Mount Tom Road, Mio, Mich. 48647 (517/826-3211).

3. Roscommon Forest Area (Roscommon Field Office), Box 218, Roscommon, Mich. 48653 (517/275-5151).

Hunters can sometimes get further information by contacting DNR personnel at these locations (they may not be staffed full time):

1. Grayling Field Office, 4895 West County Road, Grayling, Mich. 49738 (517/348-6271).

2. Harrison Field Office, 708 North Clare Ave., Harrison, Mich. 48625 (517/539-6411).

3. Houghton Lake Field Office, Box 158, Houghton Lake Heights, Mich. 48630 (517/422-5522).

4. Lincoln Field Office, 408 Main St., Lincoln, Mich. 48742 (517/736-8336).

5. Sanford Field Office, 118 North Saginaw Road, Sanford, Mich. 48657 (517/687-7385).

6. Standish Field Office, 527 North Main, Standish, Mich. 48658 (517/846-4104).

7. West Branch Field Office, 2389 South M-76, West Branch, Mich. 48661 (517/345-0472).

Michigan DNR

Michigan DNR

Ottawa National Forest

THE Ottawa National Forest spans 927,426 acres in four western Upper Peninsula counties. The forestland, all of which is open to hunting, contains six ranger districts (addresses at end of this report). Counties with national forest holdings include Iron, Houghton, Gogebic, and Ontonagon (*all of which see*). The national forest contains over 700 lakes and 2,000 miles of streams.

Upland hardwoods comprise 406,900 acres, a whopping 43 percent, of the total land base. Other forest types include aspen (174,700 acres), swamp conifers (62,300 acres), balsam fir (59,850 acres), lowland shrubs (53,400 acres), red and white pine (49,850 acres), jack pine (24,600 acres), hemlock (23,300 acres), paper birch (16,350 acres), lowland hardwoods (14,200 acres), and spruce (8,950 acres). Very small amounts of oak and upland shrubs are included, and open areas comprise some 26,000 acres.

Hunters seek deer, black bear, coyotes, bobcats, snowshoe hares, raccoon, squirrels, ruffed grouse, woodcock, and waterfowl. An occasional timber wolf (protected) is sighted. The Ottawa National Forest does not maintain specific "game-management" areas. Instead, wildlife welfare is incorporated into each of the management prescriptions of the land.

Three of the six districts, however, do maintain grouse-hunter walking trails. Check with local rangers to see if they are marked and to obtain maps. Here are the hunter walking trails, with districts in parentheses: Pelkie Creek (Ontonagon), Davidson Lakes and Interior (Kenton), and Cooks Run (Iron River).

Hunters can obtain maps and general information by writing directly to the Forest Supervisor, Ottawa National Forest, East Cloverland Drive, Ironwood, Mich. 49938 (906/932-1330 or toll-free in the Upper Peninsula: 1-800-561-1201). Some maps are free; others have a nominal charge (make out checks to USDA Forest Service). Here is a listing:

1. *Forest Visitor Guide (mini-map)*. Scale of one inch equals six-and-a-half miles, this map is designed as a guide to the location of national forest recreation areas, facility types, and other points of interest. It shows highways and access roads to recreation areas. Cost: none.

2. *Forest Visitor Map*. This is a map of the entire forest at a scale of quarter-inch equals one mile. It shows the road system, lakes, streams, camp and picnic grounds (with site index), winter sports areas, points of interest, and other information. Cost: $1.

3. *Secondary Base Series Map*. A map of the forest is printed on two sheets with a scale of one-half-inch equals one mile. It is the standard administrative map of the national forest, showing more detail than the Forest Visitor Map but excluding the recreation site index. The East Half Map is 28 inches x 34 inches, and the West Half Map measures 29 inches x 40 inches. Cost: $1 per map.

4. *Primary Base Series Map*. These maps are at a scale of two inches equals one mile and are in a township format covering approximately 36 square miles. They were derived from the U.S. Geological Survey topographic quadrangles, are highly detail-ed, and serve as the base for all other national forest maps. There is a total of 73 15-inch x 20-inch maps, which cover the entire forest. Of special interest to hunters is that topography is shown with a contour interval of 20 feet. Order by township name and range. Cost: $2 per sheet.

The Ottawa National Forest has 25 campgrounds containing about 500 campsites. Most are rustic areas located on a scenic lake. Facilities include hand pumps, vault toilets, picnic tables, and fire rings. Electrical hookups and showers are not provided. Current charges vary from $3 to $5 (several are also free), but after fall closing dates no fees are collected (they are, however, still open to hunters and other recreationists). Closing dates vary from September 10 to November 30. Camping is permitted throughout the national forest free of charge; however, facilities are available only at designated sites.

Here is a listing of the campgrounds by county:

Name of site	County	Number of campsites
Bobcat Lake	Gogebic	12
Black River	Ontonagon	41
Langford Lake	Gogebic	11
Henry Lake	Gogebic	11
Moosehead Lake	Gogebic	13
Pomeroy Lake	Gogebic	19
Golden Lake	Iron	22
Lake Ottawa	Iron	32
Lake Ste. Kathryn	Iron	25
Perch Lake—West	Iron	20
Sparrow Rapids	Houghton	6
Norway Lake	Iron	28
Tepee Lake	Iron	17
Sturgeon River	Houghton	9
Lower Dam	Houghton	7
Courtney Lake	Houghton	21
Bob Lake	Houghton	17
Imp Lake	Gogebic	22
Marion Lake	Gogebic	41
Sylvania	Gogebic	83
Blockhouse	Iron	2
Burned Dam	Iron	6
Matchwood Tower	Gogebic	5
Paint River Forks	Iron	3
Paulding Pond	Ontonagon	4
Robbins Pond	Ontonagon	3
Taylor Lake	Gogebic	21

A special area within the Ottawa National Forest may interest hunters who want a quality, remote experience. The 21,000-acre Sylvania Recreation Area in southeastern Gogebic County offers virgin timber and pristine wilderness where motorized vehicles and equipment are off-limits. Primitive camping is allowed at designated sites by permit only (available from the Sylvania Visitors Center, corner US-2 and US-45 in Watersmeet or from the visitor information station at the entrance to the tract off USFS-535).

The best way to get specific information regarding hunting in the Ottawa National Forest is to stop in at a district ranger office. There are six:

1. Bergland Ranger District, Bergland, Mich. 49911 (906/575-3441).

2. Bessemer Ranger District, Bessemer, Mich. 49910 (906/667-0261).

3. Iron River Ranger District, Iron River, Mich. 49935 (906/265-5139).

4. Kenton Ranger District, Kenton, Mich. 49943

(906/852-3500).

5. Ontonagon Ranger District, Ontonagon, Mich. 49953 (906/884-2085).

6. Watersmeet Ranger District, Watersmeet, Mich. 49969 (906/353-3551).

Hiawatha National Forest

THE Hiawatha National Forest spans some 881,000 acres in five eastern Upper Peninsula counties. The forestland, all of which is open to hunting, contains two distinct regions. Eastern holdings in Chippewa and Mackinac counties (*both of which see*) are represented by ranger districts located at Sault Ste. Marie and St. Ignace. Lands in Schoolcraft, Delta, and Alger counties (*which also see*) are administered from ranger districts at Rapid River, Munising, and Manistique.

Although some lands were acquired early in this century, the national forest was not formally established until 1931. Today it includes dense stands of woods, intermittent swamps, and scattered, rolling hills—all interwoven by streams and lakes.

Maple-birch-beech hardwoods comprise 172,018 acres of the forest (about 20 percent) followed by aspen (123,809 acres), jack pine (89,320 acres), red pine (83,173 acres), swamp conifers (80,278 acres), open areas (78,670 acres), northern white cedar (57,439 acres), black spruce (46,811 acres), spruce fir (30,169 acres), lowland shrubs (23,790 acres), paper birch (23,195 acres), and white pine (12,909 acres). Hunters seek deer, black bear, coyotes, bobcats, snowshoe hares, raccoon, squirrels, ruffed grouse, sharp-tailed grouse, woodcock, and waterfowl. An occasional moose, Canada lynx, and timber wolf (all protected) are sighted.

Hunters may obtain maps and general information by writing directly to the Forest Supervisor, Hiawatha National Forest, 2727 North Lincoln Road, Escanaba, Mich. 49829. Some maps are free; others have a nominal charge (make checks out to USDA Forest Service). Here is a listing:

1. *Forest Visitor Guide (Mini-map)*. Scale of one inch equals six-and-a-half miles, this map is designed as a guide to the location of national forest recreation areas, facility types, and other points of interest. It shows highways and access roads to recreation areas. Cost: none.

2. *Forest Visitor Map*. This is a map of the entire forest at a scale of one-quarter inch equals one mile. It shows the road system, lakes, streams, camp and picnic grounds (with site index), winter sports areas, points of interest, and other information. Cost: $1.

3. *Secondary Base Series Map*. A map of the forest is printed on two sheets with a scale of one-half inch equals one mile. It is the standard administrative map of the national forest, showing more detail than the Forest Visitor Map but excluding the recreation site index. The East Half Map is 28 inches x 34 inches, and the West Half Map measures 29 inches x 40 inches. Cost: $1 per map.

4. *Primary Base Series Map*. These maps are at a scale of two inches equals one mile and are in a township format covering approximately 36 square miles. They were derived from the U.S. Geological Survey topographic quadrangles, are highly detailed, and serve as the base for all other national forest maps. There is a total of 73 15-inch x 20-inch maps, which cover the entire forest. Of special interest to hunters is that topography is shown with a contour interval of 20 feet. Order by township name and range. Cost: $2 per sheet.

The Hiawatha National Forest has 21 campgrounds containing about 700 campsites. Most are rustic areas located on a scenic lake. Facilities include hand pumps, vault toilets, picnic tables, and fire rings. Electrical hookups and showers are not provided. Current charges vary from $3 to $6, but after fall closing dates no fees are collected (they are, however, still open to hunters and other recreationists). Closing dates vary from September 30 to December 1. Camping is permitted throughout the national forest free of charge; however, facilities are available only at designated sites.

Here is a listing of the campgrounds by county:

Name of site	County	Number of campsites
Bay View	Chippewa	24
Monocle Lake	Chippewa	59
Brevoort Lake	Mackinac	69
Carp River	Mackinac	44
Foley Creek	Mackinac	54
Lake Michigan	Mackinac	38
Soldier Lake	Chippewa	64
Three Lakes	Chippewa	48
Au Train Lake	Alger	19
Bay Furnace	Alger	53
Camp 7 Lake	Delta	47
Colwell Lake	Schoolcraft	35
Corner Lake	Schoolcraft	9
Flowing Well	Delta	10
Haymeadow Creek	Delta	16
Hovey Lake	Alger	4
Indian River	Schoolcraft	11
Island Lake	Alger	24
Little Bass Lake	Schoolcraft	12
Petes Lake	Alger	20
Widewaters	Alger	34
Pole Creek Lake	Delta	8

The best way to get specific information regarding hunting in the Hiawatha National Forest is to stop in at a district ranger office. There are five:

1. Sault Ste. Marie Ranger District, 2901 I-75 Business Spur, Sault Ste. Marie, Mich. 49783 (906/635-5311).

2. St. Ignace Ranger District, Ferry Lane, St. Ignace, Mich. 49781 (906/643-7900).

3. Rapid River Ranger District, US-2, Rapid River, Mich. 49878 (906/474-6442).

4. Munising Ranger District, Cedar St., Munising, Mich. 49862 (906/387-2512).

5. Manistique Ranger District, US-2, Manistique, Mich. 49854 (906/341-5666).

Huron-Manistee National Forest

THE Huron-Manistee National Forest comprises some 940,000 acres in 14 counties of the northern Lower Peninsula. This federal land, all of which is open to hunting, is represented by seven ranger districts (addresses at end of this report). Actually two separate national forests, the Huron-Manistee is managed as one with headquarters at Cadillac. The eastern portion (Huron National Forest), totaling about 415,000 acres, was established in 1909. It is administered by three ranger districts, and the following counties contain portions: Ogemaw, Oscoda, Iosco, Crawford, and Alcona (all of which see).

The western portion (Manistee National Forest) comprises about 525,000 acres, is managed by four ranger districts, and has parcels in the following counties: Mason, Newaygo, Oceana, Wexford, Lake, Manistee, Montcalm, Muskegon, and Mecosta (all of which see). It was established in 1938.

Red-pine forests totaling 172,763 acres lead a long list of forest types. A total of 165,719 acres of aspen is followed by jack pine (135,726 acres), red oak (86,468 acres), black oak-hickory (72,847 acres), maple-birch (56,713 acres), mixed oak (55,088), jack pine-oak (24,131 acres), elm-ash-soft maple (17,762 acres), mixed swamp conifer (17,596 acres), red pine-oak (17,258 acres), and white pine (15,899 acres). Lowland shrubs account for 15,534 acres, and open areas comprise 32,753 acres.

Hunters seek deer, black bear (in counties with open seasons), coyotes, foxes, bobcats (in counties with open seasons), snowshoe hares, raccoon, fox and gray/black squirrels, wild turkeys, ruffed grouse, woodcock, and waterfowl. The Huron-Manistee National Forest does not maintain specific "game-management" areas. Instead, wildlife welfare is incorporated into each of the management prescriptions for the land and resource management.

Hunters may obtain maps and general information by writing directly to the Forest Supervisor, Huron-Manistee National Forest, 421 South Mitchell St., Cadillac, Mich. 49601 (616/775-2421). Some maps are free; others have a nominal charge (make out checks to USDA Forest Service). Here is a listing:

1. *Forest Visitor Guide (mini-map).* Scale of one inch equals six-and-a-half miles, this map is designed as a guide to the location of national forest recreation areas, facility types, and other points of interest. It shows highways and access roads to recreation areas. Cost: none.

2. *Forest Visitor Map.* This is a map of the entire forest at a scale of one-quarter inch equals one mile. It shows the road system, lakes, streams, camp and picnic grounds (with site index), winter sports areas, points of interest, and other information. Cost: $1.

3. *Secondary Base Series Map.* A map of the forest is printed on two sheets with a scale of one-half inch equals one mile. It is the standard administrative map of the national forest, showing more detail than the Forest Visitor Map but excluding the recreation site index. The East Half Map is 28 inches x 34 inches, and the West Half Map measures 29 inches x 40 inches. Cost: $1 per map.

4. *Primary Base Series Map.* These maps are at a scale of two inches equals one mile and are in a township format covering approximately 36 square miles. They were derived from the U.S. Geological Survey topographic quadrangles, are highly detailed, and serve as the base for all other national forest maps. There is a total of 73 15-inch x 20-inch maps, which cover the entire forest. Of special interest to hunters is that topography is shown with a contour interval of 20 feet. Order by township name and range. Cost: $2 per sheet.

The Huron-Manistee National Forest has 32 campgrounds containing about 700 campsites. Most are rustic areas located on a scenic lake. Facilities include hand pumps, vault toilets, picnic tables, and fire rings. Electrical hookups and showers are not provided. Current charges vary from $3 to $6 (some are free), but after fall closing dates no fees are collected (the campgrounds, however, are still open to hunters and other recreationists). Closing dates vary anytime after Labor Day. Also, camping is permitted throughout the national forest free of charge; however, facilities are available only at designated sites.

Here is a listing of the campgrounds by county:

Name of site	County	Number of campsites
Kneff Lake	Crawford	27
Wagner Lake	Oscoda	12
Island Lake	Oscoda	17
Mack Lake	Oscoda	42
Luzerne Trail Camp	Oscoda	10
Horseshoe Lake	Alcona	9
Jewell Lake	Alcona	5
Pine River	Alcona	11
South Branch Trail Camp	Iosco	25
Rollways	Iosco	19
Lumberman's Monument	Iosco	20
Round Lake	Iosco	33
Hemlock	Wexford	15
Peterson Bridge South	Wexford	20
Seaton Creek	Wexford	17
Ravine	Wexford	6
Udell Rollways	Manistee	23
Pine Lake	Manistee	12
Dorner Lake	Manistee	8
Bear Track	Lake	16
Driftwood Valley	Lake	21
Sand Lake	Wexford	45
Lake Michigan Recreation Area	Mason	98
Old Grade	Lake	20
Bowman Bridge	Newaygo	16
Highbank Lake	Newaygo	9
Timber Creek	Lake	4
Nichols Lake	Newaygo	28
Benton Lake	Newaygo	24
Pines Point	Oceana	33

Hunters looking for a quality, remote experience might be interested in two special areas which may be entered only one foot. Both the 3,000-acre Reid Lake and the 10,600-acre Hoist Lakes foot-travel areas are located in Alcona County. The former includes six miles of gently rolling trail around Reid Lake, once part of a northern Michigan farm. The

Hoist Lakes Foot-Travel Area includes 20 miles of trails through pine, aspen, and hardwood forests with plenty of pothole lakes, marshes, and areas of beaver activity. Hunters may camp anywhere if they remain at least 200 feet from trails and exercise minimum-impact rules (no large fires, no cutting of standing timber, etc.). Both areas provide good opportunities for hunting deer, black bear, raccoon, red fox, coyotes, squirrels, grouse, woodcock, waterfowl, and wild turkeys.

Free maps are available from national forest headquarters in Cadillac. Hunters also can obtain them and additional information from the Harrisville Ranger District.

In fact, the best way to get specific information regarding hunting in the Huron-Manistee National Forest is to stop in to a district ranger office. There are seven:

1. Mio Ranger District, Mio, Mich. 48647 (517/826-5386).

2. Harrisville Ranger District, Harrisville, Mich. 48740 (517/724-5431).

3. Tawas Ranger District, East Tawas, Mich. 48730 (517/362-4477).

4. Cadillac Ranger District, Box 409, Cadillac, Mich. 49601 (616/775-8539).

5. Manistee Ranger District, Manistee, Mich. 49660 (616/723-2211).

6. Baldwin Ranger District, Baldwin, Mich. 49304 (616/745-4631).

7. White Cloud Ranger District, White Cloud, 49349 (616/689-6696).

J. Michael Klemens

GUIDE·TO HUNTING BY COUNTIES

227

Alcona County

ALCONA County in northeastern Lower Michigan contains large areas of loamy soils interspersed with sandy soils. The 693-square-mile county features a diverse mix of habitat too, which, overall, produces good hunting for deer, bears, bobcats, grouse, woodcock, hares, squirrels, and wild turkeys.

The southwestern region and a portion of the northeastern area contain large blocks of the Huron Manistee National Forest (*which see*), totaling over 103,000 acres or about 24 percent of Alcona County's land mass. These federal lands are completely open to hunting. In addition, scattered parcels of the Au Sable State Forest (*which also see*) in southeastern and northeastern Alcona County provide another 8,500 acres of hunting opportunity. Hunters are also welcome on nearly 1,800 acres of Negwegon State Park and a small portion of Sturgeon Point State Park site (*both of which see*), along the shores of Lake Huron.

Hunters are fortunate to have this broad base of public land at their disposal since large portions of game-rich Alcona County are tied up in farmlands and hunt clubs. The former are located west of US-23 and west of Lincoln on M-72 where farmers grow hay and corn for dairy/livestock operations. Hunt-club lands ring Hubbard Lake and spread westerly to the Oscoda County border. Club lands are off-limits, even to hunters making a courteous request. On the other hand, such a request can land permission to enter farmlands, especially if hunters seek landowners experiencing deer crop-damage problems.

I mentioned a moment ago that Alcona County contains a diverse habitat mix. About 72 percent is wooded with commercial forest species, led by aspen, which at 103,800 acres totals nearly one-fourth of the county surface area. Other key forest types of value to hunters include oak-hickory (87,300 acres), maple-birch (34,900 acres), jack pine (18,500 acres), red pine (15,600 acres), northern white cedar (14,800 acres), elm-ash-soft maple (8,800 acres), and white pine (5,900 acres). Smaller amounts of balsam fir, black spruce, paper birch, and tamarack contribute to the total.

Deer numbers are fairly good although best concentrations occur on private land in southern and western regions. Caledonia, Hawes, and Millen townships currently have high deer populations, according to a five-year DNR survey. The national forest lands produce good deer hunting too, especially in mixed areas of aspen with lowland hardwoods. For best results, hunt young growths of these species or mixed stands of jack pine with oak. During high mast-production years they pay off. Mixed-stand woodlots in the farming belt are also good if you can get access.

Alcona County deer hunters kill three to four bucks per square mile for a success ratio of about 20 percent, a little above the state average. Pressure overall is quite high at 20 to 30 hunters per square mile. This is especially true on public lands. The county has produced 13 trophy bucks so far, according to Commemorative Bucks of Michigan,

and the deer herd appears to be in good shape. About 200 animals become highway statistics each year, and during tough winters some even starve.

Sportsmen looking for a remote hunting experience should consider the Hoist Lake area west of the M-72/M-65 intersection. ORVs are not allowed; hunters will have to hike in to this roadless area, which produces deer and some bear as well as small game. Another remote area is Reid Lake, three miles southeast of the intersection mentioned. Yet a third isolated area is the Buel Tract southwest of Mikado along the Pine River.

Alcona County usually produces about half the bear tagged annually in the eight-county district headquartered at Mio. This number can range from 20 to 40 animals. Opportunities are scattered in mixed-stand forests of hardwood and aspen near thick swamps containing conifers, such as the Lincoln Swamp in the east-central region and the Block House Swamp in the west-central area. The county is open to bobcat hunting too, but unfortunately some of the best habitat for both bear and cats is west of Hubbard Lake on club lands. Hunters might also try public lands along the Au Sable River in the western portion of the county.

The wild-turkey kill is generally highest in the northern region although turkeys continue to drift south to farm areas in winter for food handouts. An upcoming outstanding area for turkeys and deer is federal land in the northeastern region where several new timber sales are sure to improve habitat. Southwest of Curran, a huge cutover which abuts the Block House Swamp is another prime turkey-hunting area. It is also favorable for bear, grouse, and deer.

The high amount of aspen in varying age classes makes for excellent grouse and woodcock habitat. Grouse are ready to stage a comeback after being down somewhat in this county. Hunter-cooperators reported 1.59 to 1.67 average flushes per hour for two years of records checked. That figure should easily double when the population cycle swings upward. Woodcock for these same two years were 1.20 and 4.29 birds per hour.

Try young aspen stands with an understory of brush and shrubs for grouse and either aspen slashings or alder covers in moist-soil areas for woodcock. Good lowland covers exist north of USFS-4431 along the southern border with Iosco County. Another prime area of tag alders and aspen cuttings near Pine River drainages is south of M-72 on either side of Stout Road for two or three miles. The block of federal forest land a couple miles southwest of Lincoln has also been recently cut. Further, hunters can try the Comstock Lake area northwest of Jewell Lake although overall pressure is quite high.

Other current cuts that produce good hare hunting in addition to grouse, woodcock, and deer include the Hoist Lake and Sunny Lake areas and the aspen clearcuts east of the Block House Swamp. Also, try swamps along the Pine River for hares as well as bobcats. Swamp-flanked tributaries of the Thunder Bay River in the northern region also produce cats.

Raccoon hunting is limited to drainages and mixed forest/croplands in the farming region. This area also produces red fox. Coyotes, on the increase in Alcona County, can be found in poor-soil sandy areas and open brushlands after jack pines have been cut. Best coyote hunting in the district, however, occurs in southeastern Kalkaska, northwestern Ogemaw, western Oscoda, and most of Crawford counties.

Good numbers of fox and gray/black squirrels are found throughout Alcona County, thanks to the high frequency of oak-type cover. Best bets for fox species are farmland stands of oaks bordering crop fields. For the shier grays/blacks hunt mixed forests of oak-pine. The Hoist Lake area is exceptional most years for squirrels.

Alcona County offers limited waterfowling opportunities. Best bets are jump shooting for wood ducks and mallards on beaver ponds and along drainages.

OTHER SHOOTING OPPORTUNITIES

None known at this time.

FURTHER SOURCES OF HUNTING INFORMATION

1. DNR District Office, 191 South Mount Tom Road (M-33), Mio, Mich. 48647 (517/826-3211).
2. DNR Lincoln Field Office, 408 Main St., Lincoln, Mich. 48742 (517/736-8336).
3. Harrisville Ranger District, Forest Service, USDA, Harrisville, Mich. 48740 (517/724-6471).
4. Topographic, county, and lake maps may be ordered from the Michigan United Conservation Clubs. For information, refer to the beginning of this book.
5. Plat books are available from the Alcona County Cooperative Extension Services, County Building, Harrisville, Mich. 48740, for $9 each (add $1 if mail ordering).
6. Alcona County ASCS Office, 215 South Second St., Lincoln, Mich. 48742.

Also, refer to the following elsewhere in this book:
1. Au Sable State Forest
2. Huron-Manistee National Forest

Alger County

LOCATED in the north-central Upper Peninsula along Lake Superior, Alger County contains 584,320 acres or about 913 square miles, most of which are open to hunting. About 18 percent of the land base falls into the Escanaba River State Forest and the Au Train Basin Waterfowl Project (both of which see). Another 20 percent constitutes the Pictured Rocks National Lakeshore and portions of the Hiawatha National Forest (both of which see) and are therefore under federal management. When added to 180,000 acres of company-owned lands enrolled in the Commercial Forest Act plan, Alger County hunters have some two-thirds of the land base, or over 400,000 acres, to enjoy.

The public lands are easily located in the MUCC publication "Michigan County Maps and Outdoor Guide." To pinpoint company lands, use this reference along with a current county plat book. You can also get legal descriptions by contacting the DNR Forest Management Division, Box 30028, Lansing, Mich. 48909 (517/373-1275), but be sure to limit your request to a specific area in the county.

Sportsmen wanting a remote, quality hunting experience can find it in Alger County, large areas of which are unbroken wilderness. Visiting hunters seek bear, deer, coyotes, bobcats, snowshoe hares, sharp-tailed and ruffed grouse, woodcock, and waterfowl. More on those opportunities and best areas to go in a moment.

The northern part of Alger County is a sandstone plateau, and the southern and central regions are actually a cuesta underlain by limestone and having a northward-facing escarpment. Overall, the county contains a number of distinct topographic divisions, the result of both glacial action and post-glacial erosion. The northwestern region contains few lakes although it is cut by streams, has bodies of wetland, and is terraced near the lake shore. The southwestern part features a few low, gravelly

ridges and a large swamp area. The north-central portion, south and southwest of Munising, is rolling land—hills and with smooth-rounded slopes—characterized by deep sandy drift. The southeastern region contains dry, sandy hardwood and pine plains, two areas of hilly uplands, and a six-square-mile swamp. The eastern and northeastern portions are mainly a level plain dotted with low isolated hills and ridges. East and northeast of Shingleton is a large swampy, marshy area dotted with islands and low ridges of sand. Smaller, wet areas are found south and southwest of Grand Marais.

All the Alger County streams flowing northward into Lake Superior are short and have a rapid fall. Having cut narrow gorgelike valleys, ranging from 100 to 150 feet in depth, they are characterized by rapids and waterfalls. Those streams running southward into Lake Michigan are larger and longer, but they have not cut deeply into the land and they usually originate in or flow through swamps.

About 85 percent of Alger County is covered with commercial-forest species. A whopping 313,000 acres is in maple-birch. Other significant cover types include northern white cedar (43,800 acres), elm-ash-soft maple (25,800 acres), red pine (21,900 acres), aspen (21,100 acres), black spruce (16,600 acres), balsam fir (14,400 acres), white pine (11,000 acres), jack pine (10,400 acres), paper birch (3,500 acres), and white spruce (3,000 acres).

Alger County gets low firearm deer-hunting pressure (about six hunters per square mile), yet yields one-of-six success ratios on bucks. Forty to 50 percent of the bucks shot are two-and-a-half-year-olds toting racks of eight points or more. The fact that 27 of the state's 1,150 biggest bucks, thus far located by Commemorative Bucks of Michigan, came from Alger County supports this big-buck contention. Hunters may spend the entire two-week season without seeing another hunter.

Deer are found throughout the county but are most sparse along the Lake Superior shoreline and most plentiful near the Delta County border. In the western region hunters concentrate in the Trenary-to-Chatham farming belt and in northern hardwoods west of Munising.

As deer move from the Lake Superior watershed to more protected areas, late-season hunters sometimes intercept them along river-valley migration routes. Wintering areas include the Au Train Basin, Powell Point, southwest of Trenary, and north of Deerton (all in the western portion). Eastern county yarding areas include Grand Marais Swamp and the Shingleton Swamp.

Alger County hosts good numbers of black bear, which frequent hardwood areas mixed with openings and fruit-bearing trees and shrubs. Bear are also found in old orchards and near croplands. Because bear are opportunistic and eat nearly everything, they are ubiquitous. Few places in Alger County do not get bear visitations, and so both baiters and dog hunters target them throughout.

Ruffed-grouse hunting is fair to good except on open farmlands or in extensive hardwood areas. Aspen, birch, and mixed types along with brushy areas produce the most grouse. Those habitats, as well as lowland brush and alder, also yield local and migrant woodcock throughout October. Try such covers along the Taylor Dam Road, Petrel Road south of Melstrand, and cutover lands south of Kingston Lake. Hunter-cooperators who furnish annual hourly flush-rate records reported consistent statistics of one bird flushed per hour on the average for three random years that we checked. Woodcock flush rates for those same seasons were 2.50, .49, and 1.15.

Part of Alger County is open to sharp-tailed grouse hunting too. For best bets on these prairie game birds, work large, open areas containing grass or other low cover. The DNR manages several Alger County openings for sharptails. They include the Kingston Plains, Stanley Lake, Danaher Plains, Prairie Creek, and Whitewash Plains.

Snowshoe hares have been down for the past few years but now appear to be staging a slow comeback. Select areas of new hardwood cuttings near conifer swamps. Some of the more remote spots experience no hare-hunting pressure all winter. In the more open places of young growth, predator hunters can find coyotes; in thick conifer swamps, they are likely to encounter bobcats. Alger County has a good supply of each, particularly coyotes.

There are a few black and gray squirrels in isolated pockets throughout the county, but very few hunters seek them. On the other hand, fair to good waterfowling occurs near the Au Train Basin Waterfowl Project, in western-county farm fields (for geese), and on lakes and potholes fronting Lake Superior. Best of these are Deer Lake and 16-Mile Lake although the latter is not as productive as it once was.

OTHER SHOOTING OPPORTUNITIES

None known at this time.

FURTHER SOURCES OF HUNTING INFORMATION

1. (Eastern Alger County) DNR District Office, 309 West McMillan Ave., Newberry, Mich. 49868 (906/293-5131).

2. (Western Alger County) DNR District Office, 1126 North Lincoln Road, Escanaba, Mich. 49829 (906/786-2351).

3. Forest Supervisor, Hiawatha National Forest, 2727 North Lincoln Road, Escanaba, Mich. 49829 (906/786-4062).

4. Hiawatha National Forest, Munising Ranger District, Cedar St., Munising, Mich. 49862 (906/387-2512).

5. Alger County Chamber of Commerce, Box 405, Munising, Mich. 49862 (906/387-2138).

6. Topographic, county, and lake maps may be ordered from the Michigan United Conservation Clubs. For information, refer to the beginning of this book.

7. Plat books are available from the Alger County Cooperative Extension Services, Municipal Bldg., Room 1, Munising, Mich. 49862. The cost is $10 (add $1.25 if mail ordering).

8. Alger/Marquette County ASCS Office, Box 166, Chatham, Mich. 49816.

Also, refer to the following elsewhere in this book:
1. Au Train Basin Waterfowl Project
2. Escanaba River State Game Area
3. Hiawatha National Forest
4. Pictured Rocks National Lakeshore

Allegan County

COVER types and land-use practices in 535,000-acre Allegan County result from what glaciers did to this area in southwestern Lower Michigan several thousand years ago. End moraines of glacial till coupled with wave action for thousands of years formed sand dunes along Lake Michigan. This is now orchard/vineyard country for several miles inland where fruit grows abundantly, thanks to its closeness to the big lake This is also a good deer hunting area, particularly in high-number years when farmers complain about crop damage.

However, access to private lands is difficult.

The south-central to southwestern portion of Allegan County is mostly outwash plains where rivers and the retreating glaciers left sandy to loamy soils over gravel. A large amount of the county's 25 percent of forested cover is found here, mostly in the 45,000-acre Allegan State Game Area (which see). The Kalamazoo River, entering the county near Plainwell, flows northeasterly through this area to empty into Lake Michigan at Saugatuck. The old alluvial floodplain is well timbered as is its tributary, the Rabbit River, which flows across the northern tier of townships. Eastern county lands between these rivers as well as those below the Kalamazoo River are largely cash-crop and dairy farmland mixed with brush and woodlands. The northern third of Allegan County is prime agricultural land, with larger farms and more intensive small-grain, cash-crop operations. Here the land is flat, the soil fertile.

This prime farmland used to hold great numbers of pheasants and still produces some hunting opportunities for pockets of wild birds. There is no state land in this region although 4,300 acres of Public Access Stamp Program lands are leased from some two dozen farmers scattered throughout the county. Many of these farms are located east of the game area in Watson, Martin, Dorr, and Monterey townships. This area also holds remnant pheasant and quail (although the season is currently closed on quail) populations as does the southern portion. DNR district headquarters at Plainwell as well as officials at the game area have available PASP land directories.

Much of Allegan County's forests are in northern hardwoods—oak, hickory, maple, and birch—with some lowland hardwoods interspersed with aspen along the river bottoms and in the game area. Included are scattered understory stands of jack pine, red pine, and white pine.

Deer hunting throughout the county rates poor to fair with best success coming on private lands in the fruit belt and also in the south-central and eastern areas. Hunters score at a nine percent success rate (one to two bucks per square mile), about half the statewide average. There are reasonable numbers of deer in Allegan County as evidenced by the annual road kill of some 300 animals. One reason that the buck kill is low is that only 11 hunters per square mile on the average participate in the shotgun-only firearm season.

Raccoon hunting is excellent in farm fields that abut to waterways. Fox are coming back in good numbers and offer untapped hunting potential. Fox squirrel hunting (occasional grays too) is excellent throughout the county, providing another underutilized resource. Find upland hardwoods next to cropped fields. Cottontails are plentiful, serving up best opportunities when hunted near woodlot and stream edges in conjunction with brush and grasslands. Michigan's wild turkey flock was restored 30 years ago on the Allegan State Game Area. Birds have now spread north and northwest along the Rabbit River. Currently, about half the hunting opportunity occurs on private land. Area L, which covers 90 percent of Allegan County, offers several week-long hunts in April and May for about 100 permit holders each. At this time it is the only area in southern Michigan where turkeys may be hunted.

Southwestern Lower Michigan is not noted for good woodcock and grouse hunting, yet pressure in Allegan County runs medium to high. Cooperating hunters report grouse flush rates in normal population years of 1.5 to 2.0, with woodcock flushes about half that figure. Find upland aspen stands or gray dogwood with tag alder lowlands for best results. Good habitat exists within the game area, along river bottomlands, and again in isolated farm covers.

Waterfowl hunters get sporadic action from migrating diving ducks along the Lake Michigan shoreline. Floating the Kalamazoo River from Plainwell to Allegan is popular with some waterfowlers (who key at impoundments below Plainwell, Otsego, and Trowbridge dams) as well as a few squirrel and deer hunters. Put-in and take-out access is good at county roads along this route. The Rabbit River is an underused float stream, which also offers jump-shooting possibilities if you can secure river access on private property. And some of the finest duck and goose hunting in Michigan occurs on managed units within the game area. In addition, the state has access on eight other lakes in this county. Enterprising hunters might check them for ducks and geese leaving the game area sanctuary. It is quite possible that in the future this region might get an extended goose hunting season similar to that in southeastern Michigan.

OTHER SHOOTING OPPORTUNITIES

Fowler Farms in Casco Township near South Haven is a shooting preserve open to the public. Sportsmen can hunt pheasants here on 640 acres. For details, contact Charles E. Fowler, Route 2, Box 298, South Haven, Mich. 49090 (616/637-4381). Also, 123-acre Collins Lodge in Clyde Township is open for club shooting by invitation only. For information, contact William F. Collins, 2652 Lake Drive, Route 2, Fennville, Mich. 49408 (616/857-2192).

FURTHER SOURCES OF HUNTING INFORMATION

1. DNR District Office, Box 355, 621 North 10th St., Palinwell, Mich. 49080 (616/685-6851).
2. Allegan Field Office, 4120 Dam Road, Route 3, Allegan, Mich. 49010 (616/673-4747).
3. Allegan State Game Area, 4590 118th Ave., Route 3, Allgean, Mich. 49010 (616/673-2430).
4. Allegan Area Chamber of Commerce, 227 Hubbard St., Allegan, Mich. 49010 (616/573-2479).
5. Otsego Chamber of Commerce, 100 West Allegan St., Otsego, Mich. 49078 (616/694-6880).
6. Plainwell Chamber of Commerce, Box 95, Plainwell, Mich. 49080 (616/685-8877).
7. Fennville Chamber of Commerce, Box 68, Fennville, Mich. 49408 (616/571-2036).
8. Wayland Chamber of Commerce, 160 West Superior St., Wayland, Mich. 49348 (616/792-2265).
9. Holland Area Chamber of Commerce, 7 East 8th St., Holland, Mich. 49423 (616/392-2389).
10. Topographic, county, and lake maps may be ordered from the Michigan United Conservation Clubs. For information, refer to the beginning of this book.
11. Plat books are available from the Allegan County Cooperative Extension Service, 108 Chestnut St., Allegan, Mich. 49010. The cost is $10 each (add $1 if ordering by mail).
12. Allegan County ASCS Office, USDA, M-40 South, 545 Jenner Drive, Allegan, Mich. 49020 (616/673-6940).

Also, refer to the following elsewhere in this book:
1. Allegan State Game Area

Alpena County

ALPENA County in northeastern Lower Michigan offers hunters the following opportunities: very good for deer; good for snowshoe hares, grouse, woodcock, and raccoon; and poor to fair for wild turkeys, bear, bobcats, squirrels, and waterfowl. The 562-square-mile county has over 44,000 acres, or about 12 percent of the land area, in state ownership. These lands comprise scattered portions of the Mackinac State Forest (*which see*) and are completely open to hunting.

Fronting Lake Huron is a nearly level plain from two to seven miles wide. Varying in height from 580 feet to 730 feet above sea level, this plain is an old bed of the ancient lake. The northern two-thirds of Alpena County is mostly level with some slightly rolling land. A half-mile south of Lachine is a sharply defined hill that stands at over 900 feet above sea level. Two miles southeast of Beaver Lake the altitude varies from 800 to 925 feet.

In the northeastern portion the glacial drift which covers nearly all of Alpena County is thin, thus exposing underlying limestone bedrock in many places. The thinnest drift is in Alpena and Maple Ridge townships; consequently, the soil here is poor. In the southern part of the county—mostly in Ossineke Township—land features include bold, hilly areas with plateau-shaped ridges penetrated by deep-valley plains and swampy bases.

A major farming area begins in the southeastern region and runs northwesterly to county center (defined by M-32, which cuts the county east to west). Another lies west of Long Lake in Maple Ridge Township. Farming practices include dairying and cropping for corn and alfalfa. The southwestern region, around Fletcher Floodwaters, is club country, with access difficult if not impossible to obtain. Artificial feeding of deer during Alpena County's normally tough winters keeps the herd in this region unusually high—up to 50 deer per square mile, which is one reason that Alpena County deer hunters often lead the state in buck-hunter success—30 percent or better. That success translates to five bucks or more for the 20 hunters per square mile, the overall rate of pressure.

Other than club country (mostly in Green Township), the best deer hunting occurs in the northwestern region, including state-owned swampy lowlands, and in Wilson Township. The northeastern portion with its limestone base grows good deer foods (aspen and mixed hardwood browse shoots) and is yet another good region to hunt. Thus far, Commemorative Bucks of Michigan has uncovered 10 Alpena County trophy deer for its all-time record book.

One reason for Alpena County's plentiful game is the abundance of aspen. Nearly half (106,300 acres) of the 230,000 acres of commercial forestland is aspen in varying stages of growth. Grouse, woodcock, deer, and snowshoe hares are game animals in particular that thrive in young aspen. Elm-ash-soft maple (23,400 acres), maple-birch (21,900 acres), and northern white cedar (19,900 acres) are other types that figure strongly in the commercial-forest species that cover 61 percent of Alpena County. Included are smaller amounts of oak-hickory and many types of spruce, fir, and pine.

Bear numbers are highest in the western half of the county, but, as already stated, access can be difficult. One good area of state land to try is Long Swamp in Wellington Township. Another is dense lowland cover along the North Branch of the Thunder Bay River in Long Rapids Township. A third is Wolf Creek Swamp southeast of Beaver Lake.

Bobcat numbers are among the lowest in the eight-county DNR district. For coyotes, try young aspen stands near lowland covers of brush and conifers. These same areas produce snowshoe hares. Alpena County has a high water table, and so hunters who target aspen stands with an understory of shrubs and brush adjacent to lowland hardwoods and conifers can be very successful at finding many types of game.

For example, grouse and woodcock hunting is sometimes exceptional around edges of swamps and along creek bottoms, especially those featuring nearby timber cuttings. Tag alder and wild-fruit areas are also productive. Hourly flush rates compiled by hunter-cooperators are pretty uniform, at least for the three years that we checked. For grouse, the rates varied from 1.45 to 1.86 and for woodcock they ranged from 1.55 to 2.40. Alpena County has fair to good rearing habitat for woodcock, but the area also gets heavy visitation by migrant birds. October 5-10 is generally the peak time for flight-bird passage, but hunting can remain good throughout October.

Fair to good wild turkey hunting occurs in southern Alpena County, mostly on private land. Not surprisingly, the better turkey range includes club country and farm lands where birds gather in winter for food handouts.

Alpena County with its network of streams (mostly flowing into the Thunder Bay River, which empties into Thunder Bay at Alpena) and abundance of swamps hosts high numbers of raccoon most years. Pressure is moderate to high. Squirrel hunting is only fair at best due to limited amounts of oak and hickory. Best bets are to target farm woodlots and to ask permission of landowners. Some of these farms also contain fair to good numbers of cottontails as well as red fox.

Opening-day waterfowl hunting on Squaw Bay can be an exciting affair except that pressure is usually high. Shoreline duck hunters can expect mallards and teal early in the season and various diver species later. Fletcher Floodwaters, the western half of which lies in Montmorency County, can be a real sleeper for ducks off and on all season. I have hunted the 10,000-acre impoundment at times when more waterfowlers were needed to move birds. Canada geese occasionally drop in here too as well as at Long Lake.

The Thunder Bay River affords good floating opportunities for deer and waterfowl hunters. They can put in at Lake Fifteen southwest of Atlanta in Montmorency County and get a fast float in shallow water for 15 miles before having to portage at Atlanta. Another portage is required at Hillman and at two logjams just below. Throughout Alpena County itself—other than tricky rapids a half-mile downstream from Long Rapids and again five miles farther—the float is a leisurely one with portages required at Seven- and Four-Mile dams.

OTHER SHOOTING OPPORTUNITIES

None known at this time.

FURTHER SOURCES OF HUNTING INFORMATION

1. DNR District Office, 1732 West M-32 (Box 667), Gaylord, Mich. 49735 (517/732-3541).

2. DNR Alpena Field Office, 4343 M-32, Alpena, Mich. 49707 (517/354-2209).

3. Alpena Area Chamber of Commerce, 133 Johnson St., Box 65, Alpena, Mich. 49707 (1-800-582-1906 toll-free).

4. Topographic, county, and lake maps may be ordered from the Michigan United Conservation Clubs. For information, refer to the beginning of this book.

5. County plat books are available from the Alpena Area Chamber of Commerce (see address above) for $10 each postpaid. Make out checks to the chamber.

6. Alpena/Montmorency County ASCS Office, 815 West Miller St., Alpena, Mich. 49707.

Also, refer to the Mackinac State Forest elsewhere in this publication.

Antrim County

ANTRIM County in northwestern Lower Michigan offers fair to good hunting opportunities for deer, bear, coyotes, raccoon, snowshoe hares, squirrels, grouse, woodcock, and waterfowl. Topographic features include the Jordan River Valley and over 28,000 surface acres of water forming Lake Bellaire, Torch, and Intermediate lakes and a portion of Elk Lake. These deep lakes all have a north-to-south orientation and were carved from the land when glaciers last covered the region several thousand years ago.

Lying along a similar axis are dozens of drumlins, streamlined hills of glacial till from one to two miles long and also shaped by the moving wall of ice. Most of Antrim County is rolling hardwood hill country, very beautiful during fall hunting season.

Of great importance to hunters is the fact that nearly 44,000 acres, or about 14 percent of the land base, is state-owned and open to hunting. Mostly eastern-county holdings of the Mackinac State Forest (which see), these lands afford good hunting for deer, bear, and small game. In addition, nearly 5,000 acres of company-owned lands have been enrolled in the Commercial Forest Act (CFA) plan. They are also open to hunting. A current plat book will indicate the location of such company property. To determine if certain parcels are enrolled in the CFA, check with DNR district headquarters at Gaylord or contact the DNR Forest Management Division in Lansing (Box 30028 or call 517/373-1275).

About 54 percent of Antrim County is timbered with commercial-forest species. Northern hardwoods (sugar maples, birch, beech, and basswood) lead the list with 111,800 acres. Aspen (22,800 acres), northern white cedar (12,900 acres), and elm-ash-soft maple (4,700 acres) also occur in pure and mixed stands.

The region between Grand Traverse Bay and Torch Lake is mostly farmed for fruit. Deer-damage complaints are ocasionally high here, and enterprising hunters might check with DNR biologists or farmers themselves to see if responsible sportsmen are welcome on private land. Along Grand Traverse Bay itself forested sand dunes containing juniper thickets afford some surprisingly good deer and snowshoe-hare hunting.

On the eastern side of Torch Lake and extending east of Lake Bellaire and Intermediate Lake is a farming belt keyed to livestock and some cropping operations. The lakes themselves are largely ringed with resorts and cottages. Cottontails live near many of the farm buildings, whereas heavy patches of cover are home range for snowshoe hares. Raccoon- and fox-hunting opportunities also exist in this farming belt. There are some excellent squirrel-hunting opportunities presently going untouched in this region. Fox squirrels (along with some grays/blacks) occur in stands of mature hardwoods containing beech and oak, especially those near corn fields.

The county center from north to south is a collection of hardwoods, conifer swamps, and abandoned farms. Brushy areas are reverting to natural-forest succession and, as such, offer good hunting for deer, grouse, woodcock, and some hares. The northeastern corner of Antrim County contains the Jordan River Valley. This area of hardwoods and aspen is popular with grouse and woodcock hunters. The river valley itself is a good place to try for a December deer as whitetails yard in lowland swamps. The Jordan River is floatable from Graves Crossing to East Jordan in Charlevoix County although it flows through portions of private land.

The southeastern portion—also mostly state land—contains fair to good numbers of coyotes, deer, grouse, and woodcock as well as hares on pine plantations. Sand plains interspersed with jack pine and red pine may hold a remnant population of sharp-tailed grouse, but there is no open season on this species here.

Overall, Antrim County rates low for deer-hunting pressure (15 hunters per square mile) and a little under the state average with 14 percent buck-hunter success (one to two deer per square mile). As mentioned, best bets are in the fruit belt west of M-66. The county is open to bear hunting, with prospects generally poor to fair each fall. Bobcat hunting is not allowed at this time.

Good numbers of fox and coyotes are largely ignored by sportsmen other than deer hunters. Raccoon are also plentiful, with moderate hunting pressure. Snowshoe hares frequent pine plantations and poplar slashings near conifer swamps throughout the county.

Antrim County features good to excellent hunting for grouse and woodcock although pressure is on the increase. According to three years of hunter-cooperator flush rates that we checked, numbers of birds moved ranged from 1.30 to 2.70. Woodcock varied widely from 1.87 to 6.50 flushes per hour, the high-end figure no doubt a year of heavy flights that stopped over. Woodcock hunters should cover worm-rich soils on abandoned farmlands (orchards and pastures especially), moist bottomlands containing alder, and wrist-thick aspen fringes during wet falls. For grouse, try along the brushy edges of streams and in areas of thick, young aspen.

Waterfowlers have been known to overlook diving-duck-hunting opportunities on the bigger lakes as flight birds stop to rest and feed. Antrim County also contains many small lakes where local production of mallards, wood ducks, and teal could yield early-season hunting potential. A lack of public land along Grand Traverse Bay limits shoreline hunting potential. On the other hand, a local population of giant Canada geese in the Bellaire area is just now beginning to cause nuisance problems.

The Jordan River float mentioned earlier may produce a few local puddle ducks. Turkey populations, although expanding, are still small.

Best hunting potential occurs in the northwestern portion of the county.

OTHER SHOOTING OPPORTUNITIES

The Elk Rapids Sportsman's Club on US-31 North in Elk Rapids operates a shooting range open to the public at varying times on a sometime-free basis. Facilities include one outdoor station each for pistol, centerfire and rimfire rifle; a trap field; and archery targets. The club offers shooting instruction and state hunter-education programs. For details, call 616/264-9476.

FURTHER SOURCES OF HUNTING INFORMATION

1. DNR District Office, 1732 West M-32 (Box 667), Gaylord, Mich. 49735 (517/732-3541).

2. DNR Bellaire Field Office, 701 Cayuga St., Bellaire, Mich. 49615 (616/533-8341).

3. Bellaire Chamber of Commerce, Box 205, Bellaire, Mich. 49615 (616/533-8917).

4. Elk Rapids Area Chamber of Commerce, Box 854, Elk Rapids, Mich. 49629 (616/264-8202).

5. Topographic, county, and lake maps may be ordered from the Michigan United Conservation Clubs. For information, refer to the beginning of this book.

6. Plat books are available from the Antrim County Cooperative Extension Services, Box 427, County Building, Bellaire, Mich. 49615. The cost is $10 each (add $1.22 if mail ordering).

7. Antrim-Otsego County ASCS Office, 110 Grove St., Bellaire, Mich. 49615.

Also, refer to the Mackinac State Forest elsewhere in this book.

Arenac County

ARENAC County lies in the east-central part of the Lower Peninsula along the shore of Lake Huron. Most of its 368 square miles is an old lake bed, and small portions consist of moraines from the last period of glaciation 8,000 to 12,000 years ago. Deep deposits of sandy soil occur throughout the lake bed and are predominant in the northwestern part of the county. Elevation of the lake bed ranges from slightly less than 600 feet to 750 feet above sea level. Low-ridge ground moraines occur in northern Clayton, northeastern Mason, northern Whitney, and west and south of Sterling.

The groundwater table is relatively high throughout much of the county. Streams, which flow year-round, are partially fed by springs. Major flows include the Au Gres River in the eastern portion, the Rifle River in the central region, and the Pine River to the southwest.

About 58 percent of Arenac County is timbered with commercial-forest species. Aspen leads the types with 38,400 acres, followed by maple-birch (15,800 acres), oak-hickory (15,700 acres), elm-ash-soft maple (13,500 acres), and paper birch (2,200 acres). Stands, however, are mostly second-growth trees of poor quality. Aspen, scrub oak, and jack

pine are trees on sandy plains where virgin white pine once grew. Over 30,000 acres of these woodlands are found on farms scattered throughout the county.

Arenac County can be divided into three general cover types that are important to hunters. The area east of M-65 to Lake Huron is intensively farmed for beans, corn, carrots, and potatoes. Very little state land is found here and access to private lands is difficult although a courteous request costs nothing.

West of M-65 to I-75 the land is a mixture of farms and woods. Aspen is widespread along with a large quantity of oak. Stand ownership is particularly heavy north of Omer. West of I-75 to the Gladwin County line lie thick cover and a high-water table area, much of which (on state land at least) is inaccessible to all but the most determined hunters. Whereas hunting pressure tends to cull big bucks early throughout Arenac County, this remote area gets little pressure and has been known to produce trophy racks. Predominant forest species are aspen, maple, oak (especially in the northern portion), and jack pine, along with lowland brush and alders.

State land totals about 12 percent, or 28,696 acres, most of which falls into the Au Sable State Forest (which see).

Another 400 acres of Commercial Forest Act land is open to hunting, by law, in an agreement between the state and companies who own lands. In exchange for offering hunting privileges and a share of stumpage value when trees are cut, the companies realize a cut in local property taxes.

A large deer herd used to roam the eastern-end farmland; in recent seasons, however, the herd has been trimmed back and, in fact, only a small portion of the northern boundary is currently open to antlerless hunting. Pressure runs about 20 hunters per square mile, with three to four bucks killed per square mile for a success ratio of about 23 percent, several points higher than the state average. According to a five-year survey recently released by the DNR, Moffatt Township produces exceptionally high numbers of deer. Northern Au Gres Township also rates high.

As mentioned, access to private land is difficult, especially for firearm hunting. An enterprising bowhunter, though, might check around for a landowner who could be happy to see another deer removed from his crop fields.

Wild turkeys have been slowly creeping into Arenac County from Ogemaw and Roscommon counties. The DNR recently translocated 54 live-trapped birds from its northern flock to Mason, Clayton, and Standish townships. In due time, linkage of the birds will likely result in a hunting season.

Few pheasants inhabit Arenac County. Best bets would be south of Omer and Standish to the Bay County line and along cattails bordering farm fields next to Lake Huron and Saginaw Bay. Private-land access to hunt pheasants is difficult to obtain. There are also a few birds in Deep River and Clayton townships on farm property sandwiched by the two major portions of state land. Landowners, however, are equally protective of their ringnecks.

Grouse hunting rates fair to poor overall. Best spots are state land containing cutover aspen parcels now regenerated and from five to 15 years of age. Interestingly, Arenac County has the highest counts of woodcock peenting (male spring mating calls) of any of the eight counties in the DNR district and is among the highest in the state. Birds are best found in high-water table regions of alder cover bordered by openings (including cultivated lands). Peenting surveys are traditionally run in Au Gres, Arenac, and eastern Turner townships.

Squirrel hunting for fox species is fair throughout the county. Work stands of mature oak next to farm fields of corn. Rabbits appear to be on the upswing,

especially on cutover areas of the state-owned blocks. There are also a few snowshoe hares north of Maple Ridge Road (northernmost highway running east to west) in conifer swamps bordered by cutover aspen stands.

Coyotes have been increasing in the past eight to 10 years, and there are good numbers of red fox. Trappers exact a fair toll during high pelt-price years. A few landowners post known fox runways while hounds run the animals by them, but hunters could more fully use this resource. In addition, Arenac County supports good numbers of raccoon, with the best hunting—and highest pressure—occurring west of M-65.

A small but productive hunting area open to the public is Wigwam Bay Wildlife Area (*which see*) on Saginaw Bay. Waterfowlers check numerous beaver ponds throughout state land and jump-shoot along the Au Gres, Rifle, and Pine rivers. The Au Gres marshes have been largely depleted in recent years due to high-water levels but still produce fair to good waterfowling in early season. Some hunters score on late-season divers by layout shooting in Lake Huron with 100-block stools.

OTHER SHOOTING OPPORTUNITIES

The Eastern Arenac Sportsman's Club, 2392 West Main St. in Twining, has a shooting range featuring 12 outdoor stations for rimfire-rifle practice. It is open to the public for fees on a limited basis. Call 517/867-4265 for information.

FURTHER SOURCES OF HUNTING INFORMATION

1. DNR District Office, 501 Hemlock, Clare, Mich. 48617 (517/386-7991).
2. Au Gres Chamber of Commerce, Box 367, Au Gres, Mich. 48703 (517/876-8313).
3. Standish Chamber of Commerce, Box 458, Standish, Mich. 48658 (517/846-4595).
3. Topographic, county, and lake maps may be ordered from the Michigan United Conservation Clubs. For information, refer to the beginning of this book.
4. Plat books are available from the Arenac County Cooperative Extension Services, Box 745, County Courthouse, Standish, Mich. 48658. The cost is $9 each (add $.88 if mail ordering).
5. Arenac County ASCS Office, 806 West Cedar St., Standish, Mich. 48658 (517/846-4565).

Also refer to the following elsewhere in this book:
1. Au Sable State Forest
2. Wigwam Bay Wildlife Area

Baraga County

BARAGA County's location in the western Upper Peninsula is a long drive for downstate hunters. That is one reason the 578,000-acre county (about 900 square miles) receives low hunter pressure. Another could be that some feel the five-county DNR district is game poor. While there may be better places to hunt deer, grouse, and woodcock, Baraga County

contains excellent Canada goose numbers, plenty of bear, and good opportunities for bobcats, coyotes, and snowshoe hares.

And that is not to say that deer or upland bird hunting is not worth the effort. As we shall see, Baraga offers fairly good potential, especially for sportsmen wishing a remote, wilderness experience.

Much of Baraga County is dominated by sandy or

loamy soils on bedrock-controlled uplands. Lowlands are largely glacial outwash areas and include the 5,380-acre Baraga Plains Waterfowl Management Area (which see) that lies about 10 miles south of Keweenaw Bay. About 1,000 acres is share-cropped with rye, oats, buckwheat, alfalfa, and birdsfoot trefoil, which attracts up to 25,000 Canada geese en route to the Horicon National Wildlife Refuge in Wisconsin. Opportunity is tremendous, and hunting pressure is low.

Lying within the county is a portion of the Sturgeon River Sloughs Wildlife Area (which also see), another wildlife migration rest stop currently being developed. The sloughs are located between Portage and Otter lakes in Baraga and Houghton counties.

Geese visit farm fields in the Skanee, Herman, and Pelkie areas. They also use Honkers Pond on the southern edge of the Baraga Plains as well as the Net River Flooding in the southern county. Beaver ponds and streams throughout offer some jump-shooting opportunities for local ducks. Waterfowlers also should try Keweenaw Bay for divers.

A solid block of western-county lands from north to south, along with scattered holdings in the northern portion and a southeastern-area chunk, are Ottawa National Forest (which see) lands. They total about 39,000 acres. Some 73,000 acres of the Copper Country State Forest (which also see) are sprinkled throughout the central region. Both state and federal forest holdings are open to hunting. So are an additional 216,358 acres of Commercial Forest Act land, owned mostly by paper companies. Altogether, over half, or some 328,000 acres, of Baraga County is open to public hunting.

To find the public lands, refer to a copy of "Michigan County Maps and Outdoor Guide," available from the Michigan United Conservation Clubs. Legal descriptions of the company lands can be obtained from the DNR Forest Management Division, Box 30028, Lansing, Mich. 48909 (517/373-1275). Be sure to give the town and range numbers of the area you wish to hunt. County plat books are also a good reference.

Although most (93 percent) of Baraga County is covered with commercial-forest species, about 85 percent amounts to mature stands of sawtimber or poletimber. This factor, plus a shortage of aspen (40,700 acres total), make for poor game production overall, even though about 70 percent of the annual allowable cuttings on state lands in the seven-county DNR forestry district is being met. About 65 percent, or 335,000 acres, of the cover type is northern hardwoods (maple-birch). Other types represented—besides aspen—include 41,400 acres of balsam fir, 28,900 acres of northern white cedar, 20,000 acres of black spruce, 18,000 acres of elm-ash-soft maple, 10,000 acres of paper birch, and smaller amounts of tamarack, jack pine, red pine, and white spruce. There is no appreciable amount of oak.

Firearm deer-hunting pressure is very low at about four hunters per square mile. One of six tags his buck for a 12 percent success rate, a few points under the state average. The deer herd is not large—only about 60 car-deer accidents are reported annually—and the buck kill overall is under one animal per square mile.

Best areas to hunt are in the northeastern and west-central county and in the Baraga Plains. A severe snow belt begins at Herman in the county center. North of here the amount of snow is somewhat less due to the protection of Keweenaw Bay. Deer take advantage and as winter descends yard in jack-pine dunes and hardwoods east of Skanee, at the tip of the Abbaye Peninsula, in northern hardwoods and swamps due south of Baraga/L'Anse, and along the hardwood-covered gorge of the Sturgeon River north and south of M-38 in the western county. Valleys and river bottoms are good late-season places to shoot a buck heading for these yarding areas.

And there are some huge bucks in Baraga County. A new list of 1,150 all-time, record-book deer, just released by Commemorative Bucks of Michigan, contains 20 Baraga County whitetails.

Bear numbers throughout the district are holding up in spite of increased hunting pressure. About 200 to 300 bear are shot each year and although most come from Ontonagon and Gogebic counties to the west, Baraga County hunters will tag 50 to 60 bruins each fall. It is hard to pinpoint good areas to hunt since bear are such opportunistic animals. For best results, try baiting in dense conifer openings or on the fringe of lowland conifers and upland hardwoods, especially in slashings. Also, keep an eye open for available mast, chokecherries, apple orchards, and other food sources.

Good numbers of coyotes and a few red fox are underharvested. Apparently there are few bobcat hunters in the western U.P. as well. DNR district sealing records for the past five years show a range of only 26 to 54 cats killed each winter. Likely, more could be taken.

Raccoon are apparently on the increase, but snowshoe hares are currently down. Try waterways near farm fields for the former and cutover areas of sapling growth near pine plantations, alder mixed with willow, and lowland conifers for the latter. Few hunters pay any attention to gray squirrels and their black phase although there are huntable numbers in Baraga County.

Ruffed grouse are down at the present but expected to come back shortly. Hunter-cooperator hourly flush-rate averages of 1.06, 1.19, and 3.90 for three years that we checked at random, must be considered with discretion since samples were light. Corresponding woodcock flush-rate figures were .60, 1.16, and .28. Look for aspen cutover areas, alder swales, and brushland edges for both grouse and woodcock.

OTHER SHOOTING OPPORTUNITIES

None known at this time.

FURTHER SOURCES OF HUNTING INFORMATION

1. DNR District Office, North US-41 (Box 440), Baraga, Mich. 49908 (906/353-6651).

2. Forest Supervisor, Ottawa National Forest, East Cloverland Drive, Ironwood, Mich. 49938 (906/932-1330 or 1-800-561-1201 from the U.P.).

3. Upper Peninsula Travel and Recreation Association, Box 400, Iron Mountain, Mich. 49801 (906/774-5480).

4. Topographic, county, and lake maps may be ordered from the Michigan United Conservation Clubs. For information, refer to the beginning of this book.

5. Plat books are available from the Baraga County Cooperative Extension Services, 5 Baraga

Ave., L'Anse, Mich. 49946 (906/524-6300). The cost
is $10 each (add $1.15 if mail ordering).

6. Baraga/Houghton/Keweenaw County ASCS
Office, American Legion Building, L'Anse, Mich.
49946.

Also, refer to the following elsewhere in this book:
1. Baraga Plains Waterfowl Management Area
2. Copper Country State Forest
3. Craig Lake State Park
4. Ottawa National Forest

Barry County

BARRY County in southwestern Lower
Michigan is in the third tier of counties
from the Indiana boundary line. The
365,000-acre county features good soil
for livestock, dairy, and cash-crop farming. The
better soils of loam occur in the east-central and
northeastern portions and include much of the
Freeport area in Carlton Township. These flat-to-
rolling farmlands include patches of timber, low
swells, and broad, shallow swales but few streams
and practically no lakes. The western and
northwestern parts of Barry County include a plain
with a narrow arm extending eastward to Hastings.
Soils here are largely sand containing heavy
coverage of oak-hickory and birch-maple woods,
predominate forest species that cover 33 percent of
Barry County.

The county contains about 250 lakes varying in
size from potholes to four-square-mile Gun Lake in
the west-central region. Together, surface water
constitutes about 10 square miles. Surface land
features result from glacial action. The level sandy
plains are glacial sand plains, the rolling or hilly
areas are morainic, and the gently rolling areas are
glacial till plains. Most of the county is drained by the
Thornapple River and its tributaries. The southeastern part drains through Wanadoga, Wabascon,
and Crooked creeks into the Kalamazoo River, and
the area around Gun Lake drains through Gun Creek
to the Kalamazoo.

Cash-crop farming for soybeans, corn, wheat, and
oats is the main agricultural practice in the better
soil areas. In much of the rest of the county, smaller
farms tend to feature livestock and dairy operations.
The entire county, however, is picturesque and has
the look of game cover.

These topographic features and resulting areas of
farmland and forests provide good hunting
opportunity, some of the best in southern Michigan.
Although a large portion of Barry County is under
cultivation, brushlands and woodlands are mixed in
with farm areas, resulting in game habitat. Hunting
access is fairly good too, with 23,300 acres of state
land open in the Barry and Middleville state game
areas and Yankee Springs Recreation Area (all of
which see). In addition, about 7,200 acres of Public
Access Stamp Program lands are leased from some
20 participating farmers (hunters can get directories
from the Barry State Game Area or from DNR
district headquarters in Plainwell). These farms are
scattered throughout all the county but the southern
one-quarter. A courteous request from considerate
hunters may also yield access to other private
holdings.

Deer hunters enjoy success comparable to the
statewide average (17 to 18 percent) with moderate
pressure at 20 hunters per square mile. However,
the game areas get heavy pressure, particularly
during the shotgun-only firearm season. County-
wide buck kill runs three to four animals per square
mile, quite high for southern Michigan. And there
are some very large deer. Commemorative Bucks of
Michigan lists two all-time record whitetails as
Barry County bucks.

Also, this county is home to plenty of deer; in fact,
the annual car-deer accident tally is usually above
500 and is always the highest in the seven-county
DNR district. Although deer-damage complaints are
usually low, due to the type of farming, the DNR has
received complaints from Hastings' homeowners
about deer eating yard shrubbery.

Good raccoon and fox populations offer some
untapped hunting opportunity. This is partly
because most nonresident dog hunters stop at
counties farther south and is also due to the
excellent mix of good farmland and natural cover.
Barry County could take considerable more squirrel
hunting pressure too, especially outside the game
areas. Oak stands next to grain fields are the best
places to key efforts, but always ask permission first
on private land. Hunters will find cottontails in good
supply too, particularly in the central and southern
regions. Try lowland brushy areas next to crop fields
and grasslands.

Best pheasant hunting occurs in the northeastern
and east-central area below Nashville. There are
scattered pockets of wild birds elsewhere in the
county too, but opportunities overall are way down
from former years. Grouse and woodcock hunters
will fare much better, thanks to excellent habitat
along waterways and nestled in hill crotches
throughout the county. The aspen count is higher in
Barry County than elsewhere in the district. Look for
stands of aspen saplings and gray dogwood thickets,
especially when found near lowland tag alders. In a
normal year grouse hunters move 2.0 to 3.2 birds
per hour. Woodcock flushes are considerably less
(.75 to 1.1 per hour) but still offer bonus shooting,
especially when late October migrants stop over.

Although Gun Lake used to be tops for diving duck
hunting, it has gone down in recent years. Other
lakes worth trying include Wall, Pine, and Fine.
Hunters might also check out any of the other dozen
Barry County lakes with public access or ask
landowners for hunting permission on others. A
float trip on the Thornapple River can produce ducks
as well as squirrels and an occasional deer. A good
put-in spot is at M-66 near Thornapple Lake or the
lake itself. About five miles below Hastings is Irving
Dam; take out on the left bank for a short portage. A
canoe-access site is found at Irving Bridge, but
Middleville Dam will require another portage.

Incidentally, camping facilities and canoe rentals are available at the town of Middleville. Duck hunters might also consider jump shooting along the Little Thornapple and Coldwater rivers and High and Cedar creeks.

Barry County offers good to excellent field hunting with decoys for geese, especially in the southeastern region. Gull Lake acts as a sanctuary for birds that venture out to farm fields. In addition, Crooked Lake near Delton holds a small resident flock. Canada geese are growing to nuisance proportions throughout the county and may provide an extended season (as in southeastern Michigan) in the near future.

Eighteen Pennsylvania wild turkeys recently released in the southern portion of the Barry State Game Area will, it is hoped, increase to produce future hunting opportunities.

FURTHER SOURCES OF HUNTING INFORMATION

1. DNR District Office, 621 North 10th St. (Box 355), Plainwell, Mich. 49080 (616/685-6851).

2. Barry State Game Area, 1805 South Yankee Springs Road, Middleville, Mich. 49333 (616/795-3280).

3. Yankee Springs Recreation Area, 2104 Gun Lake Road, Route 3, Middleville, Mich. 49333 (616/795-9081).

4. Topographic, county, and lake maps may be ordered from the Michigan United Conservation Clubs. For information, refer to the beginning of this book.

5. Hastings Area Chamber of Commerce, 115 South Jefferson St., Hastings, Mich. 49058 (616/945-2454).

6. Nashville Chamber of Commerce, 113 North Main, Nashville, Mich. 49073 (517/852-1551).

7. Bellevue Chamber of Commerce, 115 North Main St., Bellevue, Mich. 49021 (616/763-9418).

8. County plat books are available from the Barry County Cooperative Extension Service, 301 South Michigan Ave., Hastings, Mich. 49058. The cost is $10 (add $1 if mail ordering).

9. Barry County ASCS Office, USDA, 535 West Woodlawn Ave., Hastings, Mich. 49058 (616/948-8037).

Also, refer to the following elsewhere in this book:
1. Barry State Game Area
2. Middleville State Game Area
3. Yankee Springs Recreation Area

Bay County

BAY County is in the east-central part of the Lower Peninsula along the shore of Saginaw Bay. The county is quite flat and due to its use as a lake bottom for millenia, the rich soils grow excellent crops of corn, soybeans, navy beans, sugar beets, wheat, and oats. There are some dairy enterprises in Bay County, but most of the crops are grown for cash sale. Only about eight percent of its 451 square miles is wooded with commercial-forest types in fairly equal mixtures of aspen, maple-brich, and elm-ash-soft maple. These are distributed throughout farm woodlots with a particularly heavy sprinkling in the northwestern portion.

The county features many miles of frontage on Saginaw Bay, and although there are no inland lakes, many small ponds and borrow pits near highway overpasses and interchanges provide mini-habitats for wildlife and, in some cases, limited hunting opportunities. The largest body of water in the county is the shallow marsh and lagoon in the Tobico Marsh State Game Area (which see). The mighty Saginaw River with its collective waters from a dozen southern Michigan streams moves slowly toward Saginaw Bay in the southern region. Also important to drainage (and to hunters) are the Quanicassee River near the eastern edge of the county, the Kawkawlin River and its tributaries in southwestern and central regions, and the Pinconning and Saganing rivers in the northern portion.

Best hunting in Bay County occurs in two general areas. First is the Saginaw Bay shoreline, which produces ducks and geese along with a few deer, squirrels, rabbits, raccoon, and pheasants. High-water levels of Lake Huron in recent years have destroyed much of the marsh along the bay, but

there is some indication that vegetation is now creeping back. Continued marsh development will increase hunting potential.

In addition, various blocks of state land—Quanicassee Wildlife Area, Tobico, Nayanquing Point Wildlife Area (which features waterfowl hunting by permit), portions of Pinconning State Park, and five Bay County mini-game areas (all of which see)—provide hunting opportunity.

The second area of potential is the northern stack of townships along the western border with Gladwin County. Gibson and Mount Forest townships in particular have a considerable amount of woodland. West of Garfield Road and near Crump, Willard, and Bentley are good hunting areas although near the southwestern end of Garfield Township wooded cover types tend to thin out.

Game populations are poor to fair. There is some deer-hunting opportunity in northern Gibson Township. Rabbits, grouse, fox squirrels, and woodcock are found in huntable numbers, but sportsmen will have to focus on key habitats and be willing to knock on a few doors to gain permission to enter. There are no Public Access Stamp Program lands enrolled in Bay County, and only 1.5 percent of the land base is publicly-owned.

Pheasant populations have fallen on hard times in this once-productive county. In fact, a special pheasant-hunting day at Nayanquing Point was dropped recently. Townships mentioned offer some limited opportunities as do Portsmouth and Merritt townships southeast of Bay City. The Munger area continues to get opening-day pressure for pheasants, but hunters usually do not fare well. A return later in the season when crops are harvested and available cover reduced to hunting size can put a ringneck or two in the game pouch.

In addition to the shoreline, waterfowl hunting is surprisingly good for hunters willing to set out big spreads of decoys and lie under tarps or hide in pit blinds on farm fields. Limited sharecropping at Quanicassee and Nayanquing Point drives birds inland for food, especially later in the season. Jump-shooters can also score on mallards, teal, and wood ducks along the Kawkawlin River except that they will first need permission to enter private lands.

Deer-hunting pressure runs under five hunters per square mile, due mostly to the lack of public land. Buck-hunter success is quite high—around 30 percent or nearly double the state average. On the other hand, the county serves up less than one buck per square mile, and the deer herd is not very large. This is due to a lack of good habitat. Bay County does serve up an occasional trophy buck, however. Commemorative Bucks of Michigan has uncovered three such record-book racks to date.

The DNR intends to release wild turkeys in western Bay County. If the birds are left alone to propagate, hunters might be able to cash in on future potential.

OTHER SHOOTING OPPORTUNITIES

Bay County sportsmen have at least two shooting ranges to visit. The Bay City Bowmen, 2245 Eight-Mile Road in Kawkawlin, has 99 indoor/outdoor archery targets open to the public on a sometime-fee basis. The club also offers competitive shooting. For information, call (517/684-3173).

The Bay County Conservation and Gun Club on Rodgers Road in Crump has three skeet and two trap fields open to the public for fees. Shooting instruction and competitive shooting are also offered. For details, call 517/667-0011.

FURTHER SOURCES OF HUNTING INFORMATION

1. DNR District Office, 501 Hemlock, Clare, Mich. 48617 (517/386-7991).
2. Nayanquing Point Wildlife Area, 1570 Tower Beach Road, Pinconning, Mich. 48650 (517/697-5101).
3. Bay Area Chamber of Commerce, Box 838, Bay City, Mich. 48706 (517/893-4567).
4. Auburn Area Chamber of Commerce, 1491 West Midland Road, Auburn, Mich. 48611 (517/662-4001).
5. Pinconning Area Chamber of Commerce, Box 856, Pinconning, Mich. 48650 (517/879-5888).
6. Topographic, county, and lake maps may be ordered from the Michigan United Conservation Clubs. For information, refer to the beginning of this book.
7. Plat books are available from the Bay County Cooperative Extension Services, 309 Second St., Bay City, Mich. 48706. The cost is $11 each (add $1 if mail ordering).
8. Bay County ASCS Office, 1213 South Euclid Ave., Bay City, Mich. 48706 (517/686-0430).

Also, refer to the following elsewhere in this book:
1. Bay County Mini-Game Areas
2. Nayanquing Point Wildlife Area
3. Pinconning State Park
4. Quanicassee Wildlife Area
5. Tobico Marsh State Game Area

Benzie County

A T 341 square miles, Benzie County in northwestern Lower Michigan may be among the smallest in size of Michigan's 83 counties, but it is certainly not short on hunting opportunity. A good variety of forest types in varying age classes and an abundance of public lands open to hunting make Benzie County a good bet for deer, hare, squirrel, grouse, and woodcock hunters.

Sixty-five percent of its land base is covered with commercial-forest species. Maple-birch leads the way with 75,100 acres, followed by 16,200 acres of aspen, 12,000 acres of elm-ash-soft maple, 9,100 acres of red pine, 4,300 acres of northern white cedar, and 2,200 acres of oak-hickory.

Over 59,000 acres, or 29 percent of Benzie County, is state land. Holdings in the eastern two-thirds are part of the Pere Marquette State Forest (which see). The only state land in the western region is the Betsie River State Game Area (which also see). In addition, about 15,000 acres of the Sleeping Bear Dunes National Lakeshore lie along Lake Michigan north of Crystal Lake. Altogether, about 45 percent of Benzie County is public land open to hunting.

Further, another 2,347 acres of company-owned land is enrolled in the Commercial Forest Act program, which makes it open to hunting. For legal descriptions, write to the DNR Forest Management Division, Box 30028, Lansing, Mich. 48909, or call 517/373-1275.

Most of Benzie County is sandy soils interspersed with loamy soils. These are largely glacial outwash areas of sand and gravel. Topography is gently rolling to fairly steep in places, such as the Lake Michigan dune belt and the Platte River valley near Honor.

Overall, the county receives moderate deer-hunting pressure of 10 to 20 sportsmen per square mile, whose success at tagging bucks during the firearm season varies from 12 to 18 percent. That usually figures out to an average of one to two bucks per square mile.

One good deer hunting area is north of US-31 and east of CR-671. This is an upland area of mixed hardwoods and aspen with a considerable amount of public ownership. DNR cutting programs in aspen make for varying age classes, important for high game production. The sand dunes are another good spot for driving deer early and late in the season. Hardwoods cover portions of the dunes, the mainland side of which seems to be natural passageways for deer.

West of US-31 are orchards, hardwoods, and scattered parcels of aspen. Easy winters help sustain a healthy deer herd, which includes some animals with good racks. However, much of the land is in private ownership. South and east of US-31 is a blend of swamps, aspen, and a few hardwoods. This is also good deer habitat, with moderate hunting pressure. These wild, remote lands are cut by many creeks and swamps, and a large percentage is in public ownership. However, tougher winters on deer here are reflected by smaller antler size.

Although gray/black squirrels are scattered throughout the county, best hunting occurs in the oak belt around Turtle Lake in Inland Township. There are a few fox squirrels here too. Occasional bear and bobcats are sighted in Benzie County, but the season is currently closed and will likely remain so. Fox are down from former high-number years, and there are scattered numbers of coyotes. Raccoon afford hunting opportunities along waterways; pressure is moderate. Wild turkeys are scarce and only the south-central region is open to hunting at this time.

Benzie County has good hare habitat—cutover aspen, young pine planations, and conifer swamps—and populations vary according to their cyclic nature. Numbers recently appear to be creeping back after a few "down" years. Duck hunting used to be good at Grass Lake Flooding but has fallen off in recent years. For puddle-duck hunting, stick to beaver ponds and small lakes as well as stream bottoms. There are some diving-duck hunting opportunities with layout boats on larger lakes like Crystal and Platte. These lakes also host small numbers of geese, but hunting potential is severely limited due to development.

Grouse and woodcock hunting is good in Benzie County, thanks to lots of aspen cutover areas and much edge, as well as two rivers (the Platte and the Betsie), many small streams lined with brush, and a fair amount of fruit-bearing shrubs. Gray dogwood and thornapple are particularly abundant. Three years of hunter-cooperator records that we spot-checked showed average hourly flush rates of 1.37, 1.13, and 1.80 for grouse and 2.19, 1.05, and 1.12 for woodcock. Hunting pressure is heavy.

OTHER SHOOTING OPPORTUNITIES

The Benzie Sportsman Club in Thompsonville has shooting range facilities open to the public on a sometime-fee basis. Included are five outdoor stations each for centerfire and rimfire rifle and pistol as well as a skeet field. The club sponsors state hunter-education programs. For details, call 616/378-2377.

OTHER SOURCES OF HUNTING INFORMATION

1. DNR District Office, 8015 South 131 Road, Cadillac, Mich. 49601 (616/775-9727).

2. Platte River Field Office, 15200 Honor Hwy., Beulah, Mich. 49617 (616/325-4611).

3. DNR Traverse City Field Office, 404 West 14th St., Traverse City, Mich. 49684 (616/946-4920).

4. Benzie County Chamber of Commerce, Box 505, Beulah, Mich. 49617 (616/882-5802).

5. Topographic, county, and lake maps may be ordered from the Michigan United Conservation Clubs. For information, refer to the beginning of this book.

6. Plat books are available from the Benzie County Cooperative Extension Services, Government Center, Box 307, Beulah, Mich. 49617. Call for the price of a new book being compiled as we went to press, or send $5.05 (includes postage and handling) for a copy of the old directory.

7. Benzie County ASCS Office, 107 Benzie Blvd., Beulah, Mich. 49617.

Also, refer to the following elsewhere in this book:
1. Betsie River State Game Area
2. Pere Marquette State Forest

Berrien County

BERRIEN County in the extreme southwestern corner of Lower Michigan was totally covered by glaciers some 12,000 years ago. When the ice melted, it left deposits of raw soil material that range from 100 to 400 feet in thickness. These deposits cover all of 373,000-acre Berrien County, whose present surface features are largely the result of that glacial action.

Four topographical divisions lie roughly parallel to the 42 miles of Lake Michigan shoreline. The first is an old glacial lake plain covered by sand dunes to 200 feet high and in turn by scattered cover of oak and other hardwoods. A six- to eight-mile-wide band of level plain, the remnant floor of glacial Lake Chicago, lies behind this dune strip. This slightly higher region includes intermittent layers of sand over a clay/loam base, giving the plain an intricate pattern of wet and dry soils.

Broad swells, smooth ridges, and detached high plains containing morainic till are slightly higher again and extend farther inland. The fourth division covers the eastern two-thirds of Berrien County and is a broad plateaulike highland with swells of 100 to 200 feet. Portions of Berrien County have been tiled and drained, yet only slightly more than half the land area is in active farming. Most of the agricultural practices are for orchard and vine fruit, especially throughout the northern two-thirds and within a few miles of the Lake Michigan shoreline from the Indiana boundary line north. Small-scale southern county farms grow corn, wheat, oats, and soybeans as a cash crop or as food supplements for dairy and livestock operations.

Most of Berrien County features gently sloping moraines and till plains with flat to nearly level lake plains and outwash plains. There are 86 lakes scattered throughout. Deeply entrenched drainageways dissect the county—the largest being the St. Joseph River—with streams flowing westerly to Lake Michigan. The Paw Paw River in the northern half and the Galien River in the southern region run southwesterly. Major creeks from north to south include Blue, Hickory, Pipestone, McCoy, and Dowagiac. Most contain trout and/or salmon and feature timbered bottomlands.

Public access land is limited in Berrien County. The state owns 1,100 acres in the form of three state parks along Lake Michigan. A 557-acre portion of one, Warren Dunes, is open to hunting. A dozen participating farmers in the Public Access Stamp Program have about 2,400 acres also open to hunting. These lands are mostly found in the southern region, especially in Weesaw and Buchanan townships. A courteous request can sometimes result in being invited to hunt other private lands as overall pressure is light in Berrien County.

Deer hunters, for instance, average only about six sportsmen per square mile, among the lowest of southern Michigan intensity. Limited access is one reason; a small deer herd is another. Annual car-deer accidents are usually under 200 animals. Consequently, buck-hunter success runs under 20 percent and the annual take is less than one buck per square mile.

But Berrien County does have big deer. Each year it seems that one or more qualify for Commemorative Bucks of Michigan's record book, and in 1982 an Illinois hunter shot the state's finest typical-antlered whitetail, a monster buck that scored 170 and 5/8 Boone and Crockett Club points. If access can be granted, hunters should key along edge cover of farm woodlots and brushy areas in wet lowlands.

About 18 percent of Berrien County is forested with commercial species, mostly upland hardwoods — oak-hickory, ash-soft maple-elm, birch-maple — interspersed with lowland hardwoods and some aspen. Cottontails are plentiful throughout, with concentrations in brushland areas near wet spots. There are good numbers of red fox in this county too, with a scattering of gray fox and even a few coyotes. Raccoon hunting is good in lowland areas that abut corn fields and fruit farms. Fox squirrels are an underhunted species along stream bottomlands and in farm woodlots.

Berrien County used to feature some of southwestern Michigan's best pheasant hunting, but populations have fallen on hard times although remnant pockets of birds still offer some hunting opportunity. Best area to try is the central portion south of I-94. There is excellent potential habitat for a wild-pheasant comeback, however, should the state and private landowners elect to work together on a reintroduction program.

There are no wild turkeys and no DNR plans to introduce any at this time. Sporadic waterfowling opportunities exist along Lake Michigan for migrant diving ducks and Canada geese. The St. Joseph River offers hunters a splendid float for squirrels, ducks, geese, and possibly deer among picturesque scenery. Road access abounds but hunters will have to portage around dams at Niles, Buchanan, and Berrien Springs. The Galien River offers some floating opportunities too, especially in downstream reaches before it empties into Lake Michigan at New Buffalo. Another drift possibility is on the Paw Paw River upstream from the twin cities. In addition, Paw Paw Lake has diving ducks and is the only Berrien County lake with present public access. Enterprising hunters can get both jump-shooting and decoy-hunting action on small streams and private lakes, respectively, if they are careful to request permission before entering private land.

Berrien County is sparsley populated with the exception of St. Joseph/Benton Harbor metropolitan area. Hunters in this region should check with local municipalities for special regulations.

OTHER SHOOTING OPPORTUNITIES

The Berrien County Sportsman's Club on East Linco Road in Berrien Springs has extensive shooting facilities open to the public at certain times on a fee basis. Featured are 29 pistol stations (indoor and outdoor), 99 rifle centerfire stations (outdoor), and 99 rifle rimfire stations (indoor and outdoor), plus two skeet and five trap fields for shotgunners. There are also seven areas for shotgun handtrap and 26 indoor/outdoor archery targets. The club offers competitive shooting and shooting instruction. For information, call 616/429-3792.

Two sportsman's clubs with shooting facilities currently open to the public without fee are the Grand Mere Rifle Club on Ridge Road in Stevensville and the Coloma Rod and Gun Club in Coloma. The Grand Mere group allows use of its indoor pistol and rifle rimfire ranges (eight stations each) at certain times. The Coloma Club has outdoor stations for pistol, centerfire and rimfire rifles (four stations each), and archery (15 targets). In addition, there are two shotgun trap fields, and the club offers shooting instruction and shooting competition, plus a state hunter education program. Call 616/468-5651 for details.

Further, the Howard Township Conservation Club in Niles (2601 Terminal Road) has outdoor facilities for pistol and centerfire and rimfire rifle (eight stations each) as well as two shotgun trap fields all open to the public. Shooting instruction and shooting competition are also provided. Call 616/684-7500 for fee schedules and other information.

FURTHER SOURCES OF HUNTING INFORMATION

1. DNR District Office, 621 North 10th St. (Box 355), Plainwell, Mich. 49080 (616/685-6851).
2. Warren Dunes State Park, Red Arrow Hwy., Sawyer, Mich. 49125 (616/426-4013).
3. Twin Cities Area Chamber of Commerce, Box 1208, Benton Harbor, Mich. 49022 (616/925-0044).
4. Four Flags Area Chamber of Commerce, 321 East Main St. (Box 10), Niles, Mich. 49120 (616/683-3720).
5. Buchanan Area Chamber of Commerce, 119 Main St., Buchanan, Mich. 49107 (616/695-3291).
6. Topographic, county, and lake maps may be ordered from the Michigan United Conservation Clubs. For information, refer to the beginning of this book.
7. County plat books are available from the Southwestern Michigan Abstract and Title Co., 811 Ship St. (Box 380), St. Joseph, Mich. 49085. They are free when picked up (include a check or money order for $3 when mail ordering).
8. Berrien County ASCS Office, USDA, 3830 M-139, St. Joseph, Mich. 49085 (616/983-5634).

Also, refer to the following elsewhere in this book:
1. Warren Dunes State Park

Branch County

CENTRAL county in a tier of seven that border Indiana and Ohio is 517-square-mile Branch County. This is a game-producing county with farmland cropped for small grains and pastured for livestock and dairy cattle. It is one of southern Michigan's least populated counties, vying with eastern neighbor Hillsdale for that distinction. About 40,000 people live in Branch County on farms or in small communities like Coldwater, the county seat. US-12 splits the county east to west, and US-27 runs north and south. These are the major roads; most others are gravel, county-section roads.

Banch County has soils of sandy loam underlain by glacial outwash plains of sand and gravel. Some of this glacial till is coarse-textured, containing rocks from cobblestone size to boulders. Much of this till is in the form of fans and sheets flanking end moraines and as deltas along glacial lake margins. The county also contains several drumlins, streamlined hills of glacial till ½ mile to one mile long that were deposited and shaped by moving ice sheets. The glaciers of 8,000 to 12,000 years ago left lake clusters in the northwestern corner, in the north-central area above Coldwater (Randall Chain of Lakes), and in the southeastern region (Marble and Coldwater chains). There are no major rivers but rather an intricate mosaic of small streams.

The bad hunting news about Branch County is that it contains no public land. The good news is that with 9,400 acres of Public Access Stamp Program land enrolled by nearly four dozen farmers, Branch County leads the nine-county DNR district. DNR district headquarters at Jackson or the field office at Waterloo Recreation Area in Jackson County have free directories for the asking. Also, Branch County landowners are often agreeable to allowing hunters on their land if they are responsible and considerate.

And this is a county well worth hunting. About 16 percent is covered by commercial forest species. Maple and birch predominate with scattered mixtures of elm, ash, soft maple, oak, and hickory. Included are small pockets of red and white pine and white spruce. In addition, stream bottoms often contain lowland hardwoods, and there is a considerable amount of brush as well as less valuable species—tulip poplar, basswood, and cottonwood.

In spite of its low population and lack of busy highways, Branch County tallies more than '300 car-deer accidents each year, a figure which testifies to a sizable deer herd. Buck hunting success is usually near the state average of 15 percent, and Branch County hunters often kill big deer. Commemorative Bucks of Michigan, which began scouring the state for record bucks a few years ago, have turned up five Branch County trophies so far, three of which were tagged in a recent hunting season. Pressure is low to moderate with 10 to 12 hunters per square mile.

Applicant success on securing a hunter's-choice permit can run over 90 percent, again, largely due to the lack of state land.

Deer are well scattered. So are Public Access Stamp program lands, with every township represented. The heaviest concentration, however, appears to be in the central region east to west. Branch County also offers good raccoon hunting with fair to good populations. There is some later-season competition from Indiana and Ohio hunters, though. Fox, mostly reds with a few grays, are an underhunted species.

So are squirrels and rabbits, both of which are in ample supply and well distributed. Look for fox squirrels (and a few grays) in upland timbered areas, especially when corn fields can be found adjacent to oak-hickory woodlands. Rabbits are lovers of the edge—openings in brushy or thick vine areas in association with idle grasslands. Look for these near woodlot edges, stream edges, ditches, hedgerows, marsh areas, and abandoned farms. An abundance of brush piles and woodchuck holes provides excellent cover, and rabbits are often abundant in these areas. Nearly all small farms in Branch County are home to cottontails.

There are few if any grouse and no turkeys. However, Indiana DNR biologists have released both turkeys and ruffed grouse in the Pigeon River State Game Area in that state, and, conceivably, these game species could move into Branch County in the future. Fair to good waterfowling for both local puddlers and migrant divers shapes up each fall on the lake chains.

OTHER SHOOTING OPPORTUNITIES

I-69 Shooting Preserve, 7720 Bennett Road, Quincy, Mich. 49082, in Batavia Township is a 467-acre preserve specializing in pheasants. It is open to the public for those taking memberships. Contact Edwin E. Geishert (517/639-4937) for details.

FURTHER SOURCES OF HUNTING INFORMATION

1. DNR District Office, 3335 Lansing Ave., Jackson, Mich. 49202 (517/784-3188).

2. Waterloo Game Office, Route 3, 13578 Seymour Road, Grass Lake, Mich. 49240 (517/522-4097).

3. Chamber of Commerce Bronson, Inc., 863 West Chicago, Bronson, Mich. 49028 (517/369-7322).

4. Greater Coldwater Area Chamber of Commerce, 20 Division St., Coldwater, Mich. 49036 (517/278-5985).

5. Quincy Chamber of Commerce, 102 East Jefferson, Quincy, Mich. 49082 (517/639-8056).

6. Topographic, county, and lake maps may be ordered from the Michigan United Conservation Clubs. For information, refer to the beginning of this book.

7. Plat books are available from the Branch County Treasurer's Office, Courthouse Bldg., Coldwater, Mich. 49036, for $7 each (add $1.50 for mail orders).

8. Branch County ASCS Office, USDA, 1123 West Chicago Road, Coldwater, Mich. 49036 (517/278-2725).

Calhoun County

AT 715 square miles, Calhoun County lies in the second tier of counties from the Indiana/Ohio border. This south-central Lower Michigan county contains major cities (Marshall, Albion, and Battle Creek); plenty of farms with both cash-crop and dairy/livestock operations; and a fair to good amount of wildlife cover. Deer are the No. 1 game species sought, but there is also fair to good hunting for waterfowl, ruffed grouse, squirrels, rabbits, raccoon, and fox.

Heavy glaciation thousands of years ago carved Calhoun County into its present shape of gently-rolling swells and level plains. The soil is largely sandy loam underlain by deposits of gravel. There are plenty of lakes scattered throughout, and intricate stream patterns provide for plenty of bottomlands. All in all, Calhoun County affords a good mix of woodland, farmland, and brushland throughout. Small wonder that it looks like game country.

The southern portion is drained by the St. Joseph, which enters in the southeast and runs westerly through Tekonsha, Burlington, and Union City. Portions are floatable. The Nottawassepee River, a tributary to the St. Joe, drains the southwestern portion. The Kalamazoo enters the county outside Albion and collects the South Branch flow at this point. Then it meanders westerly through Marshall to Battle Creek. Here, the south-running Battle Creek River joins, and the combined flow runs on into Kalamazoo County.

The Kalamazoo is an excellent river to float. You can put in at Homer off M-60 and either run or portage the small dam just north of town. At Albion the river comes out of a swampy lake and flows under two bridges. There is a dam, which must be portaged, just past the second bridge. Several more dams require portaging en route to Kalamazoo. There are plenty of places to camp, and wildlife—squirrels, ducks, geese, and even deer are abundant. This river is best scouted first by hunters who then seek permission to enter private lands along the way. They should also check for local hunting closures in the cities en route.

As mentioned, Calhoun County is well covered with mixed stands of trees and brush. About 18 percent features commercial forest species: oak, hickory, hard and soft maple, ash, elm, birch, and aspen. Fox squirrels (along with the infrequent gray squirrel) live in mature groves of oak and hickory. Seek them anywhere in such farm woodlots, especially near crop fields of corn. Rabbits frequent edge cover of brushlands, grasslands, and woodlands, especially in low areas. They too benefit from farm practices unless cultivation is fencerow to fencerow. Of course, you will have to ask permission, which Calhoun County farmers have been fairly good about giving to considerate, responsible sportsmen.

It's especially important to cultivate good hunter/landowner relations here because there is no public land, except for a small part of the Fort Custer Recreation Area (*which see*) spilling over from Kalamazoo County. Lack of public land is the reason DNR wildlife biologists have enrolled some two dozen farmers in the Public Access Stamp Program. More than 4,500 acres, open to hunting, are currently in this program, and they are well distributed throughout. For a free directory, contact DNR officials at district headquarters in Jackson or at Fort Custer.

Calhoun and its eastern neighbor, Jackson County, are two of the best deer hunter counties in southern Michigan. They rate third and second, respectively, in the number of car-deer accidents (Kent County leads the state), sad statistics of over 600 deer annually killed but a statistic that is nevertheless indicative of a healthy deer herd. One of six hunters (15 to 19 percent) tags a buck at the rate of one to two animals per square mile. Pressure is reasonably low in this county too (mostly because of the lack of public land), about 12 hunters per square mile. And not all the deer shot are bucks.

Applicant success rates at getting a permit to hunt antlerless deer run about 90 percent.

Calhoun County grows rack deer too. Of 1,150 all-time huge bucks turned up thus far by Commemorative Bucks of Michigan, 24 were Calhoun County homegrown. Five and three of those bucks from two recent hunting seasons, respectively, were recognized as trophy deer. Continued searching by CBM will surely turn up others. Deer seem plentiful throughout with best concentrations perhaps in the northern half and southwestern portions.

Raccoon are plentiful along wooded river bottomlands adjacent to corn fields. Calhoun County is popular with 'coon hunters, many of whom come from Indiana and Ohio during the later season shared with nonresidents. Red fox is another abundant game species and one which is currently underharvested.

Pheasant hunting is very poor; Calhoun is usually among the lowest in the nine-county DNR district for both crowing counts and pheasant chick surveys. The mix of brushlands/woodlands, though, has apparently been good for ruffed grouse, which appear to be increasing numbers slowly. Hunting pressure, however, has also increased. During a recent season cooperators said they moved 3.7 grouse per hour, an unusually high figure for southern Michigan. However, this figure is reflected in less than 50 hunting hours and may not be indicative of high numbers throughout.

Waterfowlers key along river bottoms, either by floating or by jump-shooting. Mallards, wood ducks, and early-season teal or primary targets. Public access is available on some of the lakes, and hunters might want to check them later in the season for migrant divers, particularly Duck Lake in the northeastern corner. The southeastern corner east of M-99 falls into the special late season for Canada geese. However, hunting opportunities are very limited. The nuisance giant Canadas are increasing in both the Battle Creek area and the eastern portion of the county. Future boundaries for the late season may eventually claim more of Calhoun County.

OTHER SHOOTING OPPORTUNITIES

Feiler Farms Preserve (633 acres), 19425 Homer Road, Marshall, Mich. 49068, is open to the public daily for those who wish to hunt pheasants, quail, and chukar partridge. For fee schedules and other information, contact Laurence G. Feiler III at 616/781-7116.

Another preserve, Eaton Corporation, is open to those who take memberships. The 320-acre preserve, featuring pheasants and quail, is located at 1101 West Hanover St., Marshall, Mich. 49068. For more information, contact John J. Quigley, 616/781-0313.

The Albion Conservation Club, Inc., 11450 25½ Mile Rd., Albion, Mich. 49224 (517/629-4410), has shooting facilities open to the public at certain times on a sometime-fee basis. Featured are 30 indoor/outdoor pistol stations, 10 outdoor stations each for centerfire and rimfire rifle, two indoor archery targets, and two shotgun trap fields. The club offers both shooting instruction and hunter certification programs.

The Battle Creek Gun Club on Helmer Road in Battle Creek has shotgun trap and skeet fields open daily to the public for fees. Competitive shooting is available. For details, call 616/962-7715.

FURTHER SOURCES OF HUNTING INFORMATION

1. DNR District Office, 3335 Lansing Ave., Jackson, Mich. 49202 (517/784-3188).

2. Fort Custer Recreation Area, 5163 West Fort Custer Drive, Augusta, Mich. 49012 (616/731-4200).

3. Battle Creek Area Chamber of Commerce, 172 West Van Buren St., Battle Creek, Mich. 49016 (616/962-4076).

4. Marshall Area Chamber of Commerce, 308 East Michigan Ave., Marshall, Mich. 49068 (616/781-5163).

5. Greater Albion Chamber of Commerce, Box 288, Albion, Mich. 49224 (517/629-5533).

6. Topographic, county, and lake maps may be ordered from the Michigan United Conservation Clubs. For information, refer to the beginning of this book.

7. Plat books are available from the Calhoun County Clerk-Register, 315 West Green St., Marshall, Mich. 49068, for $10 each (add $1.50 if mail ordering).

8. Calhoun County ASCS Office, USDA, 120 West Drive North, Marshall, Mich. 49068 (616/781-4263).

Cass County

CASS County in southwestern Lower Michigan is on the Indiana state line. This farming county has a low population and offers fair to good hunting opportunities for deer, rabbits, raccoon, fox, and squirrels. Although it is popular with Indiana hunters as well as county residents, pressure remains moderate.

Most of the 323,000-acre county is level to gently rolling and shows the results of heavy glaciation during the last Ice Age 8,000 to 12,000 years ago. Major portions are glacial outwash plains containing loamy soils underlain by sand and gravel deposits. A portion of the northeastern region, including much of Volinia Township, contains wet, organic, and loamy soil. The northwestern corner features sandy/loamy soils that are alternately wet and dry. About 17 percent of Cass County contains commercial forests of oak-hickory, elm-ash-soft maple, and maple-birch. Beech, tulip, and aspen stands are interspersed throughout.

Areas of major forestation include two wide bands. One begins in the south-central region between Adamsville and Edwardsburg, proceeds northeasterly to Marcellus, and varies from two to eight miles wide. The second cuts east and west across the northern tier of townships—from Nicholsville past Cass County Memorial Airport. The rest of Cass County is heavily farmed for cash-crop small grains and livestock (primarily hogs) and dairy cattle. Many of these farmlands contain brush and wooded areas. A small fruit belt from Berrien and Van Buren counties extends into the northwestern portion.

State land totaling only 3,500 acres is in the form of several scattered parcels which make up the east-side Crane Pond State Game Area and a portion of the Three Rivers State Game Area (both of which see). Another 4,000 acres of Public Access Stamp program land is leased from a dozen cooperating farmers, mostly in the north-central and northeastern regions. Descriptions are available from DNR district headquarters in Plainwell or the field office at Crane Pond. Access to additional private land can result from a courteous request by considerate hunters.

Deer hunting success varies throughout the county with best reports coming from wooded townships in the northern region. Overall pressure runs about 10 hunters per square mile who kill one to two deer per square mile for a moderately low success rate of 10 percent (statewide average is about 17 percent). Deer numbers are presently not high as is also evidenced by the relatively low car-deer kill figure of about 200 animals annually. The region does produce big-racked bucks, however. Commemorative Bucks of Michigan currently shows 10 Cass County whitetails on its all-time records list of big deer. Three of those bucks were shot during the 1981 season alone.

Squirrel populations are excellent throughout the county with much untapped potential for fox squirrels and some blacks and grays. There is a fair amount of raccoon hunting pressure from both Michigan and nonresident dog men. Cass County is well traversed with streams—southeastern waterways flow into the St. Joseph; the Dowagiac River and its tributaries wander southwesterly toward Niles. Best bets for raccoon are stream bottomlands adjacent to cropped fields. Rabbit hunting is good throughout the county in lowland areas featuring brush and wooded openings. The Marcellus area is the best cottontail producer year after year. There is a good population of red fox (some grays too), with hunters bagging an occasional coyote.

Bird hunting is only fair, with best opportunities coming in the orchard belt and surrounding fields of crops and brush covers. Grouse are widely scattered in farm woodlots with aspen and along lowland areas containing brush. Hunters pocket the occasional woodcock, but there seem to be no concentrations of the long-billed birds. There are presently no turkeys in Cass County although the DNR has a long-range plan to stock them in the Crane Pond State Game Area.

Magician and Diamond lakes offer public access and good diving-duck hunting. Another good bet is to key along potholes and small streams for jump shooting mallards, teal, and wood ducks. Crane Pond State Game Area lakes and impoundments are worth checking, especially on weekdays. Float hunting on the St. Joseph River is popular, and the Dowagiac River offers drift-hunt possibilities too. Hunters get occasional geese when they set up in farm fields toward St. Joseph County.

OTHER SHOOTING OPPORTUNITIES

Rolling Hills Bird Farm, a 275-acre shooting preserve is open to the public who wish to hunt pheasants, quail, and chukars. Contact Curt C. Johnson, 17025 McKenzie St., Marcellus, Mich. 49067 (616/646-9164) for information.

The Edwardsburg Conservation Club, 26524 Pine Lake St., Edwardsburg, Mich. 49112, is open to the public every day on a fee basis. The club has outdoor stations for pistol, rimfire rifle and centerfire rifle, and two shotgun trap fields. Shooting instruction and state hunter education programs are offered too. For more information, call 616/663-2776.

FURTHER SOURCES OF HUNTING INFORMATION

1. DNR District Office, 621 North 10th St. (Box 355), Plainwell, Mich. 49080 (616/685-6851).
2. Crane Pond State Game Area Field Office, 60887 M-40, Jones, Mich. 49061 (616/244-5928).
3. Dowagiac Area Chamber of Commerce, 205 South Front St., Dowagiac, Mich. 49047 (616/782-8212).
4. Four Flags Area Chamber of Commerce, 321 East Main St., Niles, Mich. 49120 (616/683-3270).
5. Cassopolis Area Chamber of Commerce, Box 343, 139 North Broadway, Cassopolis, Mich. 49031 (616/445-2445).
6. Edwardsburg Chamber of Commerce, Box 109, Edwardsburg, Mich. 49112 (616/663-8502 or 616/663-8840).
7. Topographic, county, and lake maps may be ordered from the Michigan United Conservation Clubs. For information, refer to the beginning of this book.
8. County plat books are available from the Abstract and Title Co. of Cass County, 103 North Broadway, Cassopolis, Mich. 49031, for $5 each (add $1.50 if mail ordering).
9. Cass County ASCS Office, USDA, 110 Spencer Road, Cassopolis, Mich. 49031 (616/445-8641).

Also, refer to the following elsewhere in this book:
1. Crane Pond State Game Area
2. Three Rivers State Game Area

Charlevoix County

LOCATED in northwestern Lower Michigan, Charlevoix County is an interesting mix of privately-owned resorts and vacationland and mixed farming enterprises for fruit and livestock. Included are fair to good hunting opportunities for deer, bear, raccoon, waterfowl, turkeys, snowshoe hares, grouse, and woodcock.

About 21 percent, or 57,000 acres, of 414-square-mile Charlevoix County is state-owned. The public lands are found mostly in eastern-county holdings of the Mackinac State Forest (which see) and large portions of four Lake Michigan islands that make up the Beaver Islands Wildlife Research Area (which also see). Public land includes the 2,762-acre Fisherman's Island State Park (which also see) along Lake Michigan. All these lands are open to hunting. Further, over 5,400 acres of company-owned timberlands are enrolled in the Commercial Forest Act program and are therefore open to hunting. For legal descriptions and locations, stop in at DNR district headquarters in Gaylord or contact the DNR Forest Management Division in Lansing (Box 30028 or call 517/373-1275) and make a request for a specific portion of the county you wish to hunt. An updated county plat book will also help.

About half the land area in the county is wooded, three-fourths of which is owned by companies and individuals. The forest-cover mix is dominated by maple-birch (86,200 acres) but includes smaller amounts of aspen (13,700 acres), northern white cedar (9,000 acres), paper birch (9,000 acres), white pine (4,700 acres), and elm-ash-soft maple (4,200 acres). Missing is any appreciable quantity of oak-hickory.

Originally, northern hardwoods and pines grew on Charlevoix County uplands and swamp hardwoods and conifers grew on lowlands and bottomlands. Cutting of pines began in 1860 and ended in 1900 when the lumberman's attention shifted to hardwoods. Today sugar maples—along with smaller amounts of beech, elm, and basswood— cover large portions of the county. They grow on well-drained soils. Both quaking and largetooth aspen occur naturally in pure stands or in mixtures with pines and hardwoods. They tolerate a wide range of soil conditions and are scattered throughout. However, a big problem is that they are mostly even-aged. Selected cuttings to produce varying stages of growth would help wildlife. Without cutting, they will eventually convert to pine or a mixture of pine and hardwoods. Aspen is the key to improved numbers of grouse, woodcock, deer, and hares.

Most of Charlevoix County's jack pine, red pine, and white pine are in plantations although some exist in mixed stands. They offer habitat for wild turkeys, coyotes, snowshoe hares, and some deer.

Conifer swamps containing tamarack, black spruce, white cedar, balsam fir, hemlock, and white pine occur largely on state land. They provide habitat for bear, deer, and snowshoe hares.

Topographically, Charlevoix County is largely a series of drumlins. Drumlins are streamlined hills of glacial till one to two miles long with local inclusions of outwash deposited and shaped by moving ice during the last period of glaciation 8,000 to 12,000 years ago. These drumlins lie in a northwestern-to-southwestern orientation, and lakes and streams in the eastern two-thirds of the county are shaped along a similar axis. Frequently small creeks, potholes, and swamps lie at the base of drumlins, which in themselves offer some diversity to the landscape.

The area to the east of Lake Charlevoix and its South Arm is marginal farmland, with some of the county's best hunting opportunities occurring on private land that has been abandoned and that is now growing back to brush and trees. Hunters must first get permission, of course; once again, a county plat book is helpful to locate landowners.

Charlevoix County deer don't receive as much pressure as most other areas in the state. About 13 to 15 hunters per square mile is the norm. Buck-hunting success approximates the state average of 15 to 18 percent, and the county does produce an occasional trophy buck. One good deer hunting area is on state land in the Chandler Hills region in Chandler Township. Sand dunes fronting Lake Michigan are another good bet as are orchards where farmers might be experiencing deer-damage problems.

Bear hunting is poor to fair with best opportunities occurring in hardwood swamps in the northeastern corner and south of Boyne Falls. Bobcat hunting is currently not allowed although the animals frequent Charlevoix County conifer tracts. Fairly good numbers of snowshoe hares occur in pine plantations and in cutover stands of hardwoods and aspen near conifer lowlands. The same two areas mentioned for bear produce the county's best snowshoe-hare hunting.

Raccoon are found throughout Charlevoix County with pressure only moderate. The wild-turkey range appears to be expanding north to Charlevoix and south to Kalkaska County with some movement to the east as well.

Although Charlevoix County is not noted as a high producer of squirrels, hunters who work mature hardwoods containing beech and oak or woodlots near corn fields in the western portion of the county will score on both grays/blacks and fox species. Oak stands in the northeastern region also yield bushytails.

Fox and coyotes occur throughout the county. Potholes and stream bottoms produce a few wood

ducks and mallards for jump hunters. Lake Charlevoix—especially South Arm—affords fair to good diver hunting in late season. Lake Michigan shoreline hunters (at Fisherman's Island State Park) also shoot a few ducks, but for the most part this resource goes unused.

As mentioned, a lack of aspen cutting hampers a big increase in numbers of grouse and woodcock. Still there are some fairly good opportunities for woodcock in tag alder thickets near streams and for both grouse and woodcock in farmlands reverting to natural succession. Three years of hunter-cooperator hourly flush rate records checked show that grouse numbers varied from 1.28 to 2.31. Woodcock flush rates ranged from a low of .53 to 1.46 per hour.

OTHER SHOOTING OPPORTUNITIES

The Charlevoix Rod and Gun Club in Charlevoix has a shooting range open to the public on a limited basis without fees. Facilities include two indoor/outdoor pistol stations, four outdoor centerfire rifle stations, two outdoor rimfire rifle stations, a trap field, and outdoor archery target. Competitive shooting is featured. For details, call 616/547-2785.

The Jordan River Sportsmen Club on East Jordan Advance Road in East Jordan operates outdoor shooting ranges also open without fees to the public on a limited arrangement. Facilities include 10 stations each for pistol, centerfire and rimfire rifle, and an archery target. The club offers shooting instruction. Call 616/536-7714 for information.

FURTHER SOURCES OF HUNTING INFORMATION

1. DNR District Office, 1732 West M-32 (Box 667), Gaylord, Mich. 49735 (517/732-3541).

2. DNR Boyne City Field Office, 303 North Street, Boyne City, Mich. 49713 (616/582-6681).

3. Charlevoix Chamber of Commerce, 408 Bridge St., Charlevoix, Mich. 49720 (616/547-2101).

4. Boyne City Chamber of Commerce, 28 South Lake St., Boyne City, Mich. 49712 (616/582-6222).

5. East Jordan Area Chamber of Commerce, Box 137, East Jordan, Mich. 49747 (616/536-7351).

6. Topographic, county, and lake maps may be ordered from the Michigan United Conservation Clubs. For information, refer to the beginning of this book.

7. County plat books are available from the Charlevoix County Cooperative Extension Services, 319 North Lake St., (Box 119), Boyne City, Mich. 49712. The cost is $7 each (add 75 cents if mail ordering).

8. Emmet/Charlevoix County ASCS Office, 441 Bay St., Petosky, Mich. 49770.

Also, refer to the following elsewhere in this book:

1. Beaver Islands Wildlife Research Area
2. Fisherman's Island State Park
3. Mackinac State Forest

Cheboygan County

NEARLY 40 percent, or over 180,000 acres, of 803-square-mile Cheboygan County is state-owned. That's one plus that hunters visiting this county, at the top of the northern Lower Peninsula, can expect.

Another is fair to good hunting opportunities for deer, bear, bobcats, coyotes, grouse, woodcock, snowshoe hares, squirrels, and ducks. A lot of sportsmen go right on past Cheboygan County en route to the Upper Peninsula.

They might want to take a second look.

In addition to scattered holdings in the Mackinac State Forest (*which see*), there are a total of 1,644 acres of Commercial Forest Act (CFA) land in Cheboygan County. These are company-owned lands (mostly by the Abitibi Corporation) which are open to hunting in exchange for reduced property taxes. The DNR Forest Management Division in Lansing or the district office headquarters in Gaylord has legal descriptions of CFA lands enrolled. Other property open to hunting includes portions of Cheboygan and Burt Lake state parks and Bois Blanc Island (*all of which see*).

Topographically, two large natural divisions occur within Cheboygan County. The northern region is a broad, lowland plain which extends back from Lake Huron in a series of undulating old lake plains. Broad, flat areas, both wet and dry, characterize these plains, along with some large lakes (Black, Burt, Mullett, and Douglas—total 78 square miles) and valley swamps. The Black, Pigeon, and Indian rivers and their tributaries, all of which eventually wend their way to the Cheboygan River, drain this northern area by way of narrow, trenchlike valleys.

The southern region, especially the bottom two tiers of townships, appears more hilly in spots (partly due to steep banks dropping to stream bottoms), yet is overall a high plateau region. Most of this region is well drained but contains a few swamps and wet glacial valleys.

Originally, dense forests of hardwoods, pine, and swamp conifers covered most of the county. Today second-growth aspen, white pine, and red pine grow on the better land while jack pine, scrubby aspen, and oak sprouts manage on the poorer sites. About 84 percent of the land area is now timbered with commercial-forest species. Led by maple-birch (112,000 acres) and aspen (109,900 acres), these include northern white cedar (45,100 acres), jack pine (20,800 acres), paper birch (16,800 acres), elm-ash-soft maple (15,800 acres), and red pine (13,100 acres). Also included are smaller amounts of white pine, balsam fir, white and black spruce, tamarack, and oak-hickory.

The southeastern and northwestern portions seem to produce big bucks with fairly consistent hunting opportunities throughout the county. Cheboygan County has thus far yielded nine all-time trophy deer for Commemorative Bucks of Michigan's record book.

Most farming occurs south and west of Cheboygan in Inverness and Mullett townships. This is another good deer area which contains scattered parcels of state ownership throughout. Buck hunting success at 13 percent runs under the state average; however, this is also a low-pressure county with only 10 to 15 hunters per square mile.

The two corners mentioned contain some remote areas for deer hunters wanting a quality experience or for bear and bobcat hunters who wish to improve their odds. A high percentage of black bear killed in the eight-county DNR district headquartered at Gaylord are Cheboygan County bruins. During a recent hunting season, one of those bear dressed at 440 pounds. Hunting pressure is moderate to heavy for both bear and bobcats.

The southeastern portion also contains elk. For coyotes, target farmland brushy areas or cutover jack-pine stands. Also look for coyotes in snowshoe-hare country, which is likely to be young pine plantations and poplar slashings just growing

back, near conifers. One major area of recent clear-cutting is just north of Stoney Creek Flooding, which is southwest of Black Lake.

The area between Black Lake and Stoney Creek Flooding contains plenty of oaks and is a good spot to try for deer and squirrels (both fox and gray/black species are found in Cheboygan County) during falls of heavy mast production. Squirrel hunters might also want to try oak stands along Goose Creek Road southeast of the DNR field office at Indian River.

A high amount of aspen in varying age classes helps many wildlife species to increase in numbers. Grouse in particular offer fairly good hunting opportunities in Cheboygan County. Hunter-cooperators averaged 1.62, 2.29, and 2.70 grouse flushes per hour, respectively, during three seasons of records checked. Those same cooperators reported 2.17, 1.75, and 2.11 woodcock flushes per hour. Hunting pressure, though, along the northern tier of Lower Peninsula counties (Emmet to the west and Presque Isle to the east) is quite high.

A few wild turkeys live in southern Cheboygan County, but the season is currently closed. The number of large lakes and intricate network of rivers and streams makes for excellent float-hunting opportunities. About 45 miles of the Black River may be run by experienced canoeists. Many put in at Clark's Bridge on the Upper Black River just north and west of the old Black River Ranch State Forest. Rocks and logjams, plus the swift stream itself, sometimes make for tough going, but the effort is worthwhile as much of the river runs through state land with good hunting prospects.

As hunters float north, they must portage at Tower and Kleber Pond dams and then, after paddling through Black Lake, will have to portage once again at Alverno Dam. A little beyond are backwaters of the dam at Cheboygan, itself a good duck-hunting area. En route, hunters are likely to see deer, squirrels, and ducks. Jump-shooters can score on mallards and wood ducks throughout the county by sneaking along streams, beaver dams, and potholes. Dog Lake, Stoney Creek, and Cornwall Creek floodings in the southeastern region need rehabilitation to once again produce good waterfowl hunting; however, they're still worth checking out on opening day.

The Indian River slough region between Burt and Mullet lakes affords some early-season puddle-duck and late-season diving-duck hunting. Layout hunters in Duncan Bay and along Lake Huron itself can get fairly good hunting at times. For geese, try the Dingman Marsh Flooding just south of the Straits of Mackinac.

Raccoon numbers are usually high in Cheboygan County, but there is considerable hunting pressure.

OTHER SHOOTING OPPORTUNITIES

The Circle M Shooting Preserve, 13957 South Straits Highway in Wolverine, is open to hunting for those willing to take memberships. The preserve is 313 acres in size and features hunting for pheasants, quail, and chukar partridge. For more information, contact Otto Milbrand at 616/525-8216.

Sportsmen have at least two ranges where they may sight-in weapons and practice shoot. The Indian River Sportsman Club in Indian River is open daily to the public without fee. Facilities include outdoor stations for pistol, centerfire and rimfire rifle, archery targets, a trap field, and a shotgun handtrap area. Call 616/238-8570 for details.

The Cheboygan Sportsman Club on Siffern Road in Cheboygan is open on a part-time basis to the public for fees. Facilities include five outdoor stations each for pistol, centerfire and rimfire rifle; a skeet field; a trap field; and 15 outdoor archery targets. Call 616/627-5704 for more information.

FURTHER SOURCES OF HUNTING INFORMATION

1. DNR District Office, 1732 West M-32 (Box 667), Gaylord, Mich. 49735 (517/732-3541).
2. DNR Indian River Field Office, 6984 M-68, Indian River, Mich. 49749 (616/238-9313).
3. Cheboygan Area Chamber of Commerce, Box 69, Cheboygan, Mich. 49721 (616/627-2770).
4. Indian River Resort Region Chamber of Commerce, 3435 South Straits Highway (Box 57), Indian River, Mich. 49749 (616/238-9325).
5. Topographic, county, and lake maps may be ordered from the Michigan United Conservation Clubs. For information, refer to the beginning of this book.
6. Plat books are available from the Cheboygan County Cooperative Extension Services, Box 70 (County Building), Cheboygan, Mich. 49721. The cost is $9.50 each (add $1 if mail ordering).
7. Cheboygan County ASCS Office, M-33 South, Onaway, Mich. 49765.

Also, refer to the following elsewhere in this book:
1. Bois Blanc Island
2. Burt Lake State Park
3. Cheboygan State Park
4. Mackinac State Forest

Chippewa County

LOCATED in the northeastern Upper Peninsula, sprawling Chippewa County contains over one million acres, or about 1,580 square miles. Only Marquette County to the west is bigger. A large portion of Chippewa County is open to hunting since 23 percent of the land base is in state ownership—mostly through huge, scattered holdings of the Lake Superior State Forest (which see)—and another 21 percent constitutes a large, western-county block of the Hiawatha National Forest (which also see). Thus, over 440,000 acres of public land are open to hunting.

When added to 54,000 acres of company-owned land that is enrolled in the Commercial Forest Act plan and therefore open to hunting, nearly a half-million acres are available to sportsmen in Chippewa County. To locate these company lands, contact DNR district headquarters in Newberry or write or call DNR Forest Management Division, Box 30028, Lansing, Mich. 48909 (517/373-1275). Be sure to limit requests to a specific area. Once you obtain legal descriptions, it is a simple matter to find the unposted lands with the help of a current county plat book and county map.

Chippewa County topography includes level, lake-bed plains; gently rolling plateaus intersected and pitted by broad, swampy valleys and lakes; isolated low, rounded ridges or hills that rise above adjacent plains; and lakeshore features consisting of beach ridges, low sand dunes, marshland, and bluffs. A large number of small, flat, stony islands that lie off the southeastern coast include Drummond Island (which see).

The northern lakeshore is bordered by a low plain, with alternating swamp areas and dry sandy and gravelly ridges, lying from 10 to 40 feet above the lake level. This plain varies from one to six miles wide and is marked by a sudden rise, ranging from 20 to 50 feet, to the higher land. Central and eastern portions of the county consist of a level plain, composed of glacial river clays, sands, and silts through which stony and sandy ridges and hills protrude.

Southeastern Chippewa County includes plains and plateaulike hills, strewn with boulders and limestone blocks and interspersed with swamps. The somewhat higher western region is a plateaulike plain cut by broad swamp valleys. Northwestern Chippewa County, north of the Tahquamenon River, is a low, level, sandy plain interspersed with swamp and low, sandy ridges. A body of higher hills lies right on the Luce County border and actually joins part of a morainic plateau there.

About 705,000 acres of Chippewa County are covered with commercial-forest species and, when coupled with noncommercial forests, total about 76 percent of the land base. Commercial-forest cover types are led by maple-birch at 163,500 acres, closely followed by aspen at 155,700 acres, then jack pine (87,900 acres), northern white cedar (76,700 acres), black spruce (69,900 acres), balsam fir (40,000 acres), elm-ash-soft maple (35,400 acres), red pine (132,400 acres), and paper birch (18,800 acres). Smaller amounts of white pine, white spruce, oak-hickory, and tamarack also appear.

What appears to be an excellent forest mix conducive to good game production, however, is not actually the case in Chippewa County. This is a depressed economic region with few markets for the abundance of mature timber that, instead of being cut on an aggressive culling schedule, has reverted to a climax forest more beneficial to species like long-eared owls, red squirrels, and porcupines.

That is not to say that Chippewa County does not contain hunting opportunities. In fact, some excellent potential for several game species lies throughout. But if cutting quotas could be met at 100 percent instead of 20 to 30 percent as they currently are, then game species and hunters alike would greatly benefit.

The DNR District 4 area headquartered at Newberry, which, along with Chippewa, includes three other counties and a portion of a fourth, yields an annual harvest of some 3,000 bucks (antlerless hunting has not been allowed since 1972). These are usually big, healthy Upper Peninsula deer, as evidenced by the fact that 22 have thus far made it into the Commemorative Bucks of Michigan all-time record book.

Entering the hunting season each fall are some 55,000 to 60,000 deer in District 4—no great number considering that this administrative unit is the largest in the state. In fact, deer are widely scattered throughout the district and in Chippewa County contribute to less than 100 car-deer accidents each year. Hunting pressure is very light at an average of six sportsmen per square mile. They average one-of-six success on bucks, however, or about 13 to 18 percent.

During the most recent firearm season, Michigan's third-best nontypical buck was a Chippewa County deer. The 17-point buck, shot by a Paradise hunter, scored 192 2/8 Boone & Crockett points. During a typical season 35 to 50 percent of the District 4 bucks checked by DNR biologists carry eight points or more. However, severe winters can deplete the deer herd by 60 percent of its fawns and 20 percent of the adults. A continuing problem in the eastern U.P. is the spruce budworm, which destroys spruce and balsam trees, thus reducing the quality of thermal protection for yarding deer.

As mentioned, deer hunting is fairly uniform throughout the county. An exceptional area is in the Cedarville region on mostly private land. Yarding areas also produce late in the firearm season and during December when heavy snow forces deer to migrate. Areas of concentration include north of M-134 in the Prentiss Bay region, along the Munuscong River and small streams northwest of Kelden, on federal lands in the vicinity of the U.S. Fish and Wildlife Service Trout Rearing Station south of Rexford, the Hulbert Swamp region east of Hulbert along the East Branch Tahquamenon River, and along both sides of M-28 west of Hulbert near the Luce County border. Deer on the migratory move often use river valleys en route to these southern yarding areas.

The district produces from 125 to 150 black bear each fall. Bear are found throughout Chippewa County except in eastern farmlands (the season is currently closed on Drummond Island). Best bets are hardwoods along swamps since these areas produce food in the form of berries, apples, grubs, and wild cherries.

Coyote populations are high and growing throughout the county, with few sportsmen other than deer hunters taking advantage. Seek out jack-pine areas and swamp edges containing snowshoe hares. Bobcats are another predator frequently found in lowland coniferous cover. There are some fox in Chippewa County, but for the most part they are limited to farmlands in the eastern region. There are also a few raccoon along rivers and feeder streams, but not many hunters pursue them.

Snowshoe hares offer reasonably good hunting even during their current "down" cycle. Try cutover areas next to conifer swamps throughout the county. Good hunting occurs on the edge of such "green" cover along the Lake Michigan shoreline. What few cottontails are shot come from farmlands. A very light population of gray squirrels with a few black squirrels occurs in Chippewa County. Several released on Drummond Island (currently closed to squirrel hunting) appear to be increasing and may provide future hunting potential.

Open, grassy areas throughout the district constitute the last remaining stronghold for sharp-tailed grouse, now thought to number some 10,000 birds in the eastern Upper Peninsula. The continuing reversion to a climax forest threatens their fragile habitat. In Chippewa County largest numbers are found in the eastern farming belt, mostly on abandoned farmlands, although the state manages two large, open areas called the Maxton Plains and the Big Burn on Drummond Island where sharpies are currently protected. In central Chippewa County try south of Sault Ste. Marie on both sides of I-75 and in the Pickford and Rudyard regions (again, this is private land). In the western region try the national forest land around Rexford.

Ruffed grouse and and woodcock are fairly abundant throughout Chippewa County and receive moderate to high hunting pressure. We checked three years of hourly flush-rate records of hunter-cooperators and learned that they moved an average of 1.43, 1.36, and 1.14 grouse. The same sportsmen reported corresponding flush rate averages of 1.64, 2.06, and 2.84 for woodcock. The region gets some flight woodcock from Canada, but most of the birds are locally reared or drift in from the western U.P. as food supplies there give out due to freezing weather.

Waterfowl hunting in Chippewa County is as good as, or better than, elsewhere in the U.P. Hunters will find dabblers and divers off Brimley State Park (which see) in Waiska, the Shelldrake Flowage, and Isaac Walton bays, along Lake Nicolet between Sugar Island and the mainland, in Munuscong Lake, and in Lake George. Canada geese often feed in the same fields with sharptails. Goose hunting, however, is currently closed in the Munuscong Waterfowl Management Project (which see).

The eastern Upper Peninsula is an important stopping area for migrating divers with spectacular concentrations often occurring in fall. On an aircraft flight check late in November during the most recent fall, DNR officials estimated 2,000 scaup using the Lake George area. Munuscong Lake held 1,000 ring-necked ducks, 500 redheads, 200 scaup, and 50 goldeneyes; a raft of 150 old-squaws was in the Raber Bay area; and St. Martins Bay held 10,000 redheads in addition to large groups of scaup, goldeneyes, and buffleheads. It is not uncommon to see huge rafts of divers in the Straits area as one crosses the Mackinac Bridge in October and November. Here is tremendous hunting opportunity going unused by many waterfowlers.

Crows and woodchucks are Chippewa County species that may be hunted year-around. Both are in good supply (the larger ravens, however, are protected), and yet few hunters take advantage.

OTHER SHOOTING OPPORTUNITIES

The Chippewa County Shooting Association in Sault Ste. Marie has a firearms range open to the public at certain times on a sometime-fee basis. Facilities include 12 outdoor stations each for pistol, centerfire and rimfire rifle, and two each skeet and trap fields. Shooting instruction and shooting competition are offered. For details, call 906/632-3122.

FURTHER SOURCES OF HUNTING INFORMATION

1. DNR District Office, 309 West McMillan Ave. (Box 445), Newberry, Mich. 49868 (906/293-5131).
2. DNR Sault Ste. Marie Field Office, Box 798, Sault Ste. Marie, Mich. 49783 (906/635-5281).
3. DNR De Tour Field Office, M-134 (Box 92), De Tour Village, Mich. 49725 (906/297-2581).
4. Hiawatha National Forest Headquarters, 2727 North Lincoln Road (Box 316), Escanaba, Mich.

5. Hiawatha National Forest, Sault Ste. Marie Ranger District, 2901 I-75 Business Spur, Sault Ste. Marie, Mich. 49783 (906/635-5311).

6. Sault Ste. Marie Chamber of Commerce, 2581 I-75 Business Spur, Sault Ste. Marie, Mich. 49783 (906/632-3301).

7. Topographic, county, and lake maps may be ordered from the Michigan United Conservation Clubs. For information, refer to the beginning of this book.

8. Plat books are available from the Chippewa County Clerk's Office, Court St., Sault Ste. Marie, Mich. 49783. The cost for the 1981 edition is $5 (add $1.73 if ordering by mail). A new edition due to the published soon will likely sell for $10 to $12. Call 906/635-6300 for the actual cost.

9. Chippewa County ASCS Office, 2901 I-75 Business Spur, Sault Ste. Marie, Mich. 49783.

Also, refer to the following elsewhere in this book:
1. Lake Superior State Forest
2. Hiawatha National Forest
3. Drummond Island
4. Munuscong Waterfowl Management Project
5. Brimley State Park

Clare County

CLARE County, in the central portion of the Lower Peninsula, has a land area of 576 square miles. Located midway between southern agricultural lands and northern hardwoods forestlands, Clare County is often called the "Gateway to the North." At one time the county was covered with virgin white pine; now it features mixed stands of conifers and hardwoods interspersed with farmlands.

A hilly moraine that runs diagonally from southwest to northeast divides the county into natural watersheds. The Muskegon River and its tributaries drain the sandy jack-pine plains of the northeastern portion and ultimately empty into Lake Michigan. The southern and eastern parts of the county are drained by a network of small streams, two branches of the Cedar River, and three tributaries of the Tobacco River. These waters flow easterly into Lake Huron.

In addition, Clare County boasts 153 named lakes, 20 of which feature public access. Farming occurs on about one-third of the land base. Feed grains—oats, wheat, corn—and hay are the principal crops, grown mostly for dairy and beef cattle. Cash-crop farming is also practiced. The county contains about 24,000 people.

Hunting opportunities are very good although pressure, for the most part, is high. That is largely because Clare and its sister counties in DNR District 8 are the first stop north for downstate hunters. Also, habitats here produce an abundance and variety of game. Over 60 percent of the land base supports the growth of commercial-timber species. Aspen leads all types with 73,400 acres, followed by maple-birch (38,300 acres), oak-hickory (29,300 acres), jack pine (28,800 acres), elm-ash-soft maple (26,300 acres), red pine (11,400 acres), and smaller amounts of northern white cedar, tamarack, and paper birch.

A drawing card for hunters is that 48,000 acres, or more than 13 percent, of the county is state-owned and open to hunting. State land is in scattered parcels (mostly in the northern and western portions) of the Au Sable State Forest (which see). Further, another 719 acres of Commercial Forest Act land, owned by forest-industry companies but open to hunting by law, can be utilized. The DNR Forestry Division in Lansing will provide legal descriptions upon request. Hunters can also get this information from district headquarters in Clare.

Northern portions of the county run heavily to jack pine and are not solid producers of game. Private deer-hunting clubs claim some ownership in the northeastern corner and again in an area between M-115 and Lake George. A major farming belt lies in the southeastern quarter, with other scattered farming practiced elsewhere throughout the county.

Heavy deer-hunting pressure occurs on public land; not surprisingly, the best hunting comes on private lands. Overall pressure exceeds 30 hunters per square mile. The deer herd is quite large, however (over 300 annual car-deer accidents reported to the State Police), and winter losses are usually slight. This is because snow depths and winters are normally not severe and because deer find farmland crops to eat instead of having to depend upon poor-fare yarding browse. Buck hunter success runs 15 to 20 percent, a little above state average.

Although not noted as a big-rack area, Clare County does produce occasional trophy deer. Commemorative Bucks of Michigan currently has 15 Clare County bucks on its all-time record list. According to a five-year survey by the DNR, northeastern Hamilton, southern Arthur, southern Surrey, and most of Greenwood townships are the best deer-producing areas.

Some black bear are reported in heavily-wooded regions of the northern-tier townships, but the animals may not be hunted presently in Clare County. Hunting is permitted, however, in the next northern counties (Roscommon and Missaukee). Three-dozen wild turkeys released in central Clare County around 1979 have expanded to a flock of 400 to 500. A portion of the county is now open to hunting (check the current "Wild Turkey Gobbler Season" brochure for details). Further, the DNR has recently continued to translocate turkeys in southern Clare County from other regions of northern Michigan where they are well established.

The Muskegon River affords excellent float-hunting possibilities for deer, squirrels, and waterfowl. Heavy stands of maple, oak, ash, and mature lowland hardwoods line streams throughout the county, making for tough access but also quality hunting. Many of the flows also provide good to

250

excellent jump-shooting for wood ducks and mallards early in the season. On the negative side, several of the lakes with public access are too developed to support good duck or goose hunting. Waterfowlers might do better to check out some of the impoundment areas (Town Line Flooding, Old Fur Farm Flooding) as well as beaver ponds sprinkled throughout the county.

Cottontails are plentiful in Clare County, and there are some surprisingly good numbers of snowshoe hares during high-cycle years. An excellent swamp worth putting a hare hound into begins on the west side of the Farwell Mill Pond and runs for six miles into Isabella County near Rosebush. The state owns about 1,700 acres of this swamp.

Squirrels are plentiful in oak-hickory groves scattered throughout the county. Seek out mature oaks along cropped fields of corn. Hunters will mostly find fox squirrels with a mixture of grays/blacks in denser woods containing conifers. Dog hunters at night will also jump raccoon in corn fields bordering lowlands and along timbered stream bottoms. Pressure is moderate to high for ringtails.

Clare County rates high as a producer of ruffed grouse and woodcock too. Cooperators reported 1.6 to 2.6 grouse moved hourly during two random seasons checked. Hourly woodcock flushes for the same years were 1.23 and 1.95. Try stands of wrist-sized aspen with an understory of wild raisin, witch hazel, and dogwood. Alder pockets also host Clare County woodcock. There are even a few pheasants, but ringneck hunters will have to do their homework to find huntable populations. The other problem is getting access on private land (mostly in the farm belt of the southeastern region) to hunt. Clare County farmers tend to be more protective of their pheasants than their deer.

OTHER SHOOTING OPPORTUNITIES

There are no known sportsmen's clubs or commercial businesses with shooting range facilities open to the public.

FURTHER SOURCES OF HUNTING INFORMATION

1. DNR District Headquarters, 501 Hemlock, Clare, Mich. 48617 (517/386-7991).

2. Greater Clare Area Chamber of Commerce, 114 West Fifth St., Clare, Mich. 48617 (517/386-2442).

3. Harrison Area Chamber of Commerce, Box 682, Harrison, Mich. 48625 (517/539-6011).

4. Lake George Chamber of Commerce, Box 117, Lake George, Mich. 48633 (517/588-9463).

5. Topographic, county, and lake maps may be ordered from the Michigan United Conservation Clubs. For information, refer to the beginning of this book.

6. Plat books are available from Clare City Hall, 202 West Fifth St., Clare, Mich. 48617. The cost is $9 each (add $1.50 if mail ordering).

7. Clare County ASCS Office, 225 Main St., Room 140 (County Building), Harrison, Mich. 48625 (517/539-7892).

Also refer to the Au Sable State Forest elsewhere in this book.

Clinton County

NEARLY 80 percent, an unusually high amount for even southern Michigan, of 571-square-mile Clinton County is in active farms. Operations are split about evenly between small grain/cash crop and dairy/livestock practices. Although some of these farms contain woodlots, less than 10 percent of the overall county is commercial-timber forested, and wildlife cover is at a premium. This is especially so in the southern portion where streams are likely to be field drainage ditches devoid of cover.

But that is not to say that this south-central Lower Michigan county is poor for hunting. River bottomlands of the Grand (southwest corner), the east-west running Looking Glass (southern region), the Maple (northeastern and northwestern corners), and central-county Stony Creek concentrate wildlife. So do the Maple River State Game Area (which see) in the county's northwestern corner, the 2,680-acre Sleepy Hollow State Park (nearly all of which is open to hunting), and Rose Lake Wildlife Research Area (which see) in the southeastern corner. Cover types in these forested areas are mostly oak-hickory, ash-elm-soft maple, and maple-birch interspersed with brushlands and aspen. State land totals about 8,800 acres.

Clinton County is a series of glacial plains and moraines that are nearly level to rolling. Old lakebed plains extending westward from Saginaw Bay make up a small region in the northeastern part. Areas of nearly level soils occur on these old lake plains, till plains, and outwash plains, but the greater part of the county is characterized by slightly rolling land. Numerous swampy depressions and small lakes occur in the more rolling country, especially in the southeastern region. Some of these wet areas feature organic soils where mint, vegetables, and lawn sod are important crops.

Farmers in this county are often amenable to a courteous request to hunt. Also, 15 landowners have currently enrolled 2,800 acres of farmland in the Public Access Stamp Program. These farms are clustered in three areas: (1) between St. Johns and Maple Rapids, (2) near Wacousta, and (3) in the Rose Lake area. DNR personnel at district headquarters in Grand Rapids and at Rose Lake have free maps showing exact locations.

Clinton is not a high-kill deer county although it produces some big bucks on occasion. Commemorative Bucks of Michigan currently lists 10 Clinton County rack whitetails on its all-time list of big Michigan bucks. Pressure is low to moderate with about 16 hunters per square mile whose success rate averages six percent (far below the state average of 17 percent). Hunter's-choice permit holders average 20 to 25 percent success on bucks/does combined. Deer numbers appear to have peaked in this county and have actually been falling off in recent years.

Car-deer accidents account for 200 to 300 animals each year. Best hunting opportunities (shotguns only during firearm season) come in the game areas (where pressure is highest too) and along river bottomlands.

Fox hunting is an underutilized activity in Clinton County. Populations of fox as well as raccoon are at medium to high levels. Fox and some gray squirrels are scattered throughout farm woodlots and bottomlands. Seek rabbits here too and in brushy areas of good cover near farmland. Abandoned farms gone to seed are especially productive when they and their owners (to secure hunting permission) can be found.

Pheasant hunting is spotty although isolated populations of wild birds still exist. For best results, try farmland covers within the triangle formed by connecting DeWitt, St. Johns, and Westphalia. Grouse and woodcock numbers are low with best hunting coming in the northwestern portion of the county in brush, thick woodlots, and wet soils.

Float trippers concentrate on ducks (deer and squirrels too) on the Looking Glass, Grand, and Maple rivers where road access is available. Rose Lake offers some goose and duck hunting, and Ovid Lake—within Sleepy Hollow State Park—serves up good to excellent hunting for puddlers and late-season divers. The Maple River State Game Area is also popular with waterfowlers. Two-hundred-acre Muskrat Lake Mini-Game Area in the county center is sharecrop-managed for waterfowl. The DNR is currently trying to acquire more land along the west shoreline so it can build a lowhead dam, flood the area, and turn it into a cattail marsh. Hunting could only improve from such efforts.

Iowa and Pennsylvania wild turkeys released on the Rose Lake Wildlife Research Area are doing well and could provide future hunting opportunity. Maple River State Game Area is another likely site for future turkey releases.

OTHER SHOOTING OPPORTUNITIES

Rose Lake Wildlife Research Center, 8562 East Stoll Road, East Lansing, Mich. 48823, has a shooting range open to the public without fees. Outdoor stations for pistol (10), rimfire rifle (18), and centerfire rifle (18) are provided along with an outdoor archery target. The DNR, which supervises the range from a field office here, also offers state hunter education programs. For more information on this and range-use hours, call 517/373-9358.

Thorny Acres Sportsman Club is open to the public on a fee basis for archery enthusiasts wishing to practice or shoot competitively on 28 indoor/outdoor targets. Club address is 219 East Pine, Elsie, Mich. 48831. Call 517/862-9612 for details.

FURTHER SOURCES OF HUNTING INFORMATION

1. DNR District Office, State Office Bldg. (350 Ottawa NW), Grand Rapids, Mich. 49503 (616/456-5071).

2. Rose Lake Field Office, 8562 East Stoll Road, East Lansing, Mich. 48823 (517/373-9358).

3. DNR officials at Sleepy Hollow State Park, 7835 Price Road, Laingsburg, Mich. 48848 (517/651-6217), may be helpful.

4. St. Johns Area Chamber of Commerce, Box 61, St. Johns, Mich. 48879 (517/224-7248).

5. Topographic, county, and lake maps may be ordered from the Michigan United Conservation Clubs. For information, refer to the beginning of this book.

6. County plat books are availble for $12 each (add $1.50 if mail ordering) from Clinton County Extension Office, 306 Elm St., St. Johns, Mich. 48879.

7. Clinton County ASCS Office, USDA, 306 Elm St., St. Johns, Mich. 48879 (517/224-3720).

Also, refer to the following elsewhere in this book:
1. Maple River State Game Area
2. Rose Lake Wildlife Research Area
3. Sleepy Hollow State Park

Crawford County

CRAWFORD County is located in the north-central part of the Lower Peninsula. On the county's western edge flows the Manistee River, which eventually runs 65 miles to Lake Michigan. Through sand plains of the county center pass the Au Sable River and its tributaries. Forty-five miles later, as the crow flies, it empties into Lake Huron. It is perhaps ironic that 561-square-mile Crawford County is drained by two of the nation's finest trout streams.

Much of the terrain is nearly level or gently rolling, and most changes in elevation vary by 100 feet or less. Three broad plateaus with a north-south orientation and three corresponding sandy valleys characterize the northern portion. The southern region features several ridges that are irregular in outline but have a general east-west bent. The more level areas throughout the county are glacial outwash plains, and what hills are found are moraines. Swamps occur along both glacial features,

and lakes are very few. Lake Margrethe near Grayling is the only one of significant size.

A soil survey performed years ago estimated that dry sand plains comprised about half the total county area, hilly or rolling lands made up about 40 percent, nine percent was swamp, and only one percent consisted of surface water. Crawford is a very dry county.

Vast stretches of white pine brought lumbermen to the area by 1875 and with the pine depleted by the end of the century, active lumbering of hardwoods began. Forest fires then ravaged much of the county. Today about 84 percent is covered by commercial-forest species led by jack pine with 85,200 estimated acres, closely followed by some 76,500 acres of oak-hickory. Other forest types of importance to hunters include 36,400 acres of aspen, 35,600 acres of elm-ash-soft maple, and 19,100 acres of red pine. There are also scattered mixtures of white pine, balsam fir, black spruce, and northern white cedar.

The county currently offers fair to good hunting for deer, limited bear and turkey hunting opportunities, some excellent squirrel and woodcock hunting along with late-season waterfowling, and poor to fair grouse and snowshoe-hare hunting.

A big plus for hunters is that about 70 percent of Crawford County is publicly owned and open to hunting. This includes a large portion of the Huron-Manistee National Forest in the southeastern quarter and vast expanses of the Au Sable State Forest (*both of which see*) scattered elsewhere throughout the county. About 29,000 acres of public land is called the Hanson Military Reserve where the National Guard holds maneuvers. Off-limits areas (about 5,000 acres) for recreationists, including hunters, are posted. In addition, over 8,400 acres of Hartwick Pines State Park (*which also see*) is open to hunting.

Deer hunting prospects are fairly uniform throughout Crawford County although the northeastern corner of mixed pine and aspen probably rates best and, generally speaking, the western portion falls a little under the average. Except for winter yarding along river bottoms, the whitetail herd appears to be well scattered. High hunting pressure—40 hunters per square mile—results in a high buck kill (five bucks or more per square mile) but only 10 to 15 percent success. Most are yearling animals and few bucks get the chance to grow trophy headgear. Fewer yet will sport gray muzzles.

Even so, Commemorative Bucks of Michigan has thus far identified three Crawford County bucks as record-book deer. Best bet for a racked animal is in the Lovells area.

The county is open to bear hunting, but numbers appear to be rather low. Best places include swamp conifers around the northern two-thirds of Lake Margrethe, for several miles northeast of Grayling along the East Branch of the Au Sable, and between I-75 and the railway in Beaver Creek Township. Also, try the oil fields in the southwestern portion of the county.

One underutilized hunting resource is coyotes, increasing faster in Crawford County than anywhere else in the eight-county DNR district headquartered at Mio. Deer hunters shoot a few coyotes; predator callers and dog hunters could take more animals. For red fox, try abandoned farmlands north of the state park. Raccoon are abundant along the two rivers and their tributaries.

The county also supports excellent populations of squirrels—fox species in oak stands (especially in the southern region) and grays/blacks in mixed growths of oak and pine. Pin, black, red, and scrub oaks are the dominant species.

For best turkey-hunting results, look for aspen/alder pockets along drainages within jack-pine forests. But Crawford County turkey hunters tend to work for their birds.

Best grouse-hunting spots include (1) the South Branch Au Sable River area from Chase Bridge to Smith's Bridge, (2) in Sections 26 and 27 of Beaver Creek Township, (3) between Seven- and Five-Mile roads west of US-27, (4) southeast of the old Conservation Corrections Camp within Hartwick Pines State Park, (5) Sections 7 and 18 of Frederic Township along the Manistee River, (6) east of Bluegill and Horseshoe lakes in Maple Forest Township, and (7) east of K.P. Lake along Wakely Bridge Road.

Overall, hunter-cooperators report an average of 1.0 to 2.0 grouse flushed per hour in Crawford County. However, hunters in prime habitats such as 10- to 15-year-old aspen with an understory of wild raisin, dogwoods, thornapples, or blackberries can do better. Woodcock hunters, keeping in mind that Crawford County is very dry, will do at least as well in the areas mentioned and along drainageways. Some of northern Michigan's best woodcock hunting occurs from early to mid-October when passage birds concentrate in young aspen stands flanking the rivers.

Although snowshoe-hare numbers have slid in recent years, plenty of good habitat is available, and for the most part hares are underhunted, even during years of high populations. Try young pine stands, early-stage aspen, and pine plantations around swamp edges. Hunters might also want to check out the 8,000-acre Bald Hill area south of Lovells as jack-pine regrowth from a fire there in 1974 is just now providing good habitat.

Opening-day duck hunters might move a few birds off the old Conners Marsh Flooding northwest of McMasters Bridge. Best duck hunting, however, occurs during late season on the main branches of the Au Sable and Manistee. Floating by canoe (several liveries in Grayling have canoes for rent) can produce good hunting for mallards, blacks, goldeneyes, and Canada geese. Late-season waterfowlers might also want to try Lake Margrethe for diver hunting with layout boats.

OTHER SHOOTING OPPORTUNITIES

None known at this time.

FURTHER SOURCES OF HUNTING INFORMATION

1. DNR District Office, 191 South Mount Tom Road (M-33), Mio, Mich. 48647 (517/826-3211).

2. Grayling Field Office, 4895 West County Road, Grayling, Mich. 49738 (517/348-6371).

3. Grayling Regional Chamber of Commerce, 103 James St., Box 406, Grayling, Mich. 49738 (517/343-2921).

4. Topographic, county, and lake maps may be ordered from the Michigan United Conservation Clubs. For information, refer to the beginning of this book.

5. Plat books are available from the Crawford County Clerk, 200 West Michigan Ave., Grayling, Mich. 49738 for $10 each (add $1.05 if mail ordering).

6. Crawford/Roscommon/County ASCS Office, 2170 South Morey Road, Lake City, Mich. 49651.

Also, refer to the following elsewhere in this book:
1. Au Sable State Forest
2. Hartwick Pines State Park
3. Huron-Manistee National Forest

Delta County

DELTA County with 755,200 acres (1,180 square miles) is located in the central Upper Peninsula. Its blend of forests, farmlands, swampy regions, 514 miles of rivers and streams, 148 inland lakes, and 144 miles of Lake Michigan and Green Bay shoreline combine to provide a variety of hunting opportunities. This potential increases dramatically when one considers that over 236,000 acres of the Hiawatha National Forest, some 62,000 acres of the Escanaba River and Lake Superior state forests (all of which see), and over 72,000 acres of Commercial Forest Act (CFA) program land are open to hunting in Delta County.

Taken together, this means that hunters have over 372,000 acres, or nearly half of the total land base, in which to roam. To find public lands, refer to the Michigan United Conservation Clubs' publication, "Michigan County Maps and Outdoor Guide." To get legal descriptions of the unposted, company-owned CFA lands, contact the DNR Forest Management Division, Box 30028, Lansing, Mich. 48909 (517/373-1275), but be sure to request a specific part of the county by town and range numbers. A good plat book and your book of county maps will help you to pinpoint their locations.

About 77 percent of Delta County is forested with commercial-forest timber species. Looking at the breakdown quickly shows the high game-producing potential. Aspen leads with 129,600 acres but is closely followed by northern white cedar at 117,100 acres and by 104,000 acres of maple-birch. Other types include 55,600 acres of balsam fir, 46,100 acres of black spruce, 32,300 acres of elm-ash-soft maple, 27,300 acres of paper birch, 26,200 acres of red pine, 24,800 acres of jack pine, and smaller amounts of oak-hickory, white pine, white spruce, and tamarack.

Also improving wildlife living conditions is the fact that about 70 percent of the allowable forest harvest on state land in the four-county DNR forestry district is being met annually. As mature, climax forests are leveled, many types of game animals and birds multiply due to the increase in food and forest edge.

About nine percent of Delta County is actively farmed for hay, oats, and potatoes. Most of the farming activities occur in the southern and western regions on the Garden and Stonington peninsulas, in the Rock area, and north and west of a line from Gladstone to Escanaba to Bark River. Heavy forestation and a lack of great topographic relief throughout the county contribute to slowly meandering rivers that wind their southerly way to Lake Michigan and Green Bay. Moving from east to west, these rivers include the Fishdam, Sturgeon, Ogontz, Whitefish, Rapid, Tacoosh, Days, Escanaba, Ford, and Bark rivers. Many of the corresponding lowland areas through which they flow feature heavy swamps.

Headquarters for the three-county DNR wildlife district (Delta, Marquette, and western Alger counties) is at Escanaba. The average annual snowfall decreases as one goes south from Lake Superior, which gets about 130 inches each year. In northern Delta County the total usually runs about 100 inches and decreases to about 55 inches along Lake Michigan. This information is of value to hunters wanting to try for late-season deer.

The district deer herd, after falling to an all-time low of about 30,000 animals around 1974, has been coming back steadily, to the present figure of about 50,000 animals. In a good season, hunters will shoot about 5,000 bucks, some 40 percent of which are yearling (one-and-a-half-year-old) animals. Of 207 bucks shot during a recent hunting season, 80 touted racks of eight points or better.

In fact, Delta County with 73 trophy deer, now leads Commemorative Bucks of Michigan's all-time record list of 1,150 boss Michigan bucks, moving from its former status as No. 5. Not all these Delta County deer were shot years ago either, as evidenced by the fact that six trophies during the most recent season made it to the list, tying Delta with Lenawee County for third place that year. Deer occur throughout the county, but best hunting comes in the eastern portion on federal forest lands and in the western half as close to Menominee County as one can get. Bow hunters might want to scout southern Delta County too in the vicinity of farm fields and orchards.

As deer migrate to winter yards late in the season, they provide opportunities for hunters along river valleys. Eastern county yarding areas include Garden Peninsula's Portage Bay, Sucker Lake, and north and east of Fairport. Others are found in the southern Stonington Peninsula, from St. Vitals Point to the middle of Ogontz Bay, and river-bottom lands along the Whitefish River and its tributaries. In the western county look to swamplands in southern Ford River Township, along the Tacoosh River and Inman Creek east of Rock, and in the Hendricks area.

Supporting the contention that Delta County contains good numbers of deer is the annual grim statistic of car-deer accidents. Delta County usually follows adjacent Menominee in the 15-county Upper Peninsula for numbers killed. Other evidence of fairly high deer numbers is a continuing problem with crop damage and cedar depredation, the latter during the winter yarding period. Overall, hunters generally kill one to two bucks per square mile for a 22 percent average, above the state norm. Pressure at under 10 hunters per square mile is considered low.

Bear registration in the district has been inching close to 200 animals each fall. Bruins frequent both river bottom and orchard country, but the opportunistic animals can be found anywhere there is an abundance of food. A heavy beechnut or choke-cherry crop will attract them as do farming operations near cover. Swamp regions are good for baiting.

These same swampy areas, including the western county deer yards already mentioned, attract bobcats. Try along the Bark and Ford rivers and in the region around Hyde. The Stonington Peninsula is also worth checking out. During the past five seasons, hunters have presented from 38 to 63 Delta County cats at DNR offices for sealing.

A few red fox live near farms, and coyotes are on

the increase although a recent outbreak of mange has discouraged some hunters and trappers from seeking them out. Try the winter deer yards or jack-pine areas containing hares. One of these is in the Ensign region; another is located in the Gooseneck Lake area. Those places plus hardwoods and cutover aspen areas next to green cover (conifer swamps) also produce hares. Populations were excellent until recently when they appear to be down somewhat. Delta County also has cottontails around its communities and on its farmlands. In addition, the western half contains good populations of raccoon. The current state record, a 45-pounder, was shot in October of 1978 by Milo Peacock of Perkins in the Rock vicinity.

Delta County hunters are missing the boat by ignoring good gray and black-phase squirrel hunting. Vast stretches of northern hardwoods, sprinkled with oaks, produce mast and therefore house bushytails. Wooded regions around Escanaba, Gladstone, in the Stonington Peninsula, around Nahma, and along Forest Service Highway 13—paralleling the Sturgeon River—are best producers. Hunters will find little competition.

As for bird hunting, Delta County contains ruffed grouse, sharptails, and spruce grouse, but the latter—which, as the final species in the grouse family, likes jack pine growths and swampy, coniferous areas—is protected. A lack of large openings has sharptail numbers falling off—from 32 to merely three sightings over a recent four-year period.

On the other hand, ruffed grouse populations, although presently down, are certainly high enough to warrant hunting efforts. We randomly checked three years of hunter-cooperator hourly flush-rate records and learned that an average of 1.40, 2.74, and 1.87 grouse were moved. There is some fair to good woodcock hunting potential too on these same edge covers of brush swamp, and hardwoods, as well as swamp and old orchards and aspen slashings. Woodcock flushes over a three-year period were 1.50, .69, and 2.14.

Several hunter walking trails, from two to eight acres each, feature seeded openings to attract game. You can locate them on a county map or ask DNR wildlife or forestry personnel as to their locations.

Descriptions include:

T41N, R24W, Section 16, SW NE, one opening, two acres.

T42N, R21W, Section 4, SW ¼ W ½ SE ¼, three openings and walking trail, eight acres.

T42N, R21W, Section 7, SE SE, two openings, two acres.

T42N, R21W, Section 17, NW NW, one opening, one acre.

T43N, R22W, Section 20, N ½ NW ¼, two openings, eight acres.

Occasional reports of turkeys in the Rapid River area are probably from an illegal release. Turkeys noted in the Bark River vicinity are likely Menominee County birds dispersing to the east. Turkeys are currently protected in Delta County, and to get a cooperative winter feeding program to build the few birds here to huntable numbers would require the aid of farmers.

Interior lakes are not noted for high waterfowl production. Shallow Moss Lake with its mucky bottom is probably the best choice. The Garden Peninsula gets heavy migrant goose visitation, but finding a place to hunt in farm fields that attract them is very hard to do. Waterfowlers might better concentrate around Big Bay de Noc islands or in the Portage Marsh south of Escanaba. The open bay is good for migrant divers and geese while the marsh features fair to good hunting for mallards, teal, baldpates, gadwalls, and occasionally pintails and redheads. Pressure is high on opening day, however.

OTHER SHOOTING OPPORTUNITIES

The Civic Center, 225 North 21st St. in Escanaba, is a public shooting range open without fees. Facilities include seven indoor stations each for pistol and rimfire rifle plus seven indoor archery targets. For information, call 906/785-3551.

FURTHER SOURCES OF HUNTING INFORMATION

1. DNR District Office, 1126 North Lincoln Road (Box 495), Escanaba, Mich. 49829 (906/786-2351).

2. Forest Supervisor, Hiawatha National Forest, 2727 North Lincoln Road, Escanaba, Mich. 49829 (906/786-4062).

3. Hiawatha National Forest, Rapid River Ranger District, US-2, Rapid River, Mich. 49827 (906/474-6442).

4. Delta County Area Chamber of Commerce, 230 Ludington St., Escanaba, Mich. 49829 (906/786-2192).

5. Topographic, county, and lake maps may be ordered from the Michigan United Conservation Clubs. For information, refer to the beginning of this book.

6. Plat books are available from the Delta County Cooperative Extension Services, 118 North 22nd St., Escanaba, Mich. 49829. The cost is $12 each (add $1.50 if mail ordering).

7. Delta County ASCS Office, 2805 North Lincoln Road, Escanaba, Mich. 49829.

Also, refer to the following elsewhere in this book:

1. Escanaba River State Forest
2. Fayette State Park
3. Hiawatha National Forest
4. Lake Superior State Forest

Dickinson County

DICKINSON County in the west-central Upper Peninsula offers diversified terrain, large amounts of prime wildlife habitat, and fair to good hunting opportunities for deer, bear, bobcats, coyotes, hares, squirrels, grouse, woodcock, and waterfowl. Ridges of northern hardwoods are interspersed with swamps and plenty of aspen in varying age classes. Criss-crossed by a multitude of streams, including the broad Menominee River, which forms the

southern boundary with Wisconsin, Dickinson County offers relatively undeveloped areas to attract hunters wanting a quality, remote experience.

Her 485,000 acres (about 760 square miles) feature some 220,000 acres—about 45 percent of the land base—of the Copper Country State Forest (*which see*), all open to hunting. When added to 62,373 acres of private land currently enrolled in the Commercial Forest Act program—and therefore open to hunting—nearly 60 percent of the county is waiting for sportsmen to roam. To find these largely unposted private lands (mostly owned by timber companies), contact DNR Forest Management Division, Box 30028, Lansing, Mich. 48909 (517/373-1275), but be sure to give town and range numbers of the area you wish to hunt. Your "Michigan County Maps and Outdoor Guide" and a current plat book will also help.

About 78 percent of Dickinson County is timbered with commercial-forest species. Aspen leads with about 30 percent of the total at 116,400 acres. It is followed by maple-birch (103,600 acres), northern white cedar (46,700 acres), balsam fir (41,500 acres), black spruce (20,800 acres), paper birch (13,400 acres), elm-ash-soft maple (13,000 acres), and smaller amounts of white spruce, red pine, oak-hickory, tamarack, jack pine, and white pine.

Aspen cutting, one key to high numbers of many game species, is occurring—at least on state land—at the rate of full allowance. That effort, plus the fact that the southern one-third of Dickinson County is 20 to 30 percent open, is a big reason for outstanding deer, grouse, and woodcock hunting.

Dickinson County does not produce huge bucks at the rate that neighboring Iron County does, yet 23 whitetails are listed in Commemorative Bucks of Michigan's all-time tally of 1,150 big Michigan bucks. Most of the animals shot are yearlings; in fact, during a recent season only 6.5 percent of those examined by DNR biologists were three years of age or older. But the deer herd here is in fine shape and apparently still growing.

One piece of evidence to suggest growth is the grim statistic of annual car-deer accidents. It usually surpasses 200 animals. Another is the continuing increase of crop-damage complaints reported by farmers. Southern portions of Dickinson County have been opened to antlerless hunting, but some farmers claim that more liberalization must be allowed. One Foster City area potato farmer, for instance, reported $12,000 damage to just 12 acres of potatoes in a single year. Others report losses of 25 percent of their potato crops, claiming that deer not only eat the potatoes but scar and gouge them with their hooves and pull up others that then are exposed to the sun. Foraging deer also consume corn, cabbage, oats, barley, and alfalfa. Electric shock fences, at least around potato fields, are an expensive although effective measure to check the damage.

Controlled hunting is another. DNR biologists have issued up to 200 deer-kill tags annually in the three-county district, which includes Iron County to the west and Menominee County to the southeast. Deer crop depredation is especially high in Menominee County where biologists estimate the herd to average 50 animals per square mile.

Containing only 19 percent of the entire Upper Peninsula land base, District 2, based at Crystal Falls, produces about 40 percent of the entire U.P. deer kill each fall (however, it is the only one of four districts where antlerless hunting is allowed). In a normal autumn, 60 to 70 percent of the archery kill occurs here too.

Hard-hit Dickinson County potato farming areas are located north of Norway and Quinnesec, between Felch and Randville in the old Groveland Mine vicinity, and in the Foster City region. Enterprising hunters, especially archers, might ask some of these beleagured farmers for permission to shoot a deer.

Other good spots for deer, especially trophy animals, include aspen-covered swells interlaced with swamps south of the Turner Truck Trail and west of Gene's Pond and in the north-central portion of the county north of the Turner Truck Trail almost to Marquette County. Late-season hunters have learned that Marquette County deer migrate along rivers and valleys to cedar swamps where they yard for the winter. Deer move slowly along, feeding as they travel, covering perhaps three or four miles daily. Some of these whitetails range up to 30 miles, but most average 10 to 15 miles. An especially good area to try for a late-season buck is the east-central portion of the county east of Ralph.

Overall firearm hunting pressure is light to moderate at about 14 hunters per square mile. They kill three to four bucks per square mile for a 25 percent success ratio, nearly double the state average.

The northern tier of townships also produces good bear hunting, and there is enough state land here to enable hound men to run their dogs without fear of landowner problems. The northeastern corner contains heavy conifer swamps, good spots for starting (or baiting) bear. Northern county scatterings of red oaks also attract bear (and deer) during years of high mast production. One 800-acre area of oaks is east of Flat Rock Creek along the Marquette County border. Another similar size spot is located just west of O'Neil Lake. The district has been producing about 120 bear each fall for the past few years. Some of these are trophy animals in the 300-pound and up range and most (about 70 percent) are shot early in the season in September.

Dickinson County may yield the state's finest woodcock hunting. When upland covers of aspen begin to freeze by early to mid-October, woodcock stage both here and later in lowland habitats of alder mixed with conifers. Flush rates of several dozen in a single day are then possible. These are mostly local longbills that drift east and west, then later south, as earthworms—their principal food—dwindle. Presently, researchers at Northern Michigan University are studying woodcock migrations in Dickinson County. The supposed reason they chose this county is because of the large number of birds available. Average hourly flush-rate records from hunter-cooperators show 3.60, 3.47, and 2.13 for three years that we randomly checked.

Ruffed-grouse hunting is also very good, especially during years when the population cycle is high. Currently it is down somewhat. Grouse flush-rate averages from the hunter-cooperators were .70, .85, and 1.54. Upper Peninsula grouse do not concentrate in food areas as they are apt to do in downstate regions. That is largely because food supplies are not as concentrated. By all means, however, hunt the food crops—thornapples, acorn drops, chokecherries, etc.—when you can find them; but also check out logging roads, mixtures of young aspen and alder, lowland edges, and

256

brushlands containing hazel.

Hunters who don't want to bust the brush might consider one of several hunter walking trails that are maintained by the DNR for openings and seeded to clover and other grouse foods. Here are the names and locations of those found in Dickinson County:

The Oaks—T44N R27W, Section 6 and 7.

Snakey—T44N R27W, Section 6 and T44N R28W, Section 1.

Sand Hill—T44N R27W, Section 6 and T44N R28W, Section 1.

Old Tower—T44N R28W, Sections 1,2, and 12.

Gravel Pit—T41N R29W, Section 30.

Hoskings Creek—T41N R30W, Section 36.

Silver Lake Tower—T44N R29W, Section 19.

Strahav—T44N R30W, Section 24.

DNR foresters and wildlife biologists can also help hunters to pinpoint these productive areas.

Excellent snowshoe-hare hunting occurs north of Felch and Foster City in slashings near conifer cover. Some of these areas pass the entire winter without hearing the baying of hounds. There are a few squirrels, mostly grays and their black phase, scattered throughout the county. For best results, target the oak forests mentioned earlier. Lowland brush conifers along waterways are likely places to start a bobcat with hounds. Dickinson County is not as productive, however, as northern Menominee and Iron counties.

Overall DNR sealing records for the past few years indicate a kill of 52 to 101 cats each winter. There are a few red fox in farming country and good numbers of coyotes throughout the county. Raccoon are available along waterways, especially those near cultivated fields. Southern Dickinson County also hosts good numbers of woodchucks, but few hunters take advantage of these challenging targets.

About 1,500 Canada geese can be found in Dickinson and eastern Iron counties in fall. Giant Canadas introduced from southern Michigan nuisance-problem areas to the Hardwood Impoundment are protected, however, until numbers increase. Elsewhere, geese may be hunted. Because potato farmers usually rotate their crops with rye, geese are especially attracted. Waterfowlers might ask permission to hunt the former mine ponds at Groveland where farming now occurs. The Vulcan area is another good bet as is the farming belt north of Norway and Quinnesec and in the Foster City region.

The Ford River in central Dickinson County produces some jump-shooting opportunities for lcoal puddlers. It also courses through excellent grouse and woodcock habitat, making a mixed-bag float possible. Bergen Backwaters in the southeastern region is one of 30 wilderness recreation areas developed by the Wisconsin Electric Power Company. Duck and goose hunting can be very good here, as well as at Hancock Creek and Blomgreen Flooding, both in this same locale. In central Dickinson County try the Felch Mountain Flooding. Beaver floodings and potholes throughout the county are also productive.

All in all, Dickinson County affords good hunting opportunities. Another unique feature is that its beech forests are the last major ones in the Upper Peninsula as one moves westerly.

OTHER SHOOTING OPPORTUNITIES

The United Sportsman's Inc. in Merriman has a shooting range open daily to the public on a sometime-fee basis. Facilities include indoor/outdoor stations for pistol, centerfire and rimfire rifle, two trap fields, and archery targets. The club offers both shooting instruction and competitive shooting. For details, call 906/774-3700.

The Sagola Township Sportsmen's Club in Channing has an outdoor centerfire rifle range and a skeet field that are open to the public. For information, call 906/542-3538.

FURTHER SOURCES OF HUNTING INFORMATION

1. DNR District Office, US-2 West (Box 300), Crystal Falls, Mich. 49920 (906/875-6622).

2. DNR Norway Field Office, US-2 (Box 176), Norway, Mich. 49870 (906/563-9247).

3. DNR Felch Field Office, Highway 569 (Box 96), Felch, Mich. 49831 (906/246-3245).

4. Dickinson County Area Chamber of Commerce, Iron Mountain, Mich. 49801 (906/774-2002).

5. Topographic, county, and lake maps may be ordered from the Michigan United Conservation Clubs. For information, refer to the beginning of this book.

6. Plat books are available from the Dickinson County Cooperative Extension Services, 800 Crystal Lake Blvd., Kingsford, Mich. 49801. The cost is $10 each (add $1.50 if mail ordering).

7. Dickinson/Iron County ASCS Office, 639 Industrial Park Drive, Iron Mountain, Mich. 49801.

Also refer to the Copper Country State Forest elsewhere in this book.

Eaton County

THE major drawing card of 567-square-mile Eaton County, located in south-central southern Michigan, is a wide-ranging deer herd scattered throughout the county. This farmland region (73 percent of Eaton County is actively farmed) produces healthy, big-beamed bucks, seven of which made Commemorative Bucks of Michigan's all-time big deer record list during the 1982 season alone.

Countywide buck hunting success runs about 12 percent, higher when one adds antlerless deer shot in the hunter's-choice area, which covers nearly all of the county. In a recent season 97 percent of applicants received permits.

A big reason for that and light to moderate hunting pressure (13 hunters per square mile) is that there is no state land on which to hunt. Some farmers, however, are very good about granting access to considerate sportsmen making courteous requests. In addition, about 20 landowners have some 2,900 acres currently enrolled in the Public Access Stamp program. These parcels are scattered

throughout the southern region with concentrations in Bellevue, Brookfield, and Hamlin townships. For a complete directory, contact the DNR district office in Jackson.

Deer numbers appear to have stabilized at a sizable population. Evidence includes crop-damage complaints in the Vermontville area where wintering deer consume most of the browse along the Thornapple River. Another clue includes road accident figures which account for about 400 deer lost each year.

Several sheets of ice that advanced and then retreated over Eaton County during the glacial period gave this region its level to rolling nature. Three morainic ridges containing sand and gravel cut across the county in a southeasterly direction after entering in the northwestern portion. Sandstone bedrock occurs in the Grand River valley at Eaton Rapids and limestone bedrock is prominent in the Battle Creek River valley at Bellevue. The Grand and its tributaries—Sebewa, Sandstone, Carrier, and Willow creeks and Spring Brook—drain the eastern half. The mile-wide Thornapple River valley drains the central portion. It too has many tributaries, including the Little Thornapple River. The Battle Creek River flows southwesterly and receives feeder streams from Brookfield Township west.

Therefore, Eaton County contains intricate stream patterns, important to hunters because stream bottomlands are often wooded and provide both wildlife habitat and hunting opportunity. There are only a few lakes, which are mostly scattered throughout the southern region, but include a cluster in Sunfield Township in the southwestern corner. Most have mucky, marl bottoms. The Grand River offers an especially attractive and productive float for squirrels, ducks, and some deer. The Thornapple is best drifted from Vermontville south. Road access on these rivers is good; however, be advised that they run 100 percent through private property. Float once for scouting purposes, then seek out landowners for permission to hunt the excellent habitats you find en route.

Although Eaton County is intensively farmed for cash-crop grains, alfalfa, dairy, and livestock operations, about 12 percent of the land contains commercial-forest timber including soft and hard maple, birch, ash, elm, and some oak and hickory. Most stands are along stream bottoms and scattered second-growth woodlots on farmlands. There are increasing areas of brushlands, however, including thorny undergrowth on some pasturelands. This is particularly so in the western one-quarter toward Barry County. Overall this region has the most game.

Deer hunting rates fair to good throughout the county. Raccoon are plentiful along stream networks and are best hunted in these wetland areas adjacent to corn fields. Raccoon hunting clubs exert moderate to high pressure. Fox are another abundant game animal, one which receives light to moderate hunting pressure from landowners who band together to hunt with dogs. Stand-hunting with predator calls is an underused method. Cottontails provide good sporting opportunities when sought in edge cover of brushland/grassland areas next to crop fields and woods. There are current underutilized hunting resources for fox squirrels in scattered upland hardwood stands.

Eaton used to be a good pheasant-hunting county and still provides some opportunity in Brookfield and Eaton townships east and south of Charlotte. Isolated pockets of birds turn up elsewhere throughout the county. A habitat-improvement program between the state and landowners could have a good chance at success here. Grouse and woodcock hunting rate poor to fair with best sport coming from wet tangles of brush and young, second-growth covers. Western townships especially bear looking into. As mentioned, waterfowl hunting is limited to the river systems. There are no wild turkeys in Eaton County and no plans to introduce them.

The only state land open to hunting in Eaton County is the 39-acre Eaton Township Mini-Game Area located three miles south of Charlotte. Its specific location is E ½, W ½, NE ¼, Section 31, T2N, R4W. The tract was acquired by the Department of Transportation when the I-69 freeway was built. The area is marked with signs. Hunting opportunities are severely limited, because of its size, for rabbits and squirrels and an occasional pheasant.

OTHER SHOOTING OPPORTUNITIES

The Ingham County Conservation League, 7534 Old River Trail, Lansing, Mich. 48917 operates shooting facilities in Delta Township (northeastern Eaton County) that are open to the public on a sometime-fee basis. Included are six outdoor stations for centerfire rifle, seven indoor stations for rimfire rifle, 50 indoor/outdoor archery targets, and three skeet and two trap fields for shotgunners. The league also sponsors competitive shooting and state hunter education programs. For information, call 517/627-6982.

The Bellevue Conservation Club, 8484 Butterfield Hwy., Bellevue, Mich. 49021, is open daily to the public on a sometime-fee basis for use of its pistol (10 stations), centerfire-rifle (one station), and rimfire-rifle (10 stations) ranges. Also available are five indoor-outdoor archery targets, skeet and trap fields (two and four, respectively), and three shotgun handtrap areas. The club offers both shooting instruction and competitive shooting. For information, call 616/763-9261.

Chief Okemos Sportsmen's Club in Dimondale (4533 Gunnell Road) allows limited public use of its shooting facilities on a sometime-fee basis. Included are indoor/outdoor stations for rimfire rifle and pistol (10 each) and five outdoor stations for centerfire rifle. There is one trap field, and programs include (1) competitive shooting, (2) shooting instruction, (3) hunter-certification courses. For more information, call 517/646-6753.

FURTHER SOURCES OF HUNTING INFORMATION

1. DNR District Office, 3335 Lansing Ave., Jackson, Mich. 49202 (517/784-3188).

2. Mason State Game Farm Field Office, 1219 Hawley Road, Mason, Mich. 48854 (517/676-4600).

3. Charlotte Chamber of Commerce, 207 South Cochran Ave., Charlotte, Mich. 48813 (517/543-0400).

4. Grand Ledge Area Chamber of Commerce, Box 105, Grand Ledge, Mich. 48837 (517/627-2383).

5. Olivet Chamber of Commerce, 101 South Main, Olivet, Mich. 49076 (616/749-9674).

6. Vermontville Chamber of Commerce, Box 202, Vermontville, Mich. 49096 (517/726-1040).

7. Topographic, county, and lake maps may be

ordered from the Michigan United Conservation Clubs. For information, refer to the beginning of this book.

8. County plat books may be ordered from the Eaton County Cooperative Extension Service, 126 North Bostwick, Charlotte, Mich. 48813, for a cost of $10 each (add $1.50 when mail ordering).

9. Eaton County ASCS Office, USDA, 200 North Bostwick Ave., Charlotte, Mich. 48813 (517/543-1512).

Emmet County

TUCKED away at the northwestern tip of the Lower Peninsula is Emmet County. Although many think of this region—which includes Petoskey and Harbor Springs—as resort country, it also features good hunting opportunities. For most game species, hunting pressure is low to moderate with potential for deer, bear, bobcats, snowshoe hares, grouse, woodcock, and waterfowl running fair to good.

Emmet County contains about 460 square miles. A soil survey done 10 years ago indicated that 27 percent of the land base was farmed with roughly two-thirds in harvested crops and one-third in pasture. Those figures are still reasonably valid. An active farming belt exists east of Petoskey in Bear Creek Township. Bliss, Carp, Center, and McKinley townships in the northern half also contain farmlands—both active and abandoned. Some deserted sites are now reverting to natural forest succession and offer good hunting potential for deer, hares (and a few cottontails), grouse, and woodcock. A fruit-farming belt extends inland from Lake Michigan as well.

Another reason that Emmet County is not overrun with hunters is because many downstate sportsmen shoot past, figuring perhaps that if they are this close to the Upper Peninsula, they may as well cross the bridge and hunt there. They might want to reconsider Emmet County. Over 70 percent of the land base is covered with commercial-forest timber. Northern hardwoods (beech, basswood, sugar maple, and birch) constitute 109,800 acres and are found mostly in the northern half of the county. Northern hardwoods provide habitat for deer, bear, squirrels, bobcats, and hares.

Another 48,000 acres are in aspen, productive for grouse, woodcock, hares, and deer. Mixed and pure stands of aspen are scattered throughout. Other forest species include northern white cedar (17,500 acres), elm-ash-soft maple (10,400 acres), red pine (4,000 acres), white spruce (3,000 acres), and oak-hickory (2,500 acres). Many of the oaks are found near Lake Michigan, and what limited squirrel hunting is available in Emmet County (both fox and gray/black species) occurs here.

Besides the habitat diversity, another plus feature of Emmet County is that over 25 percent of the land base is state-owned and open to hunting. Included are both solid chunks and small parcels of the Mackinac State Forest (which see) scattered throughout the county, as well as the 7,553-acre Wilderness State Park (which also see) at the northern tip. Further, 3,443 acres of company-owned land is presently enrolled under the Commercial Forest Act. These lands are also open to hunting. A current plat book will help you find these properties, and you can obtain legal descriptions by contacting the DNR Forest Management Division in Lansing (Box 30028 or call 517/373-1275).

Emmet County deer populations are lowest in the eight-county DNR district. Best areas to hunt are in the Maple River watershed and along dune cover near Lake Michigan. Enterprising hunters might also check with fruit farmers to see if they are suffering deer damage to their crops. As mentioned, pressure is low (under 10 hunters per square mile) with one of eight tagging bucks (one buck or less per square mile) for a 12 to 15 percent success ratio.

Bobcat and bear hunting is best in cedar swamps of the northern region, north of a line from Paradise (Carp) Lake to Sturgeon Bay Point. This includes the Wilderness State Park region mentioned earlier. For raccoon, look to southern farmlands cut by small drainages. Fox numbers are low to moderate, but there is an apparent increase in coyotes. Few hunters take advantage of these predators.

Fair to good snowshoe-hare hunting occurs throughout the county in pine plantations, poplar slashings, and conifer swamps. One top area is around French Farm Lake Flooding just south of Mackinaw City. Also, consider juniper cover along Lake Michigan sand dunes.

Emmet County offers some waterfowling potential currently going unrecognized. Goose and duck hunters along the Wilderness State Park shoreline all the way to Waugoshance Point can enjoy both pass-shooting and decoy-hunting. Sturgeon Bay affords good layout-hunting opportunities during northeastern blows. In this region are many isolated pockets of water located behind the sand dunes. These are good places for jump-shooting early-season puddlers (mallards, wood ducks, teal) and for late-season migrants, especially when the bay is wind-lashed.

Some potential duck hunting exists along the southern shore of Little Traverse Bay although hunters will have to ask permission before entering private lands. The farming belt east of Petoskey affords some opportunities for field-hunting for geese. Crooked, Pickerel, and Round lakes east of Petoskey all feature public access and are potential resting spots for both migrant puddlers and divers. In the northern region I have successfully hunted shallow Paradise Lake for late-season divers. Also, this area gets visited by foraging geese from Dingman Marsh in Cheboygan County to the east. O'Neal Lake and French Farm floodings, although old and in need of rehabilitation, are two other places worth scouting for waterfowl.

The southern portion of Emmet County is currently open to turkey hunting, but numbers are presently light. Scattered pockets of grouse habitat (mostly varying age classes of aspen) provide fair to good hunting. One area to try is in the southeastern region on state land. Another is along the Maple River northwest of Pellston although hunting pressure can be intense here. Woodcock also frequent these areas as well as worm-rich soils throughout the county. Good places to look for longbills include old orchards, pastures, and tag alder creek bottoms.

Hunter-cooperators report good hourly flush rates for both grouse and woodcock. We checked three years at random and found averages of 1.85, 2.26, and 1.75 for grouse and 3.60, 1.43, and 2.45 for woodcock.

Emmet County is not only a good place to hunt, it is also beautiful in fall. The hilly, western portion comes ablaze with fall hardwoods in color and is worth the drive alone just to see.

OTHER SHOOTING OPPORTUNITIES

The Wycamp Hunting and Fishing Club, Inc., Route 2, Pleasantville Road in Harbor Springs 49740, is a 640-acre shooting preserve open to the public. Located in Bliss Township (northern Emmet County), the club offers hunting for pheasants and ducks. For information, call Dean Shorter at 616/526-2641.

Emmet County sportsmen also have at least two places to practice shooting. The Mackinaw City Range, 102 South Huron in Mackinaw City, is a publicly-owned facility open without fees. Included are outdoor stations for pistol (10), centerfire rifle (two), and rimfire rifle (two) as well as three outdoor archery targets, a trap field, and a handtrap area. For information, call 616/436-7861.

The Emmet County Sportsmen's Club, US-31

North in Petoskey, has range facilities open to the public for fees. Featured are five indoor pistol stations, two outdoor centerfire rifle stations, five indoor rimfire rifle stations, two skeet fields, a trap field, and four indoor/outdoor archery targets. The club offers both shooting instruction and state hunter-certification programs. Call 616/347-4521 for details.

OTHER SOURCES OF HUNTING INFORMATION

1. DNR District Office, 1732 West M-32 (Box 667), Gaylord, Mich. 49735 (517/732-3541).

2. DNR Pellston Field Office, 304 Stimson, Pellston, Mich. 49769 (616/539-8564).

3. Petoskey Regional Chamber of Commerce, 401 East Mitchell St. (Box 306), Petoskey, Mich. 49770 (616/347-4150).

4. Greater Mackinaw City Chamber of Commerce, Box 475, Mackinaw City, Mich. 49701 (616/436-5574).

5. Topographic, county, and lake maps may be ordered from the Michigan United Conservation Clubs. For information, refer to the beginning of this book.

6. Plat books are available from the Emmet County Cooperative Extension Services, 441 Bay St., Petoskey, Mich. 49770. The cost is $10 each (add $1 if mail ordering).

7. Emmet/Charlevoix ASCS Office, 441 Bay St., Petoskey, Mich. 49770.

Also, refer to the following elsewhere in this book:
1. Mackinac State Forest
2. Wilderness State Park

Genesee County

BECAUSE I grew up and still live in rural Genesee County, I know the hunting potentials of this area better than any other in the state. At first glance they appear to be poor: the city of Flint sprawls from county center like a cancerous growth that links several satellite communities and small cities. Because local hunting closures prevail, sportsmen will want to check for regulations. There is no state land open to hunting. The 10,000-acre Genesee County Parks System affords plenty of recreation for all except hunters, to whom it is off limits.

But there are both game animals and birds and places to hunt them in Genesee County for those willing to take a second look. Over 6,000 acres of farmland are currently enrolled by about a dozen landowners in the Public Access Stamp program. Most of these are located in the northern half of the county; to find them contact the DNR district office in Imlay City for a free directory. In addition, I have found Genesee County farmers to be responsive to hunters who ask permission first before entering their lands.

Relief of Genesee County ranges from nearly level to steep. About a third of the county is flat to slightly rolling, cut by steep banks of the Flint River and its tributaries. The most level areas are found in the western and central portions. The southwestern

region, on the other hand, is quite hilly, and rolling landscape featuring low hills is found along the eastern side fronting Lapeer County. Gouging and scraping of several ice sheets during glaciation periods shaped the land and left it covered with glacial drift. The retreating ice floes also created most of the county's lakes found mostly in the northeastern and southwestern portions.

Less than half the county is farmed. Cash-crop fields of corn, soybeans, and wheat are interspersed with pasturelands and woodlands. The Flint River, which enters from Lapeer County in the Columbiaville area and then twists its way through Flint and Flushing to exit downstream from Montrose in the northwestern corner, is wood-fringed. So are its many tributaries as well as the Shiawassee River which drains the southwestern corner. These flows join later in Saginaw County and march on to Saginaw Bay as the Saginaw River.

Altogether, about 14 percent of Genesee County is wooded with commercial timber species. Birch-maple dominate, followed by oak-hickory and elm-ash-sugar maple types. Small stands of aspen appear to be on the increase. Clusters of oak, hickory, and butternut abutting corn fields draw fox squirrels, which are largely underhunted in this county. The woods also host good raccoon populations, and raccoon hunting is a popular sport with moderate to high pressure along waterways flanked by farm fields. Trappers take most of the red fox harvested each year; hunters are missing out on sporting possibilities.

Pheasants have fallen on hard times although small populations of birds still make hunting worthwhile. Best bets are (1) south of Davison in the Goodrich/Atlas area, (2) west of a line from Flushing/Swartz Creek/Linden toward Shiawassee County, and (3) in the northeastern corner from Otisville north to Millington in Tuscola County. To find ringnecks, target set-aside acres and abandoned farms that have grown up with weeds or brushlands. These same areas produce cottontails too. Other good places to try for rabbits are grasslands, marshlands, and edges of stream bottomlands with openings.

I have enjoyed fair grouse hunting throughout brush pockets and brief aspen stands in Genesee County. According to DNR flush records from cooperating hunters, Genesee County gets fair pressure from hunters who average 1.5 to 3.0 grouse flushed per hour in good years. Few woodcock are raised locally, but it is not unusual for hunters to move a dozen or two flight birds in late October when they key along lowland covers of alder and upland covers of sumac, dogwood, and aspen. There are no wild turkeys in the county and no DNR plans to release any.

There are more deer in Genesee County than many people realize, and the herd appears to be slowly increasing. Car-deer accidents have passed the 200 animals-per-year mark. However, hunter success is very low for bucks (five percent or under) with increased pressure each successive fall. Overall, that pressure seems low at about four hunters per square mile, except when one considers that half the county is urbanized.

Genesee County does produce some monster bucks, however, as evidenced by the fact that, thus far, Commemorative Bucks of Michigan has turned up eight record whitetails shot here. As the search continues, others will no doubt be registered. Deer are found throughout the county, with best concentrations along the Flint River and in the four corners farthest from Flint.

Waterfowling opportunities are fair to good in Genesee County with hunters concentrating on (1) jump-shooting mallards and wood ducks from lakes and streams (the Flint River, however, is closed to hunting from Holloway Reservoir Dam through Flint city limits); (2) blind-hunting for both puddlers and migrant divers on Holloway Reservoir and the southwestern-region lakes of Ponemah, Lake Fenton, and Lobdell (all have public access); and (3) goose hunting in farm fields of the southern county. This latter sport can be quite effective during the late season for nuisance Canada geese (open in Genesee County from M-21 south). Mid-December aerial surveys by the DNR have shown that geese congregate on Lobdell, Ponemah, Shiawassee, and Fenton lakes among others.

A comment on Holloway Reservoir waterfowling: hunters must obtain permission from the Genesee County Parks and Recreation Commission at G-5055 Branch Road in Flint (near Mott Lake) before erecting or anchoring offshore blinds.

Genesee County has some serious shortcomings with respect to bountiful populations of game animals and places to hunt them. However, hunting potential is generally better than most sportsmen realize.

OTHER SHOOTING OPPORTUNITIES

There are four sites open to the public for practice shooting:

1. Williams Gun Club at G-5389 Lapeer Road in Davison offers shooting instruction, competition, and hunter certification courses as well as fee use of the following facilities: skeet (four fields), trap (five fields), centerfire and rimfire rifle (nine fields), and pistol (five fields). Call 313/653-2131 for information.

2. Genesee Sportsman Club, 8482 North Seymour Road in Flushing, offers fee use of shotgun skeet and trap fields (four each) and also provides shooting instruction and competition. Call 313/639-7597 for information.

3. Flushing Rifle and Pistol Club, 134 South Maple St. in Flushing, has eight indoor stations each for centerfire and rimfire rifle practice. The club also features shooting instruction and competition and sponsors hunter certification courses. Fees are charged. Call 313/659-9238 for details.

4. Grand Blanc Huntsman's Club, 9046 South Irish Road in Grand Blanc, has the following facilities open for fees: outdoor stations for pistol, centerfire and rimfire rifle; three skeet fields; four trap fields; and 28 outdoor archery targets. The club features shooting instruction and competition and it sponsors hunter certification courses.

5. Ed's Archery and Sporting Goods, 4483 East Vienna Road (M-57), between Clio and Otisville, has both an indoor and outdoor archery range open to the public for fees. Call 313/686-6494 for details.

FURTHER SOURCES OF HUNTING INFORMATION

1. DNR District Office, 715 South Cedar St., Imlay City, Mich. 48444 (313/724-2015).

2. Flint Area Chamber of Commerce, 708 Root St., Suite 123, Flint, Mich. 48503 (313/232-7101).

3. Davison Area Chamber of Commerce, 334 North Main St., Davison, Mich. 48423 (313/653-6622).

4. Fenton Area Chamber of Commerce, 207 Silver Lake Road, Fenton, Mich. 48430 (313/629-5447).

5. Flushing Area Chamber of Commerce, 133 East Main St., Box 44, Flushing, Mich. 48433 (313/659-4141).

6. Mount Morris Area Chamber of Commerce, Box 222, Mount Morris, Mich. 48458 (313/686-1560).

7. Swartz Creek Area Chamber of Commerce, Box 267, Swartz Creek, Mich. 48473 (313/635-9643).

8. Topographic, county, and lake maps may be ordered from the Michigan United Conservation Clubs. For information, refer to the beginning of this book.

9. Plat books are available from the Genesee County Cooperative Extension Services, G-4215 West Pasadena, Flint, Mich. 48504. The cost is $5 each (add $1 if mail ordering).

10. Genesee County ASCS Office, USDA, 3505 West Coldwater Road, Mount Morris, Mich. 48458 (313/787-5111).

Gladwin County

GLADWIN County lies in the north-central part of the Lower Peninsula. About 40 percent of its 503 square miles are farmed and the balance is timbered with commercial-forest types. Principal crops are corn, wheat, oats, and hay grown mostly as food for dairy and livestock operations, with the balance sold as cash crops. A whopping 129,000 acres of aspen in varying age classes leads the cover types. It is followed by elm-ash-soft maple (22,900 acres), oak-hickory (18,400 acres), maple-birch (11,400 acres), paper birch (6,800 acres), and jack pine (1,800 acres).

Aspen on state land is ideally rotated in 40-year cutting cycles whereby 25 percent is leveled every 10 years. Proper management results in four age classifications, which in turn provide ideal habitat for grouse, woodcock, deer, and rabbits. About 26 percent, or 86,643 acres, of Gladwin County is state-owned, mostly in the form of the Au Sable State Forest (which see).

Generally speaking, the eastern half of Gladwin County is state-owned. This is a high-water table area of poor-soiled land which produces mostly aspen and plenty of upland and lowland brush, along with some pure oak and small patches of jack pine.

High hunting pressure culls bucks in Gladwin County's deer herd, and rack size runs small (plenty of spikehorns and four- and six-pointers) since most deer don't live to old age. The western side of Gladwin County is farm country mixed with aspen and red-maple woods. This is particularly true in the western stack of townships (Sherman, Sage, Grout, and Beaverton). To the south the farm belt extends into Gladwin and Tobacco townships. Bigger-bodied deer sporting heavy racks—although not the rule—are nevertheless produced in this region. According to a recent five-year survey by the DNR, Bourret and Buckeye townships produce exceptionally high numbers of deer. Southern Hay and Grim townships also are big deer producers.

Overall, Gladwin County rates high for whitetails. The buck kill usually exceeds five deer per square mile, but because of intense pressure (41 hunters per square mile during a recent season), the harvest falls off to about 15 to 20 percent success, or the state average. Gladwin joins Roscommon and Lake counties as the hardest-hit deer hunting counties in the state. This is due to three reasons: (1) good numbers of deer (in a county with less than 50,000 citizens 200 to 300 deer annually lose their lives on highways), (2) a high amount of state land open to hunting, (3) proximity to southern Michigan.

Pressure is also high for raccoon, especially during seasons when pelts fetch high dollar. There are good 'coon populations throughout Gladwin County, however, along both the Tittabawassee and Tobacco rivers as well as the many smaller drainages. Red fox are another game animal that rise and fall with fur prices. Currently there are fairly good populations and hunting pressure is light. Coyotes are increasing in the county.

Another point about big game: occasional bear complaints are received in the northwestern and southeastern regions of the county (the season is closed). Also, increasing numbers of bobcats in the northeastern corner had the DNR considering an open season. That is not likely, however, since nearby Roscommon and Ogemaw counties are both closed to cat hunting. An open season in Gladwin County would subject the predators to too much pressure.

The DNR has been trying to expand wild turkeys in Gladwin County for several years. Recently 44 birds were released in several western-county areas. The northern half is currently open to hunting with the exception of Bourret and Grim townships. About 300 to 400 turkeys live within the hunting boundary and apparently survive winters, thanks to feeding by private landowners. By spring hunting season the birds disperse and many reenter state land.

Cottontail numbers are good throughout Gladwin County. About 20 percent of the rabbit bag, however, is actually snowshoe hares. Hunters concentrating on conifer swamps with nearby aspen cuttings fare the best. East-side state land north of M-61 features plenty of such cuttings near swamps. Another good bet is Sherman Township south of the Gladwin Field Trial Area, which is closed to all hunting except firearm deer (which also see). In addition, try the Geesy Marsh area in Clement Township. A point about the field trial area: long recognized as a beautiful and top-rate site, it has hosted the Grand National Grouse Trials for several years.

Fair to high populations of ruffed grouse and woodcock are found in scattered locations of aspen canopy with shrub understories. North of M-61 in Grim Township is a fine area to try. During two years surveyed, hunter-cooperators reported 1.0 to 2.0 grouse flushes per hour with woodcock flush rates actually a little higher. Gladwin County also hosts good numbers of squirrels (80 percent fox, 20 percent gray/black). Try the southeastern corner in particular (southern Grim and most of Bentley townships).

Crowing pheasants appear to be on the upswing, especially in the southern half of Butman Township, northeastern Gladwin Township, the southern third of Sherman Township, and in scattered areas of Sage Township. However, numbers are very low and since birds are almost always found on private land, hunters will find landowners reluctant to grant pheasant-hunting permission. Indeed, some Gladwin County residents are as protective of their ringnecks as other landowners may be with deer.

Although the put-take pheasant hunting program has been scrapped, it is likely that some form of rear-and-release program will continue, at least at the old Gladwin County put-take site northeast of Wooden Shoe Village. That is because hunter utilization was especially high and because few wild pheasants are available.

Duck hunters score on many of the numerous beaver ponds and along rivers and feeder streams by jump-shooting. The Tittabawassee River allows ideal float hunting, and some waterfowlers even set up decoys in bayous and hunt from boats. In addition, nuisance giant Canada geese from southeastern Michigan, translocated on Molasses River floodings, have been reproducing and providing good hunting potential.

OTHER SHOOTING OPPORTUNITIES

None known at the present.

FURTHER SOURCES OF HUNTING INFORMATION

1. DNR District Office, 501 Hemlock St., Clare, Mich. 48617 (517/386-7991).

2. DNR Gladwin Field Office, 801 North Silver-leaf, Box 337, Gladwin, Mich. 48624 (517/426-9205).

3. Gladwin County Chamber of Commerce, 608 West Cedar St., Gladwin, Mich. 48624 (517/426-5451).

4. Topographic, county, and lake maps may be ordered from the Michigan United Conservation Clubs. For information, refer to the beginning of this book.

5. Plat books are available from the chamber of commerce for $10 each (if mail ordering, add $1.50 and make out checks to the Gladwin County Cooperative Extension Services).

6. Gladwin County ASCS Office, 742 West Cedar St., Gladwin, Mich. 48624 (517/426-9461).

Also, refer to the Au Sable State Forest and Gladwin Field Trial Area elsewhere in this book.

Gogebic County

GOGEBIC County in the far western Upper Peninsula shares its southern boundary with Wisconsin while its northern boundary lies along southern Ontonagon County. Thirty-six miles of Gogebic County is wild, picturesque Lake Superior shoreline. It may be hard for a downstate sportsman to believe that Gogebic County lies as far west as St. Louis, Missouri, that it contains over 30 waterfalls, 1,200 miles of running stream, a portion of the U.P.'s largest inland lake (Lake Gogebic), a tremendous scattering of inland lakes along its boundary with Wisconsin, and some of the best hunting opportunities in both peninsulas.

Hunters come to Gogebic County seeking deer, bear, bobcats, snowshoe hares, ruffed grouse, and woodcock. They will also find ducks, geese, coyotes, and gray squirrels.

And they will have plenty of places in which to seek their quarry. Over 60 percent of the 711,000 acres (about 1,100 square miles) is open to public hunting. Eastern-county lands are heavily enrolled in the Ottawa National Forest and there are a few scattered parcels of the Copper Country State Forest and about 10,000 acres of the 58,000-acre Porcupine Mountains State Park (all of which see). Further, 171,496 acres of private land is currently enrolled in the Commercial Forest Act program and therefore may be hunted.

To find the private holdings (mostly company-owned timberlands), contact the DNR Forest Management Division, Box 30028, Lansing, Mich. 48909 (517/373-1275), and ask for legal descriptions. Be sure to furnish the town and range numbers of the area you wish to hunt, however. Helping you will be a "Michigan County Maps and Outdoor Guide" or a current county plat book.

The five-county DNR district, headquartered at Baraga, is not noted for its high deer kill—about 2,000 to 2,500 bucks each fall. Whitetails have a fairly tough go of it in Gogebic County, which has some 85 percent of its forests (92 percent of the overall land base) in sawtimber or poletimber stands—largely beyond the stage where it will greatly benefit deer (and many other game species).

Also, Gogebic County gets 150 inches or more of snow each winter.

Still, it produces 22 percent buck-kill success for the average five hunters per square mile who seek them. Some of these deer are big-racked whitetails, as evidenced by the fact that Commemorative Bucks of Michigan lists 20 Gogebic County kills in its all-time record book of 1,150 boss bucks. Best bets include south of US-2 in the west and throughout the eastern region. The swamp country along the Wisconsin border affords good wilderness hunting opportunities as does the 21,000-acre Sylvania Recreation Area within the national forest.

Late-season and December muzzleloader and archery hunters who can tough the snow and cold conditions can sometimes shoot bucks heading for winter yarding areas. In the eastern county those are apt to be around Imp Lake, throughout much of the Sylvania Tract, along CR-531 between Cisco and Beatons lakes, west along US-2 from its junction with USFS-378 to CR-525, and within the triangle formed by US-2, CR-525, and M-64 at the southern end of Lake Gogebic.

Western-county deer yards shape up along Lake Superior at Little Girls Point and in the southern Porkies. In the southern county try west of CR-519 in the McDonald Lake region.

Typical of the western U.P., over 60 percent (386,500 acres) of the commercial-forest cover types in Gogebic County is hard maple-birch. This is followed by 68,700 acres of aspen, 48,500 acres of balsam fir, 36,800 acres of elm-ash-soft maple, 33,200 acres of black spruce, 12,900 acres of northern white cedar, and 11,100 acres of paper birch. Smaller amounts of jack pine, red pine, oak-hickory, and tamarack are also represented.

In addition to trophy buck hunting, Gogebic County yields excellent numbers of black bear for baiters and hound hunters alike. The district generally furnishes 200 to 300 bruins, or about 30 to 40 percent of the entire U.P. kill, each fall. It is difficult to pinpoint good bear-hunting spots because the animals range freely in search of food and because the habitat is so diverse. Best bets are to seek food sources (farm crops, chokecherries, acorns) in areas near security cover (conifer lowlands and hardwood uplands).

Gogebic County also yields good numbers of bobcats (eight to 17 sealed during each of the past five winter seasons) and would likely furnish more if more hunters took advantage. There are also good numbers of coyotes, a few red fox and raccoon, some gray/black squirrels in oak stands mixed with conifers, and fair to good populations of snowshoe hares. The latter, however, appear to be down somewhat at this writing. Best bets are lowland swamps adjacent to young hardwood cover; also, check out USFS pine plantations under 10 feet tall.

Best duck hunting occurs in the maze of lakes along the southern boundary. Lake Gogebic itself can be layout-hunted for divers as can Lac Vieux Desert in the western county. Geese stopping to rest after crossing Lake Superior furnish some hunting opportunities too, but the other four counties in the district rate better for honkers.

Low returns from hunter-cooperators regarding hourly flush-rate records on grouse and woodcock are presented here but should be considered with discretion. Of three years checked at random, we found grouse flush statistics of 1.10, .83, and 1.08 with corresponding woodcock flushes of .07, 1.83, and .01. It is true that woodcock hunting is rather sporadic, with better opportunities in counties to the east. In Gogebic County, seek the longbills in lowland cover along streams. For grouse, try cutover hardwoods and aspen that have grown back to 10 to 15 feet as well as brushlands and the edge of heavy cover.

About 21,000 acres of the Ottawa National Forest in Gogebic County along the Wisconsin border is a wilderness area. Entrance to the Sylvania Recreation Area, also called the Sylvania Tract, is by permit only. Hunters are welcome except that wheeled vehicles and motors are not allowed. This is pure wilderness hunting, camping, and fishing. Twenty-nine wilderness-type campgrounds are provided.

The best entry is from US-2. Four miles west of Watersmeet turn south on CR-535, the Thousand Island Lake Road. You can obtain more information from the district ranger at Watersmeet (*see below*).

OTHER SHOOTING OPPORTUNITIES

The ROTC range at the L. L. Wright High School on East Ayer Street in Ironwood is open to the public without charge. Facilities include four indoor stations each for pistol, centerfire rifle, and rimfire rifle. Shooting instruction is offered. For information, call 906/932-3920.

FURTHER SOURCES OF HUNTING INFORMATION

1. DNR District Office, North US-41 (Box 44), Baraga, Mich. 49908 (906/353-6651).
2. DNR Wakefield Field Office, US-2, Wakefield, Mich. 49968 (906/224-2771).
3. Forest Supervisor, Ottawa National Forest, East Cloverland Drive, Ironwood, Mich. 49938 (906/932-1330 or 1-800-561-1201 from the U.P.).
4. Ottawa National Forest, Bessemer Ranger District, Bessemer, Mich. 49911 (906/667-0261).
5. Ottawa National Forest, Watersmeet Ranger District, Watersmeet, Mich. 49969 (906/353-4551).
6. Ironwood Chamber of Commerce, 100 East Aurora St., Ironwood, Mich. 49938 (906/932-1122).
7. Bessemer Chamber of Commerce, Bessemer, Mich. 49911 (906/663-4542).
8. Topographic, county, and lake maps may be ordered from the Michigan United Conservation Clubs. For information, refer to the beginning of this book.
9. Plat books are available from the Gogebic County Cooperative Extension Services, 104 South Lowell St., Bessemer, Mich. 49911. The cost is $12 each (add $1.50 to mail orders).
10. Gogebic/Ontonagon County ASCS Office, Cedar Street, Ewen, Mich. 49025.

Also, refer to the following elsewhere in this book:
1. Copper Country State Forest
2. Ottawa National Forest
3. Porcupine Mountains State Park

Grand Traverse County

GRAND Traverse County in northwestern Lower Michigan offers fair to good hunting for deer, grouse, woodock, snowshoe hares, squirrels, raccoon, and ducks. Although the Traverse City area is fast growing as one of Michigan's and the nation's premier vacation spots (a big reason that county lands continue to be subdivided and sold to absentee landowners), Grand Traverse County still affords a good mixture of cover types.

About 53 percent of the land base supports various types of commercial-forest species. At 38,800 acres, maple-birch leads, but it is closely followed by aspen (37,900 acres), oak-hickory (23,500 acres), and red pine (19,300 acres). Smaller amounts of jack pine, northern white cedar, elm-ash-soft maple, white pine, and tamarack are also found.

The eastern half contains most of the red and white oak forests; consequently, the better deer hunting is found here. A good mix of varying-age aspen, young plantation pines, and conifer swamps occurs throughout the lake district southwest of Traverse City and offers productive hunting for deer, hares, grouse, and woodcock. Besides Traverse City itself, a general recreation magnet that attracts many people is southeast of the city in the Spider Lake area. Hunting for the above-named species here is only fair, and although some lake hunting for ducks exists, it is very limited.

About 22 percent, or 65,752 acres, of 464-square-mile Grand Traverse County is state-owned. These are scattered parcels of the Pere Marquette State Forest (*which see*) and the Petobego State Game Area (*which also see*) in the northern region next to Antrim County. The rest of the county is evenly split between farmland (orchards, some dairy, and crops) and privately-owned parcels. Although farmers are occasionally amenable to a courteous request from sportsmen to enter their lands, hunters will have a tough time gaining access to the other private land. This is because the parcels are small and because their absentee owners use the land for hunting themselves.

An exception is about 2,000 acres of company-owned land that is enrolled in the state Commercial Forest Act plan. Therefore, it is open to hunting. Sportsmen armed with a current plat book and a good county map can locate these blocks of forestland if they first get legal descriptions. These are available from DNR district headquarters in Cadillac or from the DNR Forest Management Division in Lansing. That address is Box 30028, Lansing, Mich. 48909, phone 517/373-1275.

When the last ice sheet melted several thousand years ago, it left glacial deposits in Grand Traverse County called the Manistee Moraine. This moraine partly bounds Traverse City and extends northerly into Leelanau County and easterly from Acme to the junction of the Kalaska County line and Round Lake. The ridge-like mass of gravel, sand, and other glacial drift is three to four miles wide. The older, Port Huron Moraine crosses the county north of Fife Lake (southeastern corner) and exits in the southwestern corner.

Between these two moraines lie great glacial spillways and outwash plains. North of the Manistee Moraine, separated only by the East Arm of Grand Traverse Bay, are two large ground moraines. From these rise a number of well-rounded hills—drumlins—a quarter to two miles long and about one-eighth-mile wide. Along Grand Traverse Bay itself are lake benches, at one time the bottoms of glacial Lakes Algonquin and Nipessing. Escarpments next to the lake benches were formed by waves cutting into glacial deposits from 100 to 500 feet deep.

Early settlers found northern hardwoods (sugar maples, beech, elm) on better soils; stands of white and red pine on soils of low fertility; and white cedar, balsam fir, and black spruce in swamps. As we have seen, an excellent mix of tree species also covers much of the county today. Also, ground cover in wooded areas consists of bracken, sweetfern, dogwood, sumac, and many other plants.

Blueberries, raspberries, blackberries, and strawberries thrive in unburned, cutover areas. Junipers grow on sandy soils near Grand Traverse Bay, and openings in woodland are frequently covered with big bluestem and Canada bluegrass. All in all, the county is not only beautiful, but it produces a variety of game and nongame species.

Whitetails in particular can be greatly influenced by severe winters as this is a snowbelt region. During a recent firearm deer-hunting season, hunters shot three to four bucks per square mile for a 20 percent success ratio. The next season their harvest tumbled to only one to two bucks per square mile with corresponding success under 10 percent. In lean and fat years hunter pressure is usually moderate, about 15 to 20 guns per square mile.

The best deer hunting and habitat occurs south of Williamsburg. There is much public land in this region, but there are apt to be plenty of hunters too. South of Kingsley is also good, but these are largely privately-owned farmlands. There are a few bear and bobcats in Grand Traverse County; however, they are currently protected and will likely remain so

for a long time. A few red fox use forest openings and farmland. Deer hunters bag a few coyotes from jack-pine forests, and the animals could likely stand more hunting pressure.

Most of the squirrels shot in Grand Traverse County are grays or blacks. Seek them in mixed stands of oak and pine. There are fox squirrels in pure oak stands containing mature trees. This is especially true on state land.

Snowshoe hares appear to be ending a low-end cycle at this time and should rebound during upcoming seasons. Seek them in cutover areas just growing back, along hardwood edges of swamps, and in pine plantations under 15 years old. A few cottontails live near farm buildings to provide localized sport.

What few turkeys live in Grand Traverse County are contained to the southwestern corner. There is no open season at this time.

Small resident flocks of Canada geese provide limited, localized hunting on county lakes. Migrant passage of geese offers further opportunity, but it too is unpredictable and incidental at best. There is some duck hunting potential, however. For wood ducks, mallards, and teal, work beaver ponds and stream bottoms. For divers, look to Lake Skegemog which spills over into Kalkaska County. Long and Duck lakes are other possibilities, but apparently there is no public access. An enterprising hunter, however, might find a landowner for permission to enter.

Grouse are scattered throughout the county in cutover aspen stands, dogwood thickets, and brushy stream bottomlands. Hunters will also find them in fruit-bearing shrubs other than dogwood. We checked three years of hunter-cooperator records and learned that 1.74, 1.59, and 1.73 grouse were moved on the average each hour. Although few woodcock nest in Grand Traverse County, plenty of flight birds stop to rest from early October through the month. Those same hunter-cooperator records show 2.35, .41, and .95 woodcock moved on the average each hour.

OTHER SHOOTING OPPORTUNITIES

Grand Traverse County sportsmen have at least two shooting ranges, where they may practice and sight in weapons. The Duck Lake Gun Club, 3120 County Road in Grawn, is open to the public for fee use of its outdoor pistol, rimfire, and centerfire rifle stations and two trap fields. The club also offers competitive shooting. There is no phone.

The Camp Greilick Range, 4754 Scout Camp Road in Traverse City, is open 150 days annually to the public for fees. Outdoor firearm stations include eight each for pistol and rimfire rifle. There are four archery targets. Call 616/946-4263 for information.

OTHER SOURCES OF HUNTING INFORMATION

1. DNR District Office, 8015 South 131 Road, Cadillac, Mich. 49601 (616/775-9727).
2. Traverse City Field Office, 404 West 14th St., Traverse City, Mich. 49684 (616/946-4920).
3. Traverse City Area Chamber of Commerce, 202 Grandview Parkway, Traverse City, Mich. 49684 (616/947-5075).
4. Traverse City Area Convention and Visitors Bureau, 202 East Grandview Parkway, Traverse City, Mich. 49684 (616/947-1120).
5. Interlochen Area Chamber of Commerce, Box 13, Interlochen, Mich. 49643 (616/276-7141).

6. Topographic, county, and lake maps may be ordered from the Michigan United Conservation Clubs. For information, refer to the beginning of this book.

7. Plat books are available from the Grand Traverse County Cooperative Extension Services, 4-H Dept., Third Floor Governmental Center, 400 Boardman Ave., Traverse City, Mich. 49684. The cost is $10 each (add $1.50 if mail ordering).

8. Grand Traverse County ASCS Office, 1222 Rennie St., Traverse City, Mich. 49684.

Also, refer to the following elsewhere in this book:
1. Pere Marquette State Forest
2. Petobego State Game Area

Gratiot County

RESULTING from glaciation 8,000 to 12,000 years ago, Gratiot County land features fall into two general types. The western half is a series of glacial moraines, till and outwash plains, and old channels caused from retreating ice. The eastern half is a level lake plain, the former bed of glacial Lake Saginaw which includes a mucky swamp southeast of Ashley. The swamp, about a quarter-mile wide and three miles long, is the former head of the old Grand River channel and now carries waters of the Maple River. The Owosso Moraine, a three- to five-mile-wide range of rolling hills 50 to 100 feet high, runs north and south through the county center. These ridges are comprised of sandy soil covering gravel. Overall, much of Gratiot County is loamy soil with wet areas over clay and silt, particularly in the eastern half.

Gratiot County is one of Michigan's most intensively farmed regions with over 80 percent of the land base into active agriculture. Population is small and, therefore, farms are often rented out by landowners who work in Saginaw and Bay City factories. There is some dairy and livestock farming, but most of Gratiot County's acres grow white beans, soybeans, corn, and wheat for cash-crop purposes.

The county is quite dry with only two natural lakes—Half Moon and Madison—both in private ownership. Other lakes are man-made impoundments, also privately owned. The Pine River in the northern part of the county flows northeasterly, and the Maple River, in the southern region, runs westerly. Other watersheds are mostly drainage ditches with little or no adjacent cover for wildlife.

As might be expected, 570-square-mile Gratiot County offers limited hunting lands and opportunity. Only a little more than 10 percent is commercially forested with swamp oak, soft maple, ash, cottonwood, elm, basswood, and aspen being the principal species. Although woods patches exist on farms throughout the county, the best wildlife cover is found along stream bottoms and on two state wildlife areas: Maple River State Game Area and Gratiot-Saginaw State Game Area (*both of which see*).

Public land at these two locations amounts to 12,200 acres (about three percent of the county land base) and does provide fair to good hunting opportunities for deer, squirrels, raccoon, rabbits, grouse, and woodcock. Another 550 acres of Public Access Stamp program lands have been leased from a half-dozen participating farmers. Most of these lands are west of Ithaca near the Montcalm County line. For a free map and descriptions, contact DNR district headquarters in Grand Rapids or the Gratiot-Saginaw field office. Considerate hunters making a polite request can sometimes gain access to additional private lands in this county.

Gratiot County is not noted for huge bucks, but it does produce fairly good hunting (14 percent success) for a light amount of pressure (11 hunters per square mile) except on the public lands where hunting intensity is high during firearm season. Car-deer accidents amount to 200 to 250 animals each year, and the firearm buck kill is one to two deer per square mile. The northern region of the county has the heaviest farming and consequently the lowest deer numbers. Even so, hunters average 25 percent success on bucks and does combined. Eighty-five percent of the county is above the rifle line (M-57) for firearm deer hunting. Hunters below M-57 must use shotguns with slugs or buckshot.

These same public lands get considerable grouse hunting pressure too, but flush rates continue to be reasonably high (3.0 per hour or better in high-cycle years). Woodcock are a game-pouch bonus when found in migrations during mid- to late October. Apparently the worm-rich soils of the eastern county hold them until ground freeze. River bottomlands are also worth checking for grouse and woodcock. Gratiot County pheasants have fallen on hard times; still, a working hunter can find scattered populations. One good place to try might be the Carson City area (southwest portion).

Raccoon hunters do very well in Gratiot County although once again the game areas get the most pressure. Foxes are abundant throughout the county as are rabbits and fox squirrels. Key efforts along lowlands and brushlands adjacent to crop fields for cottontails and try still-hunting along river bottomlands and on farm woodlots for squirrels. A few gray squirrels (and mutant blacks) are shot in Gratiot County each fall. Both Maple River and Gratiot-Saginaw state game areas are likely spots for future wild turkey releases. However, no turkeys are present in Gratiot County at this time.

Best bets for waterfowl are the state lands and jump shooting for mallards and wood ducks (some teal in early season) along the Maple and Pine rivers. Portions of these streams are floatable in high-water years, but use a light canoe and carry waders to make portaging easier.

OTHER SHOOTING OPPORTUNITIES
None known at this time.

FURTHER SOURCES OF HUNTING INFORMATION
1. DNR District Office, State Office Bldg. (350

Ottawa NW), Grand Rapids, Mich. 49503 (616/456-5071).

2. Gratiot-Saginaw Field Office, 23350 South Meridian Road, Brant, Mich. 48614 (517/643-7000 or 517/373-9358).

3. Ithaca Chamber of Commerce, 147 East Center St., Ithaca, Mich. 48847 (517/875-2640).

4. Alma Chamber of Commerce, Box 506, 310 Gratiot, Alma, Mich. 48801 (517/463-5525).

5. St. Louis Chamber of Commerce, 208 North Mill St., St. Louis, Mich. 48880 (517/681-3825).

6. Topographic, county, and lake maps may be ordered from the Michigan United Conservation Clubs. For information, refer to the beginning of this book.

7. Plat books are available for $10 each (add 95 cents if mail ordering) from the Gratiot County Cooperative Extension Services, 204 South Main St., Ithaca, Mich. 48847.

8. Gratiot County ASCS Office, USDA, 125 South Maple St., Ithaca, Mich. 48847 (517/875-3900 or 875-4537).

Also, refer to the following elsewhere in this book:
1. Gratiot-Saginaw State Game Area
2. Maple River State Game Area

Hillsdale County

WITH only about 41,000 people, Hillsdale County, along the Ohio border, is the least-populated county in southern Michigan. No major expressways cut through the rolling farmland with wooded parcels. Hunting is good for deer, rabbits, and squirrels and although public land is limited (about 2,400 acres total), 14 landowners currently have enrolled some 2,700 acres in the Public Access Stamp program. More importantly, Hillsdale County farmers are reasonably amenable to allowing hunters on their land (especially for small game) when they ask first and are considerate.

Overall, the county is gently rolling to moderately hilly, particularly in the northeastern portion (Somerset, Moscow, and Wheatland townships), results of heavy glaciation a few thousand years ago. The county has the rolling or billowy surface, smooth rounded slopes, sandy or gravelly knobs and ridges, numerous lakes and swamp depressions, sandy and gravelly plains, and nearly level clay plains—all characteristic of glacial-origin land.

The southeastern portion features a gently sloping to nearly level clay plain which includes long, narrow winding strips and small areas of wetland. The rest of the county, more diversified, contains a great number of lakes and peat swamps and patches of sandy and gravelly plains pitted by dry depressions, lakes, and swamps. Most of the elevations vary by only a couple hundred feet, yet Bundy Hill in Somerset Township is nearly 500 feet higher than low, southern regions.

Small streams originate in lakes or swamps. Some of them are headwater tributaries to major southern Michigan rivers: the Raisin and Maumee, which flow into Lake Erie, and the St. Joseph, Kalamazoo, and Grand, which run to Lake Michigan. Lakes vary from potholes to long, elongated bodies of water covering 200 to 300 acres. Some have clean shores; others feature swamp and muck.

About 18 percent of the county supports the growth of commercial timber species, principally maple (hard and soft), birch, ash, and elm. Also present are oak, beech, sycamore, aspen, butternut, wild cherry, tulip poplar, even red cedar. Farms are small in size, due partly to the poorer soils of sand and gravel and due also to a poorer economic level than is found elsewhere in southern Michigan.

Livestock rearing is a bigger enterprise than cash-crop farming.

Now, for hunting prospects. The entire county is good for deer. Consider the indicator of car-deer accidents—nearly 300 whitetails die each year in a county lacking major cities and expressways. Consider too that 90 percent plus of hunter's-choice applicants get any-deer tags. About one of every eight hunters kills a buck, a ratio close to the state average. Pressure is light to moderate, about 10 hunters per square mile.

Consider too that Hillsdale County produces big bucks. Of 1,150 all-time trophy Michigan bucks thus far discovered by Commemorative Bucks of Michigan, 34 are Hillsdale County deer. Nine and six of those deer, respectively, were registered in two recent seasons. But the better deer come off private land, and in order to gain access, a hunter will have to meet landowners well before season openers. A good place to try for a December deer might be Hog and Sand creeks, which provide wintering cover. There are found in the northwestern to north-central area.

Public land gets the most pressure. It is limited to Lost Nation State Game Area (which see) between Pittsford and Hillsdale. The Public Access Stamp program lands are mostly in the western row of townships fronting Branch County, which, incidentally also offers good hunting and has the best access enrollment of the nine-county DNR district.

Hillsdale County is closed to Sunday hunting with firearms or dogs, except in the game area.

Fox squirrel populations are good throughout. Here is a challenging game species that is currently underharvested. You'll find bushytails in the game area and in farmland woodlots of oak and hickory when they abut to corn fields. Rabbits are also plentiful. Seek them in openings near brushlands and grasslands or in the wooded fringe around wet lowlands. There is untapped fox hunting potential for reds and a few grays found in southern-tier townships. Raccoon, too, provide good hunting opportunity for both Michigan and nonresident hunters.

Pheasants have fallen on hard times as they have elsewhere in southern Michigan. Better farmland exists in southern townships and here is where best opportunities can be found. Hillsdale used to be a

popular quail hunting county and although there are still scattered numbers, counts are currently low and the season is therefore closed. There are no wild turkeys in this county, and the DNR has no immediate plans to introduce any.

Waterfowl hunting is limited to potholes and stream-jumping on private land or floating the St. Joseph River in the northwestern section. Woodies, mallards, and the odd Canada goose are target species. There are no major lakes to attract large numbers of migrants although hunters might check Hemlock, Long, and Round lakes which feature access. Because Hillsdale County is getting an increasing number of nuisance giant Canada geese, a special late season is in effect north of M-34 and east of M-99 (consult the "Waterfowl Hunting Guide" for full details). LeAnn and Somerset lakes in the northeast corner usually contain Canada geese during mild winters.

No grouse are found in Hillsdale County although the DNR hopes to release some in Lost Nation State Game Area if it can get a hunting closure approved by area residents. Woodcock hunting done incidentally for other species can be fair, especially in late October for migrants.

OTHER SHOOTING OPPORTUNITIES

Hillsdale County Bowmen, 12397 Pulaski Road, Jonesville, Mich. 49250, has shooting facilities open to the public daily on a sometime-fee basis. Those facilities include 28 outdoor pistol stations, 14 indoor centerfire rifle stations, three shotgun handtrap areas, and 40 outdoor archery targets. The club offers both shooting instruction and shooting competition. For details, call 517/524-7171.

Lost Nation State Game Area has pistol, centerfire rifle, and rimfire rifle outdoor stations (two each) open to the public without charge. There is also a shotgun handtrap area. The game area is not staffed; however, DNR personnel at 517/784-3188 can answer questions.

Heritage Muzzleloaders, 8200 Haldron, Jerome, Mich. 49249, allows infrequent use of its range on a sometime-fee basis. Shooting instruction and competitive shooting are also featured. For information, call 517/688-3300.

FURTHER SOURCES OF HUNTING INFORMATION

1. DNR District Headquarters, 3335 Lansing Ave., Jackson, Mich. 49202 (517/784-3188).

2. Waterloo Game Office, Route 3, 13578 Seymour Road, Grass Lake, Mich. 49240 (517/522-4097).

3. Hillsdale County Chamber of Commerce, 65 North Howell St., Hillsdale, Mich. 49242 (517/439-5384).

4. Topographic, county, and lake maps may be ordered from the Michigan United Conservation Clubs. For information, refer to the beginning of this book.

5. Plat books are available from the Hillsdale County Cooperative Extension Services, 3371 Beck Road, Hillsdale, Mich. 49242. The cost is $10 each (add $1.25 if mail ordering).

6. Hillsdale County ASCS Office, USDA, 337 Beck Road, Hillsdale, Mich. 49242 (517/439-1496).

Also, refer to the following elsewhere in this book:
1. Lost Nation State Game Area
2. Hillsdale County Mini-Game Area

Houghton County

ALTHOUGH tucked away in the remote western Upper Peninsula, Houghton County has much to offer hunters. Plenty of public land, unpeopled wilderness beauty, and opportunities for trophy bucks and big bears, plus predators, snowshoe hares, waterfowl, ruffed grouse, and woodcock are reasons why sportsmen might want to look to the Copper Country.

Rugged hills stretch along its backbone, which fingers into Lake Superior as the southern portion of the Keweenaw Peninsula. About 50 miles of Lake Superior to the west and Keweenaw Bay to the east lap Houghton County shores. These two bodies of water are linked by the Portage Canal waterway. Inland lakes abound and many rivers cut across glacial outwash plains, morainic ridges, and exposed bedrock of some of earth's oldest geologic formations.

Nearly half of Houghton County's 659,000 acres (about 1,030 square miles) is open to public hunting. Thes lands include huge blocks of the Ottawa National Forest (which see) in the southern portion, as well as scattered parcels of the Copper Country State Forest (which also see) in northern-half holdings. They further include 116,783 acres of company-owned lands that are presently enrolled in

the Commercial Forest Act program. These properties are located throughout the county. To find them, contact the DNR Forest Management Division, Box 30028, Lansing, Mich. 48909 (517/373-1275), but be sure to include town and range numbers in your request.

A copy of "Michigan County Maps and Outdoor Guide" and a current plat book will also aide in finding these and other places to hunt.

Houghton County has light to moderate numbers of deer. The annual kill is low due to this and slight hunter pressure, about four sportsmen per square mile. They tag less than one buck per square mile for 14 percent success, near the statewide average. Altogether, the five-county DNR district yields from 2,000 to 2,500 bucks each fall, not very many when compared to other districts. Some of these deer, however, are big-bodied, trophy animals. Commemorative Bucks of Michigan currently has identified and added eight Houghton County monster bucks to its all-time list of 1,150 record Michigan deer.

Lakeshore lowlands of cedar near limestone bluffs in the northern county on the Keweenaw Bay side attract wintering deer. So do Sturgeon River bottomlands of hardwoods and cedar. Another popular, southern-county wintering yard is centered at the junction of USFS-204 and Federal Forest

Highway 16. The shipping channel cuts off north and south whitetail migration. The county averages 180 to 200 inches of snow each winter, and so snow is almost always on the ground for all of the firearm deer season. Hunters who can tough the wintry conditions have learned to post deer migration routes along river bottoms and valleys. A patient wait can often result in a fine buck.

The southern county produces more deer. In addition to the yards mentioned, try the western region merging to Ontonagon County for a ruggedly-remote hunt. Southern Houghton County also contains rugged hills covered with hardwoods.

In fact, northern hardwoods of maple-birch constitute most of the commercial-forest types that smother Houghton County to the extent of 82 percent coverage. A whopping 345,200 acres, or two-thirds, is maple-birch. It is followed by 57,500 acres of aspen, 20,900 acres of balsam fir, 17,000 acres of elm-ash-soft maple, 13,500 acres of northern white-cedar, 12,000 each of jack pine and red pine, 10,700 acres of paper birch, and 9,700 acres of black spruce. Smaller amounts of white pine, white spruce, oak-hickory, and tamarack are also represented.

A continuing problem, however, is that over 80 percent of the commercial forest is in maturing growths of sawtimber- or poletimber-size stands. Aggressive cuttings would help most game species to increase in number.

The district yields about 30 to 40 percent (200 to 300 animals) of the annual Upper Peninsula bear harvest, and of the 60 to 70 bruins shot in Houghton County, many are trophy size. Good places to hunt occur nearly everywhere that food (old orchards, chokecherries, acorn drops, and fruits and berries in season) can be found.

There is a good coyote population in the county. These predators, as well as bobcats, are largely underhunted. Only four to eight Houghton County cats are sealed each winter by DNR biologists. Populations of both predators depend a great deal on the availability of snowshoe hares, which are currently somewhat depressed in the district. Gray/black squirrels offer some hunting potential in oaks mixed with conifer, but few hunters take advantage. Limited numbers of raccoon are found along waterways, especially near farming areas.

Good to excellent hunting for flight puddlers and divers occurs at Portage Lake near Chassell. Food patches and other habitat improvements in the 32,000-acre project area of the Sturgeon River Sloughs Wildlife Area (*which see*), between Portage and Otter lakes in Houghton and Baraga counties, attract and hold plenty of Canada geese. Lakes and streams in the southern portion of the county are

also good places to hunt.

Central and southern regions offer good ruffed grouse and woodcock hunting. Try brushy farmland edges south of Houghton and Chassell, aspen slashings and pockets of lowland alder and willow. In northeastern Houghton County many abandoned farms are reverting to willow and other brush, as well as wild apple. These are also good places to try for grouse.

Grouse numbers have fallen off somewhat during the past couple of years. According to hourly flush-rate records, hunter-cooperators averaged only .94 birds during a recent season as compared to 1.70 and 1.55 during seasons of average abundance. Woodcock flush rates for these same years (from oldest to most recent) were 1.30, .27, and .23, indicating perhaps another drop.

OTHER SHOOTING OPPORTUNITIES
None known at this time.

FURTHER SOURCES OF HUNTING INFORMATION
1. DNR District Office, North US-41 (Box 440), Baraga, Mich. 49908 (906/353-6651).
2. DNR Calumet Field Office, M-26, Calumet, Mich. 49913 (906/337-1700).
3. DNR Twin Lakes Field Office, Route 1, Box 234, Toivola, Mich. 49965 (906/288-3321).
4. Forest Supervisor, Ottawa National Forest, East Cloverland Drive, Ironwood, Mich. 49938 (906/932-1330 or 1-800-561-1201 from the U.P.).
5. Ottawa National Forest, Kenton Ranger District, Kenton, Mich. 49943 (906/852-3500).
6. Copper Country Chamber of Commerce, Box 336, Houghton, Mich. 49931 (906/482-5240).
7. Calumet-Laurium Chamber of Commerce, 1197 Calumet Ave., Calumet, Mich. 49913 (906/337-4579).
8. Torch Lake Chamber of Commerce, Box 55, Lake Linden, Mich. 49945 (906/296-0948).
9. Topographic, county, and lake maps may be ordered from the Michigan United Conservation Clubs. For information, refer to the beginning of this book.
10. Plat books are available from the Houghton/Keweenaw County Cooperative Extension Services, 1500 Birch St., Hancock, Mich. 49930. The cost is $8 each (add $1 if mail ordering).
11. Baraga/Houghton/Keweenaw County ASCS Office American Legion Building, L'Anse, Mich. 49946.

Also, refer to the following elsewhere in this book:
1. Copper Country State Forest
2. McLain State Park
3. Ottawa National Forest
4. Sturgeon River Sloughs Wildlife Area

Huron County

CONSIDERING both game populations and hunting opportunity, 828-square-mile Huron County scores reasonably high marks. The deer herd has increased to sizable numbers in recent years, grouse and woodcock hunting is slowly improving, pheasants not only are holding their own but continue to provide fair to good hunting, and good waterfowling exists both along the 90-mile Lake Huron shoreline and on inland crop fields.

One key to abundant game populations is the relatively low number of people living in Huron County (under 40,000 or less than 50 people per square mile). Largest community is Bad Axe, the county seat, with about 3,000 citizens. Another key is farming practices. Although in 1980 fully 91 percent of the land base was farmed (the leading Michigan county in terms of dollar value of crops raised), many of the soils are underlain by limestone-bedrock, sand, and gravel deposits from ice-sheet action during the glacial period several thousand years ago. This means that small scattered portions of farmland which may not be easily cropped allow the encroachment of trees, weeds, and brush—all good wildlife habitat.

Farming practices include both cash-crop (sugar beets, corn, oats, navy beans, soybeans) and livestock (dairy/beef cattle and hogs) enterprises. Set-aside fields also contribute to wildlife habitat.

Originally much of Huron County was covered with white pine and hardwoods along with tamarack and cedar growths in swamp regions. Lumbermen cleared much of the forests, and raging forest fires soon after destroyed the rest. Today roughly 11 percent of Huron County is forested with commercial-timber species. About half is aspen, a rapidly-regenerating tree. The rest is mostly elm-ash-soft maple with some mixed stands of hard maple-birch.

The southern and central parts of the county consist of a gently undulating to hilly moraine. Extending out beyond the moraine toward Saginaw Bay and Lake Huron is a broad, nearly-level till plain. Small streams that transect this till plain drain toward Saginaw Bay and Lake Huron.

Public lands total about 5,000 acres, most of which are open to hunting. They include the Wildlife Bay Wildlife Area and Gagetown and Rush Lake state game areas (all of which see). Also, portions of Port Crescent (544 acres) and Albert Sleeper (680 acres) state parks (both of which see) are open to hunting for those with state park stickers. Further, small pockets of state land are DNR-managed (see under Huron County mini-game areas). About 6,000 acres, enrolled in the Public Access Stamp program by two dozen landowners, are also open to hunting. Most are found in the northeastern quadrant of the county—north of M-142 and east of M-53. For a free directory, contact DNR district headquarters in Imlay City.

Many hunters have found that Huron County farmers are agreeable to letting responsible sportsmen, who ask first, permission to hunt their lands. And these lands are well worth hunting.

Deer hunters meet or exceed the state average of 15 percent success. Huron is a high-kill county for southern Michigan with one to two bucks tagged per square mile. The DNR recently began issuing hunter's-choice permits by lottery when annual car-deer accidents topped 400 animals in a single year. Although that figure has now leveled off, Huron still leads the seven-county DNR district with its grim statistic.

Big bucks live in Huron County. In fact, the state's third-best nontypical whitetail—scoring 165-1/8 Boone and Crockett points—tagged in a recent season was shot here by a Bad Axe hunter. A check of 24 Huron County deer examined by the DNR showed that 10 sported racks of eight points or more. These deer are killed throughout the county although, not surprisingly, many come from

forested dunes along Lake Huron.

A definite drawback is that Huron County is closed to all Sunday hunting except for state lands and for offshore waterfowling on Lake Huron. That closure puts undue pressure on public lands.

Squirrel hunters will find untapped opportunities for foxes (with a few grays and black-phase animals) wherever stands of oaks or hickories can be found. Best bets are isolated farm woodlots and the forest dune belt. Rabbits are fairly plentiful throughout, and grouse hunters can expect to flush 1.0 to 2.0 grouse per hour during a season of average populations. Woodcock hunting, fair throughout lowland areas and aspen edge cover, improves with the appearance of migrant birds from mid-October until November 14, last day of the season.

No major rivers traverse Huron County; consequently raccoon populations are fair at best. There are some good fox hunting opportunities, however, a fact well known by an Ubly-area fox hunters club. There are no wild turkeys in the county and no plans at this point to introduce any.

A recent mail-carrier pheasant survey revealed that an average of 3.7 broods per route was seen. While not especially high, the figure indicates that pheasants do exist in huntable numbers. For best bets, locate set-aside or abandoned farmland that has reverted to weeds, or concentrate on brushlands adjacent to crop fields. Ringneck populations seem to be well scattered.

Excellent Huron County waterfowl hunting shapes up for both local birds and migrants. Mallards and Canada geese are the primary species, but hunter bags also contain ringnecks, teal, scaup, widgeon, baldpates, spoonbills, scoters, buffleheads, and mergansers among others. Some waterfowlers field-hunt with decoys for mallards and geese that disperse daily from the Fish Point refuge in Tuscola County. Others report good hunting offshore, depending upon availability of both wind and flight birds. Moving from east to west, launch sites are located at Harbor Beach, Port Hope, Grindstone City, Port Austin, Port Crescent State Park, Oak Beach (shallow water ramp), Caseville, Filion Road, Bay Port, Pigeon Road, Geiger Road, and Sebewaing. In addition, private businesses have launch sites just south of Geiger Road (Pop's Marina) and at Kilmanagh Road (Bud's and Charlie's marinas).

OTHER SHOOTING OPPORTUNITIES

There are no public shooting opportunities at this time. The Grindstone-Port Hope Sportsmen's Club and the Harbor Beach Gun Club have private shooting ranges for members only.

FURTHER SOURCES OF HUNTING INFORMATION

1. DNR District Office, 715 South Cedar St., Imlay City, Mich. 48444, (313/724-2015).
2. Port Crescent State Park, 1775 Port Austin Road, Port Austin, Mich. 48467 (517/738-8663).
3. Albert Sleeper State Park, 6573 State Park Road, Caseville, Mich. 48725 (517/856-4411).
4. Bad Axe Chamber of Commerce, Box 87, Bad Axe, Mich. 48413 (517/269-7011).
5. Harbor Beach Chamber of Commerce, 132 State St., Harbor Beach, Mich. 48441 (517/479-6450).
6. Pigeon Chamber of Commerce, Box 460, Pigeon, Mich. 48755 (517/453-3531).
7. The Greater Port Austin Area Chamber of

Commerce, Box 274, Port Austin, Mich. 48467 (no phone).

8. Sebewaing Chamber of Commerce, Box 622, Sebewaing, Mich. 48759 (517/883-3000).

9. Topographic, county, and lake maps may be ordered from the Michigan United Conservation Clubs. For information, refer to the beginning of this book.

10. Plat books are available from Huron County Cooperative Extension Services, Court House Bldg., Bad Axe, Mich. 48413. The cost is $10 each (add $1.50 for mail orders).

11. Huron County ASCS Office, USDA, 46 Westland Drive, Bad Axe, Mich. 48413 (517/269-9549).

Also, refer to the following elsewhere in this book:
1. Gagetown State Game Area
2. Huron County mini-game areas
3. Port Crescent State Park
4. Sleeper State Park
5. Rush Lake State Game Area
6. Wildfowl Bay Wildlife Area

Ingham County

DESPITE Lansing and its urban sprawl, 558-square-mile Ingham County offers fair populations of game species and corresponding hunting opportunity on private and limited public lands. The county is a mix of human urban populations and farms, criss-crossed by US-127 and I-96 as well as other busy highways. Traffic accounts for over 400 deer kills annually, which puts Ingham County behind only Calhoun and Jackson (to the south and west) for the nine-county DNR district headquartered at Jackson.

Deer, however, are in fairly good abundance throughout this south-central Michigan county. Buck-hunter success, however, is among the lowest in the state at only five percent. That is largely due to low overall pressure figures of 12 hunters per square mile, since a good share of hunting intensity comes on the 4,300-acre Dansville State Game Area (which see), the only public hunting land in Ingham County. Success ratios increase when antlerless deer are counted in. In a recent hunting season, 76 percent of applicants, mostly private landowners, received hunter's-choice permits. The deer herd appears to be expanding in the eastern portion.

Ingham County might not contribute much to the overall state deer kill, but it does serve up some big farmland bucks with trophy headgear. Commemorative Bucks of Michigan has turned up 14 all-time record Michigan rack deer shot in this county. Four of those were tagged in the 1982 season alone. The best area to kill a trophy buck is farm around Stockbridge in the southeastern corner.

Ingham County features rich loamy soils throughout with a sand and gravel base in the southwestern and southeastern portions, site of formal glacial outwash plains. Gentle rolling farmland is capped with a dozen or so eskers, sinuous ridges containing stratified deposits of gravel and sand drift left by flowing streams beneath glaciers thousands of years ago. Some of these low ridges offer wildlife habitat.

The only major natural lake is Lake Lansing, the former site of good duck and goose hunting. Now it is largely ringed with cottages but does feature a county park with boat access on the western shore. Several smaller, private lakes dot the southeastern part of the county, but most are surrounded by muck soils.

There are two major streams in Ingham County. The Grand River flows northward along the western side, and the Red Cedar River, in the northern portion, runs westerly. These two rivers join at Lansing and then flow out of the county at its northwestern corner. The rivers provide some float hunting and jump shooting opportunities for ducks, but adjacent lands are in solid private ownership.

About half of Ingham County is in active farmland where cash cropping for corn, wheat, soybeans, oats, and alfalfa is the main practice. Portions of these farms feature woodlots and brushlands which offer good hunting when sportsmen are allowed access (for best results, ask well in advance of when you plan to hunt). A major part of that access comes from 10 landowners currently enrolling 2,700 acres of Public Access Stamp program lands. Most of this land is found in southern-tier townships, especially Onondaga and Bunkerfield, with another block in heavily populated Meridian Township. These access lands produce rabbits, squirrels, some deer, and pheasants. For a complete directory, contact the DNR field office at the State Game Farm in Mason or district headquarters in Jackson.

Raccoon and red fox populations are moderate to good throughout Ingham County, but hunting pressure, especially for raccoon, runs quite high. There are fair to good numbers of fox squirrels and rabbits, especially in the Williamston area, according to the chamber of commerce there. Find mast-producing woodlots (oak, hickory, butternut) adjacent to crop fields for best squirrel hunting success. Rabbits like edge openings around thick-growth areas (brushlands, dense grasslands, thickets, and wet bottomlands).

Ingham County produces pockets of good pheasant hunting too, especially in the eastern portion, but hunters will have to key proper habitat (brushy areas, including heavy weed fields near croplands) and then hunt hard for a two-cock limit. Wild turkeys recently released at the Rose Lake Wildlife Research Area in Clinton County may someday spread south to provide hunting opportunity for Ingham County gobbler hunters. There are no turkeys available now, and the DNR has no immediate plans to introduce them.

Because Ingham County is quite dry, woodcock populations are very low. This situation also makes for highly limited duck hunting; however, resident flocks of nuisance Canada geese appear to be on the increase. Currently they provide extended-season opportunities for sportsmen willing to put in the time to track flight patterns and then knock on doors for permission to hunt feed fields. Check the "Waterfowl Hunting Guide" for dates and regulations.

More good news. Ingham County is home to huntable populations of ruffed grouse. Cooperating sportsmen report hourly flush rates of 1.7 to 2.0 during medium- to high-population years. Pressure is moderate to high. Overall, this county is worth looking into for small game and deer hunting opportunities.

OTHER SHOOTING OPPORTUNITIES

The Capitol City Rifle Club, 6305 Skyline Drive, East Lansing, Mich. 48823, has outdoor shooting facilities open to the public on a sometime-fee basis. Shooting stations include 36 pistol, 10 centerfire rifle, and 30 rimfire rifle. There is one shotgun trap field and one handtrap area. The club offers shooting instruction, competitive shooting, and hunter certification courses. Call 517/332-6652 for more information.

The DNR has three outdoor stations each for rifle centerfire and rimfire practice at the Dansville State Game Area. There is no fee for using the range, open daily. Contact DNR officials at the State Game Farm, 1219 Hawley Road, Mason, Mich. 48854 (517/676-4600) if you have questions.

Hogsback Archery Range is commercially-owned and open to the public on a fee basis. The location is 5654 Harper Road, Holt, Mich. 48842. Call 517/699-2439 for information. Facilities include 28 outdoor targets; shooting instruction is offered.

An Ingham County shooting preserve offers extended-season sport for those who become members. Hunter's Hollow, 740 Plains Road in Veevay Township near Mason, has hunting for pheasants, quail, and chukar partridge on its 475 acres. For more information, call Elwynn Collar at 517/676-1323.

FURTHER SOURCES OF HUNTING INFORMATION

1. DNR District Office, 3335 Lansing Ave., Jackson, Mich. 49202 (517/784-3188).

2. Mason State Game Farm Field Office, 1219 Hawley Road, Mason, Mich. 48854 (517/676-4600).

3. Mason Area Chamber of Commerce, 148 East Ash St., Mason, Mich. 48854 (517/676-1046).

4. Williamston Area Chamber of Commerce, Box 53, Williamston, Mich. 48895 (no telephone listed).

5. Lansing Regional Chamber of Commerce, Box 14030, 510 West Washtenaw, Lansing, Mich. 48901 (517/487-6340).

6. Leslie Chamber of Commerce, 144 South Main St., Leslie, Mich. 49251 (517/589-9510).

7. Topographic, county, and lake maps may be ordered from the Michigan United Conservation Clubs. For information, refer to the beginning of this book.

8. Plat books are available for $10 each (add $1.50 if ordering by Mail) from the Ingham County Register of Deeds, South Jefferson St., County Courthouse Bldg., Mason, Mich. 48854.

9. Ingham County ASCS Office, USDA, 313 North St., Mason, Mich. 48854 (517/676-4644).

Also, refer to the following elsewhere in this book:

1. Dansville State Game Area

Ionia County

IONIA County in west-central Lower Michigan has level to gently rolling land, the result of near-total glaciation some 12,000 years ago. Concentric patterns of moraines, caused from melting glacial till, extend from northeast to southwest. They run from a quarter-mile to one-and-a-half miles wide and are 10 to 40 feet high. The glacier carved out a few lakes in the western portion—namely Odessa, Morrison, Woodward, and Long (all have public access)—but for the most part, Ionia County is short on lakes. A glacial trench between Matherton and Saranac once connected old Lake Saginaw and Chicago. Today it forms the channel for the Grand and Maple rivers.

Soils are mostly sandy loam with some pockets of wet, organic loam that together produce good crops as well as good natural food for wildlife. Eighty percent of Ionia County is farmed, much of it intensively so (especially south of the Grand River) for cash-crop corn, soybeans, and white beans. Fencerow-to-fencerow farming is the norm; creeks are mostly drain cuts without cover for wildlife. Many of the farms support dairy cattle and livestock operations; others specialize in fruit (mostly apples, along with raspberries, strawberries, some pears, and peaches). Sandy soils of the northwest portion are good for potato growing. Small areas of organic soils in the central region are used to grow mint,

celery, and other vegetables. There are occasional deer-damage complaints throughout Ionia County although deer numbers seem to have fallen off after all-time highs in recent years. Still, this is a good deer county.

Only 10 percent of the 575-square-mile county is in commercial timber species, and much of this is in the extreme northern portion. However, there are scattered woodlots throughout. About half of the wooded cover type is hard maple and birch. Other northern and lowland hardwoods mixed with aspen constitute the rest. Consequently, the better hunting is in the northern region.

Hunting opportunity on state land is limited to just under 10,000 acres on one recreation area (must have a state-park access sticker) and portions of three state game areas. Consequently, these areas get pressured. Ionia County farmers, however, are good about granting access to considerate sportsmen who ask first. In addition, about 4,800 acres of Public Access Stamp program lands are currently leased from over two dozen farmers. These lands are well scattered with pockets in Ronald Township (north-central), on both sides of the Grand River, and near Clarksville. DNR personnel at district headquarters in Grand Rapids or at the Flat River State Game Area (which see) have free maps and descriptions for the asking.

At 14 percent, buck-hunter success runs a little under the state average. Pressure is moderate to high with about 20 hunters (shotguns only allowed) per square mile. They take one to two bucks per square mile, including some very large-antlered animals. Ionia ranks among the highest counties in Michigan for all-time big deer tagged. According to Commemorative Bucks of Michigan, 24 Ionia County deer have made the Michigan record book. Best deer hunting is found in northern and eastern portions along the Grand River.

Holders of hunter's-choice permits average 30 percent success (bucks and does combined). Annual car-deer accidents have run 400 or more.

The Flat River State Game Area (which see) received 26 Missouri wild turkeys in 1984. If these birds increase as expected, they should provide future hunting opportunity. Another likely site for future releases is the Portland State Game Area (which see) north of Muir. Pheasant populations in Ionia County are spotty with best bets coming north of the Grand River due to more fallow fields and wild grasslands there. Squirrel and rabbit populations are good to excellent. Try isolated farm woodlots and stream bottomlands for best results. Fair to good woodcock and grouse hunting opportunities exist, especially in the northern half, although aspen is in short supply at little more than 4,000 acres county-wide. Hunting pressure on these two species is moderate.

Raccoon are plentiful. Try wooded river bottomlands adjacent to corn fields. Ionia County has no shortage of fox either. Duck hunters are limited due to a lack of water. Best bets include jump-shooting for mallards and wood ducks along streams or float-tripping on the Flat (in the game area or from Belding south) and Grand rivers. As mentioned, there is public access to the bigger lakes where one might try layout hunting. The best of these is Long Lake east of Belding. This is a shallow lake with plenty of weed beds. If the state returns to a late season for certain diving duck species, Long Lake will probably be included.

OTHER SHOOTING OPPORTUNITIES

The Ionia Fish and Hunt Club, Bertha Brock Park,

Ionia, Mich. 48846 (616/527-9855), has indoor pistol and rimfire rifle stations open to the public at limited times on a fee basis. The club also features trap and skeet fields and a shotgun handtrap area. Shooting instruction and competitive shooting are offered too.

The Oakhill Gun Club on Pline Road in Lyons (517/647-7303) has three shotgun trap fields open to the public at certain times without change. The club offers competitive shooting as well as hunter certification classes.

FURTHER SOURCES OF HUNTING INFORMATION

1. DNR District Office, State Office Bldg. (350 Ottawa NW), Grand Rapids, Mich. 49503 (616/456-5071).

2. Flat River State Game Area, Route 2, 6640 Long Lake, Belding, Mich. 48809 (616/794-3658).

3. Ionia Recreation Area, 2132 West Riverside Drive, Route 4, Ionia, Mich. 48846 (616/527-3750).

4. Ionia Chamber of Commerce, 428 West Washington St., Ionia, Mich. 48846 (616/527-2560).

5. Portland Area Chamber of Commerce, 1419 East Grand River, Portland, Mich. 48875 (517/647-2332).

6. Belding Area Chamber of Commerce, 120 Covered Village, Belding, Mich. 48809 (616/794-2210).

7. Lake Odessa Chamber of Commerce, Box 492, Lake Odessa, Mich. 48849 (616/374-7181).

8. Topographic, county, and lake maps may be ordered from the Michigan United Conservation Clubs. For information, refer to the beginning of this book.

9. County plat books are available for $8.50 (add $1.50 if mail ordering) from the Ionia County Cooperative Extension Services, 110 East Washington St., Ionia, Mich. 48846.

10. Ionia County ASCS, USDA, 1200 South State Road, Ionia, Mich. 48846 (616/527-2098).

Also, refer to the following elsewhere in this book:
1. Flat River State Game Area
2. Ionia Recreation Area
3. Lowell State Game Area
4. Portland State Game Area
5. Ionia County Mini-Game Area

Iosco County

FRONTING Lake Huron in northeastern Lower Michigan is 563-square-mile Iosco County. Large portions are sandy-soiled but in the southern region at least have become reasonably productive for alfalfa, corn, soybeans, and potatoes. Knolls and ridges throughout contain gravel deposits, the result of glaciation thousands of years ago. Underground veins along Lake Huron, especially in the Alabaster area, contain vast deposits of gypsum.

The famed Au Sable River winds its way across the top of Iosco County en route to Lake Huron at Oscoda. Five Channel, Cooke, and Foote dams make for impoundments that offer early-season duck hunting for puddlers and late-season action for divers. Not many waterfowlers take advantage of

this resource. A second water system involves an intricate network of small streams that drain the central portion of the county. They empty into Tawas Lake whose overflow is the Tawas River, which makes a short run before emptying into Tawas Bay (Lake Huron). The southern region is drained by the Au Gres River system whose East Branch discharges into Lake Huron south of Alabaster (also called Whitney Drain) at the Singing Bridge. The Au Gres River itself continues southerly through Arenac County, exiting the land at Au Gres.

Since Iosco County soils are sandy and dry, these waterways and clusters of lakes in the central and northwestern regions are important to hunters. Deer, grouse, woodcock, raccoon, squirrels, bear, and hares use mixed habitats along these flows.

Much of northern Iosco County falls into the Huron-Manistee National Forest (*which see*), all open to hunting. Federal ownership is about 103,000 acres, or 29 percent of the land base. In addition, northeastern and southern portions are part of the Au Sable State Forest (*which also see*). About seven percent, or 25,000 acres, of Iosco County is thus state land, also open to hunting.

The farm belt parallels north-south-running M-65, through Whittemore and Hale, and includes most of Iosco County south of M-55. This farmland is mixed with aspen and lowland hardwoods. The lakes region northwest of Hale is mostly recreational land, privately-owned and difficult to gain access to. That is generally true of the farmland as well. Several private hunting clubs are located west of Alabaster and again west of US-23 between East Tawas and Oscoda.

Roughly two-thirds of Iosco County is timbered with commercial-forest species in a diverse mix that helps make this county a game producer. Jack pine and red pine with a little more than 40,000 acres each head the list. They are followed by aspen (39,500 acres), maple-birch (33,900 acres), oak-hickory (26,900 acres), northern white cedar (19,000 acres), elm-ash-soft maple (9,200 acres), paper birch (4,500 acres), and tamarack (4,100 acres). Smaller amounts of black spruce, white pine, and balsam fir also appear.

A large amount of conifer cover borders the Au Sable River drainage and provides good habitat for black bear and wintering yards for deer. The southern side of the river between Loud Dam and Cooke ponds is heavy with green growth. Another dense area containing bear and wintering deer is Seven-Mile Swamp west of Van Ettan Lake. North and west of this swamp are a series of oak ridges which make for good deer hunting and fair squirrel hunting during falls of heavy mast production.

This northern portion of Iosco County also features many pine plantations which afford good snowshoe-hare hunting. Cutover areas of aspen and young hardwoods growing back also produce hares. The central region north of M-55 is largely mixed oak and jack pine. Farther south in the farm belt there are mixed stands of aspen, maple-birch, and oak. State land west of Alabaster contains large blocks of swamp hardwoods and is a good area for hares too.

Iosco is a good deer county although the best hunting occurs on private land. Five-year DNR surveys gathered for this book indicate that deer numbers are exceptionally high in Baldwin, Wilbur, and Au Sable townships. Overall pressure is fairly intense (about 30 hunters per square mile), but buck-hunting success runs about 20 percent—a few points above the state average—or five antlered deer per square mile. Attesting to a large deer herd are (1) numerous crop-damage complaints from the farm belt, (2) the current arrangement of portions of six hunter's-choice areas within county boundaries, and (3) an annual car-deer accident rate exceeding 300 animals, highest (along with Ogemaw, the next county west) of the 21 northernmost counties in the Lower Peninsula.

Iosco County has a fairly good population of wild turkeys, which appear to be spreading throughout the farming region (especially during winter) although the season is currently closed below M-55. One good concentration point is the Sand Lake area. Another is north and west of Oscoda, especially along those oak ridges west of Seven-Mile Swamp.

Turkeys also appear to be building in the mixed oak-jack pine forests north and west of Tawas Lake.

Fox-squirrel hunting is good in oak woodlots abutting farm fields in the southern portion. For grays/blacks, try mixed northern-county stands of oaks and pines. After several poor hunting years snowshoe hares appear to be rebounding. Try plantations and cutover areas in the northern region. For cottontails, hunt along brushlands and grasslands in the farming belt. Red-fox numbers are moderate to high in farmland habitat and offer an underused resource. Coyotes also appear to be increasing, especially in northern jack-pine areas. For best raccoon hunting, try along Au Gres River tributaries and crop fields fringed with woods.

I have enjoyed exceptional ruffed-grouse hunting in the Sand Lake and National City regions even though Iosco is not rated as a good grouse county. Flush rates of under two grouse per hour are the norm. On the other hand, woodcock hunting can be superb when flight birds drop into aspen slashings and moist-soil alder covers along drainages. Don't overlook sumac-covered knolls and hillsides in this county either, especially during wet falls.

Iosco offers good waterfowl hunting for a northern Michigan county. In addition to the Au Sable River impoundments already mentioned, consider shallow, marshy Tawas Lake (especially on the northern end) for early-season mallards, teal, and black ducks and for late-season divers. A big blow on Lake Huron tends to stack up ducks both here and on Van Ettan Lake. Further, a growing number of Canada geese in the Tawas area often move into Tawas Lake and then disperse to feed on nearby crops. And there is layout shooting potential in Tawas Bay offshore from city limits and off Tawas Point State Park.

OTHER SHOOTING OPPORTUNITIES

Iosco County sportsmen have at least two shooting ranges where they can sight in and practice firing their weapons. The Iosco Sportsmen Club, Inc., 1600 North US-23 in East Tawas, has firearm and archery facilities open to the public for fees. They include one outdoor station each for centerfire and rimfire rifle, a trap field, and outdoor archery targets. Shooting competition is featured. For details, call 517/362-5184.

Wolverine Range and Guns, Inc., 5676 F-41 in Oscoda, is a commercial enterprise with eight indoor pistol stations and six indoor rimfire-rifle stations open for fee use. Shooting instruction and competitive shooting are offered along with state hunter-education programs. For information, call 517/739-3131.

FURTHER SOURCES OF HUNTING INFORMATION

1. DNR District Office, 191 South Mount Tom Road (M-33), Mio, Mich. 48647 (517/826-3211).

2. Oscoda-Au Sable Chamber of Commerce, 100 West Michigan, Oscoda, Mich. 48750 (517/739-7322).

3. Tawas Area Chamber of Commerce, Box 608, Tawas City, Mich. 48763 (517/362-8643).

4. Tawas Ranger District, Forest Service, USDA, East Tawas, Mich. 48730 (517/362-4477).

4. Topographic, county, and lake maps may be ordered from the Michigan United Conservation Clubs. For information, refer to the beginning of this book.

Iron County

IRON County in the western Upper Peninsula offers tremendous hunting variety and opportunity. Low hunting pressure; plenty of remote, wilderness area to roam; over 475,000 acres open to public hunting; and good populations of deer, bear, hares, coyotes, ruffed grouse, and woodcock are hunter attractions.

Iron County produces huge, trophy bucks for veteran sportsmen who know how and where to find them. Commemorative Bucks of Michigan lists 47 all-time, record-book deer as Iron County animals from its master list of 1,150 Michigan whitetails. That figure puts Iron in the No. 5 spot among the 83 counties in the state. More on deer and other hunting opportunities in a moment.

About 1,200 square miles, or 766,000 acres, lie within Iron County's boundaries. Much of the western region, about 165,000 acres, is Ottawa National Forest land (*which see*). Eastern-county scattered holdings of the Copper Country State Forest (*which also see*) total 84,000 acres. When added to 226,000 acres of private land currently enrolled in the Commercial Forest Act (CFA) program, over 60 percent of the land base is open to public hunting. To get legal descriptions of these private lands, which are mostly unposted, contact DNR Forest Management Division, Box 30028, Lansing, Mich. 48909 (517/373-1275). Be sure to offer town and range numbers of the area you wish to hunt. Armed with your "Michigan County Maps and Outdoor Guide," as well as a current plat book, you should be able to find plenty of unpressured hunting spots.

A thin covering of glacial drift lies over Iron County preglacial rock formations, and surface features show the relief characteristic of the glacial action itself. The general effect is that of a high plain, including broadly rolling hills, depressions, and valleys, locally interrupted by sharply rising, rounded hills and rock outcroppings, together with many scattered swamps and some 200 lakes. For the most part, wet areas occupy depressions and old glacial valleys and contribute to about 20 percent of the land mass. Small rivers and streams are headwaters of the Menominee River, which drains about 4,100 square miles in Michigan and Wisconsin before emptying into Green Bay in Menominee County.

The greater part of Iron County lies at an elevation ranging from 1,500 to 1,700 feet above sea level or 900 to 1,100 feet above the level of Lake Superior. A plains south and east of Crystal Falls averages about 1,350 feet whereas Sheridan Hill, southwest of Iron River, reaches a height of 1,840 feet.

Nearly 90 percent of Iron County is covered with various types of commercial forest. Led by 294,100 acres of maple-birch (northern hardwoods), the cover types include 149,800 acres of aspen, 80,600 acres of balsam fir, 36,000 acres of black spruce, 23,800 acres of paper birch, 14,100 acres of white pine, 7,200 acres of jack pine, 6,500 acres of red pine, 6,700 acres of white spruce, and 6,900 acres of elm-ash-soft maple.

Deer hunting is good. It is no secret that the three-county DNR district (Menominee and Dickinson counties are included with Iron County) yields some 40 percent of the annual Upper Peninsula whitetail killed (includes both sexes since the district is the only one of four in the U.P. where antlerless hunting, by permit, is allowed) although only 19 percent of the land base is found here. During some autumns 60 to 70 percent of the U.P. archery kill also occurs in the district. In Iron County about 55 to 60 percent of the bucks tagged are yearling animals (one-and-a-half years old); however, during a recent season 12 percent were three years of age or older. From a 1972 low, deer have increased steadily and now appear to be stabilized in good numbers. Iron County hunters exert low overall pressure (about seven hunters per square mile) during the firearm season. They kill one to two bucks per square mile for a success ratio of about 25 percent.

Northern portions that extend into Houghton and Baraga counties feature poor access but pure wilderness hunting. That is where wildlife biologists suggest that inquiring hunters, who are up to the rigors of a remote hunt, seek big bucks. A large portion of the northeastern region is owned by American Can Company and since it is CFA-enrolled land, it may be hunted. The region is mostly northern hardwoods with bogs, swamps, and creek bottoms featuring dense growths of black spruce. Big bucks frequenting the fringe of these deep-woods areas are pushed into them by hunters.

Western Iron County has northern hardwoods—the largest forest in the western U.P.—mixed with swamp conifers and some hemlock. The northern portion contains a few oaks. In addition to deer and bear, the area contains fishers and a few pine martens (both protected), which prefer the dense cloak of conifer cover.

Late-season hunters who can tolerate snows and cold weather can kill a buck along migrating routes (valleys and river bottoms) en route to wintering deer yards. In eastern Iron County these are found on state forest lands from the Hemlock River north beyond the Porter and Cable lakes region, dense swamplands on the northern side of the Michigamme Reservoir, and around Peavy Lake. In western Iron County try national forest lands around Perch Lake, north and west of Paint Lake, south of Golden Lake, and between Hagerman and Brule lakes.

The bear kill in District 2 is currently running about 120 animals each fall, and, over the past few years, includes several bow-killed trophies. Apple trees, chokecherries, and ridges containing mast trees are best places to hunt. Try in the Crystal Falls and Amasa area of the eastern county and in the LaCross-Pathic Lake area of the western county. Limited roads and access throughout much of Iron County make it tough for dog hunters, and so baiters have the most success. About 70 percent of the annual bear kill occurs in September.

Bobcat hunters score in many of the deep-woods swamps where trophy bucks and bear are found. DNR district biologists have sealed from 52 to 101 cats during each of the past five seasons. Raccoon-hunting opportunities are pretty much limited to waterways near farm fields. Coyotes, however, seem to be everywhere and offer underutilized potential. Both fox and gray/black squirrels are found in Iron County hardwoods containing mast but not in large concentrations. Try oaks in the southeastern region west of the Brule River from Florence to Penola.

The Penola Goose Area utilizes old sharptail management grounds to provide openings for planting rye and clover, which will attract geese. The Peavy Backwaters, Michigamme Reservoir, and Paint River areas all contain opportunities for hunting geese, local puddlers, and migrant divers. In the western county, Perch Lake is the best waterfowling bet. Early-season floats on the Net and Paint rivers can be productive as can Chicagon Slough north of Lake Emily, Camp 5 and Camp 6 creeks in southeastern Iron County, and beaver floodings throughout.

A ruffed-grouse management area in eastern Iron County has helped serve as a model for producing more grouse throughout the state. Biologists have experimented with cutting mature forests—mostly aspen—along typelines instead of squares or rectangles. The practice provides more edge not only for grouse but for hares, deer, and woodcock. The high frequency of aspen, especially in the eastern county, produces good to excellent grouse and woodcock habitat, and it does not appear that hunting pressure has affected the birds to any extent at this writing.

One underhunted area is west of Peavy Pond and north of the Brule River in T41 and 42N and R31 and 32W. In addition to grouse management on state lands, at least two timber companies have sought DNR advice on managing their forestlands for wildlife as well as wood. Wisconsin Electric in the southern county and American Can Company near Amasa are the two. Both have lands enrolled in the CFA.

According to hourly flush-rate records compiled by hunter-cooperators, Iron County yielded averages of 1.97, 3.18, and 1.30 during three years we randomly checked. Try old logging roads, forest areas with mast, fruit-bearing shrubs and trees, cutover areas of aspen that have grown back to 15 to 20 feet, lowland edges, and brushlands containing hazel. Several hunter walking trails are maintained for openings and seeded to clover and other grouse foods. Here are the names and locations of those

found in Iron County:
Way Dam—T43N R31W, Section 14
Mansifled—T43N R31W, Section 19
Camp Five—T42N R31W, Section 24.
Buck Lake—T45N, R32W, Section 31.
Lake Ellen—T44N R31W, Section 35.
Skunk Creek—T42N R28W, Section 14, 15.
DNR wildlife biologists and foresters can also help you to pinpoint these areas.

Those same hunter-cooperator records revealed average hourly flush rates of 1.50, 1.32, and 1.99 for woodcock. These are mostly local birds that eventually migrate south through Wisconsin or drift eastward into Dickinson County when worming grounds freeze. This will begin in upland areas in early October and extend to lowland covers late in the month or in November. If you are coming to Iron County to hunt woodcock, it is best to do so before October 20.

OTHER SHOOTING OPPORTUNITIES

Smoky Lake Reserve, 1 Lake St., Box 100, Phelps, Wis. 54554, is a 240-acre hunting preserve located in Stambaugh Township on the Wisconsin state line 17 miles due west of Iron River. Members may shoot mallards and train their dogs. For information, contact P.C. Christiansen at 715/545-2333.

There are two Iron County shooting ranges open to the public. The Hiawatha Gun Club in the Camp Gibbs Recreation Area near Iron River allows use of its two trap fields for fees. Shooting instruction and competitive shooting are also featured. Call 906/265-2451 for details.

Ojibway Archers has 44 indoor/outdoor archery targets also in the Camp Gibbs Recreation Area for use on a sometime-fee basis. Shooting instruction and competitive shooting are likewise offered. For information, call 906/265-2280.

FURTHER SOURCES OF HUNTING INFORMATION

1. DNR District Office, US-2 West (Box 300), Crystal Falls, Mich. 49920 (906/875-6622).
2. Forest Supervisor, Ottawa National Forest, East Cloverland Drive, Ironwood, Mich. 49938 (906/932-1330 or 1-800-561-1201 from the Upper Peninsula).
3. Ottawa National Forest, Iron River Ranger District, Iron River, Mich. 49935 (906/265-5139).
4. Iron County Chamber of Commerce, 1 East Genesee St., Iron River, Mich. 49935 (906/265-3822).
5. Iron County Chamber of Commerce, Box 68, Crystal Falls, Mich. 49920 (906/875-4454).
6. Topographic, county, and lake maps may be ordered from the Michigan United Conservation Clubs. For information, refer to the beginning of this book.
7. Plat books are available from the Iron County Cooperative Extension Services, Iron County Courthouse Annex, Crystal Falls, Mich. 49920. The cost is $12 (add $1.50 if mail ordering).
8. Dickinson/Iron County ASCS Office, 639 Industrial Park Drive, Iron Mountain, Mich. 49801.
Also, refer to the following elsewhere in this book:
1. Copper Country State Forest
2. Ottawa National Forest

Isabella County

ISABELLA County, located in the center of the Lower Peninsula, contains 572 square miles and is 24 miles square. This is a game-producing county of mixed agricultural lands and forests, but a major drawback is the lack of public land. Only 1,878 acres, or about .5 percent of the land base, is state-owned. Further, less than 600 acres of Public Access Stamp program land is open to hunting through just two landowners, both in Rolland Township (southwestern corner).

Yet Isabella County farmers are amenable to letting considerate, responsible sportsmen on their land when the hunters ask first. If allowed access, hunters will find good numbers of deer along with grouse, pheasants, rabbits, squirrels, and woodcock in their proper habitats.

The surface features of Isabella County are of glacial origin. Principal divisions occur in belts extending in a general north and south direction. The eastern part of the county lies in the lake plain adjoining Saginaw Bay. The central belt is mainly gently rolling upland. The western part is more diversified—gently rolling or hilly uplands associated with smooth outwash plains.

Most of the county is in the drainage basin of the Chippewa River, which is near its headwaters and is therefore not a very big stream. The southwestern part is drained by the headwaters of the Pine River. River flow is uniform thanks to a fairly rapid fall. These two rivers flow easterly and finally join the Tittabawassee River at Midland. Eventually, they empty into Saginaw Bay and Lake Huron.

The elevations of the lake plain reach a peak of about 780 feet above sea level (200 feet above the level of Lake Huron). The central plains rise from this elevation to a general maximum height of about 900 feet in their western part. The western portion of the county is higher yet, featuring an elevation of about 1,200 feet in the northwestern corner.

When Isabella County was first settled, dense stands of hardwoods grew on its heavier soils and pine covered the sandy-soiled regions. Today about 25 percent of the county is forested with commercial-timber species. Because nearly half is aspen in varying age classes, Isabella County produces good numbers of game (deer, grouse, rabbits) that depend upon forest regeneration for growth. Maple-birch is the second most common type, followed by equal amounts of oak-hickory and ash-elm-soft maple. In addition, the county supports growths of northern white cedar and red pine.

The southeastern portion of Isabella County is heavily farmed yet contains wooded portions. The Rosebush and Coleman regions are still good pheasant-hunting locations. So is the triangle formed by connecting Winn, Shepherd, and Mount Pleasant. East of Mount Pleasant, land along the Chippewa River for several miles both north and south is largely aspen with gray dogwood understory. Best deer hunting occurs west of Winn Road as this area is a prime mixture of farmland and forest. It also contains good fox numbers as well as plenty of raccoon along drainages. Grouse hunting is fair to good here, and flight woodcock find it to their liking. Best bet for fox squirrels is in scattered oak woodlots adjacent to cultivated fields. The northwestern corner of the county runs heavily to oak woods.

Buck-kill success averages 20 percent or higher in Isabella County. With the exception of Bay County, hunter numbers (about 14 per square mile) are lowest of the eight-county DNR district headquartered at Clare. This is a reflection of the lack of public lands open to hunting. Lack of pressure holds the buck kill to one or two animals per square mile. Yet proof of high deer numbers is the annual grim statistic of 300-plus animals killed by cars (.56 deer killed per square mile during a recent year). This is quite high when one considers that Isabella County contains only 54,000 people, nearly half of whom reside in Mount Pleasant.

During a recent firearm season 980 hunter's-choice permit holders shot an estimated 784 deer. Farming is intensive within this unit, and there have been deer-damage complaints. December hunters might want to look to the eastern portion as deer winter there.

At this time there is no wild-turkey hunting in Isabella County, but that may change rather soon. A flock of 35 birds released in central Clare County (to the north of Isabella County) expanded to 500 to 600 within five years and now provides hunting opportunity. About 50 turkeys recently translocated from the Mio district to northwestern Isabella County are expected to do equally well.

Annual grouse flush rates as compiled by hunter-cooperators have ranged from 1.65 to 4.27 birds per hour, depending upon local production. Woodcock flush rates have varied from 1.31 to 2.24. As mentioned, Isabella County contains excellent dispersal of aspen in varying age classes and therefore produces good numbers of grouse and woodcock.

There is some local production of mallards, teal, wood ducks, and Canada geese; and enterprising waterfowlers can jump-shoot along small drainages, decoy-hunt on scattered lakes throughout the county, or float the Chippewa River. Float hunters should be careful to get permission, however, before trespassing on private land. Also, the shallow eastern end of Stevenson Lake provides some duck-hunting opportunity.

No one knows how many pheasants are found in Isabella County, but hunters who cover abandoned farms or even active ones containing set-aside ground and brushlands do surprisingly well on ringnecks. Key to a two-bird limit is hunter access. In short, if you can get on the land in Isabella County, you may be well rewarded with just about any game bird or animal you seek. I have personally proved this to my own satisfaction in the Weidman and Oil City regions.

OTHER SHOOTING OPPORTUNITIES

Hunters have at least two ranges where they can practice shooting. The Isabella County Sportsmen's

Club, 2980 West Millbrook Road in Mount Pleasant, does not charge for use of its outdoor pistol, centerfire rifle (10 stations each), rimfire rifle (six stations), archery targets (15), two shotgun handtrap areas, or trap field. In addition, the club offers both competitive shooting and state hunter-education programs. Call 517/866-2264 for details.

The Chippewa Archery Shop, 5598 South Mission Road, also in Mount Pleasant, has a commercial range open to the public for occasional fees. Both shooting instruction and competitive shooting are featured. For information, call 517/773-9895.

FURTHER SOURCES OF HUNTING INFORMATION

1. DNR District Headquarters, 501 Hemlock St., Clare, Mich. 48617 (517/386-7991).

2. Mount Pleasant Area Chamber of Commerce, 300 East Broadway, Mount Pleasant, Mich. 48858 (517/772-2396).

3. Topographic, county, and lake maps may be ordered from the Michigan United Conservation Clubs. For information, refer to the beginning of this book.

4. Plat books are available from the Isabella County Cooperative Extension Services office, 200 North Main St., Mount Pleasant, Mich. 48858. The cost is $8 each (add $1.50 if mail ordering).

5. Isabella County ASCS Office, 200 North Main St., Mount Pleasant, Mich. 48858 (517/772-5927).

Jackson County

JACKSON County, located in the south-central part of the Lower Peninsula, is an excellent hunting county for downstate Michigan. Over 14,000 acres of public land in the Sharonville State Game Area and the Waterloo Recreation Area (*both of which see*) may be hunted. Also, over 3,800 acres—mostly in the northwestern region—are enrolled in the Public Access Stamp program by 16 farmers (directories are available from the district office in Jackson and from the staffed Waterloo Recreation Area). About 55 percent of Jackson County is in active farmland for cash crop, dairying, and other agricultural enterprises. Many of the landowners are receptive to a considerate request to hunt from responsible sportsmen.

And Jackson County is well worth looking at. Deer numbers are high, as evidenced by the average annual road kill of more than 600 animals, second highest in the state (behind Kent County). Grouse hunting is generally good and there is ample opportunity for raccoon, fox, squirrels, rabbits, ducks, and geese. Twenty-two percent of the county is commercially forested with oak-hickory, elm-ash-soft maple, and hard maple-birch species. And there are considerable brushlands and river bottomlands of lowland hardwoods. About eight percent of the land base is idle, some in the form of abandoned farms.

Most of the topographic features are the result of erosion and deposition during the Wisconsin glaciation period of 8,000 to 12,000 years ago. When the ice melted, a mantle of glacial drift was left on beds of sandstone, limestone, and bedrock. This glacial drift varies in thickness and forms present-day outwash plains, moraines, till plains, and gravel ridges called eskers. Gently rolling to very steep is the Kalamazoo Moraine, which runs east and west through the northern half of the county. Other moraines in the southwestern and extreme southeastern parts are generally rolling.

Rolling till plains are found in the western and northeastern portions, and a large, rolling outwash plain lies toward the southeast. The Grand, Portage, Raisin, and North and South branches of the Kalamazoo are rivers flowing through valleys cut by much larger glacial rivers in the past. Many of the 700 lakes in Jackson County (varying in size from potholes of three acres to some beyond 800 acres) are glacial in origin.

The Grand River drains all but the southwestern and southeastern parts of the county. It begins in a marsh southwest of Grand Lake and flows northerly until it leaves the county in Tompkins Township. Major tributaries include the Portage River, Sandstone Creek, and Spring Brook. The North and South branches of the Kalamazoo drain the southwestern part of the county. These streams also flow to the north. The River Raisin has its source in Novell Township and flows easterly to Washtenaw County and eventually to Lake Erie.

These rivers provide excellent opportunities for float hunters who wish to try for ducks, geese, squirrels, and even the chance at a deer. However, nearly all the land along river routes is privately owned. The Grand River in particular affords an excellent float from the access site at Maple Grove Road north of Jackson to Dixon Road a few miles downstream or even into Ingham County. About 10 miles of the Grand here were channelized years ago and the river is just now growing back. Float possibilities also exist below Jackson, and canoeists are likely to see beaver from a remnant population. Smaller streams that are forested with brush and timber throughout the county provide excellent jump-shooting opportunities for sportsmen able to secure permission to hunt private land.

Many Jackson County potholes and lakes host local and migrant waterfowl. Center Lake Chain and Portage Lake in the recreation area are popular with diving-duck hunters. Also, the Schlee Waterfowl Production Area on Page Road, southeast of Leoni, is open to hunting. Recently bought with duck-stamp dollars, the 160-acre parcel is within 2,500 acres of marsh and prairie pothole country and is currently managed for duck production.

All but the northwestern portion of Jackson County is currently open for late-season Canada goose hunting. Populations are very good, particularly in the southeastern corner on privately-owned Thorn Lake, which hosts up to 5,000 geese, according to mid-December DNR aerial surveys.

Hunting is not permitted on the lake, but hunters have learned to follow birds as they disperse to corn and winter-wheat fields, such as in the Cement City area. Then they ask permission of landowners. Other Jackson County lakes worth checking for wintering Canadas include Pleasant, Browns, Ackerson, Stony, Clark, Cascades, Rounds, and Columbia.

Deer hunters currently enjoy 10 to 14 percent success (one of eight) on bucks in Jackson County with moderate pressure (about 16 hunters per square mile). Deer are scattered throughout with crop damage complaints coming from corn and fruit farmers in the northeastern corner. Some of these bucks grow handsome racks, as evidenced by Commemorative Bucks of Michigan records recently compiled. Of 1,150 all-time big Michigan bucks thus far uncovered, a whopping 49 were Jackson County deer, five of which were shot in a recent season.

Applicants for hunter's-choice permits in four areas within the county currently stand about a 90 percent chance of getting an any-deer tag.

Groves of oak, maple, and hickory, especially when hunted near standing corn fields, produce plenty of fox squirrels and the odd gray squirrel. A few mutant black squirrels are found in the western county toward Albion. Raccoon, plentiful in lowland hardwoods with farm fields nearby, get moderate to high pressure augmented by Ohio and Indiana hunters. Fox hunting is popular with members of the Waterloo Hunt Club. There is also ample opportunity for hunting with predator calls. Rabbit hunting is generally good in mixed brushlands and grasslands, especially on abandoned farms and idle land.

When settlers first arrived, Jackson County was home to good populations of prairie chickens. Of course, they are now extinct. In their place are good numbers of ruffed grouse. In fact, Jackson is probably the best of the nine-county DNR district for grouse. Hourly flush rates in high-population years will run 2.0 to 3.0 birds. Seek grouse in upland hardwoods sprinkled with aspen and in lowland brushy areas containing gray and red-osier dogwood. Grouse hunters take incidental woodcock in these same areas and along stream bottom cover. Pheasant hunting is marginal at best.

About three dozen Iowa wild turkeys recently released in the Waterloo Recreation Area may someday provide hunting opportunity.

OTHER SHOOTING OPPORTUNITIES

The Jackson County Sportsmen's Club, 500 Mantle Ave., in Jackson, has range facilities open daily to the public for fees. Included are indoor pistol and rimfire rifle stations (12 each), two skeet, and six trap fields. Competitive shooting is offered. For more information, call 517/782-6727.

The Jackson County Outdoor Club has range facilities at 3550 Hart Road, Jackson, that are also open to the public for fees. Included are six stations each for pistol (indoor), rimfire rifle (indoor/outdoor), and centerfire rifle (outdoor). There are six

indoor archery targets and 28 archery-hunter rounds, as well as three shotgun trap fields. The club features both competitive shooting and hunter certification courses. Call 517/764-3415 for details.

Sharonville State Game Area has free outdoor stations for pistol and rimfire and centerfire rifle (three each) along with four shotgun handtrap areas. If you have questions, call the DNR district office at Jackson (517/784-3188).

Jackson Bowmen, 8757 Jennings Drive, Jackson, has 82 outdoor archery targets that nonmembers may use at certain times for occasional fees. Competitive shooting is also featured. The phone number is 517/522-4624.

Munith Rod and Gun Club on Fitchburg Road in Munith offers competitive shooting on its outdoor pistol and centerfire and rimfire rifle ranges (one station each). There are also four shotgun trap fields. Call 517/596-2186 for information.

The Grass Lake Rifle Club has three indoor/outdoor rimfire rifle stations that are open to the public at no cost. The club, 10600 Phal Road in Grass Lake, sponsors shooting instruction and hunter certification courses. For details, call 517/522-8979.

Superior Archery Equipment Company is a commercially-owned archery range with 200 hunter rounds open to the public for fees. Shooting instruction and competitive shooting are featured. The address is 315 Fifth St., Michigan Center, and the phone number is 517/764-5307.

FURTHER SOURCES OF HUNTING INFORMATION

1. DNR District Office, 3335 Lansing Ave., Jackson, Mich. 49202 (517/784-3188).

2. Waterloo Game Office, Route 3, 13578 Seymour Road, Grass Lake, Mich. 49240 (517/522-4097).

3. Waterloo Recreation Area, 16345 McClure Road, Route 1, Chelsea, Mich. 48118 (313/475-8307).

4. Greater Jackson Chamber of Commerce, 401 South Jackson St., Box 80, Jackson, Mich. 49204 (517/782-8221).

5. Brooklyn Area Chamber of Commerce, 160 South Main St., Brooklyn, Mich. 49230 (517/592-2122).

6. Topographic, county, and lake maps may be ordered from the Michigan United Conservation Clubs. For information, refer to the beginning of this book.

7. Plat books are available from the Jackson County Drain Office, 120 West Michigan Ave., Jackson, Mich. 49202. The cost is $10 each (add $1.50 if mail ordering).

8. Jackson County ASCS Office, USDA, 211 West Granson St., Jackson, Mich. 49201 (517/789-7716).

Also, refer to the following elsewhere in this book:
1. Sharonville State Game Area
2. Waterloo Recreation Area
3. Cambridge Historic State Park
4. Schlee Waterfowl Management Area

Kalamazoo County

AT first glance Kalamazoo County would not appear to be worth hunting. I-94 and US-131 bisect the 567-square-mile county into four quadrants, the city of Kalamazoo sprawls from the central portion, and metropolitan areas—including all of Portage Township except for the Gourdneck State Game Area (*which see*)—are closed to firearm discharge. Yet Kalamazoo County does offer hunting opportunities for deer (including some big bucks) and a variety of small game.

Forested areas are confined to the southeastern corner, the north-central portion of Cooper Township, and a band flanking the river from Fort Custer Recreation Area (*which see*) to the city itself.

Most of Kalamazoo County is intensively farmed for cash crop grains. Hog, beef, and dairy farming also figure and, on a lesser scale, commercial orchards, vineyards, and truck crops such as onions, tomatoes, potatoes, and celery. This intensive farming occurs most heavily in glacial outwash plains of the south-central and southwestern regions as well as in Richland Township north and east of Kalamazoo. The Gull Lake area (northeastern), the southwestern region except for the Fulton State Game Area (*which see*), and the northwestern township of Alamo are also farmed but not as intensively. Mixed stands of woodlands and brushlands in these areas produce game along with fair to good hunting opportunity.

Lakes lie scattered throughout the county except for the southeastern region. The Kalamazoo River flows from east to west before turning north at Kalamazoo and eventually leaving the county. It and its tributaries drain the northern portion. The southern region is drained by streams flowing south to the St. Joseph River. Hilly terrain in the northern portion of the county are moraines of sandy/loamy soil over gravel and sand, created thousands of years ago from retreating glaciers. Smaller till and outwash plains are found throughout with ponded areas lying along the Kalamazoo and in Pavilion and Alamo townships.

About 23 percent of the land base is currently growing commercial timber, mostly hard maple and birch, with scattered stands of oak, hickory, ash, elm, and soft maple. Aspen, tulip poplar, red and white pine, cottonwood, and some white spruce are also found along with areas of brush. Public lands already mentioned total 5,600 acres. They may be hunted along with 1,000 acres of Public Access Stamp program land from a half-dozen cooperating farmers scattered throughout the county. Thus, there is limited hunting access, but a courteous request can go a long way toward securing hunting privileges on private lands.

Kalamazoo is not a high deer-kill county, but there are fair numbers scattered throughout. The annual car-deer kill average of 350 to 400 animals is due to traffic patterns more than an overabundane of deer. Pressure is light to moderate (about 10 hunters per square mile) with 11 percent buck-kill success recorded. That translates to one to two bucks per square mile, some of which grow nice racks as evidenced by the fact that Commemorative Bucks of Michigan has entered eight Kalamazoo County whitetails on its record list of all-time Michigan big bucks. Best hunting comes in the northern half (with the exception of Richland Township).

Fort Custer Recreation Area gets intense pressure (hunters must have a state park sticker, however), which sends deer to refuge on federal military-use lands not open to hunting. Deer hunters on state property enjoy a good success ratio but can't kill enough deer. Up to a thousand animals winter in this area and because the range can't support them as many as 100 annually starve.

Raccoon populations are moderate to high with corresponding pressure. Foxes are on the increase, especially in the southern region, and afford untapped hunting potential. These are mostly red fox with an occasional gray fox sighted. A fair to good rabbit population offers sport for dog and snow-tracking hunters who work brushy fence rows, woodlot and stream edges, and abandoned farms. Fox squirrels offer further opportunity and are currently underhunted. Farm woodlots and river bottomlands are likely sites to try.

Although southern Kalamazoo County has a historical basis for pheasants, birds have hit the skids. Best areas would be farms less intensively cropped. Try those with mixed brushlands grasslands in Wakeshma Township and in the west-central and north-central region. This county produces fair to good grouse and woodcock hunting in wetland areas of brush mixed with aspen. The southeastern portion is perhaps best with some opportunity north of the Kalamazoo River. Pressure runs medium to high. Wild turkeys live in the Kellogg Sanctuary on Gull Lake (no hunting allowed anywhere on Gull Lake). The DNR also has plans to release them in the Waterloo Recreation Area and possibly along the Kalamazoo River downstream from Kalamazoo.

Growing numers of giant Canada geese are reaching nuisance proportions and may soon provide late-season hunting opportunity as they do in southeastern Michigan. Birds disperse from the Kellogg Sanctuary, from the Portage area, and from private lakes elsewhere throughout the county. Nuisance proportions are especially high in the vicinity of Gourdneck State Game Area, but urban development and the Portage Township hunting ban limit opportunities to the game area. Morrow Pond and the Kalamazoo River provide some hunting chances as well as farm fields of winter wheat and corn when access can be obtained. The same is true with mallards, wood ducks, and early-season teal along wooded waterways and potholes on private land.

OTHER SHOOTING OPPORTUNITIES

Twin Pines Shooting Preserve, four miles northeast of Augusta on M-89, is open to the public for pheasant hunting and dog training on its 160 acres. For more information, contact Roy A. Kerbs,

Route 1, Augusta, Mich. 49012 (616/731-4632).

The Kalamazoo Rod and Gun Club, 7241 North 23 St., Kalamazoo, Mich. 49004, is open to the public on a fee basis for use of outdoor pistol (30 stations), outdoor centerfire rifle (14 stations), and indoor rimfire rifle (eight stations) facilities. The club also has a shotgun trap field and a handtrap area and offers shooting instruction, competitive shooting, and the state hunter certification program. For more information, call 616/344-1750.

Southern Michigan Gun Club, Inc., has indoor pistol and rimfire rifle facilities (12 stations each) open to the public for fees. The club, whose address is 809 East Crosstown Parkway, Kalamazoo, Mich. 49001, also makes available competitive shooting and shooting instruction. The phone number is 616/385-9083.

FURTHER SOURCES OF HUNTING INFORMATION

1. DNR District Office, 621 North 10th St. (Box 355), Plainwell, Mich. 49080 (616/685-6851).

2. Fort Custer Recreation Area, 5163 West Fort Custer Dr., Augusta, Mich. 49012 (616/731-4200).

3. Kalamazoo County Convention and Visitors Bureau, 128 North Kalamazoo Mall (Box 1169), Kalamazoo, Mich. 49005 (616/381-4003).

4. Topographic, county, and lake maps may be ordered from the Michigan United Conservation Clubs. For information, refer to the beginning of this book.

5. County plat books are available from the Kalamazoo County Cooperative Extension Service for $10 each (add $1 if mail ordering), 201 West Kalamazoo Ave., Room 201, Kalamazoo, Mich. 49007, Attn: Marie Mahieu.

6. Kalamazoo County ASCS Office, USDA, 6127 Sprinkle Road, Kalamazoo, Mich. 49001, 616/327-0940).

Also, refer to the following elsewhere in this book:
1. Fulton State Game Area
2. Gourdneck State Game Area
3. Fort Custer Recreation Area

Kalkaska County

KALKASKA County, in the northwestern Lower Peninsula, covers 559 square miles. The county is part of a great plain, the surface features of which were constructed during the glacial period. Although some 700 feet of elevation difference occurs across the county—from about 600 feet above sea level in the northwestern portion to more than 1,300 feet in the northeastern and southeastern regions—local differences between hills and valleys amount to only 50 to 150 feet. Such relief is characterized by level plains, low hills with rounded tops, broad valleys, shallow basins, and old lake-bed plains.

The Manistee River bisects the county from northeast to southwest and drains the southeastern half. It flows southwesterly toward Manistee and Lake Michigan. The Boardman River and its tributaries drain the northwestern half on their way north to Traverse City. In addition to river resources, the northern half of Kalkaska County at least has several large lakes.

A broad belt of the county center, from southwest to north-central, is mostly farmland. Northern harwoods dominate the northern tier of townships, aspen in varying age classes largely rings the farmland, and mixed stands of pine are prominent farther outside toward county boundaries. Heavy oak forests are found in the southeastern, east-central, and extreme southwestern regions; and conifer swamps border the Manistee River in places. They also occasionally front the western side of US-131 and dominate the southeastern shores of Lake Skegemog.

In all, about 78 percent of Kalkaska County is timbered with commercial-forest species. Maple-birch leads the way with 90,500 acres. It is followed by aspen (54,400 acres), red pine (31,900 acres), jack pine (30,800 acres), oak-hickory (17,000 acres), and northern white cedar (11,600 acres). Smaller amounts of white pine and paper birch also occur.

Over half of Kalkaska County is state-owned through the Pere Marquette State Forest (which see) and therefore open to hunting. Sportsmen enjoy excellent hunting for woodcock and squirrels, good hunting for deer, grouse, and late-season waterfowl, fair hunting for snowshoe hares (at the present at least), bear, raccoon, fox, and coyotes, and poor hunting for turkeys (only the northwestern portion is currently open).

The best deer hunting occurs in the southeastern region in hilly stands of aspen mixed with oak, jack pine, and red pine. An especially good region lies between the main and north branches of the Manistee. Fair to good hunting can be found on farmlands for hunters obtaining permission. Farmers who occasionally register deer crop-damage complaints might be amenable to a courteous request to hunt. The northern and western portions of Kalkaska County have lower numbers of deer because that region falls into a snow belt. During tough winters starvation losses are high both here and along deer yards of the Manistee River north of Sharon. Cold Spring and Boardman townships produce the highest numbers of deer, according to a five-year survey recently released by the DNR.

Kalkaska County thus far has produced few trophy bucks for the all-time record book of champion Michigan deer as compiled by Commemorative Bucks of Michigan. Pressure is high (20 to 30 hunters per square mile), the buck kill only average (one to two animals per square mile), and success (10-15 percent) a little off the state norm.

Bear hunting is best in the southeastern part where large swamps are located. Deer hunters pot a few coyotes and red fox, but these predator species could withstand increased hunting pressure from both still-hunters with calls and dog hunters. Fox numbers are highest in the farmland whereas coyotes appear to be well scattered. One especially good coyote spot of heavy jack pine growth, however, is the Fletcher Area in the southeastern corner. Not surprisingly perhaps, the Fletcher Area has the county's best snowshoe-hare hunting. Hunters can also find the splay-footed hares in cutover areas next to conifer swamps and young pine plantations as well as river-bottom alder stands. When population cycles are high, Kalkaska County offers excellent hare hunting. Limited cottontail hunting occurs on farmlands.

For raccoon, try Manistee River bottomlands as well as feeder streams. The farmlands also house a fair 'coon population, and there are some opportunities along the Boardman River as well. Kalkaska County has an underhunted population of squirrels—fox species along oak-covered ridges and farmland woodlots and grays/blacks in oak mixed with pine. Numbers have been exceptionally high in recent years.

Grouse hunter-cooperators reported hourly flush rates of 1.26 to 1.85 for two randomly checked years. Hunters can do better than this rate if they concentrate on productive habitats of 10- to 20-year-old aspen with an understory of brush and shrubs. Thornapple, witch hazel, beaked hazelnut, gray and red-osier dogwood, wild currant, and wild raisin are prime grouse foods that provide this understory. A quarter of Garfield Township (nine square miles), once used as a grouse study area, still affords good hunting. Called the Sharon Unit, it includes Sections 22-36. This area and the extreme southeastern corner of Kalkaska County contain a remnant population of sharp-tailed grouse (closed to hunting, however). Numbers are probably under 30.

Here are the top grouse-hunting spots in Kalkaska County, starting clockwise from the Sharon Unit: (1) five miles south and a mile west of Sharon, (2) two miles northwest of South Boardman, (3) a mile east of the Penn Central tracks from CR-612 north four miles to Wood Road, (4) the western border of Sunset Trail Road between M-72 and CR-612 in Excelsior Township, (5) southeast of Bear Lake along Blue Lake Road, (6) along the Sunset Trail

Road south of M-72 and between the two rivers, and (7) the northern portion of the Hanson Military Reserve (*see county map*).

River bottoms and aspen cutover areas attract large numbers of migrant woodcock. In fact, the Manistee River system offers some of the best woodcock hunting in the state. Also, don't overlook Black and Portage creeks in the east-central portion. Hunter-cooperators for the same two years checked reported hourly flush rates from 2.40 to 3.67 longbills.

Float-hunters on the Manistee River and layout shooters on Lake Skegemog get good action for mallards and blacks and late-season divers. Other lakes that receive migrant-duck concentrations include Manistee, Bear, Grass, and Whealer.

OTHER SHOOTING OPPORTUNITIES

None known at this time.

FURTHER SOURCES OF HUNTING INFORMATION

1. DNR District Office, 191 South Mount Tom Road (M-33), Mio, Mich. 48647 (517/826-3211).

2. DNR Kalkaska Area Office, 605 Birch, Kalkaska, Mich. 49646 (616/258-9471).

3. DNR Kalkaska Field Office, M-72, Kalkaska, Mich. 49646 (616/258-2711).

4. Greater Kalkaska Area Chamber of Commerce, 350 South Cedar St., Kalkaska, Mich. 49646 (616/258-9103).

5. Topographic, county, and lake maps may be ordered from the Michigan United Conservation Clubs. For information, refer to the beginning of this book.

6. Plat books are available from the Kalkaska County Equalization Dept., 602 North Birch St., Kalkaska, Mich. 49646. The charge is $10 each (add $1.50 if mail ordering and make out checks to the Boy Scouts of America).

7. Kalkaska County ASCS Office, 605 North Birch St., Kalkaska, Mich. 49646.

Also, refer to Pere Marquette State Forest elsewhere in this book.

Kent County

KENT County in southwestern Lower Michigan is one of the largest downstate counties with a land area encompassing 845 square miles. Despite its inclusion of metropolitan Grand Rapids, Kent County contains a good mix of farmland/woodland habitat that produces an abundance of game animals and birds. Further, it offers good hunting opportunities for deer, waterfowl, and small game.

Land features include (1) several flat plains—the largest along the Grand River in the western portion; (2) hilly divisions that border river valleys (Grand River and its tributaries—Flat, Thornapple, Rogue); and (3) gently rolling areas between. Elevations across the county vary as much as 300 feet. Kent County is about 29 percent commercially forested with maple-birch, oak-hickory, and elm-

ash-soft maple predominating in that order. There are also about 14,000 acres of aspen mixed with hardwoods.

Although access to private land can be somewhat difficult, due to the proximity of Grand Rapids (check Grand Rapids-area municipalities for special regulations), hunters do have a considerable amount of area from which to choose. These include 7,800 acres of state land in the form of three state game areas and another 9,500 acres of Public Access Stamp program lands leased from some four dozen farmers, highest enrollments in the seven-county DNR district. These lands are well scattered throughout these farming districts: (1) cash-crop and dairy farming in the north-central region, (2) southern area (below the Grand River) of cash cropping with some dairying, and (3) fruit belts along both the western and northeastern county borders. For a free map showing exact locations and descriptions, contact the DNR district office in Grand Rapids. Getting access to other private lands is easiest in the northern quarter if you first make a considerate request.

This northern-county farmland region is interspersed with northern hardwoods and features plenty of farm woodlots and lakes—similar to Montcalm County (which see) just to the north. The southern farming belt is more open but still contains good woodlot cover.

Kent County has the highest car-deer accident rate in Michigan with kills approaching one animal per square mile. That is due to both metropolitan Grand Rapids and the fact that many deer live here. Kent County bucks grow big racks too, the result of good food supplies from natural cover types and farmland crops of corn, beans, and fruit. Commemorative Bucks of Michigan lists 17 Kent County bucks as all-time big Michigan deer. Although pressure is high on state lands, it is moderate overall (about 14 hunters per square mile) with the success rate of 13 percent a little under the state average of 17 percent. That translates to one to two bucks per square mile. Overall success on both sexes (about 16 percent) is lowest in the district. Deer are scattered throughout with best opportunities on private land and along the wooded river systems. Shotguns only may be used below M-57 during the firearm deer hunting season.

Fox and raccoon hunters do exceptionally well, due no doubt to rich farmlands, the river bottomlands, and some 15 square miles of surface water in the form of dozens of lakes. Fox squirrels, an underhunted resource, are common along cornfield edges, farm woodlots, and lowland hardwoods. From the Grand River north, oak and hickory predominate; south of the river are oak and butternut stands. Kent County has good rabbit populations too. Best bets are alfalfa field edges and lowland cover of brush.

Scattered pheasant pockets can be found throughout, with best numbers appearing in Wyoming and Byron townships to the southwest. The DNR has not released wild turkeys, yet it receives occasional sighting reports in the Byron Center area (from the Allegan County flock) and in the Rogue River State Game Area (which see), which no doubt have migrated southward from Newaygo County. Some day these remarkable game birds may provide hunting opportunity for Kent County sportsmen.

Grouse and woodcock hunting is surprisingly good, with both effort and flush rates (in high-cycle years) running moderate to high. During one recent season Kent County rated 3.26 grouse flushes per hour from reporting cooperators. That is not unusual when one considers the high percentage of woods and brushland interspersed with rolling farmland. The northern and northeastern areas are best with old orchards, thornapple fields, and gray dogwood stands in lowland areas producing pockets of good hunting.

Deer, squirrel, and waterfowl hunters will find portions of the Grand, Flat, Rogue, Thornapple, and Coldwater rivers all floatable. They are also good for jump shooting wood ducks and mallards if hunters are careful to get access permission first. The Grand River system provides excellent duck and goose hunting habitat—bayous, mucky areas with cattail stands, and lowland hardwoods flooding. In addition, many of the northeastern county lakes have fringes of bulrushes and emergent cattails. Bass, Lincoln, and Big Pine Island lakes feature public access. Shallow Pratt Lake east of Whitneyville is another good bet.

Kent County hunters are learning that they don't have to go north for either game or hunting opportunity.

OTHER SHOOTING OPPORTUNITIES

The Cannonsburg State Game Area (which see) northeast of Grand Rapids has three outdoor stations each for centerfire and rimfire rifle practice, plus an area for shotgun handtrap shooting. There is no charge to use these facilities. For information, call 616/456-5071.

Pine Hill Sportsman's Club, 8374 Ten Mile Road NE, Rockford, Mich. 49341 is a 512-acre shooting preserve open to the public. Pheasants, quail, chukars, and dog training are offered. Contact James Rypkema, 616/874-8459, for details.

The Rockford Sportsman's Club in Algoma Township (11115 Northland Drive, Rockford, Mich. 49341 [616/866-4273]) has outdoor stations for pistol and centerfire and rimfire rifle, plus an outdoor archery target and two shotgun trap fields. These are open to the public on a limited basis without charge. The club offers competitive shooting and shooting instruction as well as hunter education classes.

Qua-Ke-Zik Sportsman's Club (11400 Foreman Road, Lowell, Mich. 49331) charges fees to use its facilities: six outdoor stations each for centerfire and rimfire rifle, 28 outdoor archery targets, six indoor/outdoor pistol stations, and one skeet field. The club also offers state hunter education programs, competitive shooting, and shooting instruction. Call 616/897-8310 for details.

Sparta Hunting and Fishing Club, Long Lake Drive NW, Sparta, Mich. 49345 (616/696-0332), sometimes charges fees for public use of its outdoor stations for pistol, centerfire rifle, and rimfire rifle (five each); five outdoor archery targets; and two shotgun trap fields. Shooting instruction, competitive shooting, and state hunter education programs are also offered.

FURTHER SOURCES OF HUNTING INFORMATION

1. DNR District Office, State Office Bldg. (350 Ottawa NW), Grand Rapids, Mich. 49503 (616/456-5071).

2. Muskegon State Game Area (which see) for questions and information regarding west Kent County, 7600 East Messinger, Twin Lake, Mich. 49457 (616/788-5055).

3. Flat River State Game Area (which see) for questions and information regarding east Kent County, Route 2, 6640 Long Lake, Belding, Mich. 48809 (616/794-2658).

4. Topographic, county, and lake maps may be ordered from the Michigan United Conservation Clubs. For information, refer to the beginning of this book.

5. Grand Rapids Area Chamber of Commerce, 17 Fountain NW, Grand Rapids, Mich. 49503 (616/459-7221).

6. Wyoming Chamber of Commerce, Box 9143, 2323 DeHoop SW, Wyoming, Mich. 49509 (616/531-5990).

Keweenaw County

THE northern half of the Keweenaw Peninsula, which fingers into Lake Superior from the top of the Upper Peninsula, makes up Keweenaw County. This remote area—the smallest county in the state—features a 65-mile coastline of rocks and sandy beach, lowland soils of sand and loam covered with cedar and spruce, and bedrock-controlled uplands of northern hardwoods. Dense, mature forests (about 97 percent of the county is timbered), coupled with severe winters (an average of 200 to 300 inches of snow each winter), limit game production. Therefore, hunters are widely scattered and offer very light pressure.

That does not mean, however, that this ruggedly beautiful county, cut by waterfalls and containing some of earth's oldest geologic formations, has no hunting opportunities. White-tailed deer, black bear, bobcats, coyotes, snowshoe hares, Canada geese, ducks, ruffed grouse, and woodcock live in its swamps and forested edges. But it does mean that some of these game species pass the entire fall without confronting dogs or hunters.

Only about one percent of the 348,160 acres (about 544 square miles) of Keweenaw County is publicly owned through a half-dozen scattered parcels of the Copper Country State Forest (which see). However, an additional 94,757 acres of private land is enrolled in the Commercial Forest Act (CFA) program, thus giving hunters over 25 percent of the county to roam at will. To get legal descriptions of these company-owned, CFA timberlands, contact the DNR Forest Management Division, Box 30028, Lansing, Mich. 48909 (517/373-1275). Be sure to list town and range numbers (available from a good county map) of the area you wish to hunt.

Only about 2,500 people live in Keweenaw County, and that is certainly a big reason why annual car-deer accidents amount to 10 whitetail deaths or less. Another reason is few numbers of deer. Low pressure (under one hunter per square mile) results in a very light annual harvest with a success ratio of about 10 percent.

There are some fine trophy animals, however, for hunters wanting a tough, wilderness experience. Poor access roads means that 4WD vehicles or long hikes are in order. You will earn any buck you might tag in Keweenaw County.

Nearly half, or 99,800 acres, of the commercial-forest cover is maple-birch. Northern white cedar follows fir (16,000 acres). Aspen is a distant fifth at 15,000 acres. Smaller amounts of oak-hickory, elm-ash-soft maple, red pine, and jack pine also occur. The problem is that most (about 88 percent) of this commercial forest is mature growth in sawtimber and poletimber stands. Such climax forests don't enhance the populations of most game species.

Much cedar/balsam/spruce cover is found on the peninsula tip and in the southeastern region along the Tobacco River and other small streams. These are good places to ambush a late-season whitetail on its way to wintering yards.

Several trophy bear are shot in Keweenaw County each fall. Hunters normally tag about 30 bruins, which means that, for her size, Keweenaw County holds her own against the other four counties in the DNR district headquartered at Baraga. About 30 to 40 percent of the U.P. bear kills occurs in this district. In Keweenaw County the opportunistic bear are apt to be nearly anywhere. Try scouting the edge of lowland conifers with upland hardwoods and look for openings within the conifers themselves. Food areas such as acorn drops, chokecherries, and fruits and berries in season, are other good spots to begin baiting.

Keweenaw County also produces a couple of bobcats each fall and would likely yield more if more hunters sought them. Cat populations, however, are almost always contingent upon the snowshoe-hare population, which, at this writing, is somewhat depressed. Again, few hunters take advantage even during high-end years of the hare's population cycle.

Scattered stands of oaks produce some gray and black-phase squirrels, and there are some raccoon hunting opportunities along rivers in the southern region.

Waterfowl hunting potential is limited to central-county lakes (Gratiot, Deer, LaBelle, Medora). However, the Sturgeon River Sloughs Wildlife Area (which see), whose project boundaries cover 32,000 acres, is just being developed and is expected to lure several thousand migrant Canada geese en route to the Horicon National Wildlife Refuge in Wisconsin. The sloughs lie between Otter and Portage lakes in Houghton and Baraga counties.

Keweenaw County also contains huntable populations of ruffed grouse and woodcock. Hourly flush-rate records of hunter-cooperators showed figures of 1.70 for grouse and 2.55 for woodcock. However, consider these statistics with discretion as only a single year could be checked and the sample itself was light. For best bets, seek cutover areas of hardwoods and aspen just growing back, as well as lowland brush and alders and the edge of forested areas.

OTHER SHOOTING OPPORTUNITIES

None known at this time.

FURTHER SOURCES OF HUNTING INFORMATION

1. DNR District Office, North US-41 (Box 440), Baraga, Mich. 4990 (906/353-6651).

2. Copper Country Chamber of Commerce, Box 336, Houghton, Mich. 49931 (906/482-5240).

3. Topographic, county, and lake maps may be ordered from the Michigan United Conservation Clubs. For information, refer to the beginning of this book.

4. Plat books are available from the Houghton/ Keweenaw County Cooperative Extension Services, 1500 Birch St., Hancock, Mich. 49930 (906/482-5830). The cost is $6 each (add $1 if mail ordering).

5. Baraga/Houghton/Keweenaw County ASCS Office, American Legion Building, L'Anse, Mich. 49946.

Also, refer to the Copper Country State Forest elsewhere in this book.

Lake County

THE large amount of scrub oak and jack-pine forests in Lake County supports good populations of deer, raccoon, woodcock, wild turkeys, and squirrels as well as grouse and snowshoe hares in high-end years of their cycles. Large blocks of ownership by both the federal and state government have resulted in timbering practices that provide openings, edges, and brushy cover. Also, this county of gently rolling topography contains swamps, many small lakes (especially in the western half), and plenty of rivers and other drainages.

Main waterways include the Little Manistee and Pine rivers in the northern region, the Baldwin and Pere Marquette rivers in the central portion, and the Big South Branch and Little Pere Marquette in the southern area. Hilly sections occur in the Ward and Lincoln Hills areas. A particularly flat region extends from Irons east to the Pine River in the northern tier of townships.

Farming is limited to the extreme eastern and western sides. Most (82 percent) of 570-square-mile Lake County is covered with commercial-forest species. Oak-hickory leads the list of types with a whopping 134,300 acres. It is followed (in descending order of frequency) by aspen, red pine, maple-birch, jack pine, elm-ash-soft maple, white pine, and paper birch. These secondary types constitute another 165,000 acres of cover.

Running mostly north and south and just east of M-37 is a long string of swamps. It begins just north of Idlewild and extends north to about four miles from the Wexford County boundary. Another swamp region starts in the northwestern and north-central area and wanders into Mason County. These are good yarding areas for deer. They also contain a few bobcats and black bear (both of which are currently protected in Lake County). Look for snowshoe hares around the edges of these conifer swamps where cutover aspen and hardwoods meet the green cover.

The Manistee National Forest in the northeastern corner is mostly red pine and affords fairly good deer hunting. The eastern portion (east of the swamplands mentioned) is a mixture of aspen and oak, which contains squirrels, deer, grouse, and woodcock. The western half of Lake County runs heavily to oak and jack pine, with mostly jack-pine stands in the north-central region. This mixture is good for deer, hares, and coyotes. (The latter species, incidentally, is on the increase.)

About 16 percent, or 60,631 acres, of Lake County is state land constituting large-block holdings of the Pere Marquette State Forest (which see). These lie mostly in the central and north-central regions. Federal land amounts to some 28 percent, or 103,000 acres. This Huron-Manistee National Forest (which also see) land lies north, west, and south of the state land, wrapping it in a large C shape. As observed, east-side townships are mostly privately-owned farmlands.

An additional 1,400 acres of company-owned land is enrolled in the Commercial Forest Act program and is therefore open to hunting. Hunters armed with a current plat book and good county map can find these timbered lands if they first get legal descriptions. Those are available from the DNR district office in Cadillac or from the DNR Forest Management Division. The address is Box 30028, Lansing, Mich. 48909. Or call 517/373-1275.

Lake County is one of Michigan's top deer producers with Lake and Pleasant Plains townships probably the best. Other excellent areas to hunt include western Sauble Township, central Cherry Valley Township, and the areas north and west of Luther. Between 70 and 80 percent of the firearm deer kill in Lake County is yearling whitetails (a year and a half old). Buck-hunter success runs 12 to 20 percent and averages about five animals per square mile.

One reason for the high deer-kill statistic is the habitat that produces them. Another is the large number of hunters. There's no denying that the availability of public hunting lands and the abundance of deer attract swarms of hunters. Pressure, which can surpass 50 hunters per square mile, is matched only by Oscoda and Roscommon counties.

Turkey hunting is fairly good throughout Lake County, with best opportunities occurring along waterways and seeps among mixed-cover forestlands. Raccoon appear plentiful, with moderate to high hunting pressure. A few cottontails live in farming areas, but few hunters try for them. Instead, they turn their thoughts to snowshoe hares, plentiful in high-cycle years throughout poplar slashings, Christmas tree farms, and young hardwood areas near conifer lowlands.

Good squirrel hunting opportunities are largely ignored. Concentrate on mixed stands of oaks with lowland conifers for grays/blacks and open-oak areas for fox squirrels. Some waterfowl hunting potential exists on ponds, streams, and small lakes (mostly jump-shooting) and diving-duck layout shooting on larger waters such as Wolf, Big Star, and Big Bass lakes. Hunters may even come across an occasional pheasant in Lake County, but there aren't enough to warrant concentrating on them for sport.

On the other hand, woodcock and grouse provide good hunting potential, with grouse, in particular, due for a rebound after recent low-end years. It is not suprising that Lake County would abundantly produce these popular upland game birds since aspen is the second most plentiful cover type (39,500 acres) and there are plenty of brushy, stream bottomlands and understories of gray dogwood. Three years of hunter-cooperator records checked show hourly flush rates of 1.31, 3.21, and 2.28 for grouse and 1.37, 1.62, and 2.86 for woodcock. The latter can provide great sport when found in concentrations during their fall migrations. Peak time in Lake County is generally from about October 12 to October 20.

OTHER SHOOTING OPPORTUNITIES

None known at this time.

FURTHER SOURCES OF HUNTING INFORMATION

1. DNR District Office, 8015 South 131 Road, Cadillac, Mich. 49601 (616/775-9727).

2. DNR Baldwin Field Office, Box 2810, Baldwin, Mich. 49304 (616/745-4651).

3. Huron-Manistee National Forest, Baldwin Ranger District, Baldwin, Mich. 49304 (616/745-4631).

4. Baldwin Area Chamber of Commerce, Route #2, Box 2422, Baldwin, Mich. 49304 (616/745-4331).

5. Topographic, county, and lake maps may be ordered from the Michigan United Conservation Clubs. For information, refer to the beginning of this book.

6. Plat books are available from the Lake County Cooperative Extension Services, Box 246, Courthouse Bldg., Baldwin, Mich. 49304. The cost is $8 each (add $1.50 if mail ordering).

7. Osceola-Lake County ASCS office, 7700 South Patterson Road, Reed City, Mich. 49677.

Also, refer to the following elsewhere in this book:
1. Huron-Manistee National Forest
2. Pere Marquette State Forest

Lapeer County

LAPEER County at the base of Michigan's Thumb receives considerable hunting pressure from Port Huron, Detroit and metropolitan suburbs, and Flint sportsmen, all living within an hour's drive. Because Lapeer County is closed to Sunday hunting on the lands of others, the Lapeer State Game Area and open-hunting portions of Metamora-Hadley and Ortonville recreation areas (*all of which see*) take a pounding. Incidentally, recreation areas are administered by DNR Parks Division and therefore require a valid state parks vehicle permit for admittance.

In spite of this pressure, the 10,800 acres of public lands continue to produce fair numbers of squirrels, grouse, and rabbits as well as waterfowl and woodcock hunting for both local birds and migrants. In addition, nearly 30 landowners currently have over 8,000 acres enrolled in the Public Access Stamp program. These open-to-hunting lands are scattered throughout with twin concentrations in the North Branch area and Elba Township.

Lapeer County boasts 153 lakes and plenty of timbered bottomlands along tributary streams of the Flint River, whose south and north branches come together near Columbiaville. Beaver live along both branches and are a particular nuisance on the South Branch east of Metamora. About 22 percent of the county is forested with commercial timber species. Predominate types are split between maple-birch and soft maple-ash-elm, with oak-hickory and aspen also found.

Overall, Lapeer is a county with a good mix of farmlands, brushlands, and woodlands. Cash-crop farming belt for corn and soybeans is in the northern tier of townships; muck farming for vegetables occurs in the east-central region; and the southern portion is home to hunt clubs, hobby farmers, and horse raisers.

Several distinctive topographic features of Lapeer County resulted from the Wisconsin glacial period of several thousand years ago. Terminal moraines formed a chain of hills, now largely forested, from Dryden to Hadley and from Deanville to Columbiaville. Present-day rolling topography in Almont, Burnside, and Elba townships is the result of corresponding till plains and smaller moraines. At one time water flowed westward from Lake Huron across Lapeer County to Lake Michigan. The channel through which it flowed is the present-day muck channel east of Imlay City. It then followed Cedar Creek up the North Channel of the Flint River and along the Flint River into Genesee County. Steep sand terraces en route indicate that the waterway was a major one.

Lapeer County farmers are traditionally receptive toward responsible hunters asking permission to enter their lands.

After several years of increase, car-deer accidents indicate that the deer herd is leveling off. Annual figures show about 250 whitetails are highway statistics. Ten percent or less of firearm hunters tag bucks, but pressure overall is light at eight hunters per square mile. To repeat, public areas get heavy pressure. There are some large deer in Lapeer County, however. A check of DNR deer-station records for a recent hunting season shows that 18 of

42 bucks tagged carried eight points or more. And very recently, the third best typically-antlered deer in the state was shot near Columbiaville. The 10-pointer scored 147-5/8 Boone and Crockett points. Ten other Lapeer County monster bucks join it in the record book among Michigan's all-time trophy whitetails, compiled by Commemorative Bucks of Michigan.

The best area for deer is the southern region from Metamora to Dryden. Also rating high are Elba Township and the North Branch area. There are some big deer in Flint River bottomlands too. Good places for December hunting include thick cover along the river and a dense cedar swamp along Cedar Creek southwest of Burnside.

Other game animals include fox, an underused resource by hunters although trappers exact a high number each year. Raccoon are plentiful along waterways near crop fields; hunting pressure is moderate to high. Fox squirrels are abundant and only lightly hunted except in the game areas, where pressure is moderate. Plenty of cottontails offer sporting targets for both snow trackers and hound hunters. Try brushlands that meet bottomlands or crop fields.

Grouse appear to be slowly increasing on private lands with encroaching aspen and brush. A typical hunt will result in 1.50 to 3.0 birds flushed per hour in middle and high-end years of the birds' cycle. Some local woodcock nest in moist alders and other bottomland cover, and the county hosts good numbers of flight birds late in the season. Seek them in brushlands and small aspen stands when this favored habitat can be found.

Although pheasant numbers have tumbled in recent years, there are still huntable populations in isolated covers of set-aside land as well as in weeds and brushlands on abandoned farms. Recent rural mail carrier surveys indicate 2.2 pheasant broods per route, about double the southern Michigan average although far from being plentiful. Best opportunities are within the Clifford-North Branch-Brown City triangle. Twenty wild turkeys (four gobblers and 16 hens) from Pennsylvania were recently released in the Lapeer SGA west of M-24. If these birds increase as expected, they could produce future hunting opportunities.

Lapeer County offers good waterfowling. Jump-shooters and floaters alike key on wood ducks, mallards, and teal along the waterways and on many of the wood-fringed lakes. Also, Holloway Reservoir below Columbiaville offers open-water blind hunting (signs denote boundaries) for waterfowlers who register their blinds first with the Genesee County Parks and Recreation Commission (G-5055 Branch Road in Flint [313/736-7100]).

A goose refuge on Long Lake in the Lapeer State Game Area is open to perimeter hunting. Also, waterfowlers have learned that geese disperse to farm fields largely to the southeast from both Holloway and Long Lake concentration points. The reservoir and Lake Nepessing (which also has public access) are popular too with diving-duck hunters later in the season. The southwestern portion of Lapeer County (south of M-21 and west of M-53) is open to late-season Canada goose hunting. DNR mid-December aerial surveys have turned up honkers on game-area ponds as well as private lakes.

All things considered, Lapeer County offers fair to good hunting opportunities in a variety of cover types, including isolated, north-country type habitats.

OTHER SHOOTING OPPORTUNITIES

Three Lapeer County shooting preserves offer extended-season sport for those willing to take memberships. The Bourbon Barrel Hunt Club, Inc., at 1442 North Summers Road in Imlay City allows hunting for pheasants, mallards, quail, and chukar partridge on 521 acres. For information, call Donald R. Capman at 313/724-8135 or 724-6125.

Hunter's Creek Club, Inc., has 540 acres plus a 186-acre annex area for hunting pheasants, quail, and chukars. The club is located at 675 Sutton Road in Metamora. For more details, call Preston Mann at 313/664-4307.

The Huntsman, 3166 Havens Road in Dryden, offers pheasant, quail, and chukar hunting on 603 acres. Call Nora M. Tebben at 313/796-3962 for more information.

Hunters may shoot at several ranges in Lapeer County. The Ortonville Recreation Area features outdoor stations for pistol (two), centerfire rifle (four), and rimfire rifle (three) plus four shotgun handtrap areas. Fees are charged. For details, call 313/627-3828.

Lone Elm Service, 997 Van Dyke in Imlay City, sometimes charges fees for use of its outdoor stations for pistol and rimfire rifle (five each) and single centerfire rifle station. A shotgun handtrap area is also provided as well as shooting instruction and competition. Call 313/724-1154 for information.

The Lapeer County Sportsman's Club, 1312 North Lake Road in Attica, has 10 indoor pistol stations, three outdoor centerfire rifle stations, and 10 indoor rimfire rifle stations open to the public without charge. Facilities also include a skeet field, three trap fields, and archery targets. Services include both shooting instruction and competition as well as hunter certification courses. There is no phone.

FURTHER SOURCES OF HUNTING INFORMATION

1. DNR District Office, 715 South Cedar St., Imlay City, Mich. 48444 (313/724-2015).
2. Lapeer State Game Area, 3116 Vernor Road, Lapeer, Mich. 48446 (313/664-8355).
3. Metamora-Hadley Recreation Area, 3871 Hurd Road, Metamora, Mich. 48455 (313/797-4439).
4. Ortonville Recreation Area, 5767 Hadley Road, Ortonville, Mich. 48461 (313/627-3828).
5. Imlay City Area Chamber of Commerce, Box 206, Imlay City, Mich. 48444 (313/724-6408).
6. Greater Lapeer Area Chamber of Commerce, 350 North Court St., Suite 206, Lapeer, Mich. 48446 (313/664-6641).
7. Topographic, county, and lake maps may be ordered from the Michigan United Conservation Clubs. For information, refer to the beginning of this book.
8. Plat books are available from the Lapeer County Cooperative Extension Services, 1575 Suncrest Drive, Lapeer, Mich. 48446. They cost $10 each (add $1.50 if mail ordering).
9. Lapeer County ASCS Office, USDA, 237 Davis Lake Road, Lapeer, Mich. 48446 (313/664-0895).

Also, refer to the following elsewhere in this book:
1. Lapeer State Game Area
2. Metamora-Hadley Recreation Area
3. Ortonville Recreation Area

Leelanau County

LEELANAU County is a long finger of land that separates Lake Michigan from Grand Traverse Bay in northwestern Lower Michigan. Its sand dunes (now largely a national lakeshore), quaint towns, and offshore islands make it one of Michigan's most beautiful areas. In addition, the 344-square-mile county offers some hunting potential for deer, fox, squirrels, grouse, woodcock, and waterfowl.

Formed millions of years ago, the stalagmite shape of Leelanau County was further scoured and shaped by glaciers of the Wisconsin Period, 8,000 to 12,000 years ago. The resulting rolling topography includes drumlins, streamlined hills of glacial till that are one to two miles long and that lie in a north-south orientation. Today about 43 percent of the county is covered with commercial-forest species. Maple-birch is dominant with 59,200 acres, and there are smaller quantities (under 7,000 acres each) of northern white cedar, red pine, white pine, elm-ash-soft maple, and aspen.

Sand dunes (some containing swamps in between) line the Lake Michigan shore, and orchards wander throughout much of the Leelanau Peninsula.

A little more than five percent, or 11,657 acres, of Leelanau County is state-owned. These are mostly southern county parcels of the Pere Marquette State Forest (*which see*) and the 1,300-acre Leelanau State Park (*which also see*) at the northern tip. About 20 percent, or some 45,000 acres (including South Manitou Island—*which also see*) is federal land in the Sleeping Bear Dunes National Lakeshore. All these public lands are open to hunting.

In addition, 1,700 acres of company-owned lands are open to hunting since they are enrolled in the Commercial Forest Act plan. For legal descriptions (which hunters can then pinpoint on a current plat book), contact the DNR Forest Management Division, Box 30028, Lansing, Mich. 48909 (517/373-1275).

Due to a low whitetail population, firearm deer hunting pressure is light at about 10 hunters per square mile. Car-deer accidents are lowest in the Lower Peninsula and trail only Houghton and Keweenaw counties when compared statewide. Leelanau is a bucks-only county, but that is not to say that deer hunting is poor. On the contrary, firearm hunters enjoy one-of-six success, a little better than the state average, and tag one to two bucks per square mile.

The best deer hunting occurs on the west side, west of CR-669. Occasional crop-damage complaints from orchard owners suggest that asking permission to hunt private land might be a good idea. The sand dunes offer driving opportunities both early and late in the season as small islands of aspen hold deer. Good soils and a moderate climate with easy winters make for big, healthy deer.

There are few bear or bobcats in Leelanau County, and the season is currently closed for both species. Red-fox populations are fairly high and offer underutilized sport. A few coyotes and raccoon are found here too. Snowshoe hares are few in number, due largely to the northern hardwoods habitat. On the other hand, cottontail habitat is pretty good, and at times Leelanau County hosts huntable populations. Gray and black squirrels are scattered throughout, and there are also fox squirrels in areas of open hardwoods.

A few wild turkeys live in the southern portion but are not plentiful enough yet to warrant a hunting season. We were able to check only one year of records by grouse hunter-cooperators. Although they flushed 3.76 grouse per hour that season, the figure is probably unrealistic as good grouse habitat is spotty. Wild grape and silky dogwood are common, however, to wet areas such as creek bottoms, swamp edges, and lake perimeters. These are good places to zero in on for grouse and woodcock, but, once again, numbers are moderate at best. The same hunter-cooperators reported moving only .67 woodcock per hour.

Canada geese migrate through the county to provide some hunting opportunity and there is a small resident flock on Lake Leelanau. The lake offers limited shooting potential for both divers and dabblers all season long. The same is true on small lakes and ponds throughout the county, with overall waterfowling opportunities rated only fair.

OTHER SHOOTING OPPORTUNITIES

The Northport Sportsman Club, South Peterson Park Road in Northport, has a trap field and handtrap area open to the public without charge. The club also sponsors state hunter-certification courses. For information, call 616/386-5243.

FURTHER SOURCES OF HUNTING INFORMATION

1. DNR District Office, 8015 South 131 Road, Cadillac, Mich. 49601 (616/775-9727).
2. DNR Traverse City Field Office, 404 West 14th St., Traverse City, Mich. 49684 (616/946-4920).
3. Sleeping Bear Dunes National Lakeshore.
4. Suttons Bay Chamber of Commerce, Box 46, Suttons Bay, Mich. 49682 (616/271-3623).
5. Topographic, county, and lake maps may be ordered from the Michigan United Conservation Clubs. For information, refer to the beginning of this book.
6. Plat books are available from the Leelanau County Cooperative Extension Services, 116 Phillips St., Lake Leelanau, Mich. 49653. The cost is $10 each (no extra charge for mail orders). Make checks payable to 4-H Youth Association.
7. Leelanau County ASCS Office, Lake Leelanau, Mich. 49653.

Also, refer to the following elsewhere in this book:
1. Beaver Islands Wildlife Research Area
2. Leelanau State Park
3. Pere Marquette State Forest
4. South Manitou Island

Lenawee County

LENAWEE County was covered more than once by thick sheets of glacial ice. The ice wore away or ground up the bedrock to leave thick deposits of drift containing silt, sand, clay, gravel, boulders, and fragments of rock. Present-day surface features of the 754-square-mile county are the result of this glacial action thousands of years ago. Sand and gravel plains, ridges, and knolls in the northwestern part of the county, including the Onsted State Game Area (which see), are examples of this kind of deposit. Included is a series of lakes largely connected by streams.

Gently-rolling, rolling, and hilly moraines, deposited near the ice front at a time when it was nearly stationary, run southeasterly through the central portion. The eastern and southeastern parts of Lenawee County were once covered by glacial lakes, an extension of Lake Erie. Today, a few entrenched drainageways with steep sides occur along with narrow, low beaches; bars; and gentle swells. The River Raisin, main watercourse in the county, flows through this central lake-bed plain.

Elevations in Lenawee County span 600 feet of relief and are lowest in the eastern portion and highest in the west, particularly in the morainic uplands of the northwestern corner. About 12 percent of the county is timbered with forest species, hard maple and birch predominating. Red, white, and black oaks; sugar maples; and beech were the principal species on well-drained soils when the settlers arrived. Oak and hickory dominated sandy, gravelly soils while soils imperfectly drained supported sugar maple, beech, and elm. Although few virgin stands of timber remain, for the most part, forested areas are reproductions of original species.

Most of Lenawee County is in farmland with livestock raising the main practice. That is why much of the land is pastured. Most of the corn, wheat, and oats grown are used to fatten cattle and hogs with other crops, including soybeans, cash cropped. The southeastern portion is intensively row-cropped, with fencerow-to-fencerow cultivation the norm. This rich area of lake-bottom soils provides some of Michigan's best per-acre yields. Also, it is not surprisingly the best former pheasant range although populations are currently low here. Better opportunities occur in the northwestern region where birds may be found with the help of dogs in isolated pockets.

Access to private land is tough to obtain in this county. Only four farmers presently enroll land in the Public Access Stamp program. These are located in west-central townships (DNR district headquarters in Jackson or officials at Walter J. Hayes State Park have directories) of Rollin and Hudson but total less than 500 acres. Public land open to hunting is limited to the game area, the Lake Hudson Recreation Area (which see), and a 120-acre portion of Cambridge Historic State Park on M-50 near US-12. Sunday hunting with firearms or dogs is not permitted in the county except on state lands.

Considerate sportsmen asking permission to hunt private lands can sometimes gain access to fair hunting opportunities. One of the more sought-after game species is white-tailed deer. Moderate populations (under 300 annual car-deer accidents) improve from east to west, and the county produces some large-racked animals. Commemorative Bucks of Michigan currently lists 31 Lenawee County deer, including three shot during a recent season, among Michigan's all-time big bucks. Overall, hunter pressure is low (about seven hunters per square mile), due mainly to the lack of public land available. The eight-percent success rate is about half the state average. Those seeking hunter's-choice permits stand about an 85 percent chance of getting a tag. Still, only one deer or less per square mile is shot.

Excellent raccoon hunting exists throughout Lenawee County, the result of rich farms, scattered woods, and plenty of streams. The area is popular with nonresidents who come from as far as Tennessee to hunt the later season. Good populations of red fox also exist to provide underutilized opportunity. Brushy areas along wetlands and wood/brush stream bottoms provide excellent cottontail habitat and good hunting opportunity. Lenawee is one of the better rabbit hunting counties in the nine-county DNR district. Good to excellent populations of fox squirrels, with a few gray squirrels, are currently underhunted.

There are no turkeys in Lenawee County at this time and the DNR has no immediate plans to introduce any. Because this region is out of the grouse/woodcock range, opportunities are limited and pressure is light. For best grouse chances, concentrate on upland aspen and brush areas containing dogwood. Seek late October flight woodcock in lowland tangles of alder and brush.

There are no major marshy areas for waterfowl hunting. The northwestern corner, again, provides the best opportunities. There is public access on Devils and Sand lakes; consider too lakes and impoundments within the game area. The Raisin River offers about 40 miles of floatable scenic beauty and hunting opportunity from Clinton downstream to Deerfield. Hunters will want to check for regulations in municipalities (Clinton, Tecumseh, Adrian, and Blissfield) along the way. There are some wild stretches through interesting farmland, but all land en route is privately-owned.

Roughly the northern half of Lenawee County is currently open to late-season field hunting for Canada geese. Depending upon winter severity, many of the nuisance giant geese stay all winter. Good lakes to find concentrations include Silver, Devils, Deer, Sand, and Evans.

OTHER SHOOTING OPPORTUNITIES

The Morenci Sportsman Club, 8972 West Mulberry Road, Morenci, Mich. 49256, is open to the public on a sometime-fee basis for use of 16 pistol stations (indoor/outdoor), 10 centerfire rifle stations (outdoor), 16 rifle rimfire stations (indoor/outdoor), 29 archery targets (indoor/outdoor), and a shotgun trap field. Shooting instruction, competitive shooting, and hunter education courses are also offered. Call 517/458-2573 for information.

Also in Morenci, the Cunningham Range (15220 Mulberry Road) has 30 outdoor pistol stations open to fee-public use. Shooting instruction and shooting competition are featured. For details, call 517/286-6924.

FURTHER SOURCES OF HUNTING INFORMATION

1. DNR District Office, 3335 Lansing Ave., Jackson, Mich. 49202 (517/784-3188).

2. W.J. Hayes State Park, although closed to hunting, has DNR information and officials there may be able to help hunters with questions. The address is 1220 Wampler's Lake Road, Onsted, Mich. 49265 (517/467-7401).

3. Lenawee County Chamber of Commerce, 216 Main St., Adrian, Mich. 49221 (517/265-5141).

4. Greater Blissfield Chamber of Commerce, 102 South Lane St., Blissfield, Mich. 49228 (517/486-3660).

5. Tecumseh Chamber of Commerce, Box 265, Tecumseh, Mich. 49286 (517/423-3740).

6. Topographic, county, and lake maps may be ordered from the Michigan United Conservation Clubs. For information, refer to the beginning of this book.

7. Plat books are available from Lenawee County Register of Deeds for $10 each (add $1 if mail ordering and make out checks to the Lenawee County Cooperative Extension Services). The address is Lenawee County Courthouse, Adrian, Mich. 49221.

8. Lenawee County ASCS Office, USDA, 227 North Winter St., Adrian, Mich. 49221.

Also, refer to the following elsewhere in this book:
1. Lake Hudson Recreation Area
2. Onstead State Game Area

Livingston County

AT 571 square miles, Livingston County in southeastern Lower Michigan is one of the fastest-growing areas in the state. Gently-rolling farmland is rapidly being subdivided into 10-acre homesites to feed Detroit and Pontiac's urban sprawl. The southeastern portion of the county, a region of many lakes, is also the region of fastest growth. It includes Brighton. Howell, the county seat, is also expanding. This urban sprawl limits hunting opportunity.

About half the land is in active farming for corn, wheat, oats, and barley, both cash-crop and livestock/dairy operations. There are many small vegetables and fruit farms too. The loamy soil grows good crops and produces good wildlife cover, even in the southern half which is largely glacial outwash plains over deposits of sand and gravel.

Hunting for most species is generally good in Livingston County, but access is difficult. There are only a half-dozen participating farmers in the Public Access Stamp program with about 1,400 acres of land enrolled. Nearly all is in the northwest corner (Conway Township). State land, which totals about 16,400 acres, provides a major portion of the hunting opportunity, but most of the state game and recreation areas are in the south. Oak Grove State Game Area (which see) is in the north-central region. The Brighton, Island Lake, and Pinckney recreation areas (all of which see) require a state-park sticker to hunt within marked boundaries.

Livingston County is closed to Sunday hunting with firearms or dogs. Exceptions are the state lands mentioned and the Gregory State Game Area (which see), including the unattached Unadilla Wildlife Area in the southwestern corner (a part of Gregory State Game Area) and the Hillcrest Mini-Game Area on the Shiawassee River just outside Howell.

If you want to kill a trophy buck, Livingston County may well be the place to do it. In the few years that Commemorative Bucks of Michigan has been compiling big-deer records, the group has

turned up no less than 50 all-time record whitetails shot in this county. That figure currently ranks fourth in the state. During two recent deer seasons seven and five bucks were newly enrolled. A few of these deer come from state lands, but most are taken off private property. Permission to hunt will involve more homework and time than merely knocking on a farmer's door opening morning.

Hunter's-choice permit interest runs high and the 54 percent success in obtaining an antlerless tag is lowest in the nine-county DNR district. Overall hunting success at 10 percent or less is below the state average with the buck kill checking in at about one deer per square mile. Pressure runs about 12 hunters per square mile and is considered moderate. In spite of these low figures, there are quite a few deer as evidenced by an annual car-deer accident figure approaching 400 animals.

About 21 percent of Livingston County is forested with commercial-forest species. Oak and hickory dominate the list, and so it is not surprising perhaps to learn that squirrel hunting is very good for both fox and gray species. Some areas also host large populations of mutant black squirrels. The southeast region is one good area, especially in the hills and ridges of the Brighton Recreation Area. Oak-hickory woodlots abutting on grain fields in the northern and western portions are also top rate.

Main farm crop in Livingston County is corn. Coupled with the large number of lakes and wooded small streams (including the Shiawassee River which runs through Howell and then north), the area produces good raccoon populations. Fox are also found throughout. Some hunters enjoy success while night hunting with predator calls along powerline rights of way.

Rabbit hunting is usually very good throughout the county, especially in brushlands and wet bottomlands. Although slipping in numbers as they are elsewhere in southern Michigan, wild pheasants are still found in pockets along the northern tier of townships.

Grouse hunting is fairly good throughout, especially when aspen stands can be found. Brushlands and abandoned farms as well as pockets of gray dogwood and viburnums hold grouse too. Hunting pressure runs moderate to high with hourly flush rates of 1.0 to 2.0 the standard most years. Best woodcock hunting comes in late October from northern migrants. Look for the long-billed birds in orchards with some cover, sumac growths along hillsides, and stream bottomlands containing brush or alder.

State lands provide some duck hunting. North of Howell the Shiawassee River features plenty of five- to 20-acre potholes, but be sure to ask permission before entering the lands of another. There may be some waterfowling opportunities on privately-owned lakes too if hunters do their homework first.

Overall, the county is excellent for Canada geese and is included in a late season which usually begins about mid-December and lasts until mid-February. In fact, the current nuisance giant Canada goose problem, which triggered the late season, began in the Kensington Metropolitan Park near Kent Lake. This area is closed to hunting, but geese disperse throughout the region in search of corn fields and stands of winter wheat. Consult the chapter on goose hunting for how-to information.

It is not unusual for Livingston County lakes to host nearly 2,000 geese when DNR mid-December counts are made by airplane. Bass, Chemung, Woodland, Crooked, Brophy, Shannon, and Bennett generally have geese on them. The key is to follow geese departing from these lakes to see where they feed, then ask landowners for hunting permission.

OTHER SHOOTING OPPORTUNITIES

The 440-acre Huron Hunt Club, 7050 Munsell Road, Howell, Mich. 48843, operates an Iosco Township shooting preserve open to the public. Pheasants and chukar partridge are available. Contact Ronald L. Van Houten, 517/546-0106, for details.

Land-O-Lakes Bowmen, 1360 Mabley Hill in Fenton, has archery shooting ranges featuring 58 indoor/outdoor targets open to the public on a sometime-fee basis. Competitive shooting and hunter-certification programs are offered. There is no phone.

The Livingston Gun Club, 2472 Hunter Road in Brighton, is open to the public for fees on a limited basis. They have outdoor ranges for pistol (20 stations) and centerfire and rimfire rifle (30 stations each). The club offers shooting instruction and shooting competition. Call 517/437-2640 for information.

The Howell Gun Club has outdoor pistol (25 stations), centerfire rifle (15 stations), and rimfire rifle (25 stations) open to the public on a sometime-fee basis. Included are one skeet and two trap fields. Shooting instruction and competitive shooting are available as well as hunter education courses. For details, contact club members at 3210 Jewell Road, Howell, or call 517/546-4556.

FURTHER SOURCES OF HUNTING INFORMATION

1. DNR District Office, 3335 Lansing Ave., Jackson, Mich. 49202 (517/784-3188).

2. Mason State Game Farm Field Office, 1219 Hawley Road, Mason, Mich. 48854 (517/676-4600).

3. Brighton Recreation Area, 6360 Chilson, Route 3, Howell, Mich. 48843 (313/229-6566).

4. Island Lake Recreation Area, 12950 East Grand River, Brighton, Mich. 48116 (313/229-7067).

5. Pinckney Recreation Area, 8555 Silver Hill Road, Route 1, Pinckney, Mich. 48169 (313/426-4913).

6. Howell Area Chamber of Commerce, 404 E. Grand River Ave., Howell, Mich. 48843 (517/546-3920).

7. Greater Brighton Area Chamber of Commerce, 131 Hyne St., Brighton, Mich. 48116 (313/227-5086).

8. Pinckney Chamber of Commerce, 106½ West Main, Pinckney, Mich. 48169 (313/878-6036).

9. Topographic, county, and lake maps may be ordered from the Michigan United Conservation Clubs. For information, refer to the beginning of this book.

10. Plat books are available from the Livingston County Cooperative Extension Services, 314 East Clinton St., Howell, Mich. 48843. The cost is $9 each (add $.63 if mail ordering).

11. Livingston County ASCS Office, USDA, 3477 East Grand River, Howell, Mich. 48843 (517/548-1552).

Also, refer to the following elsewhere in this book:

1. Brighton Recreation Area
2. Gregory State Game Area
3. Island Lake Recreation Area
4. Oak Grove State Game Area
5. Pinckney Recreation Area
6. Livingston County Mini-Game Area

Luce County

LOCATED in the eastern or lowland-plains division of the Upper Peninsula, Luce County contains 584,960 acres (914 square miles). About half of this land lies in the Lake Superior State Forest and Tahquamenon State Park (both of which see) and is therefore open to hunting. Because another 120,000 acres of company-owned land is enrolled in the Commercial Forest Act plan, it is also open to hunting. To locate these company lands, contact DNR district headquarters in Newberry or write/call DNR Forest Management Division, Box 30028, Lansing, Mich. 48909 (517/373-1275). Be sure to limit requests to a specific area. Once you obtain legal descriptions, it is a simple matter to find the unposted lands with the help of a current county plat book and county map.

Thus, hunters have some 408,000 acres, or about

70 percent of the Luce County land base, upon which to roam. They come here seeking deer, bear, bobcats, coyotes, snowshoe hares, ruffed grouse, sharp-tailed grouse, woodcock, and waterfowl.

The northern portion bordering Lake Superior is largely a smooth plain covered with sand from glacial lake deposition. This section as a whole is reasonably dry although a number of small swamps and several large lakes are distributed over it.

The central and eastern parts make up a great swampy plain. A large peat swamp, ranging from four to 10 miles wide, is cut by the Tahquamenon River and its tributaries and extends entirely across the county in an east-west direction. Another broad, wet plain runs northwesterly from Newberry to the western boundary with Schoolcraft and Alger counties. A third swamp division, surrounding Betsey Lake in the northeastern region, wanders southwesterly to meet the Tahquamenon Swamp. Thus, about 40 percent of Luce County is remote swampland, difficult for hunters to reach.

Terraces, broken plains, and low islands rise from these swamp regions, but the highest areas in the county occur just south of Newberry, just south of McMillan, and from the Alger County line southeasterly toward Newberry. These high-ground regions are comprised of knobs, steep slopes, deep pit lakes, and deep valleys.

Lakes ranging in size from one-acre potholes to those several square miles are widely distributed. Northern county streams, such as the Tahquamenon and its branches, flow toward Lake Superior. Those in the southern region, such as the Fox, meander toward Lake Michigan.

About 80 percent of Luce County is covered with commercial-forest species. Over 40 percent (191,000 acres) is maple-birch hardwoods, but other types (in order of size) include northern white cedar (69,600 acres), aspen (44,600 acres), jack pine (44,100 acres), black spruce (29,400 acres), elm-ash-soft maple (21,300 acres), balsam fir (15,500 acres), white pine (15,100 acres), red pine (14,900 acres), tamarack (9,700 acres), and white spruce (5,800 acres).

Hunting pressure in Luce County is near the lowest in Michigan. This is not due to a lack of game animals or birds but rather to the huge expanses of dense swamp cover and the fact that this region is lightly populated.

Deer-hunting pressure, for example, is very low at an average of only three hunters per square mile during the two-week firearm season. Consequently, the buck kill is rather light at one animal or less per square mile. On the other hand, success rates of 14 percent or one for eight are near the state average. Deer, well scattered throughout the county, are found in light numbers. The best hunting occurs north of Murphy Creek and east of M-123 in the east-central region.

Late-season hunters are learning to post migration routes along river valleys as deer move south from the Lake Superior watershed to more protected surroundings for winter. Key concentration areas include west and south of McLeod's Corner, due west and again southeast of Watson's Corner, along the Tahquamenon River northwest of McMillan, in the Helmer region, and in the extreme southeastern border with Schoolcraft County.

There has been no doe season in District 4 since 1972. Usually each fall about 55,000 to 60,000 whitetails enter the hunting season; however, that is not a large number of deer when one considers that this DNR management unit is the largest of 13 in the state. The district produces huge bucks, however, with eight points or better racks sometimes making up half the kill. It is not surprising perhaps to note that of 1,150 trophy bucks uncovered thus far by Commemorative Bucks of Michigan, 128 were shot in the five-county district. However, to date Luce County has contributed only 14 animals, again a reflection of low hunter density rather than a shortage of big deer.

Hunters wishing to spend two weeks in northern woods without spotting another suit of blaze orange can do it here. The large number of seemingly impenetrable swamps and the general remoteness of the region make for good black-bear production. District 4 hunters usually tag from 125 to 150 bruins each fall. Luce County is popular with dog hunters who often attach radio collars to their hounds in order to find them (and the bears they may tree). A chase can last 25 miles with only two-track roads being crossed by bear and hounds. Many hunters find popple (aspen) slashings adjacent to swamp cover to leave bait sacks in trees or on the ground. Bear thus cast enough scent for strike dogs to find hours later.

One popular bear-hunting area is southwest of Little Two Hearted Lakes; another lies west of CR-407 south and east of the Two Hearted River.

These same cutover areas of aspen and other hardwoods provide habitat for snowshoe hares, grouse, and woodcock. Hares are currently in a "down" part of their cycle but should be increasing soon. You will also find hares in young conifer stands and just inside dense swamp cover. Bobcats seek them in the heavy, green cover whereas coyotes prey upon them in jack pines. District 4 hunters average 60 to 120 bobcats each winter, according to DNR sealing records. Not surprisingly, many come from Luce County. Coyotes are really on the increase throughout the eastern Upper Peninsula and provide untapped sport for dog hunters and predator callers alike. Some hunters, using scoped deer rifles, have even learned to bait coyotes in open areas and on frozen lakes in the dead of winter.

Grouse and woodcock experience wide fluctuations in Luce County, partly due to the lack of an aggressive cutting program on public lands. Hourly flush-rate records from hunter-cooperators for three years showed averages of 1.31, 1.94, and .83 for grouse and .80, 2.14, and .75 for woodcock. The last figures mentioned are the most recent available and suggest that a slump is in progress at this time.

Best best for grouse are recent popple slashings and lowland or upland brush. Keep an eye open for wild berries, clusters of white fruits, and nuts and you will likely find grouse. Woodcock congregate along the edge of lowland openings, in stream-bottom alders, and in upland areas where moist soils prevail. Sometimes good shooting occurs in October when migrating birds drift east and west in search of food.

Sharp-tailed grouse frequent large, open, plains-like areas containing short covers of grass. Luce County joins Alger, Delta, Chippewa, and Schoolcraft as the last region in the state where these prairie birds may be hunted. Populations in the eastern U.P. are now thought to number about 10,000 and as long as brush-to-climax forest succession continues to close openings, the birds will gradually dwindle even further. Two DNR management units in Luce County are Kelly Lake (northwest of Newberry) and the Danaher Plains (west-central region), shared with eastern Alger County. Hunting pressure, however, is high on both areas.

Luce County waterfowl certainly deserve mention. Early-season hunters report good shooting on potholes and small lakes throughout the county, with northern beaver floodings and small wetlands furnishing excellent sport. The blind Sucker Flooding in the northwestern region is a choice spot. So is the Dollarville Flooding west of Newberry and the Hendrie River system east of Newberry. Species include mallards, wood ducks, teal, and a few blacks and divers. A bonus is Canada geese which visit the larger wetlands, the few farm fields throughout, and even the sharptail management areas.

Luce County contains a few raccoon and gray/black squirrels, which go largely unharvested by hunters. Single animals from a small moose herd occasionally show up as do timber wolves (both protected).

OTHER SHOOTING OPPORTUNITIES

The Northern Gun Shop on Route 2 in Newberry has a rifle range open to the public without charge on a limited basis. Facilities include 10 outdoor stations each for centerfire and rimfire rifle. The business sponsors competitive shooting and shooting instruction. For information, call 906/293-8811.

FURTHER SOURCES OF HUNTING INFORMATION

1. DNR District Office, 309 West McMillan Ave. (Box 445), Newberry, Mich. 49868 (906/293-5131).

2. Newberry Area Chamber of Commerce, Box 308, Newberry, Mich. 49868 (906/293-5562 or 293-3111).

3. Topographic, county, and lake maps may be ordered from the Michigan United Conservation Clubs. For information, refer to the beginning of this book.

4. Plat books are available from the Luce County Cooperative Extension Services, Luce County Building, East Court St., Newberry, Mich. 49868. The cost is $10 each (add $1.50 if mail ordering).

5. Mackinac/Luce/Schoolcraft County ASCS Office, Melville St., Engadine, Mich. 49827.

Also, refer to the following elsewhere in this book:
1. Lake Superior State Forest
2. Tahquamenon State Park

Mackinac County

LOCATED along the Lake Michigan shore in the eastern Upper Peninsula, Mackinac County contains 648,960 acres (1,014 square miles), more than half of which is publicly owned and therefore open to hunting. About 31 percent of the land base falls into a huge eastern-county block of the Hiawatha National Forest (*which see*). Another 22 percent comprises western- and central-county portions of the Lake Superior State Forest (*which also see*).

Further, nearly 26,000 acres of company-owned land is enrolled in the Commercial Forest Act plan and therefore open to hunting. To locate these company lands, contact DNR district headquarters in Newberry or write/call DNR Forest Management Division, Box 30028, Lansing, Mich. 48909 (517/373-1275). Be sure to limit requests to a specific area. Once you obtain legal descriptions, it is a simple matter to find the unposted lands with the help of a current county plat book and county map.

Thus, hunters have some 370,000 acres to roam in Mackinac County. They come here seeking deer, bear, bobcats, coyotes, snowshoe hares, ruffed grouse, woodcock, and waterfowl. In addition, there are untapped hunting opportunities for raccoon, woodchucks, and crows.

About 87 percent of Mackinac County is covered with commercial-forest types. Aspen and maple-birch lead the list with 137,700 acres and 135,400 acres, respectively. They are followed by 82,400 acres of northern white cedar, 48,800 acres of black spruce, 43,300 acres of balsam fir, 20,100 acres of paper birch, 15,700 acres of red pine, and smaller amounts of jack pine, white pine, white spruce, elm-ash-soft maple, and tamarack. There is virtually no oak-hickory in Mackinac County.

What would seem to be an excellent mix of forest types is in fact largely climax-growth woods aged beyond their ideal carrying capacity for wildlife. Aggressive cutting programs are needed to regenerate new growths more beneficial to game species. Still, there are some pretty good hunting opportunities in this county.

The DNR District 4 area headquartered at Newberry, which, along with Mackinac, includes three other counties and a portion of a fourth, yields an annual harvest of some 3,000 bucks (antlerless hunting has not been allowed since 1972). Many of these (35 to 50 percent most hunting seasons) are big-beamed whitetails carrying eight points or more. At this writing, Commemorative Bucks of Michigan has uncovered 37 Mackinac County monster deer.

Entering the hunting season each fall are some 55,000 to 60,000 deer in District 4—no great number considering that this administrative unit is the largest in the state. In fact, deer are widely scattered throughout the district and in Mackinac County contribute to only about 100 to 150 car-deer accidents each year. Firearm hunting pressure is low (about six sportsmen per square mile), and buck-hunter success runs about one to two deer per square mile for a 12 to 18 percent average. Best places to hunt are in heavy aspen areas in the vicinity of cuttings and near swamps. Late in the firearm season and again throughout December, deer often migrate along river valleys toward cedar swamps in protected areas. Hunters can intercept them en route.

In western Mackinac County deer yards are found south of US-2 from the Schoolcraft County border to Point Patterson and again from Naubinway to

Epoufette. In the eastern county try along I-75 in Ignace Township and along M-134 from I-75 to St. Martin Point and again in the Hessel-to-Cedarville region.

The annual bear kill in District 4 averages 100 to 150 animals, with Mackinac County rated fair to good. Good areas in the western portion include Moran Township north of the Brevort River; in a large C shape north, west, and south of Rexton including the Hendrie River Branch, Dollar Lake, Garnett, and Seven Lakes; along Cranberry Lake Road from Naubinway north to the Chippewa County border; between Black Creek Flooding and the Millecoquins Trout Pond; and from Betty Doe Lake to Millecoquins Lake. In the eastern region try along open hardwoods with black-cherry groves and skirt heavy swamps bordered with young aspen and other hardwoods.

Snowshoe hares also frequent these cutover areas near swamps and although populations are somewhat depressed at this writing, hares appear to be just now staging a comeback. Hunters will also find coyotes in jack-pine habitat with hares whereas bobcats prefer the remoteness of conifer swamps where hares are available. Bobcat hunters throughout the district generally bring in from 60 to 120 animals to DNR offices for sealing. Coyote hunters don't make much of an impact as these animals are fast increasing.

A lack of openings in Mackinac County limits sharp-tailed grouse production although remnant flocks of birds can be found. The season in this county, however, is currently closed. Ruffed grouse, on the other hand, are fairly plentiful and receive moderate to high hunting pressure. Three recent years of hunter-cooperator records for hourly flush rates yielded 1.70, 2.10, and .97 averages. The .97 figure represents a low-end year of the birds' cycle. Like hares, grouse are due for a comeback.

Woodcock hunting is generally very good in Mackinac County, both as a result of fairly good local production plus drifting of migrant birds from the west as they seek additional food sources. Best hunting occurs during October. Hunter-cooperators reported hourly flush-rate averages of 2.90, 1.57, and 2.21 woodcock to correspond with the same-year grouse statistics.

Good grouse/woodcock habitat is wrist-sized aspen and lowland brush. Woodcock also prefer moist-soil areas with park-like cover—not too dense on the ground, yet affording some canopy protection. Look for alder stands and bracken under aspen. In eastern Mackinac County a good place is north of M-134 in areas of abandoned farmlands where brush is encroaching fields. In the western-county area try these spots: South Branch Carp River and Caffey Road, Bennett and Dells Mills roads, from Garnet to Rexton north to Chippewa County, between Davenport Creek and the Black River north of US-2, south of Engadine to Lake Michigan, and north and west of Gould City.

Good to excellent waterfowling is found in the Manistique Lakes area, on Black Creek Flooding, and along portions of the Lake Michigan shoreline, especially in the Les Cheneaux Islands and St. Martin Bay. Species include mallards, teal, black ducks, and pintails in early season and goldeneyes, scaup, redheads, buffleheads, mergansers, and old-squaws in late season. DNR biologists flying aerial surveys over St. Martin Bay in late November have estimated up to 10,000 redheads along with lesser quantities of goldeneyes, buffleheads, scaup, and old-squaws. Many times they can be seen resting and feeding in the Straits area from the Mackinac Bridge. Brevort, Millecoquins, and the Manistique lakes are excellent inland waters to try decoy-hunting throughout the season. Canada geese feed in Mackinac County farm fields and provide a bonus to waterfowlers.

OTHER SHOOTING OPPORTUNITIES

The Straits Area Shooting Association in Allenville has a private range open to the public at certain times without charge. Facilities include outdoor stations for pistol, centerfire and rimfire rifle, and a skeet field. For information, call 906/643-9876.

Les Cheneaux Sportsman's Club in Cedarville owns a shooting range with six outdoor stations each for pistol and rimfire rifle as well as 12 outdoor archery targets. These are open to the public without charge. The club also offers shooting instruction and state hunter-certification programs. There is no phone.

FURTHER SOURCES OF HUNTING INFORMATION

1. DNR District Office, 309 West McMillan Ave. (Box 445), Newberry, Mich. 49868 (906/293-5131).

2. DNR Naubinway Field Office (western Mackinac County), US-2, Naubinway, Mich. 49762 (906/477-6262).

3. DNR Sault Ste. Marie Field Office (eastern Mackinac County), Box 798, Sault Ste. Marie, Mich. 49783 (906/635-5281).

4. Hiawatha National Forest Headquarters, 2727 North Lincoln Road (Box 316), Escanaba, Mich. 49829 (906/573-2356 or 573-2314.)

5. Hiawatha National Forest, St. Ignace Ranger District, Ferry Lane, St. Ignace, Mich. 49781 (906/643-7900).

6. St. Ignace Area Chamber of Commerce, South State Street, St. Ignace, Mich. 49781 (906/643-8717).

7. Les Cheneaux Chamber of Commerce, Cedarville, Mich. 49719 (906/484-3935).

8. Topographic, county, and lake maps may be ordered from the Michigan United Conservation Clubs. For information, refer to the beginning of this book.

9. County plat books are available from the Mackinac County Cooperative Extension Services, Courthouse, 100 Marley St., St. Ignace, Mich. 49781. The cost is $12.50 each (postpaid).

10. Mackinac/Luce/Schoolcraft County ASCS Office, Melville St., Engadine, Mich. 49827.

Also, refer to the following elsewhere in this book:
1. Hiawatha National Forest
2. Lake Superior State Forest

Macomb County

MACOMB County is one of three southeastern Michigan counties (the other two being Monroe and Wayne) that contain Detroit and most of its urban satellites. The southern one-third of 481-square-mile Macomb County is heavily populated, with no hunting opportunity. This no-hunting zone includes the Clinton River and the state-owned Rochester-Utica Recreation Area.

On the other hand, northern Macomb County is still largely rural and, as such, offers hunting opportunities for farmland game species, including deer. About 40 percent of the total county land base is being farmed, mostly for dairy cattle operations and fruit growing and nursery enterprises. The most intensive farming belt is in the north-central region. A surprising 16 percent of the county is forested with commercial-timber species, namely elm, ash, maple, and birch. Poorly-drained mineral soils support growths of elm and red maple whereas organic soils contain aspen, white cedar, and tamarack.

There are scattered farm woodlots throughout Macomb County along with increasing brushlands, especially on reverted farmlands of the northwestern and north-central portions. These areas provide the best hunting for rabbits, squirrels, fox, raccoon, pheasants, and deer.

All except the northwestern corner was at one time a glacial lake or succession of gradually receding lakes as the ice cap melted. Soils that extend well out from the present shore of Lake St. Clair are underlain by sand and gravel and show ridges of former beachlines. A northeast-to-southwest running moraine that is gently sloping and one to three miles wide extends from Richmond into Wayne County. The west-central portion of Macomb County is covered by sandy glacial outwash. Undulating areas that cross the northern region are till plains or ground moraines. The northwestern corner contains a few natural lakes and man-made Stony Creek Lake (not open to hunting). There is a range of morainic hills here too.

The only public land open to hunting is about 85 percent, or roughly 700 acres, of W.C. Wetzel State Park (which see). Pheasant, rabbit, deer, and squirrel hunting is considered fair to good here along with incidental bags of grouse and woodcock. About 1,400 acres of Public Access Stamp program land are currently enrolled by several landowners in two townships: Bruce in the northwestern corner and Lenox in the east-central region. The DNR has free directories available at Wetzel, Rochester-Utica, and at district headquarters in Pontiac.

Some Macomb County farmers also allow access to their lands if responsible sportsmen make courteous requests. This is particularly true in the northern portion, farthest from cities. Hunters should also be aware that Macomb County enforces a no-Sunday-hunting law with firearms or dogs except on state lands and for waterfowl in border waters of Lake St. Clair.

Best deer hunting comes from the better farming

soils of the north-central and northwestern areas. Overall pressure is light (about three hunters per square mile) and success less than half the state average. About six percent tag bucks. There are a few large-racked deer, however, as evidenced by the fact that Commemorative Bucks of Michigan has thus far uncovered two trophy whitetails shot in this county.

There is some hunting opportunity for fox and raccoon, especially in the northern tier of townships. Rabbit numbers are generally fair to good throughout the farm belt where brushlands meet crop-field or woods openings. Best bets for pheasants occur in the northeastern corner abutting St. Clair County. Abandoned farms and idled acres on those farms still producing are the places to focus on, again if permission can be secured. Woodlots here as well as on the dairy and orchard farms produce fair to good numbers of squirrels. Woodcock and grouse are available but in low numbers. Hunting pressure is light.

West of M-53, Macomb County is open for late-season Canada goose hunting. A wintering population of the nuisance giants uses Stony Creek Lake as well as a few of the other lakes in this region. Hunters willing to scout for foraging geese and ask permission to get on private lands where they feed can be rewarded with late-season action. Duck hunting opportunities, however, are limited to jump-shooting wood ducks along small drainage systems through farmland. There is also some sneak-boat and diving-duck hunting on Anchor Bay in Lake St. Clair. The shoreline is privately-owned; however, several marinas along the shore have fee access sites.

Heavily-populated Macomb County is no hunter's mecca; however, it does offer fair to good possibilities for those willing to take a second look.

OTHER SHOOTING OPPORTUNITIES

Maple Grove Shooting Range, 2-4545 21-Mile Road in Mount Clemens, is a commercially-owned enterprise open daily to the public for fees. Facilities include 17 indoor/outdoor pistol stations, 40 outdoor centerfire-rifle stations, 40 indoor/outdoor rimfire-rifle stations, four fields each for skeet and trap, three handtrap areas, and six outdoor archery targets. The range offers both shooting instruction and competitive shooting as well as hunter certification courses. For more information, call 313/949-0020.

Peters Indoor Range and Gun Shop, Inc., is another commercially-owned business open to the public for fees. Located at 28631 Gratiot in Roseville, Peters offers 10 indoor stations each for centerfire- and rimfire-rifle practice. Shooting instruction and shooting competition are also featured. Call 313/773-7515.

The DNR oversees free public shotgun and archery shooting facilities at the Rochester-Utica Recreation Area at 47511 Woodall in Utica. Included are 10 shotgun handtrap areas and five outdoor archery targets. For details, call 313/731-2110.

FURTHER SOURCES OF HUNTING INFORMATION

1. DNR District Office, 2455 North Williams Lake Road, Pontiac, Mich. 48054 (313/666-1500).
2. Rochester-Utica Recreation Area, 47511 Woodall, Utica, Mich. 48087 (313/731-2110).
3. W.C. Wetzel State Park (call Algonac State Park officials at 517/322-1300).
4. Our Chamber of Commerce, 27602 Jefferson, St. Clair Shores, Mich. 48081 (313/777-2741).
5. Central Macomb County Chamber of Commerce, 10 North Avenue, Mount Clemens, Mich. 48043 (313/462-1528).
6. Northwest Macomb Chamber of Commerce, 49780 Van Dyke, Utica, Mich. 48087 (313/731-5400).
7. Romeo-Washington Chamber of Commerce, Box 175, Romeo, Mich. 48065 (no phone).
8. Topographic, county, and lake maps may be ordered from the Michigan United Conservation Clubs. For information, refer to the beginning of this book.
9. Plat books are available from the Macomb County Cooperative Extension Services, 9th Floor County Bldg, Mount Clemens, Mich. 48043 (313/469-5285). The cost is $10 each (add $1 if mail ordering).
10. Macomb County ASCS Office, USDA, 67533 Main St., Suite D401, Richmond, Mich. 48062 (313/727-1066).
11. Lake St. Clair Fisheries, 33135 South River Road, Mount Clemens, Mich. 48045 (313/465-4771) (staffed with DNR wildlife biologist).

Also, refer to the following elsewhere in this book: W. C. Wetzel State Park

Manistee County

MANISTEE County in northwestern Lower Michigan contains plenty of wild lands, large portions of which are open to hunting. A high water table with many creeks and swamps renders much of the county unfit for agriculture. Consequently, about 65 percent of its 542 square miles is covered with commercial-forest species, which in turn house good populations of many game birds and animals. Whitetail deer are especially plentiful. So are squirrels, snowshoe hares, grouse, woodcock, turkeys, and raccoon.

To many sportsmen Manistee County is "off the beaten track." For the most part, hunting pressure is only moderate at best.

Topographically, Manistee County contains a number of separate hilly divisions or ridges and a number of associated plains and flat valleylike areas whose boundaries are well defined. The hilly portions are not rugged but are characterized by smooth, softened slopes, except in a few places in the clay land directly along Lake Michigan, where the surface is quite choppy and deeply cut by streams. Plains and valleys are mostly dry due to sandy soils, but the Kaleva-Copemish plain, which covers the central part of the county, is swampy.

The northern part of the county (north of the Manistee River) contains a succession of hilly belts and level plains in an east-west orientation. South of the Manistee River the land as a whole is nearly level with only a few gentle swells of rolling terrain.

There is a wide mixture of forest types. Led by maple-birch at 68,800 acres, the list contains oak-hickory (54,000 acres), aspen (32,100 acres), red pine (20,500 acres), elm-ash-soft maple (17,100 acres), jack pine (12,500 acres), and smaller amounts of white pine, northern white cedar, and paper birch. About 23,500 acres, or 6.7 percent of the land base, is state-owned. This occurs in northern-county holdings of the Pere Marquette State Forest and in the Manistee River State Game Area (both of which see) upstream from Manistee. Another 61,689 acres, or 17.6 percent, is contained within the Huron-Manistee National Forest (which also see), mostly located in the southern half of the county.

In addition to these public holdings open to hunting, Manistee County has 5,411 acres of company-owned land enrolled in the Commercial Forest Act program. These lands may also be hunted. Sportsmen can find them with the aid of a good county map and a current plat book if they first obtain legal descriptions. These are available from DNR district headquarters in Cadillac or by contacting the DNR Forest Management Division, Box 30028, Lansing, Mich. 48909 (517/373-1275).

The mild climate west of US-31 is conducive to fruit growing. Deer that profit year around in this region occasionally become a nuisance to farmers. Deer may also be hunted on the mainland side of Lake Michigan sand dunes in places where cover affords protection. The central portion of the county around Kaleva contains many small farms of marginal quality. Although this is private land, it is also wild land and fairly good for hunting. A courteous request might gain permission to enter.

Along the Manistee River and south to the border with Lake and Mason counties, there are plenty of red and white oaks, aspen, and swamps in public ownership, which, as we have seen, is high in this area. However, winters are tougher and some deer are annually lost when conditions become harsh. Except for west of US-31, the sandy soils are not too productive. East of US-31 and north of the river, the soils are once more sandy and poorly drained. This area contains lowlands hardwoods and aspen and is interlaced with drainages.

Manistee County deer hunters score a little above the state average and during a very good year will exceed 20 percent success on bucks. That can amount to three to five bucks per square mile, a high yield, from the 20 to 30 hunters per square mile.

There are occasional bear and bobcats sighted in Manistee County although the season is currently closed on both species and will likely remain so. Coyotes scattered throughout the county are fair game. So are limited numbers of red fox.

On the other hand, raccoon are plentiful most years and face only moderate hunting pressure.

Turkeys are widespread throughout the county with greatest concentrations appearing in the southern region. Currently, the entire county east of US-31 is open to hunting by permit. There is good snowshoe hare habitat throughout much of Manistee County. Hunt cutover aspen lands near conifer swamps.

The northern hardwoods of beech, oak, and hickory make for good squirrel hunting—mostly grays/blacks with a few fox squirrels. For best opportunities, try mast-producing forests along the Manistee River and south. Hodenpyle and Tippy dam backwaters offer goose-hunting potential. Puddle ducks are found along creeks and on small lakes and beaver ponds. Portage and Bear lakes contain some potential for diving-duck hunting. And the Manistee River itself is ideal for a float trip for ducks, geese, squirrels, and deer. Several campgrounds exist along the way.

Grouse and woodcock hunting is generally very good throughout Manistee County. Varying age classes of aspen is one key. Plenty of wild raisin, gray dogwood, wild grape, and thornapple are others. You will find these favored grouse foods mixed with aspen and along creek bottoms. Hunting pressure is moderate. Hunter-cooperator records checked for three years showed 1.37, 1.42, and 2.03 average hourly flushes for grouse. For the same seasons woodcock flushes were 2.68, .51, and 3.05.

OTHER SHOOTING OPPORTUNITIES

None known at this time.

FURTHER SOURCES OF HUNTING INFORMATION

1. DNR District Office, 8015 South 131 Road, Cadillac, Mich. 49601 (616/775-9727).

2. DNR Traverse City Field Office, 404 West 14th St., Traverse City, Mich. 49684 (616/946-4920).

3. Huron-Manistee National Forest, Manistee Ranger District, Manistee, Mich. 49660 (616/723-2211).

4. Manistee County Chamber of Commerce, US-31 at Mason St., Manistee, Mich. 49660 (616/723-2575).

5. Topographic, county, and lake maps may be ordered from the Michigan United Conservation Clubs. For information, refer to the beginning of this book.

6. Plat books are available from the Manistee County Treasurer, Manistee County Courthouse, 415 Third St., Manistee, Mich. 49660. The cost is $11 each (add $1.50 if mail ordering). They are also available in Onekama at the Tri-Ag Building on Eight-Mile Road.

7. Manistee County ASCS Office, 6433 Eight-Mile Road, Onekama, Mich. 49675.

Also, refer to the following elsewhere in this book:
1. Huron-Manistee National Forest
2. Manistee River State Game Area
3. Pere Marquette State Forest

Marquette County

SPRAWLING Marquette County in the north-central Upper Peninsula is Michigan's largest county, spanning nearly 1.2 million acres, or 1,878 square miles. A varied shoreline of beaches and harbors to wilderness coastline laps Lake Superior for 78 miles. Inland, the topography ranges from flat, outwash plains and low, swampy areas to bold outcroppings of rock. Some 1,800 lakes and ponds lie within the county, which is streaked by more than 4,000 miles of rivers and streams. From the ruggedly remote Huron Mountains of the northern region to its southern boundary with Menominee County, Marquette County contains a tremendous diversity of land forms to wander and game animals to hunt.

Loons, bald eagles, spruce grouse, and ospreys (all protected) have a foothold here. Occasional tracks and sightings of wolves and moose—also protected—occur. Game species that provide fair to excellent hunting opportunities include deer, bear, coyotes, bobcats, fox, snowshoe hares, gray squirrels, raccoon, ruffed grouse, woodcock, ducks, and geese.

The northern portion of the county, which receives upwards of 150 inches of snow each year, includes highland hardwoods in the Huron Mountains, a large part of which is privately owned. South of the mountains, the Yellow Dog Plains with its scattered openings contains a remnant population of sharp-tailed grouse, the season on which was recently closed after 30 years of sport hunting. Huge swamps in the Escanaba River State Forest (*which see*), inland from Granite and Little Presque Isle, are winter deer yard areas. Even so, deer are not plentiful; however, bear, bobcats, coyotes, ruffed grouse, and hares usually are. Woodcock hunting is best in the young season since early frosts push the longbills out. South and east of the Yellow Dog Plains, the cover type is mostly northern hardwoods mixed with conifer growths.

This is tough, wild, inaccessible country, which is why it appeals to the hardy sportsman who wants a quality, remote hunting experience.

Eastern Marquette County includes farming areas around Skandia and north and south of Boney Falls Basin. Jack pines are predominant in the region north of Gwinn. A huge swampy area good for snowshoe hares and black bear lies mostly in state forest land from Gwinn southeasterly to Delta County. The southern portion, which fronts Menominee County, contains a great deal of aspen and is a good area for grouse and woodcock. It is also a top bet for late-season deer hunting as whitetails move south to yarding areas. Wells and Sands townships contain ruffed grouse, woodcock, and sharp-tailed grouse, but don't misidentify the latter because, as mentioned, the season is closed.

Much of southwestern Marquette County is mining country offering poor to fair hunting opportunities. Best bets are hardwoods to the west around Michigamme Reservoir and a pine belt on state forest land east of Republic. The southern boundary with Dickinson County contains a good aspen mix, attractive to grouse and deer. South of Witch Lake is a winter yarding area.

About 6,000 acres of the Ottawa National Forest (which see), located in the northwestern section, is open to hunting. Another 263,000 acres, or about 22 percent of the total land base, is state forest land, also fully open to hunting. Finally, nearly 280,000 more acres of private land is enrolled in the Commercial Forest Act program, which means that it too may be hunted. All totaled, over a half-million acres of Marquette County is huntable by the public.

To find the public lands, refer to the Michigan United Conservation Clubs publication "Michigan County Maps and Outdoor Guide." To get legal descriptions of CFA land, contact the DNR Forest Management Division, Box 30028, Lansing, Mich. 48909 (517/373-1275). Be sure to give town and range numbers of that portion of the county you intend to hunt.

Over a million acres, or about 88 percent of Marquette County, is timbered with a wide mix of commercial-forest species. Leading the list is maple-birch at 421,600 acres, followed by 121,700 acres of aspen, 82,600 acres of balsam fir, 79,100 acres of black spruce, 61,100 acres of northern white cedar, 55,300 acres of jack pine, 48,900 acres of paper birch, 42,100 acres of elm-ash-soft maple, 17,500 acres of white pine, and 11,700 acres of white spruce. Oak-hickory, red pine, and tamarack are also represented in smaller amounts.

Since about 70 percent of annual allowable timber cuttings on state forest land are being met, portions of Marquette County are constantly being rejuvenated. The side benefit is greater game production since more food and forest edge are produced.

The deer herd in the three-county DNR district is fairly stable at about 50,000 animals after bouncing back from an all-time low of about 30,000 ten years ago. During a recent firearm season, hunters shot 5,000 bucks. In Marquette County alone, where pressure is a low six hunters per square mile, the kill was one to two bucks per square mile for a success rate of 21 percent. Marquette County contains some big-bodied, huge-racked bucks as recently reported by Commemorative Bucks of Michigan. With 64 all-time record deer in the books, Marquette County trails only neighboring Delta County as Michigan's best trophy producer.

Bear are quite numerous throughout much of the county, especially so in the central portion. In fact, the annual kill has increased for several years and now is approaching 200 for the district. Bobcats are yet another abundant game animal here, as evidenced by DNR sealing records of 59 to 110 cats for each of the past five years. Try the southern county region. Coyote hunters too have plenty of opportunities for hound hunting and predator calling. A few red fox are found around farming regions, and there is some good raccoon hunting in the southwestern region along waterways.

Gray squirrels with a few black-phase animals may be found in hardwoods south of Marquette. Also, there are reports of fox squirrels near Watson. Snowshoe hares are currently down about 25 percent after several years on the high end of their cycle. Target lowland hardwoods, aspen, and conifers being cut for pulp. When numbers are high, hares may be found in nearly every swamp.

Such aspen cuttings in particular furnish good hunting opportunities for ruffed grouse and woodcock. Randomly checking three years of hunter-cooperator hourly flush rate records yielded averages of 1.70, 1.98, and .64 on grouse and 2.30, 2.44, and 4.72 on woodcock. Grouse are currently down somewhat, but woodcock seem to be holding their own and perhaps are increasing.

Hunters can utilize a wide variety of Marquette County habitat-improvement sites that have been cleared, fertilized, and seeded to benefit deer, bear, grouse, woodcock, and geese. These sites are on public land and include seeded openings and walking trails. The seedings are to rye, winter what, timothy, creeping red fescue, brome grass, alfalfa, crownvetch, hairy vetch, birdsfoot trefoil, medium red clover, and white Dutch clover. Here are their locations by town, range and section (you will need to consult a good county map or plat book—also DNR forestry and wildlife personnel can help you find them):

—T42N, R26W, Section 11, SE NE, S ½ SW ¼, three openings, 15 acres.

—T43N, R24W, Section 11, N ½ SW ¼, hunter walking trail, five acres.

—T43N, R24W, Section 18, NE ¼, two openings, 17 acres.

T43N, R24W, Section 18, SW SE, one opening, five acres.

—T43N, R24W, Section 31, NW NW, one opening, four acres.

—T43N, R25W, Section 7, NW ¼, one opening and hunter walking trail, four acres.

—T43N, R25W, Section 10, SE NW, NE SW, hunter walking trail, one acre.

—T43N, R25W, Section 16, NE SW, one opening, five acres.

—T43N, R25W, Section 16, S ½, Section 21, N ½ NW ¼, two openings, 10 acres.

—T43N, R25W, Section 19, E-W, walking trail through center of section, three acres.

—T43N, R25W, Section 20, SE NE, one opening, five acres.

—T43N, R25W, Section 28, NE ¼, four openings, 12 acres, Section 21, SW SE.

—T43N, R25W, Section 33, NW NE, hunter walking trail, two acres.

—T43N, R25W, Section 34, W ½ NE ¼, E ½ NW ¼, two openings, 25 acres.

—T43N, R25W, Section 35, NW SE, one opening, one acre.

—T43N, R25W, Section 36, S ½, two openings, 19 acres.

—T43N, R26W, Section 1, SWSE, one opening, five acres.

—T43N, R26W, Section 3, NW SW, Section 4, NE SE, hunter walking trail, two acres.

—T43N, R26W, Section 4, W ½ SW ¼, three openings, seven acres.

—T43N, R26W, Section 10, N ½ SW ¼, S ½ NE ¼, three openings, nine acres.

—T43N, R26W, Section 16, W½ NW¼, one opening, eight acres.

—T43N, R26W, Section 20, E ½ NW ¼, NESW, one opening, five acres.

—T43N, R26W, Section 22, W ½ SE ¼, two openings, 10 acres.

—T43N, R26W, Section 22, SW ¼, three openings, nine acres.

—T43N, R26W, Section 23, SW SW, two openings, eight acres.

—T43N, R26W, Section 24, N ½ SW ¼, N ½ SE ¼, walking trail plus three openings, eight acres.

—T43N, R26W, Section 25, N ½ NE ¼, one opening, two acres.

—T44N, R24W, Section 21, W ½, W ½ SE ¼, three walking trails, five acres.

—T44N, R25W, Section 20, SE SE, Section 21, SW SW, one opening, three acres.

—T44N, R25W, Section 21, NE SE, one opening, six acres.

—T44N, R26W, Section 6, SWNE, SENW, NESW, NWSE, one opening and walking trail, eight acres.

—T44N, R26W, Section 20, S ½, three openings, 16 acres.

—T44N, R26W, Section 20, SENE; Section 21, NWNW, one opening, five acres.

—T44N, R26W, Section 22, SENE; Section 23, NWSW, one opening, five acres.

—T44N, R26W, Section 24, W ½ SE ¼, one opening, four acres, hunter walking trail.

—T44N, R26W, Section 25, S ½ NW ¼, one opening, three acres.

—T44N, R26W, Section 26, NESE, one opening, three acres.

—T44N, R26W, Section 26, SESW, SWSE, one hunter walking trail, two acres.

—T44N, R26W, Section 27, S ½ SE ¼, one opening one acre.

—T44N, R26W, Section 29, NW SW, one opening, four acres.

—T44N, R26W, Section 31, SE NE, two openings, four acres.

—T44N, R26W, Section 32, SW NW, SW SW two openings, six acres.

—T44N, R26W, Section 33, S ½ NW ¼, one opening, seven acres.

—T44N, R26W, Section 34, SW NW, one opening, two acres.

—T44N, R26W, Section 35, NE SE, one opening, four acres.

—T44N, R26W, Section 35, N ½, one opening, five acres.

—T44N, R26W, Section 36, NESE, one opening, three acres.

—T45N, R22W, Section 5, NW SE, hunter walking trail, two acres.

—T45N, R26W, Section 29, NE NW, one opening, three acres.

—T45N, R26W, Section 33, NE ¼, three openings, 10 acres.

—T45N, R27W, Section 28, W ½ SE ¼; Section 29, S ¼, two openings, four acres.

—T45N, R27W, Section 31, S ½, one opening, two acres, one hunter walking trail.

—T45N, R27W, Section 32, five openings, 14 acres, NE ¼.

—T45N, R27W, Section 33, NE ¼, one opening, two-and-a-half acres.

—T45N, R27W, Section 34, SW NW, SE SE hunter walking trail.

—T45N, R27W, Section 34, SW NW, one opening, two acres.

—T45N, R28W, Section 21, S ½ SW ¼, two openings, five acres.

—T45N, R28W, Section 28, NW NW, two openings, three acres.

—T45N, R28W, Section 29, NE NE, one opening, two acres.

—T45N, R28W, Section 32, SW ¼, one opening, six acres.

—T45N, R28W, Section 33, SENE, NE SE, hunter walking trail, one acre.

—T45N, R28W, Section 33, SW NW, two openings, eight acres.

—T45N, R28W, Section 33, N ½ SE ¼, two openings, eight acres.

—T45N, R28W, Section 33, W ½ SW ¼, one opening, eight acres.

—T45N, R28W, Section 34, SW ¼, three openings, nine acres.

—T45N, R28W, Section 34, NW ¼, N ½ SW ¼, hunter walking trail, seven acres.

—T45N, R28W, Section 35, SE NE, SE SE, two openings, four acres, hunter walking trail.

—T45N, R28W, Section 36, SW ¼, W ½ NE ¼, NE NW, three openings, four acres, two hunter walking trails.

—T45N, R30W, Section 22, NE NW, E ½ NE ¼, three hunter walking trails, 16 acres.

—T45N, R30W, Section 34, W ½, five openings, 10 acres.

—T45N, R24W, Section 34, SESE, one opening, three acres.

—T46N, R29W, Section 24, W ½, two openings, 19 acres.

—T47N, R23W, Section 22, SE NE, one opening, one acre.

—T47N, R23W, Section 23, W ½, four openings and walking trail, 11 acres.

Harsh winters and a lack of farming rule out Marquette County for future wild-turkey releases. However, fair to good waterfowling for local Canada geese and puddle ducks, plus migrant geese and divers, occurs on many of the lakes close to Lake Superior. These include Independence, Harlow, Saux Head, and LeVasseur. The large storage basins, such as the Dead River, Silver Lake, and Deer Lake, attract good numbers of waterfowl by late October. Many of the larger rivers are floatable and can provide untapped waterfowling. Lake Independence and Greenwood Reservoir are the sites of giant Canada-goose releases from downstate areas where the big birds proved to be a nuisance.

OTHER SHOOTING OPPORTUNITIES

The Tomahawk Bowmen, Inc. on West US-41 in Ishpeming owns an archery range open to the public at times on a sometime-fee basis. Facilities include 28 outdoor targets. For information on times, fees, and competitive shooting dates, call 906/485-5802.

The Deertrack Bowhunters Archery Range on Vandenboom Road in Marquette is open daily to the public without charge. The club has 28 outdoor targets and offers competitive shooting. Call 906/249-3988 for details.

FURTHER SOURCES OF HUNTING INFORMATION

1. DNR Regional Headquarters, 1990 US-41 South (Box 190) Marquette, Mich. (906/228-6561).

2. DNR District Office, 1126 North Lincoln Road (Box 495), Escanaba, Mich. 49829 (906/786-2351).

3. DNR Champion Field Office, Box 163, Champion, Mich. 49814, (906/399-2251).

4. DNR Gwinn Field Office, M-35, Gwinn, Mich. 49841 (906/346-9201).

5. DNR Ishpeming Field Office, 632 Teal Lake Road, Ishpeming, Mich. 49849 (906/485-4193).

6. Forest Supervisor, Ottawa National Forest, East Cloverland Drive, Ironwood, Mich. 49938 (906/932-1330 or 1-800-561-1201 from the Upper Peninsula).

7. Marquette Area Chamber of Commerce, 501

South Front St., Marquette, Mich. 49855 (906/226-6591).

8. Greater Ishpeming Chamber of Commerce, Ishpeming, Mich. 49849 (906/486-4841).

9. Neagaunee Area Civic Association, Negaunee, Mich. 49866 (906/475-9814).

10. Topographic, county, and lake maps may be ordered from the Michigan United Conservation Clubs. For information, refer to the beginning of this book.

11. Plat books are available from the Marquette County Cooperative Extension Services, Courthouse Annex, Marquette, Mich. 49855. The cost is $14.50 each (add $.80 if mail ordering).

12. Alger/Marquette County ASCS Office, Box 166, Chatham, Mich. 49816.

Also, refer to the following elsewhere in this book:
1. Escanaba River State Forest
2. Hiawatha National Forest
3. Van Riper State Park

Mason County

MASON County in west-central Lower Michigan offers good hunting opportunities for deer, snowshoe hares, squirrels, raccoon, wild turkeys, grouse, woodcock, and waterfowl. Hunting pressure overall is moderate. About 18 percent of the 494-square-mile county is publicly-owned and open to hunting, and a wide variety of cover types are featured.

About half of the county land base is covered with commercial-forest species. Oak-hickory dominates with 51,000 acres, scattered throughout but running most heavily on the eastern side. Aspen with 32,300 acres follows. This cover type is also widely dispersed. Deer, grouse, hares, and turkeys benefit from both kinds of forest. Other commercial-forest types include elm-ash-soft maple (19,200 acres), maple-birch (18,400 acres), red pine (9,700 acres), jack pine (6,700 acres), and northern white cedar (3,000 acres).

Most of the pine grows across the northern tier of the townships whereas cedar and other swamp growth occurs between US-10 and USFS-5205 east of a line from Walhalla north through Round Lake to USFS-5205. This area known as Big Bear Swamp contains wintering deer, snowshoe hares in hardwood-fringed cover, and an occasional black bear and bobcat (both protected in Mason County). In conifer cover mixed with mature oak are liable to be gray and black squirrels too. Pure-oak stands and farm woodlots containing oaks harbor fox squirrels. Here is plenty of hunting opportunity going underutilized.

About 6,100 acres of Mason County are state-owned. These are scattered parcels of the Pere Marquette State Forest (which see), all of which is open to hunting, and the 4,514-acre Ludington State Park (which also see), nearly 3,400 acres of which may be hunted. Federal land amounts to 52,800 acres, or 16 percent of the land base. This is Huron-Manistee National Forest (which also see) land, located in scattered holdings throughout the eastern third of Mason County and in a solid-block ownership in the northwestern region.

In addition, a whopping 11,000 acres of company-owned timberland are open to hunting. DNR district headquarters at Cadillac has legal descriptions, or hunters may write or call the DNR Forest Management Division in Lansing (be specific in your request, however, as to what portion of the county you intend to hunt). The address is Box 30028, Lansing, Mich. 48909 (phone 517/373-1275). Armed with a good plat book and county map,

hunters may then locate these company lands, which usually are not marked with signs.

Topographically, Mason County contains three main areas, all the result of glaciation thousands of years ago. The first is a broad, smooth plain that occupies some 70 percent of the land base. It varies little in elevation and has the characteristic features of glacial outwash, lake-bed plain, terraced valleys, and level till plains.

The second feature is a line of sand dunes along Lake Michigan. The dune belt varies in width from a quarter-mile to three miles, the widest part being west of Hamlin Lake. These dunes rise from 50 to 100 feet above the lake and are mostly covered with junipers, jack pines, and oak. They afford excellent deer hunting as well as some opportunities for snowshoe hares and fox squirrels.

The third division consists of morainic areas rising above the main plain to heights of 150 feet. The highest areas occur in northern Summit and Riverton townships. Others are found in northern Victory, southwestern Free Soil, southern Logan, and central Eden townships, east of Round Lake and north of Fountain.

The county is drained by the Pere Marquette, Lincoln, Big Sable, Little Manistee, and Pentwater rivers. The Little Manistee River crosses the northeastern two sections, whereas the Pentwater River headwaters course through the south-central part of the county. The Lincoln and its branches pass through the county center.

A good deer population is concentrated along river bottomlands (especially the Pere Marquette) and in Big Bear Swamp. Also, because the central portion of Mason County is farmed for fruit, grain crops, and livestock, deer benefit. Hunters might ask farmers if they are suffering crop damage because at times the Mason County whitetail herd has grown to nuisance proportions. In fact, up to 200 animals are killed on county roads each year.

During recent seasons, firearm buck-hunter success has gone as high as 23 percent. Generally 20 to 25 hunters per square mile result in moderate to high pressure and, in a good season, tag three to four bucks per square mile.

Deer hunters bag an occasional coyote from jack-pine forests in the northern region. Red fox, another underhunted gamester, are prolific throughout farmland regions. Good numbers of raccoon that frequent waterways are best hunted along those that abut to crop fields. Snowshoe hares provide good sport on young pine plantations and in cutover aspen and jack-pine stands. For cottontails, look to agricultural lands containing brush. Wild turkeys may be hunted east of US-31, with best results coming along the Sable and Pere Marquette rivers. Local pockets of pheasants continue to hang on in Victory and Riverton townships, but there are hardly enough to warrant hunting them.

Woodcock frequent lowland shrubs and tag alders with best opportunities occurring from mid- to late October during fall migrations. Mason County affords good to excellent grouse hunting in cutover aspen, along stream bottoms containing brush and fruit-bearing shrubs, and on farm woodlots. Hunter-cooperator records reveal an average of 1.73, 2.98, and 2.79 grouse flushed per hour during each of three years that we checked. Those same sportsmen reported a respective average of 1.03, 2.77, and .44 woodcock moved per hour.

Hamlin Lake produces good hunting for dabblers early in the season and for divers later on. The rivers are mostly floatable and provide opportunities for ducks, squirrels, some geese, and an occasional deer. Smaller drainages, potholes, and beaver ponds hold local families of wood ducks, teal, and mallards for jump shooters.

OTHER SHOOTING OPPORTUNITIES
None known at this time.

FURTHER SOURCES OF HUNTING INFORMATION
1. DNR District OFfice, 8015 South 131 Road, Cadillac, Mich. 49601 (616/775-9727).
2. Ludington Area Chamber of Commerce, 102 East Ludington Ave., Ludington, Mich. 49431 (616/843-2506).
3. Scottville Chamber of Commerce, Box 152, Scottville, Mich. 49454 (616/757-2728).
4. Topographic, county, and lake maps may be ordered from the Michigan United Conservation Clubs. For information, refer to the beginning of this book.
5. Plat books are available from the Mason County Cooperative Extension Services, 102 South Main, Box 68, Scottville, Mich. 49454. The cost is $10 each (add $1.35 if mail ordering).
6. Mason County ASCS Office, West US-10 & 31, Scottville, Mich. 49454.

Also, refer to the following elsewhere in this book:
1. Huron-Manistee National Forest
2. Ludington State Park
3. Pere Marquette State Forest
4. Pere Marquette State Game Area

Mecosta County

MECOSTA County at 563 square miles lies in the west-central part of the Lower Peninsula. It is characterized by changing topography, plenty of water in the form of 101 lakes and the Muskegon River system, scattered pockets of deep woods, and considerable farming—especially in the southern portion. All things considered, this county has much to offer hunters.

Lacking are any prominent topographic features, and, in fact, a number of small areas of nearly level land occur, parts of which are well drained and parts poorly drained. Bordering the stream valleys are belts of rolling country of irregular width and slope. These belts are characterized by low ridges with smooth or rounded slopes, hummocks, and sharp knobs. Narrow filled-in valleys, potholes, and basins containing lakes and swamp areas are also characteristic features.

Associated with them are areas of moderately rolling upland, which, in turn, give way to somewhat broadly broken areas. The county is drained by the Muskegon and Little Muskegon rivers and their tributaries in the western portion (all running west to Lake Michigan) and the Chippewa River and its feeder streams in the eastern section (draining easterly to Saginaw Bay). Where the rivers have been dammed, impoundment water covers the lowland for some distance upstream to form artificial lakes. River valleys vary in width from a few hundred feet to three miles. Along some of the streams and bordering lakes are bodies of swamp and marshland, some of which are extensive.

State land in Mecosta County presently totals 12,540 acres or about three-and-a-half percent of the land base. It is mostly included in the form of the Pere Marquette State Forest, the Haymarsh State Game Area, and the Martiny Lakes Flooding (*all of which see*). Scattered parcels of the Huron-Manistee National Forest (*which also see*) are found along the western border. Federal ownership is less than one percent. In addition, hunters have about 1,400 acres of Public Access Stamp program land on which to hunt. Properties of the half-dozen enrollees are located in Mecosta, Hinton, and Millbrook townships. For a complete directory, see your license agent or stop in at a DNR office.

Also, Mecosta County landowners are fairly good about granting permission to considerate sportsmen who ask first and are responsible. One area, however, where access is difficult is on gas field lands in Austin Township.

Mecosta County is one of a tier of transition counties between southern agricultural lands and upstate stretches of northern hardwoods. About 34 percent of the land area is timbered with commercial-forest species led by aspen (40,000 acres), which is especially plentiful in the eastern portion. Maple-birch, elm-ash-soft maple, and oak-hickory follow in that order; and there are scattered stands of pine, spruce, and cedar. These varied cover types produce the gamut of huntable game—deer, rabbits, squirrels, raccoon, fox, grouse, woodcock, and waterfowl. Occasionally bear and bobcats are sighted in swamp regions and a few pheasants are found in isolated pockets of southern-tier townships. About 10 percent of the rabbits bagged by hunters are actually snowshoe hares, found mostly in pine plantations and isolated swamps north of the southern farming belt.

This portion of the county has the most intensive farming, a mixture of dairy and beef cattle enterprises along with cash cropping. Small pockets of farming also occur east of Big Rapids, the county seat, and again in the northeastern corner.

Mecosta County has good to excellent numbers of deer, evidenced by both crop damage reports from farming areas and by the 450-plus whitetails (highest of all counties in Region II—the northern Lower Peninsula) killed by cars each year. Also, the eight-county DNR district generally leads the state in buck kill with four to five bucks tagged per square mile. Pressure, however, is moderate to high at 25 to 30 hunters per square mile. Generally, one of each six hunters tags a buck. Portions of Mecosta County fall into hunter's-choice areas.

Good numbers of whitetails are found throughout the county, with best hunting occurring in young aspen and swamp conifers since deer use these areas as escape cover. Oak ridges south and north of the Muskegon River on national forest land also draw deer during years of high-mast yield. In addition, two areas of the county seem to produce big-racked bucks, probably due to a local genetic pool of trophy animals. These areas are Wheatland Township in the vicinity of Remus and in the Chippewa Lake area of Chippewa Township.

According to a five-year DNR survey recently released, the best areas for deer in Mecosta County are southern Chippewa, Big Rapids, and Colfax townships and eastern Sheridan, Wheatland, and Millbrook townships.

The Haymarsh State Game Area (about 1,000 acres in four major floodings) and Martiny Lakes Flooding (1,420 acres) are managed for waterfowl although deer, squirrel, grouse, and rabbit hunting is also good on these public state lands. Hunting for woodies and mallards is good in early season although pressure is high for the opener. Geese in particular are chased out early and generally go to Shiawassee County refuges for safety. Duck hunting improves as the season progresses and local ducks are replaced by passage birds. The Muskegon River is too well developed for good duck hunting, but that does not mean a float hunter cannot score on waterfowl, deer, or squirrels. Hunters should be careful, however, not to trespass on private lands. Potholes and small lakes also contain both local and flight birds throughout the season. Expanding beaver populations, that cause nuisance complaints, also provide nesting habitat for wood ducks. Therefore, beaver floodings are worth checking out.

The large amount of water in Mecosta County helps make for good numbers of raccoon, an underharvested species by hunters although trappers concentrate on the prolific furbearers in years when pelt prices are high. Good numbers of fox and some coyotes (which are expanding to southern portions of the county) are other underused hunting resources. Mecosta is a good fox-squirrel (with a few grays) hunting county. Again, more hunters could share the bounty.

The large amount of aspen along with lowland brush make for good woodcock and grouse populations. According to cooperators' reports, hunters can expect to move 2.0 to 4.0 grouse per hour in an average or better season—if they work proper habitat such as sapling-sized aspen. Woodcock hunters can expect to move one or more birds per hour, a figure which can soar dramatically when flight birds are down.

To date, the DNR has transplanted over 40 wild turkeys from other northern Michigan areas into Mecosta County as part of an effort to build local populations to huntable levels. Releases north of Remus have done especially well so far. Other areas to receive birds include south of Hersey, Chippewa Lake region, and east of Barryton. One reason for the eastern-county releases is that the Muskegon River seems to act as a natural barrier for turkey expansion from Newaygo County.

OTHER SHOOTING OPPORTUNITIES

Mecosta County hunters have at least two places where they can go to practice shooting and sight in rifles. The Big Rapids Armory, 15900 190th Ave. in Big Rapids, has five indoor stations each for pistol and rimfire rifle, plus indoor archery targets. Shooting instruction is offered. For details and fees explanation, call 616/796-6823.

The Barryton Rod and Gun Club, 3777 18-Mile Road in Barryton, does not charge for use of its centerfire-rifle station, two rimfire-rifle stations, archery targets, and trap field. The club also offers shooting instruction as well as state hunter-education programs. For information, call 517/382-7444.

FURTHER SOURCES OF HUNTING INFORMATION

1. DNR District Office, 501 Hemlock St., Clare, Mich. 48617 (517/386-7991).
2. DNR Evart Field Office, 2510 East US-10, Evart, Mich. 49631 (616/734-5492).
3. Mecosta County Area Chamber of Commerce, 246 North State St., Big Rapids, Mich. 49307 (616/796-7649).
4. Barryton Chamber of Commerce, Box 101, Barryton, Mich. 49305 (517/382-5581).
5. Topographic, county, and lake maps may be ordered from the Michigan United Conservation Clubs. For information, refer to the beginning of this book.
6. Plat books are available from the Register of Deeds, Mecosta County Courthouse, 400 Elm St., Big Rapids, Mich. 49307. The cost is $9 each (add $1.50 if mail ordering).
7. Mecosta County ASCS office, 18720 Chippewa Lake Road, Big Rapids, Mich. 49307 (616/796-2659).

Also, refer to the following elsewhere in this book:
1. Haymarsh State Game Area
2. Martiny Lakes Flooding
3. Pere Marquette State Forest
4. Huron-Manistee National Forest

Menominee County

ENOMINEE County in the west-central Upper Peninsula has the state's heaviest concentration of deer at an average of 50 whitetails or more per square mile. It also offers fair to excellent hunting potential for bear, coyotes, bobcats, red fox, raccoon, snowshoe hares, gray squirrels, wild turkeys, ruffed grouse, woodcock, and waterfowl.

The bad news about this game-rich, 660,000-acre (1,032 square miles) county is that only about 91,000 acres, or some 14 percent of the land base, is included in the Escanaba River State Forest (*which see*) and is therefore open to hunting. The good news is that another 114,740 acres (17 percent) is private land enrolled in the Commercial Forest Act program and may be hunted. To get legal descriptions of these largely unposted lands, contact DNR Forest Management Division, Box 30028, Lansing, Mich. 48909 (517/373-1275), and give them the town and range numbers of the area you wish to hunt.

Another positive Menominee County feature — from the hunter's viewpoint — is heavy crop damage by deer in the central farming belt. Corn and alfalfa are the main targets although the deer destroy large amounts of potatoes, oats, and barley too. The DNR issues permits to some 40 landowners in the three-county district (includes Dickinson and Iron counties as well as Menominee) each summer and fall so that they can save their crops. Hunters, particularly bow hunters, can make a courteous request to tag a deer on farms of some of these besieged landowners, but they should prepare to pay something for the privilege. One farmer charges hunters $100 each, but if they kill a buck he refunds $75. If the hunter shoots a doe, he gets a full refund. More on deer hunting in a moment.

Menominee County has three physical divisions. First is the eastern portion of poorly-drained, sandy plains fronting Green Bay. Second is a central rolling upland, which comprises about 75 percent of the land area. Most of the farming occurs here. Third are low, swampy areas occurring along streams, drainages, and lowland depressions between hills and ridges throughout.

The lakeshore division varies as to width. It is narrowest near the city of Menominee and widens as one goes north. The old beach of ancient Algonquin Lake separates it from the rolling uplands. Winding ridges of wind-blown sand, gravelly ridges, and stony, sandy elevations containing clay are scattered over it.

The central uplands are characterized by many oval or horseshoe-shaped drumlins, particularly in the northern and south-central region. These drumlins are streamlined hills of glacial till, a quarter-mile to one mile in length, and generally lie parallel to each other. In some places they are close together, forming V-shaped valleys between them, yet in still other spots they are separated by either peat deposits and swamp lands or sand/gravel deposits varying in relief from sharply rolling to quite flat. These drumlins provide excellent deer

habitat as well as good cover for other game.

Northwest of Faithorn along the Menominee River is a small area showing the strongest surface relief in the county. Tall, massive ledges and knobs of basalt rock occur above the tops of surrounding trees. Peat deposits and rough, stony, sandy soils occur between these ledges and knob outcroppings.

In Lake Township there is a dry, level sand plain of considerable extent. The line separating this plain from rolling uplands is very sharp. In the vicinity of Talbot and southeast of Wallace are several small areas of sand and gravel plains featuring many knolls.

Bottomlands along the Menominee River form a belt ranging from a few feet to more than a mile in width. Surface features consist of shallow, poorly drained swales and low, sandy ridges. This river drains the western part of the county before emptying into Green Bay. The eastern half also reaches Green Bay through the Ford River, Big Cedar River, and smaller streams. There are no large lakes in Menominee County. About 35 percent of the land base consists of poorly drained or permanently wet land, mainly peat swamps.

Except for a narrow strip running roughly north and south in the extreme western portion, the county is underlain by limestone bedrock at various depths. Outcroppings are common in the northern region, especially around Hermansville and east of Powers.

These varied land forms support a wide range of forest covers. In fact, about 75 percent of Menominee County is timbered with commercial-forest species. Northern white cedar leads with 128,000 acres. It is followed by 112,100 acres of maple-birch, 100,500 acres of aspen, 53,200 acres of elm-ash-soft maple, 21,900 acres of black spruce, 17,500 acres of balsam fir, 15,800 acres of tamarack, 15,200 acres of paper birch, 10,600 acres of oak-hickory, 10,000 acres of white pine, and smaller amounts of white spruce, red pine, and jack pine.

Broken into thirds, the eastern county contains mostly conifers with some hardwoods along the swampy lowlands mixed with ridges that were previously described. The central third is farmland. The western third is mostly open hardwoods. State lands are found in the eastern and western regions.

Another statistic that indicates how many deer are found in Menominee County is the annual car-deer accident figure, which is approaching 500 at this time. Only the downstate counties of Kent, Calhoun, Jackson, and Montcalm are higher. Mild winters with an average of 55 inches of snow normally would not overly stress deer. However, because there are so many and because hundreds of migrants arrive from Marquette County, the carrying capacity of Menominee County is taxed each winter. Drawn to the vast cedar swamps here, some of these deer actually starve when they run out of food. Commercial cutting of cedar for the sawmills has further limited food supplies. Even so, when deer disperse in spring, it is possible to count a thousand animals in 15 minutes of driving, and so drivers must be very wary.

An estimated 11 hunters per square mile (high on state land, low on private land) shoot three to four bucks per square mile for an excellent success ratio of 35 percent. In fact, the DNR district, with only 19 percent of the land mass of the Upper Peninsula, produces 55 to 70 percent of the U.P. archery kill, all of its antlerless firearm kill (due to special hunter's-choice permit areas), and some 40 percent of its overall whitetail (including both sexes) kill. Late-season hunters have learned to watch migration trails along valleys and river bottoms as deer move south. For the most part, these migrations are under 10 miles although some whitetails will travel 30 miles or more.

Although genetically these are not the biggest deer, some do grow fine racks. During a recent hunting season, 12 percent of the bucks tagged were three years or older, and, according to new figures just released by Commemorative Bucks of Michigan, 30 Menominee County deer have now made the all-time record book of 1,150 monster Michigan bucks.

Menominee County also produces a few bear each fall. They seem to concentrate along beech ridges during good mast years in the central part of Spalding Township. Apple trees and chokecherry patches are other good spots to check out. The DNR district generally produces about 120 bear each fall, with fully 70 percent being shot during the month of September. Landowner confrontations make running dogs a risky business, however, so for best results consider baiting.

District DNR biologists have sealed from 52 to 101 bobcats during each of the past four years. Menominee County with its spruce and cedar swamps produces most of the cats. The Hermansville area and other northern and eastern county state lands are best places to go. Fisher and pine marten—both protected—also are found in these conifer belts. These areas and other locations of heavy cover near slashings also yield good snowshoe-hare hunting although numbers appear to be slipping somewhat. Still, some swamps never see a wintertime hunter.

There are good numbers of coyotes in Menominee County and a few red fox as well. In addition, high numbers of raccoon are likely to blame for some of the crop-damage reports that farmers attribute to deer. Try cornfields adjacent to waterways in southern Menominee County for ringtails, but always ask the landowner first before entering private lands.

Eastern gray squirrels and their black phase with an occasional fox squirrel provide good to excellent hunting opportunities in the southwestern part of the county, west of Stephenson and south and west of the Menominee River in the Shakey Lakes region. Cottontail hunters can find targets around towns and farms throughout the county. Croplands and pasturelands also produce good numbers of woodchucks, which are largely ignored by hunters.

The original wild-turkey flock, introduced to Menominee County nearly 20 years ago, died off during the 1970-72 rough winters when there was no food. A 30-bird release in 1976-77 continues to increase with expanded hunting opportunities expected in the future. During a recent winter over 400 birds were counted at farms, considered one of the keys to northern Michigan turkey survival. Corn acreage has more than doubled in Menominee County during the past 10 years. Hunting has been permitted since 1981, and at this writing, hunters are tagging upwards of 60 gobblers each spring. Best hunting occurs in the southwestern portion of the county in the Stephenson area, but birds are expanding easterly all the way to Bark River in Delta County.

A few pheasants in the Faithorn area south of US-2 are apparently increasing and provide limited potential for local hunters. Ruffed grouse, although currently down, and woodcock provide good hunting opportunities for those hunting prime habitat—aspen slashings in areas with hazel and lowland edges of brush and woods. Leaf drop occurs between October 5 and 15, but woodcock hunters who wait too long will miss birds that have already migrated south.

Sportsmen might also want to consider several Menominee County hunter walking trails, seeded to clover (a primary grouse food in fall) and maintained for game production. Locations include Linbeck Lake (T36N R28W, Sections 22, 26, and 27); Westman (T35N R25W, Section 6); Cedar River (T36N R25W, Section 16); Pemene Creek (T37N R28W, Section 10); and DeTemple (T37N, R27W, Section 18). DNR foresters and wildlife biologists are helpful at locating these if hunters are unable to find them.

Hunter-cooperator hourly flush rate records for ruffed grouse show averages of .80, 1.45, and .50 for three years that we randomly checked. Hourly woodcock flush rates were .54, .28, and 9.25 for those same years. The uncharacteristically high 9.25 figure is probably reflective of a few individuals' outstanding success rather than a true indicator of potential throughout the county. That is because flush-rate returns for that year were quite limited.

Waterfowlers will find fair to good diving-duck-hunting opportunities along Green Bay shorelines when water levels are down. North Lake and the Hayward Lake marshes are good bets on days when Green Bay is wind-lashed. Small ponds and beaver floodings provide some jump-shooting action for wood ducks and mallards, and the Menominee River affords good float-hunting opportunities at times. Some opportunistic goose hunters get good action on private farm fields, but for the most part Canada geese fly nonstop through Menominee County en route to the Horicon National Wildlife Refuge in Wisconsin.

OTHER SHOOTING OPPORTUNITIES

Blahnik's Shooting Preserve and Hatchery, Route 1, Box 157, Carney, Mich. 49812, is open to the public for daily fee shooting without reservations (although reservations are preferred). Located in Nadeau Township, the 320-acre preserve features hunting for pheasants, quail, chukars, and ducks. For details, contact Henry J. Blahnik at 906/639-2643.

The Menominee Woods & Stream Sportsman Club, 1921 23rd St. in Menominee, has a shooting range open to the public for fees. Facilities include outdoor stations for pistol, centerfire and rimfire rifle, and two trap fields. The club sponsors state hunter-certification programs. For information, call 906/863-8720.

FURTHER SOURCES OF HUNTING INFORMATION

1. DNR District Office, West US-2 (Box 300), Crystal Falls, Mich. 49920 (906/875-6622).

Midland County

MIDLAND County is in the east-central part of the Lower Peninsula. About six percent of its 520 square miles is urban land, which, for the most part, incorporates the Midland city limits. Corn, wheat, oats, beans, and sugar beets are major crops grown in agricultural areas. About 45 percent of the county is timbered with commercial-forest species. Aspen (65,800 acres) leads, followed by maple-birch (32,100 acres), elm-ash-soft maple (25,800 acres), and oak-hickory (18,800 acres). Smaller amounts of paper birch and white pine also grow here.

About 12.5 percent, or 42,000 acres, of Midland County is state-owned, mostly in the form of the Au Sable State Forest (which see). These parcels are scattered with concentrations occurring in the northeastern, north-central, and west-central regions. An additional 492 acres of land owned by companies is enrolled in the Commercial Forest Act program. In an agreement with the state, these lands are open to hunting by law in exchange for reduced property taxes. The DNR Forestry Division in Lansing will supply hunters with legal descriptions upon request, or hunters can stop in at the DNR district office in Clare.

The northern half of Midland County is largely wooded, large portions of which have been cut over and now are in varying stages of regrowth. This is especially true with aspen, much to the delight of woodcock, grouse, and rabbit hunters. Dogwood types and wild raisin along with other shrub and brush species form an understory. Deer hunting, fairly good throughout the county, is also best in these cutover areas. Alder is another species prominent in lowland sites. There are few conifers.

South of M-20 deer populations are somewhat lower. With the exception of Greendale and northern Jasper townships, the land is mostly farmed for small grains and hay. Even so, pheasant hunting is very poor. Warren Township in the northwestern corner around Coleman and southern Jasper Township are best bets for ringnecks.

Warren Township, incidentally, provides an interesting mix of farmland and woodland. Deer numbers are high and wild turkeys are increasing. Lincoln Township northeast of Sanford has also received turkeys translocated from other northern Michigan areas. In all, about 50 birds have been released in these locations as well as other spots in western Midland County. Although at this writing the county is closed to gobbler hunting, future sporting opportunities are in store.

Overall, Midland County has good grouse and woodcock hunting although pressure is high from both Midland city hunters and from downstate sportsmen who see no need to drive farther north for a day's hunting. Hunter-cooperators report 2.0 to 3.0 grouse flushed per hour in years of average to good populations. Woodcock flushes are generally lower, yet flight birds can provide concentrated sport in mid- to late October.

Midland County supports good cottontail rabbit populations. Also, northern Edenville Township and portions of Mills Township produce snowshoe hares. Squirrel hunting (mostly for fox squirrels although some grays/blacks are also taken) is best north of M-20 and west of M-30. Also, considerable stands of oaks in Lincoln Township and the southeastern corner of Hope Township yield bushytails.

A float trip on the Tittabawassee River is often productive for mallards, teal, and a few Canada geese. Some hunters drift in canoes to jump ducks; others set up with decoys in quiet bayous. The Chippewa River as well as numerous smaller drainages provide good jump-shooting sport. Sanford and Wixom lakes are fair for divers. Some of the county's best waterfowling, however, occurs on the Kawkawlin Creek Flooding in the northeastern corner. Experiments by the DNR to draw down the 700-acre flooding just before season openers have resulted in good numbers of mallards, black ducks, wood ducks, teal, and Canada geese using the area. Further, nuisance giant Canada geese, live-trapped and removed from downstate, have nested successfully. The waterfowling picture is looking brighter all the time in Midland County.

Raccoon hunters concentrate on the northern half of the county, with pressure running moderate to high.

Midland is one of very few counties where Commemorative Bucks of Michigan has not confirmed any trophy buck kills to date. That does not mean that the county is poor for deer hunting, however. Success approximates the state average (about 16 percent) with 20 to 25 hunters per square mile tagging three or four bucks per square mile. Although crop-damage complaints have fallen off in recent years, the car-deer accident tally remains high at 300 to 400 animals per year. As mentioned, the northern portion of the county has the best deer hunting, especially Warren, Edenville, Geneva, and southern Jerome townships, according to a recently

OTHER SHOOTING OPPORTUNITIES

None known at the present time.

FURTHER SOURCES OF HUNTING INFORMATION

1. DNR District Office, 501 Hemlock St., Clare, Mich. 48617 (517/386-7991).

2. Midland Area Chamber of Commerce, 300 Rodd St., Midland, Mich. 48640 (517/839-9901).

3. Sanford Area Chamber of Commerce, Box 55, Sanford, Mich. 48657 (517/687-9944).

4. Topographic, county, and lake maps may be ordered from the Michigan United Conservation Clubs. For information, refer to the beginning of this book.

5. Plat books are available from the Midland County Register of Deeds, 301 West Main St., County Courthouse Building, Midland, Mich. 48640. The cost is $10 each. There is no charge for mail ordering. Checks must be made out to the Midland County Cooperative Extension Services.

6. Midland County ASCS Office, 1864 East Isabella Road, Midland, Mich. 48640 (517/832-3651).

Also, refer to the Au Sable State Forest elsewhere in this book.

Missaukee County

MISSAUKEE County in north-central Lower Michigan offers sportsmen a variety of game and differing habitats. The 576-square-mile county is home to good numbers of deer, bear, hares, and grouse; fair populations of squirrels, raccoon, and ducks; and some underused fox and coyote populations. A DNR long-range plan to merge turkeys from the Cadillac and Mio districts could result in future hunting potential. There are few turkeys at this time in Missaukee County.

Scattered holdings of the Pere Marquette State Forest (which see) total over 100,000 acres or about 27 percent of the land area in this county. That is a second reason that it is popular with hunters. A little-known third reason to hunt here is the availability of nearly 4,000 acres of Commercial Forest Act land. Owned by industries, the lands are open to hunting by law, as provided in a special trade-off with the state for reduced property taxes. For a legal description of these lands, contact the DNR Forestry Division in Lansing or find them yourself in a current plat book.

Dominant features of the county include the famed Dead Stream Swamp (which see) in the northeastern corner, the Muskegon River origins in the east-central region, the farm belt of the central and southeastern portions, and Lake Missaukee on M-55 at Lake City.

Deer hunting is best in the eastern one-third of the county, especially Enterprise Township, and poorest in the northwestern sector. Bigger deer inhabit the mostly inaccessible farm country—interspersed with private hunting-club lands—and remote portions of the Dead Stream Swamp. Hunter numbers are highest along the Houghton Lake Wildlife Research Area (which see). In fact, the numbers of bow-killed deer exceed those taken by firearm hunters by about double.

Missaukee County firearm hunters usually score 20 to 25 percent success on bucks (three to four bucks per square mile) while exerting moderate to high hunting pressure (15 to 20 hunters per square mile). State land, however, can take a pounding during the two-week gun season.

Bear populations remain good in spite of increased pressure by baiters and dog hunters in recent years.

Now that that Dead Stream has been opened again to hunting (after a 10-year closure), it is getting targeted heavily. However, most hunters do not leave roads and thus concentrate only on the fringes of this resource-rich habitat. Another underutilized area for both bear and deer is the seemingly impenetrable Scanion and Seafuse marshes on state land near the county center.

Nearly two-thirds of Missaukee County is timbered with commercial-forest species. Aspen with 71,700 acres leads the list and is followed by maple-birch (50,600 acres), oak-hickory (24,300 acres), elm-ash-soft maple (17,900 acres), northern white cedar (10,600 acres), and jack pine (6,500 acres). Occupying about 4,000 acres each are red pine, tamarack, and paper birch along with smaller amounts of white pine and balsam fir.

As might be expected, grouse hunting is fairly good in aspen (poplar) slashings from 10 to 20 years old, especially those containing an understory of beaked hazelnut, witch hazel, gray and red-osier dogwood, and wild currant. The Houghton Lake Wildlife Research Area and fringe covers of the Dead Stream Swamp rate high for grouse. Hunter-cooperators reported an average hourly flush rate of 1.20 and 2.25 grouse during two years of records checked. On the other hand, those same cooperators reported hourly woodcock flushes averaging 1.53 and 3.93.

Flight-bird hunting for longbills is especially good since portions of Missaukee County are moist-soiled. Try alder and aspen pockets along streams and in farmland brush.

Snowshoe hares are just now staging a comeback after several low-end cycle years. Again, aspen slashings and regeneration of sapling-sized hardwoods near conifer lowlands are good places to try. Consider pine and Christmas tree plantations too, especially those in the northwestern portion of the county. Also, try the Dead Stream and Haymarsh swamps. Cottontails are scarce, even on farms in the agricultural belt.

Raccoon are fairly plentiful along waterways although pressure is high during years of high-priced pelts. Other than the odd animals that fall to opportunistic deer hunters, few coyotes are shot. They and red fox in the farming zone offer underused potential. Best areas for squirrels (both fox and gray/black species) are oak ridges and lowland oak types mixed with conifers in the northern region.

High winds on Houghton Lake in nearby Roscommon County chase ducks and geese into the Reedsburg Flooding. Duck hunting opportunities also exist on Houghton Lake Wildlife Research Area floodings and on the Muskegon River. The latter is underutilized by float hunters. Also, plenty of beaver ponds, potholes, and Haymarsh Creek afford good jump-shooting for wood ducks and mallards as well as occasional teal and black ducks. Lake Missaukee is often good for late-season divers.

OTHER SHOOTING OPPORTUNITIES
None known at this time.

FURTHER SOURCES OF HUNTING INFORMATION
1. DNR District Office, 191 South Mount Tom (M-33), Mio, Mich. 48647 (517/826-3211).

2. Lake City Area Chamber of Commerce, Box 52, Lake City, Mich. 49651 (616/839-4969).

3. McBain Area Chamber of Commerce, Box 74, McBain, Mich. 49657 (616/825-2432).

4. Topographic, county, and lake maps may be ordered from the Michigan United Conservation Clubs. For information, refer to the beginning of this book.

5. Plat books are available from the Missaukee County Cooperative Extension Services, Box D, County Building, Lake City, Mich. 49651, for $3.50 each (add $1 if mail ordering).

6. Missaukee/Roscommon/Crawford County ASCS Office, 2170 South Morey Road, Lake City, Mich. 49651.

Also, refer to the following elsewhere in this book:
1. Houghton Lake Wildlife Research Area
2. Pere Marquette State Forest

Monroe County

LOW, flat Monroe County in southeastern Lower Michigan is caught between Detroit and Toledo. Consquently, the 557-square-mile county does not feature the wildlife habitat and game-animal populations that most other southern Michigan counties do. However, to assume that Monroe County is not worth hunting would be a big mistake.

Opportunities might be limited but nevertheless they do exist for pheasants, rabbits, squirrels, ducks, raccoon, and fox. Glacial-till soils are rich from being reworked over centuries by lake water from what is now Lake Erie. About 57 percent of the county is farmed for soybeans, corn, and wheat (in that order), grown almost completely for cash-crop enterprises. Intensive farming is practiced heavily in the northwestern region. Abandoned farmland, woodland, wetland, and urban areas make up the rest of the county's land area. These rich farmlands with pockets of natural cover provide fair to good wildlife habitat.

Nearly 12 percent of the county is timbered with commercial-forest species: oak-hickory, soft maple-ash-elm, hard maple-birch, and aspen. These mixed stands are mostly in the form of scattered farm woodlots often with brushland fringes, particularly east of US-23. The woods harbor fair populations of fox squirrels while brushy areas contain huntable numbers of cottontails.

There are scattered concentrations of pheasants in Monroe County as well as quail although bobwhite numbers are not high enough to allow a hunting season. Best bets for pheasants are idle farmlands (including abandoned farms if the owners can be contacted to obtain permission), especially those whose owners are participating in the set-aside program.

Public lands are limited to Petersburg, Erie, and Pointe Mouillee state game areas (all of which see), which, along with Sterling State Park (closed to hunting), total some 6,900 acres. An additional 5,000 acres is enrolled in the Public Access Stamp program by a half-dozen large farm operators in Dundee and Milan townships. Contact DNR offices for a free directory.

Also, if you're a responsible hunter willing to make a courteous request, you will likely find farmers agreeable to letting you on their land. This is especially true farthest from the cities. Hunters should keep in mind, however, that Monroe County is closed to Sunday hunting with firearms and dogs except on the game areas and for offshore waterfowl. Also, hunters will want to check for local closures, such as in the city of Monroe.

Duck hunting can be very good in the game areas although pressure, especially on weekends, can run heavy. There may be other hunting opportunities along the Lake Erie coast if sportsmen first seek permission from landowners. A county plat book is the place to start.

Most of Monroe County is flat land with grades under six percent. In the northeastern region the Saline River runs south to meet the River Raisin, which flows principally east through the central portion. Raccoon frequent the waterway. In some areas, though, farming activities run nearly to its bank. There are limited jump-shooting opportunities for ducks although, again, hunters will need to secure permission first. Also, the northwestern tip of Monroe County falls into the special late season for Canada geese. However, county lakes are limited to old quarries and highway borrow pits. The only large natural lake is Lake Ottawa in the southwestern region.

Deer-hunting pressure and success are minimal although there are a few deer in the county, as evidenced by the 50 to 100 animals that are hit by cars each year.

OTHER SHOOTING OPPORTUNITIES
The Pointe Mouillee State Game Area operates outdoor shooting facilities for pistol and centerfire

and rimfire rifle (20 stations each), archery (five targets), and skeet and trap (five fields each). They are open to the public for fees. For more information, call 313/379-4400.

FURTHER SOURCES OF HUNTING INFORMATION

1. DNR District Office, 2455 North Williams Lake Road, Pontiac, Mich. 48054 (313/666-1500).

2. Pointe Mouillee State Game Area, 37205 Mouillee Road, Rockwood, Mich. 48173 (313/379-9692).

3. Sterling State Park (although closed to hunting, park is staffed), 2800 State Park Road, Monroe, Mich. 48161 (313/289-2715).

4. Monroe County Chamber of Commerce, 22 West Second St., Monroe, Mich. 48161 (313/242-3366).

5. Topographic, county, and lake maps may be ordered from the Michigan United Conservation Clubs. For information, refer to the beginning of this book.

6. Plat books are available from the Monroe County Cooperative Extension Services, 1426 East First St., Monroe, Mich. 48161. The cost is $10 each (add $.50 if mail ordering).

7. Monroe County ASCS Office, USDA, 15621 South Telegraph Road, Monroe, Mich. 48161 (313/241-8540).

Also, refer to the following elsewhere in this book:
1. Erie State Game Area
2. Petersburg State Game Area
3. Pointe Mouillee State Game Area

Montcalm County

MONTCALM County in west-central Lower Michigan is one of the best game regions of the state. Sandy/loamy soils underlain by sand and gravel are outwash regions from glaciers that visited this area 8,000 to 12,000 years ago. Portions of the 712-square-mile county that are gently rolling to hilly are end moraines of glacial till where ice sheets once melted. The result of this ice-age action was to produce a county that pleases the eye with 200 lakes, rolling hardwoods and farmland, and intricate stream systems. Consider the streams: Tamarack Creek and the Little Muskegon River (northwest region) flow westerly toward the Muskegon River, the Flat River and Fish and Prairie creeks (southern half) run southerly toward the Grand River, and headwaters of the Pine River (northeast portion) meander toward Saginaw Bay. Incidentally, these are trout streams featuring good bankside cover for game animals and birds.

Thirty-two percent of Montcalm County is commercially forested with oak-hickory, ash-soft maple, and hard maple-birch evenly distributed at 32,000 to 39,000 acres per group. Of course, these hardwoods are in mixed stands along with some 23,000 acres of aspen. The northwest portion is largely oak-timbered. Much of the rest of the county is in good farmland with an unusually high percentage of woodland fringe. Agricultural practices include dairying and cash-crop farming, with beans, corn, and potatoes (about one-fifth of Michigan's total production) the staples grown. Some farmers grow fruit—mostly apples—west of Greenville and in the east-central region near McBride.

Much of Montcalm County is privately owned; however, a courteous request can result in hunting access. Portions of five state game areas, totaling nearly 20,000 acres are scattered throughout, and tracts in the Manistee National Forest (which see) in Reynolds Township are also open to hunters. In addition, the state leases about 4,100 acres from two dozen farmers through the Public Access Stamp program. About half of these are located in the triangle created by connecting the northwestern

county towns of Trufant, Pierson, and Howard City; the others are scattered throughout. For a free map and directory, contact the DNR district office in Grand Rapids or the staffed field office at the Flat River State Game Area (which see).

Montcalm County has traditionally been bypassed by Grand Rapids and other downstate hunters "heading north." Only in recent years have sportsmen come to realize that here is excellent hunting for deer, squirrels, raccoon, fox, and rabbits and good opportunities for grouse, woodcock, and waterfowl, even occasional pockets of pheasants.

Highest number of crop-damage complaints of the seven-county Grand Rapids DNR district occur here, mostly caused by deer to soybean and potato fields. Enterprising hunters might check to see which farmers are having problems and then politely ask for permission to hunt. The deer kill in Montcalm County typically runs three to four bucks per square mile with firearm hunters (shotguns only below M-57) enjoying 20 percent and better success, among the highest in southern Michigan. This success ratio can swell to 30 to 40 percent when coupled with hunter's-choice permits.

Deer apparently thrive due to good food supplies (mast and buds from forest cover and plentiful farm crops). Car-deer accidents for the entire county have not fallen below 500 annually for several years, ranking it among the highest in southern Michigan.

The Flat River is floatable, especially from Greenville or Belding downstream (or if you don't mind portages, from Langston downriver) with a takeout at Lowell in Kent County or at any of the access roads in the Flat River State Game Area. This float could provide good deer, squirrel, and duck hunting opportunity. The other streams offer fair jump-shooting for ducks and good bottomland hunting for grouse, woodcock, squirrels, raccoon, and rabbits.

Squirrel hunting is good throughout, with perhaps best concentrations occurring on private farm woodlots and in oak forests of the northwest county and in the Langston State Game Area (which see). Rabbit hunting is good just about everywhere with stream bottomlands getting the most pressure. This is also where grouse and woodcock hunters tend to exert the most pressure, but there is plenty of muck ground interspersed with gray dogwood and aspen throughout. Montcalm County hunters move two to three grouse per hour in normal population years, and woodcock are always available—particularly during mid-October migrations—for a bonus in the game pouch.

The large amount of corn acreage and the stream/lake frequency with wet bottomlands make Montcalm County ideal raccoon habitat. Foxes are also in abundance here. Waterfowlers concentrate on rivers and streams when they can get access. There is some diving-duck layout hunting opportunity on Crystal and Duck lakes, which offer public access. Most other lakes, some with marshy shorelines, are privately owned. A considerate hunter might obtain permission to launch a boat or hunt the marsh. A growing giant Canada goose flock in the Greenville and Edmore areas could provide hunting chances nearby. There is no extended season at this time, however.

Some of the district's better pheasant hunting is found scattered in farmland cover throughout the southern portion. Recently the DNR released northern Michigan turkeys at the Langston State Game Area and 26 Missouri birds at the Flat River State Game Area. In time these flocks will likely merge through Dickinson Creek to provide future hunting opportunity (the season is closed at this time).

All in all, Montcalm County has much to offer the downstate hunter.

OTHER SHOOTING OPPORTUNITIES
None known at this time.

FURTHER SOURCES OF HUNTING INFORMATION

1. DNR District Office, State Offie Bldg., 350 Ottawa NW, Grand Rapids, Mich. 49503 (616/456-45071).
2. Flat River State Game Area, Route 2, 6640 Long Lake, Belding, Mich. 48809 (616/794-2658).
3. Greenville Area Chamber of Commerce, 327 South Lafayette, Greenville, Mich. 48838 (616/745-5697 or—on weekends—616/745-4466).
4. Three other chambers are possibilities; however, they are staffed by volunteers. The addresses are Trufant Area Chamber of Commerce, Box 25, Trufant, Mich. 49347 (616/984-2142); Edmore Area Chamber of Commerce, Box 102, Edmore, Mich. 48829 (517/365-3015 or 517/427-5123); and Stanton Area Chamber of Commerce, Box 401, Stanton, Mich. 48888 (517/831-8314). Also ask at local businesses for information.
5. Huron-Manistee National Forest, White Cloud Ranger District, White Cloud, Mich. 49349 (616/689-6696).
6. Topographical, county, and lake maps may be ordered from the Michigan United Conservation Clubs. For information, refer to the beginning of this book.
7. Plat books are available for $15 each (add $1.50 if ordering by mail) from Montcalm County Extension Services, 617 North State, Stanton, Mich. 48888 (517/831-4212).

Also refer to the following elsewhere in this book:
1. Edmore State Game Area
2. Flat River State Game Area
3. Langston State Game Area
4. Stanton State Game Area
5. Vestaburg State Game Area
6. Manistee National Forest

Montmorency County

MONTMORENCY County in northeastern Lower Michigan has something to offer nearly every type of hunter. The 24-mile-by 24-mile-square county contains good to excellent numbers of grouse, woodcock, deer, bear, bobcats, snowshoe hares, squirrels, and raccoon. There also are huntable numbers of fox, coyotes, wild turkeys, and waterfowl. Hunting pressure for many of these species is on the increase, however.

Topographically, Montmorency County appears to be a body of highland fingered by broad valleys in the southern part and identified by several detached bodies of highland set in a broad plain in the northern region. Most of the land is level or gently rolling, but in a few places it is broken and rugged. Highest elevations occur in the southern and southwestern parts, which reach 1,200 feet above sea level. The lowest elevations (about 700 feet above sea level) are found along the Thunder Bay River near the eastern county line.

Swamps and lakes are widely distributed. The county contains 45 lakes larger than 50 acres in size as well as many small ponds and marshy areas. Various branches of the Thunder Bay River run west

to east. Overall soil types in Montmorency County are of low fertility, and what limited farming there is is confined mostly to dairy farms. About 35 percent of the county contains deep, dry sand soils which were originally covered by pine forests. A clay plain occurs in the northeastern portion where the land contains many wet swales and potholes.

Of particular interest to hunters is that 82 percent of Montmorency County is timbered with commercial-forest species. About 43 percent of that total, or 123,392 acres, is aspen type in varying stages of growth, thus providing key habitat for deer, grouse, and hares. Another 42,000 acres are northern hardwoods. Other cover types include swamp conifers (40,000 acres), oak (33,000 acres), jack pine (33,000 acres), and red and white pine (13,000 acres). Upland brush growth accounts for 32,000 acres, and lowland brush, marsh, and bog areas total 10,000 acres. Less than five percent of Montmorency County is actively farmed.

Another reason that hunters come here is an abundance of state land. Roughly 134,500 acres, or nearly 38 percent of the land base, is included in the Mackinaw State Forest (which see), all of which is open to hunting.

The deer herd appears to be fairly stable, with best hunting prospects occurring in cutover aspen stands near oak-covered ridges. Those are likely to be well scattered, but for a free county map that lists clearings, thickets, and regrowth areas stop in to the DNR Atlanta Field Office or the *Montmorency County Tribune* office. Each year the newspaper publishes a new edition of this map, which is paid for by local advertising. Hunters might also want to consider a December bow or muzzleloader hunt in the heavy swamp region east of M-33 between Jackson Lake and Rush Lake Flooding as this is a deer-yard area.

Crop damage complaints are limited to the northeastern corner (Metz Township) where farming is most active. According to a five-year study by the DNR, this area contains the highest numbers of deer in the county. Montmorency County also contains two areas of privately-owned club country where high numbers of deer are artificially maintained by feedings during what often shape up to be tough winters. One club-country region is the southeastern corner in the vicinity of Turtle Lake. The other is in the northwestern corner.

Attesting to high deer numbers is the current breakdown of Montmorency County into four hunter's-choice areas. Firearm pressure is quite high at 20 to 30 hunters per square mile. However, they tag three to four bucks per square mile for a success ratio of 10 to 15 percent, a little off the state average. Open to bear hunting, the county contains fair to good numbers of bruins throughout. The same is true of bobcats except that hunters should target poplar slashings near conifer cover and drainages as this is where snowshoe hares, the bobcat's primary winter food source, are found.

The northwestern quarter of Montmorency County also contains high numbers of elk. These magnificent animals, once native to Michigan, were reintroduced in 1918 from Wyoming and have continued to thrive since. Back-to-back seasons in the mid-60s helped thin the herd for 20 years. Special seasons by permit only will continue to do so.

It is not uncommon for grouse and woodcock hunters in the famed Pigeon River Country State Forest (now included as a portion of the Mackinaw State Forest) to encounter elk as the animals love to browse in aspen areas. In Montmorency County, at least, these aspen regrowth areas often serve as a compromise between hardwood-covered hills and lowland swamps.

Raccoon hunters key along drainages throughout the county, with best results coming in the eastern half, particularly along the North Branch Thunder Bay River as it winds intermittently through agricultural lands. The county contains a good mix of fox and black squirrels (with some grays too). Target pure oak stands for fox species and look for mixed covers of oaks with conifers for black squirrels. An excellent area to try for both species is the Avery Lake region.

The mixture of aspen with lowland brush makes for ideal woodcock and grouse habitat. According to the average from three annual surveys studied, hunters moved 1.57 to 2.37 grouse and .88 to 3.18 woodcock per hour. Although pressure for these upland birds is on the increase, Montmorency County offers many good places to hunt.

As mentioned, these same habitats produce fair to good snowshoe-hare hunting. Hares seem to be staging a comeback after several low-cycle seasons. What few cottontails live in the county are found around farm buildings.

Waterfowling opportunities are limited. Fletcher Floodwaters is generally good, with some pressure on opening-day weekend. Flight birds that occasionally drop in to the 10,000-acre impoundment can provide fast late-season sport. Headwaters of the Thunder Bay River branches produce a few mallards and wood ducks; however, they are usually too shallow in fall to float. Grass Lake and the Rush Lake Flooding contain some giant Canadas and a few local puddlers.

Wild turkeys are another game bird offering limited hunting opportunities in this county. Although there is some turkey expansion from southeast to northwest, severe winters and a lack of public feeding cause losses.

OTHER SHOOTING OPPORTUNITIES

None known at this time.

FURTHER SOURCES OF HUNTING INFORMATION

1. DNR District OFfice, 1732 West M-32 (Box 667), Gaylord, Mich. 49735 (517/732-3541).

2. DNR Atlanta Field Office, Route 1, Box 30, Atlanta, Mich. 49707 (517/785-4251).

3. Atlanta Area Chamber of Commerce, Box 333, Atlanta, Mich. 49709 (517/785-4251).

4. Hillman Area Chamber of Commerce, Box 89, Hillman, Mich. 49746 (517/742-4241).

5. Topographic, county, and lake maps may be ordered from the Michigan United Conservation Clubs. For information, refer to the beginning of this book.

6. Plat books are available from Montmorency County Soil Conservation District, Box 415 (Courthouse Building), Atlanta, Mich. 49709. The cost is $10 each (add $1.50 if mail ordering).

7. Montmorency County ASCS Office, Route 1, M-32 South, Hillman, Mich. 49746.

Also, refer to the Mackinaw State Forest elsewhere in this book.

Muskegon County

MUSKEGON County in the west-central Lower Peninsula has a land area of 322,560 acres or 504 square miles. Its surface ranges from nearly level to slightly rolling, varying from about 600 to 800 feet above sea level. A belt of sand dunes parallel to Lake Michigan is a half-mile or so wide and is mostly covered with oak and hickory, the dominant forest type in Muskegon County. This strip of dunes offers good opportunities for deer and squirrel hunting except that access is difficult.

Nearly half the county is forested. Northern hardwoods of the above two species and hard maple and birch constitute over 70 percent of the cover type. Ash, sugar maple, jack pine, red pine, and aspen are other species found. East of the sand dunes lies a wide plain which includes smaller dunes from old beachlines. This sandy, high-water table area is actively farmed for blueberries, especially in western Fruitport and Sullivan townships. Land-owners report occasional problems with deer. Between here and the Muskegon State Game Area (*which see*) are broken woodlots with an oak fringe. These hardwoods with an understory of white pine and hemlock extend more heavily from the Muskegon River north. They include 11,600 acres of the Manistee National Forest, all open to hunting and offering good opportunity for deer, squirrels, and rabbits. Other large, wooded portions are owned by scouting, church, and similar private organizations.

Rolling-to-slightly hilly areas are found on the county's eastern side and in the northwestern corner. The central plain area of Holton Township contains clay deposits over sandy soils and is the former bed of glacial Lake Chicago. Cash-crop farming here extends into Newaygo County. In the Casnovia area abutting Kent County are orchards. Separating them and cash-crop dairy farming to the west is a wooded fringe along Crockery Creek, a fine trout stream.

Muskegon County offers good hunting opportunity because of the availability of state, federal, and county land and because of its various cover types. About 1,400 acres of Public Access Stamp program land are leased (and open to hunting) from nine farmers in the southeastern region (Casnovia and Ravenna townships mostly). The DNR district office at Grand Rapids and the field office at the game area have free maps for the asking. Muskegon and Hoffmaster state parks are closed to hunting; however, Duck Lake State Park, just south of White Lake, has 542 of its 560 acres open. Park signs spell out boundaries. Altogether, over 10,000 acres of state land are open to hunting.

Deer populations appear stable throughout the county with moderate hunting pressure (about 10 hunters per square mile) and fairly good success (15 percent on bucks). Bucks typically are well-antlered, more resembling downstate farmland deer than northern whitetails even though much of the county reminds one of northern hardwoods deer hunting. For a trophy buck, key along the Muskegon River (consider a float trip) and in the game area.

The Muskegon County Wastewater System (*which see*) affords high-quality archery hunting by permit. Combined success for bucks and does in north-eastern Muskegon County had run as high as 50 percent but has dropped off in recent years. Soon it should approach the 20 percent success figure of the area to the southeast. The rest of Muskegon County is currently closed to antlerless deer hunting. Car-deer accidents generally amount to under 200 animals annually. Firearm deer hunters below M-46 must use shotguns; above M-46 rifles are permitted.

Grouse and woodcock hunting is spotty, especially in the northern hardwoods area, and efforts light throughout the county. That is partly because aspen frequency (15,000 acres total) is far down the list of cover types. For best results, find aspen stands in southern farmland area or key along tag alders in

any of the stream bottoms. These include the three major river systems and their tributaries: the Muskegon (and Cedar Creek), which bisects the county east and west; the White River in the northwestern portion; and Crockery Creek, running south to the Grand River. Little Black and Black creeks flow into Mona Lake south of Muskegon.

Cottontail rabbit hunting is good throughout, with best prospects along river bottoms and in the nursery and blueberry farming area. Also, there are reports of snowshoe hares along the White River system. Squirrels (mostly fox, some grays//blacks) are plentiful throughout oak/hickory forests and in farm woodlots. Limited pheasant hunting occurs on southern farms. Fox and raccoon populations are good to excellent. Northern Michigan turkeys released on the game area a few years ago are doing well and should provide future hunting opportunity.

Waterfowl hunters have outstanding opportunities in this county. The staffed Muskegon State Game Area is managed for ducks and geese, and the county wastewater project offers controlled hunts. The Muskegon and White rivers are floatable; their tributaries and other streams ideal for jump shooting. Layout hunters key on White and Muskegon lakes for scaup and other divers, and there are layout-hunting possibilities along Lake Michigan.

OTHER SHOOTING OPPORTUNITIES

The Wingshot Bird Farm, 1549 West McMillan Road, Muskegon, Mich. 49449, is a 189-acre shooting preserve open to the public. Pheasants and quail are hunted species. For more information, contact Alan D. Payne (616/766-3612).

The Ravenna Conservation Club has outdoor stations for pistol and centerfire rifle practice as well as archery targets and five trap fields for shotgunners. It is open to the public daily without fee. For more information, contact the club at 2530 Slocum, Ravenna, Mich. 49451 (616/853-9985). Muskegon Bowmen, Inc., 2380 North Central Road, Muskegon, Mich. 49445 (616/766-3447), has indoor/outdoor archery targets that are open to the public on a sometime-fee basis. Shooting instruction and competitive shooting are also held here.

FURTHER SOURCES OF HUNTING INFORMATION

1. DNR District Office, State Office Bldg. (350 Ottawa NW), Grand Rapids, Mich. 49503 (616/456-5071).
2. Muskegon State Game Area, 7600 East Messinger, Twin Lake, Mich. 49457 (616/788-5055).
3. DNR personnel at Hoffmaster, Muskegon, and Duck Lake state parks may be helpful. Here are the addresses:
A. Duck Lake State Park (see listing for Muskegon State Park)
B. Muskegon State Park, 3560 Memorial Drive, North Muskegon, Mich. 49445 (616/744-3480).
C. P. J. Hoffmaster State Park, 6585 Lake Harbor Road, Muskegon, Mich. 49441 (616/798-3711).
4. Muskegon County Wastewater System (see DNR officials at Muskegon State Game Area).
5. Huron-Manistee National Forest, White Cloud Ranger District, White Cloud, Mich. 49349 (616/689-6696).
6. Convention and Visitors Bureau of Muskegon County, 1065 Fourth St., Muskegon, Mich. 49441 (616/722-3751). Northern office (White Lake

Chamber of Commerce) located at 124 West Hanson St., Whitehall, Mich. 49461 (616/893-4585).

7. Ravenna Chamber of Commerce, 3800 Adams Road, Ravenna, Mich. 49451 (616/853-2271).

8. Topographical, county, and lake maps may be ordered from the Michigan United Conservation Clubs. For information, refer to the beginning of this book.

9. Plat books are available from the Muskegon County Building, 990 Terrace St., Muskegon, Mich. 49440 at a cost of $6 (add $1.50 if ordering by mail).

10. Muskegon County ASCS Office, USDA, 940 Van Eyck, Muskegon, Mich. 49442 (616/788-4488).

Also, refer to the following elsewhere in this book:
1. Muskegon State Game Area
2. Muskegon County Wastewater System
3. Manistee National Forest
4. Duck Lake State Park

Newaygo County

NEWAYGO County, in west-central Lower Michigan, contains good game populations and plenty of public land open to hunting. Deer hunting is especially popular in the 857-square-mile county, with high pressure (30 or more hunters per square mile) resulting in a buck kill of three or four per square mile. This translates to a success ratio of about 15 percent, or the state average.

Attesting to high numbers of deer is the grim statistic of 300 or more whitetails highway-killed each year. Also, recent DNR five-year compilations of random postcard surveys indicate that a major portion of Newaygo County is very high in deer production. Of 25 townships in the state reporting 21 or more bucks killed during this period, six townships are in Newaygo County. They include Lilley, Home, Merrill, Monroe, Lincoln, and Wilcox—comprising the central to north-central region.

Hunters also come to Newaygo County to seek grouse, woodcock, squirrels, wild turkeys, and snowshoe hares. About 18 percent of the land base, or 102,000 acres, comprises scattered holdings of the Manistee National Forest (*which see*), in all but the southern tier of counties. In addition, there are scattered parcels of state land in Bridgeton Township in the southwestern corner. They total less than one percent of Newaygo County real estate.

Topographically, Newaygo County shows considerable relief but no great changes in elevation. The glacially-influenced major divisions are rolling or hilly plateau uplands and plains. Hilly areas are typically ground moraines and shallow outwash deposits over claylike drift. The plains contain mostly glacial-outwash sand and gravel.

In the central-plain area of the county north of White Cloud are the headwaters of the White River and its tributary, Mullen Creek, both of which flow southward. Also found on this plain are the headwaters of the north-running Pere Marquette River. In Monroe Township the plain is marked by a great number of pitlike depressions, many of which are actually bogs and lakes.

A highland mass of glacial drift that runs along the western edge of the county in a southeasterly direction is cut by the White River valley at Hesperia and by the Muskegon River valley at Newaygo. Both streams flow southwesterly. The Muskegon River valley is an outstanding physical feature of the county. One to three miles wide, it is nestled between hills rising 100 or more feet on either side.

Finally, a poorly-drained plain between Ensley Center and Grant forms the headwater of the Rogue River.

Newaygo County contains 234 lakes and ponds. The southern two tiers of townships fall into DNR District 9, administered out of Grand Rapids. The northern two-thirds is managed by DNR District 6 at Cadillac. Muck farms south and east of Grant produce vegetables and receive crop damage by deer. The brushy fringe of these muck farms often yields good woodcock hunting. A good place for deer, hares, and grouse is along the Muskegon River since aspen is on the increase here. Deer also frequent the truck-farm belt in the southeastern corner (Ensley Township) and again in Sheridan Township south of Fremont Lake. Vegetables and fruit are grown in the latter, and in addition to deer is home to a few pheasants.

In fact, most of Newaygo County is a mix of agricultural lands and forestlands. About 60 percent is covered with commercial-forest species to provide an excellent mix of wildlife habitat. Oak-hickory type dominates with 124,300 acres. It is followed by 52,600 acres of aspen, 43,900 acres of maple-birch, 39,800 acres of elm-ash-soft maple, 26,400 acres of red pine, and 9,800 acres of jack pine. In addition, small amounts of northern white cedar, white pine, and tamarack also appear.

The abundance of such mast-producing trees makes for good populations of deer, turkeys, and squirrels. The Muskegon River affords good float-hunting opportunities for bushytails—both gray/black and fox species. The northern-tier townships of Home, Barton, and Lilley are other good spots to try for squirrels, as is Lincoln Township northwest of White Cloud.

Wild turkeys are found throughout the county but are most numerous in the northern two-thirds. The abundance of seeps, lakes, and bogs with plenty of hardwood cover, some conifers, and nearby farmlands makes for ideal turkey habitat. For snowshoe hares, try cutover hardwoods and aspen slashings adjacent to green cover such as swamps. Likely areas are southern Home and Monroe townships south of Jackson Corners and the region north and south of Nichols Lake. These swamp regions also contain the odd bear and bobcat, both of which are currently protected in Newaygo County.

A good place to try for coyotes is the northwestern corner, which contains a high amount of jack pine. This region also holds deer, hares, and turkeys. Newaygo County with its intricate network of rivers and streams also affords fair to good raccoon hunting although pressure is keen during seasons of high pelt prices. For red fox, try the farming areas mentioned as well as on agricultural lands in Goodwell Township. There are huntable populations of cottontails on some farmlands too.

Waterfowling is limited to floating the rivers, jump-shooting for puddlers on beaver ponds and along small streams, and some hunting with decoys for both divers and dabblers on the larger lakes. Many of those in the southern region feature public access.

Speaking of floating, this is an excellent way to hunt deer as well as squirrels and waterfowl. Hunters, for instance, can put in on the White River at Hesperia, Newaygo, or White Cloud. South of Hesperia they will find a rocky bottom and later swampland, then a few windfall portages and sharp turns. They can end the trip at White Lake in Muskegon County to the southwest, if they wish, with a takeout at the old US-31 bridge.

The South Branch of the Pere Marquette River offers a good hunting float beginning at 13-Mile Road about five miles west of Bitely. Go 25 miles to Huntley Bridge in Oceana County or take out at one of many places en route.

The Muskegon River is a champion stream to float with some 225 miles meandering through seven counties. Newaygo County hunters can put in at Newaygo State Park on Hardy Pond with a portage at Hardy Dam on the western side. They will also have to lift canoes at Croton Dam with a takeout at Newaygo or farther downstream at Bridgeton. Plenty of campgrounds lie along the river en route.

Newaygo County gets considerable grouse and woodcock hunting pressure, but hourly flush rates from hunter-cooperators indicate good populations. Records from three hunting seasons revealed grouse flush averages of 1.73, 2.26, and 1.99. Woodcock flushes during those same seasons were 1.31, 3.23, and 2.45. For both grouse and woodcock, hunt aspen stands understoried with dogwood, brushlands along stream bottoms, and regenerating forestlands.

OTHER SHOOTING OPPORTUNITIES

None known at this time.

FURTHER SOURCES OF HUNTING INFORMATION

1. (Central and northern Newaygo County) DNR District Office, 8015 South 131 Road, Cadillac, Mich. 49601 (616/775-9727).

2. (Southern Newaygo County) DNR District Office, State Office Bldg., 350 Ottawa NW, Grand Rapids, Mich. 49503 (616/456-5071).

3. Northern Newaygo County is managed by a DNR wildlife habitat biologist stationed at the Baldwin Field Office (616/745-4651).

4. Southern Newaygo County is managed by a DNR wildlife habitat biologist stationed at the Muskegon State Game Area, 7600 Messinger, Twin Lake, Mich. 49457 (616/788-5055).

5. Manistee National Forest, White Cloud Ranger District, White Could, Mich. 49349 (616/689-6696).

6. Fremont Chamber of Commerce, 101 East Main St., Fremont, Mich. 49413 (616/924-0770).

7. Newaygo Chamber of Commerce, 8406 Mason Road, Newaygo, Mich. 49337 (616/652-9298).

8. White Cloud Chamber of Commerce, 107 Charles St., White Cloud, Mich. 49349 (616/689-6607).

9. Hesperia Area Chamber of Commerce, Box 32, Hesperia, Mich. 49421 (616/854-6455).

10. Topographic, county, and lake maps may be ordered from the Michigan United Conservation Clubs. For information, refer to the beginning of this book.

11. Plat books are available from the Newaygo County Cooperative Extension Services, 6907 West 48th St., Fremont, Mich. 49412. The cost is $10 each (add $.95 if mail ordering).

12. Newaygo County ASCS Office, Box 67, Fremont, Mich. 49412.

Also, refer to the Manistee National Forest elsewhere in this book.

Oakland County

ALTHOUGH Oakland County has over one million people and increased competition for varied uses of its 899 square miles, it does offer hunting opportunities—in fact, some surprisingly good ones for small game. Many downstate sportsmen who pass up this area in their backyards may be overlooking some good hunting. Over 28,000 acres, most of which are open to hunting, are claimed by portions of state parks and recreation areas. There are an additional 2,000 acres of Public Access Stamp program land, mostly in the northwestern corner, open to hunting by landowner permit. For a free directory, stop in to DNR district headquarters near the Pontiac Lake Recreation Area (*which see*).

Glaciers gouged out many of the land forms and 1,468 lakes (more than any other county in the state) in Oakland County. Water bodies that cover more than 40 acres make up about 14,080 acres of the county. In addition, there are many marshes and bog areas throughout. Five major rivers have their headwaters within this county. The Clinton and Huron rivers begin in the north-central portion, the River Rouge has its headwaters in the southeastern region, the Shiawassee starts in the northwestern sector, and the Flint River begins in the northern part.

The southeastern portion of the county contains several Detroit suburbs on nearly-level glacial lake plains. The rest of the county consists of two gently undulating to very hilly end moraine bands separated by three major outwash plains in a northeast to southwest orientation.

Most of the farming is done on small parcels in the western and northern sections. Major crops are corn, small grain, alfalfa, and hay. Smaller fields may contain specialty crops such as sweet corn, lettuce, tomatoes, and other vegetables. The loamy soils produce good commercial sod and nursery stock. Other areas are pastured for dairy and beef cattle and for some of the over 200 horse farms ranging in size from five to 200 acres.

Oakland County's wildlife habitat is an interesting mix of brushlands, grasslands, and forestlands. Deer, squirrels, and rabbits are expanding in these cover areas. Grouse and woodcock, in particular, seem to be doing well, thanks to increasing amounts of upland brush and aspen due to abandoned farms left untilled by land speculators. About 22 percent of the county is forested with commercial-timber species including oak, hickory, ash, elm, hard and soft maple, and birch.

Deer are plentiful throughout although not found in such large numbers as to the west. Car-deer accidents claim about 200 whitetails annually; hunters take more. Overall pressure is light, probably under five hunters per square mile, although competition on state lands can be intense during firearm season in particular. Probably three to five percent of Oakland County hunters tag bucks. However, some of these bucks are very large and carry trophy headgear. Archers have killed big bucks within sight of the Silverdome. In fact, Oakland County has thus far produced 19 all-time big Michigan deer, according to Commemorative Bucks of Michigan, which began compiling statistics only a few years ago. Seven of those bucks were shot during two recent seasons. In 1983 Michigan's finest nontypical buck was a 22-point Oakland County deer that scored 188-7/8 Boone and Crockett points.

The big problem that many hunters face is one of access. Still, a courteous request from a responsible sportsman can go a long way toward getting permission to hunt private land. It is certainly worth trying. Another problem, however, is that portions of the county are closed to hunting in one form or another. For instance, a dozen scattered regions are totally closed. Avon, Bloomfield, West Bloomfield, Farmington, and Waterford townships are generally open to bow hunting but closed to firearms. Other sections are closed to migratory waterfowl and firearm hunting; some are open to bow, shotgun, and muzzleloader only; and still others are closed to all rifles and a few are closed to only centerfire-rifle hunting. The DNR has county maps color-coded to the types of closures under Public Act 159. Consult this map and/or consult local municipalities for specific regulations. To get a copy, stop in to any of the DNR offices in Oakland County (see listing at end of this section).

Raccoon are abundant in Oakland County and are sought by houndsmen and trappers alike who look for them in lowland hardwoods along stream bottoms next to corn fields. There are many red fox in the county too. Squirrel hunting is fairly good, especially in stands of upland hardwoods with mast-producing trees. Again, don't overlook corn-fields with timber cover nearby. But the cottontail rabbit is the bread-and-butter small-game target in Oakland County. Populations are generally good in brushlands and grasslands of abandoned farms and in edge cover of these habitats and woods along stream bottoms, cattail marshes, and young pine plantations.

Pheasants are becoming scarce throughout and hunting opportunity is quite limited. On the other hand, grouse and woodcock opportunities are looking up, especially in the tier of northern townships. Hunters now move 1.0 to 2.0 grouse per hour in an average season and shoot woodcock incidentally except when the long-billed migrants concentrate into hillside and stream-bottom cover. This phenomenon occurs in late October and can produce some excellent sport. A total of 26 wild turkeys from Missouri have been released in the Seven Lakes State Park area of Holly Township. If the flock expands as hoped, these birds could produce future hunting opportunities.

Waterfowl hunting is another plus in Oakland County. Streams and potholes afford jump-hunting success for those able to secure hunting permission. An especially wild area is the headwaters of the Flint River, home to beaver, wood ducks, and yarding deer in winter. County lakes produce mallards and wood ducks and some teal; many have public access and receive migrant birds. Best float trip would be along the Huron River, except that the metroparks are closed to hunting.

Nuisance giant Canada geese offer excellent hunting opportunities during both the regular waterfowl and extended goose seasons. Best honker concentrations are to the west and southwest. Hunters will find good numbers at Stony Creek and Kensington metroparks (both closed to hunting), at state recreation areas (all of which see) often managed for the giants, and around Lake Orion and Holly. On a recent mid-December inventory flight, DNR biologists counted geese on 45 Oakland County lakes. Hunters willing to (1) follow geese in their twice-daily flights to crop fields of corn and winter wheat and (2) seek hunting permission from landowners can enjoy good shooting.

OTHER SHOOTING OPPORTUNITIES

The Bald Mountain Recreation Area, 2500 Kern in Lake Orion, features a shooting range open to the public for fees. Facilities include 20 outdoor stations each for pistol and centerfire and rimfire rifle, three fields each for skeet and trap, and 12 outdoor archery targets. Manned by a concessionaire, the gun range offers both shooting instruction and competition as well as hunter certification programs. Those entering will need a state park sticker. Call 313/693-7261 for information.

Pontiac Lake Recreation Area, 7800 Gale in Pontiac, is run by the DNR. Featured are outdoor stations for pistol (six), centerfire rifle (12), rimfire rifle (18), archery (four targets), and a shotgun handtrap area. Shooting instruction is offered, and a park sticker is also required for admittance. Call 313/666-1020 for details.

The DNR also operates shooting-range facilities at the Ortonville Recreation Area. For details, consult the listing under Lapeer County.

Oakland County Sportsmen's Club, 4770 Waterford Road in Clarkston, allows fee public use of its extensive facilities. Included are 45 indoor/outdoor pistol stations, 40 outdoor centerfire-rifle stations, 55 indoor/outdoor rimfire-rifle stations, four skeet fields, four trap fields, four shotgun handtrap areas, and 50 indoor/outdoor archery targets. The club offers shooting instruction and competition and sponsors hunter certification programs. For more information, call 313/623-0444.

Detroit Archers, Inc., 5795 Drake Road in West Bloomfield, has 78 indoor/outdoor archery targets and 28 archery-hunter rounds available daily to the public for fees. Shooting instruction and competitive shooting are offered. The club also sponsors hunter-certification courses. Call 313/661-9610 for details.

Security Services, Inc., 31171 10-Mile Road in Farmington Hills, offers shooting instruction at its range for fees. Call 313/476-9600 for an explanation of facilities and services.

FURTHER SOURCES OF HUNTING INFORMATION

1. DNR District Office, 2455 North Williams Lake Road, Pontiac, Mich. 48054 (313/666-1500).

2. Bald Mountain Recreation Area, 1350 Greenshield Road, Lake Orion, Mich. 48035 (313/693-6767).

3. Dodge #4 State Park (not open to hunting; however, officials may be helpful), 4246 Parkway Drive, Pontiac, Mich. 48054 (313/682-0800).

4. Highland Recreation Area, 5200 East Highland Road, Milford, Mich. 48042 (313/887-5135).

5. Holly Recreation Area, 8100 Grange Hall Road, Holly, Mich. 48442 (313/634-8811).

6. Island Lake Recreation Area, 12950 East Grand River, Brighton, Mich. 48116 (313/229-7067).

7. Ortonville Recreation Area, 5767 Hadley Road, Ortonville, Mich. 48462 (313/627-3828).

8. Pontiac Lake Recreation Area, 7800 Gale Road, Pontiac, Mich. 48054 (313/666-1020).

9. Rochester-Utica Recreation Area, 47511 Woodall, Utica, Mich. 48087 (313/731-2110).

10. Seven Lakes State Park, 2220 Tinsman Road, Fenton, Mich. 48430 (313/634-7271).

11. Milford Area Chamber of Commerce, 371 North Main St., Milford, Mich. 48042 (313/685-7129).

12. Novi Chamber of Commerce, Box 187, Novi, Mich. 48050 (313/349-3743).

13. Oakland County Chamber of Commerce, 10 West Huron St., Suite 315, Pontiac, Mich. 48050 (313/335-6148).

14. Holly Board of Commerce, Box 214, Holly, Mich. 48442 (313/634-4761).

15. Lake Orion Chamber of Commerce, 2 West Flint St., Lake Orion, Mich. 48035 (313/693-8333).

16. Greater Ortonville Chamber of Commerce, Box 152, Ortonville, Mich. 48462 (313/627-2020).

17. Oxford Chamber of Commerce, 50 West Burdick, Oxford, Mich. 48051 (313/628-4691).

18. Greater Rochester Chamber of Commerce, 812 North Main, Box 431, Rochester, Mich. 48063 (313/651-6700).

19. Lakes Area Chamber of Commerce, 2410 South Commerce, Walled Lake, Mich. 48088 (313/624-2826).

20. Topographic, county, and lake maps may be ordered from the Michigan United Conservation Clubs. For information, refer to the beginning of this book.

21. Detailed plat books (showing ownerships of three acres and up) are available from the Oakland County Cooperative Extension Services, 1200 North Telegraph Road, Pontiac, Mich, 48053. The cost is $40 each (add $1.50 if mail ordering).

22. Oakland County ASCS Office, USDA, 8326 Highland Road, Pontiac, Mich. 48054 (313/666-2212).

Also, refer to the following elsewhere in this book:
1. Bald Mountain Recreation Area
2. Highland Recreation Area
3. Holly Recreation Area
4. Horseshoe Lake Wildlife Area
5. Island Lake Recreation Area
6. Ortonville Recreation Area
7. Pontiac Lake Recreation Area
8. Seven Lakes State Park
9. Oakland County Mini-Game Area

Oceana County

ROLLING topography, a sand-dune belt, forest cover mixed with farmlands, and more than 60 lakes combine to give 543-square-mile Oceana County in west-central Lower Michigan its scenic look. Some of these same natural conditions also provide good hunting for a variety of game animals and birds. However, Oceana County often gets bypassed by downstate hunters streaming north. They might want to reconsider.

Over half the county is timbered with an excellent mixture of commercial-forest species. Led by 35,700 acres of maple-birch, that mixture includes 35,000 acres of oak-hickory, 29,000 acres of aspen, 23,200 acres of elm-ash-soft maple, 15,400 acres of red pine, and 2,700 acres of northern white cedar. The central-county region is largely farmed with orchards beginning west of Walkerville and truck farming for asparagus, strawberries, and other crops occurring southwest of Hart, the county seat.

State land is mostly limited to the northwestern region. It includes a block of the Pere Marquette State Forest and the 2,700-acre Silver Lake State Park (both of which see), all open to hunting. Total state land ownership is about 5,200 acres or 1.5 percent of the land base in Oceana County. An additional 11.6 percent, or 41,418 acres, is in the Manistee National Forest (which also see), mostly in the eastern half. This federal land is also open to hunting.

Further, over 1,200 acres of company-owned lands are enrolled in the Commercial Forest Act program, making them open to hunting. For legal descriptions (which hunters can then locate on plat books and county maps), contact the DNR Forest Management Division, Box 30028, Lansing, Mich. 48909 or call 517/373-1275.

Surface features in Oceana County are the result of glaciation. They include broad, smooth plains; broken and pitted plains; and rough, hilly, or gently rolling areas of ridges, knobs, basins, and valleys. The sharpest changes in relief range from 50 to 200 feet above the plains. Generally, the western portion of the county is a large plain whereas the eastern half is a hilly upland area. An exception is Claybanks Township in the southwestern corner as a bluff in the northern part is the highest point in Oceana County.

Here and elsewhere along the Lake Michigan shore is a belt of dunes from one-half mile to one-and-a-half miles wide and ranging from 50 to 200 feet above the lake. Between this line of dunes and the western lake plain is a pitted plainlike area containing small moraines that run north and south.

About three-fourths of Oceana County is well-drained, with the highest areas originally containing white pine. The rest of the county supported a mixed hardwood forest, much as it does today. A lowland area on the eastern side is Leavitt Township, which has large, poorly drained swampy areas.

Several rivers traverse the county. From north to south these include the South Branch Pere Marquette, the North and South Branch Pentwater, and the North and South Branch White as well as their tributaries. Portions of the rivers are floatable, and the bottomlands of each contain game.

Deer-hunting pressure in Oceana County is moderate at 15 to 20 hunters per square mile. They take one or two bucks per square mile for a success factor of about 15 percent or near the state average. In truth deer are found throughout the county and public land is just as productive as private holdings. Heavy hardwoods—including oak and hemlock ridges—fronting the lakeshore in Benona and Claybanks townships offer good deer hunting. In recent years damage complaints have fallen off in the orchard belt running parallel to the lake, and for the most part deer are chased off by hunters here after opening day.

Greenwood Township in the southeastern corner contains jack pine, red pine, oak, and aspen and is a good deer area (with pockets of grouse and squirrels too). These same habitats exist in national forestlands in the northeastern corner. For hunting dense swampland late in the season, try southern Leavitt Township.

Turkeys frequent the eastern half of Oceana County in farmlands mixed with forests. The area north of M-20 and east of US-31 is currently open to hunting. Squirrel hunting for both gray/black and fox species is good on farm woodlots and in oak, hickory, and beech stands throughout the county. Some cottontails live in swales, abandoned fields, and farm vicinities. For snowshoes, find pine plantations, swamp edges, and poplar slashings near conifers.

There are a few pheasants in Oceana County but not enough to warrant hunting them. Fox are found countywide in forest openings and cultivated lands alike. Occasionally, deer hunters bag the odd coyote. Raccoon are generally abundant along waterways not far from farmlands. Waterfowl hunting opportunities are limited to jump shooting on scattered potholes, a few beaver pond floodings, and along streams.

Grouse and woodcock hunting pressure continues to increase, but birds appear to be holding up. Three years of hunter-cooperator records indicate hourly flush rates of 1.58, 4.37, and 2.19 grouse. Woodcock flushes for the same years were 1.08, 1.04, and .72. It is likely that sandy soils that dominate Oceana County are the reason for low woodcock numbers as the long-billed birds require a diet of worms and other invertebrates.

OTHER SHOOTING OPPORTUNITIES

The Hart Rifle and Revolver Club in Hart has three outdoor pistol stations, four outdoor centerfire rifle stations, and a skeet field open to the public daily for fees. The club also offers shooting instruction. For details, call 616/873-5133.

FURTHER SOURCES OF HUNTING INFORMATION

1. DNR District Office, 8015 South 131 Road, Cadillac, Mich. 49601 (616/775-9727).

2. DNR Silver Lake Field Office, Box 67, Mears, Mich. 49436 (616/873-3082).

3. Hart Chamber of Commerce, Drawer 113, Hart, Mich. 49420 (616/873-2178).

4. Pentwater Area Chamber of Commerce, Box 614, Pentwater, Mich. 49449 (616/869-4150).

5. Shelby Chamber of Commerce, 195 North Michigan, Box 72, Shelby, Mich. 49455 (616/861-4054).

6. Topographic, county, and lake maps may be ordered from the Michigan United Conservation Clubs. For information, refer to the beginning of this book.

7. County plat books are available from the Oceana County Cooperative Extension Services, 210 Johnson St., Hart, Mich. 49420. The cost is $10 each (add $1 if mail ordering).

8. Oceana County ASCS Office, 20 South Oceana Drive, Shelby, Mich. 49455.

Also, refer to the following elsewhere in this book:

1. Huron-Manistee National Forest
2. Pere Marquette State Forest
3. Silver Lake State Park
4. Pentwater River State Game Area

Ogemaw County

OGEMAW County in northeastern Lower Michigan has much to offer hunters in pursuit of deer, grouse, turkeys, woodcock, hares, squirrels, and waterfowl. Its 571-square-mile area is about 65 percent covered with commercial-forest species and over 80,000 acres (about one-fourth of the land area) is state and federal forest land open to hunting. Its nearness to southern Michigan, its more than 100 lakes, and its abundance of varied habitat that holds game all contribute toward making Ogemaw County a logical choice for hunters to visit.

Here is a sample of the varied habitat: aspen (83,600 acres), oak-hickory (40,400 acres), jack pine (32,900 acres), maple-birch (30,100 acres), paper birch (11,400 acres), northern white cedar (11,100 acres), and red pine and elm-ash-soft maple (4,100 acres each). The Rifle River, its West Branch, and other tributaries flow southerly to drain the county. The northeastern corner contains nearly 20,000 acres of the Huron-Manistee National Forest (*which see*). The northwestern quarter is mostly Au Sable State Forest (*which also see*), and unattached parcels (over 76,000 acres total) are scattered throughout.

Elevations vary by about 750 feet throughout the county although local differences are under 200 feet. A high sandy plain occurs in the northwestern region, largely devoid of swamps and lakes. Running from southwest to northeast and lying roughly west of West Branch and north of Rose City is a belt of hilly, sandy country. Bordering this belt on its eastern and southern portions is a rolling plain characterized by smooth slopes, swampy swales and valleys, and a number of lakes.

In the central part of the county, a lower sandy plain — 10 to 15 miles wide — is traversed by the Rifle River and its West Branch. Extensive bodies of swamp occur along the headwaters of the Rifle River, and there are wet patches along the southern county line. The southeastern portion of the county contains gently rolling land marked with bogs, clay flats, and small swamps.

Altogether, about 20 percent of the land area is either lake surface or swamp. The western region is reasonably dry whereas the central and eastern portions contain the most water resources. In addition to the drainage system, Ogemaw County contains over 1,000 flowing springs and more than 3,000 artesian wells.

Deer hunting is good throughout the county with perhaps the farm country in the southern half producing best. A recent DNR survey indicates that Rose, Goodar, Logan, Churchill, Ogemaw, and Horton townships contain fairly high numbers of deer. Hunting permission, however, is tough to come by, and that is largely due to the hunting pressure that Ogemaw County receives. Thirty to 40 hunters per square mile on the average translates to a lot of deer hunters, especially when one considers that three-fourths of the county is in private ownership.

Deer hunters here are quite successful, averaging five bucks or more per square mile in recent firearm seasons and 15 to 20 percent success, a little above the state average. Attesting to high numbers of deer in this county is the annual car-deer accident tally of over 300 animals. Only Iosco County, which borders the eastern side, claims as many highway-killed deer through the next four tiers of counties (21 total) all the way to the Straits of Mackinac.

Historically, however, Ogemaw County does not produce big bucks. The DNR manages the deer herd for maximum numbers, not trophy heads, and — coupled with high hunting pressure — bucks are culled at an early age. Most are harvested as yearling animals sporting spikehorns or small racks of four and six points.

Scattered reports of black-bear sightings occur throughout the county, but even though bear may be legally hunted, few are tagged since Ogemaw County represents the southern limits of their range.

Wild turkeys, on the other hand, appear to be increasing. Many birds winter in the Lupton area. Best places throughout the county to hunt them during spring gobbler seasons include (1) Huron-Manistee National Forest, (2) a mile either side of CR-17 between CR-22 and Peters Road, (3) in the Ogemaw Hills in the west-central part of the county, and (4) in Foster Township south of CR-26 and north of CR-22 and west of CR-15 to within a couple miles of Roscommon County. The center of each of the four mentioned hot spots also is a wintering area.

Good grouse and woodcock hunting occurs in the old Rifle River Recreation Area, in mixed stands of aspen and lowland hardwoods in the southwestern region, and in scattered poplar (aspen) slashings throughout the county. Pressure increases yearly, it seems, with hunter-cooperators reporting 1.22 to 2.52 flushes per hour during two random seasons checked. Hourly woodcock flushes during those years were .49 and 1.52. The best woodcock hunting occurs along stream-bottom hillsides and in aspen or alder stands near old pastures and abandoned orchards.

The large amount of oak-hickory forests makes for good (and underutilized) squirrel hunting, mostly for fox squirrels although a few grays/blacks frequent mixed stands of oak and pine. Raccoon utilize waters and receive moderate to high hunting pressure. Snowshoe hares are currently on the increase after several down years. Try grouse/woodcock covers abutting pine plantations and conifer swamps. For cottontails, check brushlands and grasslands of farm fields or around abandoned outbuildings. This farm country holds underhunted red fox, and there are also a few coyotes in Ogemaw County, especially in the jack-pine forests of the northwestern sector.

Scattered beaver ponds and potholes hold opening-day wood ducks, mallards, and the odd black duck or teal. There are few geese in Ogemaw County. On the other hand, lakes in the east-central and northeastern regions host fair numbers of puddle ducks early in the season and diving ducks later on. About a dozen lakes have public access. Don't overlook the Rifle River either for a productive float for ducks (squirrels and deer too). Hunters can put-in/take-out at CR-22, CR-18 (Sage Lake Road) or CR-19 and thus remain on state land the entire float. South of Selkirk the land is mostly private, and floaters will need permission to hunt riverbottom land.

OTHER SHOOTING OPPORTUNITIES

None known at this time.

FURTHER SOURCES OF HUNTING INFORMATION

1. DNR District Office, 191 South Mount Tom Road (M-33), Mio, Mich. 48647 (517/826-3211).

2. DNR West Branch Field Office, 2389 South M-76, West Branch, Mich. 48661 (517/345-0472).

3. Rose City/Lupton Area Chamber of Commerce, 113 North Warner St., Box 100, Rose City, Mich. 48654 (517/473-2275).

4. West Branch Area Chamber of Commerce, 422 West Houghton Ave., West Branch, Mich. 48661 (517/345-2821).

5. Skidway Lake Area Chamber of Commerce, 2777 Greenwood, Box 4041, Prescott, Mich. 48756 (517/873-4150 or 873-3103).

6. Topographic, county, and lake maps may be ordered from the Michigan United Conservation Clubs. For information, refer to the beginning of this book.

7. Plat books are available from the Ogemaw County Cooperative Extension Services, 806 West Houghton Ave., Ogemaw County Building, West Branch, Mich. 48661 for $10 each (add $1.50 if mail ordering).

8. Ogemaw/Oscoda County ASCS Office, 240 West Wright St., West Branch, Mich. 48661.

Also, refer to the following elsewhere in this book:

1. Au Sable State Forest
2. Huron-Manistee National Forest
3. Rifle River Recreation Area

Ontonagon County

ONTONAGON County in the far western Upper Peninsula is a long drive from Detroit, but downstate sportsmen might want to consider the long haul. Why? Ontonagon County's 845,000 acres (about 1,321 square miles) yield good hunting opportunities. Trophy bucks and a healthy black-bear population attract big-game hunters. Snowshoe hares, coyotes, bobcats, grouse, woodcock, and waterfowl beckon others.

A broad plain that extends the length of the county rises to rolling hills and rugged peaks from 1,000 to 1,400 feet high of the Copper Range in the northern region. Some 50 miles of Lake Superior touch Ontonagon County shores, quick-running rivers spill over waterfalls, and inland lakes dot the handsome interior. The northern half of the Upper Peninsula's largest lake—Lake Gogebic—lies on the southwestern boundary with Gogebic County.

About 35 percent of the land base is publicly owned through huge, scattered blocks of the Ottawa National Forest (227,000 acres), most of the 58,000-acre Porcupine Mountains State Park, and northeastern-county holdings of the Copper Country State Forest (all of which see). Adding these public lands to 186,482 acres of private forestland currently enrolled in the Commercial Forest Act program means that some 479,000 acres are open to hunting.

About 85 percent of Ontonagon County is timbered with commercial-forest species. More than half, or 386,600 acres, is northern hardwoods of hard maple and birch, but a large percentage (163,500 acres) of aspen is represented. Other forest types include balsam fir (35,100 acres), elm-ash-soft maple (29,800 acres), white spruce (14,600 acres), red pine (10,500 acres), black spruce (8,300 acres), white pine (8,200 acres), paper birch (7,200 acres), and jack pine (5,200 acres).

This forest diversity helps produce a variety of game species; however, more mature stands need cutting. In fact, about 85 percent of Ontonagon County commercial forests are in sawtimber or poletimber stands and are consequently beyond the size where they benefit most wildlife species the most.

Although deer are often stressed in winter by the lack of preferred browse types and the 180 to 200 inches of average snowfall, this county still produces good deer hunting. Low numbers of hunters (about five per square mile) shoot one to two bucks per square mile for a 22 percent success rate. That figure is several points above the state average. Many hunters head for remote areas to seek a trophy buck, which certainly are found here. Commemorative Bucks of Michigan currently lists 40 Ontonagon County deer among its all-time tally of 1,150 record Michigan bucks.

The western region is especially rugged, and although it produces big bucks, deer are not plentiful. Best bet would be to try a late-season deer yard and attempt to shoot a migrating animal en route. One such yard is located along Merriweather

Creek on the western side of Lake Gogebic. Other, less significant concentration areas include the Stanko Lake area north of Bergland, along the Big Iron River south of USFS-476, north of this road below White Pine and the Old Nonesuch Mine, and in the Porcupine Mountains State Park west of Union Bay.

In southeastern Ontonagon County, deer are more plentiful south of M-28 than north as the southern region is interspersed with more openings and contains more varied cover types. A major yarding area occurs along the Middle and East branches of the Ontonagon River east of US-45, north of Bruce Crossing, and west of a line from Craigsmere and Sleepy Hollow (USFS-177).

In northeastern Ontonagon County, best prospects are in the vicinity of the Rockland, Mass, and Rousseau areas where farming is practiced. The remote 14-Mile Point country on Lake Superior contains cedar, spruce, and balsam and attracts wintering deer. Whitetails also yard along the East Branch of the Ontonagon River between Victoria Dam Basin and Rousseau.

Ontonagon is one of the best bear-producing counties in the state. The five-county DNR district centered at Baraga generally produces from 200 to 300 bruins (about 30 to 40 percent of the U.P. kill) each fall, and Ontonagon will yield some 80 animals on its own. The Ontonagon-to-Greenland area is a good place to start a bear with hounds. So is the region around Ewen, but in actuality bear are found nearly everywhere throughout the county. Find food areas of mature fruits and nuts and you will generally find bear sign.

The county also produces excellent numbers of bobcats for the few hunters who try this rugged winter sport over dogs. During each of the past five years, DNR biologists have sealed from six to 21 Ontonagon County cats. Try dense conifers that contain a population of snowshoe hares such as at 14-Mile Point. Although hares are down somewhat at this writing, huntable numbers still exist in young cutover areas near swamps and in USFS pine plantations.

Another predator species mostly overlooked by hunters is the coyote. Again, work areas containing hares, especially those covers such as jack pine and near farming areas that would be more open.

A lack of oaks limits squirrel production although there are huntable numbers of grays and a few black-phase bushytails scattered throughout. Raccoon are fairly plentiful around waterways that course near farming centers.

Farmlands adjacent to Lake Superior often get visitations from migrating Canada geese that stop over to rest and feed. Also, farms in the Ewen-Bruce Crossing area and again at Mass, Rockland, and Matchwood are good bets for geese. Duck hunting is limited to Lake Gogebic and the Bond Falls Basin as well as scattered inland lakes and ponds in the southeastern region.

A sharptail management area at Matchwood has yielded no dancing males on spring booming grounds in the past couple of years. Ontonagon County is closed to sharptail hunting. However, fairly good ruffed-grouse hunting occurs most falls (currently, however, the population is somewhat depressed) throughout aspen slashings and along old logging trails. Hunter-cooperator hourly flush-rate records that we checked at random for three years show averages of .70, 1.49, and 1.81.

There is also some fairly good woodcock hunting along stream bottoms and cutover areas featuring moist, rich soils. Those same hunter-cooperators reported average hourly longbill flushes of .70, 1.09, and 2.40.

OTHER SHOOTING OPPORTUNITIES
None known at this time.

FURTHER SOURCES OF HUNTING INFORMATION
1. DNR District Office, North US-41, (Box 440), Baraga, Mich. 49908 (906/353-6651).
2. DNR Porcupine Mountains Field Office, Route 1, Ontonagon, Mich. 49953 (906/885-5712).
3. Forest Supervisor, Ottawa National Forest, East Cloverland Drive, Ironwood, Mich. 49938 (906/932-1330 or 1-800-561-1201 from the U.P.).
4. Ottawa National Fcrest, Bergland Ranger District, Bergland, Mich. 49911 (906/575-3441).
5. Ontonagon County Chamber of Commerce, Box 266, Ontonagon, Mich. 49953 (906/884-4735).
6. Lake Gogebic Area Chamber of Commerce, Bergland, Mich. 49910 (906/575-3265).
7. Mass-Greenland Chamber of Commerce, Mass, Mich. 49948 (no phone).
8. Topographic, county, and lake maps are available from the Michigan United Conservation Clubs. For information, refer to the beginning of this book.
9. Plat books are available from the Ontonagon County Cooperative Extension Services, 522 River St., Ontonagon, Mich. 49953 (906/884-4386). The cost is $10 each (add $1.50 if mail ordering).
10. Otonagon/Gogebic County ASCS Office, Cedar Street, Ewen, Mich. 49925.
Also, refer to the following elsewhere in this book:
1. Copper Country State Forest
2. Ottawa National Forest
3. Porcupine Mountains State Park

Osceola County

OSCEOLA County lies in the north-central part of the Lower Peninsula. Nearly square at about 24 miles, the 581-square-mile county is popular with local and downstate hunters who seek deer, grouse, woodcock, wild turkeys, rabbits, squirrels, raccoon, and waterfowl. The county seat, Reed City, is located in the southwestern portion. At 2,200 citizens, it is the largest town in this lightly-populated county.

Much of Osceola County is a hilly moraine that formed between the Lake Michigan and Lake Huron lobes of an ice sheet that covered this region as recently as 12,000 years ago. In the north-central part of the county, this moraine is estimated to be 1,200 feet thick. One glacial till plain is found in the southwestern portion and another is located in the eastern and northeastern region. One glacial outwash plain lies along the Muskegon River and another, located in the northwestern corner, extends into Wexford County.

Elevations across Osceola County vary by over 600 feet. Highest peak is the old Cadillac Fire Tower at 1,626 feet; lowest spot is in the Muskegon River valley at 1,000 feet. The Pine River and its tributaries drain the northwestern portion and the Muskegon River system drains the rest, with the exception of a small part of the southeastern corner served by the Chippewa River. Many small lakes dot the central and southern portions of the county.

About 47 percent of Osceola County is timbered with commercial-forest species. Dominant type is maple-birch, followed by aspen. Smaller amounts of oak-hickory and elm-ash-soft maple are also found along with some 8,800 acres of northern white cedar. The eastern portion of the county contains remote aspen stands with some oak woodlots blending to mixed covers of oak with jack pine as one moves closer to Clare County. The western region also contains more oak with less aspen as one approaches Lake County. The southeastern corner (along the Chippewa River) runs heavily to hardwoods mixed with pine.

Farmland parcels are scattered throughout the county. One agricultural area is around Marion, site of Michigan's last population of prairie chickens, only recently declared extinct. North-central portion of the county is farmland mixed with hardwoods. Portions of the Muskegon River in Sylvan and Osceola townships border dense swamps. There is also a swampy region north and west of the M-61 and M-115 intersection. Heavy aspen areas include regions northwest of Marion and in the Pere Marquette State Forest (*which see*) northwest of Evart. Both the state of Michigan and Packaging Corporation of America have cut aspen here, resulting in an increase in both game and hunters.

A good deer-hunting and fairly good turkey-hunting area is west of M-115 in the northwestern corner of the county. Also, in the county center—south of Sunrise and Big Long lakes—are solid stands of oak, a likely spot for squirrels and deer during years of heavy mast crops.

About 4.5 percent, or 16,438 acres, of Osceola County is state-owned and open to hunting. In addition, 1,588 acres are currently enrolled in the Commercial Forest Act plan, an agreement between the state and timber companies whereby private lands are open to hunting in exchange for reduced taxes and a state's share of the timber value. A current plat book will help hunters identify these lands, or sportsmen can contact the DNR Forest Management Division in Lansing for legal descriptions.

Hunting overall is very good in Osceola County. Main draw is a large deer herd and good buck-hunting success generally above the state average), which results annually in a firearm kill exceeding five bucks per square mile. Pressure is moderate to high at 20 to 25 hunters per square mile. Best hunting is in young aspen stands and in oak forests during years of high mast production. Current hunter's-choice areas have provided about 50 percent success for permit hunters. Deer numbers are currently high in the eight-county Clare district, and Osceola County has an annual car-deer accident tally exceeding 300 animals. Results of a recent DNR five-year survey, released for this book, indicate that deer production along southern-tier townships is good and is exceptionally high in Marion Township.

Float-tripping on the Muskegon River as well as jump-shooting on numerous potholes, streams, and beaver floodings throughout the county produce fair to good duck hunting. Lowland swamps with conifers fringed by brushlands and early stages of second-growth timber hold huntable populations of snowshoe hares. Cottontails are plentiful around farmlands and in brushland cover and woods openings.

Grouse hunting is fair to good with cooperators reporting flush rates of 2.0 to 3.0 birds per hour in average or better seasons. Locally reared woodcock appear to be fewer in number than grouse, but flight-bird concentrations in rich, moist-soil areas can make for temporary banner hunting. Good numbers of raccoon are largely underutilized as are red fox and increasing numbers of coyotes. Fox-squirrel populations fare with the acorn mast crop and are best hunted in oak-hickory stands adjacent to cropped fields. In addition, heavier forests containing conifers are home to gray squirrels and their black-phase relation.

Although hunting is not allowed, Osceola County citizens and hunters report occasional sightings of bobcats and black bear. This is not unusual since the county lies between southern agricultural lands and northern hardwoods areas. Recent wild-turkey releases are meant to bolster natural spreading of flocks.

OTHER SHOOTING OPPORTUNITIES

The Rendezvous Hunting Preserve, 17365 21-Mile Road in Big Rapids, is open daily to the public for hunting quail, chukars, and ducks on 138 acres. For more information, contact Thomas L. Proefrock at the above address or call 616/796-2390.

The Reed City Sportsman's Club on US-10 in Reed City has a shooting range open to the public at limited times on a fee basis. Facilities include five outdoor stations for pistol firing, a single outdoor station for centerfire rifle, and a field each for trap and skeet. The club also offers competitive shooting. For details, call 616/832-4481.

Spring Hill Camps in Evart has range facilities open to the public, also on a sometime basis for fees. It has an outdoor station for rimfire rifle, a trap field, and outdoor archery targets. Shooting instruction and competitive shooting are offered. Call 616/734-5256 for information.

FURTHER SOURCES OF HUNTING INFORMATION

1. DNR District Headquarters, 501 Hemlock St., Clare, Mich. 48617 (517/386-7991).

2. DNR Evart Field Office, 2510 East US-10, Evart, Mich. 49631 (616/734-5492).

3. Marion Chamber of Commerce, 115 East Main St., Marion, Mich. 49665 (616/743-2461).

4. Reed City Area Chamber of Commerce, 410 West Upton, Suite 17, Reed City, Mich. 49677 (616/832-5431).

5. Topographic, county, and lake maps may be ordered from the Michigan United Conservation Clubs. For informaiton, refer to the beginning of this book.

6. Plat books are available from the Osceola County Cooperative Extension Services, County Courthouse, Reed City, Mich. 49677. The cost is $10 each (add $.95 if mail ordering).

7. Osceola County ASCS Ofice, 7700 South Patterson Road, Reed City, Mich. 49677 (616/832-5341).

Also, refer to the Pere Marquette State Forest elsewhere in this book.

Oscoda County

OSCODA County is located in northeastern Lower Michigan about 30 miles inland from Lake Huron. Its boundaries encompass 570 square miles. Beginning about 1870, lumbermen stripped Oscoda County of its red and white pine and then its hardwood forests of maple, beech, and birch. Eventually the woodcutters tackled lowland stands of white cedar, spruce, and balsam fir.

Today about 85 percent of the county is once again covered by commercial timber. Hunters who understand habitat will readily see that Oscoda County has the potential for growing good numbers of game since 88,700 acres support aspen in varying age classes and another 67,100 acres are dominated by oak-hickory forests. Other important cover types

include jack pine (68,200 acres), red pine (32,800 acres), maple-birch (27,100 acres), and northern white cedar (7,700 acres). White pine, balsam fir, black spruce, and elm-soft maple-ash are represented in smaller amounts.

About 45 percent of Oscoda County is composed of deep, dry-sand soils that occupy the level and gently rolling plains that originally held virgin pine. Topographically, the county is part of a highland plain built up by a great thickness of glacial deposits. This highland plain is cut east and west by the famed Au Sable River, which meanders through a terraced valley averaging three miles in width and bordered by 300- to 400-foot-high hills.

Elsewhere, local relief that varies by perhaps 100 or so feet consists mostly of broad swells with long, smooth slopes. Low domes, knobs, and ridges shelter potholes, lake basins, and swamps lying in their valleys. In fact, swamps occur both on level plains and in hill basins. Most of the county's 122 lakes are found in the northern portion. They vary in size from one acre to nearly 250 acres; most are under 40 acres.

The northwestern quarter is largely Au Sable State Forest (*which see*) land, which is open to hunting. South of the Au Sable River and to some degree in the east-central region, the land is federally-owned and constitutes a large portion of the Huron-Manistee National Forest (*which also see*). State land comprises about 16 percent and federal ownership covers nearly 40 percent of the county.

The central part of Oscoda County, between these blocks of public land, is mostly farmed for dairy and livestock enterprises. The northeastern corner is largely club-owned land. Overall, the diverse habitat types and timber-cutting programs on state and federal land help Oscoda County to support good game populations. Deer, the most popular target sought, are generally widespread throughout although they like cutover areas just growing back and also tend to congregate in oak ridges during years of high acorn production. Hunting pressure is very high.

Black bear appear to be on the increase, along with snowshoe hares, the latter after a major decline a few years ago. Good numbers of grouse and woodcock provide solid sporting opportunities. Turkey hunting is among the best in northern Michigan and there is untapped hunting potential for squirrels and coyotes and, in some instances, waterfowl. Bobcats are also fair game.

Although Oscoda County produces three to four bucks per square mile, hunter success at 10 to 14 percent is below the state average. That is because pressure runs as high as 40 hunters per square mile countywide and is even more intense on federal land bordering club property just east of Fairview. To many downstate sportsmen, Mio, the centrally-located county seat, is the center of the universe during deer season. Good numbers of deer, bountiful public-land ownership, and the famed Au Sable River are other attractions to deer hunters. According to a recent five-year survey, Clinton and Elmer townships, along with forests bordering the Au Sable River to the west, have high deer populations.

The county is intensively managed by the DNR for full-capacity deer production. Corresponding high hunting pressure tends to cull the herd of big bucks, and so most deer shot are yearling animals sporting spikes or small racks. Commemorative Bucks of Michigan has thus far found only five Oscoda County bucks worthy of record-book inclusion. That is not to say that big deer don't live here—but those that are tagged usually come from private farmland.

Other key spots for deer (as well as grouse and snowshoe hares) include (1) the extreme southeastern corner where aspen cuttings under 10 years old are just growing back; (2) two miles west of Mio on the river's south side; (3) two miles due south of Luzerne; (4) in the Folly Swamp area three to five miles west of Luzerne and just north of M-72 (especially in late season as this is a deer-yarding area—also, archers tend to concentrate here); (5) hilly hardwoods just south of the Hunt Creek Fisheries Research Area in the north-central portion; and (6) the Block House Swamp area (also for yarding deer) in the McKinley area.

In addition, the northwestern portion of the county is slated to receive cuttings soon and should produce good numbers of game in the future. Jack pines here now yield both hares and coyotes. So does the Mack Lake area south and east of Mio where fire a few years ago regenerated over 24,000 acres.

Try the Block House and Folly swamps for black bear, on the increase in Oscoda County, and bobcats. Wintering turkeys congregate in the farm belt area from Mio to Fairview and again in the club country where private feedings keep them going during hard winters. By spring, birds tend to disperse along the Au Sable River both here and in the Luzerne/Red Oak area. In addition to the northeastern portion of the county, high turkey numbers exist south of M-72 in the Mack Lake area.

Good grouse and woodcock hunting spots, other than ones already mentioned, include mixed aspen stands around Muskrat Lake and moist-soil areas with edge cover along the Au Sable River and feeder creeks. Flight woodcock congregate on alder/aspen habitats here, especially during dry falls. Two years of randomly checked reports made by hunter-cooperators showed 2.05 to 2.40 grouse flushes per hour and .50 to 2.0 woodcock flushes per hour.

Heavy squirrel populations occur during years of high mast production. Fox species frequent farm woodlots and oak ridges on state and federal land whereas grays/blacks tend to favor oak stands mixed with conifers. Folly Swamp oaks just north of M-72 are a good bet most years.

The few red fox and cottontails that live in Oscoda County are generally linked to farmlands. Duck hunters can get jump-shooting action for woodies and mallards on beaver ponds and along small drainages. The Au Sable is ideal for early-season puddlers and late-season divers, and Mio Pond affords some decoy-hunting from either blinds or boats. Limited numbers of Oscoda County geese are usually found here too.

OTHER SHOOTING OPPORTUNITIES

None known at this time.

FURTHER SOURCES OF HUNTING INFORMATION

1. DNR District Office, 191 South Mount Tom Road (M-33), Mio, Mich. 48647 (517/826-3211).

2. Topographic, county, and lake maps may be ordered from the Michigan United Conservation Clubs. For information, refer to the beginning of this book.

3. Plat books are available from the Oscoda County Clerk's Office, Box 399, 311 Morenci (Main) St., Mio, Mich. 48647. The cost is $10 each (add $.89 if mail ordering).

4. Ogemaw/Oscoda ASCS Office, 240 West Wright St., West Branch, Mich. 48661.

5. Mio Ranger District, Huron-Manistee National Forest, M-33, Mio, Mich. 48647 (517/826-3717).

Also, refer to the following elsewhere in this book:
1. Au Sable State Forest
2. Huron-Manistee National Forest

Otsego County

OTSEGO County in north-central Lower Michigan is popular with deer, bear, snowshoe hare, coyote, bobcat, grouse, and woodcock hunters. Its resident elk herd was first hunted in 1964 and 1965 and is once again scheduled for future, limited harvesting by permit. Overall, northern Michigan's elk herd (the only one east of the Rockies except for a small Pennsylvania band) is thought to number about a thousand animals. Their range in Otsego County occupies the northern region with most numbers residing in the Pigeon River Country forestlands in the northeastern corner.

A good habitat mix is one reason that Otsego County produces game. About 77 percent of its 522 square miles is covered with commercial-forest species. Northern hardwoods of maple, birch, beech, and basswood lead with 120,400 acres (more than one-third the total land base). They are followed by aspen in varying age classes (63,300 acres), jack pine and red pine (21,800 acres each), white pine (8,300 acres), northern white cedar (7,800 acres), and balsam fir (6,000 acres). Smaller amounts of white and black spruce are also found.

Aspen in the Pigeon River Country forestlands has been intensively managed for elk, deer, and grouse. Consquently, hunting opportunities are very good. The southeastern portion of Otsego County is largely scrub oak and jack pine and affords good deer hunting. However, these are small deer—yearlings mostly—subjected to the same heavy hunting pressure that tightly culls the herd in Crawford and Roscommon counties to the south. Also, Gaylord, the county seat, falls into a snow belt that enters Otsego County from Kalkaska to the southwest. Deer are usually hard-stressed by winter's end and mortality rates can run rampant during a particularly tough winter.

That is not to say that Otsego County does not have good deer hunting. Generally, the best opportunities occur east of I-75 and south of M-32 although some big-racked bucks come from the northwestern sector adjacent to Charlevoix County. Pressure overall is under 20 hunters per square mile. They experience one-of-eight success on bucks or about 12 to 16 percent (just under the state average). Otsego County produces one to two bucks per square mile each fall during the two-week firearm season.

Over 90,000 acres, or about 27 percent of the land base, is state-owned, mostly in large-block and small-parcel holdings in the southern half and northeastern corner already noted. These lands constitute a portion of the Mackinac State Forest (*which see*), which includes the Pigeon River Country forest lands, and are open to hunting. In addition, another 3,000 acres of Commercial Forest Act land, enrolled by the timber companies who own them, are open to hunting. For legal descriptions, stop in at the DNR district office at Gaylord or contact the DNR Forest Management Division (Box 30028, Lansing 48909 or call 517/373-1275). Then use a current plat book and county map to find these timberlands.

Best bear and bobcat hunting potential is north of M-32 and east of I-75. The very southwestern tip of the county is also good, but keep in mind that pressure throughout Otsego County is high for both game species. Raccoon are plentiful along stream bottoms adjacent to farm lands, with hunting pressure moderate.

Otsego County is the highest spot in Lower Michigan; consequently, all streams flow away to other places. The Sturgeon, Pigeon, and Black rivers drain the northern half and flow northerly. The North Branch of the Au Sable River and the headwaters of the Manistee River move southerly. Dense cover along these streams and many other small drainages are good for snowshoe hares, deer, bear, grouse, and woodcock. Occasionally, hunters can expect to jump puddle ducks and to see fox or gray squirrels too. Floaters might try the Au Sable North Branch except they will run into plenty of brush and may have to portage frequently.

The eastern half of Otsego County contains many potholes and beaver ponds, also likely spots for ducks and woodcock. Hardwoods generally run throughout the center of the county and provide good habitat for deer, bear, bobcats, and coyotes although state land in this region is virtually nonexistent. Best hunting comes on small, private parcels, which hunters can sometimes gain access to if they first make a courteous request. Be aware, however, that the Michaywe housing subdivision east of I-75 and Otsego Lake is closed to hunting by local ordinance.

The west-central portion contains old farms in marginal production and is home to red fox. Also, those abandoned lands reverting to natural forest succession are good places to try for grouse and woodcock.

Farm woodlots contain squirrels. For best results, comb mature stands of oaks east of I-75 and south of M-32. Coyotes are on the increase in Otsego County, and there appears to be more than normal interest in hunting them, especially with dogs. A good place to try, either with hounds or with a good predator call, is jack-pine cover in the southeastern region. The old artillery range grounds in this area east of Guthrie Lake and along the Au Sable River contain a remnant population of sharp-tailed grouse (but hunting is not permitted)—probably 100 to 150 birds in all.

Although wild turkeys are slowly moving west, hunting opportunities at this time are poor. Only the southeastern corner of Otsego County is presently open to hunting.

Grouse and woodcock hunters do very well throughout the county in spite of increasing pressure. For grouse, look to poplar slashings and brush cover along streams and abandoned farms. These areas produce woodcock too and hunters can find them in tag-alder bottomlands and moist-soil areas rich in worms. These are likely to include abandoned orchards, pastures bordering stream bottoms, and wet areas around beaver dams. Woodcock hunting is especially productive during the fall migration period from about October 10 to 20. We checked three years of records submitted to the DNR by hunter-cooperators and learned that hourly flush rates for both grouse (1.79 to 1.88) and woodcock (1.70 to 2.60) were surprisingly stable.

OTHER SHOOTING OPPORTUNITIES

Sportsmen willing to become members may hunt pheasants, quail, chukars, and ducks at the 200-acre Pine Stump Hunting Club, 4601 Hayes Tower Road southwest of Gaylord. For information, contact James W. Avery at 517/732-9472.

We are not aware of any Otsego County shooting ranges open to the public.

FURTHER SOURCES OF HUNTING INFORMATION

1. DNR District Office, 1732 West M-32 (Box 667), Gaylord, Mich. 49735 (517/732-3541).
2. DNR Pigeon River Country Field Office, Route 1, Box 179, Vanderbilt, Mich. 49795 (517/983-4101).
3. Gaylord/Otsego County Chamber of Commerce, 125 West Otsego (Box 513), Gaylord, Mich. 49735 (517/732-4000).
4. Topographic, county, and lake maps may be ordered from the Michigan United Conservation Clubs. For information, refer to the beginning of this book.
5. Plat books are available from the Otsego County Soil Conservation District, 202 Livingston Blvd., Gaylord, Mich. 49735. The cost is $10 each (add $1 if mail ordering).
6. Otsego County ASCS Office, 111 Michigan Ave., Gaylord, Mich. 49735.

Also, refer to the Mackinaw State Forest elsewhere in this book.

Ottawa County

OTTAWA County is located in southwest Lower Michigan. About half of its 564 square miles is farmed, with cash-crop grains (corn, wheat, oats, soybeans), dairy, fruit, and vegetables the main crops grown. The western border along Lake Michigan is a mixture of young and old sand dunes to 200 feet high and sloping sand plains. Averaging one-half to one mile wide, these dunes are covered with maple, birch, red oak, and an understory of pine. They provide good deer and squirrel hunting with little pressure although access can be a problem.

The central-to-northwestern region features low-lying, sandy plains quite different from the rolling uplands of the northeastern area, which are dissected by two long, narrow valleys. Hilly and broken topography characterizes the southern region, and there is perhaps 200 feet of elevation difference throughout the county. Ottawa County has surprisingly few streams, especially in the western section. Main flow is the mighty Grand which meanders northwesterly until emptying into Lake Michigan at Grand Haven. Large north-to-south tributaries are Deer, Crockery, and Black creeks. Entering from the south is the Bass River and a few small flows.

About 20 percent of Ottawa County is prime farmland. Blendon, Olive, south Allendale, and north Holland townships used to be one of Michigan's prime pheasant hunting areas. Several mini-game areas here continue to be managed with sharecropping for pheasant production, but hunting pressure is intense and birds disperse to private land after the opener. They do provide some hunting opportunity in late season, however. This region is largely dairy farming fringed with nursery shrub production and blueberry farms on the western edge.

Blueberry farms that run northerly toward Grand Haven provide a buffer between dairy farming of the south-central county and sand dunes along Lake Michigan. A 50- to 100-feet-deep narrow valley, probably the old Grand River channel during glaciation, runs from Zeeland to Hudsonville, parallel to I-196, and is the site of muck farming for carrots, lettuce, and other vegetables. Cash-crop farming, the norm along the eastern edge, includes a fruit belt, especially heavy in the northeast corner.

At one time Ottawa County with its heavy forests of mast-producing trees contained one of the nation's largest passenger pigeon roosts. Now, 21 percent of its land mass is forested with commercial species: hard and soft maple, oak, and hickory the predominant species. Jack pine, red pine, and ash are also abundant.

Overall, hunting in this county is fair to good. The main problem is lack of public land, limited to about 1,800 acres in the Grand Haven State Game Area (which see) and the mini-game areas already mentioned. Holland and Hoffmaster state parks are closed to hunting although a few years ago the DNR allowed a limited squirrel hunting season by permit only in Hoffmaster when growing populations threatened to destroy maple trees. However, that is not likely to provide hunting opportunity again in the near future. Lands in the Public Access Stamp program, currently total over 5,000 acres on some 15 farms. Most are in the north-central and northeastern regions. The DNR has free maps and descriptions for the asking at the Grand Rapids district office.

A courteous request will help you gain access to private land, although landowners, particularly in the central and southern regions, are traditionally conservative. Some do not allow Sunday hunting.

Ottawa County deer populations have stabilized, even dipping somewhat, after a 10-year increase. Car-deer accidents run about 300 annually, average for southern Michigan. Buck hunters in recent years have enjoyed 14 percent success (one to two deer per square mile); those with hunter's-choice permits score about 25 percent success (buck and doe combined). There are some good-sized deer in this county, largely due to the shotgun-only law. Hunting pressure is light to moderate (10 deer hunters per square mile). Hunters might also check with farmers registering crop damage complaints in Robinson Township (nursery and blueberry growers) and in the "fuirt ridge" region of the northeast and Grand River bottoms.

Rabbit hunting is good throughout the county with abundant populations in low, coniferous cover and on nursery stock farms. Plenty of fox squirrel hunting opportunity exists throughout, with best chances coming along Grand River and tributary stream bottoms and in farm woodlots. As mentioned, some pheasant hunting exists in the south-central region, but pressure can be intense and access to private land difficult. Pheasant hunting is spotty elsewhere. Ottawa County contains only about 4,400 acres of aspen in mixed stands; therefore, it is a poor grouse and woodcock county with very very low hunting pressure. Best bets would be along stream bottoms, especially for flight woodcock in mid-October. There are no turkeys in Ottawa County at this time; however, a low-priority, long-range DNR plan does exist to introduce birds along the Grand River.

Fox are in abundance and there is apparently a good population of racoon. Diving-duck hunters along Lake Michigan and particularly on Lake Macatawa have solid opportunities. Some hunters enjoy jump-shooting success for mallards and wood ducks along county streams. Grand River bayous northwest of Allendale and south of Grand Haven (Stearns, Millhouse, Pottawattomie, Deremo, and Bruces) afford excellent opportunity for marsh and shore hunting with goose and puddle-duck decoy spreads. The Grand Haven State Game Area, through which the river flows, is managed by the DNR for waterfowl. The river itself affords great opportunity for float hunting waterfowl, squirrels, and deer with plenty of access possibilities from county roads. Riverside Park in Robinson Township and Deer Creek Park in Polkton Township are excellent put-in and take-out points.

OTHER SHOOTING OPPORTUNITIES

Michigan Sportsmen's Club, Inc., is a 450-acre shooting preserve specializing in pheasant-hunting dog training that is open to the public. For information, contact Keith S. Houghtaling, Box 277, Fremont, Mich. 49412 (616/924-6515).

The Grand Haven High School rifle range is open to the public on a sometime-fee schedule. Featuring seven indoor rimfire rifle stations, the range is located at 900 South Cutler St. in Grand Haven (phone 616/842-4600).

FURTHER SOURCES OF HUNTING INFORMATION

1. DNR District Office, State Office Bldg., 350 Ottawa NW, Grand Rapids, Mich. 49503 (616/456-5071).

2. Association of Commerce and Industry, Box 628, One Washington Ave., Grand Haven, Mich. 49417 (616/482-4910).

3. Zeeland Chamber of Commerce, 135 East Main Place, Zeeland, Mich. 49464 (616/772-2494).

4. Coopersville Area Chamber of Commerce, Box 161, 294 Danforth St., Coopersville, Mich. 49404 (616/837-9731).

5. Hudsonville Chamber of Commerce, 3467 Kelly St., Hudsonville, Mich. 49416 (616/669-1280).

6. Greater Grandville Chamber of Commerce, Box 175, Grandville, Mich. 49418 (616/531-3030).

7. County plat books are available from the Cooperative Extension Office, Room 101, Ottawa County Building, Grand Haven, Mich. 49417 (616/846-8250). The cost is $7, which includes postage.

8. Topographic, county, and lake maps may be ordered from the Michigan United Conservation Clubs. For information, refer to the beginning of this book.

9. P.J. Hoffmaster, Holland, and Grand Haven state parks (although closed to hunting) are staffed with DNR personnel who may prove helpful. Here are the addresses and telephone numbers:

A. P.J. Hoffmaster State Park, 6585 Lake Harbor Road, Muskegon, Mich. 49441, 616/798-3711.

B. Holland State Park, Ottawa Beach Road, Holland, Mich. 49423, 616/399-9390.

C. Grand Haven State Park, 1001 Harbor Ave., Grand Haven, Mich. 49417, 616/842-6020.

10. County ASCS Office, SDA, 17230 Robbins Road, Grand Haven, Mich. 49417 (616/842-5852).

Also, refer to the following elsewhere in this book:

1. Grand Haven State Game Area

Presque Isle County

PRESQUE Isle County in northeastern Lower Michigan does not receive a great deal of hunting pressure as compared to other downstate counties. Yet hunting opportunities here rate from fair to very good for deer, bear, bobcats, coyotes, snowshoe hares, raccoon, squirrels, grouse, woodcock, and waterfowl.

At 670 square miles, the county is among the largest in Michigan, and it features an unusually long stretch of Lake Huron shoreline between Alpena and Cheboygan. Over 81,000 acres, or about 19 percent of the land base, is state-owned—mostly large blocks and scattered parcels of the Mackinaw State Forest (*which see*). These lands are open to hunting. In addition, small portions of P. H. Hoeft and Onaway state parks (*both of which see*) may be hunted.

Elevations above sea level range from 578 feet at Lake Huron to more than 900 feet in the southwestern region. About 20 percent of the county's soil is fertile, well-drained loam, developed from glacial till and containing a high amount of limestone. Another 30 percent is moderately to poorly drained and includes pastures and croplands of medium fertility. The other half of Presque Isle County consists of deep, dry sands and peat and muck swamps. These soils thinly cover steep, stony till over bedrock. In the southeastern part of the county and south of Black Lake, limestone bedrock outcroppings are visible.

Extending inland five to 10 miles from the shore of Lake Huron are old lake plains, some of which are visible. Rising from 20 to 150 feet above these plains are highland hills. One three- to six-mile-wide ridge at Posen is bordered by a lowland valley plain. The towns of Millersburg and Onaway are also located on highland plains.

Black, Grand, and Long lakes were carved in bedrock by the last glacier several thousand years ago. They host potentially good flight-duck hunting in late season except for the most part they are built up with cottages. However, each has public access. Also, the southwestern portion of the county features many small lakes nestled in moraines and outwash plains. The network of rivers and creeks flows northerly and northeasterly into Lake Huron.

For the most part, Presque Isle County is a good producer of game. That is largely because about 70 percent of its land base is covered with a good mixture of commercial-forest species. Aspen with 94,000 acres leads the list. It is followed by northern white cedar (56,400 acres), maple-birch (26,000 acres), oak-hickory (22,200 acres), jack pine (18,300 acres), elm-ash-soft maple (14,700 acres), and paper birch (14,400 acres). Smaller amounts of red pine, balsam fir, black spruce, and tamarack also grow here.

State lands are mostly found in the western half although there is a large block on the northwestern side of Grand Lake and a particularly remote area containing elm, poplar, and swamp conifers in Metz Township through which the North Branch of the Thunder Bay River courses. Highest deer numbers occur in the south-central region of the county throughout a large farming belt that begins west of Long Lake and runs northwesterly nearly to Hammond Bay.

Hunting-club property occupies most of the land between Long and Grand lakes. The northwestern tip of Presque Isle County is mostly Abitibi Company lands leased to private clubs. Gaining access on club lands is almost impossible.

Deer hunters would do best to target adjacent state lands or perhaps ask farmers for permission since some crop-damage complaints occur throughout the farming belt. Aspen slashings near lowland swamps are also good for deer as well as snowshoe hares. If you want to try oak ridges for both deer and squirrels, look no farther than the southeastern tip of Black Lake just north of Onaway. This is a tough wintering area, however, for game animals, and so prospects may vary from year to year.

Buck-hunter success during a recent season ran 20 percent or one of five hunters tagging deer. There aren't really that many whitetails in Presque Isle County (one to two bucks tagged per square mile), but hunting pressure is quite low at about 15 hunters per square mile. High mineral content of some soils is perhaps one reason that Commemorative Bucks of Michigan has thus far turned up five Presque Isle County record racks.

Bear populations are high throughout the county, and bobcats are considered moderate in numbers. Hunters trying for either should concentrate on dense cover areas of regeneraating clear-cuts near swamps. An excellent coyote population exists throughout Presque Isle County, with few sportsmen besides deer hunters taking advantage. One good place to try is jack-pine stands on state land in the southwestern corner. This area also contains hares and deer.

Waterways throughout the county support fair raccoon populations. For best results, pinpoint those meandering through the farming belt. Small flocks of wild turkeys, presently numbering 200 to 300 birds, are slowly expanding from southern farmlands. The eastern portion of the county is presently open to hunting.

As mentioned earlier, duck-hunting opportunities are limited on the big southeastern lakes. Lake Huron shoreline hunters shoot some ducks but very few geese. The band of small lakes southeast of Millersburg might afford some jump-shooting potential as will larger streams like the North Branch Thunder Bay and the Ocqueoc rivers. Tomahawk Creek Flooding is also worth checking out both early and late in the season.

The high amount of aspen in Presque Isle County makes for good grouse and woodcock hunting. According to records submitted by hunter-cooperators, hourly flush rates for grouse ranged from 1.57 to 2.14 and for woodcock from 2.21 to 2.96. These statistics were for three years randomly checked. For squirrels, try stands of mature hardwoods sprinkled throughout the county—especially farm woodlots—in addition to the oak ridges near Black Lake.

OTHER SHOOTING OPPORTUNITIES

The Presque Isle County Sportsman's Club, 2876 Church Road in Rogers City, has a shooting range open to the public daily for fees. Facilities include two indoor/outdoor stations each for pistol and rimfire rifle, one outdoor station for centerfire rifle, a trap field, a handtrap area, and two indoor/outdoor archery targets. The club offers both shooting instruction and competitive shooting as well as hunter certification courses. For information, call 517/734-3041.

FURTHER SOURCES OF HUNTING INFORMATION

1. DNR District Office, 1732 West M-32 (Box 667), Gaylord, Mich. 49735 (517/732-3541).
2. DNR Onaway Field Office, M-211, Onaway, Mich. 49765 (517/733-8775).
3. Rogers City Chamber of Commerce, Box 55, Rogers City, Mich. 49779 (517/734-2535).
4. Topographic, county, and lake maps may be ordered from the Michigan United Conservation Clubs. For information, refer to the beginning of this book.
5. Plat books are available from the Presque Isle County Cooperative Extension Services, 123 South Third St., Rogers City, Mich. 49779. The cost is $11 each (add $1.50 if mail ordering).
6. Presque Isle/Cheboygan County ASCS Office, M-33 South, Onaway, Mich. 49765.
Also, refer to the following elsewhere in this book:
1. Mackinac State Forest
2. P. H. Hoeft State Park

Roscommon County

MOST of Roscommon County, located in the north-central part of the Lower Peninsula, is characterized by nearly level or gently sloping sandy plains cut with wetlands, swamps, and bogs. Included are low hills featuring rounded ridges with dry basins or swamp and lakes between them. What rolling terrain there is in Roscommon County is mostly located in the southeastern portion.

Thus, no striking relief features occur as the general elevation of the county is 1,000 to 1,200 feet above sea level. Level areas are outwash plains and till plains, and ridges are mainly moraines—all the result of glaciation some 8,000 to 12,000 years ago.

Michigan's largest inland lake, 30.8-square-mile Houghton Lake, lies in the west-central region. Higgins Lake and Lake St. Helen are other large bodies of water in the county. The three lakes command about nine percent of the total county surface of 513 square miles with various swamps—including a piece of the famed Dead Stream (*which see*) west of Houghton Lake—occupying another 10 percent. The swamps range in size from a few acres to large irregular areas covering several thousand acres and are widely distributed throughout the county. The region is also interlaced with small streams, and the headwaters for three major rivers—the Au Sable, Muskegon, and Tittabawassee—are found here.

A high amount of state land open to hunting (over 60 percent), diverse habitat, and good game populations all make Roscommon County popular with hunters. It leads the state in firearm deer-hunting pressure with 50 or more hunters per square mile yet produces many whitetails for both archers and gun hunters. Proof of that is the buck pole that annually sags at Tuck's Ace Hardware in Houghton Lake Heights on M-55.

Bear appear numerous as do grouse, squirrels, and snowshoe hares. Woodcock hunting is exceptional during early- to mid-October migrations. And Houghton Lake offers outstanding waterfowling, including some late-October opportunities going unnoticed.

Fair turkey-hunting prospects would probably improve if more farming occurred in the county since in northern Michigan these birds rely upon farmland handouts to survive the winter. The only farming going on at this time is immediately south of Houghton Lake, in the Maple Valley area, and near the junction of CR-600 and CR-602 in the northeastern corner.

About 72 percent of Roscommon County is forested with commercial forest species. Hunters familiar with cover types will quickly realize why this county produces large numbers of game since oak-hickory type leads with 85,000 acres and is followed by aspen with 67,500 acres. Other types include northern white cedar (24,900 acres), maple-birch (24,200 acres), jack pine (19,300 acres), elm-ash-soft maple (10,600 acres), and red pine (7,400 acres). Species tallying under 3,000 acres each include white pine, balsam fir, white spruce, and paper birch. Extensive cuttings insure varied age classes, especially with aspen, and the result is near-optimum game populations.

Large blocks of state land in all but the southeastern corner (which also has the highest number of deer) are mostly enrolled in the Au Sable State Forest (*which see*). In addition, hunters are welcome at the Houghton Lake Wildlife Research Area, the Backus Creek State Game Area, and a small portion (110 acres) of South Higgins Lake State Park (*all of which see*).

Whitetail numbers remain quite high throughout Roscommon County. Aspen tracts fronting oak ridges and conifer swamps west, north, and due east of St. Helen are productive. I have hunted similar cover south of M-55 and east of M-18 in Backus Township and one autumn tagged both a deer and a bear. The truth is that deer hunting in particular is quite good just about anywhere in Roscommon County. However, you're going to see plenty of hunters, especially during firearm season.

Although the buck kill generally exceeds five animals per square mile, hunter success at one for eight falls a little under the state average. Roscommon County is managed by the DNR to carry as many deer as possible. Heavy culling by hunters ensures that most bucks taken are yearling spikehorns or forkhorns, but occasionally a big deer is tagged. Commemorative Bucks of Michigan has uncovered 17 Roscommon County rack deer thus far. And David W. Fultz of St. Helen, who kindly offered some of the information for this chapter, has shot 22 bucks since 1969. His best head was a 10-point with an inside spread of 19½ inches, not bad for hard-hunted Roscommon County.

The intricate network of swamps and varied cover types tends to somewhat protect bear in Roscommon County. Only 12 to 15 bear are registered annually, and the population appears to be increasing. Best areas to hunt bear include the Backus Creek State Game Area, the Denton Creek Flooding, the Dead Stream Swamp, and the conifer swamps around Lake St. Helen.

In addition to ongoing studies at the wildlife research area, the DNR did extensive research in eight quarter-townships (nine square miles) throughout northern Michigan. Five of these are located in Roscommon County and because of former aggressive cutting programs still produce excellent habitat for deer, grouse, hares, and woodcock. The three-mile-by-three-mile-square areas and their locations include: (1) Nine-Mile (beginning four miles east of Maple Valley, then extending due east and south); (2) Lane's Lake (beginning one mile south of Maple Valley, then extending due south and west); (3) M-18 (beginning at the point where M-18 enters Roscommon County from Gladwin County, then extending due north and west); (4) Townline (beginning at the point where CR-270 enters Roscommon County from Gladwin County, then extending due north and east); and (5) Russell Lake (beginning at the point where Russell Creek enters Third Lake of Lake St. Helen, then extending due north and west).

Roscommon County is home to good numbers of fox squirrels in oak-covered ridges and grays/blacks closer to communities and in mixed stands of oaks and conifers. For the most part, squirrels are vastly underhunted. Raccoon frequent waterways, but numbers appear to have declined somewhat and hunting pressure is moderate to high. Although low at present, hares are found throughout the county in cutover areas containing sapling growth and in conifer plantations, especially those bordering cedar swamps. Cottontails are scarce. For red fox, concentrate on northeastern and southeastern parts of the county, particularly near the limited farming enterprises. Deer hunters collect a few fox as well as coyotes.

Most of Roscommon County (east of US-27) is currently open to turkey hunting. Best bets include the Backus Creek State Game Area, the region south of M-55, and the northeastern portion of the county.

Ten state-owned waterfowl floodings developed 20 to 25 years ago need rejuvenation in order to produce more ducks and geese. Besides Backus Creek State Game Area, two worth checking out on opening day are the Dead Stream and Reedsburg Dam floodings. Later, high winds that lash Houghton Lake often drive ducks into these protected areas.

The county goose flock probably numbers only 200 honkers but appears to be increasing rapidly. Impoundments and beaver ponds throughout, as well as the Au Sable River from Roscommon east, produce woodies and mallards and a few black ducks and teal. Lake St. Helen is closed (waterfowl-hunting rights are privately-owned), but Houghton Lake offers some outstanding gunning for early-season puddlers and particularly late-season divers.

The last 10 days in October generally see a good mix of passage ducks—goldeneyes, buffleheads, and mergansers, among others—and it is not uncommon for 2,000 to 5,000 ducks to stop over. Birds rarely hold here, though, and so action may last only a day or two. Few hunters take advantage of this opportunity. Best Houghton Lake places (depending upon wind direction and velocity) are North Bay, the northern shoreline of the main lake, and on the southern side between shore and the Middle Grounds. Some hunters use semi-permanent blinds while others rely on layout boats and big decoy spreads.

OTHER SHOOTING OPPORTUNITIES

None known at this time.

FURTHER SOURCES OF HUNTING INFORMATION

1. DNR Regional Office (for northern Michigan), 8717 North Roscommon Road (I-75 and M-18 South), Roscommon, Mich. 48653 (517/275-5151).

2. DNR District Office, 191 South Mount Tom Road, Mio, Mich. 48647 (51/826-3211).

3. DNR Houghton Lake Field Office, South US-27, Houghton Lake Heights, Mich. 48630 (517/422-5522).

4. Houghton Lake Chamber of Commerce, 1625 West Houghton Lake Drive, Houghton Lake, Mich. 48629 (517/366-5644 or 366-9472).

5. St. Helen Chamber of Commerce, Box 642 (Carter's IGA), St. Helen, Mich. 48656 (517/389-3725).

6. Topographic, county, and lake maps may be ordered from the Michigan United Conservation Clubs. For information, refer to the beginning of this book.

7. Plat books are available from the Roscommon County Clerk, Box 98, 507 Lake St., Roscommon, Mich. 48653, for $8.50 each (no extra charge for mail orders).

8. Roscommon/Crawford County ASCS Office, 409 Lake St., Roscommon, Mich. 48653.

Also, refer to the following elsewhere in this book:
1. Au Sable State Forest
2. Backus Creek State Game Area
3. Houghton Lake Wildlife Research Area
4. South Higgins Lake State Park

Saginaw County

ABOUT one-sixth of all Lower Peninsula drainage waters cross Saginaw County in the form of several large streams. Thus, the Bad, Tittabawassee, Shiawassee, Cass, and Flint rivers, along with their tributaries that together drain some 6,000 total square miles, flow into the county center to join in one large confluence called the Saginaw River.

The intricate waterway system is the dominant feature of 810-square-mile Saginaw County. Geographically, this low, central river valley plain is practically flat and featureless. About 75 square miles of the plain periodically flood throughout the year, and waters are then slow to recede due to the Saginaw River falling only one inch to the mile as it marches toward Saginaw Bay and Lake Huron. The river bottom, however, is heavily forested with lowland hardwoods, basswood, aspen, willow, and plenty of brush. As such, it harbors good populations of waterfowl, deer, and raccoon as well as grouse, woodcock, squirrels, and rabbits in upland stretches containing elm, ash, maple, hickory, oak, and birch trees.

This part of Saginaw County is exceptionally "gamey," and portions are nearly impenetrable for hunters. I have hunted raccoon along the river bottomlands and had we not been equipped with mules, it would have been tough going to keep up with our dogs.

About 8,900 acres of federal land is contained in the Shiawassee National Wildlife Refuge (which see), a portion of which is open to goose and deer hunting by permit. Another several thousand acres constitute the Shiawassee River State Game Area (which also see), open to permit waterfowl hunting. Together, the region in fall holds up to several thousand Canada geese, which disperse throughout the county. In fact, all of Saginaw County falls into

327

its own goose management area with an annual kill quota, and because of a surplus of birds, this quota was recently raised from 3,000 to 5,000 geese. The figure is set annually, however, and therefore is subject to change.

Much of Saginaw County outside the city itself is intensively cash-cropped for navy beans, soybeans, and corn. Where cultivation is fencerow to fencerow, there is precious little wildlife habitat and consequently poor hunting potential. On the other hand, farm fields interspersed with brushy fencerows, marsh areas, and woodlots hold small-game species and deer. About 15 percent of the county is timbered with commercial-forest species evenly split among oak-hickory, ash-elm-soft maple, and hard maple-birch types. Aspen is also evident and appears to be increasing.

Squirrels are an underhunted gamester throughout the county with heaviest pressure coming in the Gratiot-Saginaw State Game Area (which see). Mature oaks and hickories adjacent to cornfields are excellent spots to try in farm country for fox squirrels. Some gray squirrels are found along heavily-wooded river bottomlands. These wet areas of marsh and lowland timber also produce raccoon. Rabbit populations are fair to good in mixed vegetation stands, especially those with weedy and grassy openings. Red fox are moderately plentiful throughout the county.

Although pockets of pheasant hunting do exist, birds have fallen on tough times in Saginaw County. Best bets would be to target set-aside acres with weeds or cover crops and abandoned farmlands gone to seed. Public Access Stamp program land is currently quite limited—less than 800 acres on eight farms—to the southern portion of the county. For a free directory, stop in at either of the two state game areas.

Hunters kill as many if not more ruffed grouse in Saginaw County than they do pheasants. A hunter who picks his habitat carefully (aspen mixed with viburnums and other shrubs) can move 1.0 to 3.0 grouse per hour, depending upon what stage the cycle is in. Woodock flush rates are considerably lower, yet in mid- to late October moist lowland areas containing earthworms can load up with migrant long-bills.

Deer hunting on the federal refuge is excellent from both quality and quantity standpoints for those lucky in the lottery. Elsewhere it rates only fair with pressure light and buck hunter success well below the state average of about 15 percent. A growing deer herd appears to have leveled off, according to car-deer accident statistics. They peaked at 350 animals per year recently and have now dropped below 300. Commemorative Bucks of Michigan currently lists six Saginaw County deer on its all-time big-buck record list. However, that many trophy racks are taken each fall on the federal land alone. The truth is that Saginaw County does grow some monster bucks. Hunters should be advised, however, that shotguns only may be used south of M-57 and east of M-52/M-46/M-47.

Other than deer, the big drawing card is superb hunting for Canada geese on the federal refuge and both geese and ducks on the Shiawassee River State Game Area. In addition, portions of Crow Island State Game Area (which see) may be hunted during the waterfowl season (except that usually first-day hunting is by permit only). After that, it reverts to a game refuge. Saginaw County contains no natural lakes, but the rivers and their tributaries provide good jump-shooting and in some cases float-hunting for waterfowl.

OTHER SHOOTING OPPORTUNITIES

Saginaw County has at least five places open to the public for practice shooting.

1. Chesaning Area Conservation Club, 13750 Baldwin Road in Chesaning, sometimes charges fees for use of its pistol (six indoor stations), centerfire rifle (four outdoor stations), and rimfire rifle (10 indoor/outdoor stations) ranges. In addition, the club has a trap field and offers shooting instruction and state hunter education programs. There is no phone.

2. The Saginaw Gun Club at 9540 Gratiot Road in Saginaw charges fees and is open on a sometime basis. Call 517/781-2260 for times and costs. Facilities include 33 indoor/outdoor pistol stations, 17 outdoor centerfire rifle stations, 23 indoor/outdoor rimfire rifle stations, and four fields each for trap and skeet. The club offers both shooting and instruction and competition.

3. Saginaw Field and Stream Club, 1500 North Gleaner Road in Hemlock, sometimes charges fees for use of its outdoor pistol range (18 stations), centerfire and rimfire rifle range (20 outdoor stations each), skeet field, four trap fields, one handtrap area, and outdoor archery targets. In addition to shooting instruction and competition, the club sponsors hunter certification classes. For details, call 517/777-1787.

4. Freeland Sportsman's Club at 9693 Laduke Road in Freeland has two fields each for skeet and trap and two outdoor archery targets, all open to use for fees. The club sponsors hunter certification classes and offers both shooting instruction and competition. Call 517/695-2641 for information.

5. Bridgeport Gun Club, Inc., in Bridgeport has a wide range of facilities and programs open to the public for fees. Included are 12 indoor/outdoor pistol stations, four outdoor centerfire rifle stations, 12 indoor rimfire rifle stations, a trap field, and six outdoor archery targets. The club offers both shooting instruction and competition and sponsors hunter certification programs. For information, call 517/642-2106.

FURTHER SOURCES OF HUNTING INFORMATION

1. DNR District Office, 715 South Cedar, Imlay City, Mich. 48444 (313/724-2015).

2. Gratiot-Saginaw Field Office, 13350 South Meridian Road, Brant, Mich. 48614 (517/643-7000).

3. St. Charles Field Office (Shiawassee River State Game Area), 225 East Spruce St., St. Charles, Mich. 48655 (517/865-6211).

4. Shiawassee National Wildlife Refuge, 6975 Mower Road, Saginaw, Mich. 48601 (517/777-5930).

5. Saginaw County Chamber of Commerce, 901 South Washington Ave., Saginaw, Mich. 48601 (517/752-7161).

6. St. Charles Chamber of Commerce, Box 147, St. Charles, Mich. 48655 (517/865-6021).

7. Frankenmuth Chamber of Commerce, 635 South Main St., Frankenmuth, Mich. 48734 (517/652-6106).

8. Chesaning Chamber of Commerce, 220 East Broad St., Chesaning, Mich. 48616 (517/845-3055).

9. Topographic, county, and lake maps may be ordered from the Michigan United Conservation

Clubs. For information, refer to the beginning of this book.

10. Plat books are available from the Saginaw County Cooperative Extension Office, Courthouse Bldg., Court & Michigan, Saginaw, Mich. 48602. The cost is $13 each (add $1.50 if mail ordering).

11. Saginaw County ASCS Office, USDA, 265 South Graham Road, Saginaw, Mich. 48603, (517/781-1720).

Also, refer to the following elsewhere in this book:
1. Crow Island State Game Area
2. Gratiot-Saginaw State Game Area
3. Shiawassee National Wildlife Refuge
4. Shiawassee River State Game Area

St. Clair County

THE easternmost county in the state, St. Clair offers good to excellent hunting opportunities for a variety of game species. Deer are reasonably plentiful in the more heavily-wooded northern portion, good pockets of pheasant hunting exist in the central and west-central region, and the delta area known as the St. Clair Flats produces outstanding duck hunting. Sandwiched among these three general zones is fair to good hunting for fox squirrels, raccoon, and fox and poor to fair opportunities for grouse and woodcock.

Soils across the 740-square-mile county range from level to sharply sloping with greatest changes occurring along the Black River floodplain in the county's northern sector. Roughly 60 percent of the county land base is farmed, mostly for cash-crop grains and dairy and beef cattle operations. Lands to the west are more intensively farmed than elsewhere. In fact, the farther south one goes, the smaller the farms become. Many abandoned farms south of M-21 (I-69) have reverted to brush and weeds, which is one reason that pheasants are holding their own. These conditions are also responsible for a slow but steady increase of grouse and woodcock.

About 20 percent of St. Clair County is timbered with commercial-forest species, principally hard maple-birch, followed by aspen, oak-hickory, and elm-soft maple-ash in descending order of frequency. Northern portion stands include 5,000 acres in the Port Huron State Game Area (which see) and the Greenwood Property owned by Detroit Edison. Others are scattered throughout farm woodlots. Mast-producing hardwoods (particularly in lowland stands) produce fair numbers of fox squirrels with a sprinkling of grays and black-phase bushytails.

About 10,200 acres of St. Clair County are state-owned and mostly open to hunting. Included is a wide range from the 90-acre St. Clair Mini-Game Area (just west of St. Clair) to the 6,200-acre Port Huron State Game Area. Other public lands open to hunting include about 90 percent (890 acres) of Algonac State Park and the St. Clair Flats Wildlife Area (all of which see).

An additional 4,000 acres of farmland is currently enrolled in the Public Access Stamp program by 16 landowners. Most of these huntable lands flank the Port Huron State Game Area. The DNR has free directories available at district offices in Imlay City and Pontiac.

During the most recent pheasant brood count survey. St. Clair County led the state in numbers sighted (6.0 broods per route). Best pheasant hunting is in Mussey and Emmet townships although isolated pockets of ringnecks are scattered throughout the central and west-central portions. If pheasants ever make a comeback in Michigan, one of the quickest turnarounds is likely to occur in this region. The northern county area also continues to produce Michigan's highest spring counts of singing bobwhites although quail hunting season is currently closed.

Access to hunting on private lands is fairly good throughout the county when responsible hunters make courteous requests of farmers.

Cottontails are plentiful in brushlands and grasslands along edge openings. For grouse, concentrate on aspen stands with an understory of brush. Woodcock prefer moist soils of river bottomlands and orchards gone to seed. There is likely some overlooked hunting opportunity for migrant woodcock from mid-October through early November. Hunting pressure for both grouse and woodcock is light to moderate. Although no wild turkeys are currently found in the county, the Port Huron State Game Area is a potential site for future releases.

There are fairly good concentrations of deer, especially in the northern region. In recent years annual car-deer accidents have risen yearly from 100 to over 200, a figure that appears to have leveled off. Michigan's fifth largest typically-antlered whitetail shot during a recent firearm season was a St. Clair County buck. Although the region is not known for trophy-racked deer, each season one or more monster bucks are tagged. Buck-hunter success runs about 10 to 12 percent with light pressure (about seven hunters per square mile).

St. Clair County affords some fox-hunting opportunities on farmlands with an occasional coyote sighting reported. Raccoon hunting is generally fair along waterways including the Belle, Pine, and Black rivers. The latter is floatable from Croswell Dam to Port Huron (portages necessary at Sanilac County line, at Ford's Dam, and at the old Wadhams mill dam). Float hunters often see beaver and get jump-shooting chances for waterfowl as well as an occasional squirrel in lowland hardwoods abutting crop fields.

Anchor Bay on Lake St. Clair is the site of good duck hunting for early-season puddlers and late-season divers. Tactics include marsh hunting with small decoy spreads for the former and layout shooting and sneak-boating with 100-block stools for divers. A few layout hunters also work the lower St. Clair River. The Harsen's Island refuge is managed to hold 40,000 to 60,000 migrant waterfowl, mostly

pintails and mallards. Permit shooting within the unit or freelance hunting on state lands (St. Johns Marsh, Dickinson Island, Harsen's Island, and open-water areas) outside can result in a quality waterfowling experience.

Actually five wildlife refuges dot the Flats area and hunters will want to watch for signs on posts or buoys. They include Harsens Island, one in St. Johns Marsh, two in Anchor Bay, and one near the mouth of the Clinton River (also in Anchor Bay). Public access sites are located on the river at Marysville, St. Clair, Marine City, and Algonac State Park and in the North Channel at the end of Anchor Bay Drive. A fee ferry takes hunters across to Harsen's Island every few minutes. Public-access sites on Lake St. Clair are located at Fair Haven, New Baltimore, Selfridge Air Force Base, and the Clinton River mouth.

All things considered, St. Clair County should not be overlooked by the serious hunter.

OTHER SHOOTING OPPORTUNITIES

Algonac State Park, 8732 North River Road in Algonac, features three outdoor archery targets and a shotgun handtrap area open to the public on a sometime-fee basis. For information, call 313/765-5605.

The Blue Water Sportsman's Association, 4866 Ravenswood Road in Port Huron, has shooting facilities open daily to the public for fees. Included are indoor/outdoor stations for pistol and centerfire and rimfire rifle (10 each), two skeet fields, and eight trap fields. The association sponsors hunter certification classes and shooting competition and instruction. Call 313/364-9894 for details.

St. Clair Hunting and Fishing Club, 5484 Remer Road in St. Clair, has outdoor stations for pistol, centerfire rifle and rimfire rifle, an archery target and three trap fields all open to the public for fees. The club also offers hunter-certification programs. For information, call 313/329-4075.

Pine River Sportsman's Club, 714 Vine St. in St. Clair, has archery targets and hunter rounds (30 each) open to the public for fees on a limited basis. There is no phone.

FURTHER SOURCES OF HUNTING INFORMATION

1. For St. Clair County below M-21 (I-69): DNR District Office, 2455 North Williams Lake Road, Pontiac, Mich. 48054 (313/666-1500).

For St. Clair County above M-21 (I-69): DNR District Office, 715 South Cedar St., Imlay City, Mich. 48444 (313/724-2015).

3. Lake St. Clair Fisheries Station (also staffed by a DNR wildlife biologist), 33135 South River Road, Mount Clemens, Mich. 48054 (313/465-4771).

4. St. Clair Flats Wildlife Area, Harsen's Island, Mich. 48028 (313/748-9504).

5. Special Note: The DNR field office at the Port Huron State Game Area is currently closed.

6. Algonac State Park, 8730 North River Road, Algonac, Mich. 48001 (313/765-5605).

7. Lakeport State Park (although closed to hunting is staffed with DNR personnel), 7605 Lakeshore Road, Port Huron, Mich. 48060 (313/327-6765).

8. Greater Port Huron-Marysville Chamber of Commerce, 920 Pine Grove Ave., Port Huron, Mich. 48060 (313/985-7101).

9. Marine City Chamber of Commerce, Box 521, Marine City, Mich. 48039 (313/765-4501).

10. Capac Area Chamber of Commerce, 206 North Main St., Capac, Mich. 48014 (313/395-4313).

11. Topographic, county, and lake maps may be ordered from the Michigan United Conservation Clubs. For information, refer to the beginning of this book.

12. Plat books are available from (1) St. Clair County Cooperative Extension Services, 627 West St., Port Huron, Mich. 48060 and (2) St. Clair County Soil Conservation Service, 5120 Lapeer Road, Port Huron, Mich. 48060. The cost is $12 each. Direct all mail orders to the Soil Conservation Service and add $1 for postage.

Also, refer to the following elsewhere in this book:
1. Algonac State Park
2. Port Huron State Game Area
3. St. Clair Flats Wildlife Area
4. St. Clair Mini-Game Area

St. Joseph County

DOMINANT landforms in 518-square-mile St. Joseph County are the result of glaciers which covered the area several thousand years ago. In the northwest region rolling moraines cover most of the northern portion of Fabius Township and the central part of Flowerfield Township. Gently-rolling plains dominate the eastern half of the county, especially the southeastern section. Broad, nearly level outwash plains are the major feature elsewhere. Numerous small ponds and bogs throughout St. Joseph County are the result of irregular glacial melt.

This region originally featured abundant woodlands and scattered prairies. About 18 percent of the county is still in commercial stands of upland hardwoods, mostly in northern-tier townships. However, plenty of brushlands, scattered farm woodlots, and stream bottomlands provide additional wildlife habitat and hunting opportunity. There are still small areas of prairie soils, which are thought to have been part of the Great Plains of the Midwest. These prairie lands are found in three regions: (1) parts of Mendon and Nottawa townships in the northeast, (2) immediately surrounding the city of Sturgis in the southeast, (3) and in the southwest between Constantine and White Pigeon.

All streams are tributaries of the wide-running St. Joseph River, which wanders southwesterly across the county. Secondary flows of importance include the north-draining Rocky and Portage rivers, the Prairie River in the central portion, and Fawn and White Pigeon rivers, which drain the southern area. Portions of these streams can be floated for ducks, deer, and squirrels, and they all offer jump-shooting opportunity for those able to gain access to private land en route.

St. Joseph County harbors fair to good populations of game animals and birds, and although farmers have been traditionally reluctant to allow access, considerate sportsmen making courteous requests are sometimes granted hunting privileges. County-wide population is small (about 57,000) and the farms are generally small, averaging perhaps 100 acres in size. Most grow small grains for cash crop or hog and poultry feed. There are also some beef and dairy cattle operations.

The state owns a little more than 10,000 acres, mostly in west-central Constantine Township where Three Rivers State Game Area (*which see*) is located. Public Access Stamp program lands are currently limited to less than 900 acres on three farms in Mendon Township (northeast) and two in Burr Oak Township (southwest).

Best deer hunting comes in the northern townships of Leonidas, Mendon, Park, and Flowerfield, the latter reporting deer starvation during bad winters. St. Joseph County rates second to Branch among the southernmost tier of seven Michigan counties. Car-deer highway kills run around 300 animals annually. There are some big bucks raised here, two of which recently made the Commemorative Bucks of Michigan all-time record book.

Most pressure centers at Three Rivers State Game Area, but overall is considered light at under 10 hunters per square mile. They shoot one to two bucks per square mile for a countywide average of about 14 percent.

Most productive farmland centers around White Pigeon, Sturgis, and the Leidy Lake State Game Area. Not surprisingly, these areas are the rich prairie grasslands. Leidy Lake, home to a south-end goose refuge holding up to 1,000 Canadas at peak times in fall, is closed to hunting. There is excellent potential, however, for fringe shooting on private lands whose owners offer rental blinds. Hunters can also check for access to area crop fields. If southwestern Michigan gets an extended goose hunting season in the future, this region is likely to be included.

Waterfowling elsewhere is limited to St. Joseph River float trips and occasional jump shooting on private lands along wooded river bottoms and potholes. Southern stretches of the White Pigeon River sometimes serve up mallards and the odd goose. The state has public-access sites on about a dozen county lakes, but only Klinger Lake east of White Pigeon is noted for good opportunity (late-season divers mostly). Hunters putting in at Sturgeon Lake north of Colon can drift the mighty St. Joe all the way to the Indiana border but will have to portage around dams at Three Rivers, Constantine, and Mottville. Road access is good along this drift, but hunters should be advised that privately-owned farmland flanks both sides. A good idea is to drift this river in short sections to scout likely hunting areas, then seek permission from landowners.

St. Joseph County is popular with resident and Indiana raccoon hunters. Populations of raccoon and red fox (including some grays plus an occasional coyote) are good to excellent. Fox squirrels (including a few grays and mutant blacks) are usually abundant along river bottomlands and in farm woodlots that abut to croplands.

Pheasant hunters have to work hard to find birds. Likely areas are grasslands/brushlands around the three pockets of intensive farming and around Centreville. The Three Rivers State Game Area recently received 24 wild turkeys from Missouri. A growing flock could provide future hunting opportunity. Grouse and woodcock hunting pressure is very low with limited availability. Most birds that end up in the game pouch are shot incidentally to other game species sought.

OTHER SHOOTING OPPORTUNITIES

Willow Lake Sportsmen's Club on US-131 between Three Rivers and Kalamazoo is a shooting preserve open to the public daily for fees. Principal game species on the 325-acre preserve include mallards, pheasants, quail, and chukar partridge. For more information, contact Woody Thompson, 51704 US-131, Three Rivers, Mich. 49093 (616/279-7124).

FURTHER SOURCES OF HUNTING INFORMATION

1. DNR District Office, 621 North 10th St. (Box 355), Plainwell, Mich. 49080 (616/685-6851).

2. Three Rivers Chamber of Commerce, 140 West Michigan, Three Rivers, Mich. 49093 (616/278-8193).

3. Sturgis Chamber of Commerce, Box 165, Sturgis, Mich. 49091 (616/651-5758).

4. Topographic, county, and lake maps may be ordered from the Michigan United Conservation Clubs. For information, refer to the beginning of this book.

5. County plat books are availble for $7.50 each (add $2 if mail ordering) from St. Joseph County Register of Deeds, Box 386 (County Courthouse Bldg.), Centreville, Mich. 49032.

6. St. Joseph County ASCS Office, USDA, 610 West Burr Oak St., Centreville, Mich. 49032 (616/467-6336).

Sanilac County

AT 960 square miles, Sanilac, in the Thumb region, is one of Michigan's largest counties. It is not bisected with expressways and is only lightly populated. Sandusky, the county seat, vies with Croswell and Marlette for the distinction of being the largest community. Each has less than 2,000 citizens. The county is mostly farmland with cash-crop grain growing (oats, wheat, corn, soybeans) the major enterprise. It is practiced intensively in the central portion. There are some dairy and beef-cattle farms as well. About 11 percent of the county is forested

331

with commercial-timber species—mostly aspen, maple, and birch. Brushlands appear to be increasing.

These conditions—low human numbers, stands of woods, and pockets of brush mixed throughout farmlands—make for fairly good game populations. Deer, grouse, and woodcock are increasing; rabbits, fox, and raccoon are reasonably plentiful; and pheasants are holding their own to provide fair to good hunting.

Hunting opportunities rate average when compared to the rest of southern Michigan. A total of 8,250 acres of state land is open to hunting at Minden City, Sanilac, and Cass City state game areas and Sanilac County (Buskirk) Mini-Game Area (all of which see). Fifteen farmers currently have about 3,700 acres enrolled in the Public Access Stamp program. These are located mostly in the southern and northern areas. For a free directory, stop in at DNR district headquarters in Imlay City. Also, Sanilac County farmers have been traditionally receptive to responsible hunters who ask permission to enter their lands.

A big drawback to opportunities, however, is that Sunday hunting is limited to state lands and offshore waterfowling in Lake Huron. Consequently, the game areas take a Sabbath-day pounding. You will likely experience difficulty finding a place to park, but dense cover—particularly at Minden City—will swallow you once the road is left behind.

Sanilac County surface features, for the most part, result from the Wisconsin glacial period of 8,000 to 12,000 years ago. Gently rolling moraines in the south-central and southwestern parts of the county were caused by temporary halts of retreating glaciers. The rolling Port Huron moraine in the eastern portion marks the limits of a readvance of the ice mass. It rises 30 to 40 feet above the old lake plain to the west, and its maximum elevation is about 180 feet above the present Lake Huron level.

At one time all of Sanilac County, except for a small area of marshland to the north, was forest-covered. Dense stands of elm, ash, white oak, silver maple, and red maple grew on poorly drained sites; white pine and mixed hardwoods on well-drained uplands. Forest fires a century ago destroyed most of these forests, which at one time were home to elk. As mentioned, woodlands and brushlands are again on the increase, largely in the form of aspen with understories of red-osier dogwood, gray dogwood, and witch hazel.

That is one reason why Sanilac is gaining a reputation as a grouse and woodcock producer. In an average season hunters will move 1.0 to 2.0 grouse and 1.0 woodcock per hour. It pays to look for aspen and brush stands on farmlands and then ask permission to hunt because covers as small as three or four acres can hold a grouse or woodcock family. Sometimes these "pocket covers" will be surrounded by cultivated fields. Woodcock hunting improves later in the season when flight birds are down. Wet portions of the northern county produce best.

The most recent mail-carrier pheasant counts show 4.6 broods spotted per driver. While far from former peak years, this shows that pheasants are certainly worth seeking in Sanilac County. Best areas include the southern portion and the upper tier of townships fronting Huron County.

There are no wild turkeys; however, Minden City State Game Area is being considered for future releases. It is home now to a small population of snowshoe hares, released a few years ago as a cooperative effort of the DNR and a local sportsman's group. Hunters here are more likely to see cottontail rabbits, though. Small woodlots are good for rabbits too, with better populations in the southern region.

Car-deer accidents, increasing annually for the past five years, are approaching 400 animals. In fact, only recently has Sanilac County been included for hunter's-choice permits.

Overall, buck-hunting success is about 15 percent (one in six), or the state average. Pressure is lowest on private land and most intensive on state holdings. Together it averages six hunters per square mile. There are some dandy bucks roaming Sanilac County. The state's best typically-antlered archery kill during a recent season was a Sanilac County whitetail. Commemorative Bucks of Michigan lists 10 all-time big-deer for the county, three of which were shot in a recent season. A quick tally of bucks checked by the DNR showed that of 67 hunters awarded Successful Deer Hunter patches for Sanilac County kills, 24 had shot racks of eight points or better. Most of the other bucks carried headgear of four or six points.

Best hunting is in the northern portion, the extreme southern edge fronting St. Clair County, and the forested dune ridge paralleling the Lake Huron shore and extending one to two miles inland.

Fairly good raccoon hunting is found along creeks and farm field drainage ditches throughout the county. Competition from trappers and out-of-state hunters, however, can be keen. Fox numbers are good and, except for trappers, few sportsmen take advantage. Squirrel hunters do best along the dune ridge in oak stands. Scattered opportunities exist wherever hardwoods can be found.

Duck hunting is pretty much limited to the Lake Huron shoreline for early-season puddlers and geese and late-season divers. Public boat launch sites are located at Lexington, Port Sanilac, and the former Sanilac State Park south of Forestville. Jump-shooting along drainage ditches and the upper reaches of the Black River (floatable from Croswell south) is a possibility. Mallards and woodies are the target species.

OTHER SHOOTING OPPORTUNITIES

Marlette Sportsmen's Association on White Creek Road in Marlette has shooting facilities open to the public on a sometime-fee basis. Featured are outdoor stations for pistol (30) and centerfire and rimfire rifle (40 each) as well as a trap field and six archery targets. The club offers both shooting instruction and competition and sponsors state hunter certification classes. For details, call 517/635-7834.

FURTHER SOURCES OF HUNTING INFORMATION

1. DNR District Office, 715 South Cedar St., Imlay City, Mich. 48444 (313/724-2015).
2. Marlette Area Chamber of Commerce, Box 222, Marlette, Mich. 48453 (517/635-7455).
3. Sandusky Chamber of Commerce, Box 92, Sandusky, Mich. 48471 (no phone).
4. Croswell Chamber of Commerce, Box 251, Croswell, Mich. 48422 (313/679-3800).
5. Topographic, county, and lake maps may be ordered from the Michigan United Conservation

Schoolcraft County

LOCATED in the east-central Upper Peninsula, Schoolcraft County contains some 770,000 acres (about 1,200 square miles). More than half of this land lies in western-county holdings of the Hiawatha National Forest, central-county Seney National Wildlife Refuge, and scattered units—including huge unbroken blocks—of the Lake Superior State Forest (all of which see). State ownership constitutes about 38 percent of the land base, whereas federal properties amount to over 16 percent.

Adding 72,800 acres of company-owned land enrolled in the Commercial Forest Act plan (and therefore open to hunting) means that Schoolcraft County hunters have nearly a half-million acres, or some 63 percent of the land base, upon which to roam.

To locate the company lands, which are managed for timber resources, contact DNR district headquarters in Newberry or write/call DNR Forest Management Division, Box 30028, Lansing, Mich. 48909 (517/373-1275). Be sure to limit requests to a specific area. Once you obtain legal descriptions, it is a simple matter to find the unposted lands with the help of a current county plat book and county map.

Hunters looking for a remote, wilderness experience can find it in Schoolcraft County. Huge stretches of swamp, blocks of open plains with scant cover, and dense stands of pine and hardwoods run for roadless miles. Game species include deer, bear, bobcats, coyotes, snowshoe hares, raccoon, gray and black squirrels, ruffed grouse, sharp-tailed grouse, woodcock, ducks, and geese.

To a geologist, the county lies in the eastern lake section of a great plains area whose present topography was constructed during the last glacial period some 10,000 years ago. Bordering the Lake Michigan shore is a series of low sandy or gravelly ridges alternating with swales and swamps. These conifer swamps run from the water's edge to a width of three or more miles and are popular with yarding deer in winter.

From Manistique to Germfask is an area of rolling upland interspersed with swamps and lakes. Rounded hills slope gently to streams, including the Manistique River and its intricate swamp, that drain these uplands. North and west of Germfask is the sprawling, 95,000-acre Seney National Wildlife Refuge, an area at one time overlain with sand in an extinct glacial lake. Sand from this lake bed was blown into dunes which, in time, became covered with trees and brush to form a necklace of islands in the midst of a vast bog. Today Seney is character-ized by these string bogs, one of which—the 9,500-acre Strangmoor Bog—is a Registered National Landmark. For more details, including hunting opportunities in this unique area, see Seney National Wildlife Refuge elsewhere in this book.

This former lake plain now occupied by open marsh dotted with sand knolls and ridges also extends northerly and northwesterly from Indian Lake. The western part of Schoolcraft County is an area of comparatively striking and bold relief. Sharp knobs and ridges rise from 50 to 75 feet above the surrounding country, and depressions occupied by lakes and swamps are numerous.

About 75 percent of Schoolcraft County is covered with commercial-forest species. Maple-birch type leads with 140,900 acres. It is followed by 82,200 acres of aspen, 77,700 acres of northern white cedar, 50,400 acres of black spruce, 49,200 acres of jack pine, 30,400 acres of balsam fir, 27,300 acres of red pine, 25,600 acres of paper birch, 18,700 acres of elm-ash-soft maple, 18,200 acres of white pine, and 6,200 acres of tamarack. There is virtually no oak-hickory type.

One of the county's biggest attractions to hunters is several open plains areas containing prairie species of plants and sharp-tailed grouse. You can see some of these plains while traveling M-28 west of Seney; others require long walks for hunters. The DNR manages several such areas for sharptails in Schoolcraft County. They include the Thompson Plains, the Mint Farm and the High Rollways, and a portion of the West Danaher Plains with Alger and Luce counties. Others are called the Creighton Truck Trail, the Driggs River, the Diversion Ditch (in the Seney National Wildlife Refuge), and the Bullock Ranch. Most were former farming operations where owners drained the swamps and tried to make the land economically productive. They can be found on county maps.

Sharptail hunting is limited to five eastern U.P. counties (including Schoolcraft), where DNR estimates place the remaining population at about 10,000. Sharpies require huge blocks of open land with short cover of grass. Schoolcraft County has some of the best habitat left for these unusual game birds.

Unlike much of the rest of the eastern U.P., Schoolcraft County has markets for its timber—Manistique Pulp and Paper in Manistique and Mead Corporation in Escanaba—which means that timber cutting, necessary for improved wildlife habitat, will likely accelerate. Big blocks of old aspen in particular need cutting now so that deer, grouse, snowshoe hares, and woodcock (and hunters) will benefit.

Ruffed grouse and woodcock hunting already is pretty good in this county. Hunter-cooperator hourly flush-rate records for three years show averages of 1.00, 1.83, and 1.10 for grouse and 5.00, 1.00, and 2.09 for woodcock. Here are some general areas where habitat is good and where grouse, although currently down somewhat, can best be found:

Good northern-county areas include along CR-P450 and the Fox River northwest of Seney, along Driggs River Road north of M-28, nearby in the Walsh Ditch region south of M-28, along Petrel Road (CR-643) north of Star Siding to the Adams Trail, and along the Creighton Truck Trail south of Creighton.

In the southern region try north and west of the Triangle Lake area (near the junction with Alger and Delta counties); along the Smith Creek Truck Trail and nearby Big Ditch; northwest of Palms Book State Park to Murphy Creek; in the triangle formed by Indian Lake State Park, Cooks, and Thompson; in the Camp Nine Lakes area northeast of Indian Lake; southwest of Gulliver Lake along Lake Michigan; and south and east of US-2 from McDonald Lake to Mackinac County.

Deer-hunting pressure and buck kill (antlerless hunting has not been allowed since 1972) in the five-county DNR district is quite low. Harsh winters along the Lake Superior watershed and the overall climax forest are not conducive to a growing, healthy deer herd. During a severe winter it is not uncommon for 20 percent of the adults and 60 percent of the fawns to die. On the average each fall about 55,000 to 60,000 animals are available; however, that is not a large figure for the state's biggest DNR management district. Schoolcraft County deer are widely distributed and so hunters may go days without seeing one. When they do, chances are it will be a buck—quite possibly a big buck—since from 35 to 50 of the 3,000 whitetails tagged each fall typically carry eight points or more.

Thanks to timber cutting and other whitetail management, the southern-county region continues to improve and is as good as anywhere else in the district. For example, late season often finds whitetails on the migratory move through river valleys en route to winter yards. Good bets include the Manistique and Fox rivers, the swamp region north and west of Gulliver and McDonald lakes, and south and northwest of Indian Lake. In the northern county try along M-94 north of Lily and Boot lakes, along the Fox River east of Germfask, along the Creighton Truck Trail, and in Driggs Marsh as well as the national refuge itself.

Hunting pressure, at three hunters per square mile, is among the lowest in the state. The 10 percent success rate is a few points below the state average, yet Commemorative Bucks of Michigan has thus far identified 28 Schoolcraft County deer to join its list of all-time Michigan record racks. That is a good reason to consider hunting here.

This county is also a solid black-bear producer for both baiters and dog hunters. The latter often equip hounds with radio collars so that the owners can locate them in the vast swamps. Bear live throughout the county, but popular areas include the nest of lakes north of the Creighton Marsh on the Alger County border, south of Cusino, along the Creighton Truck Trail and Driggs River Road, and literally everywhere in the southern county (bear hunting with dogs or bait is not permitted in the national refuge).

Bobcat hunters with dogs work dense cedar swamps. Furthermore, plenty of coyotes afford good hunting potential with or without dogs. Raccoon are another game species that can be hunted with hounds, but, like coyotes, few sportsmen take advantage. Snowshoe hares, although currently down in population, provide winter action in lowland conifers and cutover aspen stands. Gray/black squirrels are few in numbers due to a lack of oak-hickory trees. There are, however, a few bushytails in maple and beech stands interspersed with pine and spruce.

Waterfowl hunting is productive on Indian Lake, the Lake Michigan shoreline, inland lakes in the Steuben area, and in the lower Manistique and Indian rivers. These areas produce early-season puddlers and late-season divers. A bonus is that Canada geese occasionally visit farm fields and sharptail management areas, which are often sewn to wheat and rye. In fact, in the Seney area some farmers rent blinds, and the wildlife refuge often holds several thousand migrants in fall.

OTHER SHOOTING OPPORTUNITIES

The Manistique Rifle and Pistol Club in Manistique owns a shooting range open to the public on a sometime-fee basis. Facilities include 16 indoor/outdoor pistol stations, eight outdoor centerfire rifle stations, eight indoor rimfire rifle stations, and two fields each for skeet and trap. In addition to competitive shooting, the club sponsors state hunter-certification programs. For details, call (906/341-2845).

FURTHER SOURCES OF HUNTING INFORMATION

1. DNR District Office, 309 West McMillan Ave. (Box 445), Newberry, Mich. 49868 (906/293-5131).
2. DNR Thompson Field Office, Route 2, Box 2555, Manistique, Mich. 49854 (906/341-6917).
3. Hiawatha National Forest, Manistique Ranger District, US-2, Manistique, Mich. 49854 (906/341-5666).
4. Schoolcraft County Chamber of Commerce, County Courthouse Building, Room 207, Manistique, Mich. 49854 (906/341-5010).
5. Topographic, county, and lake maps may be ordered from the Michigan United Conservation Clubs. For information, refer to the beginning of this book.
6. Plat books are available from the Schoolcraft County Cooperative Extension Services, County Courthouse Building, Manistique, Mich. 49854. The cost is $10 each (add $1.22 if mail ordering).
7. Mackinac/Luce/Schoolcraft County ASCS Office, Melville St., Engadine, Mich. 49827.

Also, refer to the following elsewhere in this book:
1. Hiawatha National Forest
2. Indian Lake State Park
3. Lake Superior State Forest
4. Palms Book State Park
5. Seney National Wildlife Refuge

Shiawassee County

SHIAWASSEE County is at the center of a triangle whose points include Saginaw, Lansing, and Detroit, and it lies about 40 to 60 miles from each. About 80 percent of the 540-square-mile county is farmed for both cash-crop small grains and beef and dairy cattle operations. Fruit, poultry, and vegetable farming are other enterprises. The county's northern half is dominated by wet loamy soils, blending to loamy soils underlain by sand and gravel as one moves south.

Overall, the soils are rich and produce both good crops and wildlife habitat. Where farming is intensive, however, woodlands and brushlands are scarce. Those farms cut by brushy fencerows and that contain pockets of woods and marshy areas are well worth checking out for small game and deer. About 17 percent of Shiawassee County is covered with commercial-forest species. Equal mixtures of oak-hickory, ash-elm-soft maple, and birch-hard maple, along with some aspen, are found on farm woodlots and upland stretches of river bottoms. Close to the waterways themselves are lowland hardwoods and basswood, sycamore, cottonwood, and some alder.

Hunting potential, therefore, is fairly good. Hunting opportunities, however, are limited. The state owns only about 900 acres in Shiawassee County, amounting to a piece of the Rose Lake Wildlife Research Area (*which see*) in Woodhull Township of the southwestern corner. In addition, only a half-dozen landowners have land currently enrolled in the Public Access Stamp program, which is open to hunting by request. These lands, totaling about 2,100 acres, are found south and west of county center (Bennington, Shiawassee, Woodhull, and Perry townships). Hunters can get a free directory at Rose Lake or from staffed DNR offices in adjacent counties.

Shiawassee farmers, however, have been traditionally receptive to courteous requests from responsible sportsmen asking to hunt their lands. Hunters will find good numbers of deer on farms with timber and brush cover and along river bottomlands. The deer herd, growing for years, has apparently peaked. One prime indicator is annual car-deer accident statistics, which recently surpassed 300 animals. Another is that buck hunters enjoy 10 to 15 percent success, not far off the state average. Pressure is moderate (about 12 hunters per square mile), and the total county land area yields one to two bucks annually per square mile.

Some bucks tote trophy racks. Commemorative Bucks of Michigan currently lists 19 Shiawassee County bucks on its all-time big-deer record list. The best typically-antlered bow kill in the state during a recent season was a Shiawassee County deer.

In order to get on private lands (closed to Sunday hunting for all but landowners), deer hunters should cultivate good landowner-sportsmen relations long before season openers. It is easier to obtain permission when the quarry is small game. Shiawassee County has underhunted populations of fox squirrels and some gray squirrels. For the former,

look for mature oaks and hickories near farmland fields of corn. Gray squirrels like heavier pockets of woods, and so river bottomlands are likely places to search.

Three major rivers course through Shiawassee County. The Looking Glass and the Maple drain the southern and west-central portions, respectively. Both flow westerly to join the Grand River later. These two tributaries are home to good raccoon populations and provide fair jump-shooting for mallards and wood ducks early in the season. The county's main waterway is the Shiawassee River, which enters in the Byron area and flows northerly through Bancroft, Corunna, and Owosso before leaving the north-central portion of the county on its journey to the Saginaw River.

Although the Shiawassee traverses private lands en route, a float trip can be productive for ducks, Canada geese, squirrels, and the occasional deer. Hunters should arm themselves with a county plat book, however, and float initially on a scouting trip, then ask permission to hunt from adjacent landowners. Dams at Byron, Shiawassee Town, Corunna, and Owosso (check for local hunting closures here) are easily portaged. In Saginaw County portions of the river flow through public lands.

Raccoon and fox populations are currently good in Shiawassee County. Hunting pressure is moderate to high for raccoon, light for fox. Rabbit numbers, although cyclical, are generally high enough to provide fair to good hunting. For best results, target brushlands and grasslands with openings. It pays to scout for abandoned farms as well as working farms whose owners are participating in set-aside programs. Such farms often have idle acres with weeds and brush—prime habitat for rabbits and pheasants.

The most recent pheasant mail carrier survey showed that brood numbers nearly doubled from the previous year, ranking Shiawassee County behind only St. Clair and Sanilac counties. However, pheasants have a long way to go before providing good hunting overall. As things now stand, birds are isolated in scattered pockets, but a hunter who does his homework can still bag a two-bird limit. A good place to try is the southeastern region in the Byron/Bancroft/Durand area. The DNR recently chose a portion of this region as one of three southern Michigan locations slated to receive intensive pheasant habitat restoration projects.

Grouse and woodcock hunting pressure is light to moderate throughout Shiawassee County. Based upon the few hunter-cooperators here reporting flush-rate information to the DNR, hunters can look for 1.0 to 3.0 birds moved per hour of effort in likely areas of brush or aspen. Woodcock flush rates are less than half that figure although at certain times in late October, migrant woodcock hold over. Try worm-rich lowlands or abandoned orchards with brush.

Southern Shiawassee County (below I-69) is open to the extended Canada goose season. However, a shortage of lakes limits the number of geese residing here. Hunters might check corn or winter-wheat fields, though, in the Byron-to-Shaftsburg region for goose feeding activity as the giant honkers disperse up to many miles in search of food.

OTHER SHOOTING OPPORTUNITIES

Coverside Shooting Preserve, 9348 South Ruess Road in Perry, has 510 acres open to pheasant and quail hunting for members only. For information, call Donald Edwards at 517/625-4502.

Durand Sportsman's Association on Prior Road in Durand has outdoor pistol (eight stations) and centerfire and rimfire rifle (four stations each) ranges sometimes open to the public for fees. For details, call 517/288-3594.

Shiawassee Conservation Club, 4247 North M-52 in Owosso, has range facilities open without fees to the public on a sometime basis. Facilities include outdoor stations for pistol, centerfire and rimfire rifle (one each), two trap fields, a handtrap area, and an archery target. Call 517/725-7588 for information.

FURTHER SOURCES OF HUNTING INFORMATION

1. DNR District Office, 715 South Cedar, Imlay City, Mich. 48444 (313/724-2015).

2. Rose Lake Field Office, 8562 East Stoll Road, East Lansing, Mich. 48823 (313/641-6000 or 373-1233).

3. Owosso-Corunna Area Chamber of Commerce, 215 North Water St., Owosso, Mich. 48867 (517/723-5149).

4. Durand Area Chamber of Commerce, 101 Clinton St., Durand, Mich. 48429 (517/288-6259 or 288-3715).

5. Topographic, county, and lake maps may be ordered from the Michigan United Conservation Clubs. For information, refer to the beginning of this book.

6. Plat books are available from the Shiawassee County Cooperative Extension Services, 701 South Norton St., Corunna, Mich. 48817. The cost is $9 each (add $1.05 in stamps only if mail ordering).

7. Shiawassee County ASCS Office, USDA, 1767 South M-52, Owosso, Mich. 48867 (517/723-8263)

Also refer to the following elsewhere in this book: Rose Lake Wildlife Research Area.

Tuscola County

TUSCOLA County is located in the heart of Michigan's Thumb. The northwest section of its 812 square miles borders Saginaw Bay. Soils throughout range from generally good in the northern section where large-scale cash-crop farming is the norm to generally poor in the southern region where farms are much smaller and soils are sandy loam.

Intensively farmed lands within a few miles of the bay are flat, cut by drainage ditches, and marked with small groves of woods. Wildlife cover is limited to these farm woodlots and to cattails in the drainage cuts. However, portions of the bay itself contain marshes that provide good duck and goose shooting, including locally-reared puddle ducks as well as migrant mallards, Canada geese, and diver species.

A 30-mile-long ridge, formed no doubt during the period of glaciation, starts in the county's northeast corner and gradually tapers away as it nears Vassar. Other sandy ridges traveling throughout the central portion in this same direction are smaller. These are old lake shorelines, forested now over blowsand soil. Rabbits, squirrels, deer, and grouse live here.

Bisecting the county diagonally is the northeast-to-southwest-flowing Cass River, a wide, slow-meandering stream featuring a three- or four-mile-wide valley. Deer, raccoon, and squirrels are abundant both here and along feeder streams. South of the Cass River, irregular steep hills are laced with swampy areas and small lakes. The highest point in the county, about 1,000 feet above sea level (420 feet higher than Saginaw Bay), is found here near Mayville.

Tuscola County has much to offer the hunter. It features more public hunting land than any other Thumb county—about 29,000 acres spread over six state game and wildlife areas. And there are 21 mini-game areas totaling about 1,800 acres, several of which are annexed to wildlife areas on Saginaw Bay. Further, about 2,500 acres of farmland are leased from a dozen landowners scattered throughout the county. These are lands enrolled under the Public Access Stamp program.

Tuscola County is closed to hunting on Sundays on lands of another. You may hunt on state lands in the county on Sundays.

About 16 percent of Tuscola County is commercially forested, with aspen (29,000 acres) the dominant species. Other major types include hard and soft maple, ash, birch, and about 9,000 acres of northern white cedar—more than anywhere else in southern Michigan. A considerable portion of southern Tuscola County is brush in varying stages of growth. This brush/aspen mix provides good woodcock and grouse habitat on both private and public lands. In high-cycle years grouse hunters move 3.0 or more birds per hour. Woodcock hunters average .50 flushes per hour, but this can increase greatly if you time a hunt to coincide with the fall migration, which normally peaks between October 15 and 30.

Pheasant hunting success, which is generally poor to fair throughout the county, depends upon the hunter's ability to find pockets of wild birds. Ringnecks do exist along with a few coveys of bobwhite quail in the southern region (the quail season, however, is dependent upon annual populations). Fox squirrels live throughout the county on state land and in farm woodlots. In addition, there is a small population of gray squirrels (including black mutants) in the Frankenmuth area.

Fox and raccoon are found in good numbers

throughout the county. If a band of wild turkeys from Pennsylvania recently released in the Deford State Game Area expand as expected, the county could offer future turkey hunting—wild turkeys were native to the Thumb as late as the last century. The Murphy State Game Area east of Millington is another area that someday might get turkey releases.

Duck and goose hunters have many options in Tuscola County. First are the bay-front marshes already mentioned. Second is a float trip down the Cass River; Caro, Vassar, Frankenmuth, and the Dixie Highway (M-54) Bridge are good put-in and take-out points. Third, some of the inland lakes and potholes offer excellent waterfowling opportunities for both migrant birds and those burned off Saginaw Bay. In most cases, though, hunters will have to get permission first from private landowners.

Deer hunting in Tuscola County rates fair to good with hunter success running 10 to 14 percent (one to two bucks per square mile) and pressure quite light for southern Michigan—about 11 hunters per square mile. Much of this pressure centers in state game areas. The whitetail population is reasonably high as evidenced by both car-deer accidents (300 to 400 annually) and hunter-tagged animals. Deer are well scattered throughout the county. Many bucks grow fine racks from eating both high-protein farm crops and sand-ridge acorns. Every year it seems that one or more Tuscola County hunters enter trophy bucks in the DNR Big Buck Contest.

OTHER SHOOTING OPPORTUNITIES

Michigan Sportsmen's Hunt Club, a shooting preserve near Vassar, is open to members. For information, contact Larry Joseph at 4242 Oak Road, Vassar, Mich. 48768 or call 517/823-2157. Trapper Jim's Hunt Club, 4300 East Sanilac Road, Kingston, Mich. 48741 (517/683-2620) is also open to the public but without membership requirements. In addition, Tuscola County Archers on Brusill Road in Caro

operates a fee indoor range with 36 targets all open to the public daily. They offer shooting instruction, state hunter education programs, and competitive shooting. For information, call 517/673-6713.

FURTHER SOURCES OF HUNTING INFORMATION

1. DNR District Office, 715 Cedar St., Imlay City, Mich. 48444 (313/724-2015).
2. DNR Field Office, 1123 Mertz Road, Caro, Mich. 48723 (517/673-3434).
3. Fish Point Wildlife Area, Ringle Road, Unionville, Mich. (517/673-5999).
4. Topographic, county, and lake maps may be ordered from the Michigan United Conservation Clubs. For information, refer to the beginning of this book.
5. Caro Chamber of Commerce, 130 West Burnside, Caro, Mich. 48723 (517/673-6144).
6. Vassar Chamber of Commerce, Box 126, Vassar, Mich. 48768 (517/823-8517).
7. Frankenmuth Chamber of Commerce, 635 South Main St., Frankenmuth, Mich. 48734 (517/652-6106).
8. Cass City Chamber of Commerce, 4861 Spruce Drive, Cass City, Mich. 48726 (517/872-2217).
9. Plat books are available from the Tuscola County Cooperative Extension Services, 420 Court St., Caro, Mich. 48723. The cost is $10 each (add $1.50 if mail ordering).
10. Tuscola County ASCS Office, USDA, 852 South Hooper St., Caro, Mich. 48723 (517/673-8173).

Also, refer to the following elsewhere in this book:
1. Murphy Lake State Game Area
2. Vassar State Game Area
3. Tuscola State Game Area
4. Deford State Game Area
5. Cass City State Game Area
6. Fish Point Wildlife Area

Van Buren County

AT 396,000 acres, Van Buren County in southwestern Lower Michigan is largely overlooked by hunters who key on state game areas in nearby Allegan and Barry counties. The truth is that Van Buren County has some of the lightest hunting pressure in southern Michigan, and it is home to overall good populations of game animals and birds. Over 30 percent of the land area is commercially forested with maple-birch, elm-ash-soft maple, and oak-hickory predominating. The most heavily wooded portion is found in the extreme southeast corner, but woodlots and mixed stands of brush and trees are scattered throughout the prime farmland of the east-central region, where cash-crop and dairy farming is the norm, and the mixed-practice farmlands in the rest of the county.

Those practices include fruit growing, with orchards and vineyards predominating in the western third and a tapering belt to Paw Paw, the county seat. Deer-damage complaints in high-number years are common in this region. Lands east and north of Paw Paw feature brushlands and woodlands mostly on

smaller farms nestled among gently rolling hills. This area is excellent for deer, grouse, rabbits, and squirrels.

Van Buren is one of southwestern Michigan's most picturesque counties. It features a unique and uniform mixture of interspersed cover types: woodlands, brushlands, farmlands. Glaciation from the last ice age of 8,000 to 12,000 years ago shaped present-day topography. Much of the central portion is old outwash plains from former rivers that scoured this region. Rolling hills are morainic deposits of glacial till formed when the ice retreated. A belt of sand dunes one-half to one mile wide skirts the Lake Michigan shoreline, and scattered pockets of sand from ancient beach shorelines exist several miles inland.

The roughly northern half of Van Buren County contains wet, sandy soils underlain by sand and gravel, whereas the southern region is mostly loamy soils with sand and gravel underneath. Glacial action also left this county with a high number of lakes scattered throughout but with concentrations in the

eastern half. Public access is available on about two dozen of these lakes.

However, overall state-land ownership in Van Buren County is slight, amounting to only 860 total acres. Pockets of hunting opportunity exist in tiny Van Buren State Park (about 250 acres—you must have a state parks sticker, however), Keeler Mini-Game Area (about 200 acres) in the southwestern region, and Fuller Woods (120 acres) near the county center. Public Access Stamp program lands total some 2,800 acres scattered throughout among 18 participating farmers. The largest concentration of PASP lands is in the northern tier of townships (Pine Grove, Bloomingdale, Columbia) and in southern townships of Hamilton, Hartford, and Lawrence. For a complete directory, contact DNR district headquarters in Plainwell.

Van Buren County farmers are also amenable to a courteous request to hunt from considerate sportsmen. As mentioned, hunting pressure overall is slight, making for untapped potential.

Perhaps the best potential is for deer hunters, especially in the fruit belt. Only about seven hunters per square mile keep countywide pressure low, yet hunter success on bucks can run above 20 percent (the state average is usually 17 percent). Annual kill amounts to one to two deer per square mile. Yearly car-deer accidents cost the lives of about 200 whitetails from a herd, that by most considerations, appears to have leveled off. Commemorative Bucks of Michigan has scored nine all-time big Michigan bucks from Van Buren County, and each fall one or more of the state's best-racked deer come from this area.

Other than the Paw Paw River and its tributaries, which drain the central portion, Van Buren County has no major waterways. Raccoon hunting is nevertheless considered good and is largely due to the high amount of forestlands and high-quality farming. Fox hunting opportunities also exist for both dog men and those who still- or stand-hunt with predator calls. Squirrel populations are good to excellent throughout, and hunting for bushytails is an underutilized resource. Find farmland woodlots with oak, hickory, or butternut trees adjacent to corn fields for best results. These areas support fox squirrels with an occasional gray. Rabbit hunting opportunities also abound in Van Buren County with populations well distributed. Find lowland habitat of brush in areas of cultivated fields and grasslands for best results.

Van Buren County used to be one of the best pheasant hunting regions in southern Michigan and continues to serve up opportunity in the northern half, particularly in Bangor Township. Populations, however, are mostly limited to isolated pockets of wild birds, but a hunter willing to seek access and

then key on brushy areas adjacent to crop fields and grasslands can still bag a two-rooster limit. The DNR has not released wild turkeys in Van Buren County and has no plans to do so. An occasional bird sighted in north-tier townships is a stray from Allegan County, which has a resident flock.

Not surprisingly, woodcock and grouse hunting pressure is light to moderate. Cooperative hunters report hourly flush rates on grouse of 1.60 to 3.30, depending upon the birds' cyclic population level. Woodcock, a bonus, can sometimes be found in small concentrations as late October migrants wing their way south.

The Paw Paw River affords floating opportunities for squirrel, deer, and duck hunters. A good drift is to put in at County Road 681 midway between Hartford and Lawrence. Upper river reaches will require portages. Waterfowlers might also check out county lakes with access or ask permission to hunt private lakes that attract ducks and geese. Plenty of water (eight square miles or more) exists in this county. A continuing nuisance problem with resident giant Canada geese provides field hunting opportunity now and may result in a future extended season such as that currently enjoyed by southeastern Michigan hunters.

OTHER SHOOTING OPPORTUNITIES

The South Haven Rod and Gun Club, Route 5, Box 312, South Haven, Mich. 49090, has shooting facilities open to the public at certain times. Call 616/637-4868 for details.

FURTHER SOURCES OF HUNTING INFORMATION

1. DNR District Office, 621 North 10th St. (Box 355), Plainwell, Mich. 49080 (616/685-6851).

2. Van Buren State Park, Ruggles Road, South Haven, Mich. 49090 (616/637-2788).

3. Greater South Haven Area Chamber of Commerce, 535 Quaker St., South Haven, Mich. 49090 (616/637-1450).

4. Greater Paw Paw Chamber of Commerce, 143 East Michigan Ave., Paw Paw, Mich. 49079 (616/657-3850).

5. Topographic, county, and lake maps may be ordered from the Michigan United Conservation Clubs. For information, refer to the beginning of this book.

6. County plat books are available from the Van Buren County Cooperative Extension Service, 226 East Michigan Ave., Paw Paw, Mich. 49079, for $10 each (add $1.39 if mail ordering).

7. Van Buren County ASCS Office, USDA, 816 East Michigan Ave., Paw Paw, Mich. 49079 (616/657-4095).

Also, refer to the following elsewhere in this book:
1. Van Buren State Park

Washtenaw County

IN spite of metropolis Ann Arbor and Ypsilanti, about 43 percent of 716-square-mile Washtenaw County is farmed for corn, wheat, oats, soybeans, and alfalfa. Both cash-crop and dairy/livestock enterprises are practiced. The county has a considerable amount of surface water, especially in the form of many lakes in the northwestern region. The River Raisin flows through Manchester in the southwestern corner, and the Huron River, entering from Base Line and Portage lakes in the north-central region, flows through metropolitan parks and urban areas on its southeasterly course. About 20 percent of the land base is forested with commercial timber species. Half is oak-hickory with the balance split between ash-elm-soft maple and birch-hard maple types. There are lowland hardwoods along streams and pockets of brush throughout.

Washtenaw County affords good hunting for deer, Canada geese, squirrels, and rabbits and fair hunting for grouse, woodcock, pheasants, raccoon, and squirrels. A big problem is a lack of access. Only 300 acres are enrolled by a handful of landowners in the Public Access Stamp program. State lands totaling over 13,000 acres amount to less than three percent of the land base. Hunting is permitted, though, on these state lands—Waterloo and Pinckney recreation areas and Chelsea and Sharonville state game areas (all of which see). Hunters will need a state park sticker to hunt Waterloo and Pinckney, however, and should pay attention to boundary signs indicating which parts are open and which aren't.

Washtenaw County's level to gently-rolling terrain is the result of heavy glaciation during the last ice age several thousand years ago. In the southeastern portion are traces of former Great Lakes shorelines, mostly small, wave-cut bluffs or low ridges of sand and gravel indicating former beaches. Soils here are mostly silt and clay. The rest of the county is largely glacial outwash sand and gravel in the form of level plains areas or hummocky reliefs that are end moraines containing coarse to fine-textured till. Soils are mostly sandy loam. A major gravel ridge extending northeast to southwest cuts through the northwestern quadrant. It generally separates poorer farmland from better soils. Not surprisingly, much of the state land is in this sector of poorer soils.

Washtenaw County contains good numbers of deer, as evidenced by the nearly 400 car-deer accidents registered each year. The western two-thirds has the most deer, including some big bucks. In fact, this county currently ranks third in the state (behind Delta and Marquette counties) for number of all-time big bucks discovered thus far by Commemorative Bucks of Michigan. Fifty-two prime heads have been turned up, 14 of which include bucks enrolled during two recent hunting seasons.

Overall, the county produces one to two bucks per square mile for 10 to 14 percent success (one of eight) for the average 10 hunters per square mile who seek them. Public lands are pressured heavily; best bucks and most opportunities come from private land. Access is difficult, however, due mainly to the proximity of Ann Arbor and Ypsilanti.

Raccoon are found in the game and recreation areas and in lowland hardwoods near water and farm fields. There are fair numbers of fox in the county too. Trappers take far more than hunters. Fox squirrels are abundant throughout, especially in woodlots containing mature oak and hickory next to corn fields. For rabbits, concentrate on lowland areas that hold brush or in grassy fields near farms and strip cover. Generally, good numbers are available.

Washtenaw used to be a good pheasant hunting county and still offers limited opportunity for ringnecks. Hunters will have to scout to find isolated pockets of birds. Key on farmlands that have acres set aside or on abandoned farms. A plat book will help

in locating owners for asking permission. Fair numbers of grouse and woodcock are found north of I-94 with hunting pressure running moderate to high. The DNR recently introduced Iowa wild turkeys to the Waterloo Recreation Area in the hope that these magnificent game birds may some day produce hunting opportunity.

Washtenaw County is closed to Sunday hunting on lands of another. State holdings, however, are open to hunting. Most of the Huron River, the cities, and all the metroparks are off-limits yet house large numbers of nuisance Canada geese. In fact, all of Washtenaw County is open to the extended goose hunting season. Hunters willing to put in time following birds that disperse to corn and winter wheat fields during morning and afternoon flights and then knock on doors in the hopes of securing hunting permission may be well rewarded. Thorn Lake west of Manchester holds up to 5,000 wintering Canadas, according to the DNR, which surveys the area from aircraft each December. Other lakes usually with goose inventories include Columbia, Pleasant, Four Mile, Cavanaugh, North, Half Moon, Whitmore, Portage, Little Portage, and Joslin. There is some float hunting opportunity on the River Raisin for ducks and geese and on Portage and Base Line lakes as well as on lakes within the state-owned properties.

OTHER SHOOTING OPPORTUNITIES

The Chelsea Rod and Gun Club, 7031 Lingane Road, Chelsea, Mich. 48118, has range facilities open to the public on an irregular basis for fees. Included are single outdoor stations for pistol, centerfire and rimfire rifle, a shotgun trap field, and outdoor archery target. Shooting instruction and hunter education programs are offered. There is no phone.

Golden Arrow Archery Range #3 at 7730 Willow Road in Milan is a commercial enterprise open to the public and offering both competitive shooting and shooting instruction for fees. Call 313/461-0266 for details.

FURTHER SOURCES OF HUNTING INFORMATION

1. DNR District Office, 3335 Lansing Ave., Jackson, Mich. 49202 (517/784-3188).

2. Pinckney Recreation Area, 8555 Silver Hill Road, Route 1, Pinckney, Mich. 48169 (313/426-4913).

3. Waterloo Recreation Area, 16345 McClure Road, Route 1, Chelsea, Mich. 48118 (313/475-8307).

4. Waterloo Game Office, Route 3, 13578 Seymour Road, Grass Lake, Mich. 49240 (517/522-4097).

5. Ann Arbor Chamber of Commerce, 207 East Washington, Ann Arbor, Mich. 48104 (313/665-4433).

6. Ypsilanti Area Chamber of Commerce, 11 Noth Adams St., Ypsilanti, Mich. 48197 (313/482-4920).

7. Chelsea Area Chamber of Commerce, Box 94, Chelsea, Mich. 48118 (313/475-1361).

8. Saline Area Chamber of Commerce, Box 377, Saline, Mich. 48176 (313/429-7380).

9. Topographic, county, and lake maps may be ordered from the Michigan United Conservation Clubs. For information, refer to the beginning of this book.

10. Plat books are available from the Washtenaw County Cooperative Extension Services, 4133 Washtenaw Ave., Box 8645, Ann Arbor, Mich. 48107. They cost $10 each (add $1 with mail orders).

11. Washtenaw-Wayne counties ASCS Office, USDA, 601 Jackson Road, Ann Arbor, Mich. 48103 (313/662-3900).
Also, refer to the following elsewhere in this book:

1. Chelsea State Game Area
2. Pinckney Recreation Area
3. Sharonville State Game Area
4. Waterloo Recreation Area

Wayne County

WAYNE County with over 2 million people in Detroit and surrounding suburbs is Michigan's heaviest population center. Consequently, hunting opportunities are severely limited. However, they do exist, especially for small game—rabbits, pheasants, and squirrels principally.

The western portion of Wayne County is a mixture of small farms featuring crop fields, wood lots, and patches of brush. Soils are largely clay-loam and often wet. There is no public land with the exception of the northern portion of the Pointe Mouillee State Game Area (*which see*). Nor are there any Public Access Stamp program lands. Permission to hunt private land, though not impossible to procure, is nonetheless difficult.

In addition, hunters must check with local closure laws in such outlying municipalities as Canton, Northville, and Plymouth. Practically all hunting opportunities exist west of I-275.

An exception is the Detroit River which affords good hunting for diving-duck species, especially later in the season when migrants are down. Specialized layout hunting boats and large stools of decoys are the order all along the river with particular emphasis downstream from Fighting Island to Pointe Mouillee. This area also hosts fair to good numbers of wintering crows, which could offer shooting sport. See the respective chapters on both crows and diving ducks for tips on how to hunt each.

Wayne County west of I-75 is included in the southeastern Michigan late season for nuisance Canada geese. Many of the giant geese stage along the Huron River. Although hunting here in the metroparks is prohibited, there are some fringe opportunities in farm fields for hunters willing to scout foraging geese and then ask permission to enter private lands. Goose-nuisance complaints are on the rise in the Northville-Plymouth area, but hunting is closed.

Throughout the county lives a small but stable population of deer. In fact, about 60 animals become road statistics each year.

All in all, Wayne affords the least hunting opportunities of the 83 Michigan counties. However, the fact that there is any hunting at all in such a heavily-populated region attests to two truths: (1) wildlife can survive if basic habitat needs are met and (2) controlled hunting is a valid recreational resource wherever wildlife is found.

OTHER SHOOTING OPPORTUNITIES

Wayne County sportsmen have at least four places to practice shooting:

1. Taylor Police Range, 11095 Pine St. in Taylor, offers free use of indoor/outdoor pistol and rimfire rifle (73 stations each), outdoor centerfire rifle (one station), and archery (30 targets) facilities. There is also a shotgun handtrap area. Programs include shooting instruction, shooting competition, and state hunter education programs. For details, call 313/287-6611.

2. Huron Sportsman's Association, 18736 Sterling in New Boston, has a trap field and archery facilities open to the public for fees. Included are shooting instruction and competition programs plus hunter certification classes. For information, call 313/753-9506.

3. The Lincoln Bowmen Archery Club, 26245 King Road in Romulus, has 99 indoor/outdoor archery targets which the public may use daily for fees. Further, the club sponsors shooting instruction and shooting competition. Call 313/782-9293 for details.

4. Tony's Gun Shop and Ranges, Inc., 23031 Pennsylvania Road in Wyandotte, is a commercial business open to the public for fees. Facilities include 14 outdoor pistol stations, 50 each indoor/outdoor stations for centerfire and rimfire rifle, 30 outdoor archery targets, a skeet field, and a trap field. Shooting instruction is offered. For information, call 313/283-0030.

FURTHER SOURCES OF HUNTING INFORMATION

1. DNR District Office, 2455 North Williams Lake Road, Pontiac, Mich. 48054 (313/666-1500).

2. Maybury State Park (staffed although closed to hunting), 20145 Beck Road, Northville, Mich. 48167 (313/349-8390).

3. Pointe Mouillee State Game Area, 37205 Mouillee Road, Rockwood, Mich. 48173 (313/379-9692).

4. Greater Detroit Chamber of Commerce, 150 Michigan Ave., Detroit, Mich. 48226 (313/964-4000).

5. Wayne Chamber of Commerce, 35816 Michigan Ave., Wayne, Mich. 48184 (313/721-0100).

6. Greater Romulus Chamber of Commerce, 35350 Goddard, Romulus, Mich. 48174 (313/941-5710).

7. Belleville/Van Buren Chamber of Commerce, 116 Fourth St., Belleville, Mich. 48111 (313/697-7151).

8. Northville Community Chamber of Commerce, 195 South Main St., Northville, Mich. 48167 (313/349-7640).

9. Plymouth Community Chamber of Commerce, 188 North Main St., Plymouth, Mich. 48170 (313/453-1540).

10. Topographic, county, and lake maps may be ordered from the Michigan United Conservation Clubs. For information, refer to the beginning of this book.

11. Plat books (1970 edition is the latest) are available from the Wayne County Cooperative

Extension Services, 5454 Venoy Road, Wayne, Mich. 48184. The cost is $5 each (add $1.20 if mail ordering).

12. Washtenaw-Wayne counties ASCS Office,

USDA, 6101 Jackson Road, Ann Arbor, Mich. 48103 (313/662-3900).

Also, refer to the following elsewhere in this book:
Pointe Mouillee State Game Area

Wexford County

WEXFORD County in northwestern Lower Michigan seems to be tailored to the needs of outdoor recreationists, including hunters. Its ideal location for downstate sportsmen, tremendous variety of forest cover types sandwiched around small belts of farming activities, and good game populations combine to attract hunters. They seek deer, raccoon, snowshoe hares, turkeys, squirrels, grouse, woodcock, and waterfowl. They find them all in Wexford County.

Two farming areas are the southeastern corner below Cadillac and a long belt between Manton and Mesick along M-42 in the northern region. These are mostly dairy- and livestock-farming operations. A fairly intensive agricultural area with some cash cropping occurs in the northwestern part near Buckley. Cornfields here attract geese and deer. These farming areas also draw wild turkeys in winter as birds search for food. By the spring hunting season the turkeys have usually dispersed up to several miles. They are found throughout Wexford County, but the southern third is best.

Topographically, 572-square-mile Wexford County is varied and interesting, with considerable areas of broken and hilly land. Bluffs ranging from 50 to 200 feet in height flank the Manistee River, which flows westerly across the northern section. Highest points occur in Springville, Wexford, and Hanover townships. Hunters will also find hilly sections in the eastern and southern parts of Cedar Creek Township, the northern and eastern parts of Haring, northern Selma, northern and western Boon, eastern Slagle, central Henderson, and eastern Clam Lake townships. The roughest part of the county is north of Harietta in Springville and Antioch townships. The elevation of Black Briar Hill is some 300 feet above the general level of the land.

About 73 percent, or 263,000 acres, of Wexford County is covered with commercial-forest species. Beginning with 80,600 acres of maple-birch, these cover types are varied and scattered throughout. Aspen at 53,600 acres is the next most prolific type. It is followed by red pine (52,700 acres), oak-hickory (16,000 acres), elm-ash-soft maple (13,100 acres), jack pine (10,100 acres), and northern white cedar (8,300 acres). Smaller amounts of white pine, white spruce, and paper birch are also found.

Much of this forestland falls into state and federal ownership where it is managed by periodic cutting, a practice which helps wildlife by providing more edge, food, and security cover. Some 38,000 acres, or about 10.5 percent, of Wexford County falls into the Pere Marquette State Forest (which see). These holdings occur along the northern and eastern portions. Another 89,000 acres, or 25.5 percent of the land base, is claimed by the Huron-Manistee

National Forest (which also see). This ownership occurs in the central and southwestern region and includes huge, unbroken blocks.

In addition, about 2,100 acres of Commercial Forest Act land, owned by timber companies, is open to hunting in a tradeoff with the state for reduced property taxes. For legal descriptions, stop in at the DNR district headquarters at Cadillac or contact the DNR Forest Management Division in Lansing. The address is Box 30028, Lansing, Mich. 48909, and the telephone number is 517/373-1275. If you have a legal description, you can easily find these timberlands (which usually are not posted) with the aid of a current county plat book and an updated county map.

Hunters will find good deer, grouse, and woodcock populations along the Manistee River and its tributaries. There is fair to good Canada goose hunting in the Mesick area along the Hodenpyle Backwaters and in nearby farm fields, if you get permission to enter. A sanctuary at Glengary on the Hodenpyle holds up to 1,100 Canadas that stage here during fall migrations.

Much of Wexford County is dry-soiled, mostly sand, which makes for good drainage. The central portion is droughty with low-fertility soils; consequently, game populations are not as high as elsewhere throughout the county. In the northeastern corner rye patches near Manton and south of Chase Creek Forest Campground in Liberty Township attract both geese and deer.

In spite of the dominant dry soils, hunters will find several swamp regions which hold wintering deer as well as black and gray squirrels and snowshoe hares along fringes where cutover lands meet the green cover. Occasional black bear and bobcats are also sighted although these game animals are currently protected and likely will remain so for a long time. One swamp region occurs west of Lake Mitchell. Another is in Section 31 of Clam Lake Township and Section 36 of Cherry Grove Township. A third is on state land in the northwestern region.

Red and white oaks are found mostly in the southern third of Wexford County. Turkeys, deer, and fox squirrels frequent the area to provide good hunting opportunities during periods of heavy mast production. Aspen is bunched throughout the county with concentrations in the east-central and southwestern regions and along Manistee River bottomlands.

Attesting to fairly good grouse and woodcock hunting are hunter-cooperator hourly flush records. While spot checking three years of those records, we learned that an average of 1.40, 1.20, and 1.60 grouse were moved—reasonably consistent statistics. Those same hunter-cooperators reported 1.07, 1.05, and 1.41 woodcock flushes. The best woodcock gunning occurs in mid-October when flight birds stop over to rest and feed. Try old pasturelands, brushy stream bottoms, gray dogwood thickets, and moist-soil alder groves.

Much of the national forest land contains scrub oak, northern hardwoods (beech, soft maple, elm, and basswood), and red- and jack-pine plantations. Deer numbers are fairly good and there is hunting opportunity for snowshoe hares, some grouse, and coyotes. Best coyote hunting opportunities, however, are in the very northern and southern regions of the county. Fair numbers of red fox are best hunted on agricultural lands and in forest openings. They appear to be scattered throughout the county.

There are a few pheasants west of Manton and south of Cadillac. Raccoon, numerous along waterways, receive moderate to high hunting pressure, depending upon the fluctuating value of their hides. Good hunting opportunities for wood ducks, mallards, and teal shape up on beaver ponds and along small drainages. Hunters floating the Manistee can score on ducks, geese, squirrels, and an occasional deer. An excellent campground awaits them at Mesick. There is some diver-duck hunting potential on Lake Mitchell (Lake Cadillac is closed to hunting), but it is considered only fair at best.

Wexford County deer hunters tag bucks at a one-to-eight ratio or 12 to 14 percent success (one to two bucks per square mile), a nudge under the state average. The deer herd, however, appears to be healthy although severe winters can knock their numbers down. About 150 to 200 animals die on Wexford County roads each year. Hunting pressure runs moderate to high with about 20 to 25 hunters per square mile.

OTHER SHOOTING OPPORTUNITIES

The Cadillac Police Department offers shooting instruction and has six outdoor stations for pistol shooting open to the public without charge. The police department is located at 200 Lake St. in Cadillac. Call 616/775-3491 for details.

We know of no other shooting opportunities open to the public in Wexford County.

FURTHER SOURCES OF HUNTING INFORMATION

1. DNR District Office, 8015 South 131 Road, Cadillac, Mich. 49601 (616/775-9727).

2. DNR Manton Field Office, 521 North Michigan, Manton, Mich. 49663 (616/824-3591).

3. Huron-Manistee National Forest, 421 South Mitchell St., Cadillac, Mich. 49601 (616/775-2421).

4. Huron-Manistee National Forest, Cadillac Ranger District, 3916 South 131 St., Cadillac, Mich. 49601, (616/775-8539).

5. Fife Lake Chamber of Commerce, 3591 South 37-Mile Road, Cadillac, Mich. 49601 (616/775-6879).

6. Cadillac Area Chamber of Commerce, 200 North Lake St., Cadillac, Mich. 49601 (616/775-9776).

7. Mesick Chamber of Commerce, Mesick Avenue, Mesick, Mich. 49668 (616/885-1340).

8. Topographic, county, and lake maps may be ordered from the Michigan United Conservation Clubs. For information, refer to the beginning of this book.

9. Plat books are available from the Wexford County Cooperative Extension Services, Box 158, Courthouse Bldg., Cadillac, Mich. 49601. The cost is $10 each (add $1.50 if mail ordering).

10. Wexford County ASCS Office, US-131 North, Cadillac, Mich. 49601.

Also, refer to the following elsewhere in this book:

1. Huron-Manistee National Forest
2. Pere Marquette State Forest

Suggested Reference Material

THE true value of a reference work such as "Hunt Michigan!" is in its compatibility with other reference materials. Two such aids are the "Michigan County Map and Outdoor Guide" and a U.S. government topographic map, both of which are available from the Michigan United Conservation Clubs. By utilizing this collateral material, a hunter can greatly improve his chances of success. For example, after you learn about the game species you want to hunt and determine its availability in a specific county, the next logical step is to refer to the "Michigan County Map and Outdoor Guide." This large, multi-colored publication contains up-to-date maps of all 83 Michigan counties, from Keweenaw to Monroe, arranged in alphabetical order. You can use this guide to narrow your hunting area down from a county-wide area to a township or even a specific section of land. State and federal lands are shaded to differentiate them from private land. (By the way, the "Michigan County Map and Outdoor Guide" is packed full of interesting information on Michigan's animals, birds, fish, and trees.)

Once you have your hunting area narrowed down, the next step is to obtain a U.S. government topographic map. These full-color topographic maps show terrain in even greater detail. All elevation contour lines, vegetation types, roads, trails, section markers, and houses are shown. By using a topographic map you can pick out the ridges, swamps, clearcuts, or any area most likely to harbor the specific game you seek. The "Michigan Map Index," a listing of more than 900 Michigan topographic maps is available, at no charge, from MUCC. This 32-page index lists over 2,500 available Michigan lake maps plus nautical charts and detailed information on structure fishing. By using "Hunt Michigan!" in conjunction with a "Michigan County Map and Outdoor Guide" and a U.S. government topographic map, you can literally plan your hunt before you take to the field.

When you return home with that brace of grouse or eight-point buck, make sure your wild game meals are as memorable as your hunt. To obtain the succulent best from your game, refer to the "Wildlife Chef Cookbook," also available from MUCC. In addition to more than 388 recipes, the "Wildlife Chef" is chock-full of tips and methods of preparation, storing, and cooking of wild game, fish, plants, breads, sauces, and desserts. Its handy 6"x9" size makes the "Wildlife Chef" perfect for both the kitchen and the camp.

While the venison stew is simmering on the stove, why not sit back and relax with a good book? "Hunters' Heritage," published by MUCC, is a fascinating manuscript chronicling hunting from before the arrival of the white man through the notorious market hunting period to the present. Written by noted Michigan historian Eugene T. Petersen, "Hunters' Heritage" is generously illustrated with over 70 historic photographs and line drawings, some published in book form for the first

time. It is *must* reading for any sportsman interested in learning how hunting and wildlife conservation progressed through the years and the circumstances and attitudes which influenced them.

All the reference materials listed above are available from the Michigan United Conservation Clubs. Prices include tax/shipping.

Michigan County Map and Outdoor Guide . . . $11.40
Wildlife Chef Cookbook . . . . $ 5.15
Hunters' Heritage . . . . $ 5.16
Additional Copies of Hunt Michigan! $11.95
Michigan Map Index . . . . FREE
(*Please send a self-addressed business envelope with 40 cents postage affixed.*)

To receive your copies of these publications, please send your check/money order to: *MUCC Books*, P.O. Box 30235, Lansing, Michigan 48909.

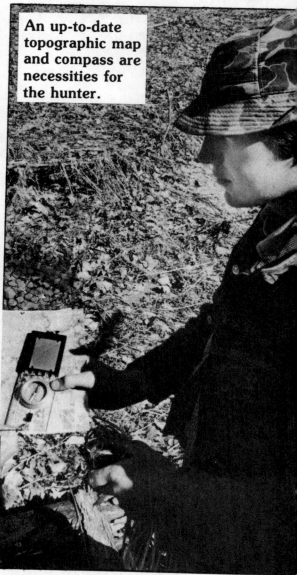

An up-to-date topographic map and compass are necessities for the hunter.

The Michigan Map Index, listing all Michigan topographic maps, is available FREE from MUCC.